A Procession of Friends
Quakers in America

BY DAISY NEWMAN

Friends United Press
Richmond, Indiana • www.fum.org

Copyright © 1972 by Daisy Newman

All rights reserved. No portion of this book may be reproduced, stored in electronic retrieval system or transmitted in any form or by means—electronic, mechanical, photocopy, recording or other—except for brief quotations in printed reviews, without the prior permission of the publisher.

Original Printing 1972
Reprinted 1980 by Friends United Press
Third Printing 1992
Fourth Printing 2007

Friends United Press
101 Quaker Hill Drive
Richmond IN 47374
friendspress@fum.org
www.fum.org

Cover design by Shari Pickett Veach

Library of Congress Cataloging-in-Publication Data

Newman, Daisy, 1904-1994
A Procession of Friends
  Includes references and index.
  ISBN 0-913408-59-X
  ISBN 978-0-913408-59-9

79-160875

For James, Nancy, and Carol
"Let your lives speak"

Other books by Daisy Newman

I Take Thee, Serenity
Indian Summer of the Heart
The Autumn's Brightness
Diligence in Love

PERMISSIONS

Grateful acknowledgment is made for the use of the following copyrighted material:

Random quotes from the series of letters entitled *Prisms* by Dr. Majorie Nelson. Reprinted by permission of American Friends Service Committee.

Excerpts from *The Story of Quakerism Through Three Centuries* by Elfrida Vipont Foulds. Published by Bannisdale Press. Reprinted by permission of the author.

Excerpts from *The Journal of George Fox*, edited by John L. Nickalls, and *The Second Period of Quakerism* by William C. Braithwaite. Reprinted by permission of Cambridge University Press.

Excerpts from Bliss Forbush: *Elias Hicks*, Quaker Liberal. Reprinted by permission of New York: Columbia University Press, 1956. Pp. 129–31.

Excerpts from *The Voyage of the Golden Rule* by Albert S. Bigelow. Copyright © 1959 by Albert S. Bigelow. Reprinted by permission of Doubleday & Company, Inc.

Excerpts from *God Is My Landlord*. Reprinted by permission of Dynamic Kernels Foundation, Inc.

Excerpts from *Me and My House* by Walter R. and Myrtle M. Williams. Reprinted by permission of William B. Eerdmans Publishing Co.

All material from *Friends Journal* reprinted by permission of the publisher.

Excerpt from *A Testament of Devotion* by Thomas R. Kelly. Reprinted by permission of Harper & Row Publishers, Inc.

Excerpts from the book *Windows for the Crown Prince* by Elizabeth Gray Vining. Copyright 1952, by Elizabeth Gray Vining. Reprinted by permission of J. B. Lippincott Company.

Excerpts from *For More Than Bread* by Clarence E. Pickett. Reprinted by permission of Mrs. Clarence E. Pickett. Published by Little, Brown & Company.

Excerpts from *The Life and Adventures of a Quaker Among the Indians* by Thomas C. Battey. New edition copyright 1968 by the University of Oklahoma Press. Reprinted by permission of the University of Oklahoma Press.

Excerpts from *The Hill of Vision* by Levinus K. Painter. Reprinted by permission of the author.

Excerpt from *Quakers on the American Frontier* by Errol T. Elliott. Reprinted by permission of *Quaker Life*.

Excerpts from *The Later Periods of Quakerism* and *The Quakers in the American Colonies*, both books by Rufus M. Jones. Reprinted by permission of The Joseph Rowntree Charitable Trust.

A portion of the poem "A Letter to the Chinese People" by Emily Greene Balch from *Improper Bostonian: Emily Greene Balch* by Mercedes M. Randall. Copyright © 1964 by Twayne Publishers, Inc., and *Beyond Nationalism: The Social Thought of Emily Greene Balch*, edited by Mercedes M. Randall. Copyright © 1971 by Twayne Publishers, Inc. Reprinted by permission of the publisher.

Excerpts from *The Journal and Major Essays of John Woolman* edited by

Phillips P. Moulton. Copyright © 1971 by Oxford University Press, Inc. Reprinted by permission of the publisher.

Excerpts from *Quakers in California* by David C. Le Shana. Copyright © 1969 by David C. Le Shana. Reprinted by permission of the author.

Excerpts from *A Garden of the Lord* by Ralph K. Beebe. Copyright © 1968 by The Barclay Press. Reprinted by permission of the publisher.

Foreword

In the Meeting for Worship after the manner of Friends, it sometimes befalls that a person who feels moved to break the silence and share a fresh insight unknowingly expresses the thoughts of those listening. The speaker is not speaking *to* the Meeting; the gathered Meeting is speaking *through* one member.

So may the company of people with whom, over the years, the writer has worshiped and worked out concerns speak through this book. Like "many candles, lighted and put in one place," they have made the light "more to shine forth." They have added their scholarly achievements, their loving concern and that characteristic humor with which Friends make little of the weightiest assignments. To name them would require another volume. It would not be acceptable, since preference for anonymity is also one of their endearing traits.

The writer has no way of expressing her gratitude to them; to her children and intimate friends for their support; to her corps of kindly, exacting, prepublication critics on either side of the Atlantic; nor to the Cottonwood Foundation and the American Section of the Friends World Committee, which facilitated visits to Yearly Meetings from the Atlantic to the Pacific. Like William Penn she can only exclaim, "O that they that read me could but feel me!"

Silence is practiced by Friends because silence alone can perceive and communicate the ineffable. They know that any attempt to give adequate verbal expression to inward experience is doomed to failure at the outset. Not even this whole bookful of words can project the Quaker vision, merely the activity which that vision set in motion.

From the year 1656, when the ship *Swallow* landed at Boston with two women on board who called themselves "friends in the Truth"—it was the unsympathetic authorities on shore who called them "Quakers"—until the present, the Friends or Quakers in America have been characterized by faithfulness to certain testimonies: sincerity, simplicity, equality, community and peace.

Quaker history is the story of individuals living out these testimonies in the context of their own times. Varying only with the general outlook of a given period, the testimonies have always been the same. They derive from the premise that there is something divine in every human being. Each person is, therefore, sacred. Each is capable, unassisted, of coming into communion with God. No creed can contain the Quaker faith since God continues to make Himself known in every generation. Outward sacraments and rites are irrelevant because the whole of life is sacramental.

That spark of divinity binds all men together so that none are free while any are ill used, none can be comfortable while any are in want. Although a social order based on this belief demands a perfection which Friends themselves never approximate, it remains the persistent, corporate dream of what they wish themselves and their nation to become.

Early Friends laid themselves open to persecution by demanding freedom of worship and justice for all, by refusing to bear arms and by dramatizing their belief in the equality of all persons, of whatever race, sex, religion, nationality or social position; by adhering strictly to the truth without taking oaths and by practicing simplicity in speech, dress and mode of living.

The physical toll exacted of those early Friends for their nonconformity—"both the spoiling of their goods and the abusing of their bodies"—is a matter of record. But the emotional destruction has not been assessed. Until we understand more about this, we cannot fully comprehend the change in the Quaker character after the persecutions subsided. During their sufferings, Friends were virtually single-minded. Later, having acquired a colony of their own and freedom to worship after their manner, they presented baffling contradictions.

Why was it that, unlike seventeenth-century Friends, who forfeited their goods and risked their lives in order to "publish Truth" to the whole known world, the majority of these later Friends asked only that they be permitted to live quietly on their farms or in their plain but imposing town houses, often becoming by their plainness and industry among the richest people in America?

Why were eighteenth-century Friends increasingly fanatical about their speech and dress, when the people around them no longer cared how they spoke or what they wore? With so many individuals and Monthly Meetings opposing slavery, how was it that the Society of Friends did not corporately renounce slaveholding until the 1770s? Yet it was during the siege of Boston in 1775 that American Quakers established their principle of feeding the hungry and clothing the naked "without distinction of sects or parties." And it was the eighteenth century that produced John Woolman, the most lovable, consistent and influential American Quaker of any age.

How could nineteenth-century Friends have driven away thousands of valued members simply because they acquired a piano or "married out"? Why was it that when they were at their best during the anti-slavery campaign and Reconstruction Friends were also at their worst, quarreling among themselves? Why did those who migrated westward, just when the theory of evolution expanded man's view of the universe, shift from the original Quaker emphasis on God's continuing revelation to a literal interpretation of the Bible?

We have no answers to these fascinating questions. This narrative is only an attempt to intimate what living as a Quaker in America has meant and what it continues to demand. The story begins with Friends' response to world events, which some of us can remember, shortly before the outbreak of the Second World War—a turning point, not only in secular but in Quaker history. A sense of new identity emerged from the Friends World Conference of 1937, when a greater number of races and nationalities assembled in Swarthmore, Pennsylvania, than had ever come together, representing Friends. The Conference "brought a vivid realization that Quakerism was no longer merely an Anglo-Saxon sect but a worldwide movement."

Present-day Friends are preoccupied with twentieth-century problems. But it is impossible to dissociate their concern from expressions of the same concern in earlier periods.

This is not strictly a history. Only representative people and events could be mentioned, in the limited space, while others of equal importance have regretfully been omitted. This is rather a *montage,* an aggregation of occasional pictures, taken from various periods and superimposed one on another. Out of the composite emerges a people who have sometimes been sadly narrow, inconsistent and petty, as well as stirringly prophetic and heroic, renouncing war and championing the poor and the oppressed.

All who cherish our national culture, which Quakers helped form, can learn from their failures and achievements. "We are one with those who preceded and those who will follow after," Errol Elliott reminds us. "If we are not aware of this we shall be like people who do not know where they are going because they do not know where they have been!"

America has not found Friends easy to live with. Gentle, serene, upright—yes. But, at their finest, they present the continual challenge, reaffirmed at their World Conference in the year before this story opens, by Henry Cadbury: "We shall apply to the nation as to the individual the searching question, What shall it profit a man if he gain the whole world and lose his soul?"

Contents

Foreword   vii

1. Quaker Meeting in the Gestapo   1
    The Day of Broken Glass • The Mission to Hitler • Silent worship in the headquarters of the German Secret Police

2. The Lion's Den   7
    The *Swallow* • The *Speedwell* • The *Woodhouse* • Nicholas Upsall

3. Why Did You Remember Me?   12
    "Questions to the President" • The British Blockade • France appeals to American Friends • Missions and service at home and abroad • European refugees

4. One That Can Speak to Thy Condition   20
    George Fox • Robert Fowler builds the *Woodhouse* • Mary Fisher visits the Sultan of Turkey • "A True Relation of the Voyage of the *Woodhouse*"

5. The First Publishers of Truth   29
    Mary Dyer • John Copeland • Humphrey Norton • William Brend • Sarah Gibbons • Dorothy Waugh • Mary Weatherhead • Christopher Holder • Samuel Shattuck • Laurence and Cassandra Southwick • John Rous • Thomas Harris • Josiah Coale • Thomas Thurston • Robert Hodgson • William Robinson • Nicholas Phelps • Joshua Buffum • Josiah Southwick • Nathaniel Sylvester • Daniel and Provided Southwick

6. Hell's Gates   37
    William Robinson and Marmaduke Stephenson hanged on Boston Common • Mary Dyer reprieved • Thomas Macy hurries to Nantucket • Mary Dyer hanged • William Leddra hanged • Wenlock Christison sentenced to hang • The King's Missive • George Wilson dies in Jamestown jail • George Rofe, Robert Hodgson and Robert Stage paddle from the Chesapeake to Narragansett • First session of New England Yearly Meeting

7. Jars and Strife, Marriage, Trial, Travels
   and Colonization   47

   Dissension · Fox sets up Monthly and Quarterly Meetings · Marriage of Margaret Fell and George Fox · Margaret imprisoned in Lancaster Castle again · Penn-Meade Trial · Fox in Barbados and Jamaica · Death of Elizabeth Hooton · Fox travels from Maryland to New England and back · Return to England · Imprisonment at Worcester · *Griffin* lands in West Jersey · *Kent* arrives · *Welcome* reaches Delaware

8. The Holy Experiment   60

   Philadelphia settled · Keith controversy · Death of Fox · Quakers on Nantucket and Rhode Island · Ralph Sandiford · Benjamin Lay · James Logan · The Bartrams · Walking Purchase · Acadians · Friends resign from Pennsylvania Assembly · Friendly Association for Gaining and Preserving Peace with the Indians · John Woolman · Anthony Benezet · Friends give up their slaves

9. Loyalists and Patriots   75

   Meetings for Sufferings · The siege of Boston · Moses Brown · William Rotch · Philadelphia Friends exiled to Virginia · British troops commandeer Friends Meetinghouse in New York · Non-resistance of Nantucket saves the town · Loyalists move to Canada · Rotch and other Nantucketers at Dunkirk · George Logan · Quaker migrations begin · Help for the Shawnees

10. Orthodox and Hicksites   86

    Elias Hicks as recalled by Walt Whitman · Quietism · Friends schools · Hannah Barnard disowned · Ralph Waldo Emerson on Bible societies · The Great Awakening · Separations of 1827-28

11. Paul Cuffe and Prudence Crandall   95

    Cuffe brothers petition General Court of Massachusetts for relief from taxation · Cuffe calls on President Madison · Cuffe takes Blacks to Sierra Leone · Edward Stabler · William Lloyd Garrison · Charles Osborn · Elihu Embree · Benjamin Lundy · Prudence Crandall opens her school to young ladies of color · Connecticut Black Law · Half a century later, Connecticut makes amends

12. Wilburites and Gurneyites   103

    Joseph John Gurney in America · John Wilbur · Separation in New England · R. H. Macy · Joel and Hannah Bean · Charles Perry and Ethan Foster wait on President Lincoln · Eli and Sybil Jones · Nereus Mendenhall · John Greenleaf Whittier

CONTENTS   xiii

13. The Tower of Babel   117

   The Baltimore Association·Quaker Indian Agents·Revivals·Canada
   Yearly Meeting·A garden of the Lord·Joel and Hannah Bean re-
   tire from the conflict·Rufus Jones gets a Prince Albert coat·The
   College Park Association·Founding of Whittier, California·California
   Yearly Meeting·Friends General Conference·Five Years Meeting·
   First Friends World Conference·Howard and Anna Brinton·Pendle
   Hill·Wider Quaker fellowship·Second World Conference·Estab-
   lishment of independent Meetings

14. The Seed   132

   Perry Hayden begins Dynamic Kernels project·The Peace testimony
   ·The Queries·Alternative service

15. Now Is the Time   140

   Thomas Kelly·The British blockade·"Letters from the Past"·Revised
   Standard Version of the New Testament·Civilian Public Service·
   The first camps·A Call to Persons of Good Will·Civilian Training
   Center for Women·Quaker Outposts·Attack on Pearl Harbor

16. Someone to Lean Upon   151

   Friends in Japan·In China·Japanese-Americans evacuated from west
   coast·Jamaica Yearly Meeting·First Japanese-American released

17. The Way Quakers Always Guard People   160

   Rufus Jones recalls twenty-five years of the American Friends Service
   Committee·American Quaker workers interned in Germany·COs become "guinea pigs"·National Mental Health Foundation·Friends'
   concern for the mentally ill

18. Towards the Present and Future Peace   169

   Friends Committee on National Legislation·Mr. Henry Ford becomes
   interested in Dynamic Kernels·Famine in India·Concern for German POWs in the U.S.A.·Interracial Youth Camps·Quaker Service
   in Mexico

19. A Habitation Fit to Dwell In   177

   Three hundredth anniversary of the birth of William Penn·Henry
   Ford withdraws from Dynamic Kernels project·Death of President
   Roosevelt·San Francisco Conference·Quaker relief in Europe, India,
   Middle East·Missionaries in Nepal·Opposition to conscription

20. The Bridegroom Kissed the Bride 184
    Massachusetts offers to pay reparations to Mary Dyer's grandson · Reunion of New England Yearly Meeting · "A Concern for a Just and Durable Peace" · COs undergo starvation experiments · Alice Shaffer goes to Germany to find Quakers · Explosion of atomic bomb

21. A Cubic Inch of Grain 191
    Jessamyn West's *Friendly Persuasion* · Theodore Dreiser's *The Bulwark* · Penal reform · John Bellers · Stephen Grellet · Service Committee work for war victims overseas · Dynamic Kernels' final harvest · Pacific Yearly Meeting

22. The Crown Prince of Japan and the People of China 202
    Elizabeth Gray Vining leaves for Tokyo to tutor the Crown Prince · Esther Rhoads · Emily Balch

23. Happy in the Real Possession 209
    East Africa Yearly Meeting · AFSC receives the Nobel Peace Prize · Concern for the people of Russia · Quaker Work Camps

24. Events at Flushing and Two Journeys to the Holy Land 218
    The Flushing Remonstrance, 1657 · Quakers in Flushing · Robert Lea · Quaker House · Rufus Jones appeals for a Truce of God in Jerusalem · Emissaries to Palestine · Eli and Sybil Jones

25. A Call to What Is Vital 227
    Lucretia Mott · James Michener · Death of Rufus Jones

26. Delegates at Amsterdam, Beethoven in Acre, Missionaries in China 237
    First Assembly of World Council of Churches · Quaker workers overseas · Service Committee undertakes work with Arab refugees in Gaza Strip · Friends Service Unit and missionaries in China

27. Prophets—True and False 248
    Interracial Work Camps · Fair employment practices and open housing · Helen Griffith · Work with Indians · Missionaries in Alaska · Quaker House · *The United States and the Soviet Union, Some Quaker Proposals for Peace* · COs · Meeting with Prime Minister Nehru · Bayard Rustin at Mount Holly · Edward Hicks

CONTENTS

28. Venturing in Where Diplomats Fear to Tread   259
    Retirement of Clarence Pickett and appointment of Lewis Hoskins to Secretaryship of AFSC · Mission to Yugoslavia · Quaker observers at Fifth UN Assembly · Quakers in Cuba · Elizabeth Vining leaves Japan

29. Quakerism's Fourth Century   267
    Third World Conference · Young Friends Gathering

30. A Great People to Be Gathered   274
    American Friends visit the Birthplace of Quakerism

31. A Reaffirmation of Faith   284
    Davis House · Washington Seminars · Conferences for Diplomats · Quaker team in Korea · A Reaffirmation of Faith · *The Quiet Eye* · Scull vs. Virginia · *Integration of Washington Schools* · Integration of Friends schools

32. Speak Truth to Power   294
    Quaker mission to Russia · Reunion of Philadelphia and New York Yearly Meetings · Friends in the Middle East · Quaker mission to Montgomery, Alabama · Three hundredth anniversary of the arrival of Friends in America

33. The *Golden Rule* and the *Phoenix*   306
    Voyage of the *Golden Rule* · Sputnik's Questions · Meeting for Worship in Honolulu jail · The *Phoenix*

34. To Stand Like a Trumpet   316
    Friends in Little Rock · John Woolman windows · Statue of Mary Dyer · Green Circle Program and SAS · Quaker Theological Discussion Group

35. The Two Oceans   326
    Friends in the Middle East · Friends in Cuba · Work with refugees in Miami · The Dalai Lama · Help for Algerian refugees · Wedding of the Crown Prince of Japan · Evacuees from Farmville, Virginia · Quaker House in Atlanta · Charlotte Friends Fellowship · Meeting with Premier Khrushchev · Quaker Peace Witness, 1660–1960 · Quakers in Bolivia

36. Love Measured by Its Own Fulness   339
    Interview with President Kennedy · Interview with President Hoover · Earlham School of Religion · Are Quakers Puritans? · Quaker education · *The Hospital* · *Quaker Profiles* · William Bacon Evans · Service to prisoners · Statement on Vietnam and World Peace · Evangelical Friends Alliance · Douglas Steere in St. Peter's · The Pope in New York · Norman Morrison · The Mohonk Conferences

37. Peace Bridge   354
    Quakerism, A View from the Back Benches · *Phoenix* sails for Vietnam · Friends' efforts to send medical supplies to both sides · Fiftieth anniversary of the AFSC · Vandalism at Conscience Bay

38. The Time Is This Present   361
    Marjorie Nelson · Fourth Friends World Conference

39. Joined to All the Living   369
    Quaker Service-Vietnam · Capture and release of Marjorie Nelson

40. A Loaf of Bread   381
    Friends General Conference · Poor People's Campaign · Stephen Cary's testimony · Euell Gibbons · Friends relief in Nigeria and Biafra · *An Uncommon Controversy* · Maine Indians · New Swarthmoor · The Lamb's War

41. Quaker Hospitality   391
    Support and hospitality of AWOL soldier in the Friends Meeting at Cambridge, Massachusetts

42. Who Shall Live?   403
    Death of Courtney C. Smith · Inauguration of Richard M. Nixon · Nigeria-Biafra relief · *Search for Peace in the Middle East* · Board of Missions, Friends United Meeting · "Man and the Economy" · *Who Shall Live?* · Support of AWOL soldiers in Atlanta and Pasadena · Joan Baez · Quaker educators · CRASH · Quaker Service-Vietnam

43. Fair to the Present   415
    Concerns for prisoners and Blacks · Moratorium March · Friends in Korea · Anna Brinton · Reunion of Baltimore Yearly Meeting · "The Future of Friends" · Young and nonagenarian Friends

44.	So Long as We Both Shall Live A Quaker wedding	424
	References	430
	Index	444

1 Quaker Meeting in the Gestapo

The crowd pressing into Downing Street was singing jubilantly "For he's a jolly good fellow" when Neville Chamberlain returned to London from his encounter with Adolf Hitler at Munich.

"I believe," the Prime Minister shouted from an upstairs window of Number 10, "it is peace in our time."

Less than a year from that day, the Second World War would break out. But for the moment, hostilities seemed to have been averted and there was rejoicing in the streets of England and France.

A few weeks later, in the streets of Germany, there was anguish. On November 10, 1938, the "Day of Broken Glass," Jewish shop windows were shattered, Jews were killed and thirty-five thousand were taken to concentration camps. It was impossible for a Jew to buy food.

Across the Atlantic, members of another faith, who had been helping the victims of Nazi persecution both in the United States and through their workers in Vienna and Berlin, hurriedly met together in Philadelphia to consider what more they might do.

Only the previous day, Clarence E. Pickett, Executive Secretary of the American Friends Service Committee, had had a conversation with President Franklin D. Roosevelt.

"I wish," Clarence Pickett said fervently, "that it had been you, sitting across the table from Hitler, instead of Chamberlain."

Was it possible that the President might yet have a talk with Hitler face to face?

"He then told me that he had considered trying to arrange such a conference, both of them traveling to the Azores. But at the moment, he was more concerned about building up a strong United States air force.

"I reminded him that Hitler had said he was prepared to discuss disarmament, and that, even though it might not be said sincerely, the German people thought it was and were themselves in deep dread of another war. It seemed to me that one of the best ways to give them a chance of expression would be to take seriously the statement of their leader. The President agreed with this in principle."

Reflecting on that conversation later, during the Korean war, Clarence Pickett observed, "Then, as now, I questioned in my innermost heart whether one can with one hand prepare the instruments of war and with the other hand the instruments of peace."[1]

The Friends who met in consultation after the Day of Broken Glass decided to make a direct appeal to Hitler.

On December 2, three Quakers quietly boarded the *Queen Mary* in New York: Rufus M. Jones, Chairman of the American Friends Service Committee, D. Robert Yarnall, Clerk of Philadelphia Yearly Meeting (Orthodox), and George A. Walton, Clerk of Philadelphia Yearly Meeting (Hicksite).

They were not clergymen, empowered with ecclesiastical authority, nor diplomats, trained in the art of negotiation and backed by military might. They were a philosopher, an engineer and an educator, who simply took seriously Isaiah's charge that they must share their bread and help the oppressed, if their light was to break forth as the morning.

American Friends were already preparing to send relief to the victims of Japanese bombardment in China. They were educating Arab children in Palestine and Africans in Kenya. They were helping unemployed miners in Pennsylvania to build homes; they were maintaining a Health Service in West Virginia, where they initiated a family planning program; they were working with American Indians on the reservations and with sharecroppers in the Mississippi Delta.

All across the United States, Quaker farmers were contributing wheat for victims of the Spanish Civil War. Bales of clothing were being shipped every week from Philadelphia to American Friends Service Committee workers, who distributed relief both in Loyalist and Nationalist Spain, disregarding party lines, responding only to suffering—to the thousands of starving children and the refugees in the mountains, who had no protection from the cold.

Now this Quaker Mission proposed to call on Hitler, hoping to arrange with him for the emergency feeding and more rapid emigration of the Jewish population.

Looking back, one may think the plan naive. But Friends were not underestimating Nazi ruthlessness. They simply clung to the hope that it still might be tempered by an impartial, personal appeal. And from the middle of the seventeenth century, when farmers and servant girls, weavers and shoemakers pleaded for religious toleration before Oliver Cromwell, Governor Endicott of Massachusetts, the Pope, the Sultan of Turkey, even before five-and-twenty flabbergasted Portuguese bishops in the Palace of the Inquisition, Friends never were afraid to "speak truth to power."

Nor was this the first time they felt called to bring food to Germany. They were old hands at it. In the summer of 1919, the American Friends Service Committee, then only two years old, sent Carolena Wood, a New York Friend, Dr. Alice Hamilton and Jane Addams, both "friends of Friends," to Berlin to determine the extent of relief needed. They found that due to the war and the blockade one million German children were likely to die from starvation.

With the help of Herbert Hoover, who was then Chief of the American Relief Administration, Friends succeeded in sending workers and food to centers throughout Germany, where the Service Committee's red and black star, painted on the door, signified love and a meal.

Quäkerspeisung, these meals were called by the pathetic young recipients, whose parents found it hard to believe that citizens of a nation which had vanquished them would rescue their children purely from motives of love. There must be a catch in it somewhere. Obviously, this was a typical American advertising stunt, probably sponsored by the Quaker Oats Company! In reality, the cereal firm had no connection with the Quakers.

But many, many people who were not Quakers backed this program. They contributed the bulk of the funds. The two governments undertook the shipment of supplies and facilitated travel for personnel. These volunteers were not necessarily members of the Society of Friends. They were men and women of various backgrounds, trained in many fields, whose chief qualification for this job was the depth of their concern—their caring.

Like all other American Friends Service Committee undertakings, this was no missionary endeavor. The workers themselves drew strength from worshiping together; their decisions were arrived at after the manner of Friends, with full expectation that through corporate seeking they would sense divine leading. But they did not preach the Gospel to the folk they came to help. Children were hungry, therefore they were fed; they were cold, so they were clothed. Older people were in need of kindness, therefore they were offered sympathy and love. These acts alone witnessed to the Quaker faith.

In several German cities, the streets where Child Feeding Centers were established during the 1920s still are affectionately called "Quäkerstrasse." Thus, ironically, the name, which a seventeenth-century English judge foisted in scorn on Friends who bade him tremble at the word of God, became, in the course of time, beloved. And Friends, who had patiently suffered being called Quakers, now began to use the name themselves, making it interchangeable with the one their forerunners had chosen.

The first Quaker Child Feeding Program in Germany continued until 1925. In its last phase, the work was overseen by Elizabeth and Robert Yarnall of Philadelphia. When he received the Hoover Medal, it was with this citation: "Humanitarian, engineer, and a leader in the engineering profession, who rendered outstanding service as a member of a mission that fed the children of Germany at the end of the World War."

Now, fourteen years later, just before a second World War, Robert Yarnall was going back to Germany to do the job again.

A Meeting for Worship was held before the Mission sailed. In the living silence, Rufus Jones felt moved to say, "We can almost certainly accomplish some practical things which need personal attention. Whether we can influence minds or soften hearts or make spiritual forces seem real—that remains to be seen. We shall do our best and wisest and we shall go in the strength of God."[2]

He spoke not only for himself and his companions but for all the American Quakers in whose name they undertook the Mission.

Later he wrote, "Our minds were so occupied with the desire to get help and relief to those who were suffering that we gave almost no thought to the dangers which confronted us on this visit."[3]

He was nearly seventy-six years old and not in the best of health. Yet he communicated enormous vitality. It emanated from his serene faith and the breadth of his vision. Humor gave buoyancy to his concern. In the hearts of his students at Haverford College and the thousands of people who heard Rufus Jones give an address or speak in Meeting, something was kindled, an aspiration which has kept his spirit alive to this day.

With no armor but the rightness of the errand, this elderly Friend crossed a turbulent ocean in midwinter to call upon Adolf Hitler. That Elizabeth Jones, his wife, and their daughter Mary did give some thought to the dangers, as his biographer intimates, is scarcely surprising.[4]

He had been obliged to cancel a trip to the Middle West, scheduled for the days which he was now spending on the Atlantic. Crossing out the earlier commitments, he wrote in his pocket diary for December 5, "We need the note of adventure, of the heroic and costly, not the twittering of birds over a volcano."[5]

The third member of the Mission, George Walton, was the principal of George School in Newtown, Pennsylvania. In that quiet corner of Bucks County, long ago, a Quaker minister and painter, Edward Hicks, illustrated the prophecy of Isaiah with his "Peaceable Kingdom": "The wolf shall also dwell with the lamb, and the leopard shall lie down with the kid: and the calf, and the young lion, and the fatling together, and a little child shall lead them."

But in Berlin, when the three American Quakers arrived at the end of 1938, greeted by the worst weather in eighty years, it was the Führer who was doing the leading.

Joseph Goebbels, the Nazi Minister of Propaganda, satirically announced the coming of "The Three Wise Men."

"We hope they will make themselves known when they are here. Then we will know, you see, when to begin to quake—quake duly before the Quakers from U.S.A. They want to formulate plans for curing us and ameliorating the situation in Germany. Don't expect us to take them seriously. We can't help it, we must laugh."[6]

The Quakers from the U.S.A. were met by their Berlin workers, by German Quakers and others who came from England and Holland to add the weight of their concern.

Seeing Hitler, it was immediately evident, was out of the question. Perhaps Goering—but this failed, too. In the end, after the Mission had tried every other avenue of approach, it resolved to seek an interview with the Chief of the German Secret Police, Richard Heydrich, better known as the Hangman. The Friends appealed to Raymond Geist, the American Consul General, to arrange such an interview.

"If ever there was a good man," Rufus Jones recalled later, "he was one. He said, 'I will do what a man can.' He put on his hat and went into the storm. In about half an hour, we were summoned."[7]

Six soldiers in black shirts with helmets and rifles escorted the three pacifists to the headquarters of the Gestapo, the German Secret Police. Great iron doors swung open. Through seven corridors, up five flights of stairs—at last, the Friends reached a room where the Consul General of the United States awaited them.

"I have done it," he announced. "Two chief officers of the Gestapo have been delegated to hear your plans."

Heydrich was visible through a window, but the Friends could only speak with his subordinates, to whom they gave this statement: "We represent no governments, no international organizations, no parties, no sects and we have no interest in propaganda. . . . We came to Germany in the time of the Blockade. . . . We were the first to arrive in Vienna after the war. We do not ask who is to blame. . . . Our task is to support life and to suffer with those who are suffering."[8]

The two "hard-faced, iron-natured men" read the statement and listened while Friends outlined their plans. Finally, the officers left the room to consult their chief, promising to return in about twenty-five minutes with the decision.

Rufus Jones has left a moving account of what happened then.

"During this awesome period we bowed our heads and entered upon a time of deep, quiet meditation and prayer—the only Quaker Meeting ever held in the Gestapo!"

To believe in "that of God in *every* man," even the most unlovely, must have demanded great faith; to remember that violence violates the divinity in the aggressor as well as the victim, so that we are obligated to act in love toward both, must have taken great strength in that unique Meeting.

"It proved to have been rightly ordered," Rufus Jones recalled. "The two men returned at the announced time and the leader said: 'Everything you have asked for is granted.' I said, 'That is splendid. We should like to have the report in writing.' 'No,' the leader said, 'the Gestapo does not give its decisions in writing.' 'What will be the evidence, then,' I asked, 'that this decision has been made?' 'Every word,' he said, 'that has been spoken in this room has been recorded by a mechanism and this decision will be in the record.' We were glad then that we had kept the period of hush quiet and had uttered no words for the record!"[9]

The Quaker silence, that "knowledge of things beyond what words can utter,"[10] had, in all innocence, outmaneuvered the German Secret Police.

2 The Lion's Den

On Christmas Eve, the Three Wise Men sailed from Cherbourg aboard the S.S. *Franconia*. They were happily taking back to Philadelphia authorization for the dispatch in January 1939 of American Quaker Commissioners to Germany and Austria with funds for relief of the persecuted people. These commissioners were to oversee the distribution of food and facilitate emigration.

As they steamed into New York Harbor, returning from a nation of concentration camps, the Three Wise Men must have been filled with emotion when they passed the Statue of Liberty. The loving welcome that awaited them contrasted sharply with the rude reception accorded the first Friends who landed on this continent.

The *Swallow* sailed into Boston in July of 1656 with two women on board, Mary Fisher and Ann Austin. Mary was young, "a Maid whose Intellectual Faculties was greatly adorn'd by the Gravity of her Deportment."[1] She had been a servant in Yorkshire. Hearing George Fox, the founder of the Quaker Movement, preach, she became "convinced of the Truth." She was brutally whipped at the University of Cambridge, when she presented the Quaker testimony against "preaching for hire and filthy lucre" to the students, who were preparing to enter the Church. Two years of imprisonment in York Castle did not discourage her from crossing the ocean to communicate "Truth" to the Puritans of Boston. Ann came from London. The mother of five children, she was "stricken in years."[2] Yet she, too, felt called to sail to the New World, bringing the news of God's universal love.

The women had come from England by way of the island of Barbados. When their luggage was searched in Boston, it was found to consist chiefly of books. These recorded the spiritual experiences of the people who called themselves Friends or Publishers of Truth.

Richard Bellingham, the Deputy Governor, convened a special council of the magistrates. It declared that the books "contained most corrupt, heretical, and blasphemous doctrines, contrary to the truth of the gospel here professed amongst us,"[3] and on a summer's day, the hangman burned the books in the Boston market place.

While there was as yet no law making it a punishable offense to be a Quaker—one would soon be enacted—Mary Fisher and Ann

Austin were hustled off to the jail. Their bodies were searched for tokens of witchcraft.

So fearful were the magistrates of the Quaker "doctrine" that they threatened to fine anyone five pounds who would endeavor to speak with the prisoners. An elderly colonist, Nicholas Upsall, hearing that the women were being starved, bribed the jailer to furnish them with food.

When Mary Fisher and Ann Austin had been imprisoned for five weeks, Simon Kempthorn, the master of the *Swallow*, was put under a bond of one hundred pounds to take the women away again, "he defraying all the charges of their imprisonment."[4]

Why was it, a contemporary demanded scornfully of the Boston magistrates, that "two poor Women arriving in your Harbour . . . so shook ye . . . as if a formidable Army had invaded your Borders?"[5]

Two or three days after the *Swallow* sailed out of Boston, the *Speedwell* sailed in, bringing a second band of Friends from England—four men and four women. At New Amsterdam the *Speedwell* stopped and picked up one more passenger, Richard Smith, who lived in Southampton, Long Island. While on a visit to England, he had met Friends and had become convinced of the Truth. Upon his return home, he was cited in the Records of the town of Southampton as "an emissary of Sathan, a Quaker." He would be more graciously cited by posterity for the distinction of having been the first Friend on the continent of North America. According to the Records, Richard Smith was "banished out of the town . . . for his unreverend carriage toward the magistrates," which probably means that he refused to take off his hat.

The Boston authorities lost no time in sending Richard Smith back where he came from, by boat rather than over land—which would have been more convenient—to guard against his infecting their colony with "his Poysonous Doctrine."[6]

Meanwhile, the other *Speedwell* Friends were imprisoned. At the end of two months, they were shipped home to England.

The window of the jail had been boarded up to prevent their talking to anyone. Somehow, the spirit of God, which they proclaimed, must have leaked out through a crack, for it touched the heart of Nicholas Upsall, the old man who rescued Mary Fisher and Ann Austin from starvation. He became the first Friend in Massachusetts Bay. Brought before the Court, he reproached the magistrates "in tenderness and love" for the "law made and published against the Quakers."[7] He was fined twenty pounds and banished.

In Sandwich on Cape Cod, he was befriended by Indians. "What a God have the English," their chief observed, "who deal so with one another over the worship of their God."[8]

Eventually Nicholas Upsall reached Rhode Island, that haven of persecuted people.

Back in England, George Fox and two other Friends were in prison at Launceston, Cornwall. The chief complaint against them was that they *"thee* and *thou* all people without respect, and will not doff their hats or bow the knee to any man."[9]

From prison Fox sent his followers an awesome yet heartwarming exhortation: "Let all nations hear the word by sound or writing . . . be valiant for the Truth upon earth. . . . Live in it . . . do not abuse it. . . . And this is . . . a charge to you all in the presence of the living God: be patterns, be examples in all countries, places, islands, nations, wherever you come; that your carriage and life may preach among all sorts of people, and to them. Then you will come to walk cheerfully over the world, answering that of God in every one."[10]

At about the same time, Elizabeth Harris, another London Friend, arrived in Maryland, having also come to America by way of Barbados. She encountered no opposition, although within a few years, Maryland would pass An Act for Suppressing Quakers. In the Puritan settlements around Annapolis and along the Patuxent River as well as on the Eastern Shore, Elizabeth Harris convinced such influential colonists as William Fuller, commander of the military forces; William Durand, one of the governing commissioners; Robert Clarkson, member of the House of Burgesses from Anne Arundel County; and Charles Bayly, who later became governor of the Hudson's Bay Company.

Bayly returned soon after that to England and was imprisoned under the Quaker Act in Newgate. There, recalling the little Friends community that sprang up on the Chesapeake as a result of Elizabeth Harris's visit, he wrote: "And then when I found this beloved life and people, I was like a man overjoyed in my heart . . . because . . . God had raised up such a people . . . in a short time we became . . . as one entire family of love . . ."[11]

Six of the *Speedwell* Friends, who had been deported from Boston, made another attempt to enter—this time by way of Rhode Island—the following year. With the addition of five fresh volunteers, they sailed from London for Newport in June 1657, on board the *Woodhouse,* far too small a vessel for crossing the Atlantic.

Massachusetts Bay made every effort to keep out this "cursed sect of *heretics* . . . who take upon them to be immediately sent of God and infallibly assisted by the Spirit."[12] But after they were banished and whipped out of the colony at the cart's tail, they came back. William Brend, "an ancient and venerable man," who had arrived first in the *Speedwell,* then in the *Woodhouse,* was whipped so furiously in "the Lion's Den, called Boston prison" that "his flesh was beaten black and as into jelly."

Yet nothing stopped the preaching of these humble plowmen and weavers and—scandalous!—these *women.* They needed no church, no pulpit, no ecclesiastical vestments, only the roadside or a chimney corner.

God, they claimed, spoke directly to all people, even simple countrymen and womenkind. Therefore they did not need a clergy. He dwelt in every human being. Therefore they would not harm any man. All of life was a sacrament. Therefore they would not partake of outward sacraments. They would not take oaths, citing the Sermon on the Mount: "Swear not at all . . . But let your communication be Yea, yea; Nay, nay." And even his opponents knew that a Friend's word sufficed.

Quaker men removed their hats when they offered prayer. Since this "hat honor" belonged to God, they refused to bare the head before magistrates. When speaking to persons in power, they would not use titles, calling all men and women by their full names, no more. At a time when it was customary to address an inferior as "thou" and a superior as "you"—the plural conveyed greater respect —Quakers testified to equality by addressing everybody in the singular.

How offensive this testimony of equality must have been to the Puritans can be imagined when one considers the catechism entitled *Spiritual Milk for Boston Babes,* published by John Cotton in 1646. In it, regarding the fifth commandment, children were taught to answer the question "Who are here meant by Father and Mother?" with "All our Superiors, whether in Family, School, Church and Commonwealth."

Increasingly severe punishments were inflicted on Quakers for entering Massachusetts until by 1660 there was none left to resort to but hanging. Marmaduke Stephenson, William Robinson, Mary Dyer and William Leddra gave up their lives on Boston Common.

Twice, Mary Dyer was offered a reprieve if only she would stay away.

"Nay, I cannot," she answered as she went to her execution, "for in obedience to the will of the Lord I came, and in his will I abide faithful unto death."[13]

The eleven Friends on board the *Woodhouse* in 1657, who knew they would end up in the Lion's Den of Boston, and the three on the *Franconia* in 1938, who were returning home after daring to enter the Gestapo in Berlin, were emboldened by the same overpowering concern to publish Truth; to plead for religious toleration and the humane treatment of all people.

Accepting George Fox's charge from Cornwall; mindful of the one delivered on the Mount; of Micah's query, "What doth the Lord require of thee, but to do justly, and to love mercy, and to walk humbly with thy God?" American Quakers sent commissioners to Europe early in 1939, hoping to rescue the persecuted.

James G. Vail of the American Friends Service Committee staff, Robert W. Balderston, who had done Quaker relief work in the 1920s, and Martha, his wife, went to Germany. Harvey C. Perry, a Rhode Island businessman, and his wife, Dr. Julianna Perry, also veterans of overseas missions, went to Austria.

They brought more than physical sustenance. Their very presence was a message of friendship and caring from multitudes of unknown people across the ocean, Friends and friends of the Friends.

For I was an hungred, and ye gave me meat: I was thirsty and ye gave me drink:... Naked, and ye clothed me:... I was in prison, and ye came unto me.

But the hearts which the Quakers had hoped to soften soon became petrified. Extermination replaced emigration. Measured in lives, the Mission to the Gestapo all but failed, though Friends had done their "best and wisest."

How could they have done less, inheritors, as they were, of a faith handed down by men and women who filled the colonial jails of Massachusetts, New Hampshire, Connecticut, New York, Maryland and Virginia; whose cows and bedding were distrained; who were likewise branded, whipped and even executed by their own countrymen because of their religion?

3 Why Did You Remember Me?

According to the United States Census Bureau, in 1940 there were fewer than one hundred thousand members in the Society of Friends. But the friends of Friends—people who were in sympathy with their concerns—were countless.

Contributions poured in for the Service Committee's relief program, from the Red Cross, the American Joint Distribution Committee, the American Christian Committee for Refugees, the Committee on Foreign Relief Appeals in the Churches, the Mennonite Central Committee, the International Committee for the Assistance of Child Refugees, and the Coordinating Council for French Relief. That year, almost a million dollars were channeled through the Service Committee to people in need. Mrs. Dorothy Canfield Fisher, a friend of Friends, organized a Children's Crusade, which awarded $22,500 to Quaker relief work in France.

Mrs. Eleanor Roosevelt announced that the proceeds from her radio broadcasting contract would be given to the Service Committee.

The President, meanwhile, was asking Congress for an additional billion dollars so that our Army and Navy might become the most powerful in the world.

"Have we, now, turned away from the great task of making democracy work?" Fred Eastman, a Friend on the faculty of the Chicago Theological Seminary, asked in an article entitled "Questions to the President." "Of solving our problems concerning the distribution of wealth and of labor, so that no one shall starve and no one be forced to remain idle? For every dollar we put into a war machine means a dollar that cannot be used for relief or education or housing or any work of peace. Must we turn our plowshares into swords and our pruning hooks into spears?"[1]

On May 10, 1940, the Germans invaded Holland, Belgium and Luxembourg. Two days later, they crossed the French frontier, determined to push the French and British forces into the sea. During the week of May 26, 345,585 men were evacuated from Dunkirk. Then, France's request for an armistice made it necessary for the thirty British Quakers who were caring for refugees from the Spanish Civil War in the south of France to return home. But

American Quakers could still administer relief in both occupied and unoccupied zones. "Food, food!" they cabled to Philadelphia. The children were hungry "all the time."

Marshal Pétain sent a personal emissary to President Roosevelt and American Friends, asking for increased assistance. The Service Committee had already decided to send relief into unoccupied France at the rate of fifty thousand dollars a month. But shipping permits could not be procured.

The British Government believed that Hitler would have to capitulate, as the Kaiser had done in 1918, if no ships were allowed to supply food to Germany and the countries she occupied. It insisted that a blockade was the quickest way to end hostilities and liberate the vanquished people of Europe.

Friends, on the other hand, still remembered going into Germany in 1918, when a blockade forced the signing of the Treaty of Versailles. They recalled the misery they had observed then—rickets, pellagra, all the diseases of undernourished children, as well as emotional scars. Those veterans of Quaker service felt that this old bitterness, festering in the German people, had encouraged Hitler's violent drive for revenge.

"No brave new world could be built by a generation whose childhood had been starved and left without kindness and mercy."[2]

Friends pleaded with their nation to increase the immigration quota so that more of the persecuted could flee to the United States—if not adults, at least some of the children. But they pleaded in vain.

"The Jews are being smashed against a wall," wrote a Quaker worker from Berlin. "It is an agonizing spectacle."[3]

The victims themselves implored, "For the love of God, get us out!"[4]

Even when these unfortunate people were eligible for the quota, they had to wait, often until the concentration camp claimed them, because the overworked staffs of the U.S. consular offices in Germany and Austria could not process the applications for visas fast enough.

Clarence Pickett pleaded with the State Department to increase their consular staffs, offering to send over qualified representatives with a knowledge of German whose job it would be to help the officials so that visas could be issued more speedily. These representatives would be paid by the Service Committee with money contributed for the purpose. The offer was rejected.

"It was a hard blow," Clarence Pickett admitted.[5]

Drew Pearson and Robert S. Allen wrote in their syndicated column "Washington Merry-Go-Round" on March 14: "If and when new Ambassadors are exchanged between the United States and Germany—as now seems probable—the man most likely to go to Berlin as U.S. envoy is a Quaker named Clarence Pickett . . . head of the American Friends Service Committee. . . . Pickett's appointment is being promoted on the ground that the United States needs someone in Berlin who is in touch not merely with Nazi officialdom, but with the German people."

No one was more surprised by this disclosure in the press than Clarence Pickett himself. In *For More than Bread* he explains that during the conversation he had had with President Roosevelt in 1938, he had spoken about the need for strengthening our embassy in Germany.

"It seemed to me that the ambassador was taking too lightly the seriousness of the situation in Germany and the possibility that it might eventually involve the United States in war. My appeal was for the President to consider placing the ablest representation possible in the German embassy, in view of the very critical relationships that were developing.

"To my amazement, he turned to me and said that he was thinking of appointing me as ambassador—which was the kind of jest of which the President was capable. I said that of course he didn't really mean that. . . . He said that seriously he had given thought to the possibility of capitalizing on the long-standing reputation of Friends in Germany due to their relief work after the First World War, and that he had not spoken in jest. . . .

"If the matter was ever carried any further by the President, I never heard anything about it. I'm sure that the State Department would have come down strongly on my incapacity to handle the undertaking. And in this case, I should have had to agree with them."[6]

Friends pleaded that summer for a durable peace, for the place of racial and religious groups in a democracy. Institutes of International Affairs, open to all, were held on college campuses: at the University of Oklahoma, at Bethel in Kansas, Grinnell in Iowa, Reed in Oregon, Manchester in Indiana, Denison in Ohio, the University of North Carolina, Mills and Whittier in California, Wellesley in Massachusetts and Muhlenberg in Pennsylvania. Quakers led these institutes and Henry Cadbury, Hollis Professor of Divinity at Harvard, addressed several of them. But most of the speakers were not Quakers. Ex-Chancellor Heinrich Brüning of Germany, Wilhelm Sollmann, who had been a member of the Reichstag, Vera Micheles Dean, of the Foreign Policy Association, Clarence Streit, author of *Union Now*—these were some of the speakers.

The Student Peace Service accepted over one hundred volunteers. They went into communities from Minnesota to Tennessee and from Kansas to Pennsylvania, armed with posters, pamphlets and high hopes. "Youth Wages Peace" was the way these students described their objective, as they courageously tried to convince the people they encountered that their country should not go to war. In the communities they visited, there were those who accused them of gross indifference to the suffering in Europe, who even questioned whether this might not be a youthful "fifth column."

Many Meetings were reaffirming their convictions that "the chief values to be preserved are the human values: life, freedom, and respect for personality; and that war, whether it be waged by our own country or any other, violates and destroys those values."

"We reaffirm our conviction of the right of the individual conscience to hold its own position in time of war, even though it be contrary to the position of the state. Without this right, freedom of religion is a mockery."

Clarence Pickett still believed that American compassion could secure peace. "Throughout our nation, either expressed or implied, ran the hunger to answer violence with a better way," he wrote later. "'Here it is,' was the theme of our plea. 'A great continent opening its doors and its hearts to those who flee violence, especially to the children—who would not flock to such leadership? How could it fail to fire the imagination of the world if it were done on a bold enough scale? How could such a worldwide movement as it could become fail in the end to isolate evil, leave it stranded for lack of disciples? . . . In the end, the real victory will go where the hearts of the people turn.'"[7]

But that summer, the evil had not been isolated.

The American Friends Service Committee representative in France received a cable from the Prime Minister: "The arrival of millions of refugees of all nationalities on the soil of France . . . has imposed on us an enormous burden . . . I entreat you to appeal immediately for the greatest possible financial assistance. . . . Paul Reynaud."

To the already overtaxed Service Committee, the needs of five million additional refugees from northern France and Belgium appeared "staggering." Half humanity seemed to be hunting for a safe haven.

Nevertheless, the Committee sent M. Reynaud the following reply:

"The American public is deeply stirred on behalf of refugees in France, every effort being made to secure large resources for their care."[8]

This response was given wide publicity in the press. On June 4, the New York *Times* said in an editorial: "Certainly the generations-old name of Quakers, which time has made honorable in all men's eyes, does not literally apply to them. They have not quaked at danger nor shrunk from hardship. Hating war, they have done their best to bind the wounds of those who innocently suffer from it."[9]

Friends gave what they could. Other organizations contributed: the Red Cross, Jewish, Protestant and Catholic agencies, and the Council for French Relief. The Service Committee prepared to send additional representatives as well as funds, believing that the presence of persons with a concern for the sufferers was in itself a kind of ministry.

While gratefully accepting funds contributed by others, the Service Committee reiterated the policy of strict impartiality, which Friends have historically upheld in every armed conflict. "Quaker relief in war-torn areas is not to be likened to partisan efforts that bolster one side against another . . . only the need of human beings and the limits of our resources determine the extent of Quaker aid."[10]

Service Committee representatives stayed at their posts in Shanghai, Rome, Lisbon and Barcelona, in Marseilles, Berlin, Vienna and Amsterdam. Emissaries of the American Friends Board of Missions continued their work in Africa, Syria and Palestine.

Errol T. Elliott, then minister of the First Friends Church in Indianapolis, reported on his return from France that although he had not been near actual fighting, "I felt as if I had shared the fellowship of men who were passing through Gethsemanes of suffering."[11]

A Quaker center was established in Mexico City and a hostel in Havana, where refugees were helped to resettle or given shelter while in transit. Quaker workers could, in some cases, reunite families separated by the war. The workers tried to foster a welcoming spirit in the Mexicans and Cubans, to interpret the potential contributions of the strangers in their midst, many of whom were highly skilled artisans, doctors or teachers.

London was bombed. Children were evacuated.

Like many other people, Friends in the United States and Canada offered a home for the duration to English children whose parents might wish to send them overseas. All English parents were torn between the fear of exposing their children to the horrors of war—perhaps invasion—and the anguish of parting with them. Quaker parents were caught in yet another dilemma. Should their children go to America, they would be obliged to sail under armed naval convoy. This was certainly not consistent with the Quaker Peace Testimony.

"If there was greater safety in remaining unarmed in the past," English Quaker parents reasoned bravely, "have we not the faith to demonstrate that truth today?"

But they were, after all, only human and they had already tasted their enemy's ruthless resolve to destroy them, armed or not.

"It would not be fair, perhaps," they rationalized pathetically, "to subject children to such an ordeal, seeing that many of them would not be old enough to have absorbed the significance of such a venture or its spiritual quality."[12]

Some Quaker parents accepted the invitations and sent their children overseas. Some, like the seventeenth-century Friends who expected their children to maintain Meeting for Worship while they themselves suffered in prison for committing this very act, decided that their children must face the dangers to which other English children were exposed.

The Friends Board of Missions was ministering on American Indian reservations as well as in Mexico, Jamaica, Cuba, Palestine and East Africa, where Kansas Yearly Meeting also had a mission. California Yearly Meeting maintained missions in Alaska, Guatemala and Honduras; Oregon in Bolivia; Philadelphia in Japan; Ohio in China and India. In the United States, Friends Meetings were helping to staff settlement houses and summer camps. The Service Committee was still contributing to the resettlement of unemployed miners and working with sharecroppers.

In Washington, D.C., the International Student House provided a home for a large number of foreign students and a meeting place for others, free from all discrimination. This was a time of world-wide tension, yet at the Student House, members of any nationality, color or religion could express their views in a relaxed atmosphere.

And the refugees—those who had got out of Central Europe in time and had actually made it to our shores—needed help. The Jewish and Catholic agencies took care of their own people. But there were many Protestants and many unchurched refugees who turned to the Friends for assistance.

"Summer is not easy for a newcomer from Germany," Eleanor Slater, of the Service Committee staff, wrote that year, "especially summer in the city—the first long summer in America . . . with the heat comes heaviness of mind. 'My bed is big with sorrows,' one Viennese explained on the first hot day of a hot Philadelphia May. Physical discomfort accentuates all the inchoate weight of anxieties, uncertainties, sorrows and nostalgias which most must carry about with them."[13]

In Bryn Mawr, Pennsylvania, at Sky Island in Nyack, New York, at Quaker Hill in Richmond, Indiana, at Scattergood in West Branch, Iowa, hostels were opened for refugees. There they were cared for during the hot weather or until permanent homes could be found. The staff and volunteers who were in charge of these hostels offered vocational counsel, endeavored to find employment for the refugees, gave them instruction in English and explained American customs. Above all, these Quaker workers communicated to the badly bruised victims of hatred a healing friendliness and resurrected hope.

I was a stranger, and ye took me in.

Under the direction of Professor Hertha Kraus of Bryn Mawr College, a group of scholars spent the summer at Wolfeboro, New Hampshire, preparing themselves to teach in American schools. In the fall, Swarthmore and Haverford colleges arranged workshops for foreign professors.

Yale University offered honorary fellowships to refugee scholars. Members of the New Haven Friends Meeting saw to their needs, supplying English lessons, helping with housing, medical care and personal problems. This Friends University Center was designed to give newly arrived teachers, who were authorities in their particular fields but not quite employable because of their European teaching methods, insight into American ways and the thinking of American students.

Quaker women and their friends all across the country sewed and sewed. They collected used clothing, cleaned, mended and then shipped it to the Service Committee storeroom in Philadelphia, where other women distributed it to the needy.

There may have been Friends who did not share this compassion. Some, while asserting that all men are children of their Father and inherit a portion of His divine nature, may even have overlooked the fact that the words mean what they say—*all* men, not just those who call themselves Christians. If there were such Friends, their indifference cannot, as fairness would demand, be cited for they did not go on record.

One tends to forget those who passed by on the other side, to remember with gratitude those who cared. And in those days, there were more significant acts of love than one could possibly recall.

Touching letters, like this one, gave evidence that the love made visible by the Service Committee was in turn proffered by the most destitute newcomer:

"You give me two such fine suits that I am without speaking. I will give one of these suits to a friend of mine. I am happy to see how glad he will be about one of these fine suits. . . . Why did you remember *me*? Such an ugly old chap?"[14]

4 One That Can Speak to Thy Condition

Why did they assume all that, these quite ordinary men and women, living fully in the world—farmers, teachers, doctors, businessmen, housewives—laboring to provide their families with physical and spiritual necessities? What drove them to regard all people as an extension of their families, a like responsibility, so that they continued restless as long as anyone in any part of the world lacked sustenance, habitation, security or friendship?

Precisely three hundred years earlier, in the English county of Leicestershire, a young shoemaker's apprentice was tending his master's sheep. For some time, George Fox had felt divinely called to "act faithfully two ways; inwardly to God and outwardly to man and to keep 'yea' and 'nay' in all things . . . and that I might not eat and drink to make myself wanton but for health . . . wherein is unity with the creation."

He kept to himself, observing that people were "strangers to the covenant of life with God . . . devouring the creation . . . and therefore I was to shun all such. . . ."[1]

"And when the time called Christmas came, while others were feasting and sporting themselves, I would have gone and looked out poor widows from house to house, and have given them some money. And when I was invited to marriages, as I sometimes was, I would go to none at all, but the next day, or soon after, I would go and visit them, and if they were poor, I gave them some money; for I had wherewith both to keep myself from being chargeable to others and to administer something to the necessities of others."[2]

Thus did a young shepherd-shoemaker lay the foundations for centuries of Quaker concern.

Feeling "the Lord's power was with me and over me," George Fox had a hunger for understanding the Scriptures and what he called Truth, by which he meant not simply honesty but that spiritual reality which is verified by inward experience. He turned for instruction to the "priests"—ministers of the Established Church —to the Separatist preachers and to "professors"—those who professed to be religious. But all proved disappointing. "I was sensible" he wrote in his *Journal*, "they did not possess what they professed."³

"Then, at the command of God, on the 9th of the seventh Month 1643, I left my relations and brake off all familiarity with young and old." He wandered from place to place, searching for someone who could speak to his condition. "A strong temptation to despair came upon me. . . . I was about twenty years of age and some years I continued in that condition, in great trouble; and fain I would have put it from me. . . .

"I went to London, where I took a lodging. . . . and I saw all was dark and under the chain of darkness. . . . I was fearful, and returned homewards into Leicestershire again . . . my relations would have had me married, but I told them I was but a lad, and must get wisdom. Others would have had me into the auxiliary band among the soldiery, but I refused; and I was grieved that they proffered such things to me. . . . The priest would come often to me, and I went often to him. . . . And this priest . . . would applaud and speak highly of me to others; and what I said in discourse to him on the weekdays that he would preach of on the First-days, for which I did not like him. And this priest afterward became my great persecutor.

"After this I went to another ancient priest at Mancetter in Warwickshire and reasoned with him about the ground of despair and temptations . . . and he bid me take tobacco and sing psalms. Tobacco was a thing I did not love and psalms I was not in an estate to sing; I could not sing. . . . And he told my troubles and sorrows and griefs to his servants, so that it got among the milk lasses, which grieved me that I should open my mind to such a one. . . .

"Then I heard of one called Doctor Cradock of Coventry, and I went to him, and I asked him the ground of temptations and despair and how troubles came to be wrought in man. . . . Now, as we were talking together in his garden, the alley being narrow, I chanced, in turning, to set my foot on the side of a bed, at which the man was in such a rage as if his house had been on fire. And thus all our discourse was lost, and I went away in sorrow, worse than I was when I came. I thought them miserable comforters, and I saw they were all as nothing to me, for they could not reach my condition.

"After this I went to another. . . . And he would needs give me some physic and I was to have been let blood . . . I could have wished I had never been born. . . .

"As I was walking in a field on a First-day morning, the Lord opened unto me that being bred at Oxford or Cambridge was not enough to fit and qualify men to be ministers of Christ; and I stranged at it because it was the common belief of people. . . . So that which opened in me, I saw, struck at the priest's ministry . . . what then should I follow such for?

"At another time it was opened in me that God, who made the world, did not dwell in temples made with hands. This, at the first, seemed a strange word because both priests and people use to call their temples or churches . . . holy ground, and the temples of God. But the Lord showed me, so that I did see clearly, that he did not dwell in these temples which men had commanded and set up, but in people's hearts. . . .

"After this, I met with a sort of people who held that women have no souls, adding in a light manner, no more than a goose. But I reproved them and told them that it was not right, for Mary said, 'My soul doth magnify the Lord, and my spirit hath rejoiced in God my Saviour.'

"And removing again to another place, I came among a people that relied much on dreams. And I told them, except they could distinguish between dream and dream, they would mash or confound all together; for there were three sorts of dreams; for multitude of business sometimes caused dreams; and there were whisperings of Satan in the night-season; and there were speakings of God to man in dreams. . . .

"Now though I had great openings, yet great trouble and temptation came many times upon me, so that when it was day I wished for night, and when it was night I wished for day. . . ."

Insight came suddenly in 1647 when Fox was twenty-three.

"Now after I had received that opening from the Lord that to be bred at Oxford or Cambridge was not sufficient to fit a man to be a minister of Christ, I regarded the priests less, and looked more to the dissenting people. . . . But . . . I saw there was none among them all that could speak to my condition. And when all my hopes in them and all men were gone, so that I had nothing outwardly to help me . . . then, Oh then, I heard a voice which said, 'There is one, even Christ Jesus, that can speak to thy condition,' and when I heard it my heart did leap for joy."[4]

Fox began walking through the Midland counties of England,

going from one market town to another, telling the people he met along the way about "the Truth in them, and the Spirit and the teacher within them."[5]

Those who had not felt uplifted by the sermons they heard in the Anglican and Puritan churches were convinced by these words. But Fox's eccentricity, his unwillingness to pay homage to men who considered themselves his superiors, and his fearlessness drew opposition from the magistrates and clergy.

In 1649, Fox was arrested in Nottingham. He was soon released. The following year he was imprisoned on a charge of blasphemy at Derby. At the end of six months, he was offered his freedom on condition that he "take up arms for the Commonwealth against the King. But I told them I lived in the virtue of that life and power that took away the occasion of all wars. . . ." So he was relegated to the felons' dungeon six months longer.

In May of 1652, while Fox was wandering through Lancashire, he "spied a great high hill called Pendle Hill, and I went on the top of it . . . and there . . . I was moved to sound the day of the Lord."[6]

He did, preaching with new power and convincing many people as he traveled northward into Yorkshire and west to the Lake District. In Ulverston he stopped at the manor house. Swarthmoor Hall, the home of Judge Fell and his wife, Margaret, was known to be a place where itinerant preachers were welcome.

That was a momentous day. Margaret Fell became convinced of the Truth and for the next fifty years Swarthmoor Hall served as a center for Friends. It was Margaret who held them together. Wherever they were, they wrote to her and she kept them in touch with one another.

Only four years after Fox climbed Pendle Hill, his followers were carrying the Quaker message to the New World. But when Mary Fisher and Ann Austin and the company on board the *Speedwell* were deported from Massachusetts at the captain's expense, shipmasters refused to take any more Quaker passengers.

In 1657, Robert Fowler, of Bridlington, Yorkshire, was building a boat, which he named the *Woodhouse*. He had been convinced by William Dewsbury, a shepherd, one of Fox's first converts. While Fowler was building his boat, he heard a voice within him. "It was said within me several times, Thou hath her not for nothing, and also New England presented before me," he wrote in his log.

"When she was finished and fraughted and . . . brought to London . . . others . . . confirmed the matter in behalf of the Lord."

But Fowler knew that he was taking great risks. "Entering into reasoning," he considered the possible "hardships and loss of my life, wife and children, with the enjoyment of all earthly things." These thoughts he says, "brought me as low as the grave." Through the ministration of George Fox, who was eager to dispatch his followers to the ends of the earth, Fowler was "raised up again" and "by the strength of God I was made willing to do His will. . . ."[7]

And so on June 3, 1657, the expedition got under way.

Six of the eleven Friends who boarded the *Woodhouse* in London were making their second westward voyage. They had come to Boston the year before in the *Speedwell*, just after Mary Fisher and Ann Austin were expelled, but they, too, had been deported.

Ann Austin and Mary Fisher were not among the little company in the crowded *Woodhouse*. Ann Austin was preaching at home, where she would shortly be imprisoned. and, within a few years, would succumb to the plague which claimed almost one hundred thousand lives in London during 1665. Mary Fisher was missing, not because the setback in New England had diminished her zeal but because she was sailing in the opposite direction, bound for Smyrna. Forced by bad weather to land on Zante, the island of Ulysses—then a Venetian possession—she made her way, alone this time, clear across Greece to Adrianople—over five hundred miles on foot—bearing a message from the Most High God to Mohammed IV, Sultan of Turkey.

The Sultan, who had a reputation for inordinate cruelty, received this young Englishwoman with the courtesy customarily accorded an ambassador, since she bore a message from another sovereign, and, through an interpreter, listened gravely to the words sent by the Most High God. When they had been delivered, the Sultan offered Mary Fisher the protection of an armed escort for her return. She declined and traveled alone safely, observing upon her arrival in England that she had been treated with greater kindness by the Sultan and his subjects than by her countrymen in Massachusetts. "The English," she declared, "are more bad."

Eventually, Mary Fisher did return to America, having, most appropriately, married William Bayly, a Quaker sea captain. They settled in Charleston, South Carolina.

Although Mary Fisher and Ann Austin were not aboard the *Woodhouse*, four of the eleven passengers were women.

Fowler records that "our dearly beloved W.D." (William Dewsbury, who had convinced him) came to see them off. He was fresh out of prison in Northampton, where he had been charged with deceiving people by telling them there is no original sin. Two days after the *Woodhouse* sailed, Dewsbury wrote to Margaret Fell concerning the voyagers, "They were bold in the power of the Lord" and predicting "many dear children shall come forth in the power of God in those countries where they desire to go."[8]

There still exists the log of this voyage, endorsed by George Fox. It is entitled "A True Relation of the Voyage undertaken by me Robert Fowler, with my small Vessel called the *Woodhouse* but performed by the Lord like as he did Noah's Ark, wherein he shut up a few righteous persons, and landed them safely, even as at the Hill of Ararat."

"Upon the first day of the fourth Moneth received I the Lord's servants aboard, who came with a mighty hand and an outstretched arm with them, so that with courage we set Sayl . . . shortly after, the South winde blew a little hard, so that it caused us to put in at Portsmouth."[9]

There, replacements were found for those crew members who had been impressed back in London. The new men signed on "for money," a local captain told Fowler, adding that, as far as he was concerned, the "Vessel was so small, he would not go the Voyage" even if the whole boat were given him in payment.

In Portsmouth, Fowler relates, his passengers seized the opportunity to go ashore and preach, convincing many. "Certain days we lay there, wherein the Ministers of Christ were not idle, but went forth and gathered sticks, and kindled a fire, and left it burning. . . ."

Finally, after another landing on the Isle of Wight, where more sticks were gathered and left burning, the *Woodhouse* put to sea. Terror struck the sailors when "presently we espied a great Ship making up towards us" but God "struck our enemies in the face with a contrary wind, wonderfully to our refreshment; then . . . we were brought to ask counsel at the Lord and the word was from him, *Cut through and steer your streightest course, and minde nothing but me.*

"When we had been five weeks at sea, in a dark season . . . having sayled but about 300 leagues, H.N. [Humphrey Norton] falling into communion with God, told me that he had received a comfortable Answer, and also that about such a day we should land in *America*, which was even so fulfilled." They saw "the Lord lead our Vessel, even as it were a man leading a horse by the head, we regarding neither latitude nor longitude, but kept to our Line which was and is our Leader, Guide and Rule. . . . Upon the last day of the fifth Moneth we made land, it was a part of the Long Island, far contrary to the expectation of the Pylot . . . there was drawing to meet together . . . and it was said, That we may look abroad in the evening, and as we sat waiting upon the Lord, they discovered the Land, and our mouths was opened in Prayer and Thanksgiving. . . ."

As they "made towards" the land, "espying a Creek," they found that "this Creek led us in between the Dutch Plantations and Long Island" and they saw the "Wisdom, Will and Power of God" because, while this landfall was "contrary to the expectation of the Pylot," it served a dual purpose. Five of the Friends on board had felt called to deliver their message to the people of New Amsterdam but had not been able to figure out a way to get there. Also, those who were aiming to enter Boston by way of Rhode Island were heartened by the "word which came to C.H. [Christopher Holder]: You are in the road to Road Island.

"In that Creek came a Shallop to meet us, taking us to be strangers making our way with our Boat, and they spoke English unto us, and informed us, and also guided us along: The power of the Lord fell much upon us, and an irresistible word came unto us, That the Seed in America shall be as the sand of the sea . . . which caused tears to break forth with fulness of joy. . . ."

The Friends who felt "the moving" toward New Amsterdam—Robert Hodgson, Richard Dowdney, Sarah Gibbons, Mary Weatherhead and Dorothy Waugh—"the next day we put safely ashore."

Fowler and Hodgson went to see Governor Stuyvesant; "he was moderate both in words and actions."[10] But this was before the five Friends whom the *Woodhouse* left behind had begun their work. Mary Weatherhead and Dorothy Waugh preached in the streets of New Amsterdam the very next day, to the outrage of the burghers, who did not share the Quaker belief in equality of the sexes. Dutch women were expected to be silent on the street.

The two Dutch Reformed ministers sent their view of this event to their superiors in Amsterdam. The date they gave does not correspond with Fowler's because the Gregorian calendar was already in use in the Netherlands while it would not be adopted in England for another century.

"On August 12th a ship came from the sea to this place, having no flag flying from the topmast, nor from any other part of the ship. . . . They fired no salute before the fort. When the master of the ship came on shore and appeared before the Director-General, he rendered him no respect, but stood with his hat firm on his head as if a goat. . . . At last information was gained that it was a ship with Quakers on board. The following morning early they hoisted anchor and sailed eastward toward Hellgate as we call it. . . . We suppose they went to Rhode Island for that is the receptacle of all sorts of riffraff people and is nothing else than the latrine of New England . . . they left behind two strong young women. As soon as the ship had fairly departed, these began to quake and go into a frenzy, and cry out loudly in the middle of the street that men should repent, for the day of judgment was at hand. Our people not knowing what was the matter ran to and fro while one cried 'fire' and another something else. The Fiscal seized them both by the head and led them to prison."[11]

On First-day of that week, Robert Hodgson called a Meeting for Worship in an orchard at Hempstead, Long Island. He was imprisoned in the magistrate's house but managed to preach from a window and "many stayed and heard the truth declared . . . and those who had been my enemies, after they had heard the truth, confessed to it."[12]

But when Governor Stuyvesant heard that this Truth was being declared in his province, he sent the sheriff, the jailer and twelve musketeers with a cart to Hempstead. Two women who had given Hodgson shelter—one with an infant in her arms—were carried the twenty miles to New Amsterdam in the cart. Hodgson was tied to the tail and dragged. Imprisoned in New Amsterdam, starved, he was hung by his hands with weights attached to his feet and unmercifully beaten. Certain townspeople tried to secure his release by offering a fat ox in payment of the fine imposed on him but the Governor insisted on six hundred guilders. When the townspeople offered to raise this sum, Hodgson declined. He was, he insisted, innocent; he had not broken any of the laws of Holland and therefore would not let himself be ransomed.[13]

Meanwhile, the *Woodhouse* was in trouble, too. This was not unexpected. Hodgson and Fowler "had several days before seen, in a vision, the Vessel in great danger . . . this was fulfilled, there being a passage between two Lands, which is called by the name of Hellgate . . . and into that place we came, and into it were forced, and over it was carried . . . rocks many on both sides; so that I believe one yard's length would have endangered loss of both Vessel and Goods; Also there were a scull of fishes pursued our Vessel, and followed her strongly, and along close by our Rudder."

The *Woodhouse* managed to make her way into Long Island Sound, continuing bravely until she reached Newport, Rhode Island, on August 3, 1657, two months after she left London. Robert Fowler declared jubilantly, "The Scripture is fulfilled in our eyes . . . Hells gates cannot prevail against you."[14]

5 The First Publishers of Truth

Suddenly they were all over America, populating the Lion's Den in Boston; penetrating Cape Cod; having their tongues bored, their ears cropped, their hands branded in New Haven Colony. Against brutal opposition, they were declaring God's love through Maryland and Virginia, southward to Albemarle Sound.

It was an inauspicious moment for Quakers to be arriving in Massachusetts. Although the colony was prospering economically, spiritually all was far from well.

The second generation Puritans were less fervent than those who had suffered persecution in the Old Country and braved the wilderness of the New World. Attendance at church might be enforced by law but the experience of conversion, which was requisite for full membership, could not be legislated. Since women and indentured servants were automatically excluded, membership dwindled. This gave the authorities anxiety enough without having outsiders appear who were loudly critical of ministers and the repressive ordinances.

The Quakers were not the first people to be unwanted by the Puritans. Twenty-one years before Mary Fisher and Ann Austin arrived, Roger Williams, the teacher of the church in Salem, was banished for asserting that the state had no jurisdiction over the consciences of men and that it was wrong to tender an oath to an unregenerate person, since the oath was an act of worship. He also claimed that the colonists had no right to land given them by the king, who did not own it; that it should be purchased from those to whom it belonged: the Indians.

Williams fled into the wilderness to the southwest and bought a tract of land from the Narragansetts. Remembering "God's merciful providence to him in his distress," he named his settlement Providence and declared that it was to be a "shelter for persons of distressed conscience."[1]

This was none too soon, for in 1644, Massachusetts passed laws against the Baptists and Rhode Island became their haven.

Two years after Roger Williams was banished, the General Court of Massachusetts passed the same sentence on Anne Hutchinson, a clergyman's daughter and the wife of a respected colonist. She was charged with "having divulged and promoted opinions that cause trouble." She had invited women to come to her house and hear her comment—not always favorably—on the Boston ministers' sermons. The Court considered this "not comely in the sight of God, nor fitting your sex." It also charged Anne Hutchinson with "having joined in affinity and affection to those upon whom the Court has passed censure."

The Church of Boston then excommunicated her.

"In the name of Christ I do deliver you up to Satan," the minister declared. "I do account you from this time forth to be a heathen and a publican . . . a leper to withdraw yourself out of this congregation."[2]

In *The Standard of the Lord Lifted Up*, Mary Hoxie Jones dramatically reconstructs the scene that followed:

"Most of Anne's former supporters were frightened and remained silent. One of them, William Coddington, dared to show that he was still her friend. Another, a young woman, rose and accompanied Anne as she made her quiet, dignified way out of the court room. A stranger who was present asked Governor Winthrop who the companion was. The Governor replied that it was Mary Dyer, the wife of the milliner, William Dyer."[3]

Roger Williams persuaded his friends, the Narragansett chiefs, to sell the island of Aquidneck, later named Rhode Island, to the Hutchinsons, Coddington, and their sympathizers for five fathoms of wampum. The Dyers also fled to Rhode Island. But Massachusetts had not seen the last of Mary. During a subsequent visit to England, she became a Friend. When she returned to Newport, the first wave of English Quakers was arriving and she joined them in challenging the Puritan laws.

A week after the *Woodhouse* landed, John Copeland sent his parents in Yorkshire an account of the voyage. "This is to let you know that I am at Rhode Island and in health, where we were received with much joy of heart; but now I and Christopher Holder are going to Martha's Vineyard in obedience to the will of God. . . . Take no thought of me . . . man I do not fear; for my trust is in the Lord."[4]

The Governor of the Vineyard promptly expelled the two Quakers, but the Algonquins took them in. "You are strangers," the Indians told them, "and Jehovah hath taught us to love strangers."[5]

When the thwarted Friends returned to the mainland, they were arrested in Plymouth, charged with being "extravagant persons and vagabonds." Under threat of being whipped if they returned, they were sent off to Rhode Island.

No sooner were the Pilgrims rid of these two than Humphrey Norton arrived, the Friend who, "falling into communion with God" aboard the *Woodhouse,* "received a comfortable answer." As Norton was being driven out of Plymouth, his shipmates William Brend and Sarah Gibbons came in. And John Copeland, who meant it when he told his parents, "man I do not fear," was already back.

One is moved to sympathize a little with the colonial authorities, even while deploring their cruelty. Their patience was sorely tried by what they called this "cursed sect of *heretics* . . . who take upon them to be immediately sent of God and infallibly assisted by the Spirit."[6]

The Governor and Magistrates of Massachusetts warned their "beloved Brethren and Naighbors of the Collonie of Plymouth" to guard against "such pests." They took the occasion to deprecate what they called "a crying downe of minnestry and minnisters" on the part of the Pilgrims themselves, exhorting them to "reinstate a pious orthodox minnestry."[7]

The Quaker message, with its comforting emphasis on God's love, was irresistibly attractive compared to the Puritan threat of hellfire, which only the Divine Elect had any hope of escaping. The Light within every man and woman was more appealing than the stern authority of the ministers and magistrates.

When Humphrey Norton, with an *H* for heresy branded on his hand, wrote about his own "convincement and call," he must have aroused envy in those who were taught to fear eternal damnation.

"My desire to live justly and to *enjoy God,* set me to inquire after this new Light and what effect it had amongst such as did believe in it. I have obtained mercy, peace with God, redemption from all filthiness of flesh and spirit. . . . His eternal rest, blessed forever."[8]

In Salem, between Roger Williams and the witches, they had Quakers. One who was not yet in New England got reports. "Some there are, as I hear, who meet in silence at a place called Salem."[9]

Dorothy Waugh and Mary Weatherhead, the two "strong young women" who had been seized by the head for preaching in the streets of New Amsterdam, were, after a short imprisonment, sent, hands tied behind them, to Rhode Island. Dorothy Waugh must indeed have been strong, for the following winter, she and Sarah

Gibbons walked from Newport all the way to Salem. "They lodged in the wilderness day and night." The whipping given them in Boston "tore their flesh."[10]

After Christopher Holder and John Copeland were expelled from Sandwich, they went to Salem, where "The Word was soon ingrafted in their hearers," who became "possessors of the same experience and fellow-sufferers with their teachers."[11]

But Holder and Copeland went so far as to preach to the minister in his own church. Holder would have been choked had not a Salem man named Samuel Shattuck intervened. He was arrested as "a friend of Quakers" and taken to Boston. The Quakers themselves were imprisoned and flogged. The "grave and aged couple" who had entertained them, Laurence and Cassandra Southwick, were deprived of their property.

Toward the end of 1657, John Rous, son of a Quaker sugar planter on Barbados, came to Rhode Island and wrote to Governor Endicott, asking for a meeting with the Massachusetts officials so that Friends might explain their faith. He got no reply.

Thomas Harris, another Barbadian Friend, was guilty not only of keeping his hat on in the presence of the Governor but—worse yet—when the hat was removed, his hair turned out to be too long. The marshal was ordered to bring a pair of shears into the courtroom and cut it off. Harris was imprisoned and starved.

The people of Boston could not countenance these outrages. Within the year, they initiated a public subscription for the relief of the sufferers. Money was quickly raised. It paid the prison fees and transportation to Rhode Island of a great many bleeding Friends.

One of these was John Rous. He was soon back. In the summer of 1658, he, John Copeland and Christopher Holder were sentenced to have their right ears cut off. When they announced that they would appeal to Oliver Cromwell, they were told that unless they were quiet, the gag would make them so.

"In the strength of God," they said after the sentence was carried out, "we suffered joyfully, having freely given up not only one member, but all, if the Lord so required."[12]

On September 3, 1658, the day that Cromwell died, Rous wrote to Margaret Fell at Swarthmoor Hall in England from the Lion's Den in Boston: "Great have been the sufferings of Friends in this land, but generally they suffer with much boldness and courage, both the spoiling of their goods, and the abusing of their bodies.

There are Friends, few or more, almost from one end of the land to the other, that is inhabited by the English."

He explained to Margaret Fell that the colonists who became Friends "do more grieve the enemy than we; for they have hope to be rid of us, but they have no hope to be rid of them. . . . The Seed in Boston and Plymouth Patents is ripe. . . . The Seed in Connecticut and Newhaven Patents is not yet ripe, but there is a hopeful appearance."[13]

By the end of 1658, Justice James Cudworth admitted that, while fines of 150 pounds were being imposed against anyone who showed sympathy with the Quakers, "almost the whole town of Sandwich is adhering towards them."[14]

A very interesting young English Friend, Josiah Coale, turned up in Sandwich at about that time, having come to New England on foot with one companion—unarmed, of course—all the way from Virginia. Before leaving his home in Gloucestershire, he had written to Margaret Fell, giving his reasons for going to Virginia:

"I have been made sensible of the groanings of the oppressed seed in that place," he explained, "unto which my soul's love dearly reacheth, and I am much pressed in spirit to go there, and to pass through the Indian's country amongst them, and to go into New England; and it is also upon my dear brother Thomas Thurston to go through with me. Dear, let thy prayers be, that in unity and love we may be preserved and kept together faithful to the Lord. . . ."[15]

Thomas Thurston was one of the *Speedwell* voyagers who tried to enter Boston in 1656, only to be shipped back to England. When he and Josiah Coale landed in Virginia the following year, the colony had legislated that there was to be "no toleration for wicked consciences."[16] Penalties were prescribed for such as Quakers, who were "so filled with the new-fangled conceits of their own heretical inventions, as to refuse to have their children baptised."[17]

The newcomers were soon imprisoned. Upon their release, they crossed into Maryland where they fared no better, for they were charged with "seducing people." The Colonial Records of Maryland state that on July 16, 1658, the Council, held at Patuxent, ". . . ordered the Sheriff of Anne Arundel to take the body of Josiah Coale and Thomas Thurston."

They must have been freed within a few months, for Coale

wrote to George Bishop, his friend at home, telling him that they set out for New England on the second of September.

"And after about one hundred miles travel by land and water, we came amongst the Susquehanna Indians, who courteously received us and entertained us in their huts with much respect . . . several of them accompanied us about two hundred miles further, through the wilderness or woods. . . . For outward sustenance we knew not how to supply ourselves, but without questioning or doubting, we gave up freely to the Lord . . . for his presence and love we found with us daily . . . opening the hearts of those poor Indians, so that in all times of need they were made helpful both to carry us through rivers, and also to supply us with food . . . we came to a place where . . . we remained about sixteen days, my fellow-traveller being weak of body through sickness and lameness; in which time these Indians . . . gave us freely of the best they could get."[18]

When the two Friends were able to move on, the Indians guided them to "the Dutch plantation . . . which was about one hundred miles further."[19] They finally reached Rhode Island.

Thomas Thurston stayed there until the following spring. Then, taking Christopher Holder with him, he returned to Maryland.

The sheriff of Severn, Maryland, had a warrant "to take Thomas Thurston and to keep him without bail or main-prise." When he was brought before the Governor and Council at Patuxent, "Tho. Thurston demanded that his accusers might be brought face to face . . . but there was no accuser appeared, nor could they lay anything to his charge, and when they saw that they had nothing to insnare him with . . . they asked him whether he would take the Ingagement; Thomas Thurston answered he could not swear . . ."[20]

Because he refused to take the oath, Thurston was sentenced to prison for a year and a day.

Christopher Holder and two other *Woodhouse* men—Robert Hodgson, who had had such a bad time in New Amsterdam, and William Robinson, who would soon give up his life on Boston Common—persisted in publishing Truth throughout Maryland.

"There are many people convinced," Robinson reported, "and some that are brought into the sense and feeling of Truth in several places."[21]

Meanwhile back in New England, Josiah Coale had left Rhode Island and gone to Martha's Vineyard. Twenty-five years old, he had already survived several imprisonments in England. But, as William Penn was to say of him, he "baulked no danger."[22] He preached "with such a grace and mode of speech, though without affectation"[23] that the Indians responded with "true breathings after the knowledge of God." Having finished this service, Coale crossed to Plymouth Patent and, together with John Copeland, visited the Algonquins.

As soon as news got around Sandwich that these two were staying at a Friend's house, they were "haled out by violence" and carried off to prison.

The Englishmen did not "love the Quakers," an Indian chief told Coale, when he was once more free to travel among them. "But . . . this is no Englishman's sea or land, and Quakers shall come here and welcome."[24]

On October 19, 1658—perhaps one of those golden days which abound in Massachusetts at that time of year, when the still warm sun shines through crimson, saffron and copper leaves, while the clear air celebrates life—on such a day, the colony of Massachusetts, having found every other punishment defeating, passed that law which decreed death: ". . . And the said person, being convinced to be of the sect of the Quakers, shall be sentenced to banishment, upon pain of death."[25]

As a deterrent, the decree was to prove no more effective than capital punishment has ever been. But in the first instances, it worked.

Old William Brend, who had almost died of beatings in the Lion's Den, was given two days to get out of Boston. He went to Providence.

Next, Salem Friends were ordered to leave. They said, "they had no other place to go to, but had their wives, children, families, and estates to look after, nor had they done any thing worthy of death, banishment or bonds."[26]

"You and we are not well able to live together," Major General Denison told them, "and at present the power is in our hands, and, therefore, the stronger must fend off."[27]

"At a General Court held at Boston, the 11th of May, 1659, It is ordered that Laurence Southwick, and Cassandra his wife, Samuel Shattuck, Nicholas Phelps, Joshua Buffum, and Josiah Southwick, are hereby sentenced . . . to banishment, to depart out of this jurisdiction . . . on pain of death."[28]

Phelps, Shattuck and Josiah Southwick sailed to Barbados and from there to England, seeking redress. Joshua Buffum fled to Rhode Island.

In haste, Laurence and Cassandra Southwick took off for Shelter Island in Little Peconic Bay near the eastern tip of Long Island. This had been purchased by three Barbadians and an Englishman for sixteen hundred pounds of sugar. Nathaniel Sylvester, one of the Barbadians, was a Friend. He soon became the sole owner and made the island a "shelter" for persecuted Quakers.

Back in Salem, the Southwick children, Daniel and Provided, who had nothing left with which to pay the fines imposed upon them for refusing to attend church, were ordered sold into slavery "to any of the English nation at Virginia or Barbadoes."[29] No sea captain would execute the order.

The frightened authorities really seem to have believed their claim that the Quakers had designs "to overthrow the Order established in Church and State."[30] This shows how little they understood the people they were opposing. Like the Puritans themselves, Friends were spiritual revolutionaries. But they were not anarchists. Their commitment to non-violence ruled out change by physical force.

They hoped to persuade; to bring about a change of heart in those who governed. They were not trying to reform but to redeem.

6 Hell's Gates

It was one thing for the *Woodhouse* to navigate safely between the rocks in the East River of New Amsterdam. It was another to plant religious toleration in the colony of Massachusetts Bay or on Plymouth Rock. Hell's gates prevailed against Friends.

For every sally they paid dearly with such inhuman punishments as only insecure men, who kept control by strict repression, could devise. Finally, on October 27, 1659, Mary Dyer, William Robinson and Marmaduke Stephenson were led to the place of execution on Boston Common.

Heavy pressure had been exerted to spare them. Governor John Winthrop, Jr., of Connecticut, pleaded with Endicott, "as on his bare knees," not to hang the Quakers. Governor Temple of Nova Scotia and Acadia offered to take them away and provide for them at his own expense. But Massachusetts stood firm.

In addition to having already been banished, Mary Dyer was guilty of the conduct that her old friend Anne Hutchinson had been charged with, which the Court deemed "not comely in the sight of God nor fitting your sex." This Quaker insistence on the equality not only of man and man but of man and woman must have been as deeply shocking to the Puritans as to the Dutch.

William Robinson was a young London merchant who felt called to sail in the *Woodhouse*. After "laboring in the cause of Truth" through Virginia and Maryland, he ventured into New England. In the Piscataqua River region of New Hampshire, around Dover and Portsmouth and what was called "the Province of Mayn," he had found many people sympathetic to the message of Friends.

The night before his execution he wrote to George Fox.

"On the 8th day of the 8th Month, 1659, in the after part of the day, Travelling betwixt Newport in Rhode Island and Daniel Gould's house, with my dear brother, Christopher Holder, the Word of the Lord came expressly to me . . . by which He constrained me, and commanded me to pass to the Town of Boston, to lay down my life, in His Will, for the completing of His Service."[1]

Marmaduke Stephenson, a Yorkshire farmer, was a recent arrival. He, too, had published Truth in the Piscataqua region. His last statement shows clearly that these men could not have circumvented their awful destiny. They both felt divinely "constrained and commanded." These were simple people and their mandate came to them with disarming simplicity.

"In the beginning of the year 1655, I was at the Plough in the east parts of Yorkshire in Old England . . . and as I walked after the Plough, I was filled with the Love and the Presence of the Living God which did Ravish my Heart . . . which made me stand still. . . . I was required of the Lord to go, and leave my dear and loving Wife and tender Children. . . . I heard that New England had made a Law to put the Servants of the Living God to death, if they returned after they were sentenced away . . . a Vessel was made ready for Rhode Island, which I passed in. So, after a little time that I had been there . . . the Word of the Lord came unto me, saying, Go to Boston, with thy Brother, William Robinson. And at his Command I was Obedient. . . . And this is given forth to be upon Record, that all people may know, who hear it, That *we came not in our own Wills, but in the Will of God . . .*"[2]

On the morning of the execution, a multitude surrounded the prison. "William Robinson put forth his Head at a Window and spoke to the People concerning the Things of God."[3]

Then, hand in hand, with Mary Dyer in the middle, the three walked to the gallows. The drummers were ordered to beat more furiously than usual so that the onlookers would not be able to hear the Quakers' last words.

After the men were executed, Mary Dyer, already bound, was reprieved. They had never really meant to hang her, only to frighten her to death. The Court order stated that she was to be "carried to the place of execution and there to stand upon the Gallows with a rope about her neck until the Rest be executed; and then to return to the prison."[4]

On the same day in Salisbury, Massachusetts, Thomas Macy, a Baptist, who had been summoned before the General Court for having entertained Quakers, wrote to explain that he was unable to travel to Boston because he was sick and could not buy a horse. He protested his innocence.

"On a rainy morning there came to my house, Edward Wharton and three men more . . . by their carriage I thought they might be Quakers and said so; and therefore desired them to pass on their way, saying to them I might possibly give offense in entertaining them; and soon as the violence of the rain ceased they went away and I never saw them since. The time they staid in the house was about three quarters of an hour. They spoke not many wo ds."⁵

Thomas Macy goes on to assure the Court that he did not speak to his uninvited guests, since he was soaked through and his wife was sick in bed; that the Quakers only wanted to know the way to Hampton.

This would indicate that they were heading for the Piscataqua region, where William Robinson and Marmaduke Stephenson, just then in the process of being hanged, had published Truth. As Thomas Macy wrote, he must have been uncomfortably mindful of the gallows.

"If this satisfy not the honoured Court, I shall submit to their sentence," he declared meekly. "I have not willingly offended. I am ready to serve and obey you in the Lord."⁶

Two days later, Mary Dyer was sent home to Rhode Island. And two weeks later, the General Court, "having considered the several offenses of those persons that entertayned Quakers," decreed that "Thomas Macy pay as a fine the sume of thirty shillings and be admonished by the Governor."⁷

He got off lightly compared to those he had "entertayned."

Macy, with several others, had just purchased Nantucket Island, purposing to settle there the following spring. Instead of waiting to be fined and admonished by the Governor, he wisely advanced the date of his departure, preferring the rigors of winter on an island thirty miles out at sea where he would be the first white settler. He hastily got his wife and five children, his friend Edward Starbuck and twelve-year-old Isaac Coleman into a small boat and lit out.

Mary Dyer stayed home that winter. But when she went over to Shelter Island to visit Friends, she told them that she must return to Boston "and desire the repeal of that wicked law against God's people and offer up her life there."⁸

Meanwhile in England, negotiations were proceeding for the return of Charles II, who was exiled in Holland. On April 4, 1660, he issued the Declaration of Breda, in which he promised "liberty to tender consciences, and that no man shall be disquieted or called in question for differences of opinion in matter of religion. . . ."

On May 21; young Charles left Holland for England to ascend the throne. Mary Dyer left Rhode Island for Boston to mount the scaffold.

"Are you the same Mary Dyer that was here before?" Governor Endicott asked her.

"I am the same Mary Dyer that was here the last general court."

"You will own yourself a Quaker, will you not?"

"I own myself to be reproachfully so called."

The death sentence was read again. "But now," the Governor said, "it is to be executed."

When she stood on the scaffold, Mary Dyer was once more offered her life, if she would only stay away.

"Nay I cannot," she declared. "In obedience to the will of the Lord God I came and in His will I abide faithful unto death."[9]

A pompous member of the General Court, who witnessed the execution, reported, "She did hang as a flag for others to take example by."[10]

To the champions of religious liberty in America she became an ensign.

One of the officers of the guard at the execution, Edward Wanton, returned home a changed man.

"Alas, Mother," he is reported to have said, "we have been murdering the Lord's people, and I will never put a sword on again."[11]

He resigned his commission in the army to become a Friend and a shipbuilder in Scituate, Massachusetts. Two of his sons, William and John, and a grandson, Gideon, became governors of Rhode Island.

But the Boston authorities were just getting warmed up. The next Quaker they hanged was William Leddra, a native of Cornwall, who had settled in Barbados and went to New England to plead for toleration. In jail with him was Edward Wharton, one of the Friends who took shelter from the rain at Thomas Macy's.

Leddra's last statement must have caused the authorities to despair of ever making an impression on the Quakers.

"The Noise of the Whip on my Back, all the Imprisonments, and Banishments on pain of Death, and the loud threatenings of a Halter did no more affright me," he declared, "through the Strength and Power of God, than if they had threatened to bind a Spider's Web to my Finger."[12]

While the Court was pronouncing sentence on Leddra, another Friend appeared, Wenlock Christison. He had already suffered severely, yet there he was in Boston again.

"Wast thou not banished on pain of death?"

"Yes, I was."

"What does thou here then?"

"I am come to warn you that you shed no more blood."

When he, too, was sentenced to be hanged, he cried, "Do not think to weary out the living God by taking away the lives of his servants. What do you gain by it? For the last man you put to death, here are five come in his room."[13]

Two old women also came to join the Quakers in the Lion's Den—Elizabeth Hooton, Fox's first convert, who had been imprisoned with Mary Fisher in York Castle, and Joan Brocksopp.

The Friends who returned to England after suffering in America used all their influence to get these persecutions stopped. Holder, Rous and Copeland, each minus an ear, furnished evidence of the treatment Englishmen were receiving in the Colonies. Humphrey Norton, who had been branded in Connecticut, and Joseph Nicholson who, with his wife, had also endured terrible suffering, published accounts of their experiences. George Bishop of Bristol collected all the reports of Friends in a book he called *New England Judged*. The King appears to have read it and to have been disturbed.

The Puritans told their side of the story. "There is more danger in this People to trouble and overcome England," Richard Bellingham warned, referring to the Quakers, "than in the King of the Scotts and the Popish Princes of Germany."[14]

When the news of the hangings reached England, Friends went straight to the King. Even before that, George Fox claimed, he had a premonition:

"And when they were put to death, as I was in prison at Lancaster, I had a perfect sense of it, as though it had been myself, and as though the halter had been put about my neck.

"But as soon as we heard of it, Edward Burrough went to the King, and told him there was a vein of innocent blood opened in his dominions, which, if it were not stopped, would overrun all. To which the King answered, 'But I will stop that vein.' Edward Burrough said, 'Then do it speedily, for we do not know how many may soon be put to death.' The King answered, 'As speedily as ye will.' "[15]

Burrough was one of Fox's first and most able companions. He knew Charles and realized that he would have to keep prodding.

"A day or two after, Edward Burrough going again to the King, to desire the matter might be expedited, the King said he had no occasion at present to send a ship thither, but if we would send one, we might do it as soon as we would. Edward Burrough then asked the King if it would please him to grant his deputation to one called a Quaker, to carry the mandamus to New England. He said, 'Yes, to whom ye will.' Whereupon Edward Burrough named one Samuel Shattuck, who, being an inhabitant of New England, was banished by their law to be hanged if he came again; and to him the deputation was granted. Then we sent for one Ralph Goldsmith, an honest Friend, who was master of a good ship, and agreed with him for £300, goods or no goods, to sail in ten days. He forthwith prepared to set sail, and, with a prosperous gale, in about six weeks time arrived before the town of Boston in New England."[16]

Friends were not above relishing Endicott's discomfort when the banished Quaker returned. The Governor was obliged to remove his hat in the presence of the royal emissary while Shattuck kept his on.

Two centuries later, John Greenleaf Whittier captured this dramatic moment in *The King's Missive*.

> Calm, sedate,
> With the look of a man at ease with fate,
> Into that presence grim and dread
> Came Samuel Shattuck, with hat on head.
>
> "Off with the knave's hat!" An angry hand
> Smote down the offense; but the wearer said,
> With a quiet smile, "By the king's command
> I bear his message and stand in his stead."
> In the Governor's hand a missive he laid
> With the royal arms on its seal displayed,
> And the proud man spake as he gazed thereat,
> Uncovering, "Give Mr. Shattuck his hat."[17]

The mandamus read: ". . . if there be any of those people called Quakers amongst you, now already condemned to suffer death or other corporal punishment; or that are imprisoned . . . you are to forbear to proceed any further therein; but that you forthwith send the said persons (whether condemned or imprisoned) over into their own kingdom of England . . . to the end such course may be taken with them here as shall be agreeable to our laws and their demerits."[18]

For one pitifully brief moment, the Quakers appeared to have in this new King Charles a much needed champion. He had reason to oppose their adversaries. The Puritans had beheaded his father. The New England colonists were already exhibiting an alarming taste for independence, disregarding the Navigation Acts, smuggling when possible. They would have to be brought into line.

Endicott did not wish to incur royal displeasure just when his own people were expressing revulsion over the hangings.

But to send the Quakers back to England, where they could air their grievances in the courts, would be downright dangerous. Of the two evils, it was more desirable to let them loose in America. So the Governor issued the order: "To William Salter, keeper of the prison at Boston, you are requested . . . to release and discharge the Quakers who at present are in your custody. See that you do not neglect this."[19]

Clearly, what the Quakers in America needed was a place of their own, where they could live unmolested and worship after their manner. But the whole Atlantic seaboard was already colonized or owned by someone. The only available territory was inland.

Late in 1660, when Josiah Coale undertook a second journey to Maryland and Virginia, he brought with him from England instructions to negotiate with his Indian friends for the purchase of land. He wrote to George Fox:

"As concerning Friends buying a piece of land of the Susquehanna Indians, I have spoken of it to them, and told them what thou said concerning it, but their answer was, that there is no land that is habitable or fit for situation."[20]

In Maryland, Coale found that Friends had "become as dry branches . . . through judging one another and clashing amongst themselves." But two months later when he was banished, he wrote Fox from Virginia: "These things are well over, and life ariseth over it all."[21]

Virginia had her martyr, too. George Wilson, a North of England Friend, had first published Truth in New Amsterdam, where he experienced, according to a contemporary account, "a line of sufferings and sharp persecution from the Dutch Governor." He then traveled in Maryland and Virginia with George Rofe. Wilson was "thrown into James Towne jail where he ended his life and finished his testimony and left a good savor behind him. . . ."[22]

George Rofe, who had been Wilson's companion, summoned all New England Friends to meet at Newport in June 1661. He and Robert Hodgson and Robert Stage set out from Chesapeake Bay for Narragansett "in a boat very small, being but fourteen foot by the keel" to attend what turned out to be the first session of New England Yearly Meeting.

The intrepid paddlers "went through the place called Helgate and got to Flushings amongst Friends and then came to Gravesend." When they finally arrived within sight of Rhode Island, "the boat turning . . . the bottom up," they almost drowned. The following year, Rofe did drown—"dear George Rofe," his contemporaries called him—"being in a small boat in Chesapeake Bay . . . and weather somewhat rough, the boat was overset . . . he lost his life."[23]

But on that June day in 1661, off Newport, all was still well. Narragansett Indians swam out and rescued the three valiant Friends, who had paddled up from Maryland.

"So we came in at Rhode Island," Rofe later wrote to Richard Hubberthorne of Yealand, Lancashire, "and we appointed a general meeting for all Friends in those parts, which was a very great meeting and very precious and continued four days together."

John Bowne and his wife had come from Flushing, where they were building a house in which they invited Friends to worship. For this, Bowne would subsequently be banished. The Bownes did not, of course, know that would be their fate when they attended the Meeting in Newport. Nevertheless, they were uneasy; their bees had not swarmed before they left home and they feared this might happen while they were gone.

It was exactly five years since Mary Fisher and Ann Austin had tried to enter New England. Now, in spite of brutal opposition, there were Friends, "almost from one end of the land to the other." They came from as far away as New Hampshire and New Amsterdam.

"And the Lord was with His people and blessed them" Rofe wrote to Hubberthorne, "and all departed in peace."[24]

But while "the Lord was with His people" in Newport, the Massachusetts authorities "made an alarm that the Quakers were gathering to kill the people and fire the town of Boston."[25]

The authorities had good reason to be nervous. A few weeks earlier Massachusetts had passed the Cart and Whip Act. This, it was hoped, would create less stir in England than hangings but would be an equally effective deterrent.

The Act provided that any person "not giving civil respect by the usual gestures, or by any other means manifesting himself to be a

Quaker, shall . . . be stripped naked from the middle upwards and be tied to a cart's tail and whipped through the town, and from thence immediately conveyed to the constable of the next town . . . and so from constable to constable till they be conveyed through any of the outwardmost towns of our jurisdiction."[26]

The Cart and Whip Act was enforced with fury. Many of those who were whipped and dragged through snow during the following winter were women. One who suffered more than one can bear to remember was Elizabeth Hooton, who was sixty when she was released from the Lion's Den after the arrival of the King's Missive. She later obtained a certificate from the King which entitled her to settle in any of his Colonies. She returned to Boston, hoping to buy a house in which Friends could worship and traveling ministers could lodge. She also wished to procure a piece of land where Friends who were put to death could be decently interred and "not be buried under their gallows in the open fields." But in spite of her royal certificate, Elizabeth Hooton was unable to settle in Boston. Instead, she was whipped through Cambridge, Watertown and Dedham and left in the wilderness at night for wolves and bears to devour. Somehow she reached Rhode Island.

James Bowden, the nineteenth-century historian, observed, "The Puritans in New England, the Episcopalians in Virginia, the Papists in Maryland, and the Calvinistic authorities of New Amsterdam, whilst differing with and persecuting each other, joined in a common effort to crush this rising and harmless people."[27]

In modern times, many have wondered why those who had themselves experienced religious intolerance were not the first to grant freedom of conscience to all. But how many downtrodden Europeans were there who, finding life, liberty and the pursuit of happiness in the New World, subsequently secured these blessings for other men?

The year the *Woodhouse* sailed to America, George Fox felt a need to write to "Friends beyond Sea, that have Blacks and Indian Slaves," pointing out that God "is no respecter of persons. . . . And he doth Enlighten every Man that cometh into the World. . . . And the Gospel is the Power that giveth Liberty and Freedom . . . to every Captivated Creature under the whole Heavens.

"And so, ye are to have the Mind of Christ, and to be Merciful," Fox reminded those Friends who had Blacks and Indian slaves, "as your Heavenly Father is merciful."[28]

No doubt they were merciful. Yet how is it possible that they, whose own freedom had been curtailed, who gladly accepted the most severe punishment for "theeing and thouing" and not doffing their hats, simply to affirm the biblical verity that God is no respecter of persons—how was it possible that these Publishers of Truth could have slaves?

But in 1661, after that first joyful Yearly Meeting on Rhode Island, George Rofe made a prophecy. He had crossed over into Massachusetts and was promptly imprisoned with six other Quakers. Released later in the summer, they went to Barbados. From there, on the eighteenth of November, Rofe wrote to Richard Hubberthorne, elatedly describing the "very great meeting and very precious" which had taken place in New England the previous June.

"There is a good Seed," he concluded, referring to Friends in America, "and the Seed will arise."[29]

7 Jars and Strife, Marriage, Trial, Travels and Colonization

"The Lord of Heaven and earth we found to be near at hand, and, as we waited upon him in pure silence . . . the Kingdom of Heaven did gather us and catch us all, as in a net, and . . . drew many hundreds to land. We came to know a place to stand in and what to wait in . . . that we often said one unto another with great joy of heart: 'What, is the Kingdom of God come to be with men?' . . . We met together in the unity of the Spirit and the bond of peace."[1]

So it appeared in the North of England to the "Valiant Sixty," the first of the people called Quakers. Having experienced this glory together, they cheerfully accepted persecution. Unity, arrived at not through external discipline but through quiet waiting on the Lord, had been their great spiritual discovery.

Yet, the very year that Friends arrived in America there was discord in London.

"An evil thing begot amongst Friends," Richard Roper wrote to Margaret Fell, "the same as was amongst the Church at Corinth, divisions and strife and contention."[2]

Fox was moved to write to "Friends everywhere . . . take heed of Jars and Strife, for that is it, which will Eat out the Seed in you."[3]

When Josiah Coale made his second visit to Maryland in 1660, he found Friends "judging one another and clashing amongst themselves." Soon after that there was havoc in Virginia, created by John Perrot, an Irish Friend opposed to organization. He split Friends by insisting that all their customs, such as going to Meeting at a specified hour and removing the hat during prayer, should be abolished. He had many sympathizers, but in Fox's opinion, he "ran out from Truth."

This dissension weakened the Society. It had other troubles. In the popular mind, Friends were confused with the Ranters, an older sect, which also believed in an indwelling God. But whereas Friends took their authority from the Light Within, perceived not alone in themselves but in their fellow worshipers, the Ranters rejected all authority and followed their individual leading without reference to the insight of a group. *Answering* that of God in everyone was the distinctive contribution of Friends.

To make this clear, Fox set up five Monthly Meetings in London during 1667 "to admonish and exhort . . . and to take care of God's glory. And the Lord opened to me . . . how I must order and establish the Men's and Women's Monthly and Quarterly Meetings in all the nation, and write to other nations, where I came not, to do the same."[4]

After writing to America, Fox decided, when way opened, to go there. But first, on October 27, 1669, he married Margaret Fell. Nine years his senior, she had been widowed since 1658. After the death of Judge Fell, she began to be harassed for her Quaker activities. In 1668, at the end of a long imprisonment in Lancaster Castle, she was freed but, as it turned out, only temporarily.

Fox had spent almost three years in the dungeons of Lancaster and Scarborough Castles, where he had been "as a man buried alive."[5] Upon his release, he traveled through England and Wales, settling Quarterly and Monthly Meetings. Then he went to Ireland. When he had, as he put it, "cleared himself of the Lord's service thataways," he returned to England, sailing in at Bristol. "And there Margaret Fell and her daughters and sons-in-law met me, where we were married. . . .

"I had seen from the Lord a considerable time before that I should take Margaret Fell to be my wife. And when I first mentioned it to her she felt the answer of life from God thereunto. But though the Lord had opened this thing unto me, yet I had not received a command from the Lord for the accomplishment of it then. Wherefore I let the thing rest, and went on in the work and service of the Lord as before. . . . But now . . . it opened in me from the Lord that the thing should be now accomplished.

"And after we discoursed the thing together I told her if she also was satisfied . . . she should first send for her children, which she did. . . . I was moved to ask the children . . . whether they were all satisfied and whether Margaret had answered them according to her husband's will . . . and if her husband had left anything to her for the assistance of her children, in which if she married they might suffer loss. . . . And the children made answer and said she had doubled it, and would not have me speak of those things. . . .

"And so when I had thus acquainted the children with it, and when it had been laid before several meetings both of the men and women, assembled together for that purpose, and all were satisfied, there was a large meeting appointed of purpose in the meeting house at Broad Mead in Bristol, the Lord joining us together in the honourable marriage in the everlasting covenant and immortal Seed of life. . . ."[6]

They had only a few days together.

"After this I stayed in Bristol about a week and then passed with Margaret . . . to Olveston, where Margaret passed homewards towards the north and I passed on in the work of the Lord. . . .

"And whilst I was in the country I heard that Margaret was haled out of her house and carried to Lancaster prison again. . . ."[7]

William Penn was not present at the marriage, having gone to Ireland to look after his father's estates. He had only lately been released from the Tower of London, where he was imprisoned for publishing a book that refuted the doctrine of the Trinity. "My prison shall be my grave," the twenty-five-year-old had declared, when pressed to recant, "for I owe my conscience to no mortal man." In Ireland, Penn found Friends "of the city of Cork, all but children being imprisoned . . ."[8] Through his influence, they were released before he returned to London in the summer of 1670.

On August 14, 1670, Penn went to Meeting in Gracechurch Street. The Friends Meetinghouse had been padlocked by the authorities. Instead of giving up and going home, Friends worshiped in the street. John Rous, who had lost an ear in New England, wrote: "As near as I could judge, several thousands were at it, but by reason of the multitude of rude people who came mostly to gaze it was more like a tumult than a solid assembly. . . . William Penn was there, and spoke . . . some watchmen with halberds and musketeers came to take him down while he was speaking; but the multitude crowded so close about him that they could not come to him . . . he promised when the meeting was done to come to them; and so he and one Meade, who is lately convinced, went to them; they carried them before the Lord Mayor, and he committed them for riot."[9]

Penn had set out that morning for Gracechurch Street simply to worship with Friends. But inadvertently he began a train of events which established once and for all the principle that a jury cannot be punished for a verdict it brings in, a principle which since that time has been an accepted part of English justice and is cherished in the United States down to the present day.

The indictment claimed that "the aforesaid William Penn and

William Meade, together with other persons . . . assembled and congregated together, the aforesaid William Penn by agreement between him and William Meade before made, and by abetment of the aforesaid William Meade, then and there in the open street did take upon himself to preach and speak . . . against the peace of the said Lord the King, his crown and dignity."[10]

Having studied law at Lincoln's Inn, Penn knew his rights. When he and Meade were brought to trial, he demanded that the law they were alleged to have broken be produced. The Recorder, or magistrate, was enraged by this request. "Take him away," he cried.

"Is this justice or true judgment?" Penn asked. "Must I therefore be taken away because I plead for the fundamental laws of England?"

The jury brought in the verdict: in regard to Penn, "Guilty of speaking in Gracechurch Street"; as for Meade, "Not guilty." Talking in the street was not a crime and the jury had refused to consider the charge of conspiring to riot.

"Gentlemen," the Recorder told the jury, "you shall not be dismissed till we have a verdict that the Court will accept; and you shall be locked up without meat, drink, fire and tobacco; you shall not think thus to abuse the Court; we will have a verdict by the help of God or you shall starve for it."

Penn faced his jury. "You are Englishmen; mind your privilege," he urged. "Give not away your right." The foreman replied, "Nor will we ever do it."

The following day, when the jury refused to budge, the Lord Mayor demanded of them, "Have you no more wit than to be led by such a pitiful fellow? I will cut his nose."

"It is intolerable that my jury should be thus menaced," Penn cried. "Is this according to the fundamental laws? Are they not my proper judges by the Great Charter of England? What hope is there of ever having justice done, when juries are threatened and their verdicts rejected?"

The Lord Mayor commanded the jailer to stop Penn's mouth. "Bring fetters and stake him to the ground."

"Do your pleasure," Penn retorted. "I matter not your fetters."

The Recorder exclaimed, "Till now I never understood the reason of the policy and prudence of the Spaniards, in suffering the Inquisition among them. And certainly it will never be well with us, till something like the Spanish Inquisition be in England. I protest,

I will sit here no longer to hear these things. Gentlemen," he told the jury, "you will find, the next sessions of Parliament, there will be a law made that those that will not conform shall not have the protection of the law. . . . I say you shall go together and bring in another verdict or you shall starve; and I will have you carted about the city as in Edward the Third's time."

"We have given in our verdict," the foreman said, "and all agreed to it, and if we give in another, it will be a force upon us to save our lives."

The jury spent the night locked up. In the morning, it returned the same verdict. When the Mayor still refused to accept it, the jury brought in the verdict "Not guilty" in respect to both prisoners. This was so enraging that each member of the jury was fined forty marks for following his "own judgments and opinions rather than the good and wholesome advice" he had been given. The jury was to be kept in prison until the fine was paid.

Penn stepped up to the bench and cried, "I demand my liberty, being freed by the jury."

But the Mayor told him that he, too, was to be imprisoned until the fine being imposed on him for contempt of court was paid.

"I ask if it be according to the fundamental laws of England that any Englishman should be fined or amerced but by the judgment of his peers or jury?" Penn countered.

"Take him away," the Recorder commanded the Sheriff, "take him away, take him out of the Court."

"I can never urge the fundamental laws of England but you cry, take him away, take him away," Penn declared, adding the famous words that were quickly quoted contemptuously by freedom-loving men all over London, "But 'tis no wonder, since the Spanish Inquisition hath so great a place in the Recorder's heart."[11]

In November the jury was brought before the Court of Common Pleas and released on bail. A year later the whole body of judges declared that a jury could not be fined for its verdict.

Penn and Meade were not released after their acquittal because they refused to pay a fine for keeping on their hats. Someone paid it for them, probably Penn's dying father.

Fox was in London trying to secure Margaret's release. "And I was moved of the Lord to speak to Martha Fisher and Hannah Stringer to go to the King and his Council and to move them for Margaret's liberty. And they went in the Lord's power. And those two women got Margaret's discharge under the broad seal. . . .

And I sent down the discharge by John Stubbs with my horse and sent her word that . . . it was upon me to go beyond the seas into America and Barbados and those countries. And I therefore desired her to come to London, for the ship was then fitting for the voyage. . . .

"Margaret and William Penn and Mary Penington and her daughter Guli and we got the King's barge and they carried us down from Wapping to the ship. . . ."[12]

Years in damp dungeons had broken Fox's health. Nevertheless, on August 13, 1671, he and twelve other Friends sailed from Gravesend in the ketch *Industry* bound for Barbados. The *Industry* was so leaky that "there were little fishes in the ship"[13] and the passengers "had to man the pumps day and night." Off the Azores Islands, they were chased by a Moorish pirate vessel "which caused a great fear among some of the passengers, dreading to be taken. . . ." Unable to decide whether to "tack about and go our old course, or to out-run him," the captain "came to George Fox to advise with him." Like the *Woodhouse* voyagers, who regarded neither latitude nor longitude, Fox calmly told the captain that "the life was over all and the power between them and us." The other Friends were practical. At nightfall, they advised the mariners to "put out all the candles but the one they steered by."[14] After a time, "the moon set . . . there came a fine gale" and the pirates gave up the chase. On October 3, the *Industry* landed safely at Barbados.

"We had many and great meetings among the whites and blacks," Fox recalled later. "And there was some opposition . . . but the power of the Lord and his glorious Truth was over all and reached most in the island."[15]

That he could exult in spiritual experiences during the three months he spent on Barbados is a measure of Fox's single-minded faith and courage, for he was very ill. "I came in weakness among those that are strong . . . but now am got a little cheery and over it. We have ordered men's meetings to be at Thomas Rous's and women's meetings next week. . . . Since I came into this island my life hath been very much burdened, but I hope, if the Lord give strength, to . . . bring things that have been out of course into better order."[16]

What burdened Fox was slavery, which he was observing for the first time. Most of his hosts were sugar planters, who depended on slave labor. When they became convinced of Quakerism, they did not immediately perceive that their consciences would not long countenance the practice of holding slaves.

"Do not slight them," Fox exhorted the planters, "to wit, the Ethiopians, the blacks now, neither any man or woman upon the face of the earth; in that Christ died for all, both Turks, Barbarians, Tartarians, and Ethiopians; he died for the tawnies and for the blacks, as well as for you that are called whites. . . . Christ, I say, shed his blood for them as well as for you . . . and hath enlightened them as well as he hath enlightened you. . . ."[17]

Fox urged Friends to educate their slaves so that they could read the Scriptures and to care for them "as Abraham did, whether they were hired, or born in his family, or bought with his money." Had Fox not been ill, had he been younger and not wearied by imprisonment, he might have gone further. He did urge the planters to treat their slaves as indentured servants. "It will doubtless be very acceptable to the Lord, if . . . masters of families here would deal so with their servants, the Negroes and blacks, whom they have bought with their money, to let them go free after a considerable term of years, if they have served them faithfully; and when they go, and are made free, let them not go away emptyhanded."[18]

Although Fox did not outspokenly condemn Friends for holding slaves, what he said was enough to make trouble. The Barbadian authorities accused the Quakers of stirring up the slaves, who did revolt later. A law was enacted prohibiting "the people called Quakers from bringing Negroes to their meetings" or into their schools.

From Barbados, Fox and his companions sailed to Jamaica. There Elizabeth Hooton, who had come along to look after him, suddenly died. "She was well upon the Sixth-day of the week," Fox wrote, "and deceased the next day . . . in peace like a lamb."

The crossing from Jamaica to Maryland in a leaky vessel, beset by storms, took six weeks. Friends passed "Florida shore where the man-eaters live, and several days we sailed forwards and backwards."[19] When they reached the Patuxent River in Maryland, they found John Burnyeat, an English farmer, waiting for them. He had called a General Meeting of Friends at West River. It lasted four days. On the Eastern Shore near Great Choptank River there was another General Meeting. William Edmundson, who had come to America with Fox, was dispatched to Virginia "where things were much out of order."[20]

"And it was upon me from the Lord to send for the Indian emperor," Fox recalled, writing about Choptank, "to come to the First-day's meeting; and the emperor came. . . . And when it was done he was very courteous and loving and came and took me by the hand, and I bade Friends take him from the meeting to a Friend's house where I was to lodge that night."[21]

A few days later, Fox and his companions started north with two Indian guides. Through the wilderness they pushed, on horseback or in boats, entertained by chiefs in their cabins even when the day's catch had been poor. At length, they reached Oyster Bay on Long Island where another General Meeting was held. Then Fox set sail for Newport to attend New England Yearly Meeting. His Quaker host there was Nicholas Easton, the Governor of Rhode Island. Fox wrote to the magistrates, declaring that there is a law of God in every man which tells him how to act toward others. He exhorted the Legislature to pass "a law against drunkenness and against them that sell liquors to make people drunk. . . . Look into all your ancient liberties and privileges," he urged, "your divine liberty, your national liberty, and all your outward liberties which belong to your commons, your town and your island Colony."[22]

In Newport, crowds came to hear Fox preach.

It was only twenty years since he had heard the Lord say, "If I did but set up one in the same spirit that the prophets and apostles were in . . . he or she would shake all the country . . . ten miles about them." In 1652 it must have seemed the Lord was indulging in hyperbole—ten miles was a long way for ideas to travel. Yet, in 1672, Quakerism was shaking not only England but all parts of the New World.

Quakerism was *being* shaken, too. Those who claimed that they took their authority from the Light Within did not perceive it the same way. It should have led them to unity as it had the Valiant Sixty. Instead, those who professed to be Friends sometimes behaved in a manner other Friends did not find consistent with Truth. Fox saw that there was need for external authority. Dead set against a clergy, he rested responsibility for the conduct of individual members in the whole group. Wherever he went in America, he established Men's and Women's Meetings to create order.

From New England, Fox and his companions returned to Long Island.

"We passed by Point Juda and Block Island and came to Fisher's Island. . . . We went at night on shore and we were not able to stay for the mosquitoes, so we went on the sloop again and put off from the shore and cast anchor. . . . The next day we went out into the Sound but our sloop was not able to live in the water so we turned in again . . . there was exceeding much rain whereby we were much wet, being in an open boat. . . . And we passed the two Horse Races, waters so called, and passed by Garner's Island and Gull's Island. . . .

"And I had a meeting at Shelter Island among the Indians. . . . Their king and his council with about 100 more Indians with him, sat about two hours, and I spoke to them by an interpreter. . . . They sat down like Friends and appeared very loving. . . . So I have set up a meeting among them once a fortnight, and a Friend Joseph Silvester is to read the Scriptures to them, negroes and Indians.

"So we came from Shelter Island . . . and as we passed Plum Island there was a very great fog. And the tide did run so strong for several hours I have not seen the like . . . there came a great rain all the night. Our sloop was open, we were very wet and were driven a great way back again, near Fisher's Island, for it was very dark . . . we passed by Falcon Island and came to the main, where we cast anchor till the storm was over.

"And then we came over the Sound . . . and hard work we had to get the land, the wind being against us. But, blessed be the Lord God of heaven and earth and of the sea and waters, all was well and we came to Oyster Bay. . . .

"James Lancaster and Christopher Holder went over the bay . . . and had a meeting the same day at Rye on the continent. . . . From Oyster Bay we passed about thirty miles to Flushing . . . we had a very large meeting at Flushing with many hundreds of people of the world. . . . A glorious and heavenly meeting it was. . . ."

But afterward there was some heckling.

"As soon as the meeting was done, there stood up a priest's son and laid down three things that he would dispute, the first was ordination of ministers, the second women's speaking, and the third that we held a new way of worship."

Reading Fox's retort, we can almost hear the tone of his voice.

"Then I said that it was like Christ's way of worship which he set up above 1,600 years ago, and was a new way of worship to him and his priests, it being in the spirit and in the truth. And as for women's speaking, such as the apostles did own I owned, and such as they did deny I did deny.

"But what was the priests of New England's ordination? For . . . they have not the same spirit as the apostles had . . . the apostles' spirit did not lead them to cut off people's ears, and to hang and banish them, and imprison, and to spoil people's goods, as they, the priests of New England had done."[23]

Then Fox and his companions boarded a sloop and "took water for the new country, Jersey, down the great bay . . . we passed by Coney Island . . . and by Staten Island . . . we passed about thirty miles in the new country through the woods, very bad bogs . . . we and our horses were fain to slither down a steep place. . . . And so we came to Shrewsbury in East Jersey, and on the first day of the week . . . we had a very large and precious meeting.[24] . . . The next day we passed on. . . . And we swam our horses over a river, and went over on a tree ourselves."[25] They slept in the woods. Finally, they reached Tred Avon [now Easton] in Maryland, and after a stay there they sailed across Chesapeake Bay to Virginia, "where we met Friends and we were refreshed in one another's company . . . we passed about thirty miles through the woods to Carolina. . . ."

They had traveled all the way from Narragansett Bay to Albemarle Sound. "Now, having visited the north part of Carolina and made a little entrance for Truth upon the people there, we began to return towards Virginia."[26]

On May 31, they set sail for home, reaching England June 28, 1673.

"Dear Heart," Fox wrote to Margaret, "This day we came into Bristol near night, from the seas; glory to the Lord God . . . who was our convoy, and steered our course . . . who hath carried us through many perils, perils by water and in storms, perils by pirates and robbers; perils in the wilderness and amongst false professors!"[27]

Margaret, her two daughters and a son-in-law came from Swarthmoor to meet Fox; William Penn and Gulielma—the lovely "Guli" whom he had married the previous spring—came from London, as well as John Rous "and many Friends from several parts of the nation. . . . Glorious, powerful meetings we had there." Fox was so elated, he was "moved to declare. . . . We can challenge all the world."[28]

On the way home, he was arrested, together with his son-in-law, Thomas Lower. For the next fourteen months, he lay in prison at Worcester or traveled to London to stand trial. At one time, "they set a little boy of about eleven years old to be my keeper."[29] After his release, Margaret reported, "We got him home to Swarthmoor, where he had a long time of weakness, before he recovered."[30]

Their troubles weren't over. Two Westmorland Friends, John Wilkinson and John Story, were critical of Fox. They opposed the Women's Meetings and the right of the group to judge its members. For a time the controversy divided Friends, but the "Separates" gradually disappeared.

Although the Declaration of Breda had given brief hope for religious toleration, Charles II's reign turned out to be ferocious for Friends. Upwards of fifteen thousand were imprisoned in England, of whom nearly five hundred died. Friends needed a refuge. It materialized in West Jersey, where Penn became one of the Proprietors. He drew up a plan of government that placed authority in the hands of the governed as Fox had done with the Meetings. "There we lay a foundation for after ages to understand their liberty as men and Christians, that they may not be brought in bondage, but by their own consent; for we put the power in the people."[31]

In 1675, the ship *Griffin* brought a group of London Quakers to West Jersey. They called the place they settled Salem because of "the delightsomenesse of the land."[32] Two years later, the *Kent* sailed from London with 230 more. Charles II "in his barge, pleasuring on the Thames, came alongside and gave them his blessing."[33] When they reached the Delaware, they settled near the place where Fox and his companion "swam our horses over a river, and went over on a tree ourselves." They named it Burlington for their old home in Yorkshire. The following year, the *Shield* brought another hundred Friends. They set up a Monthly Meeting. "Having at first no meeting-house . . . they made a tent or covert of sailcloth to meet under."[34]

They questioned whether "the selling of Rum unto Indians be lawful at all for Friends professing truth."[35] Three years later, a Yearly Meeting was established at Burlington while, back in England, Penn and eleven other Friends purchased East Jersey. Robert Barclay was elected Governor of New Jersey but never came over.

While those on board the *Kent* were crossing the Atlantic, other Friends were crossing the North Sea. As soon as Fox recovered, "It was upon me from the Lord to go to Holland, to visit Friends and to preach the gospel there, and in some parts of Germany."[36] Penn had done this while Fox was in America. He returned to the Continent with Fox, Margaret's daughter Isabel, two Scottish Friends —Robert Barclay and George Keith—and several others. Penn had no way of knowing then that some of the people convinced at this time would become the first settlers of Germantown in his province of Pennsylvania.

The idea of establishing a Quaker colony was still only a dream. But if land could be secured, it would offer a chance to demonstrate what government instituted in accordance with Truth could provide: justice, mercy, harmony and well-being. It would not only be a refuge for the persecuted; it would be "an Holy Experiment."

Charles II owed Admiral Penn a considerable sum of money. After the Admiral's death, his son William persuaded the King to repay the debt in American land—the Delaware Valley, which Josiah Coale had tried to purchase from the Susquehannas twenty years earlier.

"What!" the King is supposed to have cried when Penn made the request, "venture yourself among the savages of North America! Why, man, what security have you that you will not be in their war-kettle in two hours after setting foot on their shores? I have no idea of any security against these cannibals, but in a regiment of soldiers, with their muskets and their bayonets; but, mind you, I will not send a single soldier with you."

"I want none of thy soldiers," Penn replied. "I depend on something better than soldiers—I depend on the Indians themselves. . . ."

"But how will you get their lands without soldiers?"

"I mean to buy their lands of them."

"Why, man! you have bought them of me already."

"Yes; I know I have, and at a dear rate too. . . ."[37]

On March 4, 1681, Penn received the charter to the province of Pennsylvania. With infinite care he laid his plans, drawing up a Frame of Government that ensured religious freedom and outlawed the death penalty except in cases of murder and treason. All Christians with property might vote and hold office. Pennsylvania would be "an example to the nations."

"Mine eye is to a blessed government," Penn wrote before he left, "and a virtuous, ingenious and industrious society, so as people may live well and have more time to give ye Lord then in this

Crowded land. God will plant Americka and it shall have its day in ye Kingdom."[38]

On August 30, 1682, the *Welcome* set sail with Penn and a band of colonists on board. Thirty died of smallpox during the voyage. The ship landed at New Castle, Delaware, on October 27.

"At our arrival we found it a wilderness," one *Welcome* passenger wrote, "the chief inhabitants were Indians and some Swedes, who received us in a friendly manner. . . . Our first concern was to keep up and maintain our religious worship . . . and as we had nothing but love and goodwill in our hearts one to another, we had very comfortable meetings . . . after our meeting was over, we assisted each other in building little houses for our shelter."[39]

From England, George Fox sent the colonists a broadside, reminding them of their commitment. "My friends, that are gone, and are going over to plant, and make outward plantations in America," he wrote, "keep your plantations in your hearts, with the spirit and power of God, that your own vines and lilies be not hurt. And in all places where you do outwardly live and settle, invite all the Indians, and their kinds, and have meetings with them, or they with you; so that you may make inward plantations with the light and power of God . . . and with it you may answer the light, and truth, and spirit of God, in the Indians. . . ."[40]

Half a year after their arrival, the Friends in Pennsylvania spoke of themselves as "a family at peace within ourselves, and truly great is our joy therefore." They sent an Epistle to Friends back in England. Penn, who had left Guli and the children behind, signed it, followed by twenty-five equally homesick "tender and faithful brethren."

"Oh, remember us," they wrote, "for we cannot forget you; many waters cannot quench our love, nor distance wear out the deep remembrance of you in the heavenly Truth. . . . And though the Lord hath been pleased to remove us far away from you, as to the other end of the earth, yet we are present with you . . . our hearts are dissolved in the remembrance of you. . . ."[41]

8 The Holy Experiment

Within a year, Penn's City of Brotherly Love had eighty houses and he had made his treaty with the Indians, which Voltaire called "the only treaty not sworn to and never broken."

As for the Blacks who were brought into the colony as "servants," Penn urged that they be released at the end of fourteen years and that they pay their former owners "two-thirds of what they are capable of producing on such a parcel of land as shall be allotted to them."[1] That slaveholding was wrong, Penn did not state, although five years earlier William Edmundson, the Irish Friend, had made this abundantly clear to New England Yearly Meeting. "And many of you count it unlawful to make slaves of Indians; and if so, then why the Negroes?"[2]

To this question, Friends seemed to have no immediate reply.

But two years after the *Welcome* arrived, the little group that founded Germantown sailed in. Their ship had been pursued by Turkish pirates; they had been in terror of being captured and sold into slavery. This experience made them sensitive to the lot of the Blacks. In 1688, these German and Dutch Friends, led by Francis Daniel Pastorius, declared, "There is liberty of conscience here . . . and there ought to be likewise liberty of the body, except for evil-doers, which is another case. But to bring men hither, or to rob and sell them against their will, we stand against."[3]

The Monthly Meeting in Germantown found this concern "so weighty that we think it not expedient for us to meddle with it here" and referred it to the Quarterly Meeting in Philadelphia, which considered it "a thing of too great a weight" and referred it to the Yearly Meeting in Burlington, where "It was adjudged not to be so proper for this meeting to give a positive judgment in the case."[4] There the matter was left.

The boundary between Pennsylvania and Maryland was unclear, creating constant disputes between Penn and Lord Baltimore. It was not finally settled until almost half a century after Penn's death when Mason and Dixon drew their line, which was marked by milestones brought from England, bearing the arms of the Penns on their northern faces and of the Baltimores on the southern. Lord Baltimore went to England in 1684 to lay claim to Delaware.

Penn hurried after him to retain his hold on it, intending to return in a few months. He left Pennsylvania feeling that in spite of political disagreements between Quakers and non-Quakers, the Holy Experiment was well on its way to success. In two years, three hundred houses had been built in Philadelphia, which had a large population—twenty-five hundred. An elementary school had been opened, and Penn urged the establishment of a high school "of Arts and Sciences."

In England, Friends were being fearfully persecuted. Then Charles II died. His brother James, the Duke of York and a Roman Catholic, became King. A few months later, a decision regarding Delaware was handed down, half of the area in question going to Baltimore and half to Penn. This cleared the way for Penn's return to his province, but now other matters claimed his attention. He and James II had been friends from their youth. Penn was suddenly thrown into a position of influence at Court. He continued to administer the affairs of his colony through letters of instruction to his deputies and he kept promising to return. But he was too absorbed in politics at home. He and Robert Barclay pressed for the release of the 1460 Quakers who were languishing in English prisons. This was not effected until 1686 when the fines that had been imposed on them for not attending church were canceled. Led by Penn, a deputation carried an Address of Thanks from London Yearly Meeting to the King at Windsor.

That same year Penn wrote to his deputies, proposing the establishment of a "Public Grammar School" in Philadelphia. It was to be open to all and the poor were to be admitted without charge. This became the William Penn Charter School, which is still flourishing. Penn also made an agreement with the Delaware Indians for land in Bucks County extending northward as far as a man could walk in a day and a half or roughly thirty miles.

As an absentee landlord, Penn was having difficulty collecting the quitrents the colonists owed him. Life at Court was expensive and he was counting on a return from his investment in Pennsylvania to maintain himself and his family, but all he got from America were bills. His steward on his Irish estates was defrauding him, too. Then in 1688, after James II fled to France, a warrant was issued for Penn's arrest because he was a friend of the deposed King. His tenants in Pennsylvania weren't sure whether he was hiding or in prison. At all events, they saw no need to pay their quitrents, and Penn did not return to Pennsylvania, where he was badly needed. For, in addition to disagreements between Quakers and non-Quakers in the government, there was now also a serious rift between Friends.

They had had nothing but good will in their hearts one to another when they landed in 1682. Seven years later they had their first schism. George Keith, who had traveled to Holland and Germany with Fox and Penn, was now master of the William Penn Charter School. He charged his fellow Quakers in Pennsylvania with denying the divinity of Christ and demanded a creedal statement, which Friends refused. They had always maintained that since Quakerism is a religion of experience, ever open to fresh revelation, it cannot be contained in a creed. Keith and his followers formed a separate body, calling themselves Christian Quakers.

It was the custom for Monthly Meetings to recognize members who, under divine leading, displayed a special gift for vocal ministry. Their names were written in a book—they were "recorded" ministers. This was not an ordination but merely a way of advising other Meetings, where these Friends might visit, that they expressed views acceptable to Friends back home. Recorded ministers met together to consider the spiritual life of their Meeting. Then Friends began to feel that certain older members, who did not have a gift for speaking but who were equally concerned, should be included in the Meeting of Ministers, so it became the Meeting of Ministers and Elders. During Meeting for Worship; these Friends customarily sat in the ministers' gallery on the "facing benches." These were two or three rows of benches at one end of the Meetinghouse, raised in tiers, which faced the body of the Meeting.

George Keith was no longer welcome there. Miffed, his followers "built another gallery at the opposite end of the meetinghouse. With speakers addressing the assemblage from both galleries simultaneously, the situation became intolerable. When some men destroyed the new gallery with axes, Keithians demolished the old one as well."[5] They issued a document, printed by William Bradford, the first printer in the American Colonies, which reviled Friends in the government. Keith was charged with sedition and Bradford's press was confiscated.

Keith and Bradford left Pennsylvania; the Christian Quakers disappeared. But the Holy Experiment had been jolted.

For Friends in England, there was improvement. The Toleration

Act of 1689 made it legal for Dissenters to worship in public and gave Quakers the right to affirm instead of taking an oath. Friends had not outlived all wrath and contention nor wearied out cruelty, but George Fox did live to see the persecution subside.

On January 11, 1691, he went to Meeting at Gracechurch Street, London, where "he declared a long time very preciously." After Meeting, he complained of cold striking at his heart. "I am clear," he said when he was taken to the home of a Friend and put to bed, "I am fully clear." Penn came out of hiding and spent the next two days with him.

"I was with him," Penn wrote to Thomas Lloyd, his deputy in Pennsylvania, "he earnestly recommended to me his love to you all, and said, 'William, mind poor Friends in America.' He died triumphantly . . . 2,000 people at his burial, Friends and others. I was never more public than that day . . . that night, very providentially, I escaped the King's Messenger's hands."[6]

Penn managed to get away in time and stayed out of the Tower, but he lost Pennsylvania. King William, at war with France, saw the folly of having a colony bordering on New France which was governed by a man who would not arm. In August of 1694, the governorship was restored to Penn. He paid a high price for his reinstatement—he had to promise men and money for the defense of Pennsylvania's frontiers. His beloved Guli had died in February. In 1696, Penn married Hannah Callowhill, by whom he had three sons.

At the Yearly Meeting for Pennsylvania, New Jersey and Delaware, held in 1696, Cadwalader Morgan of the Welsh Meeting in Merion near Philadelphia told how he had ordered a slave because he needed help on his farm but then he hadn't felt comfortable. He consulted various Friends, who gave him conflicting advice. So he consulted the Lord, who "made it known unto me that I should not be concerned with them, that is, with slaves."[7] The Yearly Meeting urged "that Friends be careful not to encourage the bringing in of any more Negroes."[8]

It was not until 1699 that Penn returned to Pennsylvania for another two-year stay. He was welcomed, especially by Friends, but the colonists had managed to get along without him for fifteen years. They were getting a firm grip on their economy and their government and they didn't intend to change their habits, either by paying their quitrents or in other cases by improving their behavior, which Penn referred to as "sins so scandalous . . . I am forbid by my common modesty to relate them."[9]

"The brave dreams, the great expectations, and the deep faith which had motivated the founding of Pennsylvania as a 'holy experiment' were largely faded in 1699," Edwin B. Bronner wrote in *William Penn's "Holy Experiment."*[10]

But while many aspects of life in the colony were disappointing, the good relations with the Indians had not changed. Philadelphia Yearly Meeting continued to hold that "the practice of selling Rum or other strong Liquors to the Indians directly or indirectly . . . considering the abuses they make of it, is a thing contrary to the mind of the Lord. . . ."[11] Friends visited the Indians and three ministers from England—Thomas Chalkley, John Richardson and Thomas Story—held Meetings for Worship with them, hoping the Indians would equate the Great Spirit with the Spirit of God. The Indians listened attentively, then continued to worship in their own way.

These same ministers had greater success on the island of Nantucket. It had been settled by Englishmen who could not live in the theocracy of Massachusetts and were already disposed toward the liberal Quaker belief. In 1698, Chalkley spent a few days on Nantucket and made an impression. He was followed by Richardson, who sailed over from Newport with another Friend. The Nantucketers, fearing that they were about to be invaded by the French, rushed down to the shore. The two Friends assured them that they "came in the love of God to hold meetings among them." After hearing Richardson preach, Mary Starbuck, known on the Island as The Great Woman, "stood up, held out her hand, spoke tremblingly, and said, 'this that we have heard is the everlasting truth.'"[12] When Thomas Story went there in 1704, he had such a "concern of mind" for the establishment of a Meeting on Nantucket that he couldn't sleep. In the morning he communicated this to Mary Starbuck. She invited to her home all who wished to meet in "silent waiting on the Lord." Thus began the powerful surge of Quakerism, which was to flourish on Nantucket for almost two centuries.

It was little more than a year since Margaret Fox died in England at the age of eighty-seven. As the wife of Judge Fell and later of George Fox, she made her home, Swarthmoor Hall, a center for the first Publishers of Truth. Unknowingly, a lighted torch had been passed over the ocean from hand to hand. Mary Starbuck now made her home, Parliament House, a center for the first Nantucket Quakers.

Nantucket Monthly Meeting was established in 1708. Eight years later it declared that buying and keeping slaves—there were few on the island—was "not agreeable to Truth."[13] In 1730, these sentiments were put in writing by a Quaker carpenter, Elihu Coleman. Traveling Friends continued to visit Nantucket, linking it with Meetings in every colony and bringing news of the Quaker stand on slavery.

Those Quaker ministers, traveling "under concern" or "in the service of Truth," pushed through the wilderness, into Maine, up the east bank of the Hudson, into the back settlements of Virginia and North Carolina, carrying their message to people who were either geographically isolated or out of unity with the local church. Many of these Quaker ministers came from England. They had known Fox, Penn and other early Friends. Some had been tested by suffering. On horseback or on foot, they brought to the backwoods of America a knowledge of the world and a religious vision that expanded the narrow wilderness. They gave lonely people spiritual kinship with a large community. Through these traveling ministers, Quakers in England and all the Colonies became joined in a common identity, irrespective of borders or political loyalties. Yearly Meetings regulated their own affairs, but they looked for guidance to one another, especially to London Yearly Meeting.

By 1700, half the white population of Rhode Island was Quaker. The governors were Friends, beginning with William Coddington, who left Massachusetts for Newport after defending Anne Hutchinson. He was followed by Nicholas Easton, George Fox's host in 1672. Governor Walter Clarke outmaneuvered Sir Edmund Andros, when he came to Newport after being foiled by the episode of the Charter Oak in Hartford, Connecticut, and demanded the charter of Rhode Island.

Newport was the center for the manufacture of rum made from West Indian sugar and exported to Africa in exchange for slaves, who were sold in the southern Colonies.

But Friends were slowly rejecting the burden. In 1717, New England Yearly Meeting adopted this minute: "A weighty concern being on this Meeting concerning the importing and keeping of slaves. This Meeting therefore refers to the considerations of Friends everywhere to waite for ye wisdom of God how to discharge themselves of that weighty affair. . . ." Ten years later, the Yearly

Meeting declared flatly that the importation of Negroes was not "allowable practice and that practice is censured by this Meeting."[14]

Various Rhode Island Friends denounced the evil. Around 1730, Thomas Hazard of Peace Dale—"College Tom"—became convinced that he should only work his farm with free labor although his father, who was a large slaveowner, threatened to disinherit him. Joseph Arnold of Smithfield Meeting refused to be the guest of Friends who owned slaves when he attended Yearly Meeting at Newport in 1745. Richard Smith informed South Kingstown Monthly Meeting in 1757 that the Lord had given him "a clear sight of the cruelty of making a slave of one that was by nature as free as my own children."[15]

William Burling of Flushing, Long Island, pleaded in 1718 with his "dear brethren" of New York Yearly Meeting not to shield slavery "from the judgment of Truth."[16] His dear brethren must have pointed out the wisdom of keeping silence on this issue, for he said no more after that.

In New Jersey, where slave ships from Africa put in at Perth Amboy, John Woolman, "in the twenty-third year of my age," which would have been 1742, had an experience that was far reaching. "My employer, having a Negro woman, sold her and directed me to write a bill of sale. . . . The thing was sudden, and though the thoughts of writing an instrument of slavery for one of my fellow creatures felt uneasy . . . yet I remembered that I was hired by the year, that it was my master who directed me to do it, and that it was an elderly man, a member of our Society, who bought her; so through weakness I gave way, and wrote it. . . . Some time after this a young man of our Society spoke to me to write an instrument of slavery. . . . I told him I was not easy to write it . . . and desired to be excused. . . . I spoke to him in good will; and he told me that keeping slaves was not altogether agreeable to his mind, but that the slave being a gift made to his wife, he had accepted of her."[17]

Many Friends in Pennsylvania protested against slavery. At first, they were disowned. Ralph Sandiford wrote two anti-slavery books, which Benjamin Franklin printed before 1733, taking care not to have his name appear. And eccentric Benjamin Lay dramatized the plight of the Negro in ways that irritated sedate Friends, as when he stood in front of the Meetinghouse with his bare foot in the snow to demonstrate how slaves suffered for want of shoes in winter. Another time, in 1738, he brought a bladder of pig's blood to Meeting which he concealed until he got up to speak, telling Friends "who are contentedly holding your fellow creatures in a state of slavery" that it was as if they "should thrust a sword through their hearts,"[18] whereupon he punctured the bladder with a sword and sprinkled the blood on the Friends who were sitting near him.

The Yearly Meeting first believed that the solution to the problem lay in a ban on the importation of slaves. Friends were urged to care for such as they already had, to give them a Christian education, to keep families together and to refrain from acquiring any more. In 1711, the Pennsylvania Assembly prohibited the importation of slaves, but the British Government, involved in a thriving slave trade, vetoed the ban.

After 1720, the Yearly Meeting for Friends in Pennsylvania, New Jersey and Delaware met annually in Philadelphia and changed its name to Philadelphia Yearly Meeting. The city was now a busy commercial and cultural center. Prosperity had to learn to live with Quaker simplicity, which wasn't easy. Quaker merchants became highly influential in politics. Music, theater, gambling and other pastimes were denied them. They turned to intellectual pursuits, collected books and became self-made scholars. They founded lending libraries. Quaker emphasis on experience and the continuing revelation of truth led to the study of nature. James Logan, Penn's secretary, contributed papers to the Royal Society of London "Concerning the Crooked or Angular Appearance of the Streaks or Darts of Lightning in Thunderstorms" and "Some Thoughts on the Sun and Moon, When Near the Horizon Appearing Larger than When Near the Zenith." In 1727, Logan began studying the function of pollen in fertilizing corn. Over two centuries later, Frederick B. Tolles, director of the Friends Historical Library at Swarthmore College, declared, "Indeed it is not too far-fetched to suggest a relationship between Logan's experiments and the modern development of hybrid corn upon which much of the wealth of the American Corn Belt is based."[19]

The year after Logan began this study, another Pennsylvania Quaker, John Bartram, planted the first botanical garden in America on the banks of the Schuylkill River. Born in Darby, Pennsylvania, in 1699, John Bartram had, as a boy, turned up a daisy with his plow. Struck by its marvelous symmetry, he began studying flowers, collecting shrubs and medicinal plants, journeying as far north as Lake Ontario and southward to Florida. "It is through the telescope I see God in his glory," he said. Yet, when he was almost sixty, he was disowned by his Meeting because he maintained that while Jesus "was endowed with the power of God he was no more than a man." John's son William, whom the Seminoles called "Pucpuggy"—Flower Hunter—accompanied his father on his travels, making drawings of everything he saw. William kept the first calendar of the migration of North American birds. Later in life he described his explorations in a book entitled *Travels*. This furnished Wordsworth and Coleridge with romantic imagery for their poems.

Living among the Indians, William refuted the white peoples' assertion that the Indians "were incapable of civilization." He suggested "sending men of ability and virtue, under the authority of government, as friendly visitors into their towns: let these men be instructed to learn perfectly their languages, and by a liberal and friendly intimacy become acquainted with their customs and usages, religious and civil; their system of legislation and police, as well as their most ancient and present traditions and history." These men would, William Bartram claimed, be qualified to help the government form and offer the Indians "a judicious plan for their civilization and union with us." It would be an "atonement for our negligence in the care of the present and future wellbeing of our Indian brethren."[20]

As long as Pennsylvania adhered to Penn's policy of treating the Indians fairly there was peace. But Penn's son Thomas, who inherited the Proprietorship, was not interested in Quakerism or in making the colony holy. His father had bought land of the Indians in 1686. Described as "The Walking Purchase," the agreement covered land in Bucks County that extended as far as a man could walk in a day and a half. In 1737, Thomas wished to extend the boundaries in order to sell to certain white men land which they already illegally occupied. Thomas and his advisers saw that they could only secure the land by tricking the Indians. They arranged a "walk" which was, in fact, a swift run made by trained athletes, for whom the underbrush had been cleared in advance. Instead of the thirty miles, which would have been covered by men who were walking, they covered sixty and the surveyors threw in a few more for good measure. Thus did Penn's successors defraud the Indians, who were so angry that at the outbreak of the French and Indian War, they sided with the French against the people of Pennsylvania.

Major George Washington, aged twenty-two, was sent to the Ohio Valley in 1754 to scare off the French. "I have heard the bullets whistle," he wrote his brother after his defeat, "and believe me, there is something charming in the sound." The following year he accompanied the ill-fated General Braddock to Fort Duquesne.

At the same time, the British deported the French inhabitants of Nova Scotia—the Acadians of Longfellow's *Evangeline*—and dumped some five hundred of them, destitute and unable to speak English, in Philadelphia. Anthony Benezet, Master of the William Penn Charter School, made them his concern, collecting money from Friends to house and care for them. The Acadians, who had no reason to trust any Englishman, were sure he was only planning to sell them into slavery.

Cheated by the English, incited by the French, the Indians went on the warpath. Non-Quaker settlers on the frontier demanded protection. The non-Quaker Governor of Pennsylvania declared war on the Delawares. The Quaker Party in the Assembly refused to levy the taxes which the British required for prosecuting the war.

Friends in England, fearing that the Crown might retaliate by imposing an oath of office, effectively disqualifying Quakers from holding office in all the American Colonies, urged the Friends in the Pennsylvania Assembly to resign, which they did in 1756, leaving the government in the hands of the war party.

"Although the colonists failed to live up to the high ideals of the 'holy experiment,'" Edwin B. Bronner, Professor of History and Curator of the Quaker Collection at Haverford College, maintained, "there survived a rich inheritance from the attempt to establish a utopian community. . . . Religious toleration . . . opposition to war, humane treatment of the Indians, and the virtual abolition of capital punishment."[21]

Friends were out of power, but they were not about to give up their testimonies nor to desert their old friends. Under the leadership of Israel Pemberton, nicknamed "King of the Quakers," they immediately formed an organization that was independent of the Yearly Meeting, "neither private, public, nor part of their religious Society, but something of all three."[22] This they named "The Friendly Association for Gaining and Preserving Peace with the Indians by Pacific Measures." They agreed to support it with "a much larger part of our estates than the heaviest taxes of a war can be expected to require."[23] They raised £5000 for the reimbursement or placation of the Indians and mediated between them and the governor, who finally acknowledged that the Indians had been wronged but did nothing to make amends. While Quakers succeeded in quieting the Indians, they did not endear themselves to the militant frontiersmen, who felt threatened.

All this time, John Woolman, still in his early twenties, was being "taught by renewed experience to labour for an inward stillness; at no time to seek for words, but to live in the spirit of truth, and utter that . . . which truth opened." He remained with his employer a few years longer but he was thinking of "some other way of business, perceiving merchandise to be attended with much cumber. . . . My employer, though now a retailer of goods, was by trade a tailor . . . and I began to think about learning the trade. . . . I believed the hand of Providence pointed out this business for me and was taught to be content with it, though I felt at times a disposition that would have sought for something greater. But through the revelation of Jesus Christ I had seen the happiness of humility, and there was an earnest desire in me to enter deep into it. . . ."[24]

Woolman left his employer and began to travel under concern. In 1746, he made his first journey to the South, stopping on the way in Chester County, Pennsylvania. Friends in that area had begun protesting against slavery before Woolman was born. With a companion, he rode on through Maryland and Virginia into North Carolina. Everywhere he observed "this trade of importing slaves from their native country being much encouraged . . . and the white people and their children so generally living without much labour. . . . I saw in these southern provinces so many vices and corruptions increased by this trade and this way of life, that it appeared to me as a dark gloominess hanging over the land; and though now many willingly run into it, yet in future the consequence will be grievous to posterity."[25]

Unlike his predecessors in the anti-slavery cause, Woolman did not excoriate the slaveholders. He spoke to his hosts out of such tenderness and deep humility that they could not take offense, for it was clear that he sympathized as much with them as with the slaves.

Upon his return to Mount Holly in 1746, Woolman "made some observations on keeping slaves." But determined to utter only that which Truth opened, he didn't try to publish this essay, which he called *Some Considerations on the Keeping of Negroes*, until seven years later. Then he submitted it to the Yearly Meeting, which so warmly approved that it paid for the printing and sent the book to every Yearly Meeting in America as well as to London.

In 1755, Philadelphia Yearly Meeting determined to remonstrate with members who imported or purchased slaves, but three years later there were still a few Friends who did not wish to comply. During the Yearly Meeting sessions of 1758, John Woolman listened in suffering silence while several weighty Friends urged the Yearly Meeting to soften its stand against buying and selling slaves. They did not "openly justify the practice of slavekeeping in general," Woolman explains, but they wished to shield those who owned Negroes, asserting that if Friends would just be patient, "the Lord in time to come might open a way for the deliverance of these people."[26]

While the pious procrastinators were speaking, Woolman considered "the purity of the Divine Being and the justice of his judgments."

"Many slaves on this continent are oppressed," he told the Yearly Meeting, feeling an obligation to speak, "and their cries have reached the ears of the Most High." Friends had already been made aware of their duty toward the slaves and, Woolman declared emphatically, "it is not a time for delay."

If, knowing what God required of them, Friends should nevertheless, on account of "respect to the private interest of some persons, or through . . . a regard to some friendships which do not stand on an immutable foundation," neglect to do their duty "in firmness and constancy, still waiting for some extraordinary means" to bring about the deliverance of the slaves, God might, Woolman warned, like an Old Testament prophet, "by terrible things in righteousness God may answer us in this matter."

The slaveowners made one last attempt, suggesting that "a rule might be made to deal with such Friends as offenders who bought slaves in future." Fortunately, "many Friends declared that they believed liberty was the Negroes' right—to which, at length, no opposition was made publicly."

A committee was appointed to visit every family in the Yearly Meeting and to "treat" with those who held slaves so that Friends might be "generally excited" to the practice of the Golden Rule and might look "towards obtaining that purity which it is evidently our duty to press after." Woolman was named to this committee. He does not gloat over his triumph in the *Journal*, which merely states, "the love of Truth in a good degree prevailed."[27]

In the company of one or two other Friends, Woolman began "visiting such who had slaves. Some whose hearts were rightly exercised about them appeared to be glad of our visit. And in some places our way was more difficult, and I often saw the necessity of keeping down to that root from whence our concern proceeded."

Three years after the triumph at Philadelphia Yearly Meeting, Woolman went to New England to attend "in bowedness of spirit . . . the Yearly Meeting at Newport, where I understood that a large number of slaves were imported from Africa and then on sale by a member of our Society . . . My appetite failed, and I grew outwardly weak. . . . I was desirous that Friends might petition the Legislature to use their endeavours to discourage the future importation of them, for I saw that this trade was a great evil. . . ."

When the Yearly Meeting sessions were over, "there yet remained on my mind a secret though heavy exercise, in regard to some leading active members about Newport, being in the practice of slavekeeping . . . I . . . proposed . . . if way opened, to have some conversation with those Friends . . . we met in the meetinghouse chamber . . . After a short time of retirement, I . . . opened the concern I was under, and so we proceeded to a free conference upon the subject. . . . I was deeply bowed in spirit before the Lord, who . . . wrought a tenderness amongst us; and the subject was mutually handled in a calm and peaceable spirit."[28]

Woolman went on to Nantucket where he only stayed briefly, but judging by Monthly Meeting minutes recorded later that year, he made an impression. Captain Timothy Folger, who charted the Gulf Stream for Benjamin Franklin, was about to go "over sea." The Monthly Meeting made certain that before leaving the captain arranged to free his Black girl. In 1769, William Rotch, captain of a large whaling fleet, encouraged one of his Black crewmen to go to court and fight the claims of a man who professed to be his owner. The Nantucket court gave the Black man his freedom.

In 1763, Woolman visited the Indians at Wyalusing on the Susquehanna River. "Love was the first motion," he explained, "and then a concern arose to spend some Time with the Indians, that I might feel and understand their life, and the spirit they live in, if haply I might receive some instruction from them, or they be in any degree helped forward by my following the leadings of Truth amongst them . . . It pleased the Lord to make way for my going at a time when the troubles of war were increasing, and when, by reason of much wet weather, travelling was more difficult than usual. . . ."

The night before he was to leave, Woolman was awakened by a messenger from Friends, who had come all the way from Philadelphia to warn him "that an express arrived . . . from Pittsburgh, and brought news that the Indians had taken a fort from the English westward and slain and scalped English people in divers places." Woolman's anxious friends wanted him to know about these things, "that I might consider them." He went back to bed without telling his wife. It was, he says, a "humbling time," but he felt called to go and when he told Sarah, she "bore it with a good degree of resignation." The account Woolman gives of this hazardous journey is very touching. The Indians welcomed him warmly. One did indeed come at him with a tomahawk but soon perceived that Friend Woolman was not for scalping. The interpreters made the Meeting for Worship, which Woolman held with the Indians, so noisy that Woolman told them, "I found it in my heart to pray to God and believed if I prayed right he would hear me, and expressed my willingness for them to omit interpreting; so our meeting ended with a degree of divine love. And before the people went out I observed Papunehang (the man who had been . . . very tender) spoke to one of the interpreters, and I was afterward told that he said in substance as follows: 'I love to feel where words come from.' "[29]

On the return trip, Woolman had to pass through "the same dangerous wilderness between me and home" but he was "inwardly joyful."[30]

In Philadelphia, Woolman's friend Anthony Benezet, who had rescued the Acadians when they were evicted from the forest primeval, was publishing tracts descriptive of the horrible "Manner by Which the Slave Trade is Carried On." These tracts had a wide circulation.

Once Friends faced the evil they had either committed or condoned, they moved with all possible speed to purify themselves. From 1760 on, manumissions were arranged by slaveowners in all the Yearly Meetings and new Queries were adopted which disapproved of transferring slaves, except to freedom. But Friends went further. They compensated their freed slaves for past services, reckoning what they owed them according to the rate of wages then current.

Owning slaves was unlawful in England but transporting them

from Africa to America was another matter. English shipowners did a flourishing business. So did the shopkeepers who fitted out the ships and furnished the goods for which Blacks were traded. Woolman knew that some English Friends "mixed with the world in various sorts of traffic, carried on in impure channels." He felt moved to visit them.

He set sail from Chester, Pennsylvania on May Day, 1772, traveling in the steerage of the *Mary and Elizabeth* because of "a scruple I felt with regard to a passage in the cabin" although his friends appeared to be concerned for him "on account of the unpleasant situation of that part of the vessel."[31]

When he reached York, having walked a good six hundred miles, Woolman was welcomed by William and Esther Tuke. Falling ill almost at once, he was tenderly nursed by Friends. Far from Mount Holly, from Sarah and his beloved daughter Mary, John Woolman died of smallpox on the seventh of October 1772, twelve days before his fifty-second birthday.

At the same time, back in New England, the Yearly Meeting Woolman had labored with twelve years earlier directed that members who persisted in holding slaves were to be disowned. Philadelphia, New York and North Carolina Yearly Meetings issued the same directive in 1776, Baltimore Yearly Meeting in 1777 and Virginia in 1784.

It took time to make suitable provision for elderly slaves and to labor with recalcitrant owners. But well before the Constitution of the United States of America was ratified, no one who held a slave for whatever reason could be a member of the Society of Friends.

9   Loyalists and Patriots

Friends had barely begun to get clear of slavery before the Revolutionary War broke out, catching them in pincers between the Loyalists and Patriots. Friends were for liberty but against revolution. Each side accused them of supporting the other.

Ever since 1655 when George Fox denied "the carrying or drawing of any carnal sword . . . against thee, Oliver Cromwell, or any man,"[1] Friends had fearlessly declared their convictions before the rulers of England, asserting that all men are created equal. Quakers had died for freedom of speech and assembly, they had forfeited their livestock and household goods rather than submit to taxation for purposes that did not represent what they believed. At the same time, while the American Yearly Meetings were autonomous, they still looked for counsel to London Yearly Meeting. Quaker ministers traveled back and forth; personal friendships and family ties spanned the ocean.

But Friends would not fight; neither would they support either side. As private individuals, they had their preferences, some for one, some for the other. As a Society, they maintained strict neutrality.

A century earlier, London Yearly Meeting had appointed a body called the Meeting for Sufferings, whose function it was to support Friends imprisoned for conscience sake and to help their families. As Quakers in the American Colonies began to incur penalties for not participating in the Revolution, they also appointed Meetings for Sufferings in New England, New York and Philadelphia—the last having a concern for Friends in all of Pennsylvania, Delaware and New Jersey.

The British retaliated for the Boston Tea Party by closing the port in 1774, sending in troops and making General Gage the Governor of Massachusetts. Deprived of shipping, Boston was ruined. Many people fled to the country without any means of support. John Pemberton, Clerk of Philadelphia Meeting for Sufferings, was in New England on business. Writing home to his brother Israel, he reported that Salem and Lynn Friends were taking care of those in Boston. At the same time, English Friends, anticipating further difficulties for their brethren in Massachusetts after the First Continental Congress, encouraged Philadelphia and Rhode Island Meetings to raise a sum of money for relief.

On the eighteenth of April in 1775, General Gage sent a force to Lexington and Concord. The next day someone "fired the shot heard round the world." The Second Continental Congress convened on May 10. The Battle of Bunker Hill took place five weeks later. On July 3, the anniversary of his defeat at Fort Necessity twenty-one years earlier, General Washington sat astride his horse under an elm in Cambridge, Massachusetts, and took command of the American Army lined up on the Common. His headquarters were in Craigie House, between the Common and the Charles River.

To Craigie House on December 14 of that year came a committee of Quakers from Rhode Island, bearing a letter, which read:

> From our Meeting for Sufferings of the people called Quakers, held at Providence, 21st of Eleventh Month, 1775.
> To General Washington
> As visiting the fatherless and the widows, and relieving the distressed, by feeding the hungry and clothing the naked, is the subject of this address, we cannot doubt of thy attention to our representation and request in their behalf.
> The principle of benevolence and humanity exciting our brethren in Pennsylvania and New Jersey to contribute and send to our care a considerable sum of money, to be distributed among such sufferers . . . without distinction of sects or parties, provided they are not active in carrying on or promoting military measures (so that our religious testimony against wars and fightings may be preserved pure); and we being sensible there are many such within as well as without the town of Boston . . . desire thy favorable assistance in getting into the town,—that they may be visited and relieved in such manner as the bearers thereof . . . may think proper; and when their Christian services are accomplished, to be allowed to return to their families in safety.
> Sorrowfully affected with the present calamaties . . .
> We are
Thy Friends

Although the Meeting for Sufferings, which sent this message, had been appointed "to take cognizance of all grievances arising amongst us wherein any Friend or Friends may be affected in his person or property," it was extending help to any war victims "without distinction of sects or parties."

The Quakers from Rhode Island were shocked when they reached Cambridge. "All around the two encampments is one scene of desolation," Moses Brown noted. "Fruit, range, and other trees, fences, etc. some buildings taken smooth away . . ."[2]

General Washington received the committee kindly but said no one was allowed through the lines. Besides, there was an epidemic of smallpox in Boston. The committee would have to meet the Boston Friends on the lines.

Moses Brown was the spokesman for the committee. A Providence merchant, he had, only two years earlier, left the Baptist Church and, upon freeing his slaves, joined the Society of Friends. He told Washington that he would write to General William Howe, commander of the British forces, asking for permission to meet Boston Friends on the lines with a flag of truce so that they could be given the money needed for relief inside the town.

Washington suggested that the committee consult General Nathanael Greene, commander of the Rhode Island forces, who was also in Cambridge. "He is a Quaker," Washington said, "and knows more about it than I do."[3]

General Greene *had* been a Quaker, but when he "took arms," he was disowned. He was still, however, a friend of Moses Brown, and the way was smoothed on the American side. But General Howe would not cooperate. So the deputation went to Marblehead where there was great suffering. Accompanied by the selectmen, Friends went from house to house and in one day "helped between 60 and 70 families . . . they were very necessitous, having before been poor, when the fishery was carried on—which being now wholly stopt . . . their children . . . crawling even into the ashes to keep warm." In Salem and Gloucester, conditions were still worse. Everywhere they went, the Friends found destitute refugees. "I was at Point Shirley about 4 miles from Boston," Moses Brown wrote, "where there has been three loads of people landed from Boston." General Howe had, according to the Boston *Gazette* of November 27, 1775, "sent 300 Men, Women and Children, Poor of the Town of Boston, over to Chelsea, without any Thing to subsist on, at this inclement Season of the Year." Some of them had been exposed to smallpox. Moses Brown took care of their needs. As a daring young man he had traveled to New Jersey to be inoculated.

But "another Friend, not having had the smallpox, attended at another place in Chelsea, where were about 50 persons, that had been cleansed by smoking, most of which we made distribution to."[4]

After spending nearly three weeks and giving away about £2000, the five Friends went home to Providence. Others took over the concern. During 1776, representatives of the Meeting for Sufferings traveled between Boston and Casco Bay, distributing money along the roads where 115 years before Friends had been whipped from town to town.

Some help was sent to Nantucket, which suffered frightfully during the Revolution. Most of the inhabitants were Quakers. A century earlier, Quakers had been accused by the Puritans of designs to overthrow the government. Now, when the other colonists wished to do precisely that, they came under attack again for refusing to cooperate. William Rotch was called before a colonial courtmartial at Watertown. He had once accepted a shipment of muskets in settlement of a debt. After removing the bayonets, he sold the muskets to hunters in Canada. In 1776, a colonial raiding party discovered the bayonets in his warehouse on Nantucket. He was ordered to surrender them.

"The time was now come," Rotch explained, "to endeavour to support our Testimony against War, or abandon it. . . . I could not hesitate which to choose, and therefore denied the applicant. My reason for not furnishing them was demanded, to which I readily answered, 'As this instrument is purposely made and used for the destruction of mankind, I can put no weapon into a man's hand to destroy another, that I cannot use myself in the same way.' The person left me much dissatisfied . . . my life was threatened. . . . I took an early opportunity of throwing them into the sea. A short time after, I was called before a Committee appointed by the Court held at Watertown near Boston, and questioned amongst other things respecting my bayonets. I gave a full account . . . saying, 'I sunk them in the bottom of the sea. I did it from principle. . . . The chairman of the Committee said '. . . every man has a right to act consistently with his religious principles, but I am sorry that we could not have the bayonets, for we want them very much.'"[5]

A handful of Friends, like Betsy Ross and General Greene, who were disowned for supporting the war, formed a society of their own, calling themselves Free Quakers.

As the war began moving southward and conditions in New England improved, the Meeting for Sufferings, "Hearing of the distressed situation of the poor people in New York and the Southern Colonies,"[6] urged Philadelphia to send the money contributed for relief to those parts.

Then, as General Howe approached Philadelphia, the Continental Congress advised the Council of the State of Pennsylvania to arrest "a number of persons of considerable wealth who profess themselves to belong to the Society of people called Quakers," claiming that they were "disaffected to the American cause."[7]

On September 3, 1777, John Pemberton, who had surveyed the need for relief during his journey in New England, was seized, together with his brother Israel and eighteen others. They were transported to Winchester, Virginia, and confined there. Two of them died—John Hunt and Thomas Gilpin, an outstanding zoologist.

Washington was defeated at Brandywine on September 11, and on September 26 the British marched into Philadelphia. English Friends dispatched ships loaded with provisions to their beleaguered brethren. Irish Friends sent £2000. As Philadelphia Friends felt the need was greater in South Carolina and Georgia, they forwarded the money there.

On April 29, 1778, the Virginia exiles who survived the winter were exonerated and allowed to return to their homes. As they approached Philadelphia, they saw "the devastations committed by the English army . . . houses demolished, and left desolate . . . for some miles around the city."[8]

British troops had commandeered the basement of the Friends Meetinghouse in New York City, using it as a depot for what Friends called "their warlike stores." Rent was paid for the space. Many Friends considered this blood money and therefore unacceptable. There was such a division of opinion that the Yearly Meeting decided to appeal for advice to Philadelphia Friends, who had had similar problems with military authorities. Elias Hicks, a young recorded minister from Jericho, Long Island, was appointed to bring the question to the 1779 sessions of Philadelphia Yearly Meeting. There, Friends declared that the rent should have been refused. It was returned to the British.

That year, eight armed British vessels anchored off Nantucket and landed a small force. The Quaker authorities refused to drive off the invaders with arms. The defenseless town was plundered but, making no resistance, it was not bombarded by the fleet in the harbor, which would have reacted to force by wiping it out.

As soon as the war was over, Friends, having purged themselves of slavery, exhorted others to do the same. Anthony Benezet of Philadelphia prevailed on English Friends to place their concern before their government. In June of 1783, London Yearly Meeting, having "considered the recommendations of our brethren in America ... in favor of the poor enslaved Negroes, it is the solid judgment of this Meeting that this weighty work should begin by an address to the king."[9] Benezet added a personal appeal to the Queen, transmitted through Benjamin West, the American Quaker painter who became president of the Royal Academy.

On October 3, one month to the day after the Peace of Paris was signed, the Congress of the Confederation, meeting at Princeton, New Jersey, received a delegation of Pennsylvania, New Jersey and Delaware Friends, headed by Benezet, who presented a petition for abolition of the slave trade. The Friends addressed the members of the congress as "guardians of the common rights of mankind and advocates for liberty,"[10] but the members of the Congress took no action.

In December, Moses Brown and five other Friends presented "The Petition and Remonstrance of a Committee of the People called Quakers in New England" to the Rhode Island Assembly. Two months later, Rhode Island passed "An Act authorizing the manumission of negroes, mulattoes, and others, and for the gradual abolition of slavery."[11] Persons born after March of 1784 were to be free. Brown communicated his concern to influential non-Friends in New York and Connecticut. Friends living in New Jersey, Delaware and Maryland petitioned their legislatures. Pressure was put on the Congress again, but southern members were opposed to interference with the slave trade.

When peace was declared in 1783, Nantucket Quakers with Loyalist sympathies moved to Canada. Eager to encourage the whaling industry in the Gulf of St. Lawrence, where black whales were plentiful, the Governor of Nova Scotia offered inducements to the Nantucketers. In 1785, three brigantines and a schooner with their crews and equipment for whaling arrived and settled in the town of Dartmouth. The little Quaker colony prospered at first, but a business depression in 1792 ruined the whaling industry and most of these Friends left Nova Scotia.

Their experience was almost paralleled by Friends who emigrated to France. At the end of the war, Nantucket had little with which to rebuild its commerce. Moreover, the British imposed a tax on sperm oil transported in American ships. William Rotch sought a way to circumvent this by transferring his business to Dunkirk so that his fleet could sail under the French flag. The government of France promised not to impose duty on whale oil, provisions and fittings for the Rotch ships. The Quaker whalemen and their families, who emigrated from Nantucket to Dunkirk in 1785, were guaranteed religious freedom. They were exempt from military service, "as they are a peaceable people, and meddle not with the quarrels of Princes." They were not obliged to prove their loyalty to France by wearing the tricolor cockade or to remove their hats in the presence of authorities.

"I care nothing about your hats," the Controller of Finance replied, when Rotch explained the reason for this peculiarity, "if your hearts are right."

Lafayette, Talleyrand and Thomas Jefferson, who was then the American Minister to France, befriended the little colony. It prospered. But by 1791, the revolutionists were making things so difficult that Rotch presented a petition to Mirabeau, President of the Assembly, at Paris.

"Conscience, the immediate relation of man with his Creator, cannot be subject to the power of man. . . . We have come to implore this Spirit of Justice; that we may be suffered without molestation, to conform to some principles, and to use some forms, to which the great family of Friends called Quakers have been inviolably attached. . . . Now that France is becoming the Asylum of Liberty, of equal law and brotherly kindness . . . we hope you will extend your justice and regard to us and our children."

In his reply, Mirabeau acknowledged, "There is a kind of property which no man would put into the common stock: the motions of his soul, the freedom of his thought. . . . As Citizen, he must adopt a form of Government. But as a thinking Being, the Universe is his Country. . . . Between God and the heart of man what Government would dare to interpose?"

For the Quaker Peace Testimony, however, Mirabeau showed contempt. "Had your Brethren in Pennsylvania been less remote from the savages," he asked, "would they have suffered their wives, their children, their parents to be massacred rather than resist? My Brother, if thou hast a right to be free, thou hast a right to prevent any one from making thee a slave. . . . Consider well, whether the defense of yourself and your equals be not also a religious duty."[12]

Then English privateers began seizing French ships. William Rotch sent his vessels back to Nantucket. On January 19, 1793, two days before Louis XVI was guillotined, the American Quakers sailed out of Dunkirk. Rotch settled in New Bedford, Massachusetts. His son Benjamin and some of the others moved to Milford Haven, Wales, where, to this day, the Friends Meeting cherishes its ties with the island in America.

Many Nantucket Friends moved directly to New Bedford, a few to Vassalboro, Maine; to Hudson, New York; and New Garden, North Carolina.

But life in the South was not congenial to most Friends. For a time, it had looked as though large-scale slavery might die out. The cotton industry was not showing a profit. Then in 1793, Eli Whitney invented the cotton gin, making it possible to separate the short staple cotton from its seeds by machine. The plantations suddenly required more slaves.

That year four thousand people died of yellow fever in Philadelphia. No one understood the cause of the disease. In 1797, it struck Providence, Rhode Island. Moses Brown, who had heard of its ravages from his friends in Philadelphia, suspected that the disease was caused by stagnant water in swamps and marshes and lack of sanitation. He noticed that there were more cases in narrower streets and alleys, where air circulated less freely. He urged that Providence streets be cleaned and widened.

Cases of smallpox also increased that winter. Moses Brown had trusted immunization from his youth. Now he helped two doctor friends to introduce vaccination into Rhode Island, where it had been strongly resisted. But it was soon apparent that the vaccine was administered chiefly to wealthy patients. Moses Brown distributed it free of charge to anyone and began sending it to people in other towns and states, placing it between two pieces of glass, which he sealed at the edges with beeswax.[13]

In 1798, the United States was on the brink of war with France. Dr. George Logan of Philadelphia went to France in a private capacity and secured assurance that the French Government wished to renew amicable relations with the United States. Upon his return home, Logan was denounced as a treasonable envoy of a faction that was corresponding with a hostile nation. Congress passed the Logan Act, making it a high misdemeanor for a private citizen to interfere in a controversy between the United States and a foreign country. Nevertheless, war was averted.

Logan tried again in 1810. Congress had passed the Embargo Act, forbidding American vessels from entering foreign ports. Believing that this would starve the British population, Logan pleaded with President Madison to negotiate a treaty of friendship with Britain instead. The President replied that "manifestations of patience under injuries and indignities" could be carried too far.[14]

With Madison's knowledge, Logan sailed for England. Once more, he felt successful in his peace mission. But when he returned home, he found that his country was rapidly drifting into war. On June 18, 1812, it was declared.

Born into one of the leading Quaker families, George Logan was by then no longer a member of the Society. Some years earlier, he had joined the militia although when he was called up, he resigned. Philadelphia Monthly Meeting had reluctantly disowned him for "associating with others bearing arms." But Logan believed in the Quaker method of reconciliation. "Was it," his biographer Frederick B. Tolles asked, "a residual Quaker faith in the potential goodness of all men that led him always to look for common ground on which men could come together, where they could recognize the good in each other and the evil in the passions that kept them apart?"[15]

Early in 1800, some Pennsylvania Friends, who had migrated west of the Alleghenies, visited Friends in North Carolina and urged them to move "northwest of the Ohio River to a place where there were no slaves held, being a free country." To their hosts, these visitors seemed like "messengers sent to call us out, as it were, from Egyptian darkness (for indeed it seemed as if the land groaned under oppression) into the marvellous light of the glory of God." Scouts were sent "to view the country." Upon their return, they were persuasive. "Dear Joseph Dew . . . intimated that he saw the seed of God sown in abundance, which extended northwestward. This . . . strengthened us in the belief that it was right. So we undertook the work, and found the Lord to be a present helper in every needful time," they wrote, when they got there, to Georgia Friends, encouraging them to follow. "And thus we were led safely along until we arrived here. The first of us moved west of the Ohio in the 9th month, 1800; and none of us had a house at our command to meet in to worship the Almighty Being. So we met in the woods."[16]

Whole Meetings migrated from North Carolina, traveling over the Blue Ridge Mountains into Tennessee and northward across the Kentucky Trail into southern Ohio. From there, some of them continued to Indiana, Iowa and eventually to Kansas. How eagerly they were looking for farmland with water is revealed by the names they gave their Meetings: Lost Creek in Tennessee, Short Creek in Ohio, Whitewater in Indiana, Honey Creek in Iowa.

On the frontier, new Monthly Meetings were established under the care of the Yearly Meeting from which the Friends had come until they were considered ready to become independent. Ohio Yearly Meeting was set off by Baltimore in 1813 when the state was only ten years old. A Yearly Meetinghouse, sixty feet wide and ninety-two feet long, was built at Mount Pleasant. In the first session, Quarterly and Monthly Meetings were directed to "labor with such as make use of ardent spirits as drink." In 1816, "the descendants of Africa" claimed "the solid attention of the meeting, and an earnest solicitude . . . for discharging our duty to this deeply afflicted part of the human family." In 1818, a committee was appointed to oversee the building of a saw and grist mill at the Shawnee settlement. "The subject of inflicting *death as a punishment* for crimes being brought into view, and the meeting feeling a deep interest that this barbarous practice may be abolished . . . judges it best to encourage the meeting for sufferings to present an address to the legislature of this State."[17]

Within a few years, some Friends had gone even farther westward till they reached the east branch of the Whitewater River in Indiana, where they founded the town of Richmond and built a log Meetinghouse twenty-four feet square. By 1821, there were so many Friends in Indiana that a Yearly Meeting was set off there by Ohio Yearly Meeting.

At the request of the Shawnees, for whom the grist and saw mills had already been built, the two Yearly Meetings joined Baltimore in establishing an Indian mission at Wapakoneta. With the approval of the government, they opened a school and started an agricultural program, which was so successful that the Indians prospered. But the government, under pressure from white frontiersmen in Ohio, broke the treaties it had made with the Indians. At the onset of winter it moved the whole tribe to Kansas.

Henry Harvey, the Quaker mission worker, wrote, "They were

poorly fitted out for this journey, at that late season of the year . . . all ages and classes, from a hundred years old . . . to the infant not two days old—all had to leave at the bidding of the white man; sick or well, prepared or unprepared, this people—who were once a free people—had now to obey their masters."

The Shawnees wept as they said good-by to their friends. "We have been brothers together with you the Quakers for a long time. You took us by the hand and you held us fast. We have held you fast too. And although we are going far away from you, we do not want you to forsake us . . . we hope always to be in your hands."[18]

10 Orthodox and Hicksites

Elias Hicks, that young recorded minister from Jericho, Long Island, who was sent to Philadelphia Yearly Meeting in 1779, was destined to become the most eloquent American Quaker of his time. For the next fifty years, he traveled constantly in the ministry, feeling a concern to visit 1413 Friends Meetings and covering, his biographer Bliss Forbush estimates, 26,000 miles. Wherever Hicks spoke, crowds came to hear him. Like Woolman, he held testimonies against the accumulation of wealth and the products of slave labor. He looked to the Scriptures for inspiration but to the Light Within for authority.

The warmest recollection of Hicks's personality, the most inward and enduring evaluation of his writings come down to us not from any Quaker contemporary but from Walt Whitman who, when he was a small boy, heard Hicks preach. Hicks was then eighty-one. A month or two later he was stricken with paralysis and died. Sixty years later, when Whitman was also suffering from paralysis, he summoned the last of his creative energy to compose a touching tribute.

"Always," Whitman wrote in *November Boughs*, "E.H. gives the service of pointing to the fountain of all naked theology, all religion, all worship, all the truth to which you are possibly eligible—namely in *yourself* and your inherent relations. Others talk of Bibles, saints, churches, exhortations, vicarious atonements—the canons outside of yourself and apart from man—E.H. to the religion inside of man's very own nature . . . in a little country village on Long Island. . . . My great-grandfather, Whitman, was often with Elias . . . at merry-makings and sleigh-rides in winter over the 'plains.' "[1]

Whitman's parents, though not Quakers, communicated to him something of the peculiar character which had come down to them from their Quaker forebears. We can trace this in certain mannerisms of speech but more importantly in the poet's compassion for sufferers.

> Not a mutineer walks handcuff'd to jail but I am handcuff'd to
>   him and walk by his side . . .

Not a youngster is taken for larceny but I go up too, and am tried
and sentenced . . .
Askers embody themselves in me and I am embodied in them,
I project my hat, sit shame-faced, and beg.[2]

"Did you know," Whitman asked the friend who helped nurse him during his last illness, "that when I was a young fellow up on the Long Island shore I seriously debated whether I was not by spiritual bent a Quaker?—whether if not one I should not become one? But the question went its way again: I put it aside as impossible: I was never made to live inside a fence."

When asked whether, had he become a Quaker, *Leaves of Grass* would ever have been written, he replied, "Quite probably not—almost certainly not. . . . We must go outside the lines before we can know the best things that are inside."[3]

Nineteenth-century Quakerism could not have accepted Whitman's unconventional behavior any more than Whitman could have lived creatively inside such narrow confines. Yet, when his life was drawing to a close, he kept coming back to the one thing he still wanted to write—a "history" of Elias Hicks and George Fox. For he responded to the spiritual self-reliance of Quakerism, the identification with nature and the "religion inside of man's very own nature." In his words, "I loafe and invite my soul."[4]

> In the faces of men and women I see God, and in my own face in
> the glass,
> I find letters from God dropt in the street, and every one is sign'd
> by God's name,
> And I leave them where they are, for I know that wheresoe'er I go,
> Others will punctually come for ever and ever.[5]

There is an echo of Fox's "unity with the creation" in

> A child said *What is the grass?* fetching it to me with full hands;
> . . . I guess it is the handkerchief of the Lord,
> A scented gift and remembrancer designedly dropt . . .[6]

It was through the eyes of the child he himself had been that Whitman recalled Hicks. In Brooklyn, in November or December of 1829—Whitman wasn't sure which—he heard Hicks speak on "the last tour of the many missions of the old man's life. . . . I can remember my father coming home toward sunset from his day's work as carpenter and saying briefly, as he throws down his armful of kindling-blocks with a bounce on the kitchen floor, 'Come, mother, Elias preaches tonight.' Then my mother, hastening the supper and the table-cleaning afterward, gets a neighboring young woman . . . to step in . . . puts the two little ones to bed—and as I have been behaving well that day, as a special reward I was allow'd to go also. . . . Though . . . more than half a century has pass'd over me since then, with its war and peace . . . I can recall that meeting yet. . . . On a slightly elevated platform at the head of the room, facing the audience, sit a dozen or more Friends, most of them elderly, grim, and with their broad-brimm'd hats on their heads. Three or four women, too, in their characteristic Quaker costumes and bonnets. All still as the grave.

"At length after a pause and stillness becoming almost painful, Elias rises and stands for a moment or two without a word. A tall, straight figure, neither stout nor very thin, dress'd in drab cloth, clean-shaved face, forehead of great expanse . . . still wearing the broad-brim. A moment looking around the audience with those piercing eyes, amid the perfect stillness. . . . Then the words come from his lips, very emphatically and slowly pronounc'd, in a resonant, grave, melodious voice. . . . I cannot follow the discourse. It presently becomes very fervid, and in the midst of its fervor he takes the broad-brim hat from his head, and almost dashing it down with violence on the seat behind, continues with uninterrupted earnestness. . . . A pleading, tender, nearly agonizing conviction. . . . Many, very many were in tears."[7]

Whitman also remembered something that his father had told him about Hicks. "He said once to my father, 'They talk of the devil—I tell thee, Walter, there is no worse devil than man.'"[8]

An unregenerated poet might, in 1888, expend his last remaining energy to celebrate the memory of Elias Hicks. But during the 1820s, when Hicks was still preaching to admiring crowds, certain weighty Friends began to question his doctrinal soundness. They wanted some of those "canons" which Hicks rejected. Since they wanted them, ought not all other Friends to be subject to them, too? The fence was reinforced. Disownment became the weapon for establishing a self-destructive uniformity. It was inevitable that this should end in a series of explosions.

Friends had undergone a psychological change since the first missionaries came to America in 1656 and turned the force of their aggression on their persecutors. After 1756, when Friends in Pennsylvania, unwilling to support the French and Indian War, withdrew from public life, they concentrated more and more on their inward life. They turned their aggression upon themselves, becoming increasingly strict about plainness until by 1856 Elders were going to Quaker homes to measure the fringes on the antimaccassars. If the fringes proved too long, they were clipped, no quarter given.

In worship, for roughly a century before Elias Hicks was suddenly charged with unsoundness, Friends turned entirely inward, treasuring the silence, breaking it only under the compulsion of divine leading. "Creaturely activity," by which they meant any intellectual process, must be completely stilled before God's voice could be heard. The individual was obliged to repress all that pertained to himself if he wished to know God. This form of worship, called Quietism, demanded a painful self-examination to determine whether a message actually came from God or only from the bearer. Friends hardly dared speak. Many Meetings were totally silent.

The rejection of intellect in worship gave ministers little incentive to acquire learning. But Quietism protected the worshipers from facile sermons, more thought than felt, or theological addresses that had nothing to do with the Spirit.

Surprisingly, this introspection did not result in a wholly ingrown, self-absorbed Society. On the contrary, it sensitized the worshipers to the needs of others. It led to an early recognition of the evils of slaveholding; it enabled Pennsylvania Friends, after they had withdrawn from the government, to deal peaceably with the Indians, while the Governor could do no better than offer a bounty for Indian scalps, both male and female. Quaker energies, which had formerly gone into political activity, now focused on building humane prisons and hospitals for the mentally ill. Friends worked for the relief of debtors, for emancipation and for abolition of the death penalty. They provided schooling for freedmen.

They continued the "guarded education" of their own children. In order to give country Friends the same advantages as those who lived in the cities, they founded boarding schools. The first was opened by New England Yearly Meeting at Portsmouth, Rhode Island, in 1784, thanks to the initiative of Moses Brown, but in 1788 it closed for want of financial support. In 1796, Nine Partners School opened in Millbrook, New York. Later, it moved to Poughkeepsie and was renamed Oakwood School. Westtown School in Pennsylvania, the particular concern of Owen Biddle, George Dillwyn and John Dickinson, opened in 1799. Fair Hill Boarding School opened at Sandy Spring, Maryland, in 1819 and that same year the New England Yearly Meeting Boarding School made a fresh start in Providence. Moses Brown had donated forty-three acres of his land and had overseen the construction of the building. He wished it to be open to all, not only Friends, and to provide for poor children. Later, in recognition of his charity and vision, it was renamed Moses Brown School.

Quaker Quietism began to seem tame when, all around, evangelical enthusiasm was stirring up the Methodists, Baptists and Presbyterians. The reasonable serenity of the eighteenth-century Meetings, the quiet waiting on the Lord, was buffeted by the overpowering emotionalism of the nineteenth-century revivals in other denominations.

For Hicks, this went against the grain. "I have known some to say to a brother, pray! Now, what presumption! Should man undertake to do a single thing in God's work without the command of God? If he does, he is a fool . . . whether to promote religion or anything else," Hicks declared in Philadelphia in 1826. We must feel God's power; we must have "an evidence of His light to show us the way; and then we can go on without fear or trembling."[9]

For the first time, some Friends began to place primary importance on the Scriptures, which Robert Barclay, born just one hundred years before Hicks, called "only a declaration of the fountain, and not the fountain itself." These Friends demanded of their members conformity with doctrines of the Christian Church, as opposed to the old Quaker reliance on experience and the Light Within.

In 1801, Hannah Barnard of Hudson, New York, collided with the Elders because she denied that God could have commanded either the Hebrews to make war or Abraham to sacrifice his son. When questioned about the miraculous conception of Christ, she declared that the truth of this had not been revealed to her. She was disowned.

"Elias Hicks was much troubled by these events . . . Hannah Barnard . . . had been asked whether she could 'affirm belief in the coeval divinity of Christ,' in the miracles of Moses, and in Jehovah's commanding Joshua to kill the inhabitants of Jericho. She was also asked if she accepted the translation of the whole of the Bible as accomplished by revelation, and if Jonah had been in the belly of the whale for three days. To Elias Hicks these were not items of belief required for membership in the Society of Friends. He held that Quakers might differ in their thinking upon many religious topics; the only point of agreement required of all was the acceptance of the operation of the spirit of Truth within the soul."[10]

"This Spirit," Hicks said, "led the ancients, and it will lead us."[11]

He had no use for the newly formed Bible societies, which sent Bibles to Africa while it was illegal to teach a million and a half slaves in America to read them. Some who were not Friends shared these sentiments. Ralph Waldo Emerson was shaken when he attended a meeting of the Bible Society in the Government House at St. Augustine, Florida, and witnessed the inconsistency of Christians, who could tolerate the slave auction that was simultaneously being held in the yard outside.

"One ear therefore heard the glad tidings of great joy, whilst the other was regaled with 'Going, gentlemen, going!' And almost without changing our position we might aid in sending the Scriptures into Africa, or bid for 'four children without the mother,' who had been kidnapped therefrom."[12]

Benjamin Ferris, a Quaker from Wilmington, Delaware, took the same position as Elias Hicks. "Let us set the candle in our own candlestick, before we attempt to enlighten others," he said. As for missionary societies, "rather than send missionaries to India, which had been conquered by Great Britain at the cost of a million lives, the two Friends advocated returning civil and political rights to the Hindu."[13]

However much Quakers might keep to themselves, they were unconsciously affected by their non-Quaker neighbors, whose religious views were rapidly moving in two directions. Friends were either attracted to or frightened by the liberal theology of the Unitarians or the fervid demonstrations of the evangelicals.

In 1819, a Congregational pastor, the Reverend William Ellery Channing, was labeled "The Apostle of Unitarianism." Two years later, a Presbyterian lawyer, Charles G. Finney, experienced a conversion which resulted in fiery revivals where sinners were conducted to an "anxious" or "mourner's" bench at the front of the church and prayed over until they professed penitence.

The same year that Channing was marked for Unitarianism, Philadelphia Yearly Meeting snubbed Elias Hicks, whom it had welcomed for forty years. He had characterized those who used the products of slave labor as "thieves and murderers."[14] Friends who did not share his concern took offense. The year Finney had his conversion, Stephen Grellet, a young French refugee who had become a Friend, "wept bitterly," because, he claimed, "Elias Hicks had led many to imbibe his anti-Christian errors."[15] Grellet felt called to oppose Hicks.

A number of visiting English Friends also made it their mission to publish what they took to be defects in Hicks's Quakerism. Bent on enlightening Friends in the backwoods, they followed him around wherever he preached. Several of those who pursued the old man were women, which led his cousin, Edward Hicks, to comment on the "great importance of superior women always being right, for when they get wrong they are so difficult to manage."[16]

With time, the issue became a power struggle centered on Hicks because of his enormous popularity, especially with Friends outside Philadelphia. The plain homes and attire of those who lived in the city—merchants and professional men—often hid influential bank accounts. City Friends were urbane and better educated than those in the country, who were not getting ahead on the farm and who felt, when they traveled to the city for Yearly Meeting, that they were ignored. Country Friends resented what they felt was overbearing control on the part of the rich city Elders, who, in turn, believed that Hicks was encouraging rebellion. They could not silence him because he did not belong to their Yearly Meeting. Actually, it was not so much Hicks's preaching as the spirit of the age which impelled Friends to yearn for religious and political liberty.

Hicks calmly continued to preach the same message. He had the support of his own Yearly Meeting, New York, and of many Friends in Philadelphia and Baltimore Yearly Meetings. His chief champion was John Comly, a teacher from Byberry, Pennsylvania, who was Assistant Clerk of his Yearly Meeting. As the 1827 session approached, "My mind was opened to see," Comly recorded in his *Journal,* "that this contest would result in a separation . . . as the only means of saving the whole from a total wreck . . . it must be effected in the peaceable spirit of the non-resisting Lamb. . . ."[17]

Business was conducted at that session of Philadelphia Yearly Meeting in a manner that was un-Quakerly and unworthy. It was "a scene of confusion."

Sixty years later, Whitman reconstructed this scene out of his imagination, for Hicks was not in Philadelphia on that occasion.

But Whitman's description communicates the emotional turmoil that actually prevailed. "One who was present has since described to me the climax, at a meeting . . . with Elias as principal speaker. . . . 'The blood of Christ—the blood of Christ—why, my friends, the actual blood of Christ in itself was no more effectual than the blood of bulls and goats—not a bit more—not a bit.' At these words, after a momentary hush, commenced a great tumult. Hundreds rose to their feet. . . . Canes were thump'd upon the floor. From all parts of the house angry mutterings. . . . This was the definite utterance, the overt act, which led to the separation."[18]

Whitman's account is inaccurate. Nevertheless, separation was effected, but not in the spirit of the non-resisting Lamb. After the session adjourned, John Comly and his friends issued a statement. "God alone is the Sovereign Lord of conscience," they declared, "and with this unalienable right, no power, civil or ecclesiastical, should ever interfere." Those who considered themselves "Orthodox" called Comly and his friends "Liberals" or "Hicksites."

Whitman, in fairness, adds a "Note:" Old persons, who heard this man in his day . . . think Elias Hicks had a large element of personal ambition, the pride of leadership, of establishing perhaps a sect that should reflect his own name. . . . Very likely. Such indeed seems the means . . . by which strong men and strong convictions achieve anything definite. But the basic foundation of Elias was undoubtedly religious fervor. He was like an old Hebrew prophet. He had the spirit of one, and in his later years look'd like one. . . . The same inflexibility, intolerance, rigid, narrow-looking adherence to God's truth."[19]

The Hicksites looked on the Separation as temporary. When emotions had had time to cool, they thought, an amicable settlement would be reached. But a break had been made. It was to prove more lasting, far-reaching and tragic than anyone could have envisaged. It brought out the worst in Friends. Each body claimed to be the legitimate Yearly Meeting and therefore entitled to the property. Employing tactics no more elevated than those of the seventeenth-century Christian Quakers, who competed for the ministers' gallery, these nineteenth-century Friends locked the doors of the Meetinghouse and the gates of the burial ground on one another. Most un-Quakerly of all, to settle the question of legal ownership they took their dispute to court. It ruled in favor of the Orthodox.

The following year, Thomas Shillitoe, one of the visiting English

Quaker ministers, was present when a separation took place in New York Yearly Meeting. Shillitoe then went to Ohio, stopping along the way to warn Friends that Elias Hicks was "an impostor."[20] At Ohio Yearly Meeting in Mount Pleasant, Hicks and his sympathizers found notices posted on the Meetinghouse doors forbidding them to enter. They disregarded the notices and the Orthodox accused them of trespassing. Writs were served by the sheriff on several Ohio Friends, charging them with disturbing a religious society and gathering to commit a riot.

In Baltimore and Indiana Yearly Meetings, separations were effected with greater dignity.

What Rufus Jones was to say about the Separation which occurred nearly two decades later in New England applied equally to these earlier ones: "There never was a case in which *the way of love* would have been more effective."[21]

Friends in the separated Yearly Meetings were now typed. Henceforth, they must belong to one branch or the other. The next four or five generations would come into the world with genes immutably stamped "Orthodox" or "Hicksite": Arch or Race Street in Philadelphia; 20th or 15th Street in New York; Eutaw Place or Park Avenue in Baltimore.

The distance between their Meetinghouses was short, but they dared not traverse it. In some country places, where a Meetinghouse had two front doors and a partition down the center which was lowered when the men and women met separately, they simply pulled down the partition for good, giving each branch a side. It was only a wooden partition, very flimsy in some cases, but it might just as well have been an iron curtain.

11 Paul Cuffe and Prudence Crandall

One of the outstanding Quakers of the nineteenth century was Paul Cuffe, a sea captain, son of a freed slave and an Indian woman of the Wampanaug tribe. He was born in 1759 on Cuttyhunk, westernmost of the Elizabeth Islands off Cape Cod.

At sixteen, Paul Cuffe went to sea to learn navigation. At twenty, he sailed his own boat, an open one which he and his brother built for coastwise trade. It was intercepted by pirates. After several failures, Cuffe finally made a profit on his cargo, built a larger, covered boat and sailed to Maryland with a load of codfish, which he disposed of at a good price. This voyage opened up a large market for New England fish. Cuffe acquired bigger and bigger boats, manned by Black crews, and turned to whaling.

With the profit from his voyages, he bought a large farm on the Westport River near Dartmouth, Massachusetts, where he and his wife, Alice, who belonged to his mother's tribe, raised a family. As there was no public school in the area, Cuffe built one on his land and engaged a teacher.

In 1780, Paul Cuffe and his brother John petitioned the General Court of Massachusetts for relief from taxation. "Having no vote or Influence in the Election of those that Tax us," they wrote, "yet many of our Colour have Cheerfully Entered the field of Battle in the defense of the Common Cause."[1] The Cuffes were imprisoned at Taunton for non-payment of taxes. Eventually the taxes were reduced and paid. Within three years, Massachusetts passed the Act which gave Blacks full legal rights and privileges.

Later, sailing into Norfolk, Virginia, with a valuable cargo, Cuffe was refused clearance by the port collector on the grounds that he was a Negro. He went directly to Washington and demanded to see President Madison. A tall, handsome man with a commanding presence, Cuffe addressed the little, wizen-faced President of the United States in the Quaker manner.

"James, I have been put to much trouble and have been abused," he said. "I have come here for thy protection and have to ask thee to order thy Collector for the port of Norfolk to clear me out for New Bedford, Massachusetts."[2]

As Dolley Madison, the vivacious First Lady, had been a Friend, the President understood Cuffe's plain speech and took no offense. Clearance was granted at once.

Cuffe prospered. Soon he was sailing to Europe and rounding the Cape of Good Hope. In 1811, a concern for the religious welfare of the Africans drew him to Sierra Leone. He believed that if commerce could be developed there and trading in produce could be made more profitable than trading in human flesh, the slave traffic would end. Who was better qualified to teach the Africans agricultural and commercial skills than American Blacks, God-fearing Christians with practical experience? By helping freed slaves to emigrate from America to Sierra Leone, Cuffe would provide them with a better future and encourage the development of Africa. It seemed an excellent plan. Quakers at home and in England encouraged it and offered Cuffe the help he needed. But both governments, engaged in the War of 1812, stood in his way.

By 1815, Cuffe was able to carry out his plan. On December 10, the *Traveller* sailed from New Bedford for Sierra Leone with nine families on board. A few of the passengers paid their way, and William Rotch, who had settled in New Bedford after his fiasco at Dunkirk, contributed toward the costs but Cuffe himself spent four thousand dollars. "My hope," he said, referring to this expense, "is in a coming day."[3]

The passengers were well received. Each family was given land and a year's rations, underwritten by Englishmen who were interested in African colonization.

When Cuffe left Sierra Leone to begin the fifty-four-day voyage back to the United States, "it was like a father taking leave of his children."[4] He planned to bring another contingent of colonists to Sierra Leone the following year and was deluged by applications, but before he could make another voyage, he died, leaving an estate of twenty thousand dollars.

He had demonstrated that colonization in Africa was feasible for the American Black. Many people felt that this might be a good solution to the whole problem. Soon after Cuffe reached home, they formed the American Colonization Society. Southern politicians took up the idea with enthusiasm, which led the more radical abolitionists to suspect that the politicians saw it as a device for ridding the country of freed slaves and robbing those who were still in bondage of all hope for release.

Ten years later, Woolman's unique approach to the slavery problem was reasserted by Edward Stabler, a Friend from Alexandria, Virginia, who observed: "I have long been of the persuasion that much of the good that might have been done, has been obstructed by the attempts which have been made to abolish slavery . . . upon political instead of religious motives and convictions . . . the slaveholder has considered himself injuriously assailed,—his mind has become exasperated, and he has placed himself upon the defensive, or become an assailant in his turn . . . like all other political contentions, the conflict has been degraded into a combat of persons, instead of a contest between the principles of right and wrong.

"The latter constitute . . . true religious effort; and hence the astonishing success which attended the original movements of John Woolman and his fellow-labourers, in relation to slavery in our Society. Their attention became, in the first instance, forcibly directed to the *powers of justice, opposing the principles of injustice in themselves;* of *mercy,* arrayed against *cruelty; love* against *hatred;* and *goodness* against *evil.* . . .

"They perceived that cruelty, injustice, and oppression, were no less tyrants to the master, than when they came to operate on the slave;—and that if the slave was to be pitied for what he suffered from them, the master . . . was no less to be pitied than the slave. This made the slave-holder and the slaves the equal objects of tender solicitude."[5]

What seemed like a simpler solution to the problem than Paul Cuffe's was tried by Prudence Crandall. It turned out to be infinitely more difficult.

In 1831, Canterbury, Connecticut, was a prosperous little town. Its gracious, white homes were enhanced by classical columns, fanlights and arched windows. There was an "elegant social library" and a temperance society. Forty-six Canterbury people experienced "spiritual renewing" that year and joined the church on the Green. Across from the church stood a large house in which some leading citizens decided to establish a "genteel" school for their daughters. They advanced the money and asked Prudence Crandall to become the mistress.

Prudence was born in 1803 in Hopkinton, Rhode Island, a village that produced Quakers as hardy and steadfast as the stones in its farmers' fields. At the Friends Boarding School in Providence, she had been given an excellent education. She had already demonstrated a gift for teaching.

While she was opening the Female Seminary in Connecticut, Nat Turner and nineteen other slaves were being hanged in Virginia, and in Boston William Lloyd Garrison was publishing the first issues of the *Liberator*, a paper dedicated to the abolition of slavery.

"I am in earnest," Garrison declared. "I will not equivocate—I will not excuse—I will not retreat a single inch—and I will be heard."[6]

The stagecoach brought the *Liberator* to Canterbury. Reading it, Prudence Crandall was deeply stirred. How could she know that Garrison, who was not a Friend, was transmitting to her the ideas of three Publishers of Truth? They were the editors of the first periodicals and newspaper in America to come out for immediate, unconditional emancipation. The thinking of these Quaker editors —Charles Osborn, Elihu Embree and Benjamin Lundy—made a crusader of Garrison who, in turn, persuaded and supported Prudence.

Osborn, a North Carolina Friend, started printing the *Philanthropist* in 1816 at Mount Pleasant, Ohio. This periodical opposed all colonization schemes, claiming they were designed for the perpetuation of slavery in the South and for ridding the northern states of freedmen. Soon young Lundy joined Osborn. While an apprentice in Wheeling, he had seen coffles of slaves, chained together like animals, being bought and driven off. "I heard the wail of the captive," he recalled later, "and the iron entered my soul."[7]

In 1821, Lundy moved to Jonesboro, Tennessee, to take over the printing press of Elihu Embree, who had recently died. Embree had published the *Emancipator*, the first abolitionist newspaper. On his press, Lundy printed a monthly, which he called *The Genius of Universal Emancipation*. In 1823, Lundy decided to move to Baltimore, the center of the domestic slave trade. There he continued to publish his paper, the only one in America openly opposed to slavery.

"He was," Rufus Jones claims, "one of the first persons, if not the very first, to give public lectures against slavery."[8]

Lundy was preoccupied with finding a haven for the slaves who had formerly belonged to North Carolina Friends. The state did not sanction manumission. Any slave set free by Friends was simply picked up by some unscrupulous master. Friends had to resort to the device of turning over their slaves to the legal ownership of the Yearly Meeting, the very body which refused to countenance the practice of slaveholding. Lundy traveled to Canada, Mexico, Texas and Haiti seeking a place where these freedmen could live.

During a lecture tour in Boston in 1829, he met Garrison, who was staying in the same boarding house. Garrison was then editing a paper devoted to temperance. He was twenty-four. Meeting Lundy changed the course of his life.

"I could not know on what ground the good seed fell," the Friend said later. Within a few months he had persuaded Garrison to come to Baltimore and join him in editing *The Genius of Universal Emancipation.*

Now that Lundy had Garrison to run his paper, he went off again in search of a home for the slaves. But Garrison, like Charles Osborn, with whom Lundy had first worked, soon came to the conclusion that nothing short of immediate emancipation was acceptable. The Blacks must continue to live where they were, as free men.

When Lundy returned to Baltimore, he found Garrison in jail. A slave-ship owner had accused him of libel. Garrison was fined fifty dollars and jailed in default of payment. John Greenleaf Whittier asked Henry Clay to intercede, but before Clay could act, Arthur Tappan, a New York merchant, had paid the fine and Garrison was released.

He decided to go back to Boston and start his own paper. Together with Isaac Knapp, he issued the first number of the *Liberator* in January 1831. When the August issue appeared, proslavery sentiment was at fever pitch. Twenty slaves had murdered their masters in Virginia. More repressive laws were enacted. Georgia offered a reward of five thousand dollars for Garrison's arrest and conviction. South Carolina asked the Mayor of Boston to "ferret him out," but the Mayor refused to interfere with publication of the *Liberator.*

The November issue reached Canterbury just as Prudence Crandall was opening her school, which became an immediate success. At the close of the first year, the backers "congratulated themselves in having on Canterbury Green a school for their daughters which was conducted by a mistress of such marked ability and of such sterling character."[9]

Then, Sarah Harris, a local Black girl, came to Prudence and pleaded for an education, so that she might be enabled to teach children of her race. Prudence did not immediately accept Sarah as a pupil. The parents of many of her girls belonged to the American Colonization Society, which wanted to send the Blacks back to Africa. It claimed that they were not educable. These parents were bound to object to Sarah's presence in the Seminary.

But for some time past, Prudence had been haunted by a verse from Ecclesiastes: "So I returned, and considered all the oppressions that are done under the sun; and behold the tears of such as were oppressed, and they had no comforter; and on the side of their oppressors there was power but they had no comforter."

Sarah's request was the revelation of Truth to Prudence; she must be the comforter. She admitted Sarah as a day pupil.

The parents did indeed object. They called on Prudence, threatening to withdraw their daughters. They pleaded with her to dismiss Sarah. Like Mary Dyer, Prudence could only answer, "Nay, I cannot." And like Mary, she paid a high price. Had she been as intent on peacemaking as she was on being a comforter to the oppressed, she would have persevered in trying to convince her employers. It is doubtful whether the outcome would have been different, yet we who rejoice in her courage wish she had fought also for the hearts of her opponents.

Instead, she wrote to Garrison, asking him whether he thought she could "obtain twenty-five young ladies of color to enter a school for a term of one year at the rate of $25 per quarter including board, washing and tuition." She went up to Boston to see him. Unfortunately, the hostility of her neighbors made Prudence secretive. She told them she was going in order to buy equipment for the school. Later, she went to Providence and New York, again withholding the fact that the purpose of her trip was to find out whether she could secure Black pupils. She returned to Canterbury convinced. Then she put an advertisement in the *Liberator* for young ladies of color and dismissed her white pupils.

The Canterbury people were stunned. They felt betrayed. Had they not advanced money for the Seminary? Did that not entitle them to dictate policy? They had asked Prudence to teach their daughters, not to infest their town with colored girls, thereby lowering at one and the same time the moral standards and real estate values. Who would have thought that this genteel Quakeress would turn out to be defiant?

A special town meeting was called. The speakers predicted miscegenation. Two men appeared who were strangers to Prudence: the Reverend Samuel May, minister of the Unitarian Church in the nearby village of Brooklyn, and Arnold Buffum, a Providence Friend, agent of the recently formed New England Anti-slavery Society. They had come to defend Prudence but were barred from speaking because they were "foreigners."

Canterbury had an ancient vagrancy law. Any person who was warned by the selectmen to leave town had to post a bond guaranteeing that he would either depart or pay a fine, failing which he was to be stripped to the waist and whipped on the naked back not more than ten strokes. A writ was served on the first young lady of color to arrive. She buffaloed the selectmen by declaring that she'd rather be whipped than give in. The Reverend Mr. May, who was a friend of Lucretia Mott, posted bond for the girl and for the sixteen other Black pupils. They came from New York and Rhode Island as well as from other parts of Connecticut.

At a second town meeting, Canterbury voted to petition the General Assembly for a law forbidding schools to admit Blacks from out of the state. Known as the Connecticut Black Law, this was passed in April 1833.

Prudence's father, Pardon Crandall, was told that his daughter would be "taken up the same way as for stealing a horse or for burglaring . . . she will be put in jail. . . . There is no mercy to be shown about it."[10]

And none was. The sheriff, who thoroughly disliked doing this to a lady, took Prudence to the county jail. The cell in which she was locked had recently confined a murderer waiting to be hanged. Once more, Mr. May posted bond. Released until the next session of the county court, Prudence returned to Canterbury. Her sister Almira had bravely kept the school going in spite of stones and rotten eggs that the neighbors hurled through the windows they shattered. Local storekeepers refused to supply the school, the doctor would not tend a sick child, the church shut its doors to the girls and teachers in the Seminary. The well had been poisoned, and no one would give Prudence water. Her father had been warned to stay away, but he carried in pails from his farm on the other side of town.

The *Liberator* took up the cause. Arthur Tappan, the New York merchant who had bailed out Garrison in Baltimore, came to Prudence's rescue. He offered to pay for the finest lawyers in Connecticut and all court expenses. He came to Canterbury himself. Shocked by the conditions he found there and the fact that no newspaper dared report them, he set up a printing press in the next village and engaged Charles G. Burleigh, a young law student, to publish a paper which they called *The Unionist*. It described the Canterbury affair in detail. As the news got out, expressions of sympathy began arriving from all over the country. The issue was no longer local; it had become a battle between the Colonization Society and the Abolitionists.

During the summer, Prudence was brought to trial. The jury could not agree. When she was tried a second time, she was convicted. The case was appealed to the State Supreme Court, which had to decide the constitutionality of the Black Law: whether freed Blacks enjoyed the rights of citizens. The Supreme Court, unwilling to get involved in such a touchy question, refused on technical grounds to try Prudence.

In the end, she was vanquished not by imprisonment, not by the manure her neighbors shoveled into the school well nor by the fire with which they finally destroyed the building, but by a widower. She married the Reverend Calvin Philleo, a Baptist preacher, who took her out of the Quaker fold and carried her off to Elk Falls, Kansas, a long way from Canterbury Green.

But it was not too far for an ambitious young wheelman from Hartford out to see the sights in 1886 to drop in. George B. Thayer, traveling across the continent on his high bicycle, the latest model forty-six-inch Expert Columbia, made a detour to Elk Falls, logging on arrival 3627 pedaled miles. He had gone there to have a look at Prudence Crandall, who was by then, in his words, "of almost national renown."[11] The Connecticut State Legislature, prodded by a group of leading citizens that included Mark Twain, had just gone on record as regretting the action taken in 1833. In reparation, it voted Mrs. Philleo an annual pension of four hundred dollars. She was eighty-four years old. Her husband had long since died. She needed the money.

"If the people of Connecticut only knew how happy I am," she told Thayer, who thought the pension too small for the damage done, "and how thankful I am to them, it would make them happy too. I don't want to die yet. I want to live long enough to see some of these reforms consummated."[12]

To have had her wish, to have seen racial segregation outlawed by her country and renounced by all the members of the Society of Friends, Prudence Crandall would have had to live to be 153 years old.

12 Wilburites and Gurneyites

It was a mercy that the three Friends who paddled all the way from the Chesapeake to Narragansett in 1661 were not at Newport in 1845. They would have been heartbroken. During the 185th session of the Yearly Meeting which they had at such cost begun, it was dismembered.

Everything would have turned out differently had those who assembled in 1845 heeded the Epistle which George Fox addressed to "Friends in New-England" when the Yearly Meeting met at Newport for the second time.

"To all my Dear Friends and Brethren, whom Bonds and Death have not dismay'd," Fox wrote in 1662, "And Fetters, Irons, Whippings . . . have not daunted . . . in the Power of the Lord God . . . stand, then are ye all but One . . . in no wise abuse it through Strife and Jangling, for that eats out . . ."[1]

In 1672, Fox actually came to Yearly Meeting at Newport. He wrote that it "lasted six days together . . . And when it was ended it was hard for Friends to part, for the glorious power of the Lord . . . had so knit and united them together that they spent two days in taking leave of one another."[2]

At the Yearly Meeting in 1845, not all Friends waited until the closing session to take leave of one another. During the proceedings, a number of Rhode Island Friends walked out. John Wilbur of Hopkinton, a dedicated minister, had by extraordinary maneuvers been disowned. The underlying reason was his refusal to accept a new interpretation of Quakerism, which Joseph John Gurney, a visiting English Friend, had introduced some years earlier.

Gurney was not present at New England Yearly Meeting in 1845. He was in England at Earlham Hall, his home near Norwich. He belonged to a wealthy banking family—cultivated, fond of music, less insular than most Friends of that generation. But as a young man, Joseph John had reacted against the worldliness in which he was reared and assumed the plain Quaker dress. While he pursued the business interests of his family, he devoted a great part of his life to preaching and to working for the abolition of slavery.

The laws which excluded non-conformists from the English universities until 1871 prevented Gurney from matriculating at Oxford, but he studied there under private tutors. He made friends with Anglicans, whose evangelicalism rubbed off on him. It colored his Quakerism in such a way that some English Friends became troubled. Thomas Shillitoe, who had called Elias Hicks an impostor, declared in 1836 that Joseph John Gurney did not have "sound Quaker principles, but episcopalian ones," which had done great mischief in the Society of Friends. The following year, "under the apprehension of religious duty,"[3] Gurney came to the United States. He was already a controversial figure.

He stayed three years, preaching everywhere to Friends and others, even in the House of Representatives to President Van Buren and the Congress (which he referred to as "commons and lords").[4] He enjoyed an enormous success. Women Friends cooked so much more than Gurney could eat that to this day in certain Quaker households, leftovers are called "Joseph Johns."

In Richmond, Indiana, three thousand people came to hear Gurney preach. Forever after, this place would be the Gurneyite stronghold. The school which Gurney encouraged Friends to build there eventually was named Earlham College in honor of his home.

Pioneer Friends had more contact with the Methodists, Baptists and Presbyterians than they had ever had when they lived in tight Quaker enclaves back East. These neighbors were not only engrossed in wrestling with the soil, but with their souls. For the circuit riders and revivalists were holding camp meetings on the frontier, converting people by the thousands. The Second Great Awakening swept everyone before it, quiet Quakers and all.

"The western revivalists in the early years were dealing with a moving, floating, migrating population, and they were operating in a situation where opportunities for Christian nurture were few and often nonexistent. Consequently they had to push for a much quicker decision than their eastern contemporaries. Subjected to this coercion, the revivalists in the West tended to turn on all the heat they could and to appeal to the emotions much more than to the intellect. . . . With 'the traditionally slow cycle of guilt, despair, hope and assurance' being compressed into a few days or even hours, the emotional stress was agonizingly intensified and it cut deep into normal restraint . . . there were outbursts of weeping and shouts of joy. . . ."[5]

When Joseph John Gurney arrived in 1837, he found Friends who had witnessed and participated in revivals. These Friends were more than ready to respond to Gurney. He appealed especially to young Friends. This surprised him, since he was shocked by the way American children were brought up. "Generally the little ones are subject to but little restraint and are sadly destitute of cultivation," Gurney wrote to his own children who were in England. "The law of independence descends to the lowest grades and to the tenderest years . . . Considering how the children run wild, I am surprised to find the grown up young people so generally well-behaved and impressible. Their hearts are very open to me."[6]

Gurney preached at Yale College and was far from easy, for he noted, even then, "those outbreaks of juvenile independence, which are of not unfrequent occurrence in these institutions." Elsewhere in New England conditions were still worse. Gurney was shocked by "some dangerous sentiments" which he heard expressed "respecting the rights of women. . . . When male and female itinerant lecturers are heard declaring that women have in all respects the same civil and political rights and duties as the stronger sex . . . that wives and husbands may lawfully separate, when they are weary of each other's society . . . one cannot but tremble in view of the consequences. . . . My consolation," Gurney concluded with unwarranted optimism, "lies in the quiet assurance that the tide of these notions . . . will soon ebb, and gradually disappear."[7]

Gurney made a trip to the West Indies and assembled figures showing that the sugar crop increased after Britain freed her slaves. He returned to Washington and valiantly tried to convince Henry Clay and John C. Calhoun that emancipation was economically advantageous. "Under what stimulus has the work been effected? Solely under that of moderate wages."[8]

Gurney also continued the theological wrangle with John Wilbur of Rhode Island that had begun several years earlier when Wilbur visited England. Wilbur had been shocked to find that Gurney and other English Friends were taking part in "the formation of Bible Societies composed of Bishops, priests and people of divers other denominations."[9] In this, Wilbur simply carried on the concern of Elias Hicks, who had recently died.

But at Quarterly Meeting in Norwich, Gurney's home, Wilbur felt slighted. He had received "uncivil usage." At London Yearly Meeting in 1832, he observed that "great professions of faith in the mediation and atonement of Jesus Christ our Lord do not of themselves bring a savour of life, precious sweetness, or weight, solidity and power to a meeting."[10] Wilbur accused Gurney of so emphasizing the death and resurrection of Christ as to belittle or even deny the witness of the eternal Christ Within.

Gurney accused Wilbur of so emphasizing the Christ Within as to belittle or even deny the existence of the historic Jesus. This wrangle, begun in 1831, pursued throughout Gurney's American visit and after his return home, lasted until his death in 1846. By that time, it had created havoc.

It is easy to understand that the urbane, scholarly, charming banker, who betrayed a contemporary Englishman's patronizing attitude toward Americans, was too much for Wilbur, the homespun Rhode Island farmer, whose education had been so "guarded" that it included little beyond the study of ancient Quaker authors. Wilbur had the attributes which Walt Whitman ascribed to Elias Hicks: the "inflexibility, intolerance, rigid, narrow-looking adherence to God's truth" of an old Hebrew prophet.

At New England Yearly Meeting in 1845, those Friends who wished to adopt Gurney's form of Quakerism realized that they could never do it while Wilbur was with them. So they contrived to disown him. But his sympathizers maintained that they constituted the legitimate Yearly Meeting and they appointed a set of clerks. The Gurney sympathizers appointed another set. Both "Wilburites" and "Gurneyites" tried to conduct the business of the Yearly Meeting, each side claiming to be the official body. The unseemly and uncharitable conduct, which had been displayed nearly two decades earlier by the Friends of Philadelphia and New York, was now emulated at their 185th Yearly Meeting sessions by the Friends of New England.

They would certainly have been gentler with one another if they had only stopped to recall the one hundredth session in 1760 when John Woolman, "in bowedness of spirit went to the Yearly Meeting at Newport . . ."

But in 1845, there was no Woolman at Newport. The very strength of character which earlier made Friends heroic, willing to suffer for their convictions, now made them uncompromising and wanting in charity.

They had always maintained that "Should a difference or controversy arise among our members of such a character as cannot be adjusted by the labors of interested Friends, it should be submitted to arbitration." To take a Quaker dispute into the courts was unthinkable. Yet now there seemed no other means of determining which body was the authentic Yearly Meeting and therefore the legitimate owner of the property—the truth being, as all Friends must have known in their hearts, that neither one was, without the other. Thus did Strife and Jangling eat out.

The Massachusetts Court could hardly be expected to make sense out of the doctrinal or disciplinary charges and countercharges. But one fact stood out for non-Quakers, accustomed to deciding issues by the will of the majority: the Gurneyites claimed sixty-five hundred members; the Wilburites, five hundred. The Court declared the Gurneyites to be the legitimate body.

Wilburites and Gurneyites promptly carried their grievances around to other Yearly Meetings, which proceeded to take sides.

"If only New England Yearly Meeting had been concerned in the controversy the tragedy could have been borne," Rufus Jones reflected nearly a century later, "but New England . . . could not live unto itself, or 'separate' unto itself. All 'orthodox' Quakerism was at once involved in the tangle."[11]

Meanwhile, Gurney had been traveling again. With his sister, Elizabeth Fry, whose efforts to improve prisons were recognized all over Europe, he went to the Netherlands and was received by King William II. Gurney addressed "Dutchmen attached to their ledgers," who had investments in the West Indies, "to prove to them from facts which I had myself witnessed, the agricultural, mercantile and pecuniary advantages of the abolition of slavery."[12] In Denmark, Gurney presented the same arguments to the King, urging emancipation for the island of St. Croix.

Gurney had published an account of his journey to the West Indies in the form of letters addressed to Henry Clay. According to John Greenleaf Whittier, the book made a deep impression in the American slave states. He sent Gurney a letter of thanks "in the name of the abolitionists of America."[13]

Gurney died, like Elias Hicks, not much more than a year after the Separation took place with which his name is associated. Gurney was not altogether responsible for the subsequent changes in American Quakerism. He only promoted them, making respectably Quaker a type of religious practice which had been rejected as long as Friends kept to themselves. His emphasis on the authority of the Bible, conversion and justification through the atoning death of Jesus Christ were part of the thinking in the midst of which nineteenth-century Friends lived. Many were tired of being peculiar. It was a relief when their faith was allowed to conform more nearly to that of their non-Quaker neighbors. For, despite their determination to preserve a peculiar identity, they were, far more than they themselves appreciated, the product of their own times and localities.

The Quaker Separations took place in those years when the Unitarians were leaving the Congregationalists, the Baptists were dividing into various branches, the Lutherans were forming new synods, the Presbyterians were choosing between Old and New School, Episcopalians between High and Low Church and the Wesleyan Methodists were seceding from the Methodist Episcopal Church. At the time, among many Protestant bodies, devotion to truth, as they saw it, made schism seem preferable to accommodation just as, before long among political parties, the issue of slavery would make war seem preferable to compromise.

For two centuries after their arrival in America, the Quakers had presented their testimonies as one body. They transacted business and responded to political issues in more or less the same peculiar manner from Maine and Nantucket to the Carolinas and westward to the Pacific. Friends married Friends. Should they be so careless as to marry someone else, they were disowned. Friends spoke and dressed alike. Henry Thoreau, attending a Meeting in 1843, found the women "looking all like sisters or so many chickadees."

Quaker Meetinghouses were unadorned; Meetings for Worship uniform in their dependence on the silence. Even after they began to differ on doctrinal points, Friends continued to worship in the same way.

When, in 1852, John Greenleaf Whittier composed his *First Day Thoughts,* he was referring to his own Meeting in Amesbury, Massachusetts, where the bench which was his "old accustomed place" can still be identified. But he might have been describing a Friends Meeting anywhere in the United States.

> In calm and cool and silence, once again
> I find my old accustomed place among
> My brethren, where, perchance, no human tongue
> Shall utter words; where never hymn is sung,
> Nor deep-toned organ blown, nor censer swung;
> Nor dim light falling through the pictured pane . . .

Yet by the end of the nineteenth century, American Friends not only held various theological views; they worshiped in different ways. There were those who upheld the historic testimony against a paid ministry and those who felt the need for professional pastors; those who worshiped in Meetinghouses on the basis of silence and those who worshiped in churches with ordered services and music.

When Friends separated, they were unconsciously playing their part in the American drama of the age. But for them Separation was tragic because it was incongruous. Throughout the years of persecution, they had, as Francis Howgill said of Friends in 1652, "met together in the unity of the Spirit and the bond of peace." It was this precious experience that fused the Quakers into a people. "The Lord of Heaven and earth we found to be near at hand, and, as we waited upon him in pure silence . . . the Kingdom of Heaven did gather us and catch us all as in a net. . . . We came to know a place to stand in and what to wait in. . . ."

In the United States, two centuries later those who inherited the tradition of these martyrs were enjoying freedom of worship. They were comfortable; they were respected. How was it possible that suddenly they had not *one* "place to stand in" but *several mutually exclusive places?*

While the Gurneyites were adopting new forms, the Wilburites continued to hold that vocal ministry should come from the silence, that it be a response to the moving of the Spirit, put into words by anyone. They felt it was not fitting to pay a man for performing this act and that music, a prearranged program or the collection of money were out of place in worship.

Sometimes when they were driving to Yearly Meeting at Westerly in the southwest corner of Rhode Island, Wilburite Friends coming by way of Narragansett would stop near Perryville before a pile of stones that stood between the Old Post Road and the ocean. Those stones, people around there claimed, were the ruins of a barn George Fox preached in during the summer of 1672. Whether this was true, no one knew. But these Friends cherished the belief Fox expressed there: "And in Rhode Island we had ten glorious meetings together . . . in a justice's barn . . . an ancient justice said that if they had money enough they would hire me. So I said then it was time for me to go away, for then they would not come to their own teacher . . . we brought every one to their own teacher."[14]

Three quarters of a century after the Separation in New England, Rufus Jones compared the two Friends whose doctrinal collision brought it about. "Theologically Gurney stood in line with the Puritan opponents of Quakerism rather than with Fox and Barclay and Penington. . . . For the Quaker founders Christianity was . . .

life and experience; for him it was essentially conformity of belief with the orthodox standards of faith. For them the elemental basis of religion was God revealed in man; for him it was the historic, miraculous revelation preserved in an infallible Book. . . .

"John Wilbur supposed that *he* was in every particular precisely like the primitive Quakers. . . . He was, however, by no means as close to the original type as he thought he was. Intellectually he held strongly, stoutly, the doctrine of the inward Light as he found it formulated in the early Quaker books, and here he was much nearer the original founders than was Gurney. But original Quakerism was not something formulated in a book. It was a mighty experience of God, alive and dynamic. . . . Neither one of these two men, noble-hearted and consecrated as they both were, was the long-awaited prophet who could lead the Society of Friends to new heights of vision."[15]

Following the Separation, the Society seemed to reach new lows. On the little island of Nantucket, there were three Friends Meetinghouses so that Hicksites, Wilburites and Gurneyites could worship in antiseptic isolation.

Yet today it is clear that the two men, whose conflicting theologies brought on the trouble, also served useful functions.

If Wilbur had not stubbornly defended traditional Quaker worship, it might have disappeared from New England. What a disaster that would have been is perhaps even more evident now than it was fifty years ago when Rufus Jones made his judgment. For now, particularly in academic communities, it is to the silent Meetings that many young people of every background, who renounce violence and ecclesiastical forms, turn from the noise and press of the world to let the "still dews of quietness" drop upon their souls.

For his part, Gurney made the Quaker faith home for many who would not have been drawn to the "silent assemblies of God's people." The enclave into which Friends had been pushed by the persecutions and by the peculiarities they themselves fostered had cut them off from the rest of society. Gurney's evangelicalism bridged this chasm. It produced a type of Quaker faith and worship that other Americans could understand.

Gurney opened the door to that ecumenicity which was to become an important feature of Quakerism, reaching out during the twentieth century to people of all beliefs.

But after the Yearly Meeting was dismembered, what New England Friends had to rediscover was that "mighty experience of God," which is beyond all theology.

In 1849, countless Americans rushed to California to seek their fortunes. From Nantucket alone, fourteen ships sailed for the Golden Gate. One of the Nantucketers was a young Quaker named Rowland Hussey Macy, a descendant of that Thomas Macy who found it expedient to leave the mainland for Nantucket when William Robinson and Marmaduke Stephenson were being hanged in Boston. Rowland Macy had already spent four years on a whaler. In California, he and his brother Charles went into partnership with two merchants at Marysville, north of Sacramento. In the Marysville *Herald,* Macy and Co. advertised themselves as "general Dealers in Provisions, Dry Goods, Clothing, etc. . . . Gold Dust Forwarded to all parts of the world." Within a year, the Macys withdrew from the firm. Rowland returned to Massachusetts, where he started a dry-goods store in Haverhill.

Rowland Macy may not have contributed much to the religious life of the great West during his short stay, but from the moment he went into business he valiantly maintained the Quaker principle of a single price. It was then standard practice to ask more for goods than one expected to receive and to haggle over every sale. Friends claimed that there can only be one fair price for an article and to demand more, even with the intention of ultimately yielding, is to deviate from Truth.

In 1853, Rowland Macy began to advertise in the Haverhill *Gazette,* whose editor years before had been John Greenleaf Whittier. "Although we are proverbially modest," Macy's weekly dispatch conceded, "we cannot but feel flattered when we look back upon our four years' experience in the Dry Goods business in this town. . . . When we came here . . . there was no regular price for anything, and the most ignorant were the most imposed upon. We claim to have broken down this *cut throat* business, and by *selling goods at one price—selling them cheap*—serving all alike . . . we claim to have made the business here *respectable.* . . . Do not fail to look in at Macy's this week, for we have some GREAT BARGAINS, and no mistake.

Lowest Prices always named First. R. H. MACY"[16]

Precisely two hundred years earlier, George Fox had noted that in the beginning Quaker tradesmen lost their customers because they would not bow, take off their hats to them "nor say 'you.' . . .

But afterwards people came to see Friends' honesty and truthfulness and 'yea' and 'nay' at a word in their dealing . . . and saw that, for conscience sake towards God, they would not cozen and cheat them and at last that they might send any child and be as well used as themselves, at any of their shops."[17]

But whereas Fox claimed that Friends' reputation for honesty brought them double the business of their competitors, R. H. Macy went bankrupt in Haverhill. A second attempt to make his fortune in the West was equally disastrous. Then, in 1858, he opened yet another store, this time in New York City, way, way uptown on Fourteenth Street and Sixth Avenue. In the daily *Tribune* he advertised FRENCH FLOWERS, FEATHERS, and IMPORTED HEADDRESSES —items hardly calculated to attract the patronage of Quakeresses. Nevertheless, R. H. Macy was now on the road to greater success than he could possibly have imagined.

It was the year that the Republican nominee for the Senate from the State of Illinois was Abraham Lincoln. In his acceptance speech, Lincoln declared, "A house divided against itself cannot stand. I believe this Government cannot endure permanently half slave and half free." A national struggle was in the offing.

The same year, an event occurred that was to have far-reaching consequences in Quaker history: Joel Bean, a young teacher from New Hampshire, was recorded a Friends minister by the Monthly Meeting in West Branch, Iowa, where "the light rested, as the place for my future home, the prairie sod was broken and the little cot built to which, after two years, I brought my mother . . . the little houses of first settlers were beginning to dot the unbroken prairie. A small meeting, held in a broom-shop, had been started. . . . The meeting grew rapidly."[18] Before long, Joel Bean's whole family had come from New England to settle near him in West Branch.

The year after he was recorded a minister, he married Hannah Shipley, a Philadelphia Friend, who was also a teacher and whose "fresh enthusiasm, her ready interest and sympathy in all of the activities of the pioneer community, and her sweet charm were instantly felt," her daughter Catherine, who would inherit that sympathy, wrote of her later. "In the little quiet meeting she spoke with tenderness and feeling and aspiration."[19]

In 1861, the Beans asked their Meeting to liberate them "to visit in the love of the Gospel the inhabitants of the Sandwich islands, and to reside for some time among them."[20] With their baby they traveled to what are now the Hawaiian Islands, where they spoke to large numbers of natives. This was one of the first far-flung missionary visits undertaken by American Friends. The Beans were urged to remain in Hawaii and open a school for girls, but they felt that their place was in the Meeting at West Branch. They were welcomed back there with great affection.

By 1863, there were so many Quakers in Iowa that Indiana Yearly Meeting set off Iowa Yearly Meeting. Western Yearly Meeting for Friends in Illinois and western Indiana had already been established. That same year these three Yearly Meetings and New England, New York and Baltimore Yearly Meetings sent delegates to Baltimore to confer on the draft. The conference appointed a committee to visit President Lincoln and members of his Cabinet in the hope of securing exemption from military service for Friends. The Draft Act provided exemption but only on the payment of three hundred dollars per person.

The whole Society protested against this system. Western Yearly Meeting, addressing President Lincoln, assured him that it was impossible for Friends to "compound, by payment of money, for a service for the performance of which they feel restrained by the commands of our Saviour."[21] Since this money was to be used for the support of hospitals, many Friends were willing to pay it. Those who refused, on the ground that they could not in conscience hire a substitute to do the fighting, were jailed.

Shortly after the Battle of Gettysburg, Charles Perry and Ethan Foster of Westerly, Rhode Island, went to Washington to wait on the President.

Charles Perry had been one of John Wilbur's supporters at the time of the Separation in New England. Three years later he married Temperance Foster, Wilbur's granddaughter. The Perry home beside the Pawcatuck River, where schooners sailed in from Charleston and Savannah with stowaways, became a station on the Underground Railroad. Runaway slaves ate at the family table. After dark, Charles Perry, defying the Fugitive Slave Laws, hitched up his horse and drove the fleeing Blacks north to Hopkinton, Rhode Island, the next stop on their way to Canada.

The Meeting for Sufferings of New England Yearly Meeting (Wilburite) sent Charles Perry and Ethan Foster to Washington because three Rhode Island Friends were imprisoned at Governor's Island in New York Harbor for refusing to pay the commutation.

"President Lincoln received us kindly, but said he did not see how he could grant our friends exemption from military service, without so far 'letting down the bars' as to render nugatory all his efforts to crush the Rebellion," Ethan Foster wrote at the conclusion of the mission. "He dwelt much on the difficulties which would attend the exemption of any portion of those by law subject to draft; said that if he began there would be no stopping place. . . . At length, however, he said that he 'should be very unwilling for any truly conscientious person to be made to suffer.' . . . He finally asked, 'What *can* we do for you?' . . . I replied that our Governor suggested that he might think it would do to release these men on parole, to hold them subject to call. . . .

"The President said it would not do to make a special exemption in the case of Friends . . . we . . . expressed a hope that if any favors were granted it would be done impartially. I remarked, however, that I nevertheless thought the claims of the Society of Friends stronger . . . from the fact that they had long since abolished slavery . . . and that if every other of the religious denominations had done the same, we should not have had this war; to which he replied, 'You never said a truer thing than that.' "22

Lincoln gave Foster and Perry a note of introduction to Secretary of War Stanton who, with Secretary of State Seward, listened to the Friends' request.

Seward, "with much vehemence of manner asked, 'Why don't the Quakers fight?' Charles replied, 'Because they think it wrong and cannot do it with a clear conscience.'"

When Seward "reprimanded" them, Foster countered, "I want to ask thee one question, and I want thee to answer it: Whose prerogative is it to decide what my duty is, thine or mine?

"He did not answer the question, but . . . asked, 'Why, then, don't you pay the commutation?' We told him we could see no difference between the responsibility of doing an act ourselves and that of hiring another to do it for us."

Unsuccessful, the persistent Friends returned to the President. "After some further talk, in which his sympathy with us was plainly manifested, I think I may say, we took an affectionate leave of him."

At Governor's Island where the young men were being held, Foster and Perry pleaded with the commandant, the surgeon and the general. Back and forth they went until the men were released.

"We took the evening boat for home," Ethan Foster recalled,

"and I never remember to have spent a more joyful day and night in my life. My peace flowed as a river. . . . The young men went to their several homes. . . . No call was ever made for them by the government."[23]

Some months after the two Wilburites waited on President Lincoln, two Gurneyites, Eli and Sybil Jones of South China, Maine, also went to Washington. Eli distributed food, clothing and beds, sent by his Yearly Meeting to destitute Blacks. Sybil brought solace to the soldiers dying in the hospitals. To her, each one was their son James, who died in battle at the beginning of the war. Although it meant disownment by Friends, James had volunteered, hoping to "loose the slave's chains."[24]

> The land is red with judgments. Who
> Stands guiltless forth?

Whittier wrote. Early in the war, he had sent a letter from Amesbury "To Members of the Society of Friends," reminding them that "we owe it to the cause of truth, to show that exalted heroism and generous self-sacrifice are not incompatible with our pacific principles. . . . Let the Quaker bonnet be seen by the side of the black hood of the Catholic Sister of Charity in the hospital ward. . . . What hinders us from holding up the hands of Dorothea Dix in her holy work of mercy at Washington? Our society is rich, and of those to whom much is given much will be required in this hour of proving and trial."[25]

At no time in their history did Friends respond to need with greater devotion. They organized Women's Aid Societies to collect clothing and care for refugees. Quaker men formed Friends Associations in all the Yearly Meetings. Those who had served on the Underground Railroad now ministered to the hordes of pitiful "contrabands"—slaves who had fled or had been smuggled behind the Union lines or who were abandoned by their masters as the Union Army advanced and who had neither food nor shelter.

Friends in Virginia, North Carolina and Tennessee suffered at the hands of both armies. So many Friends had left the South that the remainder felt isolated. By 1860, the only teacher left in the New Garden Boarding School, established by North Carolina Yearly Meeting in 1837, was Nereus Mendenhall. He had decided to leave for the West. His goods were at the station, his family ready to go, when something stopped him—the realization that if he left the school would have to close and the Yearly Meeting would probably be laid down. "The baggage and trunks at the station were returned to his home and he took his place with the remnant of Friends for the duration of the storm," Errol Elliott wrote in his moving account of the man whose faithfulness saved the school which was to become Guilford College.

At last, the horror ended. On February 2, 1865, as Whittier was worshiping in Fifth-day Meeting, the sacramental silence was invaded by the joyful sound of church bells and the cannon being fired. Amesbury was celebrating the passage of the Constitutional Amendment abolishing slavery! Whittier had labored in this cause with all his strength for thirty years. In that moment, when liberation was proclaimed, his heart overflowed with praise. In the silence of the Meeting, the poem he would call *Laus Deo* "wrote itself, or rather sang itself, while the bells rang."[26]

> It is done!
> Clang of bell and roar of gun
> Send the tidings up and down
> How the belfries rock and reel!
> How the great guns, peal on peal,
> Fling the joy from town to town!
>
> Ring and swing,
> Bells of joy! On morning's wing
> Send the song of praise abroad!
> With a sound of broken chains
> Tell the nations that he reigns,
> Who alone is Lord and God!

13 The Tower of Babel

The war was over.

Friends in the South had little with which to begin a new life. Of the young men who had not gone West, many died in camp or in prison. Confederate money was worthless; farms had been destroyed by both armies. Hundreds of Quakers fled to the Northwest, hoping to reach relatives, often leaving home without any possessions. Some were stranded in Baltimore, where local Friends cared for them and helped them to reach their destination.

In this emergency, the Baltimore Association of Friends to Assist and Advise Friends in the Southern States was formed. All the northern Yearly Meetings contributed funds, which were administered by Francis T. King, a Baltimore businessman. While the war still raged, he had traveled behind the Union lines with a pass written in Lincoln's hand, bringing relief to North Carolina Friends. Now a shipload of food and farm tools was sent to those North Carolina Quakers who were trying to remain in their homes.

There was a pressing need for education. Thanks to the faithfulness of Nereus Mendenhall, New Garden Boarding School had been kept open, but it was in bad repair and had no operating funds. In 1866, the Baltimore Association came to the rescue. A normal school was added for training teachers. "There was at this time no public school system and Friends furnished, for all practical purposes, the entire public education in their area."[1]

Nevertheless, in some parts of the South, Quaker teachers were driven out, like carpetbaggers, by the Ku Klux Klan. This did not deter other teachers, sent by their Yearly Meetings in the North and Middle West, from coming in and organizing schools for freedmen. Friends were convinced that the sooner the Blacks were educated, the sooner they would be able to take their place in the main stream of American life. As the federal government assumed responsibility for the physical needs of the freedmen, the Friends concentrated on these schools.

In 1867, the ugly treatment accorded the Indian tribes on the Great Plains, who happened to be in the way when the transcontinental railroads were under construction, moved Hicksite Friends to offer their services to the government on behalf of the

Indians without compensation. Orthodox Yearly Meetings also approached the government. They urged that when Indian agents were selected, they should be "men of unquestioned integrity and purity of character."[2]

The next year President-elect Grant received a delegation of these Friends. "Gentlemen, your advice is good," he told them. "I accept it. Now give me the names of some Friends for Indian agents and I will appoint them. If you can make Quakers out of the Indians it will take the fight out of them. Let us have peace."[3]

This offer was followed by a letter from the Headquarters of the Army, assuring Friends that "any attempt which may or can be made by your Society for the improvement, education, and Christianization of the Indians . . . will receive . . . all the encouragement and protection which the laws of the United States will warrant."

The Indian agents did not immediately make Quakers out of the Indians, nor did they succeed in securing fair treatment for them at the hands of the whites. But those who volunteered to go into the dangerous Indian Territory unarmed, who opened schools and befriended the humiliated and injured tribes, were for the most part deeply dedicated men. They were constantly put in the position of having to explain the actions of a grasping Great White Father who did not always honor his promises.

The Northern Superintendency, composed of Hicksite Friends, undertook work among the Indians in Nebraska; the Central Superintendency, composed of Orthodox Friends, served the rest of the Indian Territory and Kansas.

In 1871, Thomas C. Battey, a Vermont Friend, educated at Westtown School, went to the Wichita agency as a teacher. The work was arduous but he felt relatively safe there. The following year, he "distinctly heard the question audibly addressed to me, 'What if thou shouldst have to go and sojourn in the Kiowa camps?'"[4] The thought affected him "to tears," for he considered the Kiowas "the most fierce and desperately bloodthirsty tribe of the Indian Territory . . . heretofore I had clung, with the arm of earthly love to my precious wife and children . . . the time was near in which I must forsake all."[5] Thomas Battey—Thomissey, the Kiowas called him affectionately—became their trusted friend so that when some of their tribe were taken hostage during the government's extermination of the Modoc Indians in Oregon, it was Thomissey who prevailed upon them not to "go raiding," thus preventing a war that would have ravaged the homesteads of the pioneers. He went among the Indians, he said, not as an adventurer but "travelling among them as a kind of outside conscience."

He also had an inside conscience, which was sorely troubled by the acts of some white men. He observed, "There is a gang of desperadoes, having their headquarters about . . . Waco, in Texas, who make a regular business of horse-stealing and other desperate deeds. These are furnished . . . with false hair, masks, and other Indian disguises. . . . I have no doubt, while . . . Indians have done, and are still doing, more or less raiding in that state, that a large amount of the so-called Indian depredations and barbarities, even of the darkest dye, are committed by these savages with white skins."[6]

Thomissey was ill much of the time. The Indian women cooked what they thought he could digest and "the hand of God was over him." When he was so sick that he was obliged to return home, Kicking Bird, one of the chiefs, "having had a nice robe prepared for my wife, brought it, just at leaving camp, for me to take to her." And his friend Black Beaver, the Delaware Indian who had been Audubon's guide, came to the agency to remind the Kiowas, "The Quakers are your friends; they made a treaty with the Indians more than two hundred years ago, in which both parties had bound themselves, and their children forever after them, to be friends to each other forever. This treaty has never been broken. The Indians have never taken any Quaker blood, and the Quakers have always been true friends to the Indians."[7]

Friends had had a concern for the Indians from the time they came to America. They had preached to them and organized schools—New England Friends among the Penobscots and Passamaquoddys; New York Friends among the Brothertons, Onondagas and Senecas; Philadelphia Friends among the Delawares and Monomonees; Ohio and Indiana Friends among the Shawnees. But this was the first time in their history that Quakers were acting as agents of the government and they were not fitted for the role. They served in this capacity for almost ten years with dedication, but they also made some great mistakes.

When President Hayes was elected, the policy of the government changed to such an extent that Friends found it impossible to continue. They severed the connection with the government, remaining with the tribes as missionaries. Then some Indians did become Quakers, gathered into the Kickapoo Friends Center, the Hominy Friends Meeting among the Osage Indians, Wyandotte Friends Meeting, composed of several tribes, and Council House among the Senecas and Cayugas in New York State, and Rough Rocks among the Navajos in Arizona. The fight had gone out of them, not because they were Christianized, but because their fellow Christians had corralled them onto reservations and exterminated their buffalo.

Whatever shortcomings Friends may have exhibited in their work with the Indians, their intentions were expressed by Enoch Hoag, the Iowa Friend who supervised the Quaker Indian agents working among the Kickapoos, Shawnees, Potawatomies, Kaws, Osages, Quapaws, Sacs and Foxes, Cheyennes, Arapahoes, Wichitas, Kiowas, Comanches and Apaches. Greeting the Osages in 1869, Enoch Hoag said to the assembled Nation, "My brothers! I am happy to meet you . . . I call you brothers because we all have one common Father. The Great Creator of all made the white man, the red man, and the black man equal. He gave to the white man no more natural rights than He gave to the red man; and I claim from you no rights and privileges but such as I extend to you, and you should claim from me no more than you extend to me."[8]

Within the Society of Friends, diversity increased to such an extent after the Civil War that by the 1880s innumerable divisions had taken place. Some western Meetings became highly emotional. Joel Bean, who had been recorded a minister in the days when Iowa Friends waited on the Lord in silence, found little in these innovations that could speak to his condition. "Women would fall down and roll upon the floor, as I saw in one meeting which I visited. The converts made extreme claims of perfection, so that some dear and valued members became so impressed with their superior Holiness, that they refused to shake hands with their old friends, who could not join them."[9]

Until that time, Quakers who were attracted to revivals participated in camp meetings organized by other denominations. Now the more extreme evangelicals began to hold revivals in the Meetinghouses at the close of the regular Meeting for Worship. Traditional Quaker beliefs were also being revised.

In 1867, when Joel Bean was Presiding Clerk of Iowa Yearly Meeting, two evangelical Friends, who were on their way to Kansas, stopped and preached in Bear Creek, Iowa. "Many hearts were reached and all broken up, which was followed by sighs and sobs and prayers, confessions and great joy for sins pardoned," one of them reported, "and precious fellowship of the redeemed. But, alas, some of the dear old Friends mistook this outbreak of the power of God for excitement and wild fire and tried to close the meeting, but we kept cool and held the strings, and closed the meeting orderly."[10]

That same year, on 6th Month (June) 28, Canada Yearly Meeting of Friends was established, just two days before Canada became a Dominion. New York, the "Mother Yearly Meeting," (Orthodox), sent representatives to Pickering, Ontario, to oversee proceedings. Alma G. Dale, who was then a girl of thirteen, recalled this occasion later in life: "We were early at the meeting house and watched what seemed a never-ending stream of carriages, buggies, farm wagons and people on horse-back as they turned in at the gate. I was all excitement, for I had never seen so many people gather at a place of worship . . . the meeting house was not large enough to hold them, and in the afternoon an overflow meeting was held at which William Wetherald spoke to the people as he stood in a wagon, and in his own sweet, tender manner pointed . . . to the way of salvation. . . .

"But what shall I say of the First Day morning meeting? Filled to overflowing from doors to galleries. . . . I could not see the men's gallery very well, but I had a clear view of the women's side . . . my eyes roved along each row of seats, and then slowly back and forth again and again, and I sat spellbound. The plain Quaker bonnets shading the sweet, peaceful faces, the grey and dove-coloured dresses with spotless muslin fronts, the white silk shawls. . . . Not a sound was heard . . . for the spirit of silent worship had settled over the people, and the sweet faces grew sweeter."[11]

Five years later, Kansas Yearly Meeting was set off from Indiana. Friends had come in their prairie schooners and settled in Kansas to add their vote for freedom. But the pro-slavery people came, too, and they carried guns. It was a testing place for keepers of the Peace Testimony. In *Quakers on the American Frontier*, Errol Elliott points out with amusement that in its charter from the state of Kansas, the Yearly Meeting described itself as being made up of "those called Quakers that do not hire pastors or sing hymns." Fourteen years later, the first pastor was engaged.

Meanwhile, William Hobson, an Iowa Friend, encouraged members of his Meeting to settle in Newberg, Oregon, and "make it a garden of the Lord." In 1878, they asked Honey Creek Quarterly Meeting in Iowa for Monthly Meeting status and it was granted.

By 1877, Ohio Yearly Meeting had moved so far from Friends' emphasis on the Light Within that it passed a minute deploring the "mystical views . . . in certain of our members, in opposition to the plain scriptural doctrines of man's darkness and deadness in sin by nature and his redemption therefrom by the Lord Jesus Christ, whose shed blood is the alone means of cleansing the soul from all the guilt of sin." The following year, Ohio Yearly Meeting passed another minute: "And we repudiate the so-called doctrine of the inner light, or the gift of a portion of the Holy Spirit in the soul of every man, as dangerous, unsound, and unscriptural."[12]

In Amesbury, John Greenleaf Whittier read these minutes "with more regret than surprise . . . They seem to me an entire abandonment of the one distinctive and root doctrine of our religious Society—that from which it receives all that is peculiar to it . . . and which alone gives it a right to exist."[13]

American Friends had never broken their ties with London Yearly Meeting. After the Revolution, most of the other religious bodies drifted away from their progenitor in the mother country. But right down to the end of the nineteenth century, American Quakers could echo those first settlers of Pennsylvania, who wrote to Friends in England, "Oh, remember us, for we cannot forget you; many waters cannot quench our love, nor distance wear out the deep remembrance of you in the heavenly Truth." American Yearly Meetings continued to look to London Yearly Meeting for advice and for decisions in their sibling squabbles. At every intimation of trouble, London Yearly Meeting dispatched representatives to referee, who generally upheld the evangelicals. Yet, English Friends never introduced the pastoral system or programed worship into their own Meetings.

Joel and Hannah Bean and their two little girls spent three years among Friends in England, becoming intimate with many of the most concerned. Then Joel and Hannah taught for two years at the Friends Boarding School in Providence, Rhode Island.

When the Beans returned to West Branch in 1877, there were new babies in the Meeting. Jesse Hoover, the blacksmith, and his wife, Hulda, had had another little boy—Herbert. If Herbert was like most three-year-old Quakers, he had to be reminded not to swing his legs during the tedium of Meeting for Worship. It would have been difficult for the Beans to imagine that, half a century later, this little newcomer would be on his way to the White House.

The religious enthusiasts had become more fervent during the Beans' absence. About the time that the Beans returned there was another revival at Bear Creek. After it had been going on for several days, a call was made "for all those who wish to forsake sin and lead a different life to come to the front seats." Sinners were in such a hurry that they climbed over the backs of the benches and there was great confusion. Amid shouting and hymn singing, Friends who chose to remain in their seats were pleaded with and prayed over. "To those who all along had been displeased with the revival methods," Louis T. Jones wrote in *The Quakers of Iowa*, "such a scene in their quiet meetinghouse was simply intolerable; and in utter astonishment and consternation they arose and abruptly left the meeting."[14]

Iowa Yearly Meeting convened on September 5 and Joel Bean was appointed Presiding Clerk. Two days later, the now-familiar, apparently inevitable Quaker tragedy took place: the Conservative Friends, not in sympathy with the "new doctrines," withdrew and formed another Yearly Meeting. Although Joel and Hannah Bean were theologically in accord with them, they were opposed to separation among Friends and remained. Then David B. Updegraff, the leading Quaker revivalist, who introduced the "altar of prayer" into Meetinghouses and advocated baptism by immersion, came to West Branch and conducted a series of evangelistic meetings.

"His magnetic personality and attractive theory of a short and easy way to perfection drew a large following," Joel Bean recalled. "It was an open onslaught . . . to overcome what was claimed the false teaching of the past. . . . Our meeting was left in confusion. Confidence was impaired. Fellowship was broken. Beloved neighbors became estranged. . . . Few could know what we passed through . . . of the desertion of friends, the charges of unsoundness, and of heresy." Five years later, Joel Bean felt forced to give up. "The strain wore me down and preyed upon my health. And when the way opened for it, the pointing seemed clear to remove in 1882 to California, and to retire if possible from the conflict."[15]

Within a short time, the pastoral system was introduced into Iowa Yearly Meeting. Meetings were "encouraged to call and support ministers." At the same time, the Yearly Meeting established the office of General Superintendent of Evangelistic, Pastoral and Church Extension Work.

While the Beans were going to the west coast to start a new life in San Jose, on the east coast, Rufus Jones was entering Haverford College. Three years earlier, he had arrived at the Friends Boarding School in Providence from his home in South China, Maine. He was then "within half a year of seventeen, very thin, nearly six feet tall, extremely green and awkward, but wide awake, keen, eager and ambitious. . . . I had only the dimmest notion of what I was going to be or of what I *wanted* to be. . . . When I left school for college, I was no longer a boy. I had a Prince Albert coat! Man perhaps I was not yet, but I was soon to be one."[16]

Years after he outgrew the Prince Albert coat, Rufus Jones, who had been born into a Gurneyite Meeting in the days before pastors were inaugurated, commented on one area in which this system created a transformation. "One of the most striking changes introduced was the altered attitude towards the solemnization of marriage. The Society had secured at great cost the privilege of having their members marry themselves without the mediation of any ordained person . . . pastors and other Ministers of the Society began to marry couples after the established manner of the Ministers in other churches . . . the old way of marrying was lost and forgotten with many other beautiful and precious historical customs."[17]

But there were issues on which Friends of every branch could unite—temperance and the testimony against bearing arms, dancing, secret societies and lotteries.

Although Joel Bean moved to California to "retire if possible from the conflict," the conflict pursued him. Like Elias Hicks and John Wilbur, he was regarded by many as an impediment to progress. He and Hannah Bean did not care to worship under the guidance of a pastor but they wished to remain in their Yearly Meeting. So they withdrew from the San Jose Meeting. With a number of like-minded Friends, they formed a worship group, which they asked Honey Creek Quarterly Meeting in Iowa to establish as the College Park Monthly Meeting. Honey Creek refused to recognize them. Nevertheless, they continued to worship together. In 1885, they built a Meetinghouse and in 1889 they became incorporated under the state of California as the College Park Association of Friends, independent of any Quarterly or Yearly Meeting. The

Association's members met together to "realize the Kingdom of God within the soul through the act of worship" and "to realize the Kingdom outwardly in the world."[18] Two years later, Joel and Hannah Bean's Meeting in Iowa announced that they were no longer recognized as ministers. A letter of sympathy signed by 410 English Friends appeared in Quaker periodicals on both sides of the Atlantic.

While the Beans were upholding their concept of Quakerism in the San Francisco Bay area, evangelical Friends from Iowa and Kansas were moving into southern California. Aquilla Pickering, a Chicago land and railroad promoter, and his wife, Hannah, dreamed of establishing a Quaker center. This was realized in 1887 when a colony of pioneers laid out a little town an hour by buggy from Los Angeles. They decided to name the town in honor of the poet Whittier, the foremost Quaker of their day, and they wrote to Amesbury for his consent, explaining that one of the lots was being presented to him. In his reply, the eighty-year-old Friend said of his namesake town, "I trust that its Quakerism will be of the old, practical kind, 'diligent in business and serving the Lord,' not wasting its strength and vitality in spasmodic emotions, not relying on creed and dogma, but upon faithful obedience to the voice of God in the soul."[19]

Within a few months, "the magic little city of Whittier" had eight hundred inhabitants. They dreamed of a Friends College. Enviously, they looked eastward to the Quaker colleges that had already been established: in Pennsylvania, Haverford and Swarthmore, which was named for the Fell home in England; Earlham in Indiana; Wilmington in Ohio; William Penn in Iowa and New Garden Boarding School in North Carolina, which was about to become Guilford College. Ezra Cornell and Johns Hopkins endowed non-sectarian universities. Joseph W. Taylor's bequest created Bryn Mawr College. Johns Hopkins also endowed a hospital in Baltimore to be open to all persons regardless of race or color.

Whittier Friends found that it took time to open an institution of higher learning. Within a year of their arrival, the land boom around Los Angeles became a depression. There were few jobs in Whittier. People moved away. Friends promoted a public school and temporarily scaled down their plan for a college to an academy along the lines of Friends Pacific Academy in Newberg, Oregon. When that opened in 1885, one of the first students was Herbert Hoover, who had lost both his parents and who had come to live with his uncle, Dr. H. J. Minthorn, the principal of the academy.

Whittier Friends still hoped to found a college, so they named their academy The Preparatory Department of Friends College. One of the first students to enroll was Lou Henry, daughter of the cashier at the bank, who was to become Mrs. Herbert Hoover.

At Whittier, in 1895, California Yearly Meeting of Friends Church was set off from Iowa Yearly Meeting. Delegates came from the east coast, the Middle West and from Oregon Yearly Meeting, which had been set off two years earlier. "A sweet spirit of Christian fellowship prevailed."[20]

This spirit did not extend to College Park. Three years later, all the members of the Bean family were disowned by their Meeting in Iowa because they would not contribute to the support of the pastor, even as their forerunners in colonial New England and Virginia had been imprisoned by the civil authorities because they would not support a clergy.

Back East at Chautauqua, New York, the Hicksite Friends met in 1900 to form the Friends General Conference. They continued to believe in the authority of the Inner Light and "rejected the restrictions of Christocentric orthodoxy while at the same time claiming an allegiance to Jesus Christ."[21] They held to the traditional form of Quaker worship.

The Gurneyite Yearly Meetings were striving for uniformity. Ever since 1887, when they drew up the Richmond Declaration of Faith which was evangelical in emphasis, they had been looking toward the adoption of one uniform Discipline for all Yearly Meetings. In 1902, the Yearly Meetings which adopted it—New England, New York, Indiana, Kansas, California, Wilmington, Western, Baltimore, Iowa, Oregon and Canada—met together for the first time as the Five Years Meeting.

In 1914, five years after the death of Hannah Bean, Joel died in Honolulu where, half a century earlier, they had pioneered as missionaries. Their descendants would carry forward their concern.

Friends' pressing desire to perform "a service of love in wartime" led to the formation of the American Friends Service Committee— the AFSC. On April 30, 1917, representatives of various Quaker groups met in Philadelphia and recorded this minute: "We are united in expressing our love of our country and our desire to serve her loyally. We offer our services to the Government of the

United States in any constructive work in which we can conscientiously serve humanity."

The offer was not accepted, but in France the young Conscientious Objectors of World War I found plenty of scope for their dedicated efforts. When hostilities ceased, it was clear that a service of love was still desperately needed in the prostrate countries. The Committee's representatives carried relief overseas until the victims of the war could support themselves.

Anna S. Cox, the granddaughter of Joel and Hannah Bean, went to Germany in 1920. There she met Howard H. Brinton, a Friend from West Chester, Pennsylvania, who was in charge of the American Friends Service Committee work in Upper Silesia. They were married the following summer in the College Park Meeting at San Jose.

Except for an interval of teaching at Earlham, Howard and Anna Brinton taught at Mills College in Oakland, California, until 1936, when they became directors of Pendle Hill, the Quaker center for study and contemplation in Wallingford, Pennsylvania. As long as they were on the west coast, they gave their strength to the College Park Association and even when they went East, they kept coming back on every possible occasion. By 1931, the Association included Meetings all over California, for there were many Friends who wished to worship on the basis of silence. The Brintons proposed that the College Park Association be widened to include all the unprogramed Meetings in the West. A conference was held at Mills College in 1931 and there the Pacific Coast Association of Friends was formed. It grew rapidly.

The year the Brintons met in Germany, Friends from all over the world met in England for the First Friends World Conference. Two thousand people crowded into Central Hall, Westminster, to hear Rufus Jones. He also spoke at the Conference of Young Friends, held at Jordans in Buckinghamshire, the Quaker center where William Penn is buried. The Young Friends who attended that Conference were destined to become leaders in the Quaker movement during the next fifty years.

In 1930, Pendle Hill, the Quaker center in Pennsylvania, was opened. Named for the height in England where George Fox had his vision of a great people to be gathered, this Pendle Hill, in Howard Brinton's words, "seeks to provide an education which differs from conventional schooling almost the same way that a Quaker Meeting differs from a Protestant service. Both Pendle Hill and a Quaker Meeting must pay a price for permitting the Spirit of Truth to work as it will. That price is the greater possibility of failure, but there may also be a greater measure of success when success is attained. . . . At the beginning of the first term in the autumn of 1930 some precedents were set which have persisted ever since. . . . A meeting for worship began each day. Since the Quaker form of worship unprogrammed and based on silence, interspersed sometimes by messages from anyone present, requires no creedal commitment it can be accepted by anyone, Quaker or non-Quaker, Christian or non-Christian. Experience has shown that such worship becomes a powerful bond in holding the group together and in adding a sense of depth to all pursuits."[22]

In 1936, the Brintons were appointed the directors. Of this period, Douglas Steere was to write, "when Anna and Howard Brinton decided to . . . throw their lives into the Pendle Hill experiment, we knew that we were again in the main stream of the spiritual, intellectual, and socially sensitive witness of the Society of Friends, and we could almost feel the surge forward. . . . Anna's energy, her wit, her spirit of 'nothing is impossible,' her administrative skill, her willingness to be expendable—whether in her personal strength or her own bank account—to meet someone's need, made itself poignantly felt almost from the beginning. Her confidence in Pendle Hill's future when it had so little of a 'past' was infectious, and students began to appear in larger numbers."[23]

By 1936, a considerable number of people were professing spiritual kinship with Friends although they had no wish to become members of the Society. Rufus Jones invited them to take part not in an organization but rather in a spontaneous reaching out and touching of hands. This "Wider Quaker Fellowship" was to be, he wrote in *A letter to seekers,* "a looser . . . group than the Society itself. . . . There would be no condition of membership . . . except readiness to dedicate oneself to the way of love, and a faith that man is a candle of the Lord and can become a center of radiance, an organ of the Spirit, just where he lives."[24]

The Wider Quaker Fellowship appealed not only to certain members of other denominations, who were attracted to the Quaker mode of worship and the non-violent philosophy, but it gave still other people, who would have joined the Society of Friends had they not lived too far from any Monthly Meeting to be associated with it, a sense of belonging to a spiritual community which overcomes all geographical separation. A "Fellowship of the Beatitudes," it was called by Leslie Shaffer, who took the little association under his care in its first years. It had no officers, no bylaws, no dues.

The writings of early Friends as well as modern books and pamphlets were periodically received by the members of the Wider Quaker Fellowship. In addition, letters came regularly from Emma Cadbury, a Friend who had returned to her home in Philadelphia after fourteen years of service at the Quaker Center in Vienna.

"I got from you, dear Miss Cadbury," one faraway member of the Fellowship wrote at the end of twenty years, "everything I needed—books, countless personal letters and a Bible. . . . You, dear Friend, taught me Quakerism by mail."

The Second Friends World Conference was held at Swarthmore, Pennsylvania, in 1937. All branches of Friends were represented. To Elbert Russell, Dean of the Divinity School at Duke University, as to many others, the "presence of representatives from so many races and nations brought a vivid realization that Quakerism was no longer merely an Anglo-Saxon sect but a world-wide movement."[25] The Conference decided to establish a Friends World Committee for Consultation, representing all Friends, which would enable them to cooperate. The Society of Friends in France not only sent delegates, but a letter in which it expressed concern for greater simplicity among Friends. "The amassing of worldly goods complicates our life and turns us aside from our true goal. The armament makers, who live on the suffering and deaths of their fellows, are a striking example of the evils entailed by lust for gain. And nations, driven by the same impulse to take part in the armaments race and in wars of conquest or of prestige, are another example. Thus the lack of simplicity, which perhaps seems to many to be merely a trivial defect, is, in fact, a vice, a danger both for private life and the life of nations."[26]

During the 1930s, new "independent" or "unaffiliated" Monthly Meetings, which belonged to no Yearly Meeting, began to spring up on the eastern seaboard. They were nurtured by visits from seasoned Friends like J. Barnard Walton, who traveled up and down, encouraging the little new groups, communicating love and a touching humility. These Meetings worshiped on the basis of silence "in obedience to the leading of the Spirit." Many of the members were convinced Friends, who had no Quaker antecedents to claim their loyalty and no use for bygone squabbles.

In New England the two Yearly Meetings were still estranged. The independent Meetings in Cambridge, Providence and the towns of the Connecticut Valley felt strongly that Friends should no longer tolerate the scandal of disunity. They preached reconciliation to the world, yet they couldn't get along together. What right did they have to demand good will of others? These Meetings might have joined one or another of the Yearly Meetings, but what they longed for was an end to the Separation and a new union of all Friends in New England. As Henry Cadbury put it, they didn't wish "to become the adopted children of divorced parents."

In 1937, the two New England Yearly Meetings appointed a joint committee to explore the possibility of reunion. One of the older members of this committee was opposed to all change. Nothing could be done. In 1942, a new committee was formed to which representatives from the independent Meetings were added. This second group was less hidebound. It set out to find an organizational pattern that would not only restore wholeness to the dismembered Yearly Meeting, but would embrace all Friends in New England.

This was more than a call to good will. For some, loyalty to forebears made compromise seem faithless. There were legal considerations involving property and bequests. But the chief obstacle —the one which appeared insurmountable—was the form of worship. Deeply though New England Friends might desire union, no one must be asked to renounce his own manner of coming into the presence of God.

A committee was appointed, charged with prayerfully exploring ways of emerging from this dilemma.

All the Monthly Meetings were consulted. Had they been in the habit of acting, like other bodies, according to the will of the majority, there would not have been much doubt about the outcome. But these Friends do not vote. In decision making, they believe, the majority is not necessarily wiser than the minority. Ideally, they hesitate to proceed if it is evident that even one "weighty" member is not "comfortable."

Instead, after all those present have had a chance to discuss an issue, the Clerk determines the "sense of the Meeting," that is, he or she decides whether the Meeting appears to be ready to move forward in unity. There may be members who are not in agreement with the action which is being proposed, but having stated their views and realizing that the rest of the group is comfortable, they usually withdraw their objections. If they continue to express dissent, no action can be taken.

In an impasse, Friends resort to worship. Emotions cool, separate wills yield to a higher will and occasionally a third way opens which had not been thought of before and which is acceptable to the entire group. This transcendence of individual opinion into a sense of harmony with the divine will becomes a deeply religious experience.

The New England Friends who undertook to study ways of effecting the reunion of the two Yearly Meetings hoped that it might take place within three years so that it could be accomplished on the one hundredth anniversary of the Separation. The eyes of Friends in New York, New Jersey, Pennsylvania, Delaware and Maryland were on New England. If those Friends could reverse history, what was there to prevent other separated Yearly Meetings from doing the same thing?

Could Friends of the twentieth century know that experience which Francis Howgill described in the seventeenth? "The Kingdom of God did gather us and catch us all, as in a net. . . . We met together in the unity of the Spirit and the bond of peace."

No committee, no organizational pattern, no formula—nothing less than this transcendent experience was capable of overarching such divergent traditions.

While the joint committee labored, the dismembered Yearly Meeting waited. Like the Sleeping Beauty surrounded by a prickly hedge, the Yearly Meeting waited, as it had waited nearly a hundred years, for the only measure that could restore and quicken it: the simple bestowal of a kiss.

14 The Seed

In the year 1940, a Quaker miller, Perry Hayden, of Tecumseh, Michigan, planted a cubic inch of grain—360 kernels—on a borrowed patch of land four feet wide and eight feet long.

Worshiping in the Tecumseh Friends Church one Sunday, this evangelical Friend had, he later reported, pondered "the Biblical truths regarding sowing, reaping, rebirth and tithing."[1] Clifton J. Robinson, a visiting preacher, had discussed the text from John: "Except a corn of wheat fall into the ground and die, it abideth alone; but if it die, it bringeth forth much fruit."

How much fruit?

Perry Hayden belonged to that branch of Friends who regard the Bible literally and who seek direction from its injunctions.

"When the preacher talked about wheat," he explained after the service, "he was talking directly to me about my own business. I'm going to plant a kernel of wheat and see what happens."[2]

One tenth of the small harvest he would give to the Church. The other nine tenths he would plant again. Repeating the process year after year—sowing, reaping, tithing—he would eventually have so large a crop, descended from that one little kernel, that there would not be land enough in all of Tecumseh to replant it. A time limit would have to be set on the project.

How long?

A verse from Leviticus furnished the directive: "Six years thou shalt sow thy field . . . and gather in the fruit thereof. But in the seventh year shall be a sabbath of rest unto the land, a sabbath for the Lord."

So Perry Hayden decided to conduct the experiment for six years.

Since he did not own suitable land for planting even one kernel, he appealed to the Manager of the Henry Ford farms. Almost ten thousand acres of farmland in the area belonged to the auto manufacturer. The Manager said jokingly that he guessed they could spare "a spot large enough to plant one kernel of wheat."[3] He suggested, however, starting with a larger amount, a cubic inch, in case something should happen to the one grain.

From the very outset, the experiment caught the interest of a number of people in the community, who wanted a share in furthering it. Someone made a metal container exactly one inch long, one inch wide and one inch high to serve as a cubic inch measure. Someone else contributed his soft red winter wheat. When the tiny container was filled and leveled off, it held exactly 360 kernels. These were planted by twelve boys on September 26.

Perry Hayden put a fence around the plot and a screen over the top for protection from animals and birds. He "left the rest to God."[4]

All winter long, while Perry Hayden thought anxiously about the seed he had planted, Friends everywhere were thinking of the Seed of God. "The Seed sown in the hearts of all," Robert Barclay wrote in 1678. "He is arisen to plead with the nations."[5]

Friends pleaded many causes.

The Society joined the other Historic Peace Churches—the Brethren and Mennonites—in sending a delegation to call on President Roosevelt and plead on behalf of the Conscientious Objectors, in the event that conscription should be introduced. They asked the President to appoint a civilian board whose function it would be to judge the sincerity of these men and to assign them to service projects administered by the Peace Churches. These projects would be: relief of war sufferers, reconstruction, forest reclamation and medical services.

Friends believed that all men who were opposed to fighting on conscientious grounds should be given exemption whether they happened to be, like themselves and the Mennonites and Brethren, members of Historic Peace Churches or not.

The first draft of the Burke-Wadsworth bill stipulated that only persons belonging to well-recognized sects which opposed participation in war should be exempted from duty in combatant units. Due in part to the efforts of Friends, a new draft provided exemption on the basis of individual conscience.

All persons opposed to war were to register to that effect and to have a hearing before civilian Boards of Inquiry, which might assign them to non-combatant service. If they could not conscientiously accept such service, they might be assigned to work of national importance under civilian direction.

The penalty for being unable to engage in any military work was so great that no one envisaged incurring it unless he was totally convinced. He would not, for example, be paid for the public service he might be obliged to render in place of military duty. Who, then, would maintain him, however marginally? Who would support his wife and children while he was engaged in work of national importance?

The Conscientious Objector did not have to be told that most of his fellow Americans would receive his decision with hostility; that his reasons would be misunderstood; that there would be contempt for what was generally considered to be a strange aberration. When the Selective Service Act was signed by President Roosevelt on September 16, 1940, those who felt governed by the sixth commandment would have preferred the Act passed by the Rhode Island General Assembly on August 13, 1673: "Bee it therefore enacted . . . by his Majesty's authority, that noe person (within this Collony), that is or hereafter shall be persuaded in his conscience that he cannot or ought not to trayne, to learne to fight, nor to war, nor kill any person or persons, shall at any time be compelled against his judgment and conscience . . . at the command of any officer of this Collony, civil or military . . . nor shall suffer any punishment, fine, distraint, pennalty, nor imprisonment. . . ."[6]

During the 1940s, the popular image of the Quaker—that quaint, anachronistic figure on the cereal box, that quixotic anomaly, who mops up the world after others have destroyed it—suddenly altered. In the minds of certain people, whose extravagant, sentimental praise had up to that time been embarrassing, the Quaker became overnight a coward and a threat to national security.

Preaching from his New York pulpit, one Christian minister declared that objection to war "had undoubtedly encouraged the dictators to their acts of shameless aggression." And he added, "The pacifism which has been preached so widely is unscriptural. Christ never taught that nations should not resist aggression or that they should disband their military forces."

D. Elton Trueblood, a Friend on the faculty of Stanford University, who was later to become Professor of Religion at Earlham College, tried to explain the puzzling Quaker Peace Testimony in an article that appeared in the *Atlantic Monthly*.

"There is no logical inconsistency in condemning what is patently evil and, at the same time, seeking to overcome this evil in other ways than the ways of military power.

"The Quaker opposition to war arises, not from refusal to face reality, not from the nature of the issues in a particular war, and not from fear of physical death, but from a conception of how the world is to be remade."

Once again, young Quakers faced very difficult decisions. Was it right to refuse their country's call to arms? How could any self-respecting man let another defend him—die for him, perhaps—when he was unwilling to defend himself, his family, his country? But if it was wrong to kill, was it not wrong under any circumstance? How could it be both wrong and right? At least these Friends were not, like their forerunners, threatened with disownment.

Friends have always believed that every sincere, inwardly attentive worshiper can, unassisted, ascertain the will of God, not only as it appears to him but to his fellow worshipers. It is not a solitary search. The response to God's will as Friends perceive it in themselves and in one another, rather than obedience to a traditional creed, joins them in generally living by the same testimonies.

But just as twentieth-century Quakers dropped the plain speech and attire of an earlier age while intending to keep the spirit of simplicity which these expressed, so, too, they changed their practice in respect to the Peace Testimony while still wholeheartedly committed to upholding it. They retained in membership those individuals who, in regard to military participation, sought God's will in themselves alone without reference to its operation in the other members of the Meeting or in Friends throughout the centuries and who concluded that they personally were called to support war. These members were no longer excluded from the fellowship of the Meetings as they would have been in former times, but were now held in tender concern, even though their decision was counter to the corporate testimony of Friends.

In the 1940s, young Quakers knew that whether they entered the armed forces or went to prison or to some other confinement created for their peculiar condition by the Selective Service Act, their standing in the Society of Friends would be the same. Agonized, they examined their consciences, not in fear of losing their membership, only their souls.

Older Friends tried to support the younger ones during this search without influencing them. They simply explained the provisions of the law and stood by while the arguments for and against the Peace Testimony were being weighed. It would have been un-Quakerly for those older Friends to impose their views or the Society's. Only the young man's Light Within could determine what was right for him.

Penetrating the darkness to this source of illumination must be a solitary journey. Often it proved shattering. To have a companion who had, perhaps, gone through the ordeal himself, was some comfort.

Friends felt responsible not only for their own young men but for all who took the pacifist position, even those who would not register for the draft because they believed this was the first step in military conscription.

A Philadelphia Friend, Walter C. Longstreth, acted as counsel for Arle Brooks, an ordained minister of the Disciples of Christ and a staff member of the American Friends Service Committee, at his trial in Philadelphia on January 10, 1941.

"My conscience forbade me to register under the Selective Service and Training Act of 1940," the defendant declared. "I felt it my moral duty to do all within my power to protest against conscription, which will eventually weaken and destroy democracy. I am not evading the draft. I am defending democracy."

The district attorney asked for a substantial sentence.

The Federal judge who heard the case was himself a Friend, caught between the principles of his Religious Society and the laws of the government he served. To Arle Brooks he conceded that a "thoroughly conscientious man would be torn in a situation of this kind by two loyalties, the loyalty to a Supreme Being that you have tried to serve for a number of years in a very active way and loyalty to the Goverment that gives you protection so that you are free to obey your conscience. I felt like Pontius Pilate," the judge said. "I have got to obey the law. That law commands me. I would obey it if it meant my life . . . you, having defied the law, are subject to penalty. . . . In spite of your ideals, you find yourself wearing stripes in a prison cell. You must now show charity towards us. If you were my son, I could not feel differently about it."[7]

Arle Brooks was sentenced to a year and a day in prison and deprived of citizenship rights, which could only be restored by a presidential pardon.

In the first century of their history, Friends with one accord refused to pay a militia tax. Their household goods and livestock were distrained by the colonial government. Today their automobiles will be confiscated or their bank accounts attached if Friends withhold, as some do, that portion of their income tax which is earmarked for military use. But while civil disobedience is practiced by some, who are prepared to take the consequences, most Friends, though deeply troubled, prefer to remain law-abiding citizens.

The United States had gone a long way in recognizing the rights of an individual's conscience since 1917 when Conscientious Objectors were simply given prison terms. While those who refused to submit to the draft in any form would also be sent to prison in the 1940s, those who accepted alternative service were going to be sent to camps where they would be given "work of national importance."

What did that entail? Under whose auspices would the work be carried out?

Friends joined representatives from the other Historic Peace Churches in calling on President Roosevelt, on Attorney General Frank Murphy and his successor Robert Jackson. They requested that the camps be administered by civilians; that the work be meaningful: relief of war sufferers, resettlement of refugees, reconstruction of war-stricken areas overseas, as well as medical, farm and forestry services at home.

They pointed out that while the majority of the Conscientious Objectors would welcome the opportunity to do this type of alternative service, there were those whose consciences would not permit them to accept even this, since in their eyes it denoted submission to the draft. The representatives of the Peace Churches begged officials in the government to give the consciences of such persons due recognition.

The Quakers were especially anxious to secure permission for assignment to alternative service overseas. The Friends Ambulance Unit in China, the Friends War Victims Relief Committee in England (the "War Vics") and the Quaker child feeding and refugee relief programs on the continent of Europe were all shorthanded. The Conscientious Objectors themselves were eager to be given such assignments.

Again and again, Friends returned to Washington to confer with Mr. Francis Biddle, Solicitor General of the Department of Justice, with Mr. Clarence A. Dykstra, Director of Selective Service, and later with General Lewis B. Hershey.

The men whose cause these Friends were pleading had no other champion. Few people could condone or even understand their position. In some cases, their families refused to support them.

The introduction of the draft, bringing with it the necessity for counseling men of draft age, imposed an added burden on those

Friends who, having no pastor, were already ministering to troubled members of their Meetings. In addition, they were making a living, caring for their families, assisting their neighbors when necessary and shouldering community responsibilities.

Throughout the week, these Friends tried earnestly to prepare themselves for contributing to the depth of the Meeting for Worship on First-day whether through vocal ministry or through the silence. At the same time, they served as Trustees of Friends Schools, on Committees of Peace and Social Concern, as Elders and Overseers of their Monthly or Yearly Meetings, on Finance Committees. They attended Friends Conferences, went to Washington to plead with their congressmen, dealt with problems of sharecroppers, Indians and unemployed miners, and supported overseas missions.

Those Friends who carried all these loads had needs themselves. Without leisure for inward retirement, for savoring, amid suffering, the joy of God's presence, how could they discharge their duties serenely?

In their periods of worship together, under the increasing weight of their concerns, older Friends often heard a poignant echo. Half a century earlier, John Wilhelm Rowntree, a young British Quaker, speaking to the question "Has Quakerism a Message in the World Today?" asked, "Is there perplexity? . . . Is there indifference to the higher life? Then, O Christ, convince us by Thy Spirit, thrill us with Thy divine passion, drown our selfishness in Thy invading love." The young Friend pleaded, in words that were remembered long after his untimely death, "Lay on us the burden of the world's suffering."

That part of his prayer, at least, seemed indeed to have been answered.

The Peace Testimony cannot be ignored by any practicing Friend, for it is regularly brought to his attention with the reading aloud of the Queries in his Monthly Meeting.

"Do you endeavor to 'live in the virtue of that life and power that takes away the occasion of all wars,' and to discourage all military activity as inconsistent with the teaching and spirit of Christ?" the Clerk of a Monthly Meeting inquires from time to time, reading aloud some of the Queries listed in the book of *Faith and Practice.*

Then there is a long silence. Friends are confronting their consciences.

The Quaker Queries are not regarded as a set of rules, only as a reminder of the conduct which the Society, by and large, upholds. The wording and emphasis vary from one Yearly Meeting to another, but in essence the Queries are similar, examining the spiritual quality of the Meetings for Worship and Business, personal standards of living, marriage, education, the social order and race relations.

No one, however conscientious, can feel smug when replying to searching questions such as these:

"Are your Meetings for Worship and Business held in expectant waiting for divine guidance? Is there a living silence in which you feel drawn together by the power of God in your midst?

"Do you seek to live in Christian love one toward another? Do you manifest a forgiving spirit and a care for the reputation of others? Where differences arise are endeavors made speedily to end them?

"Do you live in simplicity and sincerity and are you on your guard against worldliness and self-indulgence? Do you choose such recreations as will not hinder your spiritual growth?

"Are you free from the use of judicial oaths, from betting, and gambling? Are you free from the use and handling of intoxicants and the misuse of drugs?

"Are you punctual in keeping promises, just in payment of debts, free from defrauding the public revenue, honorable and truthful in all your dealings? Are you careful to live within your income and to avoid involving yourselves in business beyond your ability to manage? Are you helping to create political, economic, religious and social institutions which will forward the cause of brotherhood on earth?

"Do you endeavor to reverence personality in ·every human being, regardless of race or creed? Do you encourage efforts to overcome racial prejudice and antagonism, and economic, social, and educational discrimination?

"Are you endeavoring to make your home a place of friendliness, refreshment and peace, where God becomes more real to those who dwell therein and to all who visit there?"

The individual is answerable to God alone in the silence, and it is there, without the judgment of any man but supported and enlightened by the gathered meeting, that he must seek forgiveness.

15 Now Is the Time

In the seventeenth century, the Publishers of Truth declared that the Seed binds all men together. In the twentieth, this was reiterated passionately by Thomas Raymond Kelly. Beginning as a chemist, becoming a philosopher and ultimately a mystic, he inspired not only Friends but many others.

"Deep within us all there is an amazing sanctuary of the soul, a holy place, a Divine Center, a speaking Voice," he wrote in *A Testament of Devotion*. "Eternity is at our hearts, pressing upon our time-torn lives, warming us with intimations of an astounding destiny. . . . It is a seed stirring to life if we do not choke it. . . . And in brief intervals of overpowering visitation we are able to carry the sanctuary frame of mind out into the world, into its turmoil and fitfulness."[1]

Like all authentic mystics, Thomas Kelly had identified himself with those who suffer. A Conscientious Objector in the First World War, he ministered to German prisoners in England under the auspices of the YMCA. In 1924, the Service Committee sent him and his wife, Lael, to Berlin for a year to set up the Friends International Center. He went back in the summer of 1938 to visit German Friends, traveling from place to place, sharing people's crushing burdens, yet all the while "drowned in the seas of the love of God."

That fall he returned to Haverford College, where he had done graduate work, as a member of the Philosophy Department, from which Rufus Jones had recently retired. But Douglas Steere was there, a warm friend and colleague, who was to write the moving biographical preface to *A Testament of Devotion* when the book was published after Thomas Kelly's death.

As the book unfolds, Thomas Kelly exclaims joyfully, "such a discovery of an Eternal Life and love . . . makes life glorious and new. And one sings inexpressibly sweet songs within oneself, and one *tries* to keep one's inner hilarity and exuberance within bounds lest, like the men of Pentecost, we be mistaken for men filled with new wine. Traditional Quaker decorum and this burning experience of a Living Presence are only with the greatest difficulty held together."[2]

On the seventeenth day of 1941, Thomas Kelly died suddenly at the age of forty-seven. Gerald Heard, the English philosopher, who never met him but who found that the writings of this Quaker mystic spoke—as he would have phrased it, had he been a Quaker himself—"to his condition," observed at the time: "I was filled with a kind of joy when I read of Thomas Kelly. It was formerly the custom of the Winston Salem Community of Moravians in North Carolina to announce the passing of a member by the playing of three chorales by the church band from the top of the church tower. So I feel I want to sing . . . I know it is an outward loss to us . . . but I keep on feeling what it must be for a man as good as he to be able to push aside this fussy veil of the body and look unblinking at the Light. . . ."[3]

Eternity is at our hearts . . . seed stirring to life if we do not choke it.

It was fitting that only a few days before the death of this Friend, whose special concern had been for sufferers in Germany, two Quaker delegations left for Europe in the hope of getting relief through the British blockade.

The previous September, Clarence Pickett had conferred in Washington with Ambassador William Bullitt. "Mr. Bullitt ordered a cable sent to the American Embassy in France, asking whether they had any evidence of food's being extracted from unoccupied France by the Nazis . . . If we turned up no evidence of such activities on the part of Germany, Mr. Bullitt offered to go to the President and specifically ask him to request Mr. Churchill to allow relief ships to go through the blockade."[4]

It was difficult for Quaker representatives in France to ascertain whether Germany was taking food out of the "free zone." All they were sure of was the desperate need. "Can't you send more warm clothing?" they asked Friends in Philadelphia. "By no stretch of the imagination can Hitler be aided by putting a warm coat on a shivering child."[5]

The Service Committee decided to send two Friends over to assess the situation and explore possibilities for helping to end the war. President Roosevelt "warmly encouraged such a visit." The German Ambassador agreed to authorize the visas.[6]

"We felt that if children especially were allowed to starve to death in Europe, deliberately, while we were embarrassed by food surpluses," Clarence Pickett insisted, "they would not die alone, but would drag down with them into spiritual bondage those of us who participated in causing their death."[7]

On January 11, 1941, Harold Evans, a Philadelphia attorney, and James G. Vail of the Service Committee's Foreign Service Section, left for Germany. On the same day, Henry Cadbury and Robert Yarnall went to England where they arranged to forward ten thousand dollars per month in American Quaker funds to British Friends for emergency relief work in their country. The two Americans had a long session with the British Minister of Economic Warfare, but they were unable to arrange for the feeding of children in occupied parts of France. The British insisted that a rigid blockade would in the long run reduce the total suffering. Greatly disappointed, the two Friends returned to Philadelphia where, almost a century and a half earlier, George Logan had resisted the Embargo Act that was calculated to starve the British into submission.

A few weeks later, Harold Evans and James Vail returned from their mission to Germany. They reported that should the British blockade be relaxed so that relief ships could pass through, the German Government would be willing to have food sent into occupied territories but only subject to Nazi inspection. The two returning Friends felt there could be no certainty that this food would reach its intended destination. It might, as the British Government feared, be diverted to Germany.

Shortly after these missions reached home, the first of the "Letters from the Past" signed by "Now and Then" appeared in *The Friends Intelligencer*. The writer could not preserve his anonymity very long, since there was only one person in all of Quakerdom who possessed the knowledge of the Bible and Quaker history disclosed in these "Letters" and only one person with that special strain of wit, never sharp, never intended to wound, merely—and this persisted into his eighties—youthfully mischievous. He was none other than Henry Joel Cadbury.

"While the purpose of these Letters is to show modern readers the interest of Quaker history and to link that history with the present," he says in Letter 42, "no one is more conscious than 'Now and Then' of a general indifference of many Friends to their past history. 'Forbearance with forebears,' is a phrase that might express this indifference. To be sure," he adds, "too much harking back to the past, especially if tinctured with a bit of ancestor worship, may be unwise not to say boring."[8]

Genially stripping away false or sentimental notions that have crept into Quaker folklore, Now and Then shows us, through an original association of ideas, how Friends lived out their testimonies in successive generations. Here, in essence, is a lifetime of scholarship. But what impresses us, the readers, most of all, what inspires us is the evidence of a deep spiritual search quickening the historical research.

A liberal Friend, the Hollis Professor of Divinity at Harvard University, Henry Cadbury was one of the scholars who made the translation of the New Testament known as The Revised Standard Version. His concept of the place the Bible should have in our religious life is similar to that of early Friends, for whom the Scriptures constituted a corroboration of their experience.

George Fox expressed this view when he was awaiting trial at Worcester for refusing to take the Oaths of Allegiance and Supremacy. "There came three nonconformist priests and two lawyers to discourse with me; and one of the priests undertook to prove that the Scriptures are the only rule of life. Whereupon, after I had plunged him about his proof, I had a fit opportunity to open unto them . . . that the Spirit of God . . . and the grace of God, which bringeth salvation, and which hath appeared unto all men and teacheth them . . . that this is the most fit, proper and universal rule, which God hath given to all mankind to . . . order their lives. . . ."[9]

Early Friends were wary of substituting words for spiritual experience. "Why trim yourselves with the saints' words," Francis Howgill asked in 1658, "when you are ignorant of the life?"[10]

Henry Cadbury, referring to the translation of the Bible from Greek to English, observed, "Few that have not tried it know the difficulty of . . . a transfer from words to words, from one language to another. . . . The approach I have here been discussing goes much deeper than that. It is translation from language to life, from words to flesh.

"The Bible is the deposit of a long series of controversies between rival views of religion. The sobering thing is that in nearly every case the people shown by the Bible to be wrong had every reason to think that they were in the right, and, like us, they did so. Complacent orthodoxy is the recurrent villain in the story from first to last, and the hero is the challenger, like Job, the prophets, Jesus and Paul."[11]

While Friends were trying to cope with relief abroad, a new assignment devolved upon them at home, one which called for even greater resources—for imaginative leadership, dedicated personnel and supplementary funds.

The United States Government had asked members of the Historic Peace Churches—the Brethren, the Mennonites and Friends—to undertake the administration and financing of the Civilian Public Service Camps to which Selective Service would assign Conscientious Objectors. There, those prevented by conscience from bearing arms were to engage in soil conservation, reforestation and other public works. The government agreed to provide the camps, which had been used by the Civilian Conservation Corps during the depression. It also agreed to provide technical supervision and equipment. But the cost of running the camps would have to be underwritten by the church agencies.

The Brethren and Mennonites agreed, under the terms of this arrangement, to direct their camps.

Whether assuming this responsibility was appropriate for the Quakers was a decision not easily arrived at. Some Meetings felt that it put the American Friends Service Committee in the position of cooperating with Selective Service. And while the Service Committee would be nominally in charge, Selective Service reserved the right to inspect the camps. There might be serious differences of opinion in regard to policy.

Then there was the question of funds. Civilian Public Service Campers would receive no government pay for their work. They were expected to contribute thirty-five dollars a month toward their expenses but in many cases they or their families were unable to meet the cost. The deficit had to be raised by individual Friends and Meetings, even though a great many of the Campers belonged to other denominations or had no religious affiliation.

In spite of these negative considerations, the Quakers agreed to accept the responsibility. They felt that this was one way they could help the Conscientious Objectors and thereby register a protest against conscription. The undertaking turned out to be more difficult than anyone could have envisaged at the start.

A Friend, Thomas E. Jones, President of Fisk University and later of Earlham College, became the first Director of the Civilian Public Service Camps. He was succeeded by another Friend, Paul J. Furnas, a Philadelphia businessman.

General Lewis B. Hershey announced that on May 15 the first one hundred Conscientious Objectors would report to the Civilian

Public Service Camp at Patapsco State Forest near Baltimore, Maryland, which was under the care of Friends.

Paul Comly French, the Quaker who was appointed Director of the National Service Board for Religious Objectors, representing the three Peace Churches, estimated that two thousand men had been certified as being sincere in their opposition to military service. They would shortly be directed to report to camp.

The second American Friends Service Committee Camp was opened at San Dimas, California, on June 2. Three days later a third started operating at Cooperstown, New York.

At the same time, in Tecumseh, Michigan, Perry Hayden was anxiously watching the rebirth of what he called Dynamic Kernels. And in Philadelphia, Friends were earnestly pleading with the nations for what they called Dynamic Peace.

This, Rufus Jones explained, was "not a static condition, to be attained after the defeat of those who disturb it" but "a dynamic method by which to remove injustices . . . and to remedy instead of aggravating the evils that have been inflicted on the world by military aggression."

Specific proposals were embodied in *A Call to Persons of Good Will,* issued in June 1941. "The time has come," it warned, "for those who see clearly what is happening to the world . . . and who, at the same time, have a firm grasp of the divine possibilities of this human life of ours, to speak a sober, solemn word."[12]

Only four years but millions of broken lives later, another document would begin with the words: "We, the Peoples of the United Nations, determined to save succeeding generations from the scourge of war, which twice in our lifetime has brought untold sorrow to mankind, and to reaffirm faith in fundamental human rights, in the dignity and worth of the human person . . ."[13]

The *Call to Persons of Good Will* pleaded, "Is there no one in any government at the moment enough detached and above the issues of strife to call for cessation and mediation? If not, then we at least should cry aloud to those who . . . see steadily the fundamental claims of humanity to discover some way in the wisdom of God to stop this *tide of destruction.*

"It will be easier to start rebuilding the world now . . . than it can possibly ever be . . . after a still greater accumulation of hate. It is not yet a World War, but a slight turn of events now will almost certainly involve the entire world."

Dynamic Peace would require the acceptance of six principles:

1) The reduction of national armed forces with a view to universal disarmament.
2) Peaceful third party settlement of all disputes not settled by mutually satisfactory direct negotiations.
3) The freedom of all peoples to develop their own cultures and of each nation to develop the form of government its people desire.
4) Economic and social policies which affect other nations or people must be determined in international consultation, under international authority.
5) All nations should be assured equitable access to markets and essential raw materials, and should control immigration and emigration with a view to the welfare of all the nations concerned.
6) All colonies must be administered by an international authority, with the welfare and development toward self-government of the native inhabitants as the primary objective and providing equitable opportunity of access for all nations to the resources and trade of such colonies.

"There is no use expecting . . . some easy reconstruction of the world," the *Call to Persons of Good Will* concluded. "But *now* is the time."

A message similar to this one of 1941 had been published in the summer of 1917.

"The causes for which men fight—liberty, justice, peace—are noble and Christian causes. But the method of war is unchristian and immoral. . . . The peoples of every land are longing for the time . . . when the people of some great nation dare to abandon the outworn traditions of international dealing and to stake all on persistent good will.

"We are the nation and now is the time. This is America's supreme opportunity."

Down the years, these desperate pleas kept echoing: "Good will; *now* is the time."

But neither in 1917 nor in 1941 were these Quaker pleas and visionary proposals considered worthy of serious attention by a world preoccupied with conquest or survival. Four years later, after "untold sorrow to mankind," a number of the same proposals could be recognized in the United Nations Charter.

That summer, however, even some Friends began to feel that hostilities were inevitable; that only military superiority could stop Axis aggression and cruelty. While these Friends had always believed in pacifism, they began to wonder whether this war was not a moral necessity. If Britain should be unable to defend herself, the civilization they cherished would come to an end. Hitlerism had to be stopped.

Before the fateful year was out, many more American Friends were going to abandon the ancient Peace Testimony and wholeheartedly support their country's war effort. It was not an easy choice, nor a decision arrived at without much anguish.

There were still, however, a great number of Quakers who believed that military triumph carried in it the resentful roots of further conflict. One such, reflecting on the terms of the Versailles Treaty, observed that the real victors of the First World War were not Wilson, Lloyd George and Clemenceau but Mussolini, Stalin and Hitler.[14] Those who upheld the Peace Testimony were convinced that there was no higher patriotism than the guarding of their country against ever widening conflict and the loss of human values.

E. Raymond Wilson went to Washington to be Secretary of the Friends War Problems Committee. One of the efforts of this Committee was to urge defeat of the proposed Manpower bill, which would have conscripted women for work in industry.

Because many young women were eager to work for peace, the Service Committee inaugurated the Civilian Training Center for Women on Highacres Farm at Glen Mills, Pennsylvania. "To prepare women who believe in the power of constructive good will for service in their homes, in their communities, and throughout the world . . . to offer an opportunity for the deepening of spiritual resources through individual and group discipline; and to give experience in simple, cooperative, community living."

The Center was directed by a young Quaker couple, Bronson and Eleanor Clark. Bronson was destined, a quarter of a century later, to become Executive Secretary of the Service Committee.

Each day at the Civilian Training Center for Women began with meditation. There were classes in growing food, cooking and preserving, in practical nursing and first aid, the use of tools, community recreation. The cost of participation was thirty-five dollars per month.

The Friends General Conference appointed a committee to consider economic and social problems, particularly domestic, "in the light of Christian teaching." The committee agreed that, "The American people are committed to an order involving freedom of enterprise and private property . . . Our Committee is definitely committed to improving this order . . . recent experience in Europe has shown that where economic freedom is denied, other freedoms, religious and political, are not long maintained.

"It is our duty to retain the good (in capitalism) and eliminate the bad, and ultimately this must be done by changing the individuals, quickening their spirits with the inner light of a Christian conscience."

This committee asked some searching questions about the transition from a war to a peace economy when the time should come. Could a postwar depression be prevented? How could the health and strength of the people be improved? What could be done to improve housing conditions and labor legislation? How might industrial strife be prevented by arbitration, conciliation or mediation?

"We want," the committee declared, "a society of free men animated by the religious ideal of brotherhood."

At the moment, however, in most parts of the world free men and the ideal of brotherhood were rapidly being liquidated.

France had fallen, England was in desperate straits, Italy was a prisoner, Spain was prostrate from civil war, Austria, Czechoslovakia, Poland, Holland, Belgium, Denmark, Norway, Hungary, Bulgaria, Yugoslavia and Greece were in Nazi hands, and Russia was fighting for her life. North Africa was overrun, Japan had just invaded French Indochina. It was not a season of good will.

At harvest time, Perry Hayden cut his first little crop of Dynamic Kernels with a sickle hook to re-enact reaping in biblical days. His family snipped off the heads of wheat with scissors and hung them in a flour sack on the back porch to dry. After the sack was pounded with the carpet beater, it was emptied on the Haydens' dining-room table.

"The contents were then lifted into the air, a handful at a time, and dropped into pie pans, as the family blew the chaff out of the falling wheat. After two and a half hours of strenuous effort and scrupulous care, to see that not a kernel was lost, the harvest netted 18,000 kernels, or 50 cubic inches—enough to almost fill a quart jar. . . . Out of the 50 cubic inches from the first harvest, 5 cubic inches were given to the church for the tithe."

Perry Hayden observed with gentle humor, "This first tithe was very religious and went directly into the ministry."[15]

He meant the wheat was made into breakfast food which, garnished with cream and sugar, was consumed by the pastor.

The remaining forty-five cubic inches were planted a month later on another plot of land lent by the Ford farm manager. On the day of the planting, school was dismissed early so that forty-five children could take part in the ceremony. Each child received an envelope containing a cubic inch of seed. When the signal was given for the children to place the kernels in the ground and pat them down, everyone was shocked to discover that one envelope was empty. A boy had chewed up his portion and swallowed it!

This was a disaster. The loss of those 360 kernels would amount at the end of the experiment to a deficit of several thousand bushels.

Perry Hayden made a speedy trip to the farm from which he had procured the original wheat and, to the relief of those attending the ceremony, the chewed-up kernels were replaced.

In unoccupied France, twelve American Friends and a hundred European workers were distributing milk and administering feeding programs in schools, concentration camps and hospitals.

A "Quaker Outpost" was established in Lisbon, where the flood of refugees passing through the last open port was being helped. There was another Quaker Outpost in Casablanca and one in Geneva.

While Friends fanned out over the world to bring relief, they were looking to a more constructive role in the future. Their presence in the world's trouble spots brought friendship with so many people of diverse nationalities and they kept so strictly impartial, ministering to sufferers regardless of their political loyalties, that Friends hoped for a reconciling part when hostilities should come to an end.

During the first days of October, Perry Hayden was concerned about his experiment. His first crop had exceeded expectation, yielding fifty times the amount planted. If this yield continued for each of the six years, where was he going to find enough land? Before the end of the experiment, no farm in Michigan would be large enough. Then there was the problem of the government's restriction on wheat planting.

And the weather! That fall was unusually dry. Would the second crop prosper like the first? Someone else's wheat was already showing above ground. But at the end of the first week in October, Perry Hayden rejoiced. His wheat had broken through!

Two months later, when the field was covered with a cozy blanket of snow, he observed, "The Lord is working with us."[16]

The following morning at half past seven, in Pearl Harbor, Japanese bombers attacked the United States Pacific Fleet. While preparing to celebrate the birth of the Prince of Peace, Americans were overtaken by a second World War.

16 Someone to Lean Upon

Anxious cables flew from the United States to Quaker representatives stationed in Japan and Japanese-occupied China, in the countries conquered by Germany, as well as in the Hawaiian Islands, Syria, Palestine, Greece and Egypt. Representatives were given the chance to return home, but those who were not expelled remained at their posts.

Anti-American feeling in Japan had already rendered missionary activity so difficult that all but one of the Friends workers had left.

Gilbert and Minnie Bowles went to Hawaii where they continued to serve Japanese and other foreigners, helping them to find employment and introducing a unique custom of family visiting among aliens. For over half a century Gilbert and Minnie Bowles had been living symbols of American peace efforts and friendship for the Japanese. Clarence Pickett could recall the moment when this service began.

"It was a great day in my eight-year-old life when my sister Minnie Pickett left Kansas to go to Japan as a missionary," he wrote, referring to the year 1892. "One of my most vivid childhood memories is of riding in the wagon sitting on one of her big trunks as we took her to town, to put her on the train for this long journey. . . . When she returned to America after five years, it was to be married to Gilbert Bowles; and later the two of them went to Japan to spend forty-five more years in active service."[1]

Quaker concern for the Japanese people originated with the women of Philadelphia. They considered their Japanese sisters oppressed and longed to help them by sharing the Christian Gospel and Quaker testimonies, by providing education and improving the standard of living.

In 1885, the newly formed Woman's Foreign Missionary Association of Friends of Philadelphia invited two young Japanese men, who were studying at Johns Hopkins, to meet with them. One of these students was Inazo Nitobe, who would one day marry a Philadelphia Friend and become President of the Imperial College in Tokyo.

According to the report of that 1885 meeting, the two Japanese students urged the Woman's Missionary Association to send "someone now and especially desired that it might be one who would be so consecrated to the work that he would live among the people humbly as one of them, would make it his adopted country, and . . . would be willing to 'bury his bones' there."²

No missionary association could have received better counsel. Fortunately, it was taken to heart, for in 1887 when Philadelphia Quakers opened the Friends Girls School in Tokyo, a Japanese educator, Chuzo Kaifu, was put in charge, although at that time American missionaries generally were not inclined to give the people they came to help much authority.

Young men were not neglected. They were invited to come to the Shiba Meetinghouse for study of English and Western culture. Out of this emerged a school for training Christian workers. Hand in hand with religious programs went education in agricultural methods so that little farms could better support the people who depended upon them for existence.

So many Philadelphia Quakers of both sexes visited and worked in the Japan Mission or supported it from home that by 1899 the word "Woman's" had to be dropped from the name of the Association. A quarter of a century later, when it was recognized as the official missionary body of the Yearly Meeting, the name was changed to Mission Board of Philadelphia Yearly Meeting of Friends.

By 1900, there were four Monthly Meetings in Japan. By 1917, the Philadelphia Mission Board encouraged Japanese Friends to establish their own Yearly Meeting as a sign of their independence from foreign authority. Japan Yearly Meeting numbered eight hundred members at the time of the attack on Pearl Harbor.

But the only Friends missionary left was Edith Sharpless of Haverford, Pennsylvania. She was not interned. Some Japanese women, well aware of the danger, went out of their way to visit this American who had devoted her life to their service. Men were immediately suspected of subversive activity if they were discovered speaking with her. At great personal sacrifice, the Japanese cook, who had cared for the Quaker teachers since 1917, remained at her post until Edith Sharpless was repatriated.

In Japan-occupied China, Dr. W. E. DeVol, serving under the Foreign Mission Board of Ohio Yearly Meeting of Friends Church, awoke on December 7 expecting to leave Nanking for the United States. He had a permit from the Occupation authorities to travel to Shanghai the following day and join his elder brother, Charles, also a missionary, with whom he was scheduled to sail for home on December 11. Their wives and children had already left China. But on December 7, Dr. DeVol was notified that he was under house arrest. As he was of military age, he was assured that he would never see his country again.

A week later, the Japanese asked Dr. DeVol to resume his work at the University Hospital. Despite the intimidation, he was repatriated with other members of the Friends China Mission in the summer of 1942, traveling by way of Portuguese East Africa and embarking on the liner *Gripsholm*. Dr. DeVol believed that "Friends really had more generous treatment at the hands of the Japanese than did some other Americans" because the Japanese consul in Nanking had once lived in Portland, Oregon, and had attended the Friends Church there.[3]

In Shanghai, Charles DeVol, the elder brother, fared worse. He was detained, then interned for two years. It was part of a recurring pattern of terror which had overtaken Charles DeVol all his life in China. He was born there shortly after the Boxer uprising, during which his parents had had to flee from the medical mission which his mother established in 1899. They fled again at the outbreak of civil war in 1911.

In 1927, the first year of his own mission service, Charles DeVol was caught in the area of Chiang Kai-shek's army, which was hostile to Westerners. He escaped by hiding in a cistern. Eventually, he got back to the United States. Four years later, when he and his family returned to the Friends China Mission, Sino-Japanese relations were so strained that his wife and children were required to leave immediately. Now in 1941 this man, who had served the people of China all his life, was once more considered to be an enemy.

Earlier, during the Japanese invasion of China when refugees poured into Shanghai, many children lost their parents. They roamed the streets, hungry and frightened. The Municipal Council of Shanghai appealed to British and American Friends, who opened a Children's Receiving Home. But after December 7, 1941, these Friends were also subject to internment.

From Philadelphia, Rufus Jones addressed a letter to Friends in America.

"The whole world is now engaged in warfare and everybody is

concerned with adequate resources for fighting. Now, if ever, we must find adequate resources for . . . making our spiritual contribution to a world of darkness and agony.

"Our country will be swept by passion and there must be little centers of quiet and spiritual assurance in all parts of the country where we exist as a people."[4]

Rufus Jones was not mistaken in his prediction that passion would sweep the country. One of the first reactions was a demand that the Japanese cherry trees bordering the Tidal Basin in Washington be cut down. On the Pacific coast there were fears of sabotage and espionage. While Friends recognized the possibility that there might be some spies, they were convinced that most of the Japanese-Americans were honorable, loyal citizens. Like other religious groups, Friends made a point of extending the hand of fellowship.

On the Sunday after war was declared, the First Friends Church of Whittier invited the Japanese-American Friends Church to join in worship. Herschel Folger, the pastor of First Friends, and Pastor Ishikawa conducted the service.[5] "Our hearts wept in the warm atmosphere," Pastor Ishikawa recalled later.[6]

In February, the army ordered the mass evacuation of over 120,000 people of Japanese ancestry. Two thirds of them had been born in the United States and were therefore American citizens. Their parents had remained aliens because they were not permitted to become naturalized.

"All must go: old people and children, crippled and sick," an American Friends Service Committee worker in Pasadena reported. "College students are to stop their education. The economic loss alone staggers the imagination. Japanese farmers produce a very large percentage of the fresh vegetables that are grown along the West Coast, and many crops must be abandoned in the fields. A considerable amount of commercial fishing was done by Japanese crews. The stocks of Japanese-owned stores are being thrown on the market at disaster prices. Doctors and lawyers face the loss of years of effort to build up a practice. For all this, there is no prospect of compensation. But more than the financial loss is the social and personal deterioration which comes from hopes blasted, faith shaken and loyalty betrayed."[7]

From those "little centers of quiet and spiritual assurance," the Friends Meetings all over the country, more and more volunteers came out to the Pacific coast to lend encouragement. They visited their Japanese friends in the assembly centers, where they had to stand one yard outside the barbed wire fence to talk with someone inside, who had to stand another yard away from the fence.

"It is a humiliating experience for anyone to be compelled to live behind barbed wire," the Seattle Japanese Methodists declared. "It is even more humiliating to have one's essential patriotism doubted."[8]

In midwinter, some of the internees were sent from southern California to Montana and North Dakota. Clothing was a critical need. Friends supplied all that they could get their hands on.

"Think what the Japanese have been doing this past week," wrote a Service Committee worker from Seattle that spring, "standing in line first to register, then for physical exams. The last frantic arrangements, selling, storing, dispensing with precious possessions, leaving pets and gardens behind, then the last night, most of them up until four or five a.m., packing, getting everything ready for the early morning departure. Then for a few hours' sleep on the hard floor in a home empty of furniture, no beds nor mattresses. Then at six, up and get the children ready, dress in your best clothes, come down in the pouring rain, stand in line. . . .

"At each departure we have been down to see people off, helping to get family and possessions from homes down to the departure points."

The Quaker workers noted that the trains were "old ratty coaches for a two-day, two-night trip."[9]

On the other side of the world, in unoccupied France, Quaker workers were also going to the station to see people off. These were foreign Jews who were being deported to death camps. The Quakers were permitted to bring them coffee and a word of sympathy—the only token these people had of acceptance by other members of the human race. Many of the victims begged the workers to take their last possessions or cash and to see, should they never return, that these reached their heirs. Instructions were hastily scribbled on scraps of paper. To accept these possessions was illegal, but the Quaker workers felt it was the right thing to do.

"Buried in a cellar in Toulouse and transferred after the war to a safe deposit box in Paris, these objects—some pitifully humble, some of considerable value—were a real problem to French and American staff, but the joint efforts resulted, in an amazing number of cases, in finding a legitimate heir and turning over to him what often proved to be the only memento of a lost loved one."[10]

While in other parts of the world Friends witnessed tragedies that spring, in the Caribbean, they celebrated a joyful occasion. Nearly a thousand Jamaican Quakers met at Seaside, about fifty miles east of Kingston, to establish their own Yearly Meeting.

Jamaica was captured from the Spaniards in 1655 by Admiral Sir William Penn, whose son William, then eleven years old, would one day anger his admiral father by becoming a Quaker. Two years after Jamaica became an English plantation, the Acting Governor wrote, "There are some people lately come hither called Quakers, who have brought letters of credit and do disperse books amongst us."

George Fox "travelled many hundreds of miles up and down in Jamaica among Friends and the people of the world" (non-Friends) in 1671. To his wife he wrote from there, "the blessed Seed is over all."[11] By 1700, there were said to be thousands of Quakers on the island. Sickness, earthquake and persecution reduced the numbers.

In 1884, Evi Sharpless, an Iowa Quaker, had a concern for service in Jamaica. After he had preached and worked there for some time, Evi Sharpless was joined by other Quaker missionaries, also from Iowa. In this way it came about that Jamaicans who were convinced and wished to join the Society of Friends but who might never have been to the United States became members of Iowa Yearly Meeting and the Five Years Meeting.

In 1941, Jamaican Friends, feeling the time had come for independence, addressed a minute of request to these parent bodies. American representatives were sent to Seaside, empowered with minutes to effect the transfer of responsibility. Fraternal delegates from New England and Philadelphia and the Vice-chairman of the Friends World Committee for Consultation were also present.

Anna Griscom Elkinton who, with her husband, J. Passmore Elkinton, had come from Philadelphia, reported on the proceedings.

"Jamaica, Jamaica! What pictures this name evokes. Tropical beauty of rocky shore . . . flowers, profuse and brilliant; romance and the song of the Negro no longer a slave but not yet free; opportunity, poverty, ignorance . . .

"The minute of request to Iowa Yearly Meeting was read and Robert Cope read Iowa's minute of response. The minute to the Five Years Meeting and their response were also read. James

Coney, on behalf of the Five Years Meeting, then authorized the setting up of this newest of our . . . Meetings. . . . He performed this historic task with simplicity and dignity . . . as he so well said, words were not the proper medium for the blessing of this occasion but rather silent communion with the giver of all life. . . . And so a new Yearly Meeting was born and we who were privileged to be present on such a rare occasion will long remember its significance."

The odd dichotomy, which made this occasion seem a privilege in Jamaica, while it would have been unthinkable in the United States, prompted Anna Elkinton to further reflection. She had in mind the many Friends at home who, in their relations with members of other races, were still substituting paternalistic assistance for true friendship and social acceptance.

"Perhaps the part of the Yearly Meeting which was strangest but most educational and inspiring to those of us from our beloved but benighted U.S. was to have white, Negro, and East Indian members working and worshipping as one body. . . . That was a real demonstration of the Biblical truth that *there is neither Greek nor Jew, circumcision nor uncircumcision, Barbarian, Scythian, bond nor free, but Christ is all and in all.*"[12]

Perry Hayden's second crop of Dynamic Kernels was cut on the Fourth of July, 1942, in the presence of 250 people. The first crop had been harvested with a sickle to recall biblical times. This one was cut with cradle scythes to honor the pioneers.

"The wheat was stacked in two large piles, but a tremendous amount was tramped down by the crowd. Many heads were broken from stems and scattered over the field. Perry and Mrs. Hayden returned to the field after lunch and for nearly six hours they vigilantly gleaned every possible head of wheat." After the threshing, there were 881,499 kernels, weighing seventy pounds, of which seven pounds were given to the Church for the tithe.[13]

On that same Independence Day, Friends issued a statement concerning the evacuation of the Japanese from the west coast, "making it perfectly clear that we do not accept . . . or approve it. . . . The events of the past few months have caused us deep humiliation and profound concern. . . . As part of that penitence, we have felt that we should share in the relocation of students so that they may continue their preparation for a useful life among us."[14]

Milton S. Eisenhower, then Associate Director of the Office of War Information, had asked the Service Committee to relocate in educational institutions of the East and Midwest the thousands of American-born students of Japanese ancestry who had been attending schools and colleges on the Pacific coast before the evacuation.

Eager to get people out of the camps as speedily as possible, Friends undertook the task and budgeted two hundred and fifty thousand dollars for the purpose.

The first chance came to an evacuee in the camp at Tule Lake, 150 miles north of San Francisco. He had won a gold medal upon his graduation from the University of California and was admitted to the Medical School of Washington University in St. Louis, on condition that he matriculate by July 6. After that date, he would not be accepted. Consequently, he would have to remain interned.

An order for the young man's release, signed by Mr. Eisenhower, reached the San Francisco office of the Service Committee on the Fourth. One of the Service Committee workers, Thomas R. Bodine— a Conscientious Objector who would one day become Clerk of New England Yearly Meeting—rushed to Tule Lake and presented the order. The officer on duty at the camp explained that the commandant was away over the holiday and that nothing could be done until his return.

"This was to have been the first Japanese-American to be released," Thomas Bodine recalled, "and to have him lose his chance to go to medical school, after all this—"

With Quaker persistence, Thomas Bodine persuaded the officer on duty to submit the order to the second in command. Mr. Eisenhower's directive could not be ignored and the student was finally released in the care of the Service Committee representative.

The student had no way of knowing whether the stranger, who had come to take him away, really meant to help. Nevertheless, he let himself be driven at breakneck speed through the blackout to Klamath Falls in Oregon where he was to catch a train for St. Louis.

Because of the delay at the camp, it was long past departure time when the two reached the station. Fortunately, the train was late.

Thomas Bodine never forgot the eeriness of that night; the bewildered student going off in the darkened train and his own joy, as he stood watching it pull out of sight, knowing that he had helped the first Japanese-American to leave a relocation camp.

Just one, out of 120,000!

But the gates in the barbed wire fence had been opened a tiny crack, far enough to let one loyal American, who was guilty of no crime, pass through. With time, others would follow.

On the east coast, that same summer, a New England-born Japanese walked into one of the Service Committee offices and asked whether he might have a few minutes to talk to someone. He said he was twenty-two and that he expected to be inducted into the army in three days. But he had not come to discuss that. He was concerned about his parents.

"I came here to tell you about them," he said, "so I'd know that in case they should need advice or friendship while I'm away, you'll know about them and they'll have someone to lean upon."[15]

17 The Way Quakers Always Guard People

On April 30, 1942, a Twenty-fifth Anniversary Meeting was held in the Friends Meetinghouse at Swarthmore, Pennsylvania, to commemorate the founding of the American Friends Service Committee in 1917. Members and supporters of the Committee heard Rufus Jones describe its activity as "a way of life that has peace as the essence of it."

Thanks to a recording made that year, we can still hear Rufus Jones tell in his characteristic Maine accents and with his humorous asides the story of the Committee's first imaginative enterprises.

"In 1917, we picked out 100 Quaker boys . . . trained them all summer . . . in building houses . . . in handling automobiles . . . first aid work and in agriculture. In October, we sent 99 of the 100 men to France to . . . the Marne Valley, where the first great German drive had smashed every building. . . . We built two factories in the east part of France . . . the Jura region, where we manufactured portable houses. The houses were taken up to the Marne Valley and foundations were made, rubbish cleared away, house put up and then the entire roof put on it.

"And then we brought the peasant families back and started them living . . . as we built village after village, we had to take charge of the farming and we sent over a great many tractors, plows, harrows, reapers, threshing machines. And we kept feeding new men into this group . . . until it finally got up to 600. They had very quickly, of course, to establish a hospital . . . to take care of children and the women . . . a maternity hospital, because people go on having babies in wartime. And throughout the rest of the War, we stayed there and became the most intimate friends of those peasants and did everything that could be done to make their lives possible. We set out a little orchard for every family. We gave every family a pair of animals, usually two goats and if we didn't have goats, we had rabbits. But we started them off with some animals that would multiply.

"While we were at this job, we found out that five . . . American Army dumps in that region were rotting and going to pieces: millions and millions of dollars worth of material—ten thousand shovels . . . ten thousand pickaxes, a million miles of barbed wire, a million miles of telephone wire and all sorts of tools. They sold the entire dump for two hundred and fifty thousand francs.

"Well, we didn't have crew enough to move them all. So we went to the officers of the French Army and said, 'Now, here you've got a lot of German prisoners in these prison camps, doing nothing. We'd like to borrow two hundred German prisoners to help us move these Army dumps.' 'Well,' they said, 'how're you going to guard them?'"

With his hearty chuckle, a delight to all who knew him, Rufus Jones went on, "We said we'd guard them the way Quakers always guard people. Well, they wanted to know what that was and we explained. Well, strangely enough, they let us have two hundred prisoners. They worked with us magnificently. We took the dumps out into the country and sold them to the peasants for small sums, just so as not to pauperize them, and we made two million francs, which," he added with another chuckle, "is the way Quakers sometimes do.

"We took the two million francs, and built the finest maternity hospital in France in the city of Chalons-sur-Marne and presented it to the French Government. And then we photographed every one of the two hundred German prisoners, we got his home address in Germany, we sent three of our workers over to Germany—this was before the peace was signed—and hunted up every single home that any one of those prisoners came from; we gave them the photograph of the boy, we told all about him, how he looked and how he acted, then we put down on the table the amount of money he would have earned if he'd worked for wages during the whole period.

"Well, immediately after that, Mr. Hoover, who was feeding Belgian children, came over to our office and said that he supposed one million children were starving in Germany. He didn't know of anybody who could feed them. He said, 'If the Quakers will go in there and feed those children, I'll start you off with a very big gift of money and help you raise the money that you'll need for the operation.'

"Well, we settled down and thought it over. We decided that we ought to do it. We divided Germany into eight sections. We got a series of great German doctors; worked out plans for studying each child's life. And eventually we had forty thousand Germans working under our fifteen Quakers and we raised the feeding so we fed a million two hundred thousand children a day . . . we carried that on for four years.

"We were the recipients of all the cars and trucks the Red Cross had in Europe. At the end of the War, they presented us with the entire lot and we couldn't have done our work without it. So we took a lot of those trucks and cars and went into Vienna. We were the first people who got into Vienna after the War. There wasn't a drop of milk in the entire city. A city of two million people with not a drop of milk . . . practically no fires. The first thing we did was to take the trucks and go into Switzerland and buy eight hundred cows and bring them into the city and organize a milking squad and we took the milk to the babies.

"And then our boys went over into Hungary with the Ford cars and brought in coal and kept furnace fires going in the hospitals. And we stayed in Vienna through all the crises, three great revolutions that followed one after the other. . . .

"Then we came home and there came our Depression. You may have heard of it," Rufus Jones interjected ruefully. "Among those that were hardest hit were the soft coal miners. There were about five hundred thousand . . . out of work. And Mr. Hoover, who was President then, told us he had $450,000 that could be used and that he'd start us with that, if we'd undertake the care of these soft coal miners. We went into these regions . . . where coal miners lived. We took care of their families. Then we saw that it was hopeless to expect to do a permanent piece of work by just feeding children and mothers.

"And so we had the happy idea of buying land and putting the miners on small farms in a community so organized that there would be supplementary means for their livelihood. . . . started them building their houses, worked out plans for . . . furniture making. . . . In another community we had a . . . factory for knitting sweaters. And when we organized a sale of furniture and the things they had made, we had made a very striking success of these communities.

"Well, then came the Spanish War, one of the most horrible of all known civil wars . . . as usual, the people who suffered first and most were always children. We insisted that if we were going to help, we should help both sides. . . . We go where there's suffering and we don't ask what church they belong to or which side they're on. And so we got permission from Franco to come in and take care of the children on his side of the battle line.

And we told him that we were also going to be working on the other side. . . . American people raised two or three million dollars for this task."

Then Rufus Jones went on to tell about the Quaker Mission to the Gestapo.

"Well," he said in closing, "here is the past. Here are the immense needs. And God won't do it if we don't help him. If it isn't for human hands and human lips and the human heart to touch it and help bear this burden, it won't be done."

In October 1942, Rufus Jones was given the Theodore Roosevelt Distinguished Service Medal, along with Secretary of War Stimson and Booth Tarkington, the novelist. Friends were quick to note that the honor had been conferred simultaneously on the Secretary of War and on a pacifist.

That same month, Perry Hayden planted his third crop. Pheasants covered the field and threatened to devour the seed. Relying on the biblical promise "And I will rebuke the devourer for your sakes, and he shall not destroy the fruits of your ground," Perry Hayden kept his composure.

"The Lord will take care of the pheasants," he said. "Hunting season opens in five days."[1]

In the Eastern Hemisphere, the hunting season was on, too. Rommel, the Desert Fox, pushing toward the Nile, was stopped by the British at El Alamein. Hitler seized Tunisia, the Russians beat back the Germans at Stalingrad, the Italians took Corsica. General Eisenhower landed in North Africa. The Quaker Outpost at Casablanca, Morocco, which had just been opened to render assistance to refugees in internment camps, was in the midst of the fighting. In Vichy, Marshal Pétain broke off diplomatic relations with the United States. German Army units moved into unoccupied France.

Some of the officers in these units had been fed by *Quäkerspeisung* in the 1920s. This recollection made them sympathetic toward the Quaker workers, who were now behind the lines. For a time, American Quakers were still allowed to administer relief in France. Then in January 1943 they were interned at Baden-Baden. Friends feared that their relief operations would have to close down. But the Nazis allowed European Quakers to continue the work.

Gilbert F. White, one of the internees, who was a Conscientious

Objector, later recalled the frustration of this "enforced sojourn on an island of contemplation in a mounting torrent of human violence.

"One of the normal reactions to putting out fires is to turn to preventing them." That, he says, was his feeling "in the gilded cage that was Baden-Baden. Yet, when the preventive venture goes slowly and the results seem intangible, a simple involvement in human events has special satisfaction."[2]

What a comfort it would have been to him then if he could have looked into the future and seen the life of creative activity which lay before him as President of Haverford College, Chairman of the American Friends Service Committee and as a distinguished geographer!

At home, in the Civilian Public Service Camps, Conscientious Objectors were frustrated, too. Many had hoped to be sent on relief missions abroad.

A number had been trained to serve as drivers in the China Convoy. This British Friends Ambulance Unit contingent was traveling from Rangoon over the Burma Road with medical aid for war victims. American Friends were eager to help transport doctors and equipment over the long mountain route, which was menaced by bandits. This was not a "soft berth."

But the United States Government assigned the Conscientious Objectors to work at home in the Forestry and Soil Conservation Services, in the National Park Service and on dairy farms. Some of these assignments seemed important to the men, who were required to work eight hours a day without pay. Some jobs, like planting saplings in nurseries and "manicuring trees," seemed a waste of the Conscientious Objectors' skills.

The most contented assignees were the smoke jumpers, parachute-borne fire fighters. They were doing something that was badly needed and also proving that, while they would not fight, they were not afraid of danger.

Quaker representatives in Washington conferred with the Undersecretary of State, the Chinese Ambassador, officials in the Office of Foreign Relief and Rehabilitation Operations, the Secretary of War and the President himself. These all gave Friends reason to think that a large medical mission could be sent to China. Accordingly, a training course for two hundred men was set up at Earlham College in Richmond, Indiana.

When the first graduates of this course were on their way to China, a rider was attached to the Army Appropriations Bill forbidding Civilian Public Service men from leaving the country. Those who had already reached South Africa were obliged to return home.

Until their government let Conscientious Objectors go on detached service, they felt banished from "a simple involvement in human events." Saplings, cows and water holes did not provide the human contacts they craved.

Then, as Friends say, "way opened" for some of the men in Civilian Public Service. The Office of Scientific Research and Development offered them the chance to act as "guinea pigs." They served as controls for testing new drugs. They carried lice in their clothing to determine the best insecticides for use in Italy and North Africa. In the investigation of the causes and cures of diseases, they contracted hepatitis, malaria, pneumonia and poliomyelitis. One man died as a result of this.

Two took part in a study of the effects of salt water that was conducted at the Massachusetts General Hospital. During this experiment, sea water was the only liquid in their diet. At the conclusion, shipwreck rations in life boats were changed from salty foods to sweet.

One group underwent semistarvation so that researchers at the University of Minnesota could measure the consequences and determine the best methods of restoring strength to undernourished people. These experiments threw new light on the mental and spiritual as well as physical effects of malnutrition. Another group spent six to eight hours a day in 120 degrees temperature in order to discover optimum living conditions in the desert.

Later Selective Service allowed bi-racial units to work as cottage masters in an institution for Black juvenile delinquents. Five units were sent to state training schools for the mentally deficient. Here, the men felt useful.

"Each one of us, taking a sincere and unfailing interest in even one boy, can reduce the number of behavior problems considerably," one man wrote. "We have an unparalleled opportunity to prove that the love of practical Christianity is the best discipline and the best therapy there is."[3]

A large group of Conscientious Objectors relieved the acute shortage of orderlies in psychiatric hospitals.

Concern for the mentally ill was a Quaker tradition going back to Fox, who had urged Friends to procure a house "for them that be distempered." In 1671, London Friends looked for a house that would accommodate members who were "distracted or troubled in mind, that so they may not be put amongst the world's people or run about the streets."

In 1792, William Tuke, the Yorkshire Friend who entertained Woolman, proposed to his Quarterly Meeting that it build "a retired habitation . . . for members of our Society and others in profession with us, who may be in a state of lunacy, or so deranged in mind as to require such a provision." Four years later the York Retreat opened. Instead of the chains and punishments which, until modern times, were commonly used, doctors there prescribed good food, fresh air, warm baths and suitable occupations such as gardening.

In the United States, the first crude efforts to cure rather than simply confine mental patients were made at the Pennsylvania Hospital, which was founded for the purpose in 1751 by a group that included several Quakers. But it was not until 1813, when the Frankford Hospital opened near Philadelphia, that loving care without restraints was really practiced in the United States. Thomas Scattergood, a Friend who had visited the York Retreat, returned home to Philadelphia with a concern to establish a similar institution. When Friends opened the Frankford Asylum, they announced that in addition to "the requisite medical aid," they intended to give disturbed patients "such tender sympathetic attention and religious oversight as may soothe their agitated minds and . . . facilitate their restoration." The Friends Hospital, as it is now called, was the first one in the United States which never used a chain and which, from the beginning, respected the dignity of its patients.

Five years after the Frankford Asylum opened, the Bloomingdale Asylum was started in New York for the "moral management of the insane." This was the concern of Thomas Eddy, another Friend who was inspired by the humane care given at the York Retreat. Bloomingdale Asylum later became the Westchester Division of the New York Hospital, located in White Plains.

Moses Sheppard, a Baltimore Quaker, desiring that his estate "would continue to be a blessing to men and women on down through the generations," left well over half a million dollars for the establishment of an institution which would "carry forward and improve the ameliorated system of treatment of the insane."[4] The Sheppard Asylum received its charter in 1853. Later, Moses Sheppard's friend Enoch Pratt left his estate for the same purpose, and in 1896 the name of The Sheppard Asylum was changed to The Sheppard and Enoch Pratt Hospital.

It was as inheritors of this tradition that the Quaker Conscientious Objectors in World War II willingly undertook some of the most menial jobs in state hospitals. They were dismayed to find that, in some of them, conditions had improved little since the nineteenth century.

Appalled by what they saw on some of the wards, these men tried to draw the attention of the world outside to the inhuman treatment that was being given to certain patients. Laymen, with no training for the work they were doing, Conscientious Objectors, who were considered slightly deranged themselves by many of their fellow Americans or, at best, effeminate, these men found that at first no one would listen to them. Then they took photographs of patients who were not getting proper care; they made film strips. They surveyed laws in thirty states relating to mental health; wrote *A Handbook for Psychiatric Aides;* spent their time off interviewing doctors, members of the press, even Mrs. Roosevelt, in an effort to arouse public opinion. A group of these Civilian Public Service men launched a nationwide movement for reform—the National Mental Health Foundation.

"It seems fair to say," Clarence Pickett declared after the war, "that the intense concern of a few CPS [Civilian Public Service] men had measurable, permanent influence on the care of our mentally ill."[5]

Responding to the urgent call for more personnel in state hospitals, Friends organized a unit of women to serve as attendants.

While some of the Conscientious Objectors were at last feeling useful, many were still digging ditches and sodding gullies, unable to make the earth green as fast as it was being scorched overseas. They fretted in their camps.

Civilian Public Service Camps, Army camps, Relocation camps, Prisoner of War camps, Internment camps, Concentration camps—all across the world, people were confined in camps.

For those American Friends who still enjoyed the freedom and comfort of their homes, this period brought a painful awareness that they had not always been sufficiently faithful to their testimonies.

Douglas Steere movingly urged repentance. The Quakers were, he said, ridden with pride after living on old capital—the great souls and great deeds of George Fox and John Woolman. Too often the

Society has been formed by its environment instead of transforming the environment.

"We have not faced the race question squarely and made ourselves people upon whom Negroes, Jews and others can absolutely count."[6]

Medals had been awarded to Friends for service which many of their fellow members in the Society had supported and shared. Yet Friends themselves saw little cause for congratulation. Measured against the needs of humanity, their concern seemed meager and left them dissatisfied.

Out of the frustration of the Conscientious Objectors, the suffering of the "guinea pigs" and the heroic sacrifices of their contemporaries in the armed forces, out of the ordeal of the war dead on both sides, the wounded, the displaced, the hungry, the gassed, the mentally ill, a call for greater faithfulness stirred the consciences of Friends.

18 Towards the Present and Future Peace

"Governments, like clocks, go from the motion men give them," Penn observed, "and as governments are made and moved by men, so by them they are ruined too. Wherefore governments rather depend upon men than men upon governments."[1]

In 1943, the United Nations, as we know it, did not exist. There was no World Health Organization, no Foreign Aid program or Technical Assistance, no Peace Corps, only, it seemed, global conflict.

"While Germany was proposing a new order," Clarence Pickett reflected, "we—Britain and ourselves—were simply setting out to defend an old one. We did not want the order Germany outlined, but we did need to project one of our own. That was the challenge we were failing to meet."[2]

On June 11 and 12, a deeply concerned group, meeting at Quaker Hill in Richmond, Indiana, declared that Friends have a responsibility for urging the adoption of wise and right legislation.

"These critical times are bringing home to us acutely the sweeping role which government is playing in shaping life. . . . Principles and conceptions of life which Friends greatly value are opposed by the will and demands of the militarized state engaged in a great war . . . the fate of mankind depends upon the character of the peace settlement and our own government will be one of the main factors in determining what that settlement shall be."

With representatives from most of the Yearly Meetings and the unaffiliated Meetings, the Friends Committee on National Legislation was formed.

The new committee made clear in its Statement of Purpose that it did not intend "to engage in lobbying of the pressure-group character. It proposes rather to work by methods of quiet influence through personal contact and persuasion."

This committee superseded the Friends War Problems Committee organized in 1940 when the Selective Service Act was being formulated. E. Raymond Wilson, who had headed that, became Executive Secretary of the new Friends Committee on National Legislation, energetically translating religious concern into political activity.

No one expected dramatic results when the witness of Friends was laid before their representatives in Congress. But there was now a channel for presenting that witness and establishing better understanding between Friends and their government.

A month after this seed was planted, Perry Hayden cut his third crop.

Mr. Henry Ford had become intrigued by the Dynamic Kernels project. Reading an article about it in a magazine, he was amazed to discover that the experiment was being conducted on his own land. He readily accepted Perry Hayden's invitation to be present at the third harvest and offered the use of an antique horse-drawn reaper, part of his Edison Institute collection.

As the men who followed the reaper bound the wheat into sheaves, Mr. Ford pulled a Bible out of his pocket and read the text from John that had set the project in motion. "Here's the Word," he said, pointing to his Bible. "There's the wheat."[3]

One of the horses ate so much that the final harvest would be reduced by one thousand bushels. There were other troubles. Before all the wheat was shocked, a heavy rain blew much of it down. As soon as it was stacked, birds swarmed over it until Perry Hayden feared there would be nothing left for the threshers. He and Pastor Escolme knelt in the field and prayed for deliverance. Then they put up scarecrows, which proved useless. A watchman with an air rifle had to be hired to sit beside the shocks.

One thousand people witnessed the threshing. A Civil War separator, powered by ten horses in a circular sweep, had been lent by Mr. Ford, who was on hand again.

"You started this great experiment," he told Perry Hayden after the ceremony. "You're the only man who can finish it. By all means, keep it up!"

"People keep asking me where I am going to get all of the land to finish it."

Mr. Ford laughed as he drove away. "There's plenty of land around here," he called back.

Perry Hayden felt his prayer was answered. He had cause for further rejoicing: Government restrictions on wheat production were lifted.

But it was a poor crop. Kernels used for seed have to be whole and 53½ pounds were cracked in the threshing. Only 861 pounds remained after the tithe was deducted.

Then eight kernels arrived by mail. "I picked up some straw at your harvest," a Methodist minister wrote Perry Hayden, "and found eight kernels of wheat in it when I got home. I am now returning them because their loss would cheat you out of a portion of . . . God's experiment." Thanks to these eight kernels, the final harvest would be augmented by fifty thousand.[4]

The fourth planting took place on September 25, 1943. Some weeks later, Perry Hayden decided to give all the profits of the final crop to an organization that would use them to foster international good will when the war ended.

Just then, the United States, Great Britain, China and the Soviet Union were also thinking along international lines in somewhat different terms. On November 1, they issued a joint declaration from Moscow, pledging to act together against a common enemy and to establish an international organization as soon as victory was assured.

On the same day in Washington, the Friends Committee on National Legislation moved into its first office, a partitioned-off space on the lower floor of the Florida Avenue Friends Meetinghouse.

Not all American Quakers approved. There were those who felt, like their eighteenth-century counterparts, that Quakers should stay out of politics. But there was an even more time-honored precedent, as Frederick Tolles pointed out.

"Quakers have been engaged in lobbying—that is to say, in seeking to influence legislators by personal visits—ever since 1659.

"The weightiest Friends in England, including George Fox and William Penn, busied themselves buttonholing members of Parliament and appearing at committee hearings. The Yearly Meeting even rented a room in a coffee house hard by the Houses of Parliament for a headquarters—a kind of Friends Committee on National Legislation office . . . the Meeting for Sufferings urged Friends to write their Parliament men. . . . If anyone thinks the techniques of the FCNL are a modern innovation, he knows little of Quaker history."[5]

At the first General Meeting of the Committee, held in Philadelphia on January 29, 1944, certain bills pending in Congress were considered. Friends felt their religious and moral principles were involved in such issues as: shipment of food to the women and children in occupied countries of Europe; a Senate resolution for saving the Jews in those countries; repeal of the Oriental Exclusion Act; service for Conscientious Objectors in China; repeal of the poll tax; establishment of the postwar organization proposed in the Moscow Agreement.

When the Dumbarton Oaks Charter for a new world organization was released, the Friends Committee on National Legislation suggested these changes: greater powers for the General Assembly; easier amendment, elimination of the veto; the ruling out of any discrimination on account of race, color or creed; provision for limitation, reduction and eventual abolition of armaments and ultimate inclusion of *all nations*.

On top of the world-wide misery which Friends were trying to relieve and forestall, there was now famine in India. At the end of 1943, the United States Maritime Commission and the War Food Administration authorized the American Friends Service Committee to ship twenty thousand cases of evaporated milk to the Friends Ambulance Unit in Calcutta. Other religious groups as well as organizations like the CIO and AFL contributed to the cost, which came to one hundred thousand dollars.

Soon after this milk was shipped, the President's War Relief Control Board asked the Service Committee to become the agency through which other American organizations such as the India Famine Relief Committee, started by Pearl Buck and Richard J. Walsh, could send supplies. After consulting with the American diplomatic mission in India, the State Department felt that Friends would be the most acceptable people to work with the various political and religious groups in India.

The Service Committee accepted this assignment with the understanding that it would continue its traditional policy of being a non-political organization, distributing relief wherever needed.

In March of 1944, James Vail left for India to oversee this work at the same time that ten members of the Service Committee staff, who had been interned in Germany, returned home on the *Gripsholm*.

American Friends felt a concern for German civilians interned in Texas. Howard W. Elkinton, a Philadelphia Quaker, accompanied the Swiss visitor of the War Prisoners' Aid to the internment camps. He was able to take along William Reese, on furlough from Civilian Public Service, who had received a doctor's degree in music at the University of Berlin. William Reese lectured in German to the music-hungry internees, illustrating his talks with recordings.

"Upon the heels of Thursday's lecture," Howard Elkinton wrote home, "there came a sense of unity in enterprise that destroyed, for a moment, the barriers that held these persons in. . . . We had . . . beaten down the barriers that divide men. Music was the dissolving factor."[6]

To older Friends, who could still remember the (to them) incomprehensible testimony of their forebears against music, not only in worship but even in the home and school, this assurance that music could be reconciling—as they had known all along—was a measure of liberation from mistaken Quaker concepts of the past.

All across the country, Friends were laboring to "beat down the barriers that divide men" by whatever means they had at their disposal.

Young Friends and their friends went to Mexico, working as volunteers in the Clinic Service, which brought health care to people living in sparsely settled areas where less than half the babies born lived to be a year old. The volunteers had to travel on horseback. They cooked with charcoal and carried water. They introduced sanitation into the villages, beginning with the building of privies. They helped to combat malaria, smallpox, tuberculosis and venereal diseases.

These young Americans entered into the life of the Mexican villagers. They learned their songs. On moonlit nights they walked with them along the road, singing, talking, coming to understand and appreciate them.

For the first time these villagers got to know North Americans. They had been accustomed to tourists speeding by in cars. For the first time people from north of the border came to live among them and be their friends.

"When these people arrived here," a leading citizen of one village said of the Quaker Service Unit, "we could not understand why they had come. Some of us were mystified and there are some who still may be so. But I said then, 'By their fruits we shall know them.' We have seen their fruits of kindness and friendship."[7]

Aware of increasing racial tensions at home, the Service Committee gathered together an interracial and interdenominational group of educators and businessmen for "finding and sponsoring projects where members of both races can work together on an equal basis, demonstrating to their communities the ability of Negroes and whites to work together in harmony."[8]

Interracial Youth Camps brought together, for a few weeks of their summer vacation, children of all backgrounds: Indians, Blacks, Chinese, Japanese, Mexicans, as well as white Americans and refugees from Germany and Austria.

A professorship in the history and philosophy of religion was established at Howard University as a memorial to Jesse H. Holmes, a Friend who had taught in these fields at Swarthmore College. Throughout his teaching career he had labored for the removal of racial discrimination. J. Calvin Keene, a white Friend, became the first Jesse H. Holmes Professor.

While Guam and Saipan were being wrested from the Japanese at great cost of human life and the beachheads of Normandy were being widened, Friends held International Service Seminars in North Carolina and Connecticut. Living together in fellowship despite differences of color and nationality, representatives from thirty-five countries learned to appreciate each others' problems and aspirations, while they made plans for a better postwar world.

The participants often disagreed completely, but, as one of them put it, "If you had an explosion in the meeting, you worked it off over the dishpan."[9]

Meanwhile, twenty-five hundred people were gathering in Tecumseh, Michigan, to witness the fourth harvest of the Dynamic Kernels. They watched Mr. Ford, who again took part in the ceremony, drive the reaper he used as a boy.

"I never have seen better wheat in my life," he exclaimed, to which Perry Hayden replied, "That's what the Lord did for us, after our failure last year."[10]

Life magazine carried an account of the threshing ceremonies in Michigan to American fighting men everywhere in the world. An antique steam engine had been brought to the wheat field from the Edison Institute for Mr. Ford to operate. He already was thinking up elaborate schemes in connection with the planting and harvesting of the next crop, for which he offered Perry Hayden the use of 333 acres of farmland surrounding a creek.

"There's a natural beauty spot of several acres with huge trees, where we can hold the ceremonies," Mr. Ford explained. "We can dam the creek and build a mill there."[11]

The creek ran through a little valley. This formed a natural amphitheater. Mr. Ford decided to have it seeded with grass so that the following year ten thousand people would be able to watch the cutting and threshing. It was estimated that the preparations Mr. Ford envisaged would cost as much as three hundred thousand dollars.

To Perry Hayden, who had started this project with nothing but faith and the gift of one cubic inch of grain, these grandiose plans were overwhelming.

But the mill and amphitheater were already under construction when the fifth crop was planted in the little valley on September 19, 1944, just as Belgium was being liberated from her German invaders. Mr. Ford, with a grain bag around his neck, sowed a strip by hand, remarking, "This is the first time I have done this for fifty years."[12]

Then his workers, using modern machinery, planted the 321 bushels of wheat and ten tons of fertilizer which the manager of the Michigan Farm Bureau had obtained in spite of the wartime shortage.

On a smaller scale, the children of the Friends Church also sowed Dynamic Kernels—360 were planted in the yard beside the church, a replica of the first year's plot.

Mr. Ford announced that a year from then he would make five thousand acres of his land available for the sowing of the sixth and last crop. He also told Perry Hayden that he wished the money accruing from this final crop to be used for building a school and chapel in Tecumseh. For his part, he would donate a site of several hundred acres.

This request threw Perry Hayden into a quandary. He would have liked to monumentalize the tithing project. The people of Tecumseh might never forgive him if he refused to participate in the scheme. Yet he had announced publicly that the profits were to be given for the relief of the needy. Many people had contributed work and equipment on this understanding. After giving the matter prayerful consideration, Perry Hayden decided to abide by his intention.

"I couldn't feel that I was true to the original purpose of the experiment if I allowed the money to remain in Tecumseh for some selfish interest or personal whim. I want the major portion of the harvest to go to foreign lands to help bind the wounds of war. I certainly do not want to offend Mr. Ford, but I want above all else to please the Lord. Wherever God leads me in this matter, I'll follow."[13]

Mr. Ford also remained firm.

"I want to build a chapel and school in Tecumseh with the money from the final harvest of this wheat," he declared. "I have been thinking of it for a long time and I'll not change my mind."[14]

19 A Habitation Fit to Dwell In

Just five weeks after the threshing ceremonies in Michigan, festivities in Pennsylvania marked the three hundredth anniversary of the birth of William Penn.

On the afternoon of October 24, 1944, Friends assembled in the Meetinghouse at Fourth and Arch streets, Philadelphia, which stands on land given to Friends by Penn in 1693. After an impressive silence, Rufus Jones introduced representatives of other religious groups in the city.

Mr. W. David Owl, a Cherokee Indian, brought greetings from his people. He recalled Penn's extraordinary sense of justice, not manifest even in our own "enlightened" day. In drawing up the legal regulations for his province, Penn stipulated that when a jury tried a case in which a white man and an Indian were involved, the jury must be made up of six whites and six Indians.

An address by a British Friend, T. Edmund Harvey, M.P., was broadcast from London.

That same evening a civil celebration took place in the Philadelphia Academy of Music. The Governor of Pennsylvania presided. The Ambassador from Great Britain spoke of Penn's belief that peace was founded on justice. The Governor of New Jersey cited Penn's contribution to the fundamental laws of his state: civil and religious liberty, popular elections and punishment for corrupt election practices. The speaker for Delaware recalled that Penn first set foot in the New World at New Castle, Delaware, and that his spirit still lives in many of the laws and institutions of that state.

No one mentioned Penn's mistakes and misfortunes—the losing struggle to make his experiment holy; imprisonment for debt upon his return to England after the second stay in Pennsylvania; the disappointing character of his sons; loss of his faculties in his last illness. Posterity only remembered Penn's triumphs, his uncommon vision, which touched America with greatness and left her his still-untested exhortation: "Let us then try what love can do, for if men did once see we love them we should soon find they would not harm us . . . love is above all, and when it prevails in us we shall all be lovely and in love with God and one another."

Supreme Court Justice Owen J. Roberts spoke of Penn's three great accomplishments: fixing the principle of trial by jury in the English-speaking world; establishing colonial governments with fundamental civil and religious freedoms; outlining a project for the peace of Europe where "justice would be the true basis of consent."

He was referring to the *Essay Towards the Present and Future Peace of Europe,* published in 1693, in which Penn suggested a parliament of nations.

"The place of their first session should be central," Penn wrote. "To avoid quarrel for precedency, the room may be round, and have divers doors to come in and go out at . . . they (the delegates) may preside by turns, to whom all speeches should be addressed, and who should collect the sense of the debate, and state the question for a vote. . . .

"I will first give an answer to the objections that may be offered against my proposal. . . . The first of them is, that the strongest and richest sovereignty will never agree to it. . . . I answer to the first part, he is not stronger than all the rest. . . .

"The second is that it will endanger an effeminacy by such a disuse of the trade of soldiery. . . . Instruct them [youth] in mechanical knowledge and in natural philosophy. . . . This would make them men; neither women nor lions . . . the knowledge of nature, and the useful as well as agreeable operations of art, give men an understanding of themselves, of the world they are born into, how to be useful and serviceable, both to themselves and others: and how to save and help, not injure and destroy. . . . For such as the youth of any country is bred, such is the next generation, and the government in good or bad hands."

Not until three hundred and one-half years after the birth of the man who made this proposal was the United Nations Charter drawn up.

In "Letter from the Past," 52, Now and Then observed, "In celebrating the tercentenary of William Penn's birth we should not neglect his mother." He added, in his usual style, "One would suppose that in birthday celebrations the mothers would be the next person to be remembered, being in a quite literal sense the real 'next of kin.' Yet they are rarely mentioned."

In this little sketch of Lady Penn, Now and Then quotes part of a letter written to young William by one of his friends, who had just called on her. "'Full of tears she was concerning you that you should continue of that judgment [that is, a Quaker] that was so contrary to them.' She mentioned especially the Quakers' 'strange rude way of not putting off the hat,' and also the Admiral's disappointment, who had 'intended to make you a great man, but you would not hearken to him. . . .'"[1]

Penn would not hearken to his father; Perry Hayden would not hearken to Mr. Ford.

Nevertheless, in the Michigan valley where the fifth crop of Dynamic Kernels was planted, construction and landscaping continued throughout that fall. Work was being rushed for the harvest ceremonies the following July. Perry Hayden was looking ahead beyond that next harvest to the final one. He made a trip to New York, hoping to interest Herbert Hoover in coming to Tecumseh and delivering a speech on that great occasion. The former President declined.

This was a blow, yet worse was to come.

Shortly before Thanksgiving, Perry Hayden received a message from Mr. Ford, stating briefly that he wished to have nothing more to do with the Dynamic Kernels project.

Christmas was grim, too, all over the world. The Russians had encircled Budapest, Tokyo was being bombed, British troops were fighting their way up the Adriatic coast, the Nazis had completely surrounded the Americans at Bastogne. King George broadcast a message to his empire: "The defeat of Germany and Japan is only the first half of our task. The second is to create a world of free men untouched by tyranny." President Roosevelt expressed the humble thanks of himself and the nation to "those who stand in the forefront of the struggle to bring back to a suffering world the way of life symbolized by the spirit of Christmas."

When the President reached Yalta in the Crimea on February 3, 1945, Prime Minister Churchill thought he looked "frail and ill."[2]

At Yalta, Roosevelt, Churchill and Stalin agreed to divide Germany after her capitulation into East and West zones, giving the Soviet Army occupation of the East; the United States and British armies occupation of the West. In return for joining the war against Japan, Russia was promised valuable territory. As the three statesmen planned the organization which was to become the United Nations, Prime Minister Churchill tried in vain to persuade Premier Stalin to give up the veto power.

Ten weeks after the Yalta Conference, President Roosevelt died at his home in Warm Springs, Georgia, only a fortnight before the San Francisco Conference met to draw up the United Nations Charter.

At the opening session of the Conference in the San Francisco Opera House, Mr. Edward Stettinius, the host delegate, called for "one minute of silent, solemn meditation."

A message from British and American Friends was placed in the hands of all Conference delegates. "Not by coercion and penalties will the world be turned from war, but by the singleminded pursuit of the individual well-being of ordinary men and women. . . . We hope that you . . . will keep steadily before your minds the needs of all oppressed and forgotten men and women, war ravaged and starving . . . and those who have hitherto been denied the economic, cultural and spiritual benefits now available for all men. May it be given to you to meet these needs and set up for all God's people, a habitation fit to dwell in."[3]

While the Conference was opening in California, Benito Mussolini was murdered in Italy. Four days later, in the bunker under the Berlin Chancellery, Adolf Hitler shot himself.

It would be another fortnight before General Jodl surrendered to General Eisenhower and the war with Germany came to an end. In Berlin on the morning of May 9, the German High Command ratified the surrender.

In Michigan the following day, it snowed.

Beneath the thick white blanket, 5555 bushels of Perry Hayden's wheat were bravely pursuing their destiny in Mr. Ford's acres. Mr. Ford might not wish to have anything more to do with the Dynamic Kernels but his land was producing so many that were they to be laid end to end, they would circle the globe.[4]

With the cessation of hostilities in Europe, the red-and-black star actually did circle the globe. This symbol of Quaker relief was originally adopted during the Franco-Prussian War of 1870 to designate the British Quakers who were bringing food, clothing and seed corn, potatoes and cattle to the distressed people of Alsace-Lorraine and those living in a large area around Paris. Subsequently, this star became the symbol of Quaker relief work throughout the world.

Seventy-five years after the Franco-Prussian War, shipments of food, clothing, shoe leather and sewing materials, bedding and soap, all marked with the Quaker star, were once more dispatched to France, as well as to Italy and to the refugee camp operated by UNRRA in Egypt.

Before the month was out, relief workers wearing the Quaker star on their sleeves arrived in France. There they found Margaret Frawley helping the team of French Friends, *Secours Quaker*. She and Clarence Pickett had been the first Friends workers coming from the United States who were permitted to enter France after the liberation.

Two articles which appeared in the Marseilles newspaper were sent home by the American Consulate to the U. S. State Department with the comment that they represented the first friendly statement about Americans to be made publicly in that stricken city.

"A truck passes . . . A man in uniform crosses the street; on his sleeve are the words, *Secours Quaker*. We who know the meaning of that name feel a prayer mount within us, words of gratitude rise to our lips for all the Quakers have done for the children of men.

"One can sum up the activities of Quakers with one word—Love— a love the more great because it is given without reservation, and asks nothing in return."[5]

At Pendle Hill in Pennsylvania, volunteers were training for service in England, Spain, Portugal, Germany and Austria, Finland, China, India and the Middle East.

In Bengal, India, three hundred boats were being built under the care of the Service Committee. Some years earlier, the Indian Government, fearing invasion by the Japanese, had destroyed all the small craft. These new Quaker boats put the fishermen back in business and made it possible to bring medical supplies to isolated villages where 90 per cent of the famine-weakened population had been cut off from anti-malarial drugs, vitamins and sulfa.

This imaginative project was overseen by Eric Johnson, who would one day become Vice-Principal of Germantown Friends School but who, at that moment, was traveling through sodden Indian terrain on an elephant, surveying the extent of need for relief.

In Nepal, meanwhile, Everett and Catherine Cattell, evangelical Friends from Ohio, were preaching the Gospel, particularly to the untouchables who were constantly being warned by their social superiors not to dare break their caste by becoming Christians. Catherine Cattell was the sister of Charles and W. E. DeVol, the missionaries to China who were overtaken by the Japanese at the time of Pearl Harbor.

Years later, when she was asked by her co-workers, Walter R.

and Myrtle M. Williams, to write about her experiences as a missionary in the villages of Bundelkhand, Catherine Cattell described her first winter there in 1936:

"Then, for the first time, I saw the evangelists load up the oxcarts and start off for village evangelistic work. . . . I often wondered about the women in the villages and whether there would ever be an opportunity for them to hear the Gospel; also whether I would ever be permitted to go to them.

"My heart seems always to have been in the village, but there was no way to accompany it during those beginning months . . . as our men evangelists returned, telling of villager after villager who was interested in their message but whose wife had threatened to leave him if he ever considered becoming a Christian, my concern . . . became a call from heaven. Then, in 1940, came the opportunity! . . . Off we went on the forty mile trip to the camp under the big mango trees of Launri village. . . .

"Next morning the men led us about the village, introducing us, and our presence attracted immediate attention. Heretofore Christianity had been a man's religion. . . . I was too happy to sense how totally unprepared for this task I really was . . . even though I spoke in Hindi, the message still had to be interpreted. . . . What I needed was to sit 'where they sat' before I could understand them, their needs, their thought pattern and their fears. . . . Soon I realized that I needed to know something of medical treatment, for many a patient in the village would never see a real physician or hospital. . . .

"It was a long, slow process, the learning of the ways of the village. It will continue to be a process as long as one remains in India. . . . Most of the learning is unlearning in this case, in our becoming more and more simple in every way. . . . By the second season I had learned that I should give up wearing a sun helmet and don a sari, for I was often taken for a man. It seems strange now that I did not see that at once, but in those days, Americans were Americans and Indians were Indians. . . ."[6]

When Everett and Catherine Cattell went on furlough in 1945, Milton and Rebecca Coleman joined the Bundelkhand Mission.

In Washington, D.C., on June 7 of that year, D. Robert Yarnall appeared before the House Committee on Post-War Military Policy. The United States was still at war with Japan, but this committee was already holding hearings. Robert Yarnall stated the position of the Society of Friends regarding peacetime military conscription.

"We must speak out against this proposal. It is at variance not only with the principles and traditions of our Religious Society, but also . . . with the four freedoms—freedom of speech, freedom of religion, freedom from want, and freedom from fear.

"We oppose peace-time conscription because it . . . will arouse fear and suspicion in other nations . . . because it leads to further exaltation of the state as dominant over the conscience of religious bodies and of individuals."

Robert Yarnall concluded his testimony with an eloquent and pertinent reminder.

"Our own state was, to a large degree, founded by religious men and women of various sects who crossed the sea because they could not give the state their conscience, which was God's. This insistence on the primacy of conscience is a most precious American heritage, the preservation of which we do well to consider at this crisis in our history."[7]

20 The Bridegroom Kissed the Bride

In 1945, the General Court of Massachusetts (the state legislature) passed a bill which would have unhinged members of that same Court sitting nearly three centuries earlier.

The bill authorized "The state treasurer, with the approval of the governor and council, to accept, in accordance with the will of Zenos H. Ellis, of Fair Haven, in the state of Vermont . . . the sum of twelve thousand dollars . . . to provide for the construction and erection of an appropriate statue of Mary Dyer, who was hanged on Boston Common in the year sixteen hundred and sixty because she chose to suffer the death penalty rather than abandon the principles of freedom of speech and conscience, and to erect such statue on the state house grounds."[1]

Zenos Ellis, who had made this bequest, was unknown in Quaker circles. In his will, he spoke of "my ancestor, Mary Dyer."

There were many people living in Massachusetts who took an equal pride in their Puritan ancestors and who might not wish to have the misguided actions of these forebears commemorated for any passerby on Beacon Street. It was, therefore, courageous of the General Court to accept this bequest and to lay on the Fine Arts Commission the task of finding a suitable sculptor.

This was not the first time that, to its great credit, the General Court had tried to make up for past mistakes. In 1740, Governor Jonathan Belcher told it, "I should . . . be glad if there might be a Committee appointed by this court to inquire into the Sufferings of the People called Quakers in the early days of this country, as also into the Descendants of such Families as were in a manner ruined in the mistaken Management of the terrible affair called Witchcraft. I really think there is something incumbent on this Government to be done for retrieving the Estates and Reputations of the Posterity of the unhappy Families that so suffered, and the doing it, tho so long afterwards, would doubtless be acceptable to Almighty God, and would reflect honour upon the present Legislature."[2]

The committee was appointed. Two centuries later, Henry Cadbury searched records in the State House at Boston for its report but could find none. He did, however, furnish us with the ending of the story, citing what was probably a memorial to the life of Mary Dyer's grandson, Samuel, who lived on her old farm in Newport and died in 1767.

"During his life," the eighteenth-century account relates, "the Legislature of the province of Massachusetts Bay . . . being informed that one of her descendants was living, sent a deputation of their body to confer with him . . . they represented that they deeply regretted the conduct of their ancestors, or predecessors, in putting his ancestor to death; and desired to know what compensation or satisfaction they could make. . . . He received them courteously and told them . . . that no compensation could be made; he could accept nothing as the price of blood; that their sense of the injury and injustice committed, exemplified by their acknowledgment, was sufficient; and he freely forgave all the actors in that dismal catastrophe."[3]

Another reversal of history would have come as a tremendous surprise had the Friends who lived a century earlier been able to witness the joyful gathering on the elm-shaded lawns of Phillips Academy in Andover, Massachusetts, at the summer solstice, 1945. All Friends in New England had come together in order to be united into a single Yearly Meeting. Many of those present, who had suffered lifelong chagrin because of the Separation, considered this a veritable miracle.

The committee charged with overseeing the reunion of the separated Yearly Meetings and the inclusion of the new independent Meetings had labored valiantly, employing all the art of Quaker diplomacy and relying, above all, upon divine leading. It was clearly understood that the constituent Monthly Meetings would continue to worship after the manner they preferred. There was not to be uniformity, only unity. Thus, after 1945, New England Yearly Meeting consisted of both pastoral and non-pastoral Monthly Meetings. Since a large proportion of the members belonged to the Five Years Meeting and wished to retain this tie, the entire consolidated Yearly Meeting became affiliated with the Five Years Meeting. Later it also joined the Friends General Conference.

In 1845, it was estimated that there were seven thousand Friends in New England. By 1945, there were only half that number.

Since both bodies had continued to meet annually, the first reunited session of New England Yearly Meeting became the 285th.

When the grave formalities, which sealed the reunion, were

concluded and hands were shaken all around, Rufus Jones stepped to the edge of the platform and exclaimed, smiling in his infectious way, "Now! The marriage has been solemnized. The ring is on the finger. The bridegroom has kissed the bride. Now, Friends, *make it work!*"

What would, a quarter of a century later, be popularly termed a "generation gap" had been closed. But in the years to come, other issues, notably race relations, would be raised by younger members in New England Yearly Meeting, constantly challenging the older ones to act with the same courage and initiative that they, as young people, displayed in 1945.

Before adjourning, the Yearly Meeting sent the following letter:

Honorable Harry S. Truman
President of the United States:

The New England Yearly Meeting of Friends (Quakers) at its 285th annual session, held in Andover, Massachusetts, June 20-25, 1945, has a profound concern that definite peace proposals should be made to Japan immediately, in such a way that hostilities may be brought to a conclusion without entailing further ruthless destruction . . .[4]

Alas, this concern did not avert the tragedy that was shortly to fall upon Hiroshima and Nagasaki.

In the silence of worship, New England Friends, like others in the United States, asked themselves what message they, as citizens of a victorious nation, could send to the prostrate people of Europe. As speedily as possible, the necessities of life were being shipped overseas. Douglas Steere and a group of Quaker workers had already arrived in Lapland, which was devastated when the Russians forced the Finns to drive out the Germans. The retreating armies burned homes, cut down trees and sacked the countryside. Refugees from Karelia and Eastern Lapland had streamed into Finland.

But Friends knew that food, clothing and medicine were, of themselves, inadequate, however destitute people might be. The vanquished hungered for fellowship in the human family. While ministering to the physical needs, the Quakers must bring sympathy to all, regardless of their record in the conflict.

A few days after the close of this historic occasion in New England other Friends were again in Washington. On behalf of the Mission Board of Philadelphia Yearly Meeting (Orthodox),

Esther B. Rhoads and J. Passmore Elkinton, who had done mission work in Japan, visited Undersecretary of State Joseph G. Grew. They had come to present "A Concern for a Just and Durable Peace."

"Wholesale destruction, as we have seen it in Europe, and as we are seeing it now in Japan, involves not only the obliteration of civilian property but also the sacrifice of tens of thousands of human lives—men, women and children. They are American lives as well as Japanese. . . . history will condemn, we believe, the wholesale bombing and burning of the enemy's cities."[5]

Meanwhile, Perry Hayden's wheat was ripening. He set July 14 as the date for the fifth harvest.

When Mr. Ford had announced the previous November that he no longer cared about the project, the fact that he was seriously ill was a carefully guarded secret. This, of course, accounted for his unexpected withdrawal. The truth came out when his farms and hobbies were sold and the management of the company passed out of his hands. During the reorganization no one seemed empowered to make decisions.

Legal permission for cutting and threshing had to be obtained from the Ford Motor Company, which now had jurisdiction over the land where Perry Hayden's wheat stood, but repeated applications failed to bring any reply.

As the date neared and there was still no answer, it became obvious that the harvest would have to be postponed. The tension wore on everybody's nerves.

Plans for a big celebration were canceled. The idea began to circulate of staging a symbolic harvest. If permission could be secured for cutting a small segment of the field, the thousands of people who were looking forward to this ceremony would be content. A telephone call from the Ford Company's attorney blasted even this hope.

"We have given orders that not a reaper is to go into the field, not even for a demonstration," he said. "No one is to be permitted on the grounds for any kind of Dynamic Kernels affair. We will cut the wheat later and turn it over to you."[6]

It was also stated unequivocally that Ford land would not be available for the last planting. No one else owned five thousand acres. Moreover, the cost of planting, threshing, hauling and storing the final crop would come to almost one hundred thousand dollars.

So many people had become interested in the Dynamic Kernels that it no longer seemed Perry Hayden's personal project. They wished to see it carried to its conclusion. But where would the land and money come from?

While Perry Hayden was bringing all his resourcefulness and spiritual strength to bear upon the production of food, thirty-six Conscientious Objectors, also eager to make a contribution to society, were undergoing systematic starvation. They had volunteered as subjects in an experiment being conducted at the University of Minnesota. The objective was to find out what happens to a famine-stricken person and how he can be rehabilitated.

In an article which appeared in the Minneapolis Sunday *Tribune* and later was condensed in the *Reader's Digest,* Kenneth Tuttle, one of the Conscientious Objectors, reported his experience.

"As our hunger deepened, we found it even more trying to control our irritability. . . . Many men's knees and ankles swelled. . . . Concentration was all but impossible. We would sit in the library with books before us, daydreaming about the food-filled past. We were cold all the time . . . girls became merely of academic interest. . . . We were half dead. Our legs and feet were hungry, as well as our stomachs and mouths. We were eating ourselves."

At the end of six months, the men's stomachs had so shrunk that three months were required to restore them to normal.

"The first day of rehabilitation was a terrific anticlimax. The additional 400 calories we got seemed nothing. . . . It took ten days . . . before we felt any relief. It was months before I regained the energy I had lost. Regardless of how much I ate, I did not feel satisfied. The deep emotional disturbances I went through left me feeling that I am a different person than I thought I was, and not knowing quite what I am. . . . Those who do survive prolonged hunger are never going to forget it or be the same as they were before."

In Germany, when the fighting stopped, there was not only physical hunger with its emotional consequences, but terrible spiritual starvation. Innocent individuals, feeling involved in the national guilt, craved acceptance by members of nations which condemned their country's moral degeneration. They longed to return to the fellowship of the human race.

Sensitive to this hunger, a Chicago Friend flew to Frankfurt. She was Alice Shaffer, Chief of the Welfare Branch of the Division of International Labor, Social and Health Affairs of the U. S. State Department. She had taken a leave of absence to carry an American Quaker message of friendship to the German Quakers, with whom she had been working when the war broke out.

Arriving in Frankfurt, Alice Shaffer walked all day through the rubble-strewn streets. The house where she had cared for refugee children in 1939 was a heap of bricks and twisted metal. By the end of the "hard, disappointing afternoon" she had not found a single Friend. Some, she learned from former neighbors, had been killed in air raids; others were imprisoned for befriending Jews or listening to the B.B.C.

At the end of ten days, having searched Mannheim as well as Frankfurt, Alice Shaffer finally located a Friend who put her in touch with others.

"We have been hoping for and expecting word from America," one German Friend exclaimed joyfully, "but we know also what an awful name we have among the family of nations."[7]

In Berlin, a "hollow shell," Alice Shaffer found about twenty people holding Meeting for Worship on Sunday morning at the Quäker Buro. During the war, they told her, they had often worshiped together in air-raid shelters.

To the greetings from Friends in America, the German Friends replied in part: "With deepest gratitude we have received our never-forgotten Friend Alice Shaffer as your ambassador of peace. . . . Many people look upon the Quakers as their hope and ask: when will the Quakers come?"[8]

They had already come to Belsen Concentration Camp in April— a team of the Friends Relief Service which had been called in by the British Army when it entered the camp and discovered an epidemic of typhus. Arriving at Belsen, these British Quakers found that the forty thousand people there had had nothing to eat or drink for a week. Six hundred were dying each day. Ten thousand lay dead.

"Among the heaps of dead, the living wandered . . . the vast concourse of scarecrow people, bodies incredibly emaciated and faces stamped with a single expression of despair."[9]

By coincidence, the previous summer, Mr. Ford had had a vision of ten thousand people. They were not, however, these "heaps of dead," whom the British Friends discovered at Belsen. They were gay, suntanned Michigan people whom he pictured sitting on the new Ford grass in the amphitheater that surrounded the little valley—"a natural beauty spot"—and they were celebrating the fifth harvest of the Dynamic Kernels. But this never came to pass.

Instead, a simple service was conducted in the Friends Church by the pastor, Edward Escolme, with the assistance of ministers from other denominations. It was a joyful service, for in the course of the addresses, a plan was presented whereby the tithing project could be carried forward, not through the help of one powerful industrialist, but by "the people"—the farmers of Michigan and surrounding states. Each farmer would plant as much of the seed as he could accommodate. Ten per cent of the yield would go to his own church. This plan was received with great enthusiasm.

The farmers of the county assured Perry Hayden that they would "come to the rescue. You can get ten thousand acres instead of five, if you need them."[10]

After the service, the throng gathered in the yard of the church to watch representatives of the Grange, the county farmers, the local churches and the 4-H Council wield sickles and cut the tiny plot of wheat, which the children had planted the year before. Senator Elmer Porter tied the wheat into a bundle and presented it to the Grange Master of Michigan. Networks, newspapers and *Time* magazine carried reports of the symbolic harvest across the country.

A few days later, sixty-seven Ford workmen brought forty huge combines into the little valley and harvested 5555 bushels of Perry Hayden's wheat, which they turned over to him. The tithe was sold and the proceeds, $861.03, were given to the Friends Church, which in turn donated the whole sum to the Tecumseh Hospital.

But before Perry Hayden had even begun the painstaking task of distributing the seed for his last planting, the yield of which he dedicated to "foreign lands to bind up the wounds of war," atomic bombs were discharged upon Hiroshima and Nagasaki, inflicting wounds of war such as no man had ever known.

21 A Cubic Inch of Grain

At Christmas of 1945, Scribner's bookshop in New York displayed a collection of Quaker hats and bonnets. This was to announce publication of *The Friendly Persuasion,* a collection of fourteen short stories by Jessamyn West, a California Friend. With affectionate humor and insight, she brought to life Quakers who lived in Indiana a century earlier.

The book was received with appreciation, not only by Friends but by all who longed for the serenity and spiritual sturdiness of the Birdwells. Readers who could not embrace Quakerism wished somehow that they might make this simple way of life their own. Hollywood turned the book into a film.

Three days after Christmas, Theodore Dreiser, the great American novelist of the 1920s, died, leaving an unpublished novel about Quakers in Pennsylvania. Entitled *The Bulwark,* it is a story of conflict between generations in the beginning of the present century. The children of plain, upright, narrow Solon Barnes and his wife rebel against all that their parents stand for.

The Bulwark is less successful as the Quaker novel it was intended to be than as a forecast of today's conflict between generations in all sectors of American society. The essence of Quakerism is not experienced until the end of the book. "God has taught me humility," Solon Barnes, on his deathbed, tells one of his disappointing children, "and in His loving charity, awakened me to many things that I had not seen before. One is the need of love toward all created things."[1]

When the book appeared, Frederick Tolles observed that Dreiser's "conception of a Quaker meeting for worship is akin to a Methodist experience meeting or a Christian Science testimonial meeting." But "in spite of Dreiser's imperfect grasp of Quakerism," Frederick Tolles found *The Bulwark* satisfying, owing largely, he said, to Dreiser's "honesty and pity."[2] Other Friends felt that Dreiser had tried to write about their religious experience without ever having shared it. The book was unreal, they thought, even though the old-fashioned Quaker types, their plain dress and speech, might be well portrayed.

By the time these books were written, Quaker dress had died out almost everywhere. In southeastern Ohio, a few conservative Friends still wore it. The "plain language" was spoken in all parts of the country, but usually within the family or among Friends, rarely in conversation with others. Some Quaker children felt ill at ease with it, even at home, maintaining that it smacked of in-group snobbishness. Few, however, seemed to be troubled by the fact that the plain language, as American Friends have spoken it since the nineteenth century, is ungrammatical. At some point, for some unknown reason, the inflection was altered so that in place of *thou*, the correct form, which Friends used earlier, they began to use the accusative *thee* for the nominative. And to compound the injury, they gave the second person pronoun a third person verb, producing a mishmash that is hard to justify.

Friends still addressed Friends without titles, whether they wished to be familiar or formal. But when addressing non-Friends, they no longer felt called to testify to the individuality of persons, irrespective of status. In order not to sound quaint, Friends now used "Mr." and "Mrs." like everyone else. This, their children were also quick to point out, was patronizing; it made a subtle distinction between people who were members of the Society of Friends and those who were not. From the moment modern Quakers began to temper their peculiar style, they became wound in a hopeless tangle.

Rufus Jones pointed out that a more demanding peculiarity was needed now. "For a century and a half we maintained our unique type of faith by withdrawal from the world and by building hedges of protection around our members. The peculiar garb and speech, the maintenance of guarded education, the refusal to share in the work and method of other religious bodies, all tended to protect Quaker youth from the social impact of the world around them. . . .

"We live in the world. . . . We are bound to live in the world and to look and speak like the general run of people. But we must not, we cannot, give up the idea of being a *peculiar people*. Only henceforth the peculiarity must not be in outward form, it must be in *inward life and power* . . . the absolute confrontation of our lives with the reality of God."[3]

Many people humbly sought that confrontation.

From Maine to California, they worked for improvement in relations between races, between labor and management, for the resettlement of unemployed miners, of refugees and Japanese-

Americans who had been uprooted. They pleaded on behalf of the Conscientious Objectors, many of whom were still in prison or in camps, which Friends felt they could no longer administer.

They worked for a basic change in the entire penal system. "Imprisonment is . . . not reforming; it is destructive. The only solution is a spiritual one in which every person feels his share in the guilt of any person and feels responsible for anything that happens to mankind."[4]

Friends had been under the weight of this concern from the beginning. When, at the age of twenty-six, Fox was imprisoned at Derby on a charge of blasphemy, he wrote to the judges: "I am moved to write unto you to take heed of putting men to death for stealing cattle or money." He also pointed out "what a sore thing it was that prisoners should lie so long in gaol, and how that they learned badness one of another."[5]

Elizabeth Hooton, imprisoned at the same time, wrote to the Mayor of Derby. Later, confined in Lincoln Castle, she pleaded with "him in Authority to reform the Abuses of the Gaol," urging, "Either remove strong drink out of this place or remove the Gaolar."[6]

Friends handed down their concern for penal reform in a kind of apostolic succession, not effected by the laying on of hands but by a contagion of spirit which broke out all over England and wafted across the Atlantic in defiance of the prevailing wind. Three years after Fox wrote to the judges about the evils of prison life and capital punishment, a boy was born to London Quakers who was destined to make the first modern proposal for the abolition of the death penalty. The whole end of justice, John Bellers claimed, should be reform of the criminal—a completely revolutionary idea.

"How sincerely can we say the Lord's Prayer," Bellers asked at the end of the seventeenth century, "*Forgive us our Trespasses as we forgive them which trespass against us;* when for the loss, possibly of less than 20 shillings, we Prosecute a Man to Death?"[7]

As for the effects of prison life, Bellers echoed his friend Fox. To put felons into Bridewell or Newgate, he said, never "reclaims them . . . they learn but more skill in their Trade, under the Tutors they meet there." Bellers was convinced that crime was the result of poverty, illness and ignorance. Criminals should be given decent care in healthful surroundings, where they could repent; they should be taught vocational skills in prison, which would prepare them for a better life after their release.

The first step in the prevention of crime, he asserted, was care of the poor. Bellers and William Meade, Penn's co-defendant in the famous trial, disbursed a fund which kept poor Friends from becoming public charges. They bought flax and gave it to these Friends to spin, thereby making them self-supporting. "I think it as much more Charity," Bellers said, "to put the Poor in a way to live by honest Labour, than to maintain them Idle, as it would be to set a man's broken leg, that he might go himself, rather than always to carry him."

Over and over, Bellers was arrested for attending Friends Meeting. In 1684, he and twenty other London Friends were under indictment for taking part in "riotous Assembly with Force and Arms," which hardly seems an apt description of a Quaker Meeting for Worship. When the jury found these Friends guilty, "One of the prisoners said, 'We desire you would not send us to a bad Prison, where some of our Friends have been suffocated.' The Recorder answered, 'I can't build Prisons for you. You need not go to Prison unless you will. The Court has been moderate as to your Fines.' The Prisoners said, 'Whatever the Fines are, we cannot pay them, knowing we have injured no Man.'"[8]

In 1696, Bellers addressed "To the Children of Light in Scorn called Quakers" and "To the Lords and Commons Assembled in Parliament, Proposals for Raising a College of Industry of All Useful Trades with Husbandry." Later he published *Some Reasons for an European State*, similar to Penn's earlier proposal for a parliament of nations. Penn had witnessed the marriage of John Bellers to Frances Fettiplace in 1686. It is not surprising that the founder of Pennsylvania had an influence on the younger man.

To this vision of united nations, Bellers added a suggestion of his own that would one day become a near fact, though not till 1948 when his name was all but forgotten. He added "A Proposal for a General Council or Convocation of all the different Religious Perswasions in Christendom, (not to Dispute what they Differ about, but) to Settle the General Principles they Agree in: By which it will appear that they may be good Subjects and Neighbors, tho' of different Apprehensions of the Way to Heaven.'"[9]

Bellers called the attention of the Lord Mayor and other officials of the city of London to the plight of the little bootblacks and children who had no decent home, "the distress'd children called the Black Guard . . . such of them as escape being starv'd with Hunger and Cold, or some rotten or malignant Distemper . . .

frequently supply our Jayls and Gibbets. . . . Necessity hath no Law, Hunger will break Stone-Walls . . . every Day that they are neglected, they not only infest the Streets of this City, but it may be the Loss . . . of a useful Posterity . . . Reformation will be much more Glory and Honour to Magistrates, than the Power of executing Severities upon any of them when they become Criminals."[10]

Friends were reminded that "The Children called The Black Guard are . . . our Neighbours, our Flesh and Blood, our Relations, our Children, however mean and contemptible they may now appear."[11]

In a broadside addressed to "The Criminals in Prison," Bellers affirmed man's perfectibility. "Consider the Nobility of your Nature," he urged, "being of the same Species with other Men, and therefore capable by a thoro' Reformation to become Saints on Earth, and as Angels in Heaven to Reign with our Saviour there, who said to the repenting Thief on the Cross, *To-day shalt thou be with me in Paradise.*"[12]

About the time that this Friend, at the age of seventy-one, took leave of the world he had tirelessly labored to make more compassionate, a little Quaker boy across the ocean began, as he later recorded, "to be acquainted with the operations of divine love." He was on his way to a neighbor's house in Burlington, the province of West New Jersey, when he saw a robin sitting on her nest. As he came near, she fluttered about and he threw stones at her till she fell dead. "At first," he recalled, "I was pleased with the exploit, but after a few minutes was seized with horror, as having, in a sportive way, killed an innocent creature while she was careful for her young." He knew the baby birds would "pine away and die miserably" so he killed them, too, "much troubled" by the incident. Recalling it in manhood, John Woolman observed that God "hath placed a principle in the human mind, which incites to exercise goodness towards every living creature."[13]

Like Bellers, Woolman was consumed with concern for the captive and the poor—the slave who, through no fault of his own, was condemned to lifelong bondage and the indigent who, because of the greed and vanity of the rich, lacked the very necessities for survival.

From its founding, the province of West Jersey, under Quaker proprietors, did not tolerate the "bloody punishments" inflicted in England. The "Laws, Concessions and Agreements" assured religious liberty and trial by jury. Debtors were not imprisoned as they were in the mother country, but were left at large to earn so that they could pay back what they owed.

In framing the first laws for New Jersey and Pennsylvania, Penn took care to correct an abuse from which he himself had suffered when imprisoned. In the English jails, the prisoner was obliged to pay for his food. Subsistence depended on one's ability to pay without having the freedom to do a day's work, coupled with the jailer's integrity and frame of mind. "All prisons shall be free, as to fees, food, and lodging," these first laws read.

Enforced idleness irked the Friends who were locked up. Penn and Bellers maintained that prisoners should be allowed to work for their living while they were confined, thus preserving their self-respect instead of making them objects of charity. But as political power in Pennsylvania passed out of Quaker hands, these reforms were thrown out. Even the death penalty which, under Penn's Frame of Government, had only been applicable in cases of murder or treason, was later invoked for lesser offenses.

In 1776, Friends organized the Philadelphia Society for Relieving Distressed Prisoners. After the Revolution, this Society managed the Walnut Street Prison. It was intended as a place where malefactors would have a chance to meditate and repent. It was therefore known as a "penitentiary." Instead of being thrown in together, regardless of the class of crime committed or the mental condition and sometimes even without segregation of the sexes, as prisoners had been confined previously, in the new institution each offender was given a cell to himself with a little garden and was expected to work. It was hoped that solitude would help him to repent of past mistakes. That solitary confinement was as cruel as some of the antiquated punishments was not apparent to these well-meaning Friends.

Stephen Grellet, the French-born American Quaker, made a journey to Europe in 1813. In London he visited Newgate Prison. "We found many boys who, decoyed into vice by thieves and pickpockets, and now mixing in prison with older and depraved men, were likely to come out thence far greater adepts in crime," he reported. In the women's section, he "found many sick, lying on the bare floor or on some old straw, having very scanty covering over them, though it was quite cold; and there were several children born in the prison among them, almost naked. On leaving that abode of wretchedness and misery, I went . . . to my much valued friend, Elizabeth Fry, to whom I described, out of the fulness of my heart, what I had just beheld."[14]

The response of Joseph John Gurney's sister, Elizabeth Fry, to this appeal marks the beginning of a new era in penal reform.

Another American Friend who visited Europe around that time and returned with deeper awareness of the needs of prisoners was John Griscom, a teacher from New York. He established the House of Refuge, to care for children whose parents were in prison. In 1817, New York Friends founded the Society for Prevention of Pauperism, which became the Society for the Reformation of Juvenile Delinquents. Isaac T. Hopper, a Quaker who had been a conductor on the Underground Railroad, acted as secretary of the New York Prison Association. He left his estate to a home for needy women and those discharged from prison.

In Indiana, Sarah Smith, a Friends Minister, was not content with visiting prisons and preaching to the inmates. She became a matron in the penitentiary, where she sought through kindness and understanding to reform the people placed under her care.

Modern psychological insight makes some of the early Quaker concepts of dealing with prisoners seem primitive, but they represent the first efforts in America to treat those who have offended against society with love and hope rather than brutality. Concern for the prisoner—his rights as a human being and a citizen—and efforts to abolish the death penalty are still living Quaker testimonies.

"Our gracious Creator cares and provides for all his Creatures . . . and so far as his love influences our minds, so far we . . . feel a desire to . . . lessen the distresses of the afflicted and increase the happiness of the creation," Woolman wrote in *A Plea for the Poor*. "Here we have a prospect of one common interest from which our own is inseparable, that to turn all the treasures we possess into the channel of universal love becomes the business of our lives."

These words, written almost two centuries earlier, were uppermost in Friends' minds as the Second World War ended and they endeavored to help those whose lives had been broken by it.

In the handsome old Friends Meetinghouse at 20 South Twelfth Street, Philadelphia, where the Service Committee maintained its national office until the scope of its undertakings forced it to move to larger quarters, the regular Monday morning staff meetings were always preceded—as they still are—by a Meeting for Worship. While the staff members are not all Friends, they feel in sympathy with Quaker practices and testimonies and they find strength for the coming week in the period of silence. Following the Meeting for Worship, workers from the regional offices across the country or those returned from overseas report on their activities.

Every week in 1946, this succession of indefatigable men and women rose from the facing bench in the Philadelphia Meetinghouse and described, one after another, how concerns, emanating from some earlier span of worship, had been translated into visible manifestations of human solidarity.

Workers who had just returned from overseas brought reports. From Lapland, destroyed by the retreating Germans, where food and shelter were desperately needed; from China, where Madam Chiang Kai-shek felt moved to write of the Friends Ambulance Unit, "In spite of ever-present danger of death or mutilation, members of the China Convoy have carried out their work of mercy."[15] From Poland, where a million and a half destitute refugees were returning to an already impoverished country; from Italy, where Quakers were helping rebuild 150 destroyed villages; from Calcutta, where Pandit Nehru, visiting the Friends Service Unit, said in a low, gentle voice that more important than the Unit's work—"efficient as that is"—has been the psychological approach, the emotional understanding and appreciation that has gone into it.

From France, Germany, Austria, Hungary, Holland and Norway, Service Committee workers brought news of reconstruction both of buildings and of lives.

Sometimes they spoke of miracles, as when they reported that they had visited German prisoners in a hospital camp in France to assure them that someone cared, to bring them what little food was obtainable and materials for making toys. They persuaded the Germans to send the dolls and wooden animals they made not only to German children, but also to the little Jewish refugees and French children whose fathers had been prisoners of war.

"We have seen things happen in this camp," a worker recalled.[16]

Such large-scale programs could not have been mounted by the 118,000 Americans who called themselves Quakers without the help of others. People of every belief supported their efforts. Money began to pour in—as much during the first half of 1946 as in the whole of 1945.[17] Students in colleges across the country gave up meals to share with hungry students overseas.

"This kind of expression of fellowship with others in suffering is the texture out of which a life of inner security is built," Clarence Pickett observed. "It may well be that the greatest contribution our Committee has made lies in its having afforded opportunities for people to give of self and substance to meet others' needs."[18]

Two hundred and fifty-six farmers in Michigan and other states, as far away as Tennessee, expressed their fellowship with those who were suffering in the wake of war by growing the last crop of Perry Hayden's wheat. These farmers, only a few of whom were Quakers, had bought the Dynamic Kernels at market price or lower and planted them on their land, promising to give one tenth of the yield to their own churches—175 in all, representing thirty denominations. But long before the wheat was ripe, the churches transferred their rights to the American Friends Service Committee so that one tenth of the entire crop could go overseas. It amounted to 72,150 bushels. Had Perry Hayden continued his experiment for ten years, he would have grown enough wheat to cover the United States. In thirteen, it would have covered the earth.[19]

The harvest was celebrated at the Adrian Fair Grounds on August 1, declared by Governor Harry F. Kelly as Biblical Wheat Day for the state of Michigan. Merchants decorated the downtown streets with banners and filled their store windows with festive sheaves.

At 10 A.M., in brilliant sunshine, a parade took over the city of Adrian, heading for the Fair Grounds. Leading the procession were the Haydens and Mrs. Emma Clement, Mother of the Year, a Black from Louisville, Kentucky, the widow of a Methodist bishop. In the car with them was Clarence Pickett, who had come from Philadelphia to accept the gift on behalf of the Service Committee.

Next came the Drum and Bugle Corps, the Boy Scouts, Red Cross and 4-H, followed by men displaying the tools used in successive years to harvest the Dynamic Kernels: a sickle, a cradle, a reaper pulled by a pair of beautiful black horses, a binder and combine hauled by tractors and, at the finish, the self-propelled combine.

Then came the wheat, mountains of it! Led by a woman who drove a truck filled with the tithe from her entire farm, the procession stretched for more than a mile. Trucks, carrying the grain loose between high side boards, followed cars stuffed to the roof with bags or pulling trailers filled to overflowing. Some farmers brought a tithe; others their whole crop. Some, who had not planted Dynamic Kernels, contributed their own wheat. These farmers were of all races, colors, creeds and nationalities.

"It was an outpouring of the spirit."[20]

With flags flying, bands blaring, spectators cheering, the parade reached the Adrian Fair Grounds. Ten thousand people already filled the grandstand and bleachers. The cars and trucks were unloaded at the race track. Piled up before the grandstand, the bags of wheat made a mountain.

The previous fall, Dynamic Kernels had been planted on fifteen acres inside the race track. Now the wheat stood high, ready to be cut. It was flailed by hand and ground into graham flour at an old stone mill set up on the field. A helicopter immediately flew one hundred pounds of the stone-ground flour to Toledo, Ohio, where hot ovens were waiting to bake it into crackers.

At the Fair Grounds, fifty men and women, riding western ponies, were staging a rodeo when the helicopter returned, just fifty-five minutes after take-off. All eyes watched it descend. The pilot unloaded the graham crackers, 4-H girls stuffed them into little cellophane envelopes and sold them to the spectators for the benefit of the Service Committee. The crackers, which had been wheat standing on the spot only hours earlier, were consumed in still less time.

During the afternoon, Clarence Pickett addressed the crowd, expressing gratitude for the huge gift of wheat. He explained that it would be processed into Ralston Relief Cereal, which had been developed by Lucy Morgan, a Friend whose husband, Arthur E. Morgan, formerly President of Antioch College, was Chairman of the Tennessee Valley Authority.

Lucy Morgan's objective was to design a food which would provide the nourishment necessary for sustaining life while being, at the same time, easy to transport. A hundred-pound-bag of her Relief Cereal lay on the speakers' platform, ready to be shipped to people who were starving.

"This is the food," Clarence Pickett announced, pointing to the bag, "that your wheat will provide for these unfortunate people."[21]

In closing, the Reverend Clifton Robinson, whose 1940 sermon touched off the whole project, reminded the crowd that "We can make our lives what we please, either meaningless, or we can make of them something important."

He was about to make his own life important by serving as a missionary in India.

The triumphal conclusion of the Dynamic Kernels project far exceeded Perry Hayden's dream six years earlier when he sat in the Tecumseh Friends Church pondering the words *Except a grain of wheat fall into the ground and die, it abideth alone; but if it die, it bringeth forth much fruit.*

While this celebration was taking place in Michigan, in California, Richard M. Nixon, a graduate of Whittier College, was running for Congress on the Republican ticket against Jerry Voorhis, the Democratic incumbent.

A couple of weeks later in Pasadena, the Pacific Coast Association of Friends adopted a minute, composed by Howard Brinton, authorizing the formation of Pacific Yearly Meeting. It had taken 285 years from the time that the first Yearly Meeting of Friends was established in America for one that was also dedicated to "silent waiting on the Lord" to cross the continent.

"We have met in great unity," the closing minute of the Pacific Coast Association read in 1946. "Out of this unity has come the Pacific Yearly Meeting, the fruition of years of hopes and labor . . . another opportunity to increase this vital unity and to work more effectively in the service of God."

22 The Crown Prince of Japan and the People of China

A few days earlier, on a hillside in New Hampshire, another Friend was challenged to take a long leap on faith. Elizabeth Gray Vining, spending her vacation above Lake Sunapee, received an invitation to go to Japan.

An American Education Mission visiting Tokyo had been charged by the Emperor with finding a suitable tutor for his son. Upon its return home, the Mission, after careful consideration, selected Elizabeth Vining. Handsome, gracious, serene, the author of books for young people, she was—everyone who knew her agreed—the perfect choice. But she was reluctant.

"I felt myself so inadequate and inappropriate, a quiet Philadelphia Quaker at the most elaborate and mysterious court in the world, that my instant reaction was to say no. Positively no."[1]

What made her willing to accept the appointment was the chance it offered to contribute to world peace.

"That Japan had renounced war in her new constitution was to me immensely significant. Here, perhaps, was an opportunity to uphold the hands of those who were willing to risk greatly for peace, and to bring before the Emperor's son in his formative years the ideals of liberty and justice and good will upon which peace must be based if it is to endure."[2]

When the invitation from Tokyo reached New Hampshire, Elizabeth Vining wrote immediately to Rufus Jones. She received this reply:

> My dear Elizabeth,
> My first response as I read thy letter this morning, with its great news, was *Selah*, which is a profound pause of awe and wonder over some great new insight or discovery, and if you translate it, it means, "Just think of that"!! with two exclamation points . . . thee is the one to do this important thing. Thee has been getting ready for it and the task has come to meet thee. Yes, we shall give our prayers for strength and guidance and we shall go on believing in thee.[3]

Elizabeth Vining was following a long line of Philadelphia Quakers to Japan. But she was not going under the auspices of Friends, nor was she sponsored by the Occupation.

"The act of the Emperor in asking that an American woman come to Japan to teach his son the English language was a gesture of great import," Clarence Pickett observed. "Seldom has one seen the conquered express eagerness to have the language of the conqueror taught to the imperial heir so quickly after a bitter war."[4]

"On October 1, 1946, I set sail for Japan to tutor the Crown Prince."[5]

Thus begins *Windows for the Crown Prince,* Elizabeth Vining's account of her stay in a country which, only a year earlier, had been her own country's enemy.

Two cars with officials—Japanese and American Occupation personnel—had gone to Yokohama to meet Elizabeth Vining's ship when it landed in rain on October 15.

"After the introductions, handshakings, and bows, I found myself in one of the cars. . . . A low and gentle voice spoke beside me. 'I am Tane Takahashi,' it said. 'I am to be your secretary.'

"She went on to tell me that she had been educated in the United States and was herself a member of the Society of Friends. I could not see her face in the dark, but as she spoke and I felt her serene and perceptive personality, I realized that someone had put a great deal of thought and effort into finding just the right person to help me. Someone among the Japanese themselves must sincerely want this undertaking to be a happy one. From that moment the burden of uncertainty and anxiety lifted, never to return."[6]

Arriving in Tokyo, Elizabeth Vining was taken to the house that had been prepared for her use.

"People poured out to welcome me. Esther B. Rhoads was there, my friend and fellow member of Germantown Monthly Meeting. . . . Another Friend was there too, Luanna J. Bowles, a member of the Education Division of the Civil Information and Education Section (of the Occupation). Bowing on the steps were the household staff."[7]

At the close of her first exciting day, Elizabeth Vining had time to notice the homely things.

"As I lay in bed waiting for sleep, I heard the sound of wooden clogs in the street outside, a clip-clop that made me realize more keenly than any other one thing that now I was actually in Japan. Clip-clop, clip-clop, lightly yet with a little drag, the wooden *geta* passed along the lane and died away. Later in the night I felt my first earthquake, a tiny tremor from the earth's center like the flicker of a fish's tail—a catfish, the Japanese say, moving its whiskers. In the morning the rain was gone and I woke to a dazzling blue and gold October day. From the flat roof on top of the house I could see Mount Fuji, ethereal in the distance, white-shawled against the blue sky. . . ."[8]

"I saw the Crown Prince for the first time together with his father and mother. The occasion was without precedent. . . .

"He was twelve years old then, a lovable-looking small boy, round-faced and solemn but with a flicker of humor in his eyes. He wore the dark blue uniform of all Japanese schoolboys . . . his head was shaven close to the scalp; his short black fur of hair was glistening."[9]

"We want you to open windows on to a wider world for our Crown Prince," the Grand Steward of the Emperor's Court told Elizabeth Vining.

Windows were opened for her, too. "At meeting for worship one Sunday," she wrote back to Philadelphia shortly after her arrival, "I could see through the window women washing sweet potatoes and laying them out to dry in the sun on the concrete steps that are all that is left of the Friends Meetinghouse . . . sweet potatoes were just about all they had to eat. . . . The devastation from the incendiary bombs covers acres and miles. . . . Little shacks, built out of wood, if people are lucky, or of old iron and tin, are going up everywhere. There will be no way to keep them warm this winter."[10]

Esther B. Rhoads, who had taught in the Friends Girls School in Tokyo before the war, was trying against severe odds to build up the school again and to bring new hope to the Japanese people.

"The Quaker groups in Japan are scattered and much of their property has been destroyed," she reported, "but the spirit of groups and individuals is the same—earnest, sincere, and deeply affectionate. Somehow after five years of war, relationships are touched with the miraculous.

"There is first of all the miracle of endurance. . . . But the greatest miracle of all is forgiveness. Almost everyone who calls at the Friends Center has lost some member of the family, his home, or was perhaps himself injured in one of the air raids. They greet us from America with deep affection. . . . There is no trace of bitterness.

"I talked with atomic bomb victims in Hiroshima. Somehow all these people have the gift of forgiveness. If they blame anything for the tragedies through which they have passed, it is *war* and not Americans."[11]

As the representative of the American Friends Service Committee on LARA—Licensed Agencies for Relief in Asia—Esther Rhoads was working with the National Catholic Welfare Conference, securing the first relief from America. LARA communicated the concern of the victors for the people they had defeated.

"We work *with* Japanese, while the army works over or above," Esther Rhoads wrote home. "We *go to* Japanese officials; they have to go to the army. We work in cold offices, and the Japanese government is getting us fuel as a free gift. U.S. offices require fuel, and black coal-smoke pours out of U.S. used buildings and settles on fireless homes round about."[12]

Esther Rhoads kept pressing Philadelphia. "Isn't there anything that can be done to get relief supplies off from San Francisco? One can't keep going on the leaves of turnips. . . . At the orphanage the children were . . . almost lifeless . . . too undernourished to do anything but sit."[13]

These were the conditions in Japan when Elizabeth Vining arrived at the end of 1946.

Not only was she expected to tutor the Prince; she was to teach his class in the Peers School once a week. At her first meeting with the class, the principal told her, through Tane Takahashi, that he would make a speech and all she had to do was bow. But Elizabeth Vining wished to express appreciation for the welcome herself and to say something else.

"In myself I am not in the least important, but the fact that I am here this morning is a sign of something very important," she said. "That your Emperor asked me to come at this time and my government helped me to do it, is something new in the world and something hopeful.

"The chief reason why I wanted to come is that in her new constitution Japan has renounced war as an instrument of national policy. Other nations must follow. I believe that out of her great suffering and defeat Japan will draw a new strength and a new vision that will enable her to lead the world in ways of peace.

"You are the generation that will have to do it. Your job will be to create a world in which every human being can develop the best there is in him, a world in which free men can work together for the good of all. I come to you in friendship and in the hope that I can take a small share in helping your many distinguished teachers to prepare you for your great task," Elizabeth Vining concluded.

"I doubted as I looked at those childish faces, if it could mean very much to them. . . . When I left Japan four years later, some of the boys referred in their farewell letters to what I had said that day."[14]

Boys this age had never had a woman teacher, and it was suggested that a Japanese sit in the back of the room during Elizabeth Vining's lessons to keep order.

"Many students were interpreting this new 'democrashy' to mean that they could do exactly as they liked, and the teachers were afraid that I would have trouble in controlling my classes. Remembering what fiends we were to the French and German conversation teachers when I was in school, I thought it quite probable that I might have difficulty, but I did not think that having a Japanese teacher as a policeman in the room was a satisfactory solution.

"One of the fertile sources of foreign-teacher-torture, I remembered, was derision in all its varied forms of the way in which they mangled our names in pronouncing them. So I thought that I would eliminate that hazard at any rate by giving all the boys English names . . . it would be a good experience for the Crown Prince for once in his life to be on exactly the same level as the other boys, with no title and no especial treatment at all. . . .

"I marched into Section A the first morning very calm outwardly but feeling a bit adventurous within.

"The boys all stood up. 'Good morning, boys,' I said. 'Good morning, sir,' they replied with one voice. I laughed and they laughed. Then I told them that you said sir to a man but you called a woman by her name. . . .

"'My name is Mrs. Vining,' I said, and turned to the boy who sat at the first desk on the right-hand side. 'What is your name?' He told me.

"'That is your real name,' I conceded, 'but in this class your name is Adam.'

"He looked surprised, as well he might.

"'Now,' I announced, 'I am going to give you all English names.

"... In this class, your name is Adam. Please say Adam. Please say, 'In this class my name is Adam.'

"The second boy caught on more quickly and the third boy jumped up eagerly to get his name. As I worked toward the Prince, who sat in the exact center of the room, I could see the others cutting their eyes around at each other, all agog to see what I was going to do about this situation.

"I reached the Prince and said, 'In this class your name is Jimmy.' There was no particular reason for Jimmy, except that it just happened to be one of my favorite names.

"He replied promptly, 'No. I am Prince.'

"'Yes,' I agreed cordially. 'You are Prince Akihito. That is your real name. But in this class you have an English name. In this class your name is Jimmy.' I waited, a little breathless.

"He smiled cheerfully, and the whole class beamed. . . .

"I was in terror that the newspapermen would get hold of it and headlines would appear in the *Stars and Stripes:* Tutor Calls Emperor's Son Jimmy. The secret never got out—among westerners. The Japanese knew and, evidently, approved. . . .

"Incidentally, I never had any trouble with discipline."[15]

To Friends at home—indeed, to most Americans—the presence of Elizabeth Gray Vining at the Imperial Court of Japan represented a confidence in the future that had long been wanting. Now that the military men had finished leveling the cities of Japan, a pacifist woman was going into them, simply to build up a love for the best of Western culture.

The steadfast efforts of another Quaker woman to achieve peace were honored in 1946 when Emily Greene Balch, a member of the Friends Meeting at Cambridge, Massachusetts, shared the Nobel Peace Prize with John R. Mott, a leader in international church and missionary movements.

Emily Balch devoted her long life to the cause of child welfare, the improvement of working conditions for women, better understanding of immigrant problems and opposition to war. With Jane Addams, she founded the Women's International League for Peace and Freedom. She helped draft the first minimum wage bill ever put before a state legislature. In 1915, she was a delegate to the International Congress of Women held in The Hague.

When she was fifty years old, Emily Balch was dismissed from the faculty of Wellesley College for opposing American entry into the First World War. When she was eighty, her constructive efforts to win peace were recognized by the bestowal of the most coveted prize in the world.

A few years later, the *Friends Journal* reprinted a poem she had written, which read, in part:

> Dear People of China:
>
> This is a letter of love that I am sending you.
>
> Men and women with your patient faces,
> Little children with your bright eyes,
> How could I not love you?
>
> I am an American, and what you perhaps call a capitalist.
> Need that be a barrier to love?
> It does not hold back mine . . .
>
> Shall fellow men be divided by ideologies?
> No. No. They shall not be so.
> Of course, "coexistence" has great difficulties.
> Even men who have a common country,
> Who speak the same language, profess the same religion—
> Even such do not find mutual understanding, mutual
>   trust too easy.
> Yet the greatest barriers are not insuperable.
> Let us strive to learn to live together . . .
>
> Let us be patient with one another,
> And even patient with ourselves.
> We have a long, long way to go.
> So let us hasten along the road,
> The road of human tenderness and generosity.
> Groping, we may find one another's hands in the dark.[16]
>
> Emily Balch
U.S.A.

23 Happy in the Real Possession

Barely a month after Elizabeth Vining reached Japan, a momentous event took place in Kenya: East Africa Yearly Meeting of Friends was established at Lugulu.

An authorizing minute, adopted by the Five Years Meeting at Richmond, Indiana, was read in the Luragoli dialect by Petro Wanyama to twelve hundred Bantu Quaker representatives. Until that moment, the eighteen thousand Kenyan Quakers had been under the care of the Five Years Meeting. Empowered by this minute, East Africa Friends would henceforth conduct their affairs themselves.

The American Friends Board of Missions sent representatives to this solemn and joyous occasion, the Friends World Committee cabled greetings and New York Friends, in keeping with an old custom, sent a "token gift of good will" with which to start a treasury.[1]

Proceeding according to Quaker tradition, African Friends appointed a Clerk. He was Joeli Litu, who had helped the early missionaries to translate the Bible into the vernacular. What was not traditional was a gavel, which Joeli Litu wielded because African Friends speak to business with a good deal of freedom.

Reviewing the stages by which they had reached this new autonomy, they recalled with affection the first Americans who arrived at Kaimosi in 1902, "having come to Kenya under a direct sense of divine leading, possessed of a deep concern to share the gospel of Christ with backward peoples."[2] They were Willis R. Hotchkiss, Arthur Chilson and Edgar T. Hole, sons or grandsons of western pioneers.

The Africans watched incredulously as these first Quakers built a dam on the Goli Goli River. Suddenly, the water set a saw and grist mill in motion.

Such a passion for work as the Americans displayed had never been seen in those parts. But for some mysterious reason, on one day, which they called "the Sabbath"—it corresponded with the phases of the moon—the Americans knocked off completely.

The Bantu religion depended on sorcerers, incantations and sacrifices to ward off evil spirits. The missionaries told about another spirit, their God who lived not in rocks and trees but in every person.

A New York Friend, Levinus K. Painter, has gathered the recollections of some of the oldest African Quakers.

"Could the words of these men be true when they talked about God, a loving Father, whom they could not see, but who had power to change their lives inside? Who was this God? What about the story of the Christ who loved all men?

"So the inquiring Africans came again and again through the winding forest paths to hear the heart-warming words. . . . Often their arrival was heralded by drum beating and dancing, their own buoyant way of arriving at a meeting for worship."[3]

Malaria and tuberculosis were prevalent. Over half the children died before they were a year old. In 1903, Dr. Elisha Blackburn arrived at Kaimosi and, with the help of his wife, Virginia, set up a dispensary in a grass hut, performing surgery and effecting cures beyond any the witch doctors had accomplished.

The missionaries built roads and bridges. They taught the Africans carpentry, cement work, how to make and lay brick. They had a concern for the bodily needs of those among whom they had come "to share the gospel of Christ" and who were, many of them, underfed.

In certain quarters back home there was a strange lack of understanding.

"On his first return visit to America, some of Arthur Chilson's well-meaning supporters reminded him that they had sent missionaries to Africa to preach the Gospel and convert the heathen, not to build mill dams. Arthur Chilson's answer was to take a new water turbine with him when he returned to Africa. The mill on the Goli Goli River continued to saw logs into boards and to grind grain into *posho* (cornmeal)."[4]

The greatest triumph was the mastery of the Luragoli dialect. Unlike missionaries of other denominations, the Quakers were not content to use Swahili, the trade language of East Africa. It was not spoken by the tribes. Few women understood it.

"We long for the time to come when we can speak to the Africans in their own tongue," Arthur Chilson wrote in the first year. Before long, he was able to do so without an interpreter.

When Emory and Deborah Rees of Western Yearly Meeting arrived in 1904, they began to study the language, evolving an alphabet and a system of spelling and grammar so that they could put the dialect into writing.

"We made charts of unbleached muslin for use in teaching. But we had difficulty with the children, who preferred to wrap their charts around them to see how it felt to wear clothes."[5]

This led naturally to teaching the girls to sew. Soon the girls were making themselves things to wear.

The *First Reader* in Luragoli was published in 1907. Consisting mainly of Bible stories, it was used in the schools that the missionaries immediately established. Adults as well as children laboriously discovered the Scriptures in their own language.

"Young and old sat together on split logs or on the beaten earth floor and learned the marvels of the printed page, and . . . the religion that many of them had already accepted."[6]

It ceased to be something belonging to the whites. When the Africans could sing and pray and preach in their own tongue, the religion became theirs, adapted to their own particular needs.

In 1909, Emory Rees went home on leave. He took with him his Luragoli translation of the Gospel of Mark. Friends in Marion, Indiana, printed five hundred copies although, at that time, there were not one hundred people who could read the language. Emory Rees took the books back to Kaimosi, along with a small printing press that he taught the Africans to operate.

There was this young man Joeli Litu, who thirty-five years later would be appointed the first Clerk of East Africa Yearly Meeting. He knew Swahili. The New Testament had been translated into that language. Reading the Swahili, Joeli Litu could change the words into his own tongue. With his help, Emory Rees undertook the translation into Luragoli of the entire New Testament.

"We discussed each book, word by word, phrase by phrase. When we felt that we understood the passage, we made the best translation we could."[7]

It took years. Emory and Deborah Rees left Africa. But the American Bible Society completed the printing.

The arrival of the New Testaments in 1927 caused tremendous excitement at the mission stations.

"We put one of the leather-bound copies into Joseph Ngaira's hands . . . he quietly handled it over from cover to cover, very reverently. Then he said, 'O Mirembe ku'iwe Lilega Lahya.' (O peace to you, New Testament, so happy in the real possession.)"[8]

Joeli Litu and Jefferson Ford of Western Yearly Meeting, who had come out to the mission in 1914, then went to work on the Old Testament. After twenty years, they completed the translation. The manuscript was sent to America. Emory Rees checked it only weeks before he died in 1947.

At the same time, another Friend, whose name was Joel, too, and who was also a translator of the Bible—*into* not *from* English—was preparing to fly from Boston to Oslo.

The Nobel Peace Prize for 1947 was being awarded to the American Friends Service Committee and its British counterpart, the Friends Service Council. Henry Joel Cadbury, Chairman of the American Committee, had been invited to go to Norway and accept the Service Committee's share of the prize. He postponed his classes at the Harvard Divinity School for a week.

A dress suit with tails was *de rigueur* at the ceremonies. Henry Cadbury did not own one and heeding the "tender and Christian Advice" which London Yearly Meeting issued in 1691—that Friends take care to keep to plainness "and to avoid pride and immodesty in apparel and all vain and superfluous fashions of this world"—he hardly felt justified in buying a suit for the occasion.

Fortunately, workers in the Committee's Philadelphia storeroom where used clothing is collected and shipped to the needy all over the world were able to come to the rescue. They had already fitted out the members of the Budapest Symphony Orchestra with dress suits donated in various clothing drives. Now, they unearthed a magnificent garment for the chairman of the Committee.

"It seems to fit me perfectly," he wrote to his brother-in-law, Rufus M. Jones, "and I can leave it in Europe."[9]

Roland H. Bainton, Professor of Ecclesiastical History in the Yale Divinity School, who, as a young Conscientious Objector in 1917, served in the first American Quaker Reconstruction Unit, heard Henry Cadbury tell gleefully about this typically Quaker solution to a difficult sartorial problem. Thereupon, Roland Bainton drew a delightful cartoon, still treasured, of his opposite number at Harvard wearing tails. It bears the caption *Nobel oblige!*

Thus equipped, Henry Cadbury left Boston.

Flying over the Atlantic in 1947, he recalled the vision of an ocean of light and love above the ocean of darkness and death which had come to George Fox exactly three hundred years earlier.

"About the beginning of the year 1647, I was often under great temptations; and I fasted much, and walked abroad in solitary places many days, and often took my Bible and went and sat in hollow trees and lonesome places till night came on; and frequently in the night walked mournfully about by myself, for I was a man of sorrows in the times of the first workings of the Lord in me...."[10]

"The Lord shewed me that the natures of those things which were hurtful without were within, in the hearts and minds of wicked men. . . . And I cried to the Lord, saying, 'Why should I be thus, seeing I was never addicted to commit those evils?' And the Lord answered that it was needful I should have a sense of all conditions, how else should I speak to all conditions; and in this I saw the infinite love of God. I saw also that there was an ocean of darkness and death, but an infinite ocean of light and love, which flowed over the ocean of darkness. And in that also I saw the infinite love of God."[11]

High above the Atlantic Ocean, Henry Cadbury pondered on that vision of George Fox and the train of events which his spiritual search set in motion.

At Oslo, Gunnar Jahn, Chairman of the Nobel Committee, said of the Quakers in his presentation speech: "It is the silent help from the nameless to the nameless which is their contribution to the promotion of brotherhood among nations. . . . This is the message of good deeds, the message that men can come into contact with one another in spite of war and in spite of difference of race. May we believe that there is hope of laying a foundation for peace among nations, of building up peace in man himself, so that it becomes impossible to settle disputes by use of force?"[12]

Resplendent in his hand-me-down tails, the chairman of the American Friends Service Committee addressed King Haakon, the Crown Prince and the dignitaries:

"If any should question the appropriateness of bestowing the Peace Prize upon a group rather than upon an outstanding individual, we may say this: the common people of all nations want peace. In the presence of great impersonal forces they feel individually helpless to promote it. You are saying to them here today that common folk—not statesmen, nor generals, nor great men of affairs—but just simple plain men and women like the few thousand Quakers and their friends . . . can do something to build a better, peaceful world. . . . To this idea, humble persons everywhere may contribute."

The American Friends Service Committee's share of the Nobel Prize came to twenty thousand dollars. Surveying the devastated countries and the millions of sufferers all over the world, the Committee found it painful to decide where to allocate this manna.

In Poland and Hungary, where the need had been very great when the Quaker relief teams arrived, the Communists now declared that, much as they appreciated what had been done, the services of Friends were no longer required since the new government was able to undertake rehabilitation. When the Quaker workers left, they were seen off at the railway station by large numbers of people "whose honest expression of affection was accompanied by tears at seeing the departure of the last vestige of non-governmental connection between themselves and the West. . . . To be present and watch the curtain go down is a heart-rending experience."[13]

Relations between the governments of the United States and the Soviet Union were strained, and the Friends decided to spend the whole amount of the prize in a gesture of friendship from the people of America for the people of Russia.

Three hundred years earlier, George Fox, overjoyed by his discovery of God's indwelling presence, tried to communicate it to all the monarchs of Europe and Asia, including not only the mythical Prester John but the "Czar of Muscovy." He urged his friend William Caton to go to Russia because "the Lord has a vine . . . to be set up that-a-ways."

In 1917, six American Quaker women entered Russia by way of Vladivostok and from then until 1924, Quakers distributed supplies sent from America for famine relief. Alexander Panyushkin, later the Soviet Ambassador to the United States, claimed that it was the Quakers who saved his life when he was starving after World War I. In 1936, Harry and Rebecca Timbres, Baltimore Quakers, took their children to Russia and settled in a remote forest village near the Volga in order to establish an anti-malaria program. Within a year, Harry Timbres contracted typhus and died there.

It was, therefore, as part of a continuing concern that in 1948 American Friends, with the permission of their government, dispatched four thousand five-gram vials of streptomycin, then a new drug, to the Russian Red Cross for use in children's tuberculosis hospitals. Each vial bore a label, stating in Russian, "This streptomycin is a testimony of goodwill and friendship from the American Friends Service Committee to be used to promote the health of the people of the U.S.S.R."

At the same time, an advertisement appeared in several large

American newspapers, stamped with the Service Committee star and bearing the title "Not by Might, Nor by Power, But by My Spirit."

The advertisement urged that a group of leading citizens meet to formulate proposals for a general settlement of outstanding issues between the United States and the Soviet Union; that the United States strengthen the United Nations as an instrument of world law and order; that personal contacts be established through exchange of students, writers, religious leaders and industrial workers. "The world," the advertisement said, "is aghast at the dread prospect of the United States and Russia competing for military supremacy. This need not be; this must not be. . . . If America has tried and failed to find peace, now is the time to try again. . . . From the ashes of our frustration and despair, let us rise with new determination to solve our differences with Russia in peaceful ways and in terms that will build a truly united world."

Two hundred and thirty-five students, dedicated to rebuilding the devastated areas of Europe, had contributed the labor of their hands and the outreach of their hearts the previous summer as American Friends Service Committee Work Campers. From Lapland to Italy, from Belgium to the Austrian Tyrol and Poland, these students, representing twelve different countries and belonging to many religious bodies, offered their service to war-torn communities.

Few of the Work Campers spoke the same tongue. Yet when they sat down together in—for the most part—a strange land and sought ways to serve, they found solutions to the knottiest problems. During worship each day, they learned that deeply felt messages could overleap the limitations of language. Many of these young men and women, who had come simply to build houses or repair bridges, discovered that they were in the thick of a rewarding spiritual experience.

Everywhere they went, they made friends.

When those who worked in Belgium first arrived, village people were suspicious. Then, becoming convinced of the Work Campers' sincerity, the farmers brought them cherries, beans, even a little meat. School children came to the camp with potatoes, shopkeepers gave discounts, the shoemaker repaired rapidly worn-out boots free of charge.

Fifty-two Work Campers responded to this plea from Finland: "We call you, youth of the world today, to help us begin a new life. We greet and welcome you joyfully to the ruins of our homes, with the hope that we may build a new future of love and happiness in our hearts."[14]

Lokka, an isolated village, had been completely destroyed. "The Greatest Living American" was the title affectionately conferred by the people of Lokka on a Black girl from Chicago, who did the cement work. She had only been in the country six weeks when she made the welcoming speech in Finnish at a party to which the Work Campers invited the village people. In reply, a farmer said, "This is the first time in four hundred years that anyone has come to Lokka not to destroy or to take away something, but actually to give help."[15]

At first, the Finnish students thought group discussions of procedure were a waste of time. Wouldn't it be more efficient simply to elect a leader and follow his instructions? Before long, these young Finns began to see that every member was needed in the deliberations and that one could oneself be responsible for doing work well.

When the Work Campers left, they were invited to return to Lapland the following year in time for the reindeer roundup. One Finn remarked: "My country has always been known as a country which pays its debts. But we now have a debt we cannot repay. It is a debt of gratitude, a debt of love."[16]

The Work Camp concept originated in 1920 in the mind of a Swiss, Pierre Ceresole, who later joined Friends. The son of a former President of Switzerland, he had been imprisoned for refusing military service. He knew the burning urge of pacifists to contribute to society in the way that American and British Friends had done after the First World War when they went to France and undertook reconstruction.

"One gets disgusted with words," he said. "One does not get disgusted with creative service."

Pierre Ceresole presented his idea to the International Fellowship of Reconciliation and to European Friends. The response was enthusiastic. As a result, a group of volunteers from nations that had been enemies in the First World War went to northern France together and helped rebuild devastated areas.

One of the Germans in that group wrote, "For a long time, I have hoped for a chance to go and repair in France a little of what my brother (killed at Verdun) and his comrades were forced under military orders to destroy."[17]

John S. Hoyland, an English Friend, pointed out that the original international fellowship of Christianity had begun in just this way. Barriers of every kind—language, nationality, race, sex, class—were broken down as people obeyed "the command for this august sacrament of menial service, as instituted by Christ at his last supper with his disciples."[18]

The American Friends Service Committee and the Friends Service Council of Britain developed the Work Camp principle along Quaker lines. It became so popular that it was rapidly taken over by other organizations and adapted to their philosophies—not necessarily pacifist or religious—notably VISTA and the Peace Corps.

"The act of bringing people together from different nationalities doesn't mean they automatically love each other," Jean Fairfax, the Service Committee worker who organized the first Quaker Work Camps in Austria, acknowledged, "but the Work Camp provides a tough practical problem for all to work at. To finish a building job once begun becomes a common purpose; suddenly, almost with surprise, those who have thought they could never get along in the world with the others find that they like and respect them."[19]

A Swiss student who took part in a Quaker Work Camp summed up his impressions this way: "Such a life gives us the opportunity to live with other countries' men and to see in each of them our brothers. And at once we see that every man, from whatever country he may come, he has the same problems, the same interests, sorrows and pleasures. And what seems to me the most important: Love is for all human beings the same."[20]

24 Events at Flushing and Two Journeys to the Holy Land

When the United Nations General Assembly convened at Flushing Meadows in 1946, few of the delegates realized that as early as 1656 the ground they were standing on had been dedicated to those causes for which they were called there—peace, freedom, equality and justice. It had been hallowed by the sufferings of a humble people called Quakers and those who dared to receive them.

Governor Stuyvesant had decreed that Lutherans were to be denied "free liberties exercised in their houses"; that Jews were not to "infest Manhattan"; and that anyone who entertained a Quaker or allowed a Quaker Meeting to be held in his house should be fined £50.

In defiance of this last decree, thirty men of Flushing, led by the Town Clerk and the Sheriff, drew up a Remonstrance in which they declared: "If any come in love unto us, we cannot in conscience lay violent hands upon them." They wished, the signers of the Remonstrance stated firmly, "not to judge least we be judged; neither to condemn least we be condemned." They reminded the Governor that their charter entitled them "to have and Enjoy the Liberty of Conscience, according to the Custome and manner of Holland, without molestation or disturbance."[1]

Stuyvesant was not only unmoved by the Remonstrance; he abolished the town government of Flushing and imprisoned the two leading signers. One recanted and was released. The other stood his ground and was banished.

Three centuries later this judgment was reversed. The United States Post Office issued a three-cent stamp entitled "Religious Freedom in America." It depicted a beaver hat, a Bible, an inkstand holding a quill pen, and a banner bearing the inscription: "1657 The Flushing Remonstrance 1957."

But in 1657, after the arrival of the *Woodhouse*, the New Amsterdam ministers were complaining to their superiors in Holland about the Quakers, who cried "loudly in the middle of the street that men should repent." The next year, the ministers reported:

"The raving Quakers have not settled down, but continue to disturb the people of this province by their wanderings and outcries."[2]

Friends were forced to worship in the woods. When John Bowne built his house in 1661, he invited them to meet there. He was imprisoned on the charge that he had made his house a "conventicle" for Quakers and the Council threatened to banish him "if he continues pervicacious . . . to crush as far as possible that abominable sect . . . who . . . endeavor to undermine the police and religion."[3]

Since Bowne continued pervicacious in prison, he was banished. When he reached Holland, the directors of the West India Company countermanded Stuyvesant's order and sent Bowne back to Flushing a free man. "It is our opinion," they declared, "that the consciences of men, at least, ought ever to remain free and unshackled."[4]

The Bowne House is still standing at 37-01 Bowne Street in Flushing. It has been designated a Historic Landmark by the Landmarks Preservation Commission of the city of New York. A legend in the kitchen states: "In This Room An Oppressed People Found Sanctuary. Here lived John Bowne Who Suffered Arrest, Imprisonment, Separation from his Home, his Wife and Children and Banishment to the Old World so that a Then Despised People might worship God in this Room and in the New World, in the Manner of Their Own Choosing. Here Was Born Religious Freedom in the American Way of Life."

The Remonstrance Stone in the garden of the Bowne House pays tribute to "the glory of the town that had such men for its founders."

By the time Fox visited America, Flushing was "in the Duke of York's dominions." Friends were still disciplined for refusing to serve in the militia or to take oaths, but they could worship in peace. Fox went to Oyster Bay and "through the woods to Flushing where there was a large meeting at John Bowne's house, who was banished by the Dutch."[5]

After Fox rested on a couch, which is still standing in the dining room, he held a Meeting under the oaks across the way because the Bowne House could not contain the crowd. A stone bearing the inscription "Fox Oaks" marks the place where these trees stood.

William Penn came to Flushing in 1683. He advised his friend James, then Duke of York, who had been having trouble collecting taxes from his distant province, to grant the towns of Long Island a representative assembly. "Let them be governed by laws of their own making," Penn counseled, "in order that they may be free men."

Friends built the first school in Flushing "uppon the Cross-way, wch is neere ye Center of ye towne."

By 1694, they had built a Meetinghouse on land adjoining John Bowne's. The following year, New England Yearly Meeting adopted a minute stating that "ye Meeting at Longe Island Shall Bee From this time a Yearely meeting." Thus set off from New England, New York Yearly Meeting held its first session in Flushing on May 29, 1696. Only twenty-three years after the Meetinghouse was built, it had to be enlarged.

New York Yearly Meeting was held there annually until the Revolutionary War, when the building was seized by the British and used by them, first as a prison, then a hospital and finally as a barn.

In her *Story of Flushing Meeting House*, Ann Gidley Lowry cites the remarkable fact that "this simple house exemplifies not only the ideas of the Friends who built it but also of those who form the Meeting today."

By the time the United Nations convened in Flushing, the "raving Quakers" were no longer preaching in the streets. But they were still trying to publish Truth.

Friends were now thoroughly respectable—deplorably so, some of them thought. And yet, while they were well behaved and quiet in the streets, they were really up to their old tricks.

Robert Lea, a businessman who lived in Flushing, made friends with the foreign diplomats he met on his daily walks and invited them to his home for dinner. The moment the guests were seated at the Lea table, they confided that they had longed to visit an American family. They were lonely amid the ruins of the old World's Fair, weary of protocol and cocktail parties.

At the Lea home, United Nations representatives from all over the world found they could relax. People from countries that were hostile, who might otherwise never have spoken to one another, broke bread together after a Quaker silence.

Then the United Nations moved to New York. Feeling that there was need for an informal meeting place, Friends opened Quaker House near the new United Nations Headquarters, first in an apartment, then in a brownstone provided by generous contributors. A resident couple was put in charge: Philip Jessup, author of *A Modern Law of Nations,* and his wife, Lois, the American Friends Service Committee representative to the United Nations.

Quaker House became a center where Friends—political and social scientists, businessmen, teachers, housewives, welfare and religious workers—invited UN personnel, as well as non-official groups "to consider how those dedicated to maintaining the peace of the world might more effectively let their concerns be felt."[6] Meeting over tea or at an informal supper party, safe from exposure to the news media, people discussed freely what lay upon their hearts.

Trygve Lie and some of the ambassadors to the United Nations appreciated this informal, non-partisan setting. Under the auspices of people whose discretion could be trusted, meetings were arranged between sensitive representatives or envoys. Quaker House soon became a very busy place.

At the February 1948 meeting of the UN Economic and Social Council, the Friends World Committee was granted consultative status. This enabled Friends to work for the improvement of Russian-American relations, the strengthening of the United Nations and relief and refugee problems in Kashmir and Palestine.

That same month Rufus Jones and Clarence Pickett invited representatives of various religious bodies to meet with them at Quaker House in order to consider a proposal for ending the fighting in Jerusalem. The British Mandate in Palestine was due to terminate on May 15. After that date, the fighting would presumably become more intense.

Francis B. Sayre, former Assistant Secretary of State, who was then Chairman of the Trusteeship Council of the United Nations, had urged Rufus Jones to take the initiative in appealing for a Truce of God. Since Jerusalem was a Holy City to Jews, Moslems and Christians, it was hoped that religious leaders of the West might be able to persuade the religious leaders of Palestine to effect such a Truce.

On January 25, 1948, Rufus Jones had celebrated his eighty-fifth birthday. Five days later, he was desolated by the assassination of Gandhi. His fifty-fourth book, *A Call to What Is Vital,* was just ready for press. Weary and with pain in his chest, he marshaled his energies, longing to bring peace to a land which would not opt for it.

As a result of the meeting at Quaker House, he drafted a message. This was eventually signed by the Most Reverend Geoffrey

Francis Fisher, Archbishop of Canterbury; Bishop Eivind Bergraav, Primate of the Church of Norway; the Right Reverend Henry Knox Sherrill, Presiding Bishop of the Protestant Episcopal Church of America; Archbishop Athenagoras of the Greek Orthodox Church, representing the Eastern Orthodox Church; Dr. John R. Mott, leader of the International YMCA, and Dr. Harry Emerson Fosdick, pastor emeritus of Riverside Church in New York, as well as Rufus Jones himself.

He had asked Francis Cardinal Spellman to join in the appeal, identifying himself as having "worked continually with Roman Catholic people, especially in Poland and Austria and rural France, and I have all my life been studying and writing about Roman Catholic saints and mystics."[7] But the Cardinal did not feel free to participate.

The message read: "Those of us whose names are listed below, representing some of the most important Christian groups over the world, have a profound love for the land of Palestine and for the Holy City of Jerusalem. We devoutly wish that we could make peace and concord prevail over the entire land, but we are representatives of Religion, not of Politics or of Government Policies, and we can use only persuasion, in no sense the exhibition of force.

"In the spirit of Religion and in a united love for the City which is the mother of our religious faith and of the other religious faiths of the Western World, we are united in asking you to establish a 'Truce of God,' which means a holy area of peace and freedom from violence, in the City of Jerusalem, until once more this whole land which we love and cherish with devotion shall be blessed with peace."[8]

This appeal was sent to Jerusalem on March 12, addressed to Isaac Hertzog, Chief Rabbi of Palestine, and Amin Bey Abdulhadi, head of the Supreme Moslem Council.

Friends felt that while it was too much to expect peace, a truce in Jerusalem might be the beginning of wider reconciliation. Following their usual procedure, they dispatched persons to communicate their concern. James Vail, who had arranged relief in Germany and India, was at that moment in Africa on a Quaker mission. He hastened to Cairo. Edgar B. Castle, a distinguished educator, was appointed by English Friends to join him in exploring the type of Quaker service that would reconcile Arabs and Jews and in pleading for a truce.

In Cairo they met with Azzam Pasha, Secretary General of the

Arab League, who assured them that every place where Jesus walked is sacred to Moslems.

On Easter Sunday the story of the united appeal drawn up by Rufus Jones was released to the American press. The following day, this cable from Rabbi Hertzog arrived in Philadelphia: "Heartily endorse proposed Truce of God for city of Jerusalem. My heartfelt blessings for success your efforts."[9]

Meanwhile, James Vail and Edgar Castle traveled to Jerusalem. As they were being driven up the Jericho Road, past the Garden of Gethsemane and through Bethany, the driver told them to take off their hats so that they would not be mistaken for Jews and fired upon. After talking with Rabbi Hertzog and Christian leaders in Jerusalem, the two Friends were convinced that a truce was only possible if the Moslems took the initiative. Thereupon, they rushed back to Cairo and visited Azzam Pasha again.

"Will you accept the honor of assuming moral leadership and calling for a truce?" they asked him.

Azzam Pasha agreed and suggested that they help him write the document in which he called on the Arabs to observe a truce in the Old City of Jerusalem and the Mount of Olives.

"Thus," Clarence Pickett observed with well-deserved relish, "when a cease-fire order for Jerusalem became effective under the British High Commissioner early in May, with both Jews and Arabs co-operating, we had the satisfaction of knowing that, among others working for the truce, our delegates had played some part in the successful negotiations."[10]

On May 7, Mr. Andrew Cordier, who was then Administrative Assistant to the Secretary General of the United Nations, announced that the UN planned to set up a temporary administration in Jerusalem and that Jews and Arabs had united in naming Clarence Pickett as one who would be acceptable to both groups in the role of commissioner. But Clarence Pickett felt he could not leave the Service Committee.

Harold Evans, Clerk of Philadelphia Yearly Meeting (Orthodox), a lawyer with lifelong experience in Quaker work, was persuaded to accept the appointment. James Vail, just home from Palestine, turned around and went back with Harold Evans. Before their departure on May 22, Harold Evans conceded that "according to normal standards, the chances for the success of this mission are small.

"However, this is by no means a conventional mission. It is

absolutely without political bias. It is concerned only with all the inhabitants of Jerusalem as human beings. We have no military force to uphold our decision, nor as Quakers would we welcome it. Whatever we may accomplish will depend entirely upon the only force we regard as valid or capable of solving the position we face—man's good will to man."

Choosing as his text the prophecy of Zechariah at the time that the Temple of Jerusalem was rebuilt, five centuries before the birth of Christ, Harold Evans closed his farewells with a bright vision of what this mission might lead to. "If such a venture should succeed, it might be a first ray of light in a new and better day of international relationships and provide a present-day application to the call, 'not by might, nor by power, but by my spirit.'"[11]

Alas, once again the Quaker vision outstripped history. By the time the two Americans reached Palestine, might and power were the only forces invoked. With the termination of the British Mandate and the proclamation of the State of Israel, war had broken out. Count Folke Bernadotte became the UN mediator. Harold Evans and James Vail joined him in efforts to secure a truce.

It was both with concern for peace and with special ties that Friends prayerfully sent these emissaries to Palestine in 1948.

Eight decades earlier—two years and a day after General Lee surrendered at Appomattox—a moving scene took place on the wharf at Boston. Eli and Sybil Jones of China, Maine, were boarding the ship *China* for a missionary journey to the Holy Land. In addition to the Friends in plain Quaker dress, who had come from all over New England to see them off, there were two surprising well-wishers: Governor John A. Andrew and General Nathaniel P. Banks, the congressman from Massachusetts.

Eli Jones's young nephew Rufus, writing twenty years later, observed that the honor conveyed by the presence of the two politicians was "a striking contrast to the treatment which the missionary Quakers two hundred years before received at the hands of the Boston officials."[12]

John Greenleaf Whittier had hoped to accompany Eli and Sybil Jones to the Holy Land, but ill health obliged him to stay home. Instead, he sent these farewell verses:

> As one who watches from the land
>   The lifeboat go to seek and save,
> And, all too weak to lend a hand,
>   Sends his faint cheer across the wave,—

> So, powerless at my hearth to-day,
>   Unmeet your holy work to share,
> I can but speed you on your way,
>   Dear friends, with my unworthy prayer.
>
> Go, angel-guided, duty-sent!
>   Our thoughts go with you o'er the foam;
> Where'er you pitch your pilgrim tent
>   Our hearts shall be and make it home.

"Missionaries are peacemakers," Rufus Jones wrote, commenting on this journey to the Holy Land, "and it is well that members of the Society of Friends have been led to do work here. . . . To this little country . . . to this people divided into so many religions, Eli and Sybil Jones felt a call to bear the gospel first promulgated from its hills and in its valleys."[13]

British Friends had given the Joneses funds to use at their discretion. A worthy cause was immediately presented.

"While in the neighborhood of Jerusalem they visited Ramallah. There was a boys' school in this place, and here they were met by a young woman who asked that she might be helped to teach a girls' school. Eli Jones asked her if she could teach, to which she answered, yes. After consideration it was decided to use some of the money, which had been donated by the British Friends, to help this young woman—Miriam—educate the girls of the neighborhood."[14]

Upon their return home, Eli and Sybil Jones persuaded New England Yearly Meeting to make itself responsible for the Ramallah Mission. Eventually, it operated schools for both girls and boys as well as a baby clinic. It established a Friends Meeting in Ramallah—the only one ever to exist in Palestine. In 1918, the American Friends Board of Missions assumed responsibility for the work in Ramallah. Over the years, a procession of American Friends has gone there to teach.

"These little schools taught many things besides reading and writing and arithmetic. They were centers of light and love and healing."[15] This is how the work at Ramallah was described by still another Jones—Christina H. (no relation)—whose husband, A. Willard, became Principal of the Boys' School in 1942.

Eli and Sybil Jones was Rufus Jones's first book, written when he was twenty-five and just married to Sarah Coutant, his first wife. She died eleven years later, leaving Rufus with their seven-year-old son, Lowell, who did not long survive his mother.

When the book was published in 1889, Sybil Jones was no longer living. A few months later, Eli was stricken with pneumonia. In *Friend of Life*, Elizabeth Gray Vining gives this touching account: "Rufus had gone to South China to be with him. He asked to be lifted up to see the lake, and so, in Rufus's arms, he died. 'No one else can affect me as he did,' Rufus wrote. . . ."[16]

Words which Rufus Jones used to characterize his Uncle Eli are, in our eyes, equally applicable to himself. "If those men do us the greatest service who give us the clearest view of our relation to God and our duty to man, then we owe him gratitude, for he successfully helped feet that were failing to find a surer foothold on the abiding base of the Rock of Ages."[17]

25 A Call to What Is Vital

A three-cent stamp entitled "One Hundred Years of Progress of Women" was issued by the United States in 1948. The post office of first-day issue was Seneca Falls, New York, where the first Woman's Rights Convention was held in 1848. This purple stamp bears portraits of Elizabeth Stanton, Carrie Chapman Catt and Lucretia Mott, wearing her plain Quaker cap.

The emancipation of women was not the original concern of the Friend in this trio. It developed as a corollary to Lucretia Mott's compassion for the slaves. "I felt bound," she declared, "to plead their cause in season and out of season, to endeavour to put myself in their souls' stead, and to aid all in my power in every right effort for their immediate emancipation."[1]

Born on Nantucket in 1793, the daughter of a Quaker sea captain, Lucretia Coffin was descended from Thomas Macy, who hurried to the island when Governor Endicott was about to "admonish" him for entertaining Quakers. Lucretia was educated at Nine Partners School near Poughkeepsie, New York, which Elias Hicks had helped found. After her graduation, she remained there to teach and was struck by the fact that, while the girls paid the same tuition as the boys, women teachers only received half the salary given to the men.

One of those men, James Mott, "a tall, pleasant-looking youth, with sandy hair and kindly blue eyes . . . shy and grave," impressed Lucretia most favorably. She herself was, in the words of her granddaughter, "short of stature, quick in her movements, and, notwithstanding the repression of Quaker training, impulsive and vivacious in manner. She had a keen appreciation of humor, and was fond of a joke, even at her own expense. Combined with these lighter qualities . . . even at this early time, were those elements of spiritual fervor and strength which ripened into the revered character of Lucretia Mott."[2]

James and Lucretia were married in Meeting when she was eighteen and he was almost twenty-three. He entered the cotton business in New York, but after hearing Elias Hicks preach, he and Lucretia felt uneasy about living off the produce of slave labor. They moved to Philadelphia where James went into the wool trade. He was not immediately successful and for a time Lucretia did some teaching.

After the death of her second child, Thomas, she spoke so movingly in Meeting that she was recorded a Friends minister. The Separation of 1827 brought heartache, for the Motts had ties with Friends in both branches. By temperament and conviction they belonged with the Hicksites, but they suffered from the necessity of making a choice. So bitter was the feeling in some circles that twenty years later, when the Motts were on a religious visit in Indiana and Lucretia was taken ill, the Orthodox Quaker physician she consulted turned away, saying, "Lucretia, I am so deeply afflicted by thy rebellious spirit, that I do not feel that I can prescribe for thee."[3]

She was, in fact, too liberal even for the Hicksites, who almost disowned her. Forgetting the service of those seventeenth-century women Friends, whose public testimony helped to secure the liberty which nineteenth-century Friends enjoyed, Lucretia's contemporaries thought it not seemly for women to speak in public. Ministry in Friends Meeting was one thing; addressing non-Quaker gatherings was quite another. But the chief cause of Friends' dissatisfaction with Lucretia was her radical abolitionist activity, which they feared would lead to war. And they abhorred war as much as they abhorred slavery. Patience, they argued, would in the end overcome slavery without bloodshed.

In 1833, the Motts attended the first Convention of the American Anti-Slavery Society. Since women were barred from acting as delegates, a group made up chiefly of Friends formed the Philadelphia Female Anti-Slavery Society and chose Lucretia Mott for their president. She had to learn parliamentary procedure since "that was the first time in my life I had ever heard a vote taken, being accustomed to our Quaker way of getting the prevailing sentiment of the meeting."[4]

The Mason-Dixon line, drawn to settle the boundary dispute between the Penns and the Baltimores, was the watershed between the free and slave states. Runaways from Maryland, who could make it over the line into Pennsylvania, were technically free, but their masters pursued them. Pro-slavery sentiment was so strong in Philadelphia that the Anti-Slavery Societies could not rent a place for their meetings. In 1838, they built their own—Pennsylvania Hall, dedicated to "Liberty and the Rights of Man."

Three days after the dedication, during the Anti-Slavery Convention of American Women, Pennsylvania Hall was attacked by a mob. That night, it was set on fire. Leaving it flaming, the mob started toward the Motts' house. Lucretia and James, having sent the younger children to a neighbor's, sat in their parlor with the older ones and a few friends, awaiting the onslaught. It never came. The mob had decided to burn the Quaker Shelter for Colored Orphans and a Black church instead.

John Greenleaf Whittier and Benjamin Lundy, who had been printing abolitionist papers in Pennsylvania Hall, lost their press and personal possessions.

"They have not yet got my conscience," Lundy wrote the next morning, "they have not taken my heart, and until they rob me of these they cannot prevent me from pleading the cause of the slave. I am not disheartened, though everything of earthly value (in the shape of property) is lost. We shall assuredly triumph yet!"[5]

Some frightened "pseudo-abolitionists," as Lucretia called them, "seriously counseled that we gradually dissolve our Anti-Slavery Societies . . . and let things go on in the old way." They left "no means untried to induce us to expunge from our minutes a resolution relating to social intercourse with our colored brethren. . . . In Boston the bone of contention has been the admission of another proscribed class—women—to equal participation in the doings of the Convention."[6]

In 1840, the Motts went to England in order to attend the British and Foreign Anti-Slavery Society's Conference. It was a disheartening visit. London Friends refused to recognize them because they were Hicksites and the conference refused to admit women. But something that affected the lives of future generations occurred there—Lucretia met Elizabeth Cady Stanton, with whom she vowed to work for woman's rights. When they chanced to meet again eight years later at Waterloo, New York, where the Motts were attending the Yearly Meeting of Friends, they decided to call a convention at nearby Seneca Falls. Only women were supposed to attend on the first day but so many sympathetic men appeared that they were invited to participate. James Mott, "tall and dignified in Quaker costume," was made chairman.

Meanwhile, though the Elders might frown, Friends all up and down the United States were secretly helping slaves to escape. They cited Scripture in their defense: "Thou shalt not deliver unto his master the servant which is escaped from his master unto thee: He shall dwell with thee, even among you."

Henry Brown, a slave in Richmond, Virginia, was so desperate that he had himself packed in a box and shipped on the railway by Adams' Express. It was feared that he would suffocate or be injured in transit. When the box was delivered at the Anti-Slavery office in Philadelphia, it was opened by Miller McKim, a Presbyterian minister.

"Miller says we can hardly conceive the relief and excite't. to find the man alive," Lucretia wrote to friends, "and the poor fellow's happiness gratitude—singing a hymn of praise."

"Box" Brown, as they called him, was taken to the Motts' home and sent from there to safety. "This," Lucretia observed, "will tell well in history sometime hence, in the days of freedom, oh!"[7]

A few years later, Jane Johnson and her ten-year-old son were brought to Philadelphia from the South by their master. When the woman learned that she was now in a state that did not uphold slavery, she took her child and ran away. The owner went to court, charging Passmore Williamson, an Orthodox Friend, and William Still with "conspired effort" to incite the woman to escape. Those who had helped her then thought it best to let her appear and stand trial. Lucretia accompanied her to the trial and, after Jane Johnson's acquittal, took her to her home, from which the woman was conveyed to safety by the Underground Railroad. "Miller and the Slave passed quickly thro' our house," Lucretia wrote to her sister, "to the same carriage—wh. drove around to elude pursuit. I ran to the store room and filling my arms with crackers and peaches, ran after them and had only time to throw them into the carriage—and away they drove."[8]

Passmore Williamson was sentenced to one hundred days in prison because he refused to admit that he had known where the runaways were hiding. Lucretia went to visit him and—most courageous of all—she appealed to his fellow Orthodox Friends as well as to her fellow Hicksites to consider this "outrage" at their Monthly Meetings.

At heart, though, Lucretia was most of all a housewife. When she was not busy preaching, working on behalf of the slaves and the rights of woman, sitting in court and writing voluminous letters, she made carpets. Not only did she cut, sew and nail down those in her own house—"I am going to Mt. Holly in a week or two," she wrote in 1855, "to help our cousins make their carpets."[9]

Her concerns kept impinging on her domesticity.

"I had a heap of clear-starching to do on Third-day last, but one after another called, to ask about the School of Design, the Woman's Medical College, and colored beggars came in, so that I had not finished when C-P- came to dine. I brought my starching into the parlor, and between dinner and dessert excused myself to iron. . . ."[10]

Under the Fugitive Slave Law, Daniel Dangerfield was brought before the Federal Commissioner in Philadelphia, charged with being a runaway slave. A Unitarian minister present at the trial only saw Lucretia standing "by the side of the ragged fugitive . . . in her pure Quaker garb. . . . She uttered never a word, caused no interruption."

But she was not altogether silent before the trial. The Commissioner, she knew, was a birthright Friend. She approached him "and, in an undertone, expressed to him the hope that his conscience would not allow him to send this poor man into slavery. He received it civilly; but replied that he must be bound by his oath of office. . . . When the man was brought in . . . The Commissioner had an anxious countenance and looked pale. The case occupied the remainder of the day and all the night, several women remaining until morning. . . . The Commissioner . . . finally decided that as the height of the man did not agree with the testimony of the claimant, he could not be given up."

"This," Lucretia declared, when she was an old lady, "is the only case in which I ever interfered in any trial by our courts, further than to shelter the fugitives."[11]

When John Brown was awaiting execution, his wife stopped in Philadelphia on her way to see him. He wrote her that he was glad she was "under Mrs. Mott's roof." The events at Harper's Ferry threw Friends into their usual dilemma—they supported the cause but not the violence. After Brown's execution, Lucretia made her position clear. "I have no idea, because I am a Non-Resistant, of submitting tamely to injustice. . . . I will oppose it with all the moral powers with which I am endowed. . . . The early Friends were agitators; disturbers of the peace; and were more obnoxious in their day to charges which are now so freely made than we are."[12]

James and Lucretia Mott helped found Swarthmore College. Their daughter Anna was elected to the Board of Managers. In 1869, a year after the death of her father, Anna died. Lucretia pursued her concerns. With attainment of emancipation for the

Black, she labored for the Indian. She pleaded with President Grant to spare the twelve Modocs who were condemned to death following their uprising.

Thirty years after the first Woman's Rights Convention, Lucretia took part in an anniversary celebration at Seneca Falls. She was then eighty-five. One hundred years after the first convention, her country saw fit to honor Lucretia Mott by placing her portrait on a postage stamp.

Several living Friends were also singled out in 1948. The Olympic Soccer Committee chose Rolf Valtin, a student at Swarthmore College, to take part in the games about to be held in London. The Sons of the Revolution presented a medal to William T. Harris, a member of Green Street Monthly Meeting, Germantown, Pennsylvania, for his outstanding work in combating juvenile delinquency. And the Pulitzer Prize, awarded to the author of the most distinguished fiction, went to James A. Michener for *Tales of the South Pacific*.

The pleasure which Friends took in this award to one of their young men indicated the tremendous change in their attitude toward the arts. Inheritors of Puritan morality, they had, until the end of the nineteenth century, distrusted fiction as being inconsistent with truth, even as they had, to their immeasurable loss, shut music and art out of their lives. This is not to say that certain Quakers did not relish romances in private or hide a piano in an upstairs parlor where it would escape the notice of visiting Overseers. But officially, these were unacceptable. In an earlier age, the Quaker fiction writer would, at best, have been eldered—reproved by the Elders of his Meeting. In mid-twentieth century, he was appreciated.

An engaging article by James Michener entitled "A Quaker Passport" had recently described the adulation with which non-Friends often humble and embarrass those who think themselves least deserving of praise.

"Since graduating from college, I have traveled with many different kinds of passports, but none commanded more respect than the single word *Quaker*. It is a word which carries its own currency throughout the world. In Australia, in Italy, the word has won long and lasting respect. . . .

"This has naturally caused me some concern, for obviously I am not the man to whom the word—in its world-wide connotation —applies. There is some over-Quaker who is referred to in the world's mind when the word is used. He is peaceful, honest, quiet, sincere, trustworthy, helpful, generous and progressive. . . . In religious matters he is unassuming, cooperative and uncontentious . . . he is reported to spend more than the usual portion of his income on the education of his own and others' children. In politics he is sane, liberal, trustworthy, and hard working. In his daily life he is a friend to all men.

"Now this picture of Quakerism was so often thrust upon me that I cast among all my memories of all my Quaker friends and found no one who lived up to the pattern. . . .

"I therefore decided that Quakerism must be a symbol whose living reality is fed by many men, and the religion is indeed fortunate that it is the best of our best that is remembered with affection and it is from this best that we all take our color. I am not a pacifist . . . but I borrow both stature and courage from those men who are stanchly pacifist. Some of the least-educated persons I know are Quakers, yet we all borrow from the reputation of our really great educational and philosophical leaders. In the same way there are Quakers who drink too much but whose reputations are sustained by those of us who are known to be abstemious. . . .

"The word Friend is bolstered up by the good deeds of all, so that wherever one goes he takes with him a little more than he actually is. He borrows upon the deposits made by others. In a very real sense I feel that I have been fairly exclusively a borrower from the joint account, and I am glad to take this opportunity to pay my deepest respects to those Friends who have been making the contributions."[13]

James Michener's fellow members in Swarthmore Meeting must have chuckled over his mischievous reference to the fact that Friends are generally thought to be "cooperative and uncontentious" in religious matters. The two Philadelphia Yearly Meetings had been going their separate ways since 1827 and the bitterness that accompanied the schism still hung like a miasma over the present generation, which had no interest in the obsolete issues.

Lately, however, efforts had been made in both Yearly Meetings to explore the possibility of reuniting. There were more difficulties to be overcome in Philadelphia than in New England, where the differences had been not so much doctrinal as in manner of worship. New England resolved this by letting each Monthly Meeting decide whether it wished to worship on the basis of silence or according to program. In Philadelphia, both Yearly Meetings worshiped in silence, but they differed in belief. Contentiousness had, however, been left behind and it was with the greatest good will that Philadelphia Friends undertook to write a *Faith and Practice* that would, they hoped, be acceptable to both branches.

As the earliest Friends "walked after the plough" in Old England, they naturally spoke of their sense of God's presence as the Seed. "Therefore know the triumph in the Seed," George Fox wrote from Swarthmoor Hall, "in which is my love and in which I rest."[14]

Rufus Jones was also country born, but in New England, in Maine, where spring is eagerly awaited after the long winter. He coined his own expression: "the vernal equinox of the spirit." It seems part of some glorious design that it should be precisely in the latter part of March of the year 1948 that Rufus Jones began to take his leave of this life. He suffered a coronary occlusion. After a stay in the hospital, he returned home where he seemed to be making progress when he was stricken a second time.

"The heart specialist said only a miracle could save him," his daughter Mary recalled afterward. "The miracle occurred."[15]

Years later, Elizabeth Gray Vining wrote a beautiful biography of Rufus Jones, *Friend of Life,* which is both a faithful documentation and a glowing expression of thankfulness for the life of this Friend, who reverenced all life. Of those last weeks, she wrote: "He had work to finish and, indomitable, he proceeded to do it."[16]

He had promised to review a book about Emanuel Swedenborg and to give the opening address at New England Yearly Meeting in Andover, Massachusetts, on the twenty-third of June. He knew then that he would not be able to deliver the address himself, but he summoned all his remaining strength for the writing and asked Mary to go to Andover at Yearly Meeting time and read the address in his place. Did he know that he was asking his daughter to summon a superhuman measure of the heroic spirit?

"Slowly," she remembered, "he wrote what he wanted to say to his Yearly Meeting, a page each day until he completed 'A New Installment of the Heroic Spirit.' . . .

"*A Call to What Is Vital* had gone to the publishers before his illness; he and Elizabeth Jones were back at their old task of proofreading, his bed was strewn with the pages of galley proof just as his study had been for the past forty years and more. . . .

"On the morning of June 16, Rufus Jones received from his stenographer the typed copy of his Yearly Meeting address. He made a few corrections and laid it aside for his daughter to read aloud to him so that he might hear how it would sound as she read it to his friends a few days later. Picking up the last pages of the galley proof, he read these through and laid them down. His work was finished. After his lunch he took a nap, as he always had, and in his sleep he crossed over from the world that is seen to the one which is unseen."[17]

With these words from *A Biographical Sketch*, Mary Hoxie Jones has given us a glimpse of those moments which brought to a close her father's great achievement. And she quotes from a letter he had written sixty years earlier to Sallie Coutant, his first wife, shortly before their marriage. "It is my great wish exceeding all others that I may feel in the last hours of my life that I have done my work and that the Great Father is satisfied with my life, so that death may be to me like falling asleep as it is for all who faithfully walk the right road."[18]

"His work was finished." But his vital affirmation of life and God's purpose would continue to invigorate the countless people all over the world whose spirits he had touched.

Exactly a week after the completion of the opening address, and only three days after Rufus Jones was laid to rest in the little graveyard beside the Haverford Meetinghouse, Mary traveled to Massachusetts and carried out her father's last wish. Bravely, she read the address before New England Yearly Meeting, many of whose members had known Rufus Jones all their lives. "Our Rufus," he was to them.

"There is only one thing supremely important now," his last message concluded, "and that is to help build a new kind of world. The only way to be good in this crisis is to be *heroically good*."[19]

One touching response to the news of this beloved Friend's death is recalled by J. Floyd Moore, who later became Professor of Biblical Literature and Religion at Guilford College. "As a representative of the AFSC in Germany, I was issuing a special monthly food allotment for tubercular children at a Catholic hospital in Wittlich to a septuagenarian saint, Schwester Fulcedes, who explained to me in German how that morning she and the children had said a special prayer at Mass for the 'Quaker Pope, Herr Jones.' . . . This response epitomized the spirit of many for whom

Rufus Jones represented a quality of life which rose above nation or creed."[20]

In the closing pages of his last book, Rufus Jones summed up his belief, returning to one of his favorite passages of the Old Testament.

"The prophet Ezekiel saw in his creative vision a revelation of God as a divine being with many wings, but with 'the hands of a man under the wings.' This is a true figure. The work of the world will not be done from the sky or by angels. It will be done by men's hands, but, if it is well done, it will be done under divine guidance and divine inspiration. . . .

"If there is, as I believe, an *inner kingdom of spirit*, a kingdom of love and fellowship, then it is a fact that a tiny being like one of us can impress and influence the divine heart, and we can make our personal contribution to the will of the universe, but we can do it only by wanting what everybody can share and by seeking blessings which have a universal implication."[21]

26 Delegates at Amsterdam, Beethoven in Acre, Missionaries in China

The First Assembly of the World Council of Churches convened in the Netherlands in August 1948 to discuss "Man's Disorder and God's Design" almost two and a half centuries after Friend Bellers made his "Proposal for a General Convocation of all the different Religious Perswasions in Christendom."

During the Assembly, the morning services in Amsterdam's Koepelkerk were conducted by the clergy of the many faiths represented: on the first day by a minister of the Church of Christ in Japan, then by an American Methodist Bishop, then a Hungarian Lutheran pastor, an Australian Congregationalist minister, a Malagasy Dutch Reformed divine and the Bishop of the Church of South India.

On the seventh morning, it was the Quakers' turn. They issued "A Call to Worship" in English, French and German, addressed to all their fellow delegates. A leaflet giving a brief explanation of the Quaker manner of worship lay in each pew, when several hundred delegates arrived—Baptists, Eastern Orthodox, a gorgeously robed Ethiopic Bishop, a woman from the African Methodist Zion Church, Salvation Army and scores of other delegates. Missing were the Roman Catholics. The Pope did not approve of their participation.

Representing 147 different denominations in forty-four countries, some of the delegates held doctrines which were considered heresies by others. It was, for example, impossible for the various faiths to join in celebrating the Lord's Supper since they disagreed on the form of the service. As for Friends—they declined outward sacraments in any form, maintaining that communion with God is, for them, a purely inward experience. With these incompatible beliefs, the delegates had not been able to worship together as one body before.

The Quaker Meeting excluded no one, and no one could feel insincere in taking part. Yet to many of those present, the explanation in the leaflet must have been more puzzling than enlightening, for the procedure it described was hardly what they regarded as a religious service. The organ was still. Choir, processional, minister were absent.

The English version in the leaflet read: "Worship, according to the ancient practice of the Religious Society of Friends, is entirely without human direction or supervision. A group of devout persons come together and sit down quietly with no prearrangement, each seeking to have an immediate sense of divine leading and to know at first hand the presence of the living Christ. It is not wholly accurate to say that such a meeting is held on the basis of silence; it is more accurate to say that it is held on the basis of 'holy obedience' . . . Such a meeting is always a high venture of faith and it is to this venture that we invite you this hour."[1]

Unfamiliar though it was, the reverent silence took hold of the churchmen. After a time, two American Quakers spoke. Then a Lutheran pastor rose to offer prayer in German, another followed in French, an Egyptian priest prayed in the language of the ancient Copts. Before the closing silence, a moving prayer was offered by Angus Dun, Protestant Episcopal Bishop of Washington, D.C.

British Friends had not sent delegates to the Council because they were unable to subscribe to the creedal phrase in the articles of membership: Jesus Christ as God and Savior. Many American Friends felt reluctant for the same reason.

It was only the theological statement that disturbed Friends. On both sides of the Atlantic, they were heartily in favor of the ecumenical movement. They had taken part in the first attempt to establish Christian unity at the international level, beginning with the Edinburgh Conference on Faith and Order held in 1910. American Friends were represented at the Utrecht Advisory Council, the body which prepared the constitution for the World Council, by Elbert Russell, Dean of the Divinity School of Duke University and author of *The History of Quakerism*.

In 1907, the Five Years Meeting joined the Federal Council of Churches of Christ in America. The more liberal Yearly Meetings held back. In 1929, the American Friends Service Committee co-operated with the Federal Council in bringing relief to Marion, North Carolina, where mill workers had been laid off after striking. The two bodies cooperated again during the Spanish Civil War. Following the attack on Pearl Harbor, they worked together in relocating Japanese-Americans who were being evacuated from the west coast.

For differing reasons, American Quakers at the World Council in Amsterdam were not completely comfortable. Canadian and General Conference Friends proposed a theological amendment, which was voted down by the Council. On the other hand, Algie I. Newlin and D. Elton Trueblood, representing the Five Years Meeting, felt that the basic statement did not go far enough. Howard H. Brinton placed a resolution before the Council that had been drafted by Philadelphia Yearly Meeting (Orthodox). It condemned war as incompatible with Christ's teaching and urged that Christians refuse to be bound by the state's command to support war. The resolution was voted down.

Bliss Forbush, Chairman of the Friends General Conference, commented on his return home: "We are actually members but we can withdraw. If we stay, we can make many more contributions from within than would be possible from the outside. We can, for instance, present our philosophy of the use of the laity."[2]

Although most American Yearly Meetings have remained in the World Council and London has stayed out, the whole Society continues to ponder the question.

While the Council assembled, many American Friends were "walking cheerfully over the world," binding up wounds of the war just concluded and striving to help avert still another by reducing tensions between hostile groups. Some—the professors and students—volunteered their vacation; others gave years.

No account is adequate that does not cite the efforts of each one, for each helped to relieve some misery, give hope to broken spirits and create a little pocket of peace in a troubled world. But limitations of space preclude a full account. The few whose activities are mentioned here are simply examples of what many Friends were doing. They could not have accomplished this without the backing of a tireless staff at home and the host of self-effacing contributors.

Douglas Steere of Haverford College, traveling through Europe as a Friends visitor, stopped at Braunschweig, Germany. There, under the direction of a Service Committee worker, Margaret Atkinson of Wrightstown, Pennsylvania, Meeting, German Friends were laying the foundation for a barrack to house a Quaker Center.

"I certainly saw what living by faith meant," Douglas Steere wrote home. ". . . all I could see was a hole! When they laid the cornerstone . . . they would not let Peg see the stone beforehand.

When it was unveiled it had chiseled into it her initials A M A: Anna Margaret Atkinson. Peg protested . . . for they had all helped and planned. Adolf Beiss, the wonderful German Friend who was chairman, assured Peg before the crowd that AMA stood for 'love' in Latin and that it was on love that this Neighborhood Center was being built. This little incident tells . . . how much they care for Peg in Braunschweig and the spirit in which they work together."

Algie Newlin of Guilford College and his wife, Eva, directed the Friends Center in Geneva, where they helped "the refugee whose money was frozen in Germany; the girl in Bonn who needed a pair of shoes; the Austrian professor who wanted Quaker literature; the Yugoslav student who read in the Bern Library and needed an overcoat; the Greek student with TB; the Spanish refugee; the needy and elderly Austrian couple in Lausanne; the Jewish woman in Sofia whose husband was killed by the Nazis."[3]

George A. Selleck, Executive Secretary of the Friends Meeting at Cambridge, Massachusetts, and his wife, Florence, went to Finland for two years as representatives of the American Friends Service Committee, conferring with Suomen Huolto, the Finnish relief agency, about distribution of supplies; helping to organize and conduct Work Camps. They brought with them an uncommon capacity for friendship, an attentiveness to the inner lives of others that ministered lovingly to people who had endured conquest.

The Sellecks' apartment became the Helsinki Friends Center, where residents of the community were invited to meet Finnish leaders, where displaced persons from Karelia could meet fellow refugees. The Finnish Work Camp Organization, which planned both summer and winter projects, made its headquarters there. To the young Finns who went there to organize activities, the apartment became home. They could stay to dinner and talk about their problems.

George and Florence Selleck traveled around Finland, visiting small industries which had been started in 1947 at the suggestion of two other Service Committee representatives: Arthur Morgan and his wife, Lucy, the Friend who designed the relief cereal into which Perry Hayden's wheat was processed. Drawing on his exprience as Chairman of the Tennessee Valley Authority, Arthur Morgan had surveyed the resources of the country and suggested ways in which Finnish business could compete for world markets.

Another imaginative gift from American Quakers made possible the appointment of Joshua A. Cope, a Friend in the Department of Forestry at Cornell, to a visiting professorship at the University of Helsinki. He shared his expertise with foresters all over Finland.

In the local Friends Meeting, organized as a result of Douglas Steere's visit in 1938, the Sellecks communicated to the war-battered Finns that sense of God's caring, which alone can heal.

Jean Fairfax, former Dean of Women at Tuskegee Institute, spent two years in Austria working at the Quaker Neighborhood Center in Vienna and organizing Work Camps. Under her leadership, young people who had never known democracy were encouraged to plan projects themselves.

The starving young apprentices and victims of tuberculosis, to whom she brought food and clothing, called Jean Fairfax their "brown angel of mercy." Speaking fluent German, she interpreted the concern of "the people behind the packages"—those anonymous Americans who cared enough to help someone unknown.

At the Yalta Conference, the Allies had agreed that when the war ended Berlin and all of Germany would be divided into four zones of military occupation—American, Russian, British and French. But in 1948, the Russians attempted to gain control of the whole of Berlin by blockading the city. The other powers organized an airlift, transporting food and other necessities by cargo planes as long as the blockade lasted.

American Friends had planned a seminar for thirty-nine students from Denmark, England, Finland, France, Norway, Poland, Sweden, Switzerland, the United States and East and West Germany. The seminar was to be held at Mittelhof, the Quaker Community Center in Berlin. Far from abandoning the plan because of the sudden crisis, Friends decided that the tense atmosphere made it all the more imperative, even though students, faculty and food had to be flown in to the "Airlift Seminar."

With planes humming overhead, the students, among whom were Jews and former Nazis, talked all day and half into the night with the German, English and American professors, for some of the Europeans feared they might never have another chance to meet people outside their own country.

The Quaker Center at Mittelhof had been opened after the war under the leadership of Alice Shaffer, who left the U. S. State Department to make a place where bombed-out Berliners could sit in a warm room, find books, hear music, do their laundry and repair their shoes.

"We found ourselves listening hour after hour," she wrote back to Philadelphia, "as people who had been afraid to talk or who had lost their family, or their friends and their contact with sympathetic understanding, found new friends and a new approach to life."

During the blockade, negotiations with the military for food and supplies needed at Mittelhof called for that delicate Quaker diplomacy which does not rely on political leverage but on the belief that all men are children of God and that it is to the divinity in them that one must appeal.

Meanwhile, Moses Bailey, Professor of Old Testament at Hartford Seminary, took a leave of absence to communicate the Quaker concern for better understanding between Arabs and Jews in Palestine. As a young couple, he and his wife, Mabel, had taught in the Friends School at Ramallah. He spoke Hebrew and Arabic. Impartiality was his strength. What his political bias may have been, no one ever knew. Coming, like Rufus Jones, from Maine, he also leavened his concern with humor.

A month before Moses Bailey left for Palestine, Count Bernadotte was assassinated. To the Quakers who had worked with him, he had not only been a leader but a friend. That Dr. Ralph Bunche should be chosen to succeed the Count struck Clarence Pickett as "one of those blessings all too rare in political history."[4]

When Moses Bailey reached Tel Aviv, he conferred with Israeli authorities and secured permission for Quaker workers to enter Acre, a walled city where Arab refugees needed both relief and reassurance. But people in power were not the only ones to whom he turned his attention. Porters, mail clerks, refugees felt a self-esteem of which they had been too long deprived simply because this man, passing that way, looked on them as persons.

Delbert Replogle, a Quaker businessman from Ridgewood, New Jersey, with his wife, Ruth, followed Moses Bailey to Israel and organized the relief program. Meanwhile, the Headmaster of the Friends School at Ramallah, A. Willard Jones, and his wife, Christina, members of Western Yearly Meeting, were helping refugees in their area.

Then the American Quaker relief undertaking in the Middle East became greatly enlarged. The UN asked the Service Committee whether it would accept responsibility for Arab refugees in that portion of southern Palestine which came to be known as the Gaza Strip. After conferring with Egyptian government officials, with UN representatives and the U. S. Food and Agriculture Organization, the Service Committee accepted the assignment.

By the end of 1948, arrangements had been made for fifty workers wearing the Quaker star to enter the Gaza Strip.

Friends realized that this would be a challenging service. As Clarence Pickett observed, "We understood all that lay behind the setting up of the Jewish state, the long period of suffering and persecution in Europe, the high hopes and idealism connected with the return to the homeland. On the other side was the deep-seated bitterness not only of the Arab refugees but of all the Arab states surrounding the newly established state of Israel. It took little imagination to realize that this situation would test to the utmost both our administrative skill and our spiritual resources."[5]

That these resources could be relied on had already been demonstrated in Acre by a little incident, which Frederick Tolles related: "A Quaker relief worker went with an armed Israeli soldier to visit a needy Arab family. When they got to the Arab home, the soldier said he would wait outside. 'They won't want to see me,' he remarked. The relief worker went inside and in a few minutes returned with the father of the Arab family, who invited the soldier in. Surprised and touched by this gesture of good will, the soldier entered the Arab hovel, leaned his gun against the wall, and sat down to a cup of coffee with the family."[6]

Clarence and Lilly Pickett reached Cairo on January 16, 1949. The main purpose of their visit was to interpret the motivation for Quaker relief and its non-political character to Egyptian officials. The next day they flew to Gaza.

Under Quaker auspices, Dr. Jerome Peterson, a Black doctor from New York, organized a medical service in the refugee camps. The clinics ministered to two hundred thousand people each month. Dr. Abdul Hamid Zaki, Director of the Egyptian Association of Social Studies, set up tent schools for the sixty-five thousand children.

In Jerusalem, Clarence Pickett met with Martin Buber, whom he called "a prophet in the tradition of Isaiah, Jeremiah, Amos and Hosea . . . Though he feels keenly that Israel for the moment is too preoccupied with physical rebuilding to turn toward the spiritual realities which alone can make the enterprise significant, he declared . . . 'The time will come, and I must keep my faith in the persistent work of God.'"[7]

With the help of other agencies, the Service Committee continued to aid 230,000 refugees in the Gaza Strip until April 1950. Meanwhile, in Acre, where both Arabs and Jews were being furnished with the necessities of life, the Quakers, intent on peacemaking, also introduced the most irresistible of all reconciling forces.

One member of the team, Don Peretz, an American student who had served with Friends in Mexico, sent home this account: "Napoleon failed to take Acre after subjecting it to a 60-day artillery bombardment and siege. Beethoven took the town in two hours just the other Saturday evening. For the first time in two years, there was a concert in Acre. The occasion was probably the first in the town's history in which Jews and Arabs sat together at a classical concert."

The quartet of Jewish musicians had been brought over from Haifa.

"A Jewish teacher . . . who was recently discharged from an Israel commando unit, sat next to an Arab doctor whose wife is now a refugee in Beirut. In French they discovered that this was the first concert either one had been to since the start of the war. Another Arab doctor explained to one of his neighbors, who had a concentration camp number ingrained on his arm, that he had not experienced anything like this since he was a medical student in Leipzig. They spoke German. . . . Our Moslem storekeeper and our Moslem friends . . . sat at ease with Christians and Jews. Most of the Christian Arabs brought their wives. Some Christian women even came alone. . . .

"The four musicians who gave our first concert were of professional standing. . . . After the Quaker concert the leader told me, 'This performance has been one of the most enjoyable I have given!' "[8]

If music could accomplish this miracle, why could not religion? During his visit to Jerusalem, Clarence Pickett, sounding like a prophet himself, looked toward such a millennium.

"As I went about, talking with persons of different faiths, it began to seem to me not impossible that the words of the great prophets would even yet prove to be the note which alone could bring peace within this great family of kindred peoples: the call of Allah in the Koran, 'But I invite you to the Mighty, the Forgiving'; and of Micah in the Old Testament, 'And what doth the Lord require of thee, but to do justly, and to love mercy, and to walk humbly with thy God?'; and of Jesus in the New Testament, 'Love your enemies . . . do good to them that hate you, and pray for them which despitefully use you.' "[9]

On the plains of North Central China, where the most destructive battles of the Civil War were just then being fought, a valiant little band had no time to meditate on the charges of Micah and the Sermon on the Mount, so busy was it translating them into reality. The Chinese Communist Government had asked the Friends Service Unit, consisting of British and American Quakers, to send an emergency team into the Hsüchou area to care for wounded civilians and Nationalist soldiers.

Following tradition, Friends offered assistance to both sides in the conflict, disregarding political sympathies. As the fortunes of battle wavered, the Unit found itself sometimes in Nationalist territory, sometimes behind the Communist lines, where bodies lay half buried in mud, villages were razed to the ground, and children huddled together for warmth, some of them suffering from pneumonia or smallpox.

"There were old festering wounds bound in dirty ill-smelling rags. . . . The operating room was a hut with a straw ceiling and mud floor. . . . Flies were thick everywhere. We tried DDT in the operating room, but that only caused the flies to drop dead into the incision instead of flying in under their own steam, which seemed a doubtful advantage."[10]

At the end of nine months, they had cared for 35,433 patients.

On the dusty, windswept plains of Central China, kala azar was a ruthless disease that especially attacked children. One team of the Friends Service Unit, using drugs donated by the American Red Cross, undertook to wipe it out. The clinics were held in mud huts. Wheelbarrows full of sick children were brought in. A peasant carried his two suffering children in baskets hung from a pole across his shoulders, eight miles to the clinic and eight miles home again.

But the Communists were convinced that missionary service was part of a Western imperialist plot to win control of the people. As they extended their conquest, anti-American feeling became so strong that Friends withdrew.

"We have had the satisfaction of having filled—however inadequately—a space that otherwise would not have been filled," the Unit stated in its final report. "The last of our equipment has been packed, the farewell feast is over, and the ox-carts are loaded at the door ready to start on the road back."

It seemed a sad ending to American Quaker service in China that had begun in 1880 when Esther H. Butler, who had experienced conversion during a revival service conducted by Methodists and Friends at Damascus, Ohio, undertook mission work in Nanking in a house she called The Quakerage. During the Nanking riots of 1891, when many missionaries lost their lives, Esther Butler was forced to flee, but as soon as quiet was restored, she returned to start an orphanage and, with the help of other missionaries, built a hospital.

Neither the Boxer Uprising, in which 135 missionaries and sixteen thousand Chinese Christians were killed, nor the Chinese Revolution of 1911, when the Manchu Dynasty was overthrown, discouraged these dedicated missionaries from the Friends Church of Ohio. In fact, they established a dynasty of their own.

In 1898, Dr. Isabella French arrived at Luhr, north of Nanking, to carry on evangelistic work and to start a dispensary. Two years later she was joined by Dr. George F. DeVol, to whom she had been engaged while they were still in Ohio. He became her husband and co-worker. Two sons took over responsibility for the Mission when their parents' work was done. The DeVols' daughter, Catherine Cattell, was a missionary in India and their granddaughter, Barbara Brantingham, with her husband, John, carried forward the work on Taiwan into the 1970s.

Dr. William Warder Cadbury, a Philadelphia Friend, went to Canton in 1909 to teach in the University Medical School affiliated with Canton Christian College and to become Superintendent of the Canton Hospital. Although he was supported by members of his Meeting, he had not come to evangelize. Of this silent type of missionary, Rufus Jones said, "If he could make the blind see, the lame walk, the leper clean, the tumor-laden person whole, then his gospel of love and salvation would at once make its appeal to the heart."[11]

Friends united with American Baptists and American and Canadian Methodists in establishing West China Union University in Chengtu, which became a haven for students from Occupied China during the Sino-Japanese War.

Errol Elliott, in citing the "gunboat diplomacy" under which the missions existed, "as foreign countries came in to quell disturbances and enforce treaties for their own lucrative trade," remarked, "It is little wonder that the future unfolded as it did—in an enforced leaving of missions from China. In recent years the churches of other nations have learned how much they needed to hear the voice of China, not simply to lift their own voices in this centuries-old country."[12]

Quaker concern for China, pursued with more courage than insight and ending in frustration, is as old as Quakerism.

"This year, 1661, many Friends went beyond the seas," George Fox noted in his *Journal*. "John Stubbs, and Henry Fell, and Richard Scosthrop were moved to go towards China and Prester John's country, but no masters of ships would carry them. At last they got a warrant from the King; but the East India Company would not obey it, nor the masters of their ships. Then they went into Holland and would have got passage there, but no passage there could they get. And then John Stubbs and Henry Fell took shipping to go to Alexandria in Egypt, and so to go by the caravans from thence. And Daniel Baker and Richard Scosthrop took another ship to go to Smyrna; and Daniel Baker left Richard Scosthrop sick in a ship, where he died. . . ."[13]

It was not only in China that these brave Publishers of Truth hoped to proclaim "the day of the Lord." In addition to the Epistle written in Latin and English, which George Fox had addressed to the Emperor of China, the three carried with them many others intended for the King of Spain, the Pope, the King of France, the magistrates of Malta, the Sultan of Turkey and Prester John, believed to be the Emperor of Ethiopia.

Evidently feeling that these Epistles did not cover the whole territory, Fox gave the dauntless Friends who journeyed eastward one last one, addressed "To All the Nations Under the Whole Heavens."

27 Prophets — True and False

Rufus Jones used to tell about a five-year-old boy who had been bombed out of his home during the war and evacuated to the country. "Now," the little boy whimpered, "I'm nobody's nothing."

While demonstrating to the nobody's nothings of this world that they were indeed somebody's somethings and that this unknown somebody cared enough to come from a long way off with the necessities of life, Friends were simultaneously negotiating on behalf of the sufferers with government officials at home and abroad. Above all, they pleaded with those in power for legislation to avert suffering.

Clarence Pickett would shortly remind Friends that "It is not we who have to solve all the problems of the world; the heart of the Eternal is touched by the tragedy of events. . . . It is the direction in which His spirit tries to move people that we should seek."

And he declared, "I do not believe it is beyond the capacity of nations to find that sense of direction, even as it is vouchsafed to individuals. If this be true, how deeply important it is, when the lives of millions depend on actions that are being taken now by government, that we who believe in the guidance and power of the spirit of religious faith shall exercise that faith in all the phases of our life."

Interracial groups of teen-agers called upon their congressmen and found to their surprise that they were "just like anybody else." But they were dismayed over the discrimination in Washington and insisted on eating only in places which would serve them all. One youngster disclosed that this was the first time he had ever been with people in whose eyes he did not read the word "Negro" when they looked at him, the first time he ever "felt warm inside."

Conciliation and relief were needed at home, too—how desperately, it was a shock for young Americans to discover.

In foreign countries, even those which had recently considered them enemies, Quaker Work Campers received a warm welcome. Why was it that in certain sections of their own country they got a hostile reception, when they offered the labor of their hands and the outreach of their hearts?

Some white Work Campers went South to spend the summer helping Black students build a new wing on their school. After they took part in the Black Fourth of July celebration—a cruel mockery for those who had not, as yet, won their independence—the Work Campers were threatened by sheriffs and had to leave town.

A small interracial Work Camp in Texas assumed responsibility for a recreation program in a Black neighborhood. Great care had been taken to explain the Quaker philosophy in advance. Nevertheless, the idea of a group of girls, most of them white, living in a Black neighborhood was more than the white community could tolerate and the Work Camp was obliged to withdraw.

But there were gains. The Service Committee's Visiting Lectureships brought Black scholars and artists to schools and colleges. The students received them with enthusiasm and some of the institutions offered the visiting lecturers faculty appointments.

Friends all over the country were working to promote fair employment practices. In Philadelphia, Curtis and Nellie Bok gave a dinner for executives of the leading department stores to persuade them of the value of hiring on the basis of merit. A training program was introduced for job applicants of all racial and cultural backgrounds. Its aim was to supplement the education of those who desired better jobs.

Open housing was being pressed by Friends from coast to coast.

A unique self-help interracial project was undertaken in a blighted area of Philadelphia where 114 families had been crowded into a block of Civil War buildings. They had no central heating; ten families shared one bath. Some were so crowded that they had to sleep by turns.

The Redevelopment Authority of the City of Philadelphia made the property available to Friends for two hundred thousand dollars less than it cost the Authority to acquire it. The City Planning Commission laid out the area. A well-known architect drew up plans for the rehabilitation of the entire block into ninety-nine apartments with modern conveniences. Any labor not covered by union requirements was contributed by the people who looked forward to occupying the apartments. To train them for these jobs, the Friends Neighborhood Guild and the Philadelphia Board of Education opened a workshop.

The Service Committee became the redeveloper and ultimately the landlord on a non-profit basis. When the remodeling was completed, Friends turned the property over to a board that represented the occupants of the block and the city.

Many Friends were volunteering their full time, neither as missionaries nor as Service Committee workers. They simply saw a need they could fill.

Among these was Helen Griffith, of New England Yearly Meeting, who felt that Black colleges needed faculty members with advanced degrees. Upon her retirement as Professor of English at Mount Holyoke College, she spent four years replacing Mrs. Naomi Townsend, a member of the faculty of Tougaloo College in Mississippi, freeing her to acquire a Ph.D. at the University of Pittsburgh.

While Mrs. Townsend was working toward her doctorate, her students at Tougaloo had the benefit of the same English instruction that the most privileged girls in the country had received at Mount Holyoke. Yet Tougaloo's budget was not affected.

During the fiftieth reunion of her class at Bryn Mawr College in 1955, Helen Griffith marched in the academic procession. Then she went home, packed her doctor's cap and gown and shipped them to Mrs. Townsend, who was about to receive her degree. Deeply moved, Mrs. Townsend declared that now Helen Griffith's mantle had, in every sense, fallen upon her shoulders.

The plight of the Navajos in Arizona and New Mexico troubled many Americans at this time. More than half the children were dying before they reached the age of six. The tuberculosis rate was eight times higher among the Navajos than the national average. Of the twenty-four thousand school-age children, only six thousand were able to attend school.

Sharing the national guilt for this state of affairs, Friends started a program of service on the reservation. In addition, Quaker Work Campers built a hostel in Tuba City, Arizona, so that Indians coming to town from great distances would have a place to spend the night.

In the summer of 1949, Work Campers built a community house for the Hopi Indians in Arizona. Rumors went around the reservation that these young strangers were undercover agents for oil firms or looking for uranium. Then one of the Hopis exclaimed, "I catch on what this is all about! It is a tradition in the Hopi tribe that when one of the clan is in need of help with his garden, for instance, we all pitch in and help him. These people think the clan is worldwide." Another Hopi, joining the Work Campers in laying stone for the community building, commented, "This is the first time white people have come on our reservation to give instead of to get."[1] Indians who moved to the cities of California were helped by local Friends to adjust to life off the reservation and to become familiar with their new environment.

In commemoration of fifty years of mission work in Alaska, California Yearly Meeting purchased an airplane, enabling its mid-twentieth-century missionary to serve remote communities.

In 1895, Anna Hunnicutt, a Quaker student at William Penn College in Oskaloosa, Iowa, felt a concern to work with the Eskimos in northern Alaska. Although over thirty years had passed since the United States purchased Alaska, the federal government could not provide schools and health care for all the people. Missionaries filled most of these needs.

Anna Hunnicutt took her concern to her Yearly Meeting, California, which had just recently been established. As it did not feel ready to undertake so great a responsibility, it sent her instead to the mission supported by Oregon Yearly Meeting at Kake in southern Alaska. Later, Anna Hunnicutt went to Douglas Island to teach the Indians. While there, she confided to the U. S. Commissioner of Education that she still wished to serve the Eskimos in the extreme North.

The following year when the Commissioner called at Kotzebue, just above the Arctic Circle, the Eskimos there begged him to send them someone who could teach their children and tend their sick. He told them about Anna Hunnicutt. The Eskimos appointed two of their strongest men to visit her. They rowed an open canoe 250 miles through the Bering Sea to Cape Prince of Wales where they boarded a ship that took them the rest of the way.

"On Douglas Island they appealed to Anna Hunnicutt and Charles and May Replogle. The missionaries felt the hand of the Lord was leading—but how would the work be supported? They felt Charles should go to California to present the matter there, but they had no funds. Soon a letter with a one-hundred-dollar check was received, coming from a Friend in Maine. . . . That very day a steamer was in the harbor. . . . When it steamed out, Charles Replogle was aboard. Friends in California agreed to underwrite the new work and Robert and Carrie Samms proved ready to go with Anna Hunnicutt. So on June 6, 1897 they sailed for Kotzebue."[2]

The missionaries were warmly received. They set up a school and a Friends Church, giving the Eskimos Quaker names, but they also went outside the fold and named one George Washington, one Abraham Lincoln and another James Russell Lowell. They performed marriages according to the custom of California Yearly Meeting. Applicants for membership in the Friends Mission at Kotzebue promised to "do as the Lord Jesus Christ would like me to do" and not to lie, steal, gamble, drink, sell or make whiskey; to pray to Jesus every day; to have but one husband or wife; as an unmarried man or woman to live a pure life and to attend church regularly.[3]

In 1899, when Anna Hunnicutt's term of service ended, she was replaced by Martha Hadley, a Friend from Wilmington, Ohio, who kept a diary of activities at the Mission and recorded the weather—cloudy, mostly. In December 1903, when Martha Hadley's term of service was over and she was starting home on board the schooner *Corwin*, two brothers named Wright were lifting their biplane off a sand dune at Kitty Hawk, North Carolina. They kept it in the air for fifty-nine seconds. In 1949, the successors of the first brave Alaska missionaries had a plane, too, and they were flying all over their territory.

In New York, meanwhile, Philip Jessup, a member of the United States delegation to the UN, was holding private conversations at Quaker House with Mr. Malik, the Russian delegate to the UN. It was a nice peaceful place in which to discuss the Berlin blockade. By May of that year, the blockade was lifted.

When Philip Jessup was sent to the International Court of Justice at The Hague, his wife, Lois, the American Quaker representative at the UN, was replaced by Elmore Jackson, who also became the Friends World Committee's consultant to the UN Economic and Social Council.

Elmore and Elizabeth Jackson and their two daughters moved into Quaker House. In February 1949, the Jacksons held the first of their regular "at homes," which were to become significant occasions. Officials and staff of UN delegations were invited to drop in and make the acquaintance of Friends.

That same month, some Quaker political scientists and educators, troubled over mounting tension between the United States and the Soviet Union, met at Quaker House and organized a Working Party to explore possibilities for improving relations between the two countries.

The findings of the Working Party were summed up in a pamphlet and published a few months later by the Yale University Press under the title: *The United States and the Soviet Union, Some Quaker Proposals for Peace.* These were specifically: resumption of trade and normal exports, rebuilding and neutralizing Germany and invigorating the United Nations. The Quaker proposals were vastly different from the United States policy of containment.

On Sunday, June 5, the New York *Times* carried a front-page article describing these efforts to promote better understanding between prominent American citizens and officials of the Soviet Union. Andrei A. Gromyko, who was then Deputy Foreign Minister, was quoted as having expressed "confidence in the integrity of the Quakers."

A week later Henry Cadbury, Clarence Pickett and Elmore Jackson called at the Soviet Embassy in Washington to express their hope that cultural relations between the two countries might be developed. They made it clear that when travel was possible, Quakers would visit Moscow.

The Service Committee released some impressive figures at the end of that summer. Under its sponsorship, eleven hundred participants, of all races, representing sixty countries of the world, forty-three states of the Union, 224 colleges and universities, forty-one religious denominations, served in seventy-seven projects in five mental institutions, two correctional institutions, six seminars in Europe and Asia, ten seminars in the United States, fifty-seven industries and cooperatives, seven work camps in Mexico, thirty-two work camps in Europe, eleven work camps in the United States.

These young people could go home in the autumn, feeling that they had contributed at least a little toward humanity's needs. But the Conscientious Objectors who were still in prison because of their refusal to register for the draft could not go home.

On May 26, the Justice Department had authorized all United States Attorneys to register non-registrants. "Except in the most willful instances," the order read, "indictments should not be brought in future cases of religious objectors who refuse to submit for registration."

Many subsequent instances were evidently considered "most willful," for fines and long prison terms were still imposed.

Writing in braille for the *American Friend*, Guilford B. Street, Pastor of the Honey Creek Friends Meeting near New Providence, Iowa, pointed out that to the non-registrants, the issue was "clearly that of the right of government to compel its people to yield obedience above that which they owe to God and the Divine Law." He pointed out that this conflict between vested authority and the consciences of men has raged throughout recorded history, going back to the Book of Daniel. He described the founding of this nation by men who brought "to its shores ideals of freedom, of liberty of conscience, and of separation of church and state. . . .

"The obvious and the usual answer is that one should obey the law. The implication is that he should accommodate his conscience to its provisions. One should take the easy way of submission, even though it does violate his religious belief. . . . The position of our Government in the war crimes trials was that loyalty and obedience to the state did not excuse men from the requirements of moral law, which comes from God.

"In the final analysis, it is but a token submission which the state is requiring. The question of manpower is not an issue since these men would have been exempted as conscientious objectors if they had registered. . . . What, then, is the real purpose of these prosecutions? Why, in most cases, are such stiff prison sentences imposed?

"Men have never been fully able to appreciate the conscientious scruples of others in matters in which they themselves see no moral issues. Yet, here is a principle which is the very basis of our liberties and should be cherished by every American. A man's highest duty should be to God. . . . Only thus can democracy be safe."[4]

Seventy-five prominent Americans sent a joint letter to President Truman on September 14, urging immediate freedom for the Conscientious Objectors in prison. Most of the signers were not Friends —John Dewey, John Dos Passos, Harry Emerson Fosdick, John Haynes Holmes, Louis Untermeyer, Carl Van Doren, Pierre van Paassen and Thornton Wilder, among others—but they mentioned in their joint letter, the "Quaker record of service to humanity" and pointed out that "members of this group practicing its teachings are branded as felons and numbered as convicts in prisons from coast to coast."[5] Harold Evans and Clarence Pickett called on President Truman, pleading for an amnesty and release of these men. The President indicated that he would discuss the matter with the Attorney General.

Over the Labor Day weekend, fifty-four persons gathered at Camp Onas in Rushland, Pennsylvania. Half of them were Young Friends and half belonged to Catholic Youth. They had sought this opportunity to get to know each other and discuss their beliefs. On the Sunday morning they attended Mass together in Newtown. In the evening, they worshiped together after the manner of Friends. They discovered that their basic religious assumptions were so far apart that they would have to spend more time together before they could begin to understand one another.

In October, a group of Friends went to Washington to meet with Pandit Nehru at the Indian Embassy. His purpose, the Prime Minister told Friends as he had told reporters earlier, was "a voyage of discovery of the mind and heart of America, and to place before you our own mind and heart."[6]

Within a week, those rare Quaker minds and hearts which sometimes turn from politics to take cognizance of sentimental occasions quietly observed the two hundredth anniversary of the marriage of John Woolman to Sarah Ellis in Chesterfield, New Jersey.

"About this time," Woolman tells us in his *Journal*, "believing it good for me to settle, and thinking seriously about a companion, my heart was turned to the Lord with desires that he would give me wisdom to proceed therein agreeable to his Will; and he was pleased to give me a well-inclined damsel, Sarah Ellis; to whom I was married the eighteenth day of the eighth Month, in the year 1749."[7]

Just two hundred years later, in the Mount Holly house which Woolman built for their daughter Mary and her husband, a Black man addressed a group of his fellow Quakers. Bayard Rustin had been asked to deliver the annual lecture of the John Woolman Memorial Association.

He had worked with the Service Committee; he had spent much of the Second World War in federal prisons for upholding the Peace Testimony; he had received the Jefferson Award for being "one of the Americans who has done most in the recent past to better relations between colored and white citizens." A few months before he delivered the Woolman Lecture, he went to India at the invitation of Mahatma Gandhi's son. He was entertained at

Government House in New Delhi and discussed world problems with Prime Minister Nehru.

A week after his return to the United States, the Supreme Court of North Carolina upheld a lower court's decision sentencing Bayard Rustin to thirty days on a chain gang for disobeying the Jim Crow law during a bus trip two years earlier.

The year 1949 was also the one hundreth anniversary of a death or, as Friends would say, of thankfulness for a life—that of Edward Hicks, painter of the pictures he called "The Peaceable Kingdom." In his sixty-nine years, he produced, apart from a few lovely landscapes, perhaps one hundred canvases illustrating a single subject: the prophecy of Isaiah.

He had been a failure as a farmer but as a minister in the Society of Friends, he was, like his cousin Elias, greatly appreciated, until the Separation.

In his time, a Friend was recorded a minister not because he had studied in college or seminary, but in recognition of rigorous self-discipline. Edward Hicks had spent years endeavoring to distinguish between vocal ministry that is purely intellectual or self-gratifying and the true leading of the Spirit. Personal sorrow refined Hicks's perception. A minister was, like any other Friend, simply "a humble learner in the school of Christ."

By trade a sign painter and decorator of carriages, Hicks devoted his spare time to the symbolic expression of his deep belief.

"May his peaceable kingdom for ever be established in the rational, immortal soul," he prayed. "Then will be fulfilled the prophetic declaration . . . 'The wolf also shall dwell with the lamb, and the leopard shall lie down with the kid, the calf, and the young lion, and the fatling together, and a little child shall lead them: the cow and the bear shall feed, their young shall lie down together, and the lion shall eat straw like the ox. The sucking child shall play upon the hole of an asp, and the weaned child shall put its hand on the cockatrice's den. Nothing shall hurt or destroy in all my holy mountain, for the earth shall be full of the knowledge of the Lord, as the waters cover the sea.'"[8]

In "The Peaceable Kingdom" canvases, William Penn makes his treaty with the Indians against a scene of Hicks's own Bucks County or perhaps the Natural Bridge of Virginia. The Little Child, who leads with outstretched arm, has the face of a country bumpkin; the other children blandly dare the snakes to bite them. These formal little figures do not long hold our attention. It is the animals, painted in warm tones of sepia, chestnut, fawn and ocher, who capture us—the ox with his calm gaze, wise beyond the wisdom of men, for he has overcome his aggressive nature, and the lion and the leopard who are profoundly disturbing. "There is a peculiar identification of the artist with these great golden cats and their serpentine tails," Eleanore Price Mather says in her study, *Edward Hicks, Primitive Painter, His Religion in Relation to His Art.*

"As we ponder these great felines, we cannot help thinking of Blake's 'Tiger! Tiger!' particularly of the line, 'Did He who made the lamb make thee?' . . . to Hicks the leopard meant sensual beauty . . . the viewer sees in the lion not an animal but Edward Hicks staring at us with woebegone concern, as though he were the prophet himself."

Eleanore Price Mather shows how the Orthodox-Hicksite Separation "and the social tragedies left in its wake, laid a heavy imprint on both the writing and the painting of Edward Hicks."[9]

Almost two centuries after Hicks's birth, John Canaday, writing in the New York *Times,* called him "by acclamation America's greatest primitive painter and one of the great ones of any place."[10]

How Hicks would have loved Handel's *Messiah!* Had he not been a Friend, constrained from enjoying music, he could have heard Isaiah's prophecy celebrated by another master in another medium. But he was not allowed to enjoy music. Nor was he supposed to enjoy painting. Since he obviously did, he was eldered on occasion—reproved by the Elders of his Meeting.

Handel and Hicks—Handel, majestic, celestial; Hicks, homespun, zoological, giving his pictures the background not of the New Jerusalem but his native land. These two—one of the greatest composers and one of the least-known painters—set a century apart, diverse in religious tradition, both proclaimed the establishment of the Kingdom of God on earth. Despite all the evidence to the contrary, they renew our faith in its coming.

At the close of 1949, the *Friends Intelligencer* also prophesied— a risky indulgence for any but authentic prophets.

Reginald Reynolds, an English Friend, had just published a book entitled *Beards: Their Social Standing, Religious Involvements, Decorative Possibilities and Value in Offense and Defense*

Through the Ages. In announcing publication, the *Intelligencer* observed, "There seems little danger that the general public, or Friends in particular, may become interested in cultivating more facial foliage than we have been accustomed to see for the last generation or two."[11]

28 Venturing in Where Diplomats Fear to Tread

Clarence Pickett retired as Executive Secretary of the Service Committee in March of 1950. "I could not have asked for a more satisfying twenty years," he declared.[1] The Committee named him its Honorary Secretary.

Lewis Hoskins, who had been Personnel Director of the Service Committee in Philadelphia and a member of the Quaker Unit in China, was appointed to succeed Clarence Pickett. In accepting the appointment, Lewis Hoskins said, speaking for himself and the other members of the staff, "We wish to be sensitive most of all to Divine leading as we seek to implement as effectively as our resources permit, the concerns for a peaceful and just world on all levels of human relationship."[2]

Late in June, North Korean troops invaded South Korea. The UN Security Council declared North Korea an aggressor, the United States supported the resolution and, after only five years of peace, young Americans were sent overseas to fight again. In this war 33,237 would die.

General Douglas MacArthur, speaking to Elizabeth Vining in Tokyo, described the plight of the Korean people. "It is pitiful. Pitiful. Fierce fighting men pour down from the North and then up from the South, and now down from the North again. Each house has a North Korean flag and a South Korean flag, and most of the time they don't know which to wave. Both sides line them up and shoot them down."[3]

The Quaker response to this new assault on humanity was an even more dogged effort to encourage friendship and understanding between East and West. Way opened, as Friends say, most unexpectedly in Yugoslavia.

The pamphlet entitled *The United States and the Soviet Union, Some Quaker Proposals for Peace*, fell into the hands of the wife of a Yugoslav envoy in the United States. Impressed by some of its arguments and especially its tone, this lady translated the pamphlet. It was then circulated among prominent Yugoslavs at home. The Belgrade Government thereupon instructed its representative at the UN to invite an American Quaker delegation to visit Yugoslavia.

The invitation was accepted by the American Friends Service Committee on the condition that its representatives be allowed to observe without restriction the social conditions in which they were interested; that the Committee be free to issue a report of their visit; that the representatives have an opportunity to visit institutions and confer with government officials as well as private citizens; and that the Service Committee dispatch the Mission at its own expense.

On September 15, this Mission flew to Europe. The members were Harold and Sylvia Evans of Philadelphia; Colin W. Bell, who would one day become Executive Secretary of the Service Committee; and William B. Edgerton, then a member of the faculty of Pennsylvania State College. As a Service Committee worker, he had assisted Yugoslav refugees in Egypt. He spoke Serbo-Croatian and was thus able to converse with the Yugoslavs in their own language.

"We went to Yugoslavia with a good deal of hesitation because we thought that our movements would be restricted, overguided and closely watched," Sylvia Evans conceded upon the return of the Mission. "Quite on the contrary, from the time we were greeted in Belgrade until the day some five weeks later when we crossed over the barbed-wired border into Greece, we found not only freedom to go wherever we wanted to go and do whatever we wanted to do, but cooperation and help in accomplishing our ends. . . .

"First and last, we met many people—those in high government, members of the old bourgeoisie, workers in industry, young people in labor brigades, our interpreters and chauffeurs in various places, members of cooperatives, peasants. Everywhere we found interest in us as foreigners, receptivity, and a desire for friendship and exchange of ideas. . . . Even among the poorest we found a delightful, though sometimes embarrassingly generous hospitality. More than once we sat at a table in a peasant's home, where two of us were offered Turkish coffee in the only two cups in the house; then the cups were washed, refilled, and again presented with coffee and dignity. . . . Throughout our journey—and with many people—there grew friendships which were almost startling in their spontaneity, sincerity and eagerness."[4]

Only a very few Yugoslavs had heard of the Society of Friends.

These were people who remembered the work of the Friends Ambulance Unit in Yugoslavia after the war. To others, the name "Quaker" conveyed nothing until the members of the Mission interpreted their message.

The Yugoslavs listened in surprise. They had been, they explained, in the habit of thinking of organized religion as a barrier to social progress, the champion of the status quo, which had no concern for man's daily life and problems. The most ardent supporters of the Communist regime were interested to discover that religion can be a dynamic force which compels man to seek truth, work for social justice and discover means to achieve it. Characteristically, the Mission members emphasized the fact that Friends' practice falls short of their ideals.

Marshal Tito told the Mission that he had read a book on Quakerism during his long years in prison.

"There is one point on which I think the Quakers go a little too far," he said with a chuckle, patting his cheek. "This business of turning the other cheek!"[5]

In summing up its report, the Mission recommended that every possible type of contact be cultivated between Yugoslavia and the West by means of correspondence, exchange of literature, radio, tourism, trade, and the intervisitation of persons.

The report concluded, "We do believe that contacts which lead to mutual understanding of the way our minds work and the reasons that have made them work that way must lead to mutual respect and must bring real peace nearer. We believe this to be true of all men and all nations. . . ."[6]

While the Quaker Mission was in Yugoslavia, the Fifth Assembly of the United Nations convened at Lake Success.

The Service Committee had appointed as Secretary for Russian-American Relations William Huntington, a veteran overseas worker. His function was to invite Soviet representatives and Americans to meet at Quaker House and exchange views in the hope that by this means the tension between citizens of the two powers could be relaxed.

Henry Cadbury had observed that the Quaker's "faith in man's capacity to persuasion enables him to experiment and to venture in where diplomats fear to tread. He regards neither war nor injustice as inevitable." Referring to "something of God" in every man, he said, "To this he appeals by patience, by reason, by example, and if necessary, by his own suffering for the right. If he does not always succeed, his average success is not much behind that of those who use what they choose to call the 'practical' methods of fighting for their rights though the heavens fall."[7]

In this spirit, regarding neither war nor injustice as inevitable, the Friends World Committee appointed an international team of six observers to attend the Fifth Assembly of the UN.

These Friends gathered at Quaker House on October 5, 1950. Clarence Pickett and Elmore Jackson were there from the United States; Elsa Cedergren, sister of Count Bernadotte, from Sweden; Heberto M. Sein, an expert in Latin-American affairs, from Mexico; Gerald Bailey and Agatha Harrison from England. Gerald Bailey was a journalist. Agatha Harrison had lived in India and brought to the team special insight into the thinking of that country.

Early each morning, before driving out to Lake Success, these Friends worshiped together at Quaker House, praying that in all their contacts, especially those with people who put their faith primarily in military power, they might be open and sensitive to God's leading. They thought of their mission as "a denationalized, universally motivated effort to serve the cause of peace and world brotherhood."[8]

Many UN delegates, the team discovered, had heard of the Quakers. Although they did not know much about their beliefs, they knew about their activities. So the ground was prepared. Circulating among the delegates at Lake Success, the impartial Quaker observers quickly won confidence and even affection.

Heberto Sein, the Mexican Friend, who brought to every assignment an engaging sense of humor, felt obliged to explain to people, when they first met him, that he inherited his startling red hair and freckles from his American mother. In 1888, Margaretta Marriage, a young Iowa Friend, went to Mexico as a missionary to teach in the Friends School in Matehuala. There she met and married Encario M. Sein, a fellow teacher. Their son Heberto married a French Friend. With their combined knowledge of many cultures, the young Seins became valued Quaker ambassadors in many parts of the world.

"To what extent," Heberto asked himself, reflecting later on the Fifth Assembly, "does the military action taken in Korea represent the real convictions of the people in the countries whose governments voted for it? It is the United Nations, the press kept saying, that is at war. However, I felt that for some minds possibly there was this question: Which military action effected by the UN

Command was authorized by the United Nations? Which was not? . . .

"As the representatives of the great powers discussed disarmament, I felt keenly that they did not cease to think in terms of military might. Behind their seats were real or potential divisions of men under helmets obediently waiting in silence. Their life depended on decisions over which they exercised no control. . . . The more the powers arm themselves, the more they fear and mistrust each other. . . . I felt that the policy makers of the two powers had not exhausted the moral and spiritual resources that could enable them to create mutual confidence."[9]

To the Quaker observers, the political tensions of the hour made it seem imperative that there be a quiet place at Lake Success where delegates who wished to tap their spiritual resources in the course of a noisy day could withdraw. A Moslem delegate had confided to them that he shut himself in Telephone Booth Number 4, when it was time for his prayers.[10]

Friends appealed to the Secretary General's office. A quiet room was set aside to which people of many religious faiths and political loyalties repaired for their devotions.

In Cuba, meanwhile, Friends were celebrating their fiftieth anniversary. Their periodical *El Amigo Cubano* published an article on George Fox and a review of Cuban Quaker history, translated for the *Friends Intelligencer* by Samuel J. Bunting.

"Sometime before 1900, Zenas L. Martin was superintendent of the mission of Five Years Meeting Friends in the Island of Jamaica. One day Friend Martin was on shipboard coming from his station to the mainland. As the ship passed near the coast of Cuba, he and the ship's captain, a Mr. Baker, were deep in conversation, admiring the natural beauty of the landscape. Captain Baker remarked that he intended shortly to retire and start to grow bananas back there behind the shore line, and asked, 'Why doesn't your church establish missions in Cuba, too? The people there have just as much spiritual need as those in Jamaica.'

"Zenas Martin presented the plan to Friends, who received it with great enthusiasm. It was during the Spanish war. . . . On November 11, 1900, the first missionaries from the Friends Church in North America landed at the port of Gibara. . . . They soon organized a Meeting, Sunday School and day school."

The first of these missionaries, Sylvester Jones of Iowa, wisely encouraged the Cubans who became convinced of Quakerism to take responsibility for their religious affairs. United States intervention in the Cuban economy made these new Friends eager to be independent of foreign support. After the missionaries withdrew in 1942, the American Friends Board of Missions appointed Hiram and Janet Hilty its representatives in Cuba simply "to give whatever aid they can in the development of an understanding and appreciation of the Christian way of life as interpreted by Friends."[11]

At the sessions of the Five Years Meeting, convened at Richmond, Indiana, in October 1950, the delegates from Cuba were Juan Guzman, a Quaker pastor, Miguel Tamayo, an American-trained pharmacist, and Juan Sierra, also a pastor and Principal of the Friends School at Puerto Padre.

Jamaica was represented by George Minott, a pastor and teacher; Kenneth Crooks, Headmaster of Happy Grove School at Hector's River, the holder of a Ph.D. degree from Harvard; Mabel Vincent, an East Indian by birth, who had attended William Penn College in Iowa. The delegate from Mexico was a medical student, Fortunato Castillo, son of a beloved pastor, the "Quaker Saint of Mexico."[12]

During these sessions, four hundred men attended the First National Conference of Quaker Men. A counterpart to the United Society of Friends Women, which had for decades supported missions, Quaker Men dedicated their efforts to church extension. L. Glenn Switzer, who presided, D. Robert Yarnall, who discussed the ethics of business, and Archibald A. Bond, a medical missionary, were cited as "outstanding examples of the committed life."

While Friends were traveling from far and near to Indiana, Elizabeth Vining was preparing to leave Japan. She had stayed a year longer than her contract called for. All on her own, she had imparted to the Crown Prince and the rest of the Imperial Family the finest aspects of American culture. They, in turn, had reached out to her in friendship, touched by her deep caring and her poet's response to the beauty of their country.

On a rainy morning she had given the Crown Prince his last English lesson of the summer.

"When we had finished talking about *Julius Caesar*, I told him that in the autumn I was going home to the United States, not for a visit, but to stay. I had been in Japan for four years, I said; in that time he had grown from a little boy to a young man. I felt that I had taught him all I had to teach him, and that it was time for me to be in my own country.

"He looked sober. For a moment he made no comment, and then he asked; 'Will you come back to Japan some day?'

"I said that I hoped to, for I would always be a little bit homesick for Japan. I told him that I hoped also to see him in America, and his face lighted up."[13]

Before Elizabeth Vining's departure, the Japanese Government bestowed a decoration on her—the Third Order of the Sacred Crown, given only to women.

"... the order was presented on a day so full of extraordinary honors and privileges that I moved through them in a daze ... we went in to lunch, I with the Emperor, Mr. Yoshida with the Empress.... Speaking through interpreters the Emperor and Empress both thanked me for my work with the Crown Prince, and the Empress spoke especially of the atmosphere of happiness which she said I had created for him. I replied that it had been my prayer that he have a free and happy growth to his fullest capacities and that I felt he had very fine potentialities of mind and spirit. The Emperor said that he felt happy but *hazukashii* (shy) to hear his son so praised."[14]

Four years earlier, when Elizabeth Vining had entered the class of boys for the first time, she felt "a bit adventurous within." The last lesson was poignant.

"My heart was full as I sat there in the midst of my boys, every one of whom was dear to me. They had been a joy to teach, and throughout the four years I had never come away from their class without a lift of the heart ... we closed the day by standing and singing 'Auld Lang Syne.' I crossed my arms in the Scottish way and took the hand of the Crown Prince on one side and of the boy who had been master of ceremonies on the other.[15]

"Mount Fuji had withdrawn behind a cloud the day I left Japan as she had done the day I came ... my mind went back over the past four years ... I had seen a broken and bewildered nation pick itself up from its ashes ... I had seen a chubby small boy develop into a poised young man....

"I had been asked to open windows onto a wider world for the Crown Prince ... certainly many windows had been opened for me—and perhaps through me for others—both on Japan itself and on the ancient, ceremonious, hidden world within the Moat. Through windows, whichever way they face, comes light, and light, I thought, is good."[16]

29 Quakerism's Fourth Century

In 1952, Quakerism entered upon its fourth century.
Historians dated the beginning of the movement from that spring day in 1652, when a young man climbed Pendle Hill in Lancashire "with much ado, it was so steep; but I was moved of the Lord to go atop of it . . . and the Lord let me see atop of the hill in what places he had a great people to be gathered."[1]
Spiritual descendants of the people George Fox had gathered three centuries earlier assembled, nine hundred strong, for the Third Friends World Conference at Oxford, England, from July 28 to August 6, 1952. They came from five continents.
"The Vocation of Friends in the Modern World" was the subject to which they addressed themselves. Their purpose was not to celebrate past events, but to explore the contribution Friends might make in the century ahead.
Wilfrid E. Littleboy, an English Friend, served as Conference Clerk and Errol Elliott, then editor of the *American Friend*, as Assistant Clerk.
"Rather than venerating history, we now must *make* history," Errol Elliott declared. "The chief question is not how worthy were our ancestors, but rather what kind of ancestors are we to be."[2]
Some months before the Conference, the *Friends Intelligencer* published a lexicon of Quaker expressions, translated from English into the languages of those who would be coming from Asia, Africa and the continent of Europe. Thus, if any American delegate had done his homework, he knew on arrival at Oxford that *Il Quaccherismo* is Italian for Quakerism; *Ystavien uskonnollinen seura* is Finnish for the Religious Society of Friends; *Ny Fivahana mangina* means the silent Meeting for Worship in Madagascar; *Ubulavu bwo musi mwo mwoyo* denotes the Light Within to Kenyan Quakers; *Subeto-no Hito-no Uchi-ni Kami Yadoru* is Japanese for "that of God in every man."
But language turned out not to be the real barrier. Most of the delegates spoke English, no matter where they came from American Friends quickly learned to say, "Ter-centeen'erie" and "clark."
They were warmly welcomed by the people of Oxford. This

was in sharp contrast to the reception given the first Quakers who entered the city.

Convinced that all men must come, as George Fox phrased it, "to their own Teacher in themselves," those first Quakers went to Oxford in the autumn of 1654 to preach against the training of "hireling ministers." Two of them—Elizabeth Fletcher, aged sixteen, and William Simpson, twenty-seven—had a disconcerting way of going "naked through the streets of that city, as a sign against that hypocritical profession."[3]

The Friends who came to Oxford in 1952 made no such testimony. Nor did they suffer the indignities to which the unresisting seventeenth-century Friends were subjected, many of them too cruel and shocking to print.

"Our usual manner hath been to meet together to wait upon and worship God in spirit and truth . . . at which time 'twas the constant practice of the scholars there to meet us and act wickedness and abuses toward us, as pulling of Friends' hair off their heads, and beards by the roots. . . . They took one Friend by the neckcloth and held him up from the ground until they had near choked him, and stopped another Friend's mouth ready to strangle him. . . . They have brought hogs into our meeting . . . they have come . . . whooping and halloing, houghing, scoffing, swearing and cursing and . . . calling for . . . beer and tobacco, calling Friends rogues and whores, dogs, bitches and toads . . . making a noise like cats and dogs. . . ."[4]

The Friends who arrived in 1952 were privileged to worship unmolested. They took up residence in nine of the Oxford colleges, charmed by the gardens, the architectural magnificence, the scholarly associations.

The Americans joyfully embraced antiquity as if they considered innerspring mattresses and modern plumbing not really essential. And after they had been locked out a midnight or two, they accepted the fact that, like undergraduates, they must observe the rules of the college, whose gates closed on the stroke of eleven.

With the same slightly unpatriotic relish the Americans had savored when they witnessed the Changing of the Guard in London, they listened to an account of the British Quaker deputation which, in accord with ancient custom, had recently gone to Buckingham Palace to present a loyal address to Elizabeth II.

"May it please the Queen," the address began. "As representing the Religious Society of Friends commonly known as Quakers, we bring you the love and loyalty of many hearts. . . . We pray that God will enable you, through a long and happy reign, to keep your subjects united not only in loyalty to you, our Queen, but also in fresh dedication to those standards of righteousness in family and public life that alone exalt a nation. We pray too that your example and influence may continue to promote understanding and peace among all peoples."

Standing on a low dais just in front of the Duke of Edinburgh, the Queen had replied that she was "deeply moved by the . . . warmth of your good wishes towards myself, my husband and our children. I join in your prayers. . . ."[5]

Differences of language and foreign customs did not perturb the American delegates at Oxford. What they had to adjust to, in the first days, was the fact that their own delegation was disconcertingly heterogeneous in its views. Friends from one section of the United States sometimes found it difficult to share the thinking of Friends from another. American Quakers who worshiped on the basis of silence were at home in a European Meeting. Those who were accustomed to program were not, but they felt comfortable worshiping with African Quakers, who had been convinced by missionaries from pastoral meetings in the United States.

All the Americans thought of themselves as adhering generally to the Quaker testimony of simplicity in dress and standard of living. Yet they felt embarrassingly affluent when they arrived in a country which was still coping with food rationing and clothing coupons.

A German delegate urged Friends to look at their possessions for the roots of war. Possessions create envy. People who have more than they need are reluctant to part with anything.

The poverty of the African Friends and the domination of the white race on their continent challenged all who called themselves Christian.

Friends from countries close to the Iron Curtain spoke of their spiritual confusion and disillusionment. The Japanese Quakers, who had welcomed the disarmament imposed on their nation at the conclusion of the war, deplored the encouragement Japan was now being given to arm again.

The hot war in Korea and the cold war with Russia seemed more real to Americans when they lived under one roof with people who had been personally deprived of freedom by the Communists.

Intellectually, none of this came as a surprise. But it had a devastating impact when it was embodied in living persons.

There were so many opinions at this Conference, colored by such a variety of national and personal experiences, that it seemed questionable whether any deep understanding could be reached. Then Friends worshiped together and all these differences receded as they came to "know one another in that which is eternal."

"We are one at the center," Howard Brinton concluded, "however diverse we might be at the circumference; one in our searching; one in our regard for the viewpoints of one another, but even more, one in the unity of the spirit, in the bond of peace."[6]

Part of each day, the delegates met in small worship-fellowship groups.

"When I had to live for a year in the same house as the leading Nazis of a small town," a German Friend said in one of these groups, "I often felt it was very difficult. . . . But looking back, I know I have learned much. . . . If the children were to have a normal, healthy development, one had to create confidence and overcome all hostilities. There I learned to see the child of God in each person. Later on, these experiences have helped me under the Russian occupation. Often I *was* afraid, but words like those of William Penn gave quietness and helped me: 'Nor can we fall below the arms of God, how low so ever it be we fall.' "[7]

Some Friends, mainly those from the continent of Europe, questioned "the relevance of traditional Christian phraseology to the contemporary situation; some speakers almost seemed to be suggesting that in the interests of spreading the gospel of Christ, we might be well advised to drop such words as 'Christ' and 'Christians.' If one looked at such statements out of the context of the ideological battle which is raging in many parts of the world, one might have been shocked; but those who were speaking in this way were evidently filled with a passion for the Christian message."[8]

Meeting in the Town Hall of the city of Oxford, the full Conference was addressed by the Reverend Oliver S. Tompkins, Associate General Secretary of the World Council of Churches.

"You are in many ways a standing perplexity to most of us," he told Friends. "You have decided to dispense . . . with certain ordinances which we believe to be God's expressed will. . . . Yet you steadily show the fruit of the spirit in a way which continually makes us ask in what sense these things are necessary."[9]

The Conference declared itself categorically opposed to racial discrimination and impelled to take action to eradicate it. Slavery, Friends were reminded, came to an end not through one short, mighty effort, but because individual Quakers *began* to give up their slaves.

Bayard Rustin declared that the problem is not really a racial one; it is man's injustice to man. He warned of "good" people, who camouflage prejudice as moral orderliness. They refuse to face the hidden causes, such as underprivilege, which are responsible for the open violence found in a Black slum.[10]

At a public meeting in the Sheldonian Theatre, an Indian Friend, Ranjit M. Chetsingh, Principal of the Baring Union Christian College at Batala in the Punjab, spoke of the cataclysmic events, which were overtaking the peoples of Asia. As a result, the East was no longer under the spell of the white man's magic powers. People who formerly came to the East from Western countries, including some who came to preach the Christian message, had brought with them an unconscious sense of the superiority of their civilization. The white man's confidence in his superiority had been shaken to unrecognized depths, and out of this shaking of confidence grew an assertiveness, a tendency to rely more and more on weapons of destruction.

"Today there is a great urge among Friends to go out to help in such small measure as they can in building up material comfort. . . . I wish to sound a note of warning to Friends. . . . The best we have to share with the world is experience of the living God made real to us in Jesus Christ. . . . On what happens to Asiatic peoples in the next few years . . . depends the future of mankind."[11]

Margarethe Lachmund of Berlin, Recording Clerk of Germany Yearly Meeting, assured Friends that "real love comes from God and John Woolman is a living example of this. For us German Friends to whom the challenge of Communism to the Christian world comes with special gravity and urgency in the Eastern section of our country, many of John Woolman's words have become a summons to conscience."[12]

Henry J. Cadbury spoke of the independence from current standards which is an important characteristic of Quakerism.

"Such independence is looked at askance, not only in the political but in the ecclesiastical field. . . . I believe we are . . . an enigma . . . not merely to red Moscow and red Peking but also to Whitehall and the White House. . . . We are confronted with major issues of critical importance. . . . Are Friends as fearless in following their consciences in 1952 as they were in 1652?"[13]

The Conference passed a minute expressing its hope that "the willingness of the Government of India to use their good offices in the cause of peace" in Korea might be accepted. A copy of this minute was cabled to Chou En-Lai, Foreign Minister of the Chinese Peoples' Republic; Andrei Vyshinsky; Dean Acheson; Anthony Eden; the chief negotiators at Panmunjom; the Prime Ministers of North and South Korea; the Secretary-General of the United Nations and Prime Minister Nehru.

Encouragement was sent to Elmore Jackson and Dr. Frank Graham who, on behalf of the United Nations, were mediating between India and Pakistan over the question of Kashmir.

In the closing sessions, some Friends felt that a message should be sent to all men expressing Friends' shame at their own material comfort and their share in their nations' use of power. Others felt that if Friends had nothing creative to communicate, it would be better to omit the message. Feeling ran high on both sides.

Then something dramatic happened, which those who were present are not likely ever to forget. Barrow Cadbury, the beloved ninety-year-old English Friend, rose in the midst of this debate and offered prayer: "O God, we're in a fix. Please help us out of it."[14]

Silence descended on the vast Town Hall. Its vaulted ceiling and the arches in the high gallery reverberated with thundering stillness. Friends felt drawn into a unity that was beyond all issues save the will of God. In Whittier's words, they were becoming reclothed in their rightful minds.

Out of the silence, clarity slowly emerged. Friends saw that they did have something to say to the world, which encompassed the conviction of the whole body. They formulated this in "A Message to Men Everywhere."

It pleaded for an end to the "vicious circle of hatred, oppression, subversive movements, false propaganda, rearmament, and new wars. . . .

"We call upon peoples everywhere to break this vicious circle, to behave as nations with the same decency as they would behave as men and brothers. . . . Let us join together throughout the world to grow more food, to heal and prevent disease, to conserve and develop the resources of the good earth to the glory of God and the comfort of man's distress. These are among the tasks to which, in humility for our share in the world's shame, and in faith in the power of love, we call our own Society and all men and nations everywhere."[15]

When, at the close of their Third World Conference, Friends moved out of the cloistered Oxford colleges and went back into the world, they carried with them a new dedication.

They had passed beyond "intellectual argument into a place of inner certainty that lies deeper than words and doctrines," Gerald Littleboy, Headmaster of Saffron Walden Friends School, wrote in retrospect. "It was to such a place that we came again and again at Oxford. . . . Here also, Friends from all over the world and from all the traditions of Quakerism came to know a 'one-ness' in the love of God which was a deeper experience than had come to many of us before. . . . Because of this experience, those of us who were there are different people, and that difference has now to be lived as we move among our fellows."[16]

It was interesting that these afterthoughts were almost identical with those of the Young Friends, who held an International Gathering at Reading in advance of the Oxford Conference.

"We came to a conclusion," they reported, "that the most urgent thing we had found was our need to accept each other, as we are, with all our differences. We need to know a great deal more about each other, our national life, many small things that make us personal beings to one another. Then we can begin to understand the ideas we speak about, to learn to know why we are as we are. In the process, each is changed.

"How can Friends come closer together and know each other? This is not just our question but a question for the world. We are left, as a Friend down in Bristol said in Meeting, all our lives to live it out."[17]

30 A Great People to Be Gathered

Young and old came away from the International Gathering and the Friends World Conference tendered by the experience. Some returned directly to their homes. But six hundred Friends from twenty-one countries set out on a pilgrimage to the northwest of England to visit the places associated with the beginnings of the Quaker Movement.

They went with three books in their pockets: *The Journal of George Fox; The Birthplace of Quakerism, A Handbook for the 1652 Country,* by Elfrida Vipont Foulds; and *The Valiant Sixty* by Ernest E. Taylor.

Traveling in busloads along the edge of the Cotswolds, through Warwickshire, Leicestershire, Derbyshire and Cheshire, they came at last to the Lancashire side of the Pennine Chain. During the long journey, they reread Fox's account of his early wanderings, his discourses with local priests and preachers, from whom he vainly sought help.

No present-day Friend who ever tried to counsel a troubled young person could fail to be moved by Fox's pathetic "I saw there was none among them all that could speak to my condition."

Then, in 1647, "When all my hopes in them and all men were gone, so that I had nothing outwardly to help me, nor could tell what to do, I heard a voice which said, 'There is one, even Christ Jesus, that can speak to thy condition' and when I heard it my heart did leap for joy. . . . And this I knew experimentally."[1]

Overnight the world seemed changed. "And all things were new, and all the creation gave another smell unto me than before, beyond what words can utter."[2]

From a troubled, uncertain youth, George Fox became transformed into a man who felt compelled to bring others to their Teacher. In his wanderings he met men and women whom he convinced, but the great sweep that became the Quaker Movement did not begin until 1652, the year he was twenty-eight, when he climbed Pendle Hill.

"I was to bring people off from all the world's religions, which are vain, that they might know the pure religion and might visit the fatherless, the widows and the strangers, and keep themselves from the spots of the world. And then there would not be so many beggars, the sight of which often grieved my heart, to see so much hard-heartedness amongst them that professed the name of Christ.[3]

"And I was to bring people off . . . from men's inventions and windy doctrines, by which they blowed the people about this way and the other way, from sect to sect . . . with their schools and colleges for making ministers of their own making but not of Christ's; and from all their images and crosses, and sprinkling of infants, with all their holy days (so called) and all their vain traditions, which they had gotten up since the apostles' days."[4]

Rereading Fox's *Journal* during their journey to his countryside, the present-day Quakers were struck by the fact that their own concerns were identical with his—care of the poor and the oppressed, the equality of all men and women, moderation, honesty, a religion of experience, and practice of the Golden Rule. As though it had just been written, the seventeenth-century *Journal* spoke to their condition.

At the foot of Pendle Hill, between the little villages of Barley and Downham, far from any visible habitation, these twentieth-century pilgrims stepped down from their buses, breathed in the pure air and lifted their eyes.

"I spied a great high hill called Pendle Hill, and I went on the top of it with much ado, it was so steep; but I was moved of the Lord . . . and when I came atop of it I saw Lancashire sea . . . I was moved to sound the day of the Lord; and the Lord let me see . . . in what places he had a great people to be gathered."[5]

The pilgrims of 1952 began their climb with probably more ado, since many of them were considerably over twenty-eight. They crossed stiles and stone walls, encountering sheep grazing on the fell. They prevailed against the high wind until, breathless, they stood at the top, looking down on an expanse of tilled fields separated by hedgerows. They looked northward to the rugged hills of the Lake District and, like George Fox, westward to the Irish Sea, which was only visible on a very clear day.

This was the place they had heard about all their Quaker lives.

Overhead, clouds of majesty hung in the clear atmosphere. The encircling landscape presented colors which the pilgrims from overseas had only known in British paintings. Awed, clothed in silence, with the wind from the Western world blowing across them, Friends worshiped together on Pendle Hill.

From time immemorial, it had been known as a sinister place, where witches and weavers of evil spells were said to congregate. For Friends, it was purified by the vision of George Fox, turned into a mountaintop of aspiration for generations of pilgrims to climb, more often figuratively than with their feet.

Going down was almost as difficult as going up. The earth was soggy and the narrow path very steep. Many who began by walking took to sliding.

One American pilgrim, Frederick Tolles, indulged in "a brief flight of historical fancy."

"I do not wish to be taken more than half seriously. Still, I wonder whether in this vision from the top of Pendle Hill, Fox could have foreseen another harvest of souls, farther in the future, in fields remote from nothern England, but just as dramatic, just as fateful, and, in the end, vastly more extensive. Could it have been beyond the sea, beyond the Atlantic, in the half-known lands to the west and southwest, that Fox saw 'a great people to be gathered'?

"But whether or not Fox, standing on Pendle Hill that spring day glimpsed the transatlantic world in his mind's eye, it is a fact, and a momentous one, that hardly three years were to pass before adventurous 'publishers of Truth' were going over to possess that land."[6]

When George Fox came down on that May evening, he and his friend Richard Farnsworth spent the night at an alehouse. There he "writ a paper to the priests and professors concerning the day of the Lord and how Christ was come to teach people himself by his power and spirit and to bring them off all the world's ways and teachers to his own free teaching. . . . And the Lord opened to me at that place, and let me see a great people in white raiment by a river's side coming to the Lord. . . .

"And the next day we passed on among the fell countries and at night we got a little ferns or brackens and lay upon a common and the next morning . . . Richard Farnsworth parted with me and I was alone again.

"So I came up Wensleydale; and at the market town . . . I declared the day of the Lord to the priest and people, and bid them repent and take heed of deceitful merchandise . . . and afterward passed up the dales warning people to fear God and declaring his Truth to them. . . . And people took me for a mad man . . . at last I came to a great house where there was a schoolmaster . . . and they had me into a parlor and locked me in and said I was a young man that was mad and was got away from my relations and they would keep me till they could send to my relations. But . . . I convinced them . . . and they let me forth . . . and so [I] passed away and wandered in the night."⁷

Fox hurried on to find the people he had seen in his vision. The astounding thing is that, without knowing it, they were actually waiting for him "by a river's side." This river, the Lune, flowed through Westmorland and Yorkshire. It was there, near Sedbergh, that the people who called themselves Seekers were meeting when George Fox arrived on Whitsunday, the sixth of June.

"This was the place that I had seen a people coming forth in white raiment," Fox declared in the *Journal*.⁸

He had spent the night at the home of Richard Robinson in Brigflatts, a mile from Sedbergh. A Friends Meetinghouse, one of the most beautiful in England, was built at Brigflatts only thirteen years after George Fox's first visit.

The modern pilgrims stood in the garden of Brigflatts Meetinghouse, listening to an account of the grim events which took place in the days when Non-conformist meetings were still forbidden. Inside, they were intrigued with the pen for the sheepdogs, who always came to Meeting with their masters.

After worshiping at Brigflatts, the pilgrims crossed the River Lune and climbed Firbank Fell. Near the summit they came to a rock known locally as Fox's Pulpit, which has a tablet affixed to it telling the story of the Quaker Movement's beginnings.

LET YOUR LIVES SPEAK
HERE OR NEAR THIS ROCK GEORGE FOX PREACHED TO ABOUT ONE THOUSAND SEEKERS FOR THREE HOURS ON SUNDAY, JUNE 13, 1652. GREAT POWER INSPIRED HIS MESSAGE AND THE MEETING PROVED OF FIRST IMPORTANCE IN GATHERING THE SOCIETY OF FRIENDS KNOWN AS QUAKERS. MANY MEN AND WOMEN CONVINCED OF THE TRUTH ON THIS FELL AND IN OTHER PARTS OF THE NORTHERN COUNTIES WENT THROUGH THE LAND AND OVER THE SEAS WITH THE LIVING WORD OF THE LORD ENDURING GREAT HARDSHIPS AND WINNING MULTITUDES TO CHRIST.

In the Preface to the original edition of Fox's *Journal*, published three years after his death, William Penn described the dissatisfaction of these Seekers with the Puritan religion and the Anglican and Presbyterian churches. They had, Penn said, "left all visible churches and societies and wandered up and down, as sheep without a shepherd, and as doves without their mates, seeking their beloved, but could not find Him. . . . These people were called Seekers by some, and the Family of Love by others, because, as they came to the knowledge of one another, they sometimes met . . . waited together in silence, and as anything rose in any one of their minds that they thought savoured of a Divine spring, so they sometimes spoke."

One of those convinced that day on Firbank Fell was John Audland, a linen draper and farmer, who was to carry the message of Fox through the West of England.

Another was Francis Howgill, a tailor and farmer, who later wrote, "Return home to within: sweep your houses all, the groat is there, the little leaven is there, the grain of mustardseed . . . and here you will see your Teacher not removed into a corner but present when you are upon your beds and about your labour."[9] As a publisher of Truth, Francis Howgill would die in Appleby jail.

Before George Fox stood on the rock and "declared freely and largely God's everlasting Truth," these two Seekers had preached to a smaller gathering in Firbank Chapel.

This led Fox to speak his mind regarding church edifices, or steeplehouses, as he called them.

"I was made to open to the people that the steeplehouse and that ground on which it stood were no more holy than that mountain . . . that they might all come to know . . . their bodies to be the temples of God and Christ for them to dwell in."[10]

Within two weeks of his experience atop Pendle Hill, George Fox had convinced Seekers in Westmorland, Lancashire, Cumberland and West Yorkshire. Within two years, sixty or more men and women would travel from there to other parts of England, spreading the Quaker message, although they knew that they were risking their liberty, even their lives. These were "The Valiant Sixty."

They were not educated for this mission; they simply felt called. Most of them were yeomen or husbandmen; some did tailoring, glovemaking and shopkeeping. Two were gentlemen, four schoolmasters, two had been soldiers and three—Mary Fisher, Jane and Dorothy Waugh—were servants.[11]

They burst forth from these fells and dales like people suddenly released from prison—from the bonds of superstition and fear—released by firsthand knowledge of the infinite love of God.

From Firbank Fell, George Fox went home with John Audland. On Wednesday, June 16, they went to Preston Patrick Chapel where the Seekers were meeting again. John Camm, a leading Seeker, invited Fox to sit in the preacher's pew. But Fox refused and sat at the back in silent waiting upon God for about half an hour. John Camm's young son Thomas later recalled that Francis Howgill "seemed uneasy, and pulled out his Bible and opened it, and stood up several times, sitting down again and closing his book."

Finally, George Fox stood up and preached. "It was the day of God's power, a notable day indeed, never to be forgotten by me, Thomas Camm . . . I being then . . . a schoolboy of about twelve years of age."[12]

Those who became Friends that day would soon be tried in Preston Patrick Hall for non-payment of tithes. Beyond the Hall, at the end of a solitary lane, lies Cammsgill, the Camms' farm, where Fox spent the night of June 16, 1652.

Two years later, Camm and Howgill walked to London to declare to Oliver Cromwell "the message of the Lord." But they found him "too high in notion to receive Truth."[13]

To the pilgrims from Pennsylvania, the visit to Preston Patrick and Cammsgill was of special importance, for John Camm took the Quaker message to Oxford. The students received it with hostility, but a shopkeeper named Thomas Loe was convinced. In 1657, Loe went to Ireland to preach. There, on what was also to be a notable day, another boy of about twelve, the son of an admiral, heard Loe and was deeply moved. The boy was William Penn.

Eleven years later, Penn joined Friends. A quarter of a century after he heard Loe preach, Penn boarded the *Welcome,* a square rigged three-master, and set sail from England "for my country" to establish Pennsylvania "that an example may be set up to the nations . . . an Holy Experiment."[14]

At Cammsgill, in the ancient barn, redolent with hay, the pilgrims of 1952 stood together worshiping. Only birdsong and country sounds broke the deep silence. Then the pilgrims journeyed on to Kendal, following by their mid-twentieth-century means of locomotion in the footsteps of George Fox.

Preaching in Kendal during those incredible weeks of 1652, Fox convinced Edward Burrough, then a young man of nineteen. Nine years later, it would be Burrough who, pleading with Charles II, secured an end to the hanging of Friends in New England. Burrough himself died in Newgate Prison at the age of twenty-nine, "a valiant warrior who never turned his back on the Truth."[15]

The Americans were most impressed by Swarthmoor Hall at Ulverston. Isabel Ross, a descendant of Margaret Fell, welcomed the pilgrims. Beautifully restored, Swarthmoor Hall communicates even today that harmony which prevailed there when George Fox arrived, an unknown itinerant preacher. Judge Fell, the lord of the manor, was away. His wife, Margaret, and their children and some of the servants were deeply moved by Fox's preaching.

"I declared the Truth to her and her family,"[16] Fox recalled later.

Margaret Fell became troubled. What would her husband think about her being persuaded of this Truth in his absence?

George Fox left Swarthmoor, returning to Kendal and Sedbergh. A little while later, Richard Farnsworth, his companion before Wensleydale, and James Nayler, the most expressive and tragic of all the Valiant Sixty, arrived at Swarthmoor looking for Fox.

These dramatic events are beautifully described by Elfrida Vipont Foulds in *The Story of Quakerism Through Three Centuries*.

"At last word came from Judge Fell that he was on his way home, and Margaret, rejoicing, sent word to George Fox at Sedbergh to return at once, for she longed to see the two men together and have her peace of mind restored. From Lancaster Judge Fell rode down to the shore of Morecambe Bay and then set out on the last stage of his journey, which lay across the treacherous sands, only to be crossed at low tide. . . . As he neared the shore, he saw to his astonishment a little group riding to meet him. Even at a distance, they looked like the bearers of sad tidings. He spurred his horse . . . The rector and the gentlemen of the neighborhood surrounded him, their faces grave and troubled. His wife, his children, his entire household had been bewitched by a travelling preacher.

"Judge Fell rode home with an anxious mind. This news struck at the very heart of his home life. . . . At Swarthmoor Margaret met him and he saw the trouble in her eyes. She could not face the choice that might lie before her, whether to displease her beloved husband or to be disloyal to the truth. James Nayler and Richard Farnsworth came forward, assuring him that they had come to his house in love and goodwill. They offered to leave at once, but

Margaret begged them to stay. Judge Fell did not gainsay her. . . .

"That evening George Fox returned, and Margaret Fell asked her husband if he might come into the parlour where they were sitting. . . . Little by little Margaret Fell's fears were allayed. Her husband's face lighted as George Fox spoke—'and he spoke very excellently as ever I heard him.' There was something in the atmosphere of that loving home which brought out the very best in George Fox and would always do so; the very thought of it would inspire him and countless others for years to come."

Judge Fell persuaded the rector that "here was no witchcraft, but a faith men might well live by, even if he did not himself wish to embrace it."[17]

He gave Friends leave to meet for worship in the great hall. He did not join them but sat in the parlor opening out of the hall and shared the silence with them there.

"Those weeks," Elfrida Vipont Foulds observed, "began with a vision and culminated in a home; both were essential and neither in itself would have been sufficient."[18] Swarthmoor Hall furnished Friends with a stable focal point while the wayfaring Fox walked cheerfully over the world or languished in prison. This sense of community gave the movement strength. Through Margaret Fell, in those early days before she herself was condemned to the dungeons of Lancaster Castle, Friends heard which of their fellows to visit in prison, which families needed to be cared for. By 1656, books were being sent from Swarthmoor to places like Virginia. Money was collected so that Friends could publish Truth to all the nations under the whole heavens.

When the 1952 pilgrims left Swarthmoor Hall, some of the more adventuresome elected to wait for low tide and walk across the sands of Morecambe Bay to Lancaster in imitation of the early Friends, who had preferred this passage, dangerous though it was, to the long walk over land. But most of the pilgrims were glad to climb back into the buses and revisit the Lake Country.

On their way to Lancaster, they stopped at Yealand Conyers, the home of Elfrida Vipont Foulds, where they visited the seventeenth-century Meetinghouse and the school. This was built in accordance with the wishes of Robert Widders, one of Fox's companions on the journey to America, who left six pounds in his will for the education of children.

"I passed after the meeting to Robert Widders's," Fox noted in

1660, "and Friends all passed away fresh in the life and power of Christ."[19]

How convincingly Fox communicated this life and power, how deeply he was held in affection by his followers we can deduce from a letter Widders wrote while he was in Lancaster jail: "George, sometimes when I think on thee, the power rises and warms my heart. Bonds and fetters (are) ready to burst assunder, for it is not possible that they could hold me."[20]

Fox recalled that a man "whose name is Thomas, set upon six Friends going to a meeting to wait upon the Lord at Yelland. He beat them and abused them with bruising of their faces, and shed much of their blood, and wounded them sore. And they never lifted a hand against him, but gave him their backs and cheeks."

A beautiful clock on the wall of the school commemorates Richard Hubberthorne, also a Yealand man. When George Rofe wrote to him from Barbados about the great Meeting of New England Friends at Newport in 1661, saying, "There is a good Seed and the Seed will arise," Hubberthorne was in London, pleading with the House of Commons as it debated the Quaker Act.

Could Hubberthorne have guessed that this very Act, which, in spite of his efforts, was passed the next year, would lead to his own imprisonment and early death in Newgate? "Dear innocent Richard," Fox said, "as innocent a man as liveth on the earth."

The Quaker Act forbade more than five adults to assemble for worship in one place, but Friends disregarded it. "Our little children kept the meetings up, when we were all in prison, notwithstanding their wicked Justice, when he came and found them there, with a staff that he had with a spear in it."[21]

The 1952 pilgrimage to the 1652 country ended at Lancaster. Friends read in Fox's *Journal*, "I passed from Swarthmoor to Lancaster, and so through many towns, and felt I answered the witness of God in all people, though I spoke not a word."

Lancaster is dominated by the great, grim Castle, perched above the river Lune. It has been estimated that almost every seventeenth-century Friend in the district "spent at least weeks, if not months or years, in its dark and filthy gaols. . . . The Quarterly Meeting kept the prisoners supplied with fuel and candles."[22]

Margaret Fell spent four years as a prisoner in the Castle. As long as Judge Fell lived, she was safe, but after his death, she began to have difficulties. Finally, she was imprisoned for fourteen months and then sentenced under the Statute of Praemunire. This was an ancient law, designed to destroy anyone who would not conform to the ruler's religion, whatever that happened to be. The offender was outlawed and imprisoned indefinitely. His property might be confiscated.

When Margaret Fell heard her sentence, she said, "Although I am out of the King's protection, yet I am not out of the protection of Almighty God."[23]

Even a glance at the dungeons in the Castle was more than the twentieth-century pilgrims could bear. They hurried away to a more attractive place—the Friends School, whose headmaster, James Drummond, had organized the pilgrimage.

In Lancaster Meetinghouse, the visitors reverently recalled John Woolman, who stopped to worship there in 1772. He had attended London Yearly Meeting and was heading for York, traveling as a pilgrim should, on foot. He chose this means of covering the length of England in protest against the merciless speed the newfangled stage coaches demanded of their horses and the neglect of the little postboys who, as overworked as the animals, suffered greatly, he observed, "in long cold winter nights."

As the 1952 pilgrimage came to a close in Lancaster, an American Friend recalled later, "Our thoughts kept going back from the past to the present, venturing forward also into an unknown future. . . . The words . . . inscribed on a tablet on 'Fox's Pulpit' will have to become a new reality for all of us who were in England's Northwest, as well as for Friends at home. They read: 'Let your lives speak.' "[24]

31 A Reaffirmation of Faith

While Friends at Oxford and Reading and in the George Fox country were renewing their perception of the ocean of light and love flowing over the ocean of darkness and death, a young American Friend was making that vision a near reality in Israel. Patricia Hunt directed an International Work Camp. It demonstrated that people of different races, nationalities and faiths can live, worship and work together. Arab, Israeli, European and American Work Campers spent six weeks together, not only peaceably but creatively.

After visiting them, Moses Bailey commented, "One or two persons of prominence predicted that . . . the camp would break up in political argument. As a matter of fact, the results were exceptionally good. The group worked together in harmony . . . friendships were formed across every barrier . . . because the proposal of getting Arabs and Jews together was 'impossible' it was news. . . . Government officials watched it with interest and some came to observe. Finally, on the last day of camp, the Prime Minister invited the whole group to his home for supper and conversation. For many, there was a real sense of fulfillment in all this."

That fall, the Federal Republic of Germany conferred the Order of Merit on Clarence Pickett for his efforts "to fight hunger and hopelessness among the German people in one of its darkest hours. . . . It wishes to honor you and through you the Society of Friends and all those who support it . . . keeping the great humanitarian tradition of America a living reality."

Appointed by President Truman to a commission charged with recommending a policy for American immigration, Clarence Pickett observed the ferment taking place all over the world, "the growing yearning for recognition and equal treatment on the part of the darker races, together with the upsurge of nationalism. . . . These factors are not transient. They will not pass quickly or quietly."

In Washington, D.C., public housing and recreation, the fire department, hotels, theaters, barber shops and restaurants were still completely segregated, although a law passed eighty years earlier prohibited racial discrimination in restaurants.

Davis House on R Street, which had been given to Friends to provide hospitality for visitors from overseas, was one place where foreign diplomats, who could not find accommodation elsewhere because of their color, were welcomed.

There, in 1952, Friends began holding what they called the Washington Seminars. Concerned because the ninety thousand American civilians who represented their country abroad were encountering increasing unfriendliness, Friends invited government officials and specialists in social psychology, current history, international relations and public opinion to come together and exchange information. Congressmen and reporters attended. The participants reached the conclusion that one factor in building good will was the adaptability of government personnel to living conditions abroad. As a result of these seminars, the policy for appointing overseas staff was modified.

The success of the Washington Seminars led Friends to establish the Conferences for Diplomats at Clarens, Switzerland, overlooking Lake Geneva. In this beautiful spot, junior attachés from the embassies in Geneva were invited to spend ten days, getting to know their opposite numbers as people rather than as officials. This was difficult in Geneva, especially for members of delegations unfriendly to each other. Dr. Ralph Bunche and Gilbert White chaired these conferences. The diplomats walked together in the mountains. Unhindered by protocol and completely off the record, they discussed the problems that divided them.

While these young diplomats on the hillside overlooking the Lake of Geneva were taking a step toward reducing international tensions, Russia announced the explosion of a hydrogen bomb. A month later, Nikita Khrushchev became the First Secretary of the Central Committee of the Communist Party and the Japanese Government decided to establish a national defense force.

Fighting had ceased in Korea. Prisoners were exchanged at Panmunjom. At Pusan, a Quaker team began the task of caring for thirty-three thousand refugees, feeding children and pregnant mothers, distributing clothing and teaching the widows the trade which offered Korean women the best prospect of getting a job— barbering.

In Korea, Quaker workers were stuffing cardboard into the walls of bombed houses and keeping the wind out with plastic liners from powdered milk barrels. In Vietnam, Ho Chi Minh was declaring that his government would consider any French proposal which respected the country's independence and French paratroopers were taking Dien Bien Phu, only to surrender it six months later. In

Philadelphia, on June 8, 1954, the American Friends Service Committee issued a public statement urging the United States not to follow the French example of trying to deal with Indochina's problems in military terms. "Nothing but disaster lies down that road," the statement maintained.

Quakers were trying to plug up holes in their national fabric. An old enemy, the loyalty oath, had reappeared. Just as earlier Friends were barred from many professions, so now teachers in some states were out of a job because they believed that swearing does not make a more dedicated and dependable citizen. California's Levering Act required each church and other tax-exempt organization to file a declaration that it "does not advocate the overthrow of the Government of the United States or of the State of California by force or violence . . ." Rather than sign a loyalty oath, Pacific Yearly Meeting Friends forfeited their tax exemption. "We affirm our unchanging conviction that our first allegiance is to God," the Friends Meeting of Berkeley wrote to the city assessor. "And if this conflicts with any compulsion of the State, we serve our country best by remaining true to our higher loyalty."

Senator Joseph McCarthy's activities were threatening the very heart of democracy. Friends issued A Reaffirmation of Faith: "It is our deep concern to help make clear that current attacks on civil liberties strike at the roots of both American political philosophy and Friends' basic concept of man's relationship to God. . . . We join with others who have defended and increased the areas of freedom. We will support with new vigor those ways which dignify and ennoble the individual."

In 1954, "those ways which dignify and ennoble the individual" took joyous form in *The Quiet Eye: A Way of Looking at Pictures*. In this book, Sylvia Shaw Judson, a Quaker sculptor living in Lake Forest, Illinois, collected photographs of works by her favorite artists and matched them with lines by her favorite writers: Henri Rousseau with George Fox, Dürer with Woolman, Edward Hicks with William Blake, Duccio, the Sienese painter, with Whittier, Seurat with Chaucer—demonstrating the timeless and spaceless and all-encompassing nature of Truth.

"Much of the art of our own time is an art of symbol . . ." Sylvia Judson wrote in the Introduction. "I suppose that one reason for this is discouragement with ourselves as human beings, due to the current confusion and distress in the world, or a sense of our unimportance in the face of the incredible extension of our natural horizons. It is also a yearning to speak a universal language . . . but we remain human beings just the same, and living subjects still hold warmth and immediacy for us."

The first picture shows part of a Quaker Meetinghouse bench —simple, clean-cut, carefully crafted. It accompanies a passage from Philadelphia Yearly Meeting's *Book of Discipline:* "True simplicity consists not in the use of particular forms, but in foregoing overindulgence, in maintaining humility of spirit, and in keeping the material surroundings of our lives directly serviceable to necessary ends, even though these surroundings may properly be characterized by grace, symmetry, and beauty."

That Quaker concern for the brotherhood of man might have unexpectedly negative as well as good effects was foreseen by Clarence Pickett. "One has the feeling that, as Whittier's antislavery efforts seemed to help precipitate the war over slavery, so now Quakers' belief in the inherent worth of men in the sight of God, regardless of color, status, or creed, may seem to give some support to disruptive forces."

Early in 1950, David H. Scull, a white Quaker from Annandale, Virginia, who was employed in the U. S. Department of State, had entered Thompson's Restaurant on 14th Street in the District with three Blacks. They were refused service. Suit was brought against the restaurant. After a series of appeals in which the decision went first one way and then the other, the Supreme Court upheld the law of 1872, which prohibited racial discrimination in restaurants. This was the first legal success in the long battle to overcome segregation in the national capital.

Following the 1954 Supreme Court decision on school desegregation, a committee of the Virginia Legislature toured the state looking for those who were responsible for stirring up their colored people. David Scull, who had meanwhile become owner of a printing business, was subpoenaed by the committee. Because he refused to answer questions regarding his membership in interracial organizations and the support he had given to court cases on the ground that this was an unwarranted invasion of privacy, designed to harass people who were trying to advance civil rights, he was fined and sentenced to jail for contempt of court. The case was appealed. In Scull vs. Virginia, the U. S. Supreme Court unanimously reversed the lower court decision.

Friends recognized that there was need not only for legislation, but for a revision of personal attitudes. Hoping that school segregation would soon be judged illegal, the Service Committee initiated a program in 1951 that was designed to facilitate the changeover.

An interracial team set up a fact-finding center in Washington. The members conferred with school and recreation officials and met with community groups throughout the District. Two years before the Supreme Court's desegregation decision, seminars on school integration were offered to interested educators. One hundred and eighty-two of the teachers, principals and administrators who eventually integrated the District of Columbia school system had participated in the Quaker seminars.

"This is the first time we have sat down together to talk about this," a principal said, when the seminars began. And at the last one, a young teacher exclaimed, "I'm ready now; I hope they don't wait until I'm unready."[1]

After the Supreme Court decision, the Quaker Community Relations Program was even busier.

"Newly integrated P.T.A.s want help in program planning," Irene Osborne, one of the Quaker workers, reported. "Church and civic groups ask for speakers to evaluate the process. The liberals in the segregated Citizens Association (white) and Civic Association (Negro) wonder how they can achieve integration. Worried citizens call to check on rumors (most of them silly). . . .

"We've distributed 12,000 copies of our pamphlet *Integration of Washington Schools*. . . . More and more we receive requests for help from the South. How was it done in Washington and how has it worked out? A Southern farmer writes, 'We are isolated here and have no help. Can you send us all the material you have?' Citizens in Knoxville sent an SOS for help in taking the lead there. The Virginia and Maryland counties near D.C. are intensely interested; P.T.A.s ask for speakers, citizens committees seek advice, and schools want help in training teachers. . . .

"Just ahead is the period when real integration and a meaningful program of democratic education can be achieved."[2]

In 1955, the program was evaluated in a report, "Toward the Elimination of Segregation in the Nation's Capital, 1951–1955." The report concluded that "this specialized resource was helpful primarily because it helped the community to find its own resources. It is important to ask ourselves how Quaker thinking has related to the program. To what extent is a religious philosophy meaningful as a basis for a social action program?

"We found, first, that it was of the utmost importance that the case against segregation should be posed in moral terms. There is usually no lack of those who will oppose segregation as uneconomical, wasteful, inefficient, and educationally unsound. It is too seldom said that segregation is wrong, doing harm to those who segregate as well as to those who are segregated. . . . We have found much strength from the Quaker belief in the power of love. At every step, we have found that we needed to believe in human beings, to speak to the best in them, to give the best of ourselves in response. . . . We have tried to be genuine and to put our case plainly, following the Quaker ideal of living 'where the heart stands in perfect sincerity.'"

But there was a strange contradiction. Sidwell Friends School, located right in Washington, remained segregated until the fall of 1956 when it admitted "a limited number of qualified Negro students" to its kindergarten.

With all this laudable concern for the integration of other people's schools, how was it possible that Friends lagged in their own? In 1934, only two or three of all the Friends schools in the United States enrolled Black students. By 1945, eight of the seventeen secondary schools reported a token number.[8] In New York, New England and Pennsylvania, where the public schools were open to all, there were still all-white Friends schools as late as 1955.

And why beholdest thou the mote that is in thy brother's eye, but considerest not the beam that is in thine own eye?

The historic basis for Friends' tardiness in integrating their schools was not, to their way of thinking, race prejudice. During the nineteenth century, when Friends believed that the only way they could maintain their faith was to withdraw from the world, they looked on their schools as nurseries of Truth in which their young would be imbued with all the Quaker virtues and guarded from the evils outside. Obviously, the only way to attain this purity was by excluding all who were not Friends.

Academic excellence was then a secondary consideration. But as time went on, the educational standards rose. Not all Quaker children were able to meet the higher standards. Those who could not were obliged to go elsewhere. There was also a growing reluctance on the part of many concerned Quakers to set their children apart from others in the community. They considered it their duty to improve the public schools by sending their children to them and by contributing their support to Parent-Teachers Associations.

At the same time, some people who were not Friends felt eager to send their children to Quaker schools where gentleness and gentility prevailed.

As the emphasis shifted from a guarded to a good education, intellectual ability became the requirement for admission. The optimum was membership in the Society of Friends and intellectual keenness rolled into one little person.

In some of the secondary schools the pressure to get students into the best colleges soon overshadowed the fact that it takes more than a bevy of brains to create a Quaker atmosphere. As teachers and children of other faiths entered the schools, the Meeting for Worship gradually ceased to be central. In some, it disappeared altogether in favor of a non-denominational assembly supplemented, perhaps, by a few moments of silence.

Gentleness and gentility still prevailed as well as devotion to the individual child's needs. No one thought there was any discrimination. Jewish and Italian children, who were rejected by many other private schools, were accepted, scholarship aid was found for the children of refugees, Orientals were welcomed and some Blacks.

Like other independent schools, those owned by the Friends were always in need of money. The plainness which had sufficed for a guarded education was not geared to the twentieth century. Schools needed laboratories now and swimming pools. It was not right to underpay teachers and staff.

Parents and alumni who were not Friends came to the rescue. Their loyalty and generosity knew no bounds. But they also had ideas about the way the schools should be run, and these did not always coincide with the peculiar traditions of Friends.

Trustees and heads of schools tried to accommodate to the non-Friends. Judged by community standards, none of the changes were unreasonable. They were simply not Quakerly.

Friends schools prospered. Their graduates got into the best colleges and the graduates of Quaker colleges got into the best jobs. But somehow, in the squeeze and anxiety, all but a handful of Black students were left out.

Not every Quaker educator, preoccupied with inadequate faculty salaries and College Board scores, could preserve the wide vision of Rufus Jones, who said in an address at Moses Brown School in 1942, "However important it is to make a living, it is even more important to make a life."

A REAFFIRMATION OF FAITH

In 1940, the two Philadelphia Yearly Meetings between them had only one Black member and no Black children in their schools.[4]

In 1949, the two Yearly Meetings issued A Statement on Segregation. "As a religious society ... we are deeply concerned with the patterns of segregation that have developed in our communities, and with the suffering, the waste of talents, the antagonisms, the blocks to spiritual and cultural growth which they involve. . . . Even as earlier Friends set themselves to eliminate slavery from their membership, we in our generation set ourselves to overcome the evils of segregation."

By 1952, the Philadelphia Yearly Meetings had a dozen Black members. Forty Black children were enrolled in their schools.[5]

But one or two of the schools, worried about making ends meet and realizing that integration would reduce enrollment, were slow to comply with their Yearly Meeting's clear directive.

When the elders floundered, the children, untroubled by social custom or ways and means, went straight to the heart of the matter. At the 1952 sessions of Philadelphia Yearly Meeting (Hicksite) the students from George School, which is under the care of the Yearly Meeting, expressed their concern for the inclusion of Blacks in the student body so forcefully that those who were obstructing integration yielded.

By 1956, the schools under the care of Philadelphia Yearly Meeting had 106 Black pupils and eight teachers or staff members.

Friends south of the Mason-Dixon line were severely put to the test.

Bliss Forbush, Headmaster of Baltimore Friends School, explaining the situation there, confessed that the "Monthly Meeting, which holds the School property and funds in trust for educational purposes, has been opposed to integration. Many statements have been presented to the business session advocating sympathetic attention to the needs of Negroes, but it was minuted in 1950 that the Meeting had not welcomed members of the Negro race to the First-day school, into Quaker membership, or as partners in the institutions controlled by the organization. It was confessed that much education needed to be done before Negroes would be welcomed into Meeting membership; none has yet applied. The Educational Committee represents a cross section of Meeting feeling, and as late as 1945, when the School first appointed a committee to study the subject, 8 of the 12 members were opposed to integration."[6]

In 1951, Baltimore Yearly Meeting still would not go on record in favor of integration. By 1955, the question precipitated acute tension. Unity was mandatory before any action could be taken. If only one weighty member voiced opposition, a minute favoring integration could not be approved. The Quaker business method, which was intended to draw Friends together in harmonious obedience to the will of God, suddenly prevented them from doing what they knew in their hearts to be right.

In clear terms, Bliss Forbush explained the dilemma. With local variations, it was the same as the situation in every other Quaker school and most of the colleges.

"There is a larger number of children of alumni in Baltimore Friends than in any American Quaker school—109. Children of the third and fourth generation are enrolled. Although these alumni are intensely loyal to the School, they retain the Southern opinion on racial matters held by other Marylanders. Their children and their support are coveted by those in charge of the School. Baltimore Friends was one of the first Quaker schools to write a strict tenure clause into its teachers' contracts. As private conversations indicated that a change in admission policy might mean a large withdrawal of students, the Committee faced a second ethical problem: Should the teachers, a majority of whom were not Friends, be asked to pay by a salary cut for a change in policy made by the Committee?"

This time there still was not unanimity.

"After a full discussion, it was found that one quarter of the members of the Educational Committee (a body which rotates, with appointments for a three-year term, and thus accurately represents the Monthly Meeting) were opposed to the move suggested and desired postponement of any action for a minimum of three or five years."

But this time there was unity.

"Discussion continuing, the four members who did not believe in action at the present time courteously declared they would not stand in the way of the majority, and the minute was approved."

The Educational Committee in charge of Baltimore Friends School agreed "to open the Nursery School and Kindergarten to Negro children as of September 1955, and to open the first grade to them in 1956, and succeeding grades of the School one grade at a time each year thereafter. . . .

"The Baltimore Monthly Meeting has expressed its approval of the change by authorizing the Trustees to borrow money for the School if necessary to meet a temporary condition that may jeopardize the salaries of faculty members with tenure of office caused by reduced enrollment resulting from this change of policy."[7]

All over the country, Friends schools sought Black students. Southern Meetings expressed support for integration in their public schools. The Friends Meeting of Austin, concerned over the efforts of certain Texas communities to thwart school integration, announced, "While recognizing the many problems it has created, we believe that the Supreme Court decision calling for an end of segregation in our public schools is right and just, and we believe all differences of opinion as to how this should be achieved must be resolved in a spirit of love and Christian forbearance. We deplore the apathy of those who would remain silent in the present situation as giving their tacit approval to the forces of evil which reflect on the dignity of the state and its citizens."[8]

Friends could not wait to set the record straight, to make up for past wrongs. But many realized that it was not enough to do the right thing in regard to the Blacks. While energetically pursuing integration, they must also have a concern for white people whose lifelong training had conditioned them to segregation, who could not easily accept sudden change. This was a delicate undertaking, calling for patience and humility on the part of Friends. Those who felt that their fellow members and their communities were not moving fast enough did well to look back at their own history.

How was it possible that a century and a quarter had gone by since Prudence Crandall attempted to admit just one "little miss of color" to her fashionable Female Seminary in Canterbury, Connecticut? Had Friends followed her example during the intervening years?

A whole century and a quarter!

"There is a politics of time, but there is also a politics of eternity that man would ignore, but cannot. He plays with the politics of time, sees it, manipulates it, imagines it is of himself alone; but both the politics of time and of eternity are of God. . . .

"The politics of eternity works not by might but by spirit . . . the divine command to love all men. Such love is worlds apart from the expedient of loving those who love us, of doing good to those who have done good to us. It is the essence of such love that it does not require an advance guarantee that it will succeed, will prove easy or cheap, or that it will be met with swift answering love. Whether practiced by men or nations, it well may encounter opposition, hate, humiliation, utter defeat . . . It is a principle deeply grounded in the years of Quaker sufferings. . . .

"As individuals and as a nation we must literally turn about. We must turn not only from our use of mass violence but from what is worse, our readiness to use this violence whenever it suits our purpose, regardless of the pain it inflicts on others. We must turn about.

"The race is on; it may be almost run . . . The more we cling to security the less secure we feel; the more we cling to armaments and economic privilege the more frightened we become. How shall man be released from his besetting fears, and from his prevailing sense of futility?"[1]

To this question, the Quaker pamphlet *Speak Truth to Power, A Study of International Conflict* addressed itself in the spring of 1955.

"Quaker experience in the past three centuries will indicate one basis for our optimism about the practical nature of seemingly impractical concepts," the authors declared, citing as examples the humane treatment of prisoners and the mentally ill, in which 18th and 19th Century Friends pioneered, although such treatment was considered preposterous by their contemporaries. As for slavery— would that the program suggested by those Friends had been adopted!

"Believing in justice for oppressed and oppressor alike, they called for emancipation, but for remuneration of the slaveholder for his losses, where hardship would be involved. This part of the Quaker program was ignored by the more impulsive men who finally took over the abolition movement in America and the consequences were tragic. Perhaps if justice to slaveholders had been realized, and pacific methods followed, the bitterness that erupted in civil war and endured for a century, might have been avoided. . . .

"The work of Lucretia Mott in the struggle for women's rights; the concern of the more conscientious Eighteenth Century Quaker iron-masters for the protection of workers in an industrialized society, the well-known efforts of Penn for justice to the Indians— all these provided further examples of non-violence being turned to practical account. . . . We are, of course, aware that Quakers have failed . . . in many areas of life. . . . But we are convinced that our failures are due to our own unreadiness to live boldly by the faith we hold, rather than to any irrelevance or inadequacy of the faith itself."[2]

This call to "live boldly" by faith in the non-violent process seemed about to be answered at San Francisco late in June when the United Nations celebrated the tenth anniversary of the signing of its Charter.

After a period of "silent prayer or meditation," President Eisenhower declared that the armaments race was not leading to peace but to terror and pledged the United States to work to replace the clash of the battlefield with peaceful and reasonable negotiations.

"We shall reject no method, however novel, that holds out any hope however faint, for a just and lasting peace," he said.

While this celebration was proceeding in San Francisco, six American Friends deplaned in Leningrad. The American Quaker hope of a visit to the Soviet Union was at last realized.

"We intended to seek out worshipers of God, to bring them greetings and encouragement," the delegates explained upon their return. "We hoped that our journey might serve as a symbol to the Russians of the good-will and desire for peace that we believe to be deeply rooted in the hearts of Americans . . . we were conscious of our obligation to make the journey not only with open minds and open hearts but also with open eyes."[3]

During their month-long stay, the Friends covered twelve thousand miles, from Leningrad to the border of China. They were able to travel with few restrictions, although they could not go to all the places they had hoped to see. They visited in private homes, on collective farms and in factories. Russians had their opinion of the McCarthy hearings and American comics. They also had a great deal of misinformation about American life.

"The average Soviet citizen . . . fears the United States . . . pictured to him as the center of reactionary capitalism whose ruling circles insist on imposing military bases and German rearmament on an unwilling world.[4]

"Nowhere did we find anybody—whether a Party member or not—whose attitude toward his own government revealed even a trace of that sense of personal responsibility for making his voice heard on issues of policy which we consider to be a part of the very essence of democracy."[5]

Wherever they went, the Friends attended Baptist and Russian Orthodox Church services, delivering through William Edgerton, the one delegate who spoke Russian, the good wishes of Friends at home. In Kiev, they made contact with the Old-Believers, a sect of twenty-two million members.

Friends visited the synagogues in Kiev and Moscow. The rabbis assured them that Jews were enjoying religious toleration. This did not square with what the delegation understood to be the fact and seemed to indicate fear of the government as well as mistrust of strangers.

"Obviously the synagogue committee had been nonplussed by this sudden appearance of foreign Christians professing an interest in the situation of the Jews in Kiev. As we left the room after our interview, one of the Jews . . . asked, 'Did I understand you to say that you really aren't Jews at all?'"[6]

Before leaving Russia, the delegation called on Andrei A. Gromyko, Acting Foreign Minister, and presented to him a memorandum on disarmament drawn up by the Quaker United Nations Program in New York. It suggested a way out of the impasse over the question of arms inspection, which the West insisted upon and Russia would not accept. Friends proposed that the International Labor Office be authorized to inspect and report violations to the UN. The memorandum stressed that "an element of faith" was needed. Mr. Gromyko promised to study the proposal sympathetically.

"There is," the delegates observed, when they reached home, "an important injunction to feed our enemies if they are hungry.

Sometimes to sit with those who are styled enemies and eat their bread with them also develops a new attitude on both sides."[7]

While Friends were fostering international good will and racial harmony, a different kind of rapprochement was taking place in Philadelphia. Although it involved members of the same religion and race who lived side by side and whose spiritual forerunners constituted a single body, just as much openness was needed to achieve it.

In 1911, two young Friends, Henry J. Cadbury and Samuel J. Bunting, Jr., decided to invite ten others, Orthodox Friends from Arch Street and Hicksites from Race Street, to join them in studying the Great Separation of 1827. Every week these Friends met and read accounts, diaries and Meeting minutes of that period. Their hope may have been that with better understanding of the causes of separation they might effect a reunion of the two Yearly Meetings. It was eventually achieved, but not for another forty-four years. During that period, members of both Yearly Meetings worked together amicably on the Service Committee, the Friends World Committee, in the Young Friends Movement, at Pendle Hill and for the Friends Council on Education. In 1930, the Clerk of the Education Committee of the Orthodox Yearly Meeting was Morris Leeds and the Clerk of the Education Committee of the Hicksite Yearly Meeting was his wife, Hadassah Moore Leeds. It seemed to this couple highly desirable that they join forces. The result was the Friends Council on Education, which later served schools in other Yearly Meetings. It became a clearinghouse for teacher placement and exchange of views and it encouraged the religious influence in the Quaker schools.

But the Philadelphia Yearly Meetings came no closer to reunion. In 1952, one of the last "plain" Friends, William Bacon Evans, observed with his usual gentle wit, "Friends should move carefully, but I don't think waiting 125 years is moving too fast."

A committee worked for a number of years to produce a book of *Faith and Practice* which, it was hoped, would be acceptable to both branches. This was a difficult task since the differences were doctrinal. They had to do with the Light Within versus the Bible as the revelation of God and with the place of Jesus in human history. At last, a version was produced that satisfactorily overcame all objections. Friends felt comfortable with it and were now ready to move toward complete reunion.

On March 26, 1955, each Philadelphia Yearly Meeting met in its own Meetinghouse. Each adopted a minute that terminated the 128-year separation.

At Arch Street, the Meeting was deeply exercised as it framed the final minute: "Let no one of us be satisfied with any verbal statement; no words can express the infinite love of God to us. . . . Together we follow Jesus, and we are not afraid, humbly aware that we are engaged in a spiritual pilgrimage. . . .

"The Meeting united in approving the full and complete union or merger of this Yearly Meeting . . . (Arch Street), with the Philadelphia Yearly Meeting of Friends (Race Street). . . ."[8]

At Race Street a similar minute was adopted, recording that "The working out of details and certain adjustments of habit will call for tenderness and grace and constant awareness of the leadership of Jesus Christ."[9]

Both minutes closed with the same words: "We give thanks for the sense that our Heavenly Father has spoken to us that we go forward, and we rejoice that together, with diversities of gifts but the same Spirit, we are called to the service of God who is Love."[10]

To the many expressions of thanksgiving from the body of the Meeting, which followed the adoption of these minutes in each Meetinghouse, a note of gaiety was added at Race Street when "one member related that he had united with an Arch Street Friend five years ago to the day, and having never regretted the step, he surmised that the Yearly Meeting could now look forward to similar bliss."[11]

On the morning of March 28, more than eleven hundred Friends assembled in the Arch Street Meetinghouse for the first session of the reunited Yearly Meeting. It was an occasion for deep rejoicing.

Another consolidation was announced at that session. The periodicals published by each of the former Yearly Meetings—*The Friend*, edited by Richard R. Wood, and the *Friends Intelligencer*, edited by William Hubben—were to be merged and called the *Friends Journal*. William Hubben was appointed editor.

"For more than a century each of these publications has been a source of enlightenment, of inspiration, and of fellowship," the Board of Directors said, in making the announcement. "It is inevitable that many of our readers should feel regret. . . . But it is characteristic of Quakers to look forward rather than back. . . . It is a beginning, not an ending."[12] In the new *Friends Journal*, the historic Quaker custom of referring to the months of the year by number was to be dropped in favor of the names in general use—pagan deities and all. Philadelphia Friends were really going modern!

Disturbed by pressure exerted on President Eisenhower to use military force in the Far East, the Yearly Meeting directed the clerks to send him a telegram urging that he continue to resist this pressure.

Every Monthly Meeting was asked to welcome Blacks into membership and warm fellowship. Institutions under the care of Meetings were directed to treat everyone equally. Hope was expressed that individual Friends would accept all their brothers as neighbors, as equals in work relationships, in community activities, organizations and facilities.

"We have been challenged to a wider outreach and a clearer vision of God's will," the Epistle to Friends Everywhere declared.

That summer, another long-desired reunion took place at Silver Bay on Lake George in the Adirondack Mountains. After years of joint effort and setback, the two New York Yearly Meetings finally became one again. Doctrinal differences still existed, but Friends no longer felt that diversity of belief prevented them from worshiping and working together harmoniously.

"We already feel more at home in our united Yearly Meeting than we have felt for many years in our separate organizations," they declared at Silver Bay, "because we know this union is God's will."[13]

A visiting Friend, George Walton of Philadelphia Yearly Meeting, one of the "Three Wise Men," said, referring to the spirit of unity, "Dear Friends, you cannot make it, but when it is given, you can manifest it."[14]

Thomas Lung'aho brought messages from Friends in Kenya, using their greeting word *Mirembe,*—peace!

The reunited Yearly Meeting wrote to Governor Averell Harriman of New York, expressing deep concern over the rapid increase in juvenile delinquency. Friends also addressed a letter to Shinzo Hamai, Mayor of Hiroshima, Japan, expressing regret that they had not been able to send a representative to the World Conference Against Atomic and Hydrogen Weapons. "We hope," they wrote, "that as your conference shares in meditation and discussion you may find a deep faith and conviction in the conquering power of love and good will to change the spirits of men."

The Yearly Meeting sent two Epistles. The one To Friends at

Home read: "We rejoice that we can bring a special message to you this year. It happened! We are united into one Yearly Meeting!! We want to share with you how deeply we are moved by this event. . . . Of course we have our differences. But now we know that they may serve the richness of God's vast purposes, if we offer them humbly and in the spirit of prayer."

To Friends Everywhere they wrote: "We seek to recapture . . . such love as will resist evil without violence, without hatred of the wrongdoer, and without compromise. . . . To the lonely seekers in this hurried and soul-hiding world, we would say, 'Dear friends, we are walking beside you . . . seekers, too.' "[15]

Now and Then, the Quaker Janus, looked back as well as forward. "More than 25 centuries ago the prophet Ezekiel, living in exile, combined two forecasts regarding his shattered people. One is the familiar vision of the valley of dry bones, of which he prophesied that breath would come from God and the bones would live. The other has to do with the division of the nation into two nations ever since the death of Solomon over 300 years before. The prophet was told to take a stick and write upon it 'Judah and the tribes associated with him' and another stick and write upon it 'Joseph, i.e., Ephraim, and the tribes associated with him' and to join the two together that they might become one in his hand. This action is symbolic of the union which God Himself promised the prophet He would bring about between the long sundered segments of the Hebrew people, 'and they shall be no more two nations, neither shall they be divided into two kingdoms any more at all . . . so shall they be my people and I will be their God.'

"Whether reunion is the result of new life or whether the new life is the result of reunion," Now and Then reflected, "the 37th chapter of Ezekiel does not say, but it combines them both. This makes a happy omen."[16]

The Quaker faith in the power of love was severely tested on the morning of January 9, 1956, when Jordanian rioters destroyed the American Friends Service Committee village development project thirty-five miles from Amman. The project had been designed to help Jordanians cultivate their soil and improve health conditions. Paul Johnson and his wife, Jean, who were in charge, were rescued by local police before the arrival of the mob. There was every reason to believe that this was not an attack on Friends but part of the general anti-Western animosity. Nevertheless, the damage was so extensive and the political situation so unsettled that the Service Committee Board questioned the wisdom of rebuilding.

In April, Paul Johnson and Elmore Jackson conferred with government officials in Jordan and Lebanon, who urged Friends to continue serving in their countries. While this request was heartening, Elmore Jackson warned Friends that "religious and educational leadership from outside the area is likely to be less and less welcome in positions of supervisory responsibility. Are we prepared, then, to train and give increasing responsibility to nationals from the countries in which we work? Are we willing to carry this to the point where ultimate control of our projects or educationl institutions rests with those whose national loyalties lie in the Middle East?

"If Quakers are to work successfully in an area which knows so little of Quaker belief, we must, I believe, maintain a continual 'mission of interpretation' to those carrying political responsibility in the area. Otherwise, our projects will be jeopardized by the shifting fortunes of political leadership. Quakers have, I believe, a special opportunity in this region to test out our fundamental conviction that the life of the spirit can heal and unite, that it can release life instead of embittering it. . . ."[17]

At the same time, three Friends appointed by Philadelphia Yearly Meeting arrived in Montgomery, Alabama, carrying "a message of love and good will" to all the inhabitants of that city.

Before coming, they had telephoned to the Mayor and the Reverend Martin Luther King, Jr., both of whom signified their willingness to meet with these Quaker representatives.

"We are aware that there is no simple, easy answer to the problems with which you are faced," the message which Friends brought to Montgomery read. "We come in humility, to learn as much as we can from both sides, and to give support and encouragement to the creative potentialities we believe exist in both groups toward bringing about a solution which does not compromise basic human dignity."[18]

Four months earlier, Mrs. Rosa Parks had refused to give up her seat on a Montgomery bus and move to the rear.

"For a white person to take the seat I would have had to stand. I had been working all day on the job. I was quite tired. . . ."[19]

The bus driver called a policeman. Mrs. Parks was arrested and jailed. Later she was released on a $100 bond and brought to trial on December 5. The day of the trial, forty-two thousand men and women walked to work, beginning a year-long boycott of the city transportation system. Alabama's anti-boycott law was invoked. Mrs. Parks, Mr. E. D. Nixon, who organized the boycott, the Reverend Martin Luther King, Jr., and ninety other Black pastors were jailed.

The Friends who went to Montgomery assured everyone that they did not go with the hope of negotiating a settlement of the bus situation but "with the hope that we might express Friends' concern that the controversy should be non-violent and that those belonging to each side should be led to a deeper search for their responsibility in the light of their religious faith."[20]

By the time these Friends arrived, segregation in buses had already ceased to be the central issue. The Blacks' real aim was full citizen rights—school integration and voting privileges.

The visiting Friends were impressed by the as yet little-known President of the Montgomery Improvement Association, the Reverend Martin Luther King, Jr., "an able, quiet man, 27 years of age, who inspires confidence."[21]

As these Friends met with leaders of each group, they did their best to "speak the truth in love at all times."[22]

A few weeks later, at the summer solstice, 1956, New England Yearly Meeting, holding its 296th session in Auburndale, Massachusetts, sent a letter of "prayerful support to the non-violent resistance movement . . . in Alabama" and to the Roman Catholic Archibishops of New England and Louisiana, expressing "sympathetic accord with the forthright stand of their Church against racial discrimination."[23]

During this Yearly Meeting session, New England Friends learned that Sylvia Shaw Judson had been selected by the Boston Fine Arts Commission to make the statue of Mary Dyer for which Zenos Ellis had left a bequest.

A handsome residence at 6 Chestnut Street, close to the State House, was being given to New England Friends by John Greene, a friend of Friends. The Yearly Meeting authorized a Board of Directors, appointed by the Quarterly Meetings, to establish a residential and educational center there and to name it Beacon Hill Friends House.

The Yearly Meeting listened to the troubled Epistle addressed by its Young Friends to Young Friends Everywhere.

"Those of us who believe that it is wrong to kill need the support of others in our convictions . . .

"We are concerned also about how we are going to make a living which will be consistent with our Friends testimonies. We would like to know if all our years spent in school are preparing us for this occupation. . . ."

Connecticut Valley Quarterly Meeting brought forward a concern that New England Yearly Meeting, already part of the Five Years Meeting, affiliate also with the Friends General Conference, looking to the eventual unity of all Friends.

Then, over one hundred members of the Yearly Meeting, young and old, commemorated the arrival of Friends in America by reverently re-enacting some events that took place in New England during the past three hundred years. Entitled *The Business of Our Lives*, this presentation was quickly nicknamed *The Quakerama*.

In the production, Mary Fisher and Ann Austin disembarked from the *Swallow*; William Robinson, Marmaduke Stephenson and Mary Dyer were led to their execution; Samuel Shattuck returned to Boston with the King's Missive. George Rofe and his companions paddled up from the Chesapeake to Narragansett Bay in their fourteen-foot canoe to call the first Yearly Meeting of Friends in New England, and George Fox arrived eleven years later. John Woolman gently labored with the last Quaker slaveholders and Prudence Crandall opened her school to "young ladies and misses of color." Most fittingly, her part was played by Helen Griffith, whose mantle had fallen in 1955 on the shoulders of a Black educator.

Joseph John Gurney and John Wilbur, played by his great-grandson Henry Foster, argued on stage over the issues that led to the Separation of 1845, which seemed dated and inconsequential to the audience of 1956.

GURNEY: The divine origins of Holy Writ are unquestionable.
WILBUR: But the inspiration of the Holy Spirit has not ceased. Life comes to us not from the record itself, but from communion with Him of whom the record tells.
GURNEY: The perfection of religion on an evangelical foundation—
WILBUR: The old inheritance must be guarded.
LITTLE CHILD OF 1956, speaking from the audience: Why don't you two make up?
(Wilbur and Gurney refuse to yield.)

BOY OF 1956: Well, if you knew our parents like we know them, you'd stop this kind of talk. They'll never stand for it. Keep it up, if you want to. Argue, let your children argue. Keep it up a hundred years, even. But when our parents come along—

Events in 1863 were recalled. Ethan Foster and Charles Perry—played by the latter's grandsons, Thomas and Harvey Perry—pleaded with President Lincoln on behalf of the Conscientious Objectors who were in prison.

John Greenleaf Whittier was seen next, worshiping in his Meeting at Amesbury, Massachusetts, and composing a poem on the occasion of the Emancipation Proclamation. Two years later, the poet was bidding farewell to Eli and Sybil Jones as they embarked for the Holy Land.

Young Rufus Jones, declaiming in genuine Maine accents, appeared on stage wearing the Prince Albert coat which signified, in 1881, that he had become a college man. And finally, the spiritual descendants of the Friends who had separated in 1845 joyfully reunited New England Yearly Meeting a century later.

Then Wilbur and Gurney reappeared. The children in the audience went on stage, joined hands and encircled them, singing Whittier's

> Dear Lord and Father of mankind,
>   Forgive our foolish ways!
> Reclothe us in our rightful mind,
> In purer lives Thy service find,
>   In deeper reverence, praise.
>
> Drop Thy still dews of quietness,
>   Till all our strivings cease;
> Take from our souls the strain and stress,
> And let our ordered lives confess
>   The beauty of Thy peace.

Wilbur and Gurney reached out to each other tentatively. Finally, they shook hands, beaming. When last seen, they had come down from the stage and were following the Little Child, walking arm in arm through the audience, out into the world, with the happy children scampering after them.

"Friends, these are our peacemakers and publishers of Truth, remembered in our hearts and minutebooks, recorded by history for their courage and concern," the narrator declared at the end.

"But let us not forget the thousands whose names have slipped from sight, the ordinary men and women who lived out their Quaker testimonies in their fields and their kitchens, on roadsides and vessels, in town meetings and country schoolhouses, in federal penitentiaries and Civilian Public Service Camps, wherever it was that the Inner Light impelled them to state their belief. They are our heroes too, as brave and serviceable an example to us in our own time as the ones who hung as a flag.

"It is in such humble roles as theirs that most of us are called out to bear witness to that of God in every one. And this we take to be the business of our lives."

33 The "Golden Rule" and the "Phoenix"

Just three hundred years after the little coastwise vessel *Woodhouse* crossed the Atlantic, the thirty-foot ketch *Golden Rule* prepared to sail from San Pedro, California, bound for the Marshall Islands in spite of the fact that the United States had scheduled nuclear weapons tests in the area and mariners were warned to stay away.

Some months earlier in Philadelphia, a small committee had been formed, half of whose members were Friends. It called itself Non-Violent Action Against Nuclear Weapons. To dramatize and protest the danger of radioactive fallout resulting from nuclear explosions, this committee had raised funds for purchasing and fitting out the *Golden Rule*. Three of the four men who signed on as crew were Friends. All came from the east coast. A month before the boat sailed, the committee and crew addressed a letter to President Eisenhower, explaining that they did not intend to interfere with the explosions but only to call the attention of the American public to the danger for all mankind.

"We are sensitive to the great responsibility you bear," their letter assured the President. "There will be no deception in our effort. All action will be taken openly and trustingly in the Gandhian spirit of a non-violent attempt to effect needed change by speaking to the best in all men. For years we have spoken and written of the suicidal military preparations of the Great Powers. . . . We mean to speak now with the weight of our whole lives . . . to say to all men, 'We are here because stopping preparation for nuclear war is now the principal business of our lives; it is also the principal requirement for the continuation of human life.' . . . We hope our presence in the test area will speak to that which is deepest in you and in all men: that all men are capable of love."[1]

On Sunday afternoon, February 10, 1958, about three hundred supporters and well-wishers who had come to see the *Golden Rule* off held a Friends Meeting for Worship in the San Pedro boatyard.

"It was a gathered meeting," Albert Bigelow, the skipper, recalled later, using the Quaker expression for a sense of being closely knit in worship. "In the bright sunshine, we experienced together the presence of the Lord. There was a terrible awareness of our inadequacies for the work in hand, the voyage ahead. But there was a wonderful feeling, the strength, the spirit," he added, quoting George Fox, "that the Power of the Lord was over all." When the *Golden Rule* left port, "a flotilla of yachts and water taxis followed us out beyond the breakwater. One by one they turned back until the last was gone. We were alone, darkness settled over the deep."[2]

Albert Bigelow had only recently joined the Society of Friends although his wife had belonged for some time. An architect by profession, he had been a lieutenant commander during the Second World War, commanding a subchaser in the Solomon Islands and later a destroyer escort. He had been on the bridge of his ship approaching Pearl Harbor in August of 1945 when the news came through that an atom bomb had been exploded over Hiroshima. Years later, when some of the victims were brought to New York for plastic surgery, two of these "Hiroshima Maidens" stayed with the Bigelow family in Cos Cob, Connecticut.

Like many others who had been through the war, Albert Bigelow was seeking "some sort of unified life-philosophy or religion . . . I became impressed by the fact that in one way or another the saints, the wise men, those who seemed to me truly experienced, all pointed in one direction—toward non-violence, truth, love; toward a way and a goal that could not be reconciled with war."[3] He resigned his commission in the Naval Reserve and became a Friend.

The mate of the *Golden Rule*, William R. Huntington of St. James, Long Island, was a seasoned Friend and yachtsman. He had been a Conscientious Objector during the Second World War. Like Albert Bigelow, he was an architect and a grandfather. The third Friend, George Willoughby, had also been a Conscientious Objector. Chairman of the Committee for Non-Violent Action Against Nuclear Weapons but a less experienced sailor than the other two, he signed on as seaman.

When the *Golden Rule* was seven hundred miles off California, David Gale, the second seaman, became ill. Then a storm damaged the boat so badly that the skipper felt forced to return to San Pedro. Orion Sherwood, a young Methodist who had been teaching in a Friends school, replaced David Gale. The boat was repaired, and on March 25 she set sail again.

The following day, in Washington, D.C., a Quaker delegation

headed by Lewis M. Hoskins, Executive Secretary of the American Friends Service Committee, presented a petition at the White House. Addressed to President Eisenhower, it asked that he cancel the nuclear weapons tests in the Pacific "as a first realistic step toward disarmament and peace." The petition was signed by forty-seven thousand Americans. It had been circulated not only by Friends but also by the Baptist Peace Fellowship, the Methodist Board of World Peace, the Congregational Christian Pacifist Fellowship, the Church of the Brethren and several non-denominational groups.

The launching of the first Russian satellite in October of 1957 had raised for many people what Stewart Meacham of the American Friends Service Committee's Peace Education staff called "Sputnik's Questions":

"We are told that we must be prepared for economic sacrifice and belt tightening if we are to 'catch up.' If this is true, who will sacrifice what? Will airplane, rocket, and munitions makers sacrifice some of their cost-plus margins? . . . Will the oil companies sacrifice their special tax concessions? . . . Or is the sacrificing all to come from working people . . . or . . . people with fixed incomes whose small salaries and pensions shrink as prices spiral upward?

"What about diplomacy and our friends overseas? Will winning the race to the moon solve Asia's economic problems? Will it feed Pakistan's landless villagers? Will it build hydroelectric dams in India? Will it bring self-government to the people of Kenya or the Belgian Congo? Will it end the terror in Algeria? Will it solve the question of Middle East oil? Will it set the slaves of Saudi Arabia free, bring free trade unions to Spain? . . . Just who will be remembered and who forgotten as we race Russia into outer space?

"And what about that troublesome word 'morals'? What kind of morality is it where right and wrong are decided by the fastest rockets and the biggest warheads? . . . These are Sputnik's questions. But Sputnik, a man-made thing, can do no more than pose them, fling them far out into space, and fly on. The answers must come from man himself, reached in terms of faith in God and belief in humanity and justice, which alone can provide the freedom and security that the people of the world are hungry for today."[4]

Other Americans heard other questions raised by Sputnik and gave other answers. To them, freedom and security depended on nuclear supremacy. Despite marches, vigils, petitions and the four brave sailors for whom stopping these explosions had become the business of their lives, the weapons tests went off in the Pacific as scheduled.

On April 11, when the *Golden Rule* had been at sea for seventeen days, her crew heard over the ship-to-shore radio that the Atomic Energy Commission had issued an order barring U.S. citizens from entering the Eniwetok-Bikini explosion area. This changed the nature of the voyage—if it was to be completed—from one of lawful protest, as originally conceived, to an act of civil disobedience. When the four left California, they were willfully planning to endanger their lives but, to the best of their knowledge, they were not about to break the law. The United States had always upheld the fundamental principle of freedom of the sea. How could this principle be reversed without an act of Congress? Surely, the men told each other, the AEC's new regulation would be ruled unconstitutional in the courts.

They held a Meeting for Worship, seeking divine guidance. Like George Fox, they had dedicated their lives to "unity with the creation." Nuclear bombing was "devouring" it. They had embarked on this voyage as witnesses to their belief that this devouring was contrary to the will of God. They must obey His will, even at the cost of disregarding the new order of the AEC.

The *Golden Rule* was about a week from Honolulu and a month from the bomb test area. Had she not been in need of repairs and water, the crew would have bypassed Honolulu in order to avoid a possible confrontation with the authorities there, which would delay them until the tests were over. The whole purpose of the voyage was to enter the area while the tests were going on. The men considered postponing the repairs and rationing what water they had but this seemed too risky, for even if they could manage until they reached the Marshall Islands, they were not sure of being able to obtain water there. They decided to face whatever lay in store for them in Honolulu.

Back on the mainland, many groups were demonstrating against the tests.

"The atomic powers are slowly poisoning the earth and are preparing its destruction," Kenneth E. Boulding, Professor of Economics, declared during a "vigil of penitence" held at the University of Michigan. An active Friend, Kenneth Boulding confessed that "as a citizen of an atomic power I am ashamed of its policies, ashamed of reliance upon terror for defense, ashamed of the perversion of science to man's damnation, and ashamed of my own silence and inaction."[5]

On Saturday, April 19—the anniversary of Paul Revere's ride—the *Golden Rule* sailed into Honolulu at sunrise and tied up at the Alawai Yacht Basin.

"Operation Hardtack" was the name given to the Eniwetok explosions. On Monday morning, the *Golden Rule* men called on the Joint Task Force in charge of the Operation and stated their plans. They estimated that their voyage to the eastern edge of the test area would take eighteen days. During that time they promised to broadcast their position daily so that it would not be necessary to track them by ship or aircraft. As American taxpayers, they wished to avoid such unnecessary expense.

The day before they were to leave Honolulu, the Federal Court issued a restraining order against the boat and her crew. At the hearing in which the government was granted the injunction, members of the crew were not permitted to speak, but their attorney announced, "My clients wish to inform the Court that they will attempt to go despite the temporary injunction."[6]

The crew left the courtroom, drove down to the Yacht Basin and set sail. A Coast Guard cutter towed them back. In traditional Quaker style, the four men refused to post bail, so they were taken to the Honolulu jail to await trial. Six days later they were sentenced to sixty days in jail. The sentence was suspended, but the men were put on probation for a year. They did not feel that they could conscientiously agree to the terms of the probation. They appealed both the sentence and the temporary injunction, which held the *Golden Rule* fast in port.

They returned to the boat to await the outcome of their appeal. During their stay in jail, a fifty-foot, weatherbeaten ketch, *Phoenix*, had tied up in the Yacht Basin. The American family and Japanese mate on board were preparing for the last leg of their round-the-world cruise. The owner, Earle Reynolds, an anthropologist, had been working in Japan for the U. S. Atomic Energy Commission, studying the effects of radiation from nuclear bombing on the children of Hiroshima and Nagasaki. While living in Hiroshima, he had bought the *Phoenix*. Then he gave up his job and, with his wife, two teen-age children and the Japanese mate, spent four years cruising around the world.

Betraying a touch of pardonable envy for the lightheartedness of the *Phoenix* crew, the skipper of the tied-up *Golden Rule* observed, "They had been welcomed into and sped on their way from more than a hundred different ports. . . . They had had no official difficulties, indeed, officials had tried to ease their passage. They had gone where they chose, they belonged to no party or church or organization. They were on their own. They had had a glorious adventure."[7]

A chance encounter with the *Golden Rule* changed all this. Earle Reynolds and his wife made friends with the four pacifists. Suddenly, nuclear radiation was no longer a matter for objective investigation. It was people—burned people, children yet unborn who would come into the world with birth defects, a seared and eventually lifeless planet. According to Albert Bigelow, the crew of the *Phoenix* suddenly asked themselves, "Are we here for a purpose? Do we have this boat, our beloved *Phoenix*, for a purpose? Is not the final leg of our ocean adventure a higher adventure? Are we not called perhaps to have an adventure of the spirit?"[8] Even thus had Robert Fowler observed while he was building the *Woodhouse* exactly three hundred years earlier, "It was said within me several times, Thou hath her not for nothing, and also New England was presented before me . . . others . . . confirmed the matter in behalf of the Lord."

American newspapers reported on the *Golden Rule* case. People were thinking about the effects of nuclear testing. Demonstrators marched to AEC offices all across the United States. "Stop the bomb tests—U.S., Russia, Britain," the demonstrators' signs read, "Stop the tests, not the *Golden Rule*." A "vigil without food" was held at the AEC offices in Germantown, Maryland, by members of Non-Violent Action Against Nuclear Weapons in an effort to obtain an interview with the director. On the sixth day, he came out to meet the demonstrators. It was not a meeting of minds.

The third week in May the U. S. Court of Appeals in San Francisco heard the *Golden Rule* case. It refused to set aside the lower court's injunction. Now the pacifists had to make some hard decisions. Finally, they cabled the President of the United States, urging him to stop the tests and to initiate instead a vigorous constructive policy. They announced that they would continue their voyage, leaving June 4 at noon.

Another cable went to the President and to the Director of the AEC.

"The crew of the yacht *Phoenix*, believing that the attempted protest voyage of the ketch *Golden Rule* is justified morally and legally, respectfully urge the immediate termination of the Pacific bomb tests. Moreover, we urge that the recent ruling of the AEC, which closes off vast areas of the high seas, be rescinded. The *Phoenix* will sail from Honolulu in the near future, clearing for the high seas."[9]

Her course from Honolulu to Hiroshima, her home port, lay directly through the bomb test area.

On June 4, a gay crowd gathered at the Alawai Yacht Basin, waiting to see the *Golden Rule* cast off. Some of the well-wishers had hung leis around the necks of the crew. The trade wind was blowing, the engine was idling, everything was ready to go. But they had announced their sailing for noon and they felt bound not to leave a minute sooner. At 11:50, two federal marshals pushed through the crowd. They carried warrants for the arrest of Albert Bigelow on a charge of criminal conspiracy.

"What conspiracy?" he asked, "and with whom?"[10]

The judge offered to free him on his own recognizance, but Albert Bigelow refused to promise that he wouldn't try to sail again.

So he was returned to the Honolulu jail where "the turnkey and guards gave me friendly greetings. My mates—the inmates—gave me a hearty welcome."[11] Locked in his maximum security cell, Albert Bigelow had no way of knowing that that very afternoon the *Golden Rule* was heading down the harbor under full power, passing the buoy at the mouth and sailing blithely out into the Pacific. William Huntington was at the helm and Jim Peck, who had come over from the mainland, made the fourth crew member.

From the deck of the *Phoenix*, Earle Reynolds watched anxiously through his binoculars. Two Coast Guard cutters steamed out in pursuit but before they could overtake the *Golden Rule*, she was beyond the three-mile limit. She was safe! But no—when she was almost six miles out, the cutters closed in. An officer boarded the boat with a warrant for the arrest of William Huntington. The crew decided to sail the boat back to Honolulu instead of letting her be towed. By sunset, they tied up at the dock from which they had left only a few hours earlier. A U.S. marshal was waiting there to take William Huntington to jail.

He pleaded guilty. In his statement he condemned as wickedness, blasphemy and criminal insanity the "plan to use or prepare to use . . . nuclear weapons of mass extermination against our fellow man.

"All of us," he told the Court, "and all the others who have stood with us and behind us have not . . . for any petty or mischievous reason, tried to embarrass the government. But we have been trying to say with our whole being that the light of greatness which has guided our country and its greatest statesmen in the past—and will so guide it in the future—is there for the present leaders of our government to follow. They do not need to go along with the rest of the world in panic and fear down this road to senseless destruction and threatening the whole human race. They can take action in the opposite direction."[12]

Within a short time, all five of the shipmates were locked up for sixty days. They had a new cause to fight for now, one which had been a Quaker concern for three hundred years—the dehumanization of prisoners by their community. The *Golden Rule* men, who were serving only a relatively short sentence, saw that their fellow inmates felt rejected and willfully forgotten by the community which had put them away, in many cases for years and years.

By contrast, the five pacifists were held in love and concern by their sympathizers and by the members of the Honolulu Friends Meeting, who came to visit them as often as permitted. Four of these came to the prison to hold a Meeting for Worship the Sunday after the *Golden Rule* men were jailed, but although the Friends had applied in advance, they had not understood all the regulations and they were turned away. Cathy Cox, aged ninety-three, the daughter of Joel and Hannah Bean, was one of these. Another was Gilbert Bowles, eighty-nine, who had just been awarded the Order of the Rising Sun by the Emperor of Japan for his work in anthropology and international relations. When these same Friends returned the following Sunday, having complied with all the regulations, they were admitted.

"A dozen or more prisoners joined us. The long tables with plank seats permanently attached were not the best arrangement for a Friends meeting. . . . It was stifling hot. The narrow grill in the eaves let in little air. It freely admitted the din and commotion of the jailyard . . . oaths and obscenities did float through. . . . Then a wondrous thing happened. Despite the unlikely circumstances and, to many, the unfamiliar method, the meeting gathered; we were all caught up in God's net. A shared religious experience does not permit of telling very well, it has to be lived. I can only try to say that we were joined to one another and to the Lord in a living silence. Out of that stillness, a few were moved to speak to the condition of all. . . . The living presence of the Lord was among us and we knew that the power of the Lord was over all."[13]

The pacifist prisoners wrote a report based on their experiences, which they called "This Is Your Jail." It was distributed by the Honololu Friends Meeting to government and social agencies, in the hope that it would create some awareness of conditions and so develop a concern in the community.

It was clear now that the *Golden Rule* could not complete her voyage before the bomb tests were over. So the "experiment with Truth," as the shipmates called their voyage, had come to an end. On June 28, the boat was sold to a Californian, who renamed her *Puori* and sailed her to the South Seas.

From the Honolulu jail, her former crew issued this statement: "When we sailed the *Golden Rule* for the bomb test area, we stated that we would proceed as far as possible. We sailed from San Pedro to Honolulu. Twice we have attempted to sail from Honolulu to the Marshall Islands bomb test area. Twice we have been stopped by government action.

"The second time we were sentenced to sixty days in prison. We are still in jail. It is, therefore, impossible for us to sail again before the end of the present tests."[14]

But the *Phoenix*—the imprisoned pacifists liked to think that the *Phoenix* had risen from the ashes of the *Golden Rule*. A week after their boat had been stopped for the second time, the *Phoenix* was "clearing for the high seas," bound for Hiroshima. Three weeks later, as she was heading toward Bikini, she was stopped by a U. S. Coast Guard cutter. Earle Reynolds was placed under arrest. He was obliged to sail two hundred miles off his course to the U. S. Naval Base at Kwajalein. From there, he was flown to Honolulu.

PHOENIX SKIPPER MAY FACE PRISON TERM OF 20 YEARS, the newspaper headlines announced.[15]

Norman Cousins, editor of the *Saturday Review*, spoke for many Americans when he called the Reynolds protest "a matter of profound moral and political significance. His cause is not his alone; it belongs to the community of man."[16]

The case was to drag on for two agonizing years, during which time Earle Reynolds was not allowed to leave Hawaii without permission. On December 29, 1960, the San Francisco Court of Appeals set aside the conviction and reversed the judgment of the lower court.

"We have made at least a gesture for peace and for our country," Earle Reynolds declared when the case was over. "We have also discovered a sense of dedication and purpose that we never had before."[17]

During their enforced stay in Honolulu, Earle and Barbara Reynolds attended the Friends Meeting and finally "took one of the most important steps in our lives."[18] They applied for membership in the Society of Friends.

"We're glad to have you with us," Gilbert Bowles told Earle Reynolds after he was taken into membership.

"I'll probably make the world's worst Quaker," was the reply.[19]

Friends on the mainland had been generally divided in their attitude toward the men on the *Golden Rule*. A great many were so in accord with their testimony that they felt the men were, in a sense, standing in for them. They had not been able to do enough to support the voyage. The Orange Grove Friends Meeting in Pasadena engaged an attorney. Individual Friends all over the United States contributed money and moral support.

All Friends shared the men's concern for life and for an uncontaminated planet. But many wished the *Golden Rule* had expressed the concern in some other way, not by defying regulations. Quakers had been law-abiding for so long that they could not readily accept civil disobedience. They all believed in "following the leading of the Spirit." That this pursuit could drive one to collide with heads of state and their chain of command in the middle of the twentieth century just as surely as it did in the seventeenth came to some as a slow, very painful realization.

Their ambivalence was touchingly expressed by the elderly Friend, who said to one of the *Golden Rule* men, "Thee did right to follow thy leading of conscience—but thee had no right to break Ike's law."[20]

34 To Stand Like a Trumpet

To prevent Black students from entering Little Rock's Central High School in September 1957, the Governor of Arkansas called out the National Guard. To prevent the National Guard from preventing integration, the President of the United States called out federal troops. To prevent further deterioration in race relations, the Quakers of Little Rock gave a party.

It was a great success. About sixty people, Black and white, attended the reception given in honor of Lillian Smith, author of *Strange Fruit* and *Killers of the Dream*. At the same time, the Friends Meeting, with the approval of all its members, published a letter in the *Arkansas Gazette*. "As part of the Christian brotherhood," it said, "we feel that Christ's message comes to us today bidding us love our neighbors whatever color they are. He bids us put trust in our fellow men in place of fear, and supplant proud antagonism with humble, helpful friendliness."

Abusive telephone calls, calculated to intimidate, usually followed publication of letters favoring integration. But no such calls came to the Meeting. These Friends had, in their words, tried to "understand and use the spirit of John Woolman in our present context." In this spirit they wrote, "We would refrain from judging harshly the conduct of those who may seem to fall short, remembering that the ultimate victims of hate are those who hold it in their own hearts."[1] Friends tried to remember also that the ultimate victims of hate, whose attitudes make them so little lovable, need to be loved as much as—perhaps more than—those they victimize.

Quaker concern for Blacks in Arkansas went back to the Civil War, when Indiana Yearly Meeting sent relief workers to Helena where masses of refugees were concentrated. As the Union Army advanced, the slaveholders along the Mississippi fled, taking the able-bodied Black men with them and leaving behind the women and children, the sick and infirm, who found safety within the Union lines but had neither food nor shelter. The Indiana Friends ministered to these refugees, opening an asylum for children and an industrial school, which eventually became the Southland Institute. A Friends Meeting, under the care of Whitewater Monthly

Meeting in Indiana, was established at the Institute. Many members of this Meeting, who had been born slaves, became valued ministers in the Society of Friends and traveled up and down the country "in the service of Truth." For over sixty years Southland trained leaders in agricultural methods and community relations.

So when, in 1957, Little Rock Friends courageously championed their Black neighbors, they were following a long-established Quaker tradition. The contemporary attitude was different, though. Instead of relief and schooling for ignorant slaves, these Friends were offering friendship based on equality and the recognition of a common need to find solutions for problems that were undermining their city and their nation.

As always, it was the young who were bearing the brunt of the suffering. With this in mind, Little Rock Quakers planned a World Affairs Seminar for teen-agers of both races. Their concern for white youth as well as Black was very much in the spirit of Woolman.

Exactly two hundred years earlier, on a trip through the South, he had been shocked by his encounter with large-scale slavery. With rare perception, he saw that the young whites would eventually pay for the greed of their forebears and he fearlessly predicted the cost of holding slaves.

"These are a people by whose labour the other inhabitants are in a great measure supported, and many of them in the luxuries of life. These are the people who have made no agreement to serve us, and who have not forfeited their liberty that we know of. These are souls for whom Christ died, and for our conduct toward them we must answer before that Almighty Being who is no respecter of persons."

During his travels in 1757, Woolman felt moved to write to "Friends in the back settlements of North Carolina," reminding them that "where people let loose their minds after the love of outward things, and are more engaged in pursuing the profits . . . of this world than to be inwardly acquainted with the way of true peace . . . treasures thus collected do many times prove dangerous snares to their children. . . .

"And now, dear Friends and brethren, as you are improving a wilderness, and may be numbered amongst the first planters in one part of a province, I beseech you, in the love of Jesus Christ, to wisely consider the force of your examples, and think how much your successors may be thereby affected . . . children feel themselves encompassed with difficulties prepared for them by their predecessors."²

It was as though Woolman were describing the plight of America's children in 1957 and the dark gloominess that hung over the land even after integration in the schools became compulsory.

In preparation for the Teen Age World Affairs Seminar to be held the following March, Little Rock Friends formed an interdenominational Planning Committee composed of youngsters and adults. Several of the older members were ministers in city churches. As tension increased, two ministers felt obliged to withdraw. The YWCA, where Friends planned to hold the Seminar, received menacing telephone calls. Nevertheless, the Y held to its national policy of welcoming interracial groups.

The Seminar was scheduled to begin on Friday evening, March 14, 1958. Friends hoped for thirty participants but they knew that it was going to take great courage on the part of those youngsters to come. Would any of them dare? At the appointed time, twenty-four whites and eleven Blacks arrived. They belonged to Baptist, Catholic, Episcopal, Methodist and Presbyterian churches, to the Jewish Synagogue and the Friends Meeting.

That evening, they asked each other, How can we young people prepare for peace? What should be the role of the United States and Russia at the UN? What can the individual do? What function has religion in achieving peace?

Norman Whitney and Spahr Hull of the American Friends Service Committee staff joined Little Rock Friends in acting as resource persons.

On Saturday morning, the youngsters went out in pairs to interview prominent civic leaders and to pose these same questions. After lunch, they came together again and discussed the answers they had received at the interviews. They saw that there was a relation between conditions for world peace and the tension in their own city.

Sunday morning, during the closing session, members of the Seminar summed up their impressions. "We should come with an open mind, but this takes a while." "We must be honest with each other." "Non-violence cannot be used as a weapon." "One must love everybody in order to love God."

Spahr Hull spoke of creative ways to respond to fear through prayer, courage and "walking together."

"So many eggs and tomatoes have been thrown at me," one

Black girl from Central High School exclaimed, "they can't hurt me any more. But we must go on from there."

Norman Whitney urged the participants to remember that the Seminar experience had been real. "Live the kind of person you would like to be," he told them. "Continue a sharing experience. . . . Begin ripples of influence. . . . This is a time for greatness; this is a place for greatness; you can be a part of this."[3]

John Woolman seemed to be speaking to the condition of Friends now as clearly as he had two centuries earlier. At the 1958 sessions of Philadelphia Yearly Meeting, Frederick Tolles reminded Friends that, "two hundred Yearly Meetings ago, Quaker history turned a corner. The Philadelphia Yearly Meeting of 1758 was more than an event in sectarian annals: it was one of the turning points in the moral history of the Western world, for it was the moment when, for the first time, an organized Christian body considered the practice of slaveowning in the light of religious principles and not only condemned it but took decisive steps to eliminate it."[4]

The Yearly Meeting of 1758 was brought to this decisive action by a single man, who was "so truly humbled as to be favored with a clear understanding of the mind of Truth." He was John Woolman, the tailor from Mount Holly, New Jersey.

By mid-twentieth century, the "terrible things" Woolman had foretold two centuries earlier were happening to children all over the United States, even those whose ancestors had had no part of the traffic in human beings. Not alone Friends but many other Americans were discovering that Woolman's words applied to our own time: "Oppression in the extreme appears terrible, but oppression in more refined appearances remains to be oppression."[5]

A few people were also beginning to question whether the American dream of affluence and the power it provided was worthy or even desirable. Not many of these people were about to give up their possessions or refrain from acquiring new ones, but they identified romantically with the young man of thirty-six who had "learned to be content with a plain way of living . . . that on serious consideration I believed Truth did not require me to engage in much cumbrous affairs. . . . The increase of business became my burden . . . Then I lessened my outward business and, as I had opportunity, told my customers of my intention, that they might consider what shop to turn to; and so in a while wholly laid down merchandise, following my trade as tailor, myself only, having no apprentice. I also had a nursery of apple trees, in which I employed some of my time."⁶

By 1958, Woolman belonged not only to the Society of Friends but to the nation. He pointed the way to that purity which many wished for with all their hearts. He was recognized as "a genuine American saint."⁷

Two months after Philadelphia Yearly Meeting recalled the stirring events which occurred two centuries earlier, the Plymouth Congregational Church of Minneapolis, Minnesota, dedicated its Woolman Window as a memorial to a beloved deacon and his wife. There, in stained glass, stands an imposing figure dressed in an ornate eighteenth-century outfit, quite unlike any the simple Woolman would have worn—he who even refused to wear dyed clothing because dyes were produced by slaves. Nevertheless, this window does tell Woolman's life story. We see the robin he killed in his childhood, his tailor shop, the slave working the soil, the Indians he befriended, the horse he rode on his travels in the ministry and the ship he embarked on in 1772 for the voyage to England, from which he would never return.

How startled this plain Friend, who worshiped in unadorned Meetinghouses, would be, could he behold himself in all this splendor, virtually canonized! He appeared again in stained glass as part of the "Social Reform Window" on the north wall of Grace Cathedral in San Francisco, together with St. Paul, a monk, a bishop—odd company for him—and two others with whom he would have felt thoroughly at home: the prophets Amos and Jeremiah. If saints are people through whom the light shines, then Friend Woolman was indeed a saint.

In the Minneapolis window, one small feature symbolizes Woolman's whole essence—a trumpet so poised that it seems to be blown by an invisible trumpeter. It gives the key to Woolman's approach, illustrating, as it does, his words: "I waited in silence sometimes many weeks together, until I felt that rise which prepares the creature to stand like a trumpet through which the Lord speaks to his people."

Another Friend, who also struggled to win freedom but who never knew the taste of triumph, would have been surprised by a belated but eminently fitting commemoration.

In 1959, the three hundredth year after the execution of Mary Dyer, the Commonwealth of Massachusetts erected a statue of her on the south lawn of the State House overlooking Boston Common. Bronze, seven feet high, the statue portrays a woman wearing the simplest seventeenth-century dress and a small cap, sitting erect on a bench with her hands in her lap—a Quaker at worship. She seems to be gazing from the anguish of this life toward the love beyond.

"Courage, compassion and peace," Sylvia Judson said the figure was intended to represent. "I also wanted her quite simply to exist—solitary and exposed, as though the only safety was within."

Words written by Mary Dyer shortly before her death are chiseled into the base of the statue, with the antique spelling retained: "My life not availeth me in comparison to the liberty of the Truth."

When Massachusetts accepted the bequest in 1945 "for the construction and erection of an appropriate statue of Mary Dyer," the Fine Arts Commission of the Commonwealth announced a competition. Many sketches were submitted but none satisfied the judges. Years went by. The ideal sculptor did not appear. Then, one day, a Friend associated with the commission chanced upon *The Quiet Eye*. According to the jacket, the author was a sculptor and a Quaker. Here, the Boston Friend thought, might be someone who, having this particular religious insight, could catch the spirit of Mary Dyer better than the preceding competitors. Sylvia Judson was invited to submit a sketch. The one she presented was enthusiastically accepted by the Commission and she went to work in her Lake Forest studio.

No portrait of Mary Dyer exists. The problem, therefore, was to capture her personality rather than an outward likeness and to communicate her predicament. Sylvia Judson was inspired by several Quaker women she knew, whose spiritual beauty was reflected in their looks and bearing. She studied the contours of their faces and the character of their hands in repose. But the figure she finally created was wholly original. She made a plaster model, which was sent to Florence, Italy, to be cast in bronze.

Fourteen years after the bequest for it was received, the statue arrived in Boston. The Fine Arts Commission unanimously agreed that it had been worth waiting for, the best sculpture the Commonwealth had acquired in generations. The Commission arranged for its erection on the south lawn of the State House as a companion piece to the existing statue of Mary Dyer's friend, Anne Hutchinson. A tree that obscured the view from Beacon Street was moved. Three Friends took part in the unveiling ceremony and Governor

Furcolo eulogized Mary Dyer, expressing sentiments very unlike those of his predecessor, Governor Endicott. Descendants of Mary Dyer's six children witnessed the unveiling as well as representatives of Quaker organizations, other religious bodies, and the one Quaker member of the Massachusetts Legislature, Mary Newman.

When the statue appeared in its place on the crown of Beacon Hill, Sylvia Judson exclaimed, "I loved doing it."

No monuments have, as yet, been erected in honor of two colorful Quaker heroes who burst upon the scene as the 1950s turned into the '60s—Churkendoose and Rimi—but posterity will undoubtedly repair this omission.

Churkendoose is a bird—part chicken, turkey, duck, goose—who is rejected by the other barnyard fowl because he's different. "Why must I be a chicken or a goose?" he asks them. "Can't you like me as a Churkendoose?" What he craves is to get into the Green Circle, the childhood world of friendship, faith and love.

The Green Circle Program is taken to schools by a trained demonstrator who encourages the children to explore their relationships with one another, with family, neighbors, fellow countrymen and fellow human beings around the world. Cutouts of people and symbols are arranged on a flannel board inside a green felt circle. The children begin to realize—perhaps for the first time—that all of life is built on differences. To keep the Green Circle growing, the demonstrator points out, "we must accept and love one another *for* our differences because we all belong to the family of man and it is the kind of heart we have that really matters most. How big has your circle grown?"[8] she asks.

Sponsored by the Philadelphia Yearly Meeting Committee on Race Relations, the Green Circle Program was designed for use in Friends First-day Schools. Gladys Rawlins, the originator, never dreamed that it would reach out from this limited setting to all the public schools in Philadelphia. Soon hundreds of thousands of elementary school children all over the United States and in eleven foreign countries were sharing the sorrows and joys of Churkendoose.

"Have you ever been shut out from friendships that you wanted?" The eyes of second graders give a heartbreaking answer. "How did you feel?"

Churkendoose is a genuine hero—he rescues the inhabitants of the barnyard from the fox. Then he is lionized. But glory isn't what he craves. "This is not right," he tells his neighbors. "Yesterday you caused me tears. Now, today, you give me cheers. I don't want the tears, and I don't want the cheers."

"What do you think the Churkendoose wanted?" the demonstrator asks.

"To be loved! To be in the Green Circle!"

This program was eventually sponsored by the National Council of Christians and Jews, the American Association of University Women, the South Florida Desegregation Consulting Center, and Boards of Education in many cities. A Green Circle Workshop was held at Western Reserve University in Cleveland. Think of it— *Churkendoose going to the university!*

Rimi never went beyond the second grade—his head was hollow —but it was love at first sight for anyone lucky enough to know him. He came from Italy. When he arrived in America, he was wearing a forest-green tunic and a plaid neckerchief into which was knotted a tiny bell. A felt hat completed his costume—no Quaker broad-brim but a rakish fedora. His eyes were sometimes sad, for the town of Rimini, where he came from, was devastated in the Second World War and children who had lost their parents told Rimi their secret sorrows. But he always thought of ways to make them laugh.

All the schools in Rimini had been bombed flat. A wonderful lady named Signorina Margherita collected all the orphans and any other children who wanted to go to school, some dogs, a cat and rabbits. Army barracks were put up on the rubble, a garden was planted and school opened. The teachers made puppets for the children out of papier-mâché so they would have a next of kin to talk to. That was how Rimi came to be.

Way off in America, something called SAS—the School Affiliation Service of the American Friends Service Committee—heard what was happening in Rimini. Myrtle McCallin of SAS asked the faculty and students of Friends Central School in Overbrook, Pennsylvania, whether they would like to make friends with the faculty and students of the school in Italy. Soon pencils and notebooks and colored slides of life in America were arriving in Rimini. Christmas cards and valentines and class photographs and letters to individuals started going back and forth across the ocean. The children wrote in their own language, but they understood each other for the languages of friendship are many.

The Rimini children liked their distant friends so much that they decided to send them one of their treasures. So Rimi traveled to America, wearing his green tunic with the bell in his neckerchief. He had a marvelous time. Every child in Friends Central School wanted to put a forefinger up inside Rimi's head, a thumb and middle finger into his sleeves and talk with him. Mrs. Moore, the kindergarten teacher, made Rimi a Santa Claus outfit and fastened the little bell to the point of his cap. She gave him some magnificent, white whiskers. The Friends Central children bought presents for the Rimini children and Rimi took them in his suitcase when he went home for Christmas, promising to return by Groundhog Day.

Begun in 1946 as a program for sending material aid to war-stricken schools, SAS later changed the emphasis to international understanding. Three hundred and twenty elementary and secondary schools, public and private, in Africa, Belgium, England, France, Germany, Italy, Japan, Mexico, the Soviet Union and the United States participated. If understanding could replace prejudice in the classrooms of the world, tensions between nations might diminish. School administrators quickly saw the educational advantages of SAS. Partner schools exchanged students and teachers. In 1961, a teacher exchange program was arranged with the Soviet Union which proved so successful that the number of participants increased in subsequent years. Russians and Americans had their first opportunity to know one another in the classroom on a day-to-day basis. Warm relationships resulted.

Mrs. Moore went to Rimini one year and Signorina Margherita visited America. They needed no introductions. Rimi had told everyone about them. Everyone remembered him in his Santa Claus outfit, getting on the airplane with his suitcase full of presents. When he arrived, the Rimini children thought there was something just a little magical about him for none of them had ever been in an airplane. What a Christmas that was in Rimini!

A new periodical, *Quaker Religious Thought,* appeared in the spring of 1959. This was the publication of the Quaker Theological Discussion Group, which had been formed two years earlier by Friends from all branches whose purpose was "to explore the meaning and implications of our Quaker faith and religious experience through discussion and publication."

One member of the Theological Discussion Group spoke as a scientist. William D. Lotspeich was chairman of the Department of Physiology at the University of Rochester Medical School. "As a research scientist," he explained, "I find that I do not have ideas about my problem in the laboratory unless I sit down and consciously decide that I am going to have ideas. This I usually do in the quiet of my study, where all other thoughts are pushed aside. . . . Very often in such periods of concentration there springs forth in my mind a new form, a unity of ideas that were previously disparate. . . . The same thing happens in meeting for worship. We consciously decide to enter worship, clear our minds of extraneous thoughts, compose our restless bodies, and concentrate with our whole mind on the problem of discovering spiritual reality . . . we may experience a new release of spiritual energy which often leads to new ideas for understanding and action. We see in the recent events of our lives new meaning . . . there is the element of commitment . . . and in it one finds the true meaning of life. Christ said the same thing when he told us that we have to lose our life to find it."[9]

35 The Two Oceans

Those ubiquitous American Quakers seemed to be everywhere at the end of the 1950s. Relief and mission workers fanned out from Guatemala to Yugoslavia, from the Middle to the Far East, from Bolivia to Kenya. Some preached the Gospel; some proclaimed it silently through acts of love. Either way, they must have experienced what Fox felt when he saw "that there was an ocean of darkness and death, but an infinite ocean of light and love, which flowed over the ocean of darkness."

Apart from the regular overseas programs, unforeseen emergencies were breaking out so fast that no one could keep up with the need.

When Egypt seized control of the Suez Canal in 1956, 135,000 people were made homeless. In addition, Jews whose families had lived safely in Egypt for generations were now in peril. The American Friends Service Committee sent Paul Johnson to Cairo on a special mission to arrange for bringing relief to the refugees. In New York, Elmore Jackson, Director of the Quaker UN Program, and British members of that team discussed the matter with the Egyptian Foreign Minister. In Geneva, American Friends offered funds and personnel to the International Committee of the Red Cross for relief of the Egyptian Jews.

Upon his return from the Middle East, Paul Johnson went to Washington and testified before the House Foreign Affairs Committee. He stressed the need for long-range economic development programs in the Middle East, divorced from military programs and administered within the framework of the UN.

Three months after the start of the Suez Crisis, Soviet tanks and troops crushed the uprising in Hungary. Refugees fled to Austria with only what they carried on their backs. Tons of used clothing were hastily sent by American Friends. Twenty thousand Hungarians fled to Yugoslavia, which lacked resources for maintaining them. They were, moreover, trying to escape from Communism and did not wish to stay there. After Quaker workers brought in relief from their warehouse in Vienna, they helped to relocate these refugees in other countries. Local officials cooperated. Good relations had been established with Yugoslavia ever since the visit of the Quaker Mission in 1950. Many Yugoslav students had participated in the Quaker International Seminars.

At New Year 1959, Fidel Castro overthrew the Batista government, burning and bombing villages. Cuban Quakers appealed to American Quakers for help in ministering to thousands of homeless people. Hiram Hilty, Professor of Spanish at Guilford College, who had taught in Cuba, and Robert Lyon, Executive Secretary of the New England office of the Service Committee, were sent to survey the extent of relief needed. They met with Cuban Friends, virtually the only non-Batista people who deplored Castro's executions. Together the American and Cuban Friends called on the new Prime Minister to voice their concern. He gave "sober attention to their message," according to Hiram Hilty, who undertook a series of Quaker Missions to Cuba, "because Friends had spoken out for peace and justice in Cuba at a time when America and the rest of the world were noticeably indifferent to Batista's tyrannies."[1] For a while, American Friends were able to send relief through the Cuban Friends Service Committee. But in imagining that their pleas for mercy would be heeded, they proved overly optimistic. Before long, thirty Cuban Quakers had to flee. At least one was imprisoned. Then the tidal wave of refugees began to break on our shores—nineteen people so crowded in a twenty-foot boat that they had to keep their arms close to their sides during the long crossing. The U. S. Coast Guard came to the rescue when these little boats were stranded on the Florida Keys. The airlift brought a never-ending stream of penniless people. They were fed and clothed by the Church World Service Refugee Program, of which Earl Redding, a member of North Carolina Yearly Meeting, was Director, and by the American Friends Board of Missions.

"I don't sleep as well as I once did," a Friend in Miami confided. "Often I wake up thinking of the new arrivals. . . . I wonder what to do about Eva, a frail, bewildered mother who has a husband in prison and under sentence of death because he brought his large family of children to safety and then returned alone in his boat for others. How is Dorotea getting along in her factory job in New England? She showed us two bullet wounds in her leg and the crippled hand they gave her before she was let out of prison. The Underground put her on a boat. We managed to find her some clothing and a suitcase. When she left, she said, 'You are really my friends.'

"Miami is bulging at the seams. But the problem of aiding these people is not hers alone. It is one for the entire nation. It is one for the Free World."[2]

Three months after Castro ousted Batista, the monks and peasants of Tibet revolted against their Chinese invaders. This rebellion was mercilessly crushed. The Dalai Lama and fourteen thousand Tibetans fled to India. They were quartered in camps on the hot plains along the northern border. Through the Quaker International Center in Delhi, funds were raised to resettle these refugees in the hills, where the climate was more bearable and the terrain resembled their homeland.

Bradford Smith, a Friend from Shaftsbury, Vermont, who was Director of the Quaker Center in Delhi, visited the Dalai Lama. He described him as a very young man, in his middle twenties, who was dressed in a dark scarlet robe with a neck scarf of red and yellow, which showed that he belonged to both of Tibet's religious orders. Bradford Smith spoke to him through a Sikkimese interpreter.

"I told His Holiness that I brought greetings from a small religious group known as Quakers, who had at one time also known persecution in their own country, who had always had an interest in the welfare of the homeless, and who welcomed the opportunity to be in contact with people of other religions, feeling that there is essential unity in things of the spirit."

The Dalai Lama spoke of the refugee children whom Bradford Smith had been to see. There were so many, huddled into a small building, that they had to sleep five to a bed. Their education was of great concern to His Holiness. "China has taken our beloved country," he said. "Tibetan culture is being destroyed, and we must keep it alive outside Tibet."

Bradford Smith suggested that some of the Tibetan children might be sent to Quaker schools in Britain and the United States. Before leaving, he presented the Dalai Lama with Quaker books and assured him that Friends had the deepest interest in maintaining spiritual contact with him. "Though our numbers are few," he said, "we Quakers hope that in some small way we may be a channel of help to you and your people."[3]

Meanwhile, two hundred and fifty thousand Algerian refugees, most of them women and children, had fled to Tunisia and Morocco to escape the war in their country. British and American Friends sent relief workers. "I have just come from the frontier, visiting the encampments there while cannon were booming," Dr. Rita Morgan, the American Quaker representative in Tunisia, wrote to Philadelphia. "The condition of the people is so pitiful that I can find no words to tell you . . . many will surely die."[4]

The American Friends Service Committee launched a million-dollar fund drive to meet this emergency. Its regional offices throughout the United States issued a call for extra volunteers to pack used clothing. Quaker housewives turned in their trading stamps for blankets. One family donated an heirloom with purely sentimental significance—a horse blanket that had belonged to an ancestor who operated a teamster's business in Philadelphia in the 1850s. On Thanksgiving morning 1959, a Trans World Airlines plane took off from New York for Tunis with an emergency shipment, carried free of cost.

Quaker Christmas trees all across the United States were trimmed with nickels—"Blanket Nickels," intended for Algerian relief. After Christmas they were converted into eleven thousand dollars' worth of blankets and shipped overseas. Farmers in Ohio, Indiana and Iowa sent their printed cotton poultry feed bags to Philadelphia so that Algerian women, gathered in Quaker self-help centers in Tunisia and Morocco, would have material for making dresses, which not only clothed but cheered them.

The New York *Times* later referred to the Friends who were working in these Algerian refugee centers as the only "American presence" there and went on to say, "They have earned good will for their country that the State Department, out of consideration for the political sensibilities in France, has been unable to achieve. This good will is an important asset for the United States in the future independent Algerian state."

One member of this "American presence" was William Huntington, mate of the *Golden Rule*.

While hundreds of American Friends rushed to all parts of the world on missions of mercy, one traveled to Japan on a purely joyous errand. Thirteen years had gone by since Elizabeth Gray Vining first went to Tokyo to "open windows for the Crown Prince." He was then a "lovable-looking small boy, round faced and solemn but with a flicker of humor in his eyes." Now he was twenty-five and about to be married. His affection for his American tutor had not diminished after she went home. Of the more than three thousand guests who had been invited to his wedding, all were Japanese save this one. In addition to her pleasure in being able to witness the marriage, Elizabeth Vining expressed satisfaction because the Prince was allowed to break with tradition and marry the girl of his choice.

"Although his councillors for several years had been searching for a bride for him and had widened their list of possible girls to take in many who did not belong to noble families, including the daughter of Mr. Shoda, a well known industrialist, he did actually in a very real sense find his own bride. In the summer at Karuizawa, where he had more freedom than in Tokyo, he met Miss Michiko Shoda on the tennis court and fell in love with her.

"The wedding took place in the Imperial Shrine in the heart of the Palace grounds and I was privileged to be the only foreign guest. The day was glorious with April sunshine and the thousand-year-old ceremony was performed in dignity, simplicity and quiet. Only the twitter of birds in the great trees above broke the silence. In spite of the brilliant costumes and the exotic setting, it was more like a Quaker wedding than anything else I could compare it to, as the young Prince, without prompting, made for both of them promises very similar to the Quaker ones and the two sipped the ritual wine that might be said to correspond to the signing of the certificate."[5]

Back home, there were—impossible to believe—American refugees, too, that year. Children living in Farmville, Virginia, were obliged to go elsewhere and live on the charity of strangers if they were to get any education. Instead of opening its public schools in the fall of 1959, Prince Edward County padlocked them to avoid integration. The white townspeople started private academies for their children. Seventeen hundred Black children were left without any school to go to.

The American Friends Service Committee hastily sought foster homes for the handful of high school students who were willing to leave their families, brave the unknown and live among strangers, most of them white. Forty-seven Farmville youngsters, who wanted to graduate, took the chance.

None of the European emigrés, difficult though their situation was, needed to make quite the cultural leap that the Farmville children were required to take in adjusting to their white foster homes. Everything was a revelation, from the incredible experience of having a white man shake one's hand to learning how to flush an indoor toilet; from finding that, at bedtime, a white foster mother would kiss one good night along with the other children, to entering a classroom full of white students and a white teacher. This must have taken as much courage as walking on the moon.

Transplanted to more favorable educational surroundings than they had ever enjoyed, some of the Farmville children began to see that they might go on to college. They saw, too, that the denial of schooling on the grounds of a child's race was even more monstrous than they had believed when they were still back home, accustomed to being treated as inferiors. They returned to Farmville less docile than when they left in 1959. Seeing their little brothers and sisters who, at the age of ten, had never set foot inside a school, many of them became bitter.

During the four years that the Farmville public schools remained closed, children were placed in families in Massachusetts, Kentucky, Ohio, Pennsylvania and Iowa. This emergency placement was clearly not a solution. The children who were left behind had nothing but the teaching their parents were able to provide.

As no Quakers lived in Farmville, they could not personally appeal to members of the white community to consider the moral aspect of the situation. But they were able to send Service Committee representatives to Farmville from time to time to try to establish communication between the races. It strengthened the morale of the Black community to have emissaries from a concerned group visiting them regularly.

In Atlanta there were a good many Quakers. They were very successful during those years in creating better understanding. Quaker House, a place where any seeker could share religious experience and join in fostering racial harmony, opened in 1960. The first scheduled activity was a series of parties for Black and white students who that fall would be going to school together for the first time. The hope was, John Yungblut, the Director, explained, that these occasions would "improve understanding between students of the two races."[6] Later, when they met in their classrooms, they were already acquainted. An interracial group of high school students came together regularly at Quaker House for play reading. Their parents participated in art classes and seminars on "The Philosophy of Nonviolence," led by Dr. Martin Luther King, Jr., on "School Desegregation" and "Classics of Devotional Literature." Meetings of theological students and community leaders, to whom Friends interpreted their concerns, helped draw together a divided city.

That same year, North Carolina Yearly Meeting enabled the Charlotte Friends Fellowship to buy a house in the center of Charlotte where Friends could worship together and find ways to "convert world and community tensions into ties of humanity." Norman Morrison, a graduate of the Pittsburgh Theological Seminary and a deeply committed Quaker, became director of the Charlotte Friends Center. It reached out to its non-Quaker neighbors, "striving toward greater effectiveness in bringing people with differences together through small, informal meetings in an atmosphere of free discussion, where things can be said in truth rather than for popular effect."[7]

Displaying great courage, the Charlotte Friends Fellowship issued a statement supporting the Black students' non-violent protests against segregated lunch counters. This statement was sent to the manager of each of the stores that practiced discrimination and it was published in the local newspaper. "If we dismiss these protests as mere isolated events and of no importance," the statement warned, "history shall overtake us before we know the cause of our own undoing."[8]

Premier Nikita Khrushchev, then at the height of his power, was not on his best behavior when he attended the United Nations General Assembly in October 1960. He called the Security Council "worse than a spittoon" and took off his shoe to bang it on the desk with such effect that Assembly President Boland broke his gavel trying to restore order.

But Friends wished to make meaningful contact with the Premier, "to reduce the all-pervading acceptance of violence as an inevitable element in international relations." With this objective, some Friends had a private talk with him. Later, they accompanied Fritz Eichenberg, the Quaker artist, when he presented the Premier with books he had illustrated for an American edition of Russian classics. Marking the fiftieth anniversary of the death of Tolstoi and the three hundredth of the Quaker Peace Testimony, the presentation took place at the Soviet Mission in New York.

"Mr. Chairman," Fritz Eichenberg said, "please accept these books, written by great Russian writers, translated into English and illustrated by an American artist . . . presented to you by a group of Americans belonging to the Religious Society of Friends

(Quakers), which, by a tradition of 300 years, is dedicated to the cause of peace, nonviolence and conciliation, to the dignity and sanctity of human life, regardless of race, creed, or political belief. We feel these books belong in a Soviet library as a token of friendship and of the interdependence of our cultures. The bonds of kinship between Tolstoi and the Quakers were strong at a time when no world organization, devoted to the establishment of peace, existed."[9]

The Premier was in a genial mood, which was communicated by his interpreter. "He sat very close to me," Fritz Eichenberg recalled later, "looking at my work . . . but talking about the merits of revolution. I countered with ideas of my own concerning world peace and co-existence. He seemed to enjoy my stand, and he ended the interview warmly, even telling a few jokes, which made us laugh. He was earthy. I liked him very much."[10]

On Sunday, November 13, Friends from all over the United States held a solemn Meeting for Worship in the Florida Avenue Friends Meetinghouse, Washington, D.C. When the Meeting broke, over a thousand Friends walked three miles to the Pentagon to mark the three hundredth anniversary of the Declaration of 1660, in which the First Publishers of Truth set forth the Quaker Peace Testimony.

The Declaration was presented to Charles II by Friends in England, who had been accused of conspiring in an armed insurrection. It read, in part: "All bloody principles and practices, we . . . do utterly deny, with all outward wars and strife and fightings with outward weapons, for any end or under any pretence whatsoever. And this is our testimony to the whole world . . . the spirit of Christ, by which we are guided, is not changeable, so as once to command us from a thing as evil and again to move unto it."[11]

This Declaration was being reaffirmed by American Friends as they lined up on three sides of the Pentagon, young and old, parents with small children, a woman in a wheel chair, another on crutches. At intervals in the long lines of people, signs were held aloft reading simply "Quaker Peace Witness, 1660–1960."

Many of the participants had never made a public witness. They were self-conscious and uncomfortable. But as they felt themselves become part of a three-centuries-old procession, which had utterly denied all wars and fightings in fair weather and foul, they became exhilarated. Others were old hands at demonstrations—those who had kept a vigil for the past sixteen months at Fort Detrick, protesting their nation's preparation for biological warfare; those who protested the building of the Polaris submarine in New London, Connecticut, and the men who sailed the *Golden Rule*.

Except for a few friendly conversations with military policemen and with the young Pentagon official who came out to have the purpose of the Witness explained, it was conducted in silence. This was not supposed to be a show of Quaker power. The 120,000 Americans who called themselves Quakers were not likely to influence any politicians. Moreover, many modern Quakers did not uphold the traditional Peace Testimony. Those who came to Washington because they did deny fighting "first in ourselves and then in others" were there primarily to confront their own conduct and standard of living. Paraphrasing Fox's "answering that of God in every one," a speaker in the Meeting for Worship had exhorted Friends to deal with "that of the Pentagon" in their own hearts.[12]

On Monday, after a 6 A.M. Meeting for Worship, groups from the various states called on their senators and congressmen. Delegations also visited the British, French and Russian ambassadors and an official in the State Department. One delegation carried a message from the Peace Witness of 1960 and an illuminated scroll bearing the Declaration of 1660 to the White House for presentation to President Eisenhower. The whole body sent a telegram to President-elect Kennedy, requesting that he grant Friends an interview in the near future and urging him to "wage total peace" through world disarmament, general sharing of our God-given resources, and constructive use of the vigor and good will of our youth.

Friends throughout the country had followed the example of those in the Urbana-Champaign, Illinois, Meeting, who contributed 1 per cent of their gross income to the United Nations as "a token not only of our willingness to be taxed and governed by a system of world law, but also of our desire to share in the economic betterment of other peoples and areas." The first installment of the forty-six thousand dollars contributed during the Peace Witness was taken to the UN by a delegation that traveled in a bus owned and operated by an Iowa Friend.

"What will we do this anniversary year," *Now and Then* asked his readers, "about civil defense, about biological warfare, about the hidden control by the Pentagon of our minds and property, about taxes that go to war preparation, about the suppression of the truth concerning the risks of nuclear war or even of testing?"[13]

As Friends returned to their homes, they felt uplifted by the enduring faith expressed in the ancient Declaration: "We do earnestly desire and wait, that by the Word of God's power and its effectual operation in the hearts of men . . . all people, out of all different judgments and professions may be brought into love and unity with God, and one with another, and that they may all come to witness the prophet's words who said, 'Nation shall not lift up sword against nation, neither shall they learn war any more.'"[14]

Alas, that time had not yet arrived.

On June 4, 1961, missionaries from Oregon Yearly Meeting of Friends Church were attacked on the Mission farm at Copijara, Bolivia, by Indians who threatened to kill them. Fortunately, a few days earlier, the missionaries had brought their wives and children to La Paz for safety. They had moved the tractor, combine and trucks away so as to salvage at least that much if the farm was taken over. The Indians, however, wanted not only the land, but all that went with it and this was their reason for the attack.

When Oregon Yearly Meeting sent its first mission workers to Bolivia in 1930, the Aymara Indians were practically slaves. They were underfed and unjustly treated by the white landlords and mine owners, who were fabulously wealthy and controlled the political power. Only 5 per cent of the population could vote. The rest was illiterate. Although the country was nominally Roman Catholic, many Indians still worshiped the gods of their ancestors.

It was to these people that Oregon Yearly Meeting, one of the most evangelical of all the American Quaker groups, felt called to minister. At the outset, Oregon Friends cooperated with the American Bible Society to produce a translation of the New Testament in the Aymara dialect. "Almost as soon as a man receives Christ as his Savior the desire to learn to read is born in his soul," Carroll Tamplin, the first missionary, wrote back to Oregon. "But before the seed can be sown extensively we must wage war against illiteracy. . . . We must do our utmost to expel the darkness that clouds the minds of these souls."[15]

The landlords did not want their peasants enlightened. Neither did the businessmen, who even resented the missionaries' efforts to wipe out disease. "Sanitation will tempt the gringo to come in and wrest our business from us. Let our friend Yellow-jack stay," they told Carroll Tamplin, who expostulated to his Mission Board at home, "Think of it! They consider the unsanitary conditions and yellow-fever better companions. . . . May God have pity on us as a race! The missionary is suspected of being an ally of . . . the 'capitalistas de Wall Street,' and forerunners of Yankee Imperialism. They cannot imagine anyone coming to them without selfish motives! That one who is not their relative should care for them is incomprehensible!"[16]

In 1932, when Bolivia drafted men for the Chaco War, the new Quakers in Bolivia found themselves in the same dilemma as their fellow Quakers in North America. "Their hearts are torn! Has not Christ taught them to love their enemies? . . . Upon protest they are immediately dispatched to the front lines where they must either fight in self-defense or submit themselves to brutal killing."[17]

In 1947, Oregon Yearly Meeting purchased the three-thousand-acre farm at Copijara, forty miles from La Paz, as a site for a Bible school and the means of supporting it. By 1950, the Oregon Mission Board felt the time had come to establish a Bolivian National Friends Church.

Along with the land, buildings and animals that were on the farm when it was purchased came 146 Indians. The Bolivian Government was astonished when the new owners freed them and gave them the land they had worked. "Our plan of freedom for the Indians . . . saved the farm for us in 1952 when the land reform program became effective,"[18] a missionary reported after the revolution. Nevertheless, the Mission lost half the crop-producing land.

But more than land reform followed the revolution of 1952. Like oppressed peoples everywhere, the Bolivian Friends wanted to rid themselves of those who had made them self-reliant. In 1958, they demanded that the farm be turned over to them and that they be given funds for its support. Oregon Friends agreed that this should be done eventually, but they did not think the Bolivian Church was strong enough yet.

Anti-American feeling kept rising and the wealth that the farm represented, however altruistic its application, was a constant reproach. "Though our house . . . is smaller than many of theirs," one missionary observed, "we are rich. . . . We have a heater . . . a kerosene refrigerator, a sink, and beds for our whole family. These are big in their estimation."

So, on June 4, 1961, the Bolivian Friends took over the farm by force. The beleaguered missionaries agreed to return the tractor and other pieces of equipment. They were to be given half the grain and potato crops and half the sheep. "In the providence of God our missionaries escaped bodily injury and were permitted to return to La Paz," the Yearly Meeting minuted, adding, "The material loss has been considerable. . . . The spiritual gains, in which the farm played such a vital part, cannot be reckoned."

Left on their own, the Bolivian Friends soon regretted having sent the missionaries away. They begged them to come back. In a beautiful spirit the missionaries returned, acknowledging that their role was no longer that of a "loving, overseeing god-father, but a co-laborer." As one of them put it, they had a new relationship "of 'togetherness' rather than the 'colonialism' type of missionary service."[19]

Friends all over the United States were discovering that they must devise new ways of expressing their concern. The channels through which they had funneled love for three hundred years were not appropriate to the 1960s. Feeding the hungry and educating the illiterate could only be done by people with superior wealth and learning. In the case of the missionaries, converting the heathen could only be done by people who considered that they had a superior religion. Love was no longer enough. It was absolutely requisite but it was not enough. Somehow, Friends would have to break new ground.

In October 1961 an event occurred which showed American Friends that the people they had once served as missionaries could now, in turn, enlighten them. The gentle words of an East African Quaker, spoken in Kenya, helped to reverse the policy of racial segregation at Guilford College in North Carolina, making it one of the first church-related colleges in the South to open its doors to Blacks.

When the Eighth Triennial Meeting of the Friends World Committee took place in Kaimosi, Kenya, in late August, one of the seventy-nine delegates from the United States, President Clyde A. Milner of Guilford College, carried with him invitations from North Carolina Yearly Meeting and the Trustees of his college. The Friends World Committee was being invited to hold its Fourth World Conference, scheduled for 1967, on the campus of the college in Greensboro.

The invitation was received coldly. European Friends declared plainly that they did not wish to attend a conference at a racially segregated institution.

"I can recall the deep tension and feeling," J. Floyd Moore, who subsequently organized the Fourth Friends World Conference, wrote about that session in Kaimosi. "Some Friends made it quite clear that they didn't think that a world conference should be held on a campus which had been unable to integrate its student body since opening in 1837. Out of that remarkable meeting, the voice of Thomas Lung'aho spoke in a spirit of loving fellowship, saying that the acceptance of a genuine invitation might strengthen those Friends in Southern USA who were committed to the cause of racial equality. In a wonderful coming together of hearts, if not of minds, the Friends World Committee united in accepting the invitation, if way opened. Clyde Milner brought this message back to the Trustees of Guilford College. At their next meeting in October, after hours of serious and—to some—painful deliberation, they united in loyalty to a higher goal than personal or local tradition, announcing and immediately implementing their decision to integrate the College. It was the result of long years of concern, preparation and leadership, but President Emeritus Milner has made it clear that the nature and spirit of that historic meeting in East Africa was the major factor in bringing the Trustees to the point of joining in a decision."

What Woolman called the "channel of universal love" led in two directions.

36 Love Measured by Its Own Fulness

"There will be pickets," Colin Bell roguishly advised President Kennedy's social secretary, "not only outside but inside the White House."[1]

And there were. Friends found the paradox very amusing. They also gave thanks that in their country dissenters were respected.

On Sunday, April 29, 1962, over a thousand Friends converged on Washington again, pleading for an end to preparation for nuclear war. After worshiping in the Sylvan Theatre near the Washington Monument, they walked quietly in pairs up Pennsylvania Avenue, soaked by rain. For hours, they maintained a prayerful silence outside the White House, all except two of the pickets, who left to attend a dinner party inside. They were Clarence Pickett and Linus Pauling, the prize-winning chemist who, while not a Friend, felt so strongly that nuclear testing should be banned that he had joined the Quaker Vigil.

President and Mrs. Kennedy were giving a dinner in honor of all the American Nobel Prize winners. The American Friends Service Committee, which shared the Peace Prize in 1947, was represented by Clarence and Lilly Pickett. The President obviously knew that the Picketts were pickets but his manner indicated only admiration for their lifelong service to humanity.

While these pickets were eating a dinner they later described as "simple but delicious," the rest assembled in All Souls Unitarian Church, where Dr. Mordecai Johnson, President Emeritus of Howard University, challenged them to overcome racial discrimination in their communities. This, he said, was the first step in breaking the domination and exploitation that Western Europeans have practiced for the past five hundred years.

Monday morning, a Quaker delegation left for New York, taking to the United Nations a gift that was earmarked to be spent on low-cost housing. Other delegations called at the embassies, still others at the State Department or on their senators and representatives.

The following day, six of the Friends were received by President Kennedy at the White House.

Friends came here in 1862 to call on President Lincoln—women in bonnets and men with broad-brimmed hats firmly set upon their heads. They came for the purpose of encouraging the President to free the slaves. Whether they influenced him, no one knows, but a few months later he signed the Emancipation Proclamation. Was it not possible that in 1962, with God's help, Friends might encourage this eager, young President to lead the world toward peace?

He sat in his rocking chair, facing the guests seated on either side of a table. They brought him a message from all the participants in the Vigil, which affirmed their belief "that all war is contrary to the mind and spirit of Christ . . . Our consciences are revolted by the fact that the nations now are spending more on armaments than the total income of the poorer half of the world's people who suffer from chronic misery."[2]

After delivering the Vigil's message, the Friends told of their experience in offering food to unfriendly nations that were in need. They were impressed by the President's "cordial, frank and sincere welcome and by his ready response to their concerns."[3]

At the time, Friends were restrained by protocol from quoting the President. After his assassination, they felt free to divulge the fact that he had referred to the protests which many Friends Meetings sent him and Secretary of Defense McNamara when it was rumored that the new Polaris submarine was going to be named for William Penn. To the Pentagon, this seemed appropriate since Penn was one of the great Americans. To Friends, it was unthinkable that so staunch a defender of the Quaker Peace Testimony should have his name conferred on an engine of war. "Smiling wryly," Now and Then recalled a year later, the President "assured the visitors that it would not be done. . . .

"I think the main impression given by the interview, apart from his charm of manner and alertness of mind was its disclosure of a man frustrated and 'trapped.' Widely regarded as in the most powerful position in the world, the President showed awareness of the limitations of his freedom. . . . When disarmament was mentioned he said bluntly, 'The Pentagon opposes every proposal for disarmament.' . . .

"Here was a man who was ready to consider two sides of a question. I have been haunted ever since by a cryptic remark he made at the end. When it was suggested that one could not do two opposite things at the same time, he replied without hesitation, 'That is the way all life is, systole and diastole.'"[4]

Quite naturally, this visit recalled for Henry Cadbury the one he made more than thirty years earlier, when President Hoover requested him to come to the White House on a designated day. It happened to be the time when the Professor was scheduled to meet his class at Bryn Mawr College. His ingrained Quaker testimony to equality required that he decline the invitation. How could he disappoint the Bryn Mawr girls just because he had been summoned by the President of the United States? Someone managed to persuade Henry Cadbury that he had better postpone his classes and go to the White House.

When he arrived, he found that he had been called because the Hoovers were trying to find a place to attend public worship.

"I come of Quaker stock," the President had said during the campaign, when some of his supporters tried to make a political issue of the fact that Al Smith, his opponent, was a Roman Catholic. "My ancestors were persecuted for their beliefs. Here they sought and found religious freedom. By blood and conviction I stand for religious toleration both in act and in spirit. The glory of our American ideals is the right of every man to worship God according to the dictates of his own conscience."[5]

The President told Henry Cadbury that although apart from relief work he and Mrs. Hoover had had little recent contact with Quakers, they wished to attend a Friends Meeting now and were at a loss to know where to go. The problem was not that there was no Friends Meeting in Washington but that there were three— Hicksite, Gurneyite (the branch in which Herbert Hoover had been reared) and Independent.

"With the public eye so much upon him," Henry Cadbury explained, when he reported that interview, "it was embarrassing for the first Quaker President in our history to have to acknowledge the disunited condition of the Society of Friends right in the national seat of government. He asked me, as chairman of the American Friends Service Committee . . . to induce local Friends to combine.

"This request took me as much by surprise as the invitation had. I think, however, I succeeded in explaining to him that I had no papal powers, that the AFSC was a relief organization, and that for me to engage in church politics or local problems of Quaker divisions would be resented and would injure the happy cooperative working of all sorts of Friends with the Committee. So we dropped the subject."[6]

They spoke instead about peace. The President expressed his

desire to reduce naval expenditures and his hope for the success of the naval disarmament conference. Henry Cadbury asked him what aspect of their common Quaker traditions he regarded as most significant.

"Without hesitation he answered, 'Individual faithfulness.' . . . Both he and I often had heard it emphasized from the meeting galleries in our childhood . . . it seems to me a phrase descriptive of his own life and, indeed, of the somewhat characteristic social approach of Quakerism as a whole . . . our progressive social concerns begin with an individual and spread to others—not as mass movements controlled from above, but by the accumulation of responsible practice of personal fidelity. . . . Of course, not all conscientious persons construe identically what is their duty. But loyalty to it is the *sine qua non* of the good society."[7]

The Hoovers' religious problem was resolved not by Quaker "papal powers," but by the removal of two of the Friends Meetings to the suburbs and the building of a spacious Meetinghouse at 2111 Florida Avenue where the Independent Friends welcomed all Friends and friends of Friends. Here, protected by secret service men and gaped at by sightseers, Herbert and Lou Henry Hoover attended Meeting regularly as long as they lived in Washington.

In the fall of 1962, after a couple of experimental years, the Earlham School of Religion settled down confidently on the campus of Earlham College in Richmond, Indiana. It offered both the B.D. and M.A. degrees. Although some Friends Meetings had employed pastors since the end of the nineteenth century, there had been no accredited Quaker school for training them. They were graduates of institutions conducted by other denominations and inevitably brought to their Quaker pastorates some of their non-Quaker indoctrination. This had its drawbacks for Friends, as Alexander Purdy, Dean Emeritus of Hartford Seminary, where he and Moses Bailey had taught many Quaker students over the years, pointed out.

"Few seminaries of my acquaintance have not felt the impact of the current neo-orthodox emphasis. Without questioning certain real values in this return to Calvinism, one must insist that it is not congenial to Friends. The other trend is the so-called 'enrichment of worship.' Again, without questioning what this emphasis on ceremony and ritual may mean to many worshippers, I do not find it congenial to Friends. . . . Friends have always witnessed to the validity of first-hand religious experience. This affirmation is central in the Earlham School of Religion. . . . That the true flame may be lighted and made to burn more steadily in a fellowship of study, worship and work is the conviction of this venture."[8]

Wilmer A. Cooper was appointed Dean of the Earlham School of Religion. "Never before," he said, after the School was solidly established, "has a Graduate School of Religion been so needed among Friends, not only to produce needed leadership, but to help Friends appraise themselves and their proper place in the Christian Movement as a whole."[9]

In his own graduate student days, Wilmer Cooper had taken what he called "another look at Rufus Jones," whose thinking still inspired the unprogramed Meetings. "In view of his great contribution to twentieth-century Quakerism a re-evaluation of his views would now seem appropriate. . . .

"The area of Rufus Jones's thinking that has created the most discussion recently is his interpretation of the origin of the Quaker movement. A number of important studies have been made which take issue with some of his conclusions. Rufus Jones interpreted early Quakerism as having roots in two Continental movements: the Continental mystics and the Continental humanists. . . . More recent research has shown that although early Quakerism possessed mystical elements, it was primarily a 'left-wing' religious movement within English Puritanism. The claim for humanist elements in early Quakerism is even more doubtful."[10]

These views were held by two of the most distinguished contemporary church historians, both Congregational ministers, who had studied the early Quaker period: Roland H. Bainton of Yale Divinity School and Geoffrey F. Nuttall of London University. Many young American Quaker scholars found that their researches led them to similar conclusions. In *The Quakers in Puritan England*, published at this time, Hugh Barbour, Professor of Religion at Earlham College, said, ". . . Quakers showed themselves Puritans in their ideas of how God works in remaking men. Puritans had known such inward change while opening themselves to the biblical message; Friends had known this more radically in baring themselves to the Light within them."[11] T. Canby Jones, Professor of Religion and Philosophy at Wilmington College, had already spoken of Fox as a Puritan. "Like other Puritans he was determined not to believe anything that was not expressly scriptural."[12] And Edwin B. Bronner, writing at about the same time, observed: "In the past,

Friends have been unwilling to admit that they were closely related to the Puritanism of the seventeenth century, but today they are more willing to accept that fact. While early Friends rejected many Calvinistic doctrines, particularly predestination, it is obvious that Friends were puritanical in many ways."[13]

Other Friends questioned the new interpretation. "Is Quakerism mystical or evangelical?" Howard Brinton inquired on the one hundredth anniversary of the birth of Rufus Jones and immediately replied, "It is both in the best sense of these two words. However, the evangelical revival in the latter part of the nineteenth century, though it exhibited much first-hand religious experience, threw Quakerism off its base by making salvation dependent on the acceptance of a certain creed, rather than recognizing union with the living Christ within as essential. The evangelicals regressed to the very position which early Quakerism had opposed. . . . Rufus Jones has been criticised by some recent scholars because he gave Quakerism a background in mystical movements . . . rather than in Puritanism. . . . But the theory that Quakerism was simply 'radical Puritanism' would have astonished the Puritans and Quakers of the Seventeenth Century. Each repudiated the other as anti-Christian. . . . The belief that Quakerism is a form of Protestantism has completely changed the character of Quakerism in many parts of America, resulting in imitation of Protestant theory and practice."[14]

Frederick Tolles believed that "Quakerism, though rising out of the Puritan environment of Commonwealth England . . . was nevertheless in some respects neither Protestant nor Catholic, but a *tertium quid*, suspect in the eyes of Puritan and Anglican alike. In its complete reliance upon the Spirit of God manifested in the soul of every man, Quakerism revealed itself as one of the varieties of mystical religion."[15]

To the average Friend, who was not a scholar, the tangle of Quaker roots was less engrossing than the application of Quaker belief to daily life. The search for Quakerism's ancestry seemed like a discussion about which side of the family the baby takes after— a question that, as every relation knows, does not lend itself to consensus. To most Friends in the severely testing 1960s, just as in the 1660s, Quakerism—whatever its roots—was simply the discovery that their Teacher spoke to their condition.

The average Friend was more preoccupied with the draft than with theology; with the loyalty oath, where it was mandatory; with the struggle for civil rights and against civil defense, since Friends believed safety lay not in air raid shelters but in disarmament. They worried lest their investments and taxes be used to promote violence. Some questioned whether they had a right to own so much that they could invest and could be taxed.

They were troubled about prayers in public schools. "We ought not to insist on religious exercises in our schools if such acts violate the religious liberty of our fellow Americans," Edwin Bronner said, in testifying before the House Committee on the Judiciary. "We can practice our religion in our churches and in our homes, and we have the privilege of worshiping in private. . . ."[16]

At the same time, Friends did insist on the practice of religion in their own schools—not the recitation of prayers but those essential aspects of Quaker education, which Howard Brinton defined as "a family relationship between students and faculty, the education of both heart and intellect, the midweek meeting for worship, courses in the Bible as the necessary equipment of an educated person, and the teaching of history from an international point of view."[17]

Although Friends were deeply interested in improving the quality of public education, many of them still believed that Quaker schools had a unique contribution to make, too—not, as in the past, for the "guarded education" of their own children but for the enrichment of any who might wish to enroll. "They are ourselves," Francis D. Hole of Madison, Wisconsin, said of Friends schools, "our Quakerism and some of our secular culture made visible."[18]

Friends schools offered freedom to experiment with new educational concepts. When George I. Bliss started the Meeting School in Rindge, New Hampshire, he placed much of the responsibility for administrative policy in the school's Meeting for Business, which was composed of faculty and students. By taking the sense of the Meeting, the whole school community arrived at decisions affecting curriculum, living arrangements, and rules about smoking, drinking and matters relating to sex.

Although Friends came to Boston in 1656, they did not, so far as we know, start a school in the area until 1960, when Cambridge Friends School opened with Thomas Waring as headmaster. Friends located the school in a neighborhood that badly needed the friendliness and recreational facilities the school provided. Afternoon, weekend and summer programs for neighborhood youngsters became as much part of the school's program as the academic curriculum, making the school one that lives what it teaches.

Other Friends schools opened in Sandy Spring, Maryland; Westbury, New York; and Detroit. Carolina Friends School was started under the care of two Monthly Meetings, Durham and Chapel Hill, North Carolina. John Woolman School, in the foothills of the Sierras of northern California, hoped not only to train its students for full and useful lives but also for leadership in the Society of Friends, to deal with problems in Latin America and the Orient. Virginia Beach Friends School acquired a friend in a noted psychologist, who went there from time to time to consult with teachers and parents because he felt the school was developing in its students the qualities he valued—"compassion, concern, commitment and courage." When Louise Wilson, the Principal, first invited him to address the parents, she felt obliged to explain that they could not afford his usual fee. The psychologist waved the whole matter aside. He didn't want anything. "But," he said, knowing Friends' concern for the needy around the world, "if you care to send something to some poor people I know in Israel—"

A completely new departure in higher education was undertaken when Friends World College opened in Westbury, New York, with two distinct aims: that it be Quaker in spirit having at its center the Meeting for Worship, and that it be international in outreach, with a student body of all faiths, races and nationalities. "The World will be the campus," Morris Mitchell, Director of Programing, announced. "The core of study will be the problems of life."[19]

Friends were generally as backward as everyone else in providing sex education, although in the seventeenth century William Penn deplored the fact that "millions of people come into and go out of the world, ignorant of themselves and of the world they have lived in. If one went to see Windsor Castle or Hampton Court," he said, "it would be strange not to observe and remember the situation, the building, the gardens, the fountains. . . . And yet few people know themselves; no, not their own bodies, the houses of their minds, the most curious structure of the world, a living, walking tabernacle."[20]

But nineteenth- and early twentieth-century Friends were brought up to feel that sex was something one did not discuss. When a group of British Quakers published *Towards a Quaker View of Sex* in

1964, some older Friends, both in their country and the United States, experienced discomfort. Dr. Mary Steichen Calderone, a member of Manhasset, New York, Meeting, urged Friends to open communication with their young people and to repair the damage done by ignorance. "The gift of sex," she once said, "is something the American culture has abnegated." Her concern for women with unwanted pregnancies led her to become the Medical Director of the Planned Parenthood Federation of America. Then she attended the First North American Conference on Church and Family, organized by the National Council of Churches. Several of the doctors and behavioral scientists who took part in that conference saw the need for and established the Sex Information and Education Council of the United States—SIECUS—to dignify sex "by openness of approach, study and scientific research designed to lead towards its understanding and its freedom from exploitation."[21] Mary Calderone was chosen head of this council.

"The idea of a national campaign for sexual enlightenment being led by a woman, a grandmother, and a Quaker at first tended to be treated as a joke," David Mace, her colleague and fellow Quaker wrote. "Gradually, however, we all became aware that this was exactly what was needed. If a highly cultured and religious woman in her sixties felt called to chide the nation for its unhealthy attitudes to sex, this was indeed something to think about."[22]

In 1964, a book appeared which recalled the far-reaching effect of Stephen Grellet's visit to Elizabeth Fry, after he had seen the neglected people in Newgate Prison and had described "out of the fulness of my heart what I had just beheld." But the book was by a contemporary Friend and focused on the needs of the sick poor today. When the novelist Jan de Hartog and his wife, Marjorie, moved to Houston, the first thing they heard was that the city hospital was so shorthanded, there was no one to feed the infants. From that moment, the care of the indigent sick in Houston became the business of their lives. Jan de Hartog volunteered as an orderly. He found that conditions in the hospital were even worse than he had been led to expect. He and his wife persuaded other members of the Friends Meeting to volunteer, and after a time, other people in the community. *The Hospital* is the moving record of that experience. By the end of the book, two hundred Houston people are volunteering as nurses' aides and orderlies and more are being trained.

A charming book was also published that year: *Quaker Profiles, Pictorial and Biographical 1750–1850,* by Anna Cox Brinton. The words of Elizabeth Fry, which she quotes, seemed particularly timely: "Nothing is so likely to cause our Society to remain a living and spiritual body as its being willing *to stand open to improvement.* . . . My belief is, that neither individuals nor collective bodies should *stand still* in grace, but that their light should shine brighter and brighter unto the perfect day."

One of Philadelphia's last "plain" Friends, William Bacon Evans, died in 1964 at the age of eighty-eight. His invariable use of "thee" and "thy," even when speaking to flabbergasted (but usually delighted) strangers, his collarless coat and missing necktie were not simply the eccentric preservation of archaic Quaker customs. They were a living testimony to the simplicity which he believed modern Friends ought to be practicing.

"A broad-brimmed island amid the commuting throng," was how Robert W. Tucker lovingly described this gentle Friend, after meeting him at the bus terminal when William Bacon Evans came to New York to visit the United Nations. His satchel was full of those toys and puzzles he made, which children at Yearly Meeting looked forward to receiving. At the UN, the toys were gravely presented to somewhat surprised guards, to "diplomats, tourists, translators, and personnel from the Secretariat."[23] Trailing this plain Friend through the UN, Robert Tucker began to understand more clearly the "contagious saintliness" of Woolman. Because he refused to wear dyed clothing, he also "made a first impression of being an oddball, like William Bacon Evans."[24]

But this UN tour "turned into a triumphal procession." Hearing about it, a New York Friend exclaimed, "If we could just set him loose in that place, we'd have world peace within one year!"

"When you first met him," Robert Tucker had to admit, "you thought he was a nut. It was not just his garb or his speech; it was his whole approach to life, his bizarre practice of regarding every casual human contact as a chance to find a new friend. But then after about five minutes you would start to realize that *you* were the nut. For this was the way we all ought to be. This was a man who could be fully human in a world where we all frustrate much of our humanity. This was a man to whom other people truly were unique and wonderful. And he made it seem so easy and natural, he was indeed so contagiously what he was, as to make it impossible to assess him by your standards or by the world's standards, simply because you were too busy assessing yourself and the world by his standards."

Friends never miss an opportunity for celebration. On October 19, 1964, at the regular Monday morning meeting of the Service Committee staff in Philadelphia, three co-workers, who had turned eighty, and their wives were honored. It was a chance for the staff to express the very deep affection and regard in which they held Clarence and Lilly Pickett, Henry and Lydia Cadbury, Howard and Anna Brinton. Referring to the service the three men had rendered throughout their lives, Anna Brinton quoted Dag Hammarskjold: "In our era the road to holiness lies through the world of action."

Six months later, Friends felt the truth of this keenly when Clarence Pickett died. I. F. Stone, editor and Washington correspondent, wrote, "To know Dr. Clarence Evan Pickett was to know what the Friends mean by the Inner Light. It shone from that most unassuming man."[25]

"Have you a friend in prison?" Philadelphia Yearly Meeting queried its members, implying that if they didn't, maybe they ought to make one. Friends were reminded of the many forgotten prisoners with years to serve, who have no contact with their families or former associates. The regular visits of some concerned person, who is leading a constructive life in the outside world, can help inmates to become hopeful and to make plans for a better future, even though release may be years away. When the time does come, these Friends, having fostered a relationship with the offender, can help him to become re-established in society.

In 1958, the Service Committee opened Crenshaw House in Los Angeles, a home for men released on parole. Austin-McCormack House was opened in San Francisco in 1965 and the first halfway house for women on the west coast, Elizabeth Fry House, was about to open its doors to women released from prison who had no work and no place to stay. Within the year, Rufus Jones House would open in Des Moines. In addition to providing a home and new friends, these halfway houses offer family and vocational counseling. Those who need it are assisted in procuring psychiatric help.

To uphold those who were in legal difficulties for registering their objection to war or for participating in the non-violent struggle for civil rights, Monthly Meetings all over the country were soliciting pledges from their members to pay their fines or post bail.

On March 19, 1965—two days after the death of Clarence Pickett, ten days after the first American combat troops arrived in South Vietnam on a "limited mission" and forty days after the first U.S. bombers attacked North Vietnam—the Friends Committee on National Legislation held its annual meeting in Washington, D.C. The committee issued a "Statement on Vietnam and World Peace," calling for:

an end to bombing of North Vietnam;

a cease fire by United States and South Vietnamese forces for a period of four weeks, for example, to encourage a beginning of international negotiations;

negotiations for a permanent cease fire and a settlement which will be acceptable to the peoples of South Vietnam and of Southeast Asia. Recognizing that there are risks involved, this settlement should . . . be supported by effective international peacekeeping machinery;

a phased withdrawal of U.S. and other outside military forces from Southeast Asia looking toward a non-aligned status for nations in that area, coupled with full U.S. participation in a major international economic and social development program including the Mekong project to raise living standards in those countries willing to participate;

immediate efforts by our Government to remove restrictions and open communications, trade and travel with the People's Republic of China and with North Vietnam. Since Chinese cooperation is essential to the achievement of permanent peace in the Pacific, these efforts would be directed toward securing their greater participation in disarmament measures in the community of nations. . . . This would permit progress toward more stable world conditions and would enable our own and other nations to get on with the constructive task of building for the world a "Great Society."

Above the roar of bombers, winging their way to Vietnam, the Quaker "Statement" was not heard.

In the spring of 1965, the Five Years Meeting, which began in 1902, changed its name to Friends United Meeting, since it was now meeting every three years. With the new name went a rededication. "As we begin a new era in Quaker history, we must have that meeting of minds that is unique to men who have sought the mind of the Lord together."[26]

Ohio, Kansas, Oregon and Rocky Mountain Yearly Meetings, feeling that the Friends United Meeting did not express their beliefs, formed the Evangelical Friends Alliance. "The Alliance is not the Friends Church," Arthur O. Roberts, Professor of Religion and Philosophy at George Fox College, explained, "but it is a step of faith on the part of four yearly meetings who look toward a Friends Church, world-wide in scope and evangelical in nature." Many members of these Yearly Meetings "share Everett Cattell's 'passion for unity' on the basis of theological consensus rather than on the basis of heritage or name."[27]

One of the last acts of the Five Years Meeting was the handing over of its property in East Africa to the members of East Africa Yearly Meeting for their ownership and administration. Kenya had become independent and so had the Kenyan Quakers. But Friends United Meeting intended to continue supporting them with funds and personnel.

Equally concerned over the welfare of their Black brothers at home who were imprisoned for encouraging voter registration, Friends went to Selma, Alabama, and joined the non-violent march to Montgomery. James Reeb, one of their co-workers, did not return. A Unitarian minister, he had given up his church in Washington to live in the Roxbury, Massachusetts, ghetto, hoping, through the channel of the American Friends Service Committee, to secure decent living conditions for his neighbors. He went to Selma in answer to a call from the Reverend Martin Luther King, Jr. After the march, he was hit on the head with a club. He died two days later in a Birmingham hospital.

The Friends World Committee appointed observers to the Ecumenical Council in Rome. Reporting on the fourth session of Vatican II, Douglas Steere described the outward incongruity of a Quaker presence in St. Peter's. ". . . the observers were pouring in, dressed in their ecclesiastical and academic finery. (A few old pilgrims like myself were dressed in ordinary business suits.) The basilica was packed . . . I was assigned a seat in the front row of the observers and was a little startled when Bishop Willebrand, Secretary of the Commission for Promoting Christian Unity, walked up and said, 'And how are you, Bishop Steere?' "[28]

At that session, the Pope declared that "the church in this world is not an end in herself. She is at the service of all men. She must make Christ present to all . . . as widely and generously as possible." He asked the Council to support him during his coming peace mission to the United Nations.

There, in New York, on October 4, another Friends World Committee observer, William Huntington, who was now director of the Quaker United Nations Program, sat in the gallery of the General Assembly Hall, listening to the Pope. He felt as if the Pope were "speaking in a truly centered meeting for worship, bringing a message from God himself."

"No more war, never again war," the Pontiff admonished the nations. "Men cannot be brothers if they are not humble . . . it is pride that disrupts brotherhood."[29]

Would the Pope's thrilling exhortation that he had come so far to make put an end to the fighting in Vietnam?

Many Friends who deeply loved their country felt she was wrong in pursuing the fighting. One who tried desperately to make his conviction heard was Norman Morrison. He was thirty-two. He had left the Friends Meeting in Charlotte to become Executive Secretary of Baltimore Monthly Meeting, Stony Run, where he was held in deep affection. It must have come to him at this time that as a Christian, he was called to make the most compelling witness he could make. "Quakers seek to begin with life," he once observed, "not with theory or report. . . . The most important thing in the world is that our faith becomes living experience and deed of life."

By the last week in October there were 148,300 American fighting men in Vietnam. Two U.S. planes accidentally bombed a friendly South Vietnamese village. Senator Edward Kennedy, on a tour of the country, foresaw "a long and enduring struggle."

On the second day of November, Norman Morrison took his baby to Washington. He carried her to the Pentagon in his arms, put her down, doused his clothing with fuel and set himself afire.

Like Mary Dyer, he had felt that his life availed him nought "in comparison to the liberty of the Truth."

At Thanksgiving, twenty-three foreign students met together at the Mohonk Mountain House in New Paltz, New York, for a three-day conference to discuss their "dropout" problem—foreign students who come to the United States for a limited period and decide, while here, not to go home again. They gave as the chief reasons for this the fact that their families and friends found they had changed. Ideas they had acquired in the United States were resented back home and they could not find jobs which utilized the skills they had acquired in the States.

When Keith Smiley, a New York Friend and a proprietor of the Mountain House, called the conference in the hope that these foreign students, discussing their problems together, might find some solutions, he was following a family tradition. In 1883, Albert K. Smiley invited a number of Quakers and others who were influential in religious circles or active in politics to A Conference of Friends of the Indian and Other Dependent Peoples. This conference pushed for the rights of Indians to their land and to education; of Blacks to industrial and professional training as well as higher education. Later conferences discussed the needs of Hawaiian, Puerto Rican and Philippine peoples.

In 1884, Albert Smiley called the first of the Lake Mohonk Conferences on Peace and Arbitration, "To find means by which our own country may have all her disputes with foreign lands settled by arbitration, and bring other nations to join her as rapidly as possible."[30] A resolution was adopted asking the President of the United States to invite Austria, England, France, Germany and Russia to join the United States in establishing a Permanent Tribunal. Conference representatives carried the resolution to Washington but President Cleveland would not receive them. Nevertheless, the idea spread. It became reality in 1907 when the International Conference at The Hague was called for the pacific settlement of international disputes.

That mankind, addicted to warfare, did not avail itself of this machinery for living peacefully does not detract from the grandeur of the mountaintop vision at Lake Mohonk. "An act of love that fails is just as much a part of the divine life as an act of love that succeeds," an English Friend has said, "for love is measured by its own fulness, not by its reception."[31]

37 Peace Bridge

In 1967, nine years after the *Phoenix* made her remonstrance against nuclear bomb tests, she sailed again under concern, as Friends say, referring to the solicitude that their religious principles evoke. This time she left Hiroshima, bound for Haiphong. She was carrying medical supplies, worth ten thousand dollars, the gift of Friends in America to village dispensaries in North Vietnam. Since the shipping lanes were open, Earle Reynolds, the skipper, did not foresee any trouble. From her masthead the *Phoenix* flew the red-and-black star, symbol of Quaker service to suffering humanity. The star was also painted on the sides of the boat to show planes and warships in the South China Sea that she sailed on an errand of mercy.

She was under charter to A Quaker Action Group, newly formed by certain American Friends, predominantly younger, who felt that their Yearly Meetings were not radical enough in their Christian commitment. Some members of the group had helped to write the pamphlet *Quakerism, A View from the Back Benches*, which, in whimsical language, exhorted the Society of Friends to live up to its profession.

Quakers had always ministered to sufferers on both sides of a conflict. They were frustrated now by the U. S. State Department's refusal to let the Service Committee help refugees and injured civilians in North Vietnam. This restricted the Committee's scope to the sector of the country which our government was supporting. A Quaker Action Group had no connection with the Service Committee. On its own, it raised funds in the United States and assembled a Quaker crew which it sent to Japan to man the *Phoenix*. On March 1, 1967, she sailed from Hiroshima and put in at Hong Kong, where members of the crew called on the American consul general to tell him of their plan. In a kindly way he warned them of penalties attending civil disobedience. They explained that they did not wish to break their nation's law but felt their first duty was to obey the injunction "Love your enemies."

As the *Phoenix* neared Haiphong, she found herself in waters that were being bombed. She had to wait until the raid was over before she could dock. While the crew was delivering the medical supplies to the Red Cross Society of the Democratic Republic of Vietnam, on the other side of the globe members of Philadelphia Yearly Meeting, closing their 1967 assembly, issued an Epistle to Friends Everywhere.

"Almost from the very beginning of Yearly Meeting," it read, "our sessions were plunged into intense and spiritually turbulent discussions on Vietnam . . . the more painful because . . . we ourselves share the guilt and have fallen far short of following the teaching of our Master, Jesus Christ. Our Yearly Meeting was united in opposition to the military actions of our country in Vietnam. . . . Friends, in their long history, have often broken with secular governments rather than defraud their own consciences."[1]

The discussions had indeed been turbulent. In the words of the closing minute, these Friends were "caught up in great waves of deep concern"— racial discrimination, the misuse of drugs, population increases at home and abroad, capital punishment, prison conditions. But the draft and the war, especially the bombing of civilians, took precedence over all. During the sessions, Friends "heard many voices, young and eager ones and some older and more cautious."

The young and eager ones urged their fellow members of Philadelphia Yearly Meeting to support the *Phoenix* and to send additional funds for relief to North Vietnam, "regardless of any obstacles which may present themselves."[2]

A year earlier, New York Yearly Meeting had issued A Message to Friends on Vietnam, calling on them to "obey the Inner Light even when this means disobeying man's laws and to risk whatever penalties may be incurred."[3] Friends throughout the United States had been mailing parcels of bandages and antibiotics to the North Vietnamese civilians. But toward the end of 1966, the U. S. Post Office refused to accept them. Friends then sent an average of one thousand dollars per week to the Canadian Friends Service Committee, which bought medicines and shipped them in equal amounts to the Red Cross societies of North and South Vietnam and to representatives of the Viet Cong.

The Johnson administration declared this to be a violation of the Trading with the Enemy Act of 1917. It instructed fourteen thousand American banks not to honor checks made payable to the Canadian Friends Service Committee. American pharmaceutical firms with branches in Canada were forbidden to sell medical supplies to Canadian Friends. A Quaker Action Group's bank account was frozen.

The American Friends Service Committee then applied for a license on humanitarian grounds. This was first granted and later revoked.

After waiting three months for a license, New York Yearly Meeting withdrew the application and instructed its Vietnam Committee to "find ways of shipping relief materials without license," advising officials in Washington of this action. New York Friends went to Canada and turned over three thousand dollars to Friends there. Many others felt the time had arrived to follow the example of their forerunners who, just over a century earlier, obeyed the Inner Light, when this meant disobeying man's laws, and traveled to Canada with "contraband"—runaway slaves. After notifying authorities of their intention, Friends of 1967 also traveled to Canada with "contraband" bandages, which they carried across the Peace Bridge at Buffalo, New York, and handed to waiting members of the Canadian Friends Service Committee.

"Our faith has no power until it is incarnated in our lives," Philadelphia Yearly Meeting stated on the day the *Phoenix* reached Haiphong. "Most of us do little more than participate in occasional protests and support service to those our weapons have wounded. We have used the words of Christ, but we have not acted upon them."[4]

One of the "young and eager" voices which, in the words of Philadelphia Yearly Meeting's Epistle, made "more earnest and compelling" the need to "ease the suffering of human kind in Vietnam" belonged to Marjorie Nelson of Kokomo, Indiana, a doctor who was completing her residency at the Pennsylvania Hospital. It was a soft, calm voice but the Arch Street Meetinghouse reverberated with its deep feeling and authority. Marjorie Nelson urged Friends to support these causes for the sake of their religious belief. She herself, she told them, was shortly going to join the Quaker medical team in South Vietnam and her younger brother, Beryl, had signed on for the second voyage of the *Phoenix*, which was scheduled for later in the year when Friends would bring medical supplies to both the South Vietnamese Red Cross and the militant Buddhists.

Many of the "older and more cautious" members of Philadelphia Yearly Meeting were not comfortable with the exhortation that Friends refuse to pay the portion of their taxes earmarked for military expenditures. Nor did they feel easy about the implication of the statement: "We recognize the privileges and obligations of citizenship, but we reject as false that philosophy which sets the state above moral law." Breaking the law was, to them, unthinkable. Nevertheless, Albert B. Maris, the Presiding Clerk, concluded that this statement represented the sense of the Meeting. Friends who had entertained reservations also realized that the statement adhered to the Quaker tradition and they refrained from voicing further objections. The statement was therefore included in the minutes. Albert Maris carried out his duty as clerk according to Quaker custom, but the sense of the Meeting ran counter to his personal conviction. For he was not only a deeply concerned Friend; he was also a federal judge. At the close of the Yearly Meeting, he asked to be relieved of the clerkship. A man of great integrity and lifelong concern for Quaker service, he was cruelly torn by the dilemma. Nevertheless, he remained in active membership with Friends and continued to be held by them in the warmest affection and esteem.

A month after the close of Philadelphia Yearly Meeting, on April 30, 1967, the American Friends Service Committee marked its fiftieth anniversary. Dedicated to seeking peaceful solutions to national and world problems—"To see what love can do"—representatives of various Quaker groups had met on April 30, 1917, and established the Committee which came to be known all over the world as the AFSC.

The Committee's first service was wartime relief in France. "It has come to you to put your lives into this," Rufus Jones told the Quaker workers there in 1918. "They will not remember your names.... But this thing you are doing will never cease, for when you translate love into life, when you become organs of God for a piece of service, nothing can obliterate it."

The Committee's latest service was wartime relief in Vietnam. It had come to the Quaker workers there to salvage burned and broken bodies, to carry forward, in their generation, the unfinished business of translating love into life.

On April 30, 1967, during the fiftieth anniversary dinner at Haverford College, a coast-to-coast telephone hookup enabled workers and supporters of the Service Committee all over the United States to hear the addresses. Colin W. Bell, the Executive Secretary, movingly described the Committee's aspiration "to bring America nearer to the realization of her dream. . . .

"We have seen since the Second World War proliferation of AFSC attempts to improve the quality of communication and the recognition of common humanity in many directions," Colin Bell told Friends, "among little children and young people and between those young people and us older ones who may often appear to them as champions of a status quo they do not like; between those whose lives seem to be swimming against all of the tides of advantage and privilege and those of us for whom the established pattern of society is going our way; between people in positions of power and leadership who, nevertheless, need some catalyst to bring them into constructive contact with each other. . . . In brief, to bring America nearer to the realization of her dream."

Born in England, Colin Bell became Executive Secretary of the American Friends Service Committee after having been a member of the Friends Ambulance Unit in China, the administrator of Quaker relief for Arab refugees in the Gaza Strip and Director of the Quaker International Center in Geneva, where he also served as the Friends World Committee's observer at the United Nations.

In his talk at the anniversary dinner, he outlined the contribution that the Service Committee ought to make to the human family in the days to come.

"The human family is going to be very young in years," he said. "This means that the AFSC must find ways of relating in real terms to the vision and the aspiration which I believe exists in this erupting volcano of world youth . . . the human family is going to be vastly larger . . . the earth's resources can meet the needs of this huge, young world family only—*only*—if a radical revolution in men's relationships takes place among us all. Only if the totality of the earth's resources . . . are directed toward the good of men everywhere. . . . Nothing less than all we have will be enough for all we have to do. There is no other recourse before the nations but to rise above narrow self-interests, to sweep war and self-seeking and greed away in a revolution of love. God give us strength to make the AFSC, despite all its human fallibilities, one small, precious instrument in that sort of revolution."

As Friends reviewed the past fifty years, they thought with gratitude of those now gone, whose vision had enhanced life for millions of people. They recalled Clarence Pickett and listened to the recording made by Rufus Jones in 1942. "We go where there's suffering," they heard him say in his characteristic Down

East accents, "and we don't ask what church they belong to or which side they're on."

Two weeks after this anniversary, it became evident to New York Friends that such an interpretation of Christian charity was badly misunderstood by some of their neighbors, who took it for Communist sympathy. When, coming through a lane that was beautiful with apple blossoms on a bright morning in mid-May, the Friends of Conscience Bay Meeting in St. James, Long Island, gathered for worship, they found that the walls of their Meetinghouse had been defaced. Angry, blood-red letters spelled out this message: "TREASON! TRAITORS! THERE CAN BE NO COMPROMISE WITH COMMIES! $10,000 FOR V.C., A KNIFE IN THE BACK FOR AMERICAN G.I.'S! THE AMERICAN DEAD WILL BE AVENGED!" Beside the door of the Meetinghouse was painted "THIS IS A GOD-IS-DEAD SO-CALLED 'CHURCH.'"

Conscience Bay Friends had contributed a small sum toward the voyage of the *Phoenix* and had sent money to Canada earmarked for relief in North Vietnam. They had thought that their neighbors understood their position and respected it, even those who disagreed.

Sadly, Friends entered their violated Meetinghouse and considered what they ought to do. Plans for repairing the damage gave way to a discussion of the larger issue—how to respond creatively to an act of terrorism. On the one hand, Friends have traditionally suffered persecution without reacting; on the other, they have vigorously come to the defense of the persecuted. Clearly, in the eyes of those who did the defacing, they were identified with other minorities, whose places of worship were attacked— burned and bombed Black churches in the South and the synagogues in Nazi Germany. It was hoped that the present experience would give Friends deeper understanding of the plight of other minorities.

Since defacement of a house of worship constitutes a felony, they notified the police, but they decided not to prosecute should the vandals be apprehended. Reporters rushed to the scene. It was announced in the newspapers that on the following Sunday members of the Meeting would repaint the walls. Anyone who wished to help was invited to come.

Expressions of support poured in. A paint manufacturer in Brooklyn donated paint. A local painter offered to do the job over should the work party "make a mess of it." On the Sunday,

Roman Catholic priests, Protestant ministers, their parishioners, a delegation from the neighboring synagogue, members of the Civil Liberties Union and the Human Relations Commission, Friends from New York City and friends of Friends arrived on the scene—so many volunteers that they had to cue up to get in a lick with their brushes. The women of the Meeting served sandwiches and coffee. Photographers from the *Times* and *Newsweek* covered the scene.

It was estimated that two hundred people helped restore the Conscience Bay Meetinghouse to its former appearance. They did not all share Friends' views, but they stood firmly for the right of Americans to voice their testimonies.

This was stated clearly in a heartening telegram which came from the Association of Reform Rabbis of New York. It read: "The right to dissent and freedom to express one's religious convictions are basic democratic principles which must be safeguarded under any condition, regardless of one's views on the conduct of the war in Vietnam."

Before nightfall, volunteers had given the Meetinghouse two coats of paint. The Friends of Conscience Bay stood off to admire their shining walls. Everything looked fresh and beautiful, thanks to the brotherly love of those who had come to help. But these Friends had also encountered hate and they felt sad. Hate was not going to be as easy to erase as red paint.

One Friend observed ruefully, "It is going to cost much to be a Quaker again!"[5]

38 The Time Is This Present

Marjorie Nelson was about to finish her residency at the Pennsylvania Hospital when the American Friends Service Committee asked her to go to Vietnam for two years. The Committee was preparing to open a Quaker Rehabilitation Center at Quang Ngai.

All through her childhood in Kokomo, Indiana, Marjorie Nelson—Marge, to her friends—had known exactly what she intended to do when she grew up. She wanted to bring medical care to people in some faraway place like China, and to tell them of God's love. Growing up in the Courtland Avenue Meeting in Kokomo, part of Western Yearly Meeting, Marge thought in evangelical terms: She wanted to be a missionary.

Earlham College, Indiana University Medical School, internship and residency in Philadelphia—all were meant to lead to the one objective. In order to help Marge prepare for overseas work, the Pennsylvania Hospital had assigned her to a tour of duty on board the *Hope*. In June of 1965, she was in Guinea studying tropical medicine.

While she was in college and getting her medical training, she was also deeply involved in YFNA—the Young Friends of North America—serving as Chairman of the association's East-West Contacts Committee. In 1965, she represented YFNA at the Christian Youth Seminar in Prague, where she was the only American delegate, and again the next year in Stockholm.

So when the call from the Service Committee came for work in Vietnam, Marge had had experience abroad, she was twenty-six, ready professionally and deeply concerned.

This was not a call to the mission field—Service Committee workers don't preach—but Marge was convinced that God's love can be enunciated either with or without words. Her heart reached out to communicate it with an eagerness anyone could understand and her healing hands knew how to translate it into practical reality.

To those familiar with the statue of Mary Dyer, the modeling of Marge's face seemed reminiscent—the high cheekbones and resolute chin. Part of her light brown hair was cut in long bangs; the rest was piled high on her head, making her look both childlike and sedate. Mostly, her expression was thoughtful. Then, suddenly Marge would turn gay, even mischievous. But as she pictured herself in Vietnam, surrounded by fighting, she was a little frightened. Which pacifist can be sure that put to the test, he will behave in accordance with his principles? Then there was the burden of anxiety Marge would be imposing on her father. It was worrying enough, having her brother on the *Phoenix*. Moreover, Marge was very reluctant to put half the globe between herself and a certain young Friend from Minnesota. She hesitated, but only briefly.

On the first of July, 1967, she went to Pendle Hill where she had a few weeks of preliminary briefing by the Service Committee for her Vietnam assignment. She delayed leaving until September because she still had commitments at home. The first was at Guilford College in Greensboro, North Carolina, where the Fourth World Conference of Friends was being convened.

It was fifteen years since Friends had come together at Oxford—high time that the two hundred thousand in the world family should, through emissaries, have a chance to look into one another's faces and hear one another's voices again. Of the nine hundred representatives who came from thirty-eight countries on six continents, Marge was one of the youngest. She hoped the Conference would give her confidence. She needed to feel that she was being seconded in spirit. And she found what she hoped for—a clear sense of the world-wide fellowship and concern of Friends. She, was about to implement a part of this concern!

Most of the representatives needed the assurance that as they worked in their little corner of the world for peace, for the well-being and dignity of all men, they were not alone. The barrier of language made discussion slow for people coming from thirty-eight countries, but Friends could easily worship together. The living silence overleapt all language.

North Carolina seemed a fitting place to hold the Conference. The state passed a resolution welcoming the participants and recalling the arrival of the first Friends, three centuries earlier, around Albemarle Sound. In 1672, William Edmundson held the first religious service in Carolina. George Fox came a few months later. John Archdale, who became governor in 1695, had been convinced by Fox. Speaking of him, Floyd Moore said, "Archdale's creative leadership in the tension between colonists, proprietors, French and Indians places him in the high company of Penn both as a Friend and as a governor."[1]

North Carolina Yearly Meeting of Friends was established in 1698. In Guilford itself, on the site of the first Friends Meetinghouse, a marker commemorates the beginning of the Underground Railroad, which eventually helped perhaps as many as one hundred thousand slaves to escape into the free states and Canada. Three Friends, Vestal Coffin, his son Addison and his cousin Levi, were the principal leaders. All the way from that spot in Guilford to Canada and westward, other Friends manned the escape routes. But there were also many who would not participate because the activities of the Underground Railroad were surreptitious and illegal.

Guilford, the seat of a leading Quaker institution, enhanced by so much Quaker history, would seem to be the ideal place for Friends to gather. The college had been racially integrated since 1961. But there were people in the area who did not approve of the Quaker testimony to racial equality. Two years earlier, on a Sunday in May, a bomb exploded in the New Garden Meetinghouse, opposite the college. "What did we do that was wrong?" one of the children asked the pastor, who replied, "Maybe we did something that was right."[2]

The whole Friends World Conference was shaken when some representatives from overseas went off campus and experienced the unfriendliness which is the daily lot of dark-skinned Americans. On campus, a warm feeling of family prevailed. The colorful national dress of representatives from Japan, Korea, India and Africa brightened the scene. Malagasy Friends, like all Friends of bygone days, could be distinguished by their hats.

In the opening address, L. Hugh Doncaster, Lecturer in Quaker History at Woodbrooke College in England, stressed the feeling of oneness among Friends despite their diversity, yet cautioned them "not to bend over backwards for the sake of a superficial unity, but to speak the truth as we have known it . . . the only attitude which is consistent with our Quaker belief."

Hugh Doncaster frankly found flaws in the pastoral system which, he felt, leads "right away from that which I believe to be essential Quakerism." He was equally critical of his own Yearly Meeting where what he called a much more insidious mood was prevalent, a mood of vague permissiveness, "which very easily runs from Quakerism into Ranterism, which so stresses individual faithfulness and freedom that it undercuts corporate testimony. . . .

"There is only one ultimate loyalty required of us and that is to God himself," he declared with such conviction, such Woolman-like humility that his listeners were deeply moved. "It is finally at the level of spirit that you and I, whatever branch of Quakerism we come from, will find a oneness in God. And let us not allow any particular form or formulation to be a form of idolatry. Let us get behind to the love of God Himself. . . . Because—because the world as I see it is dying, literally dying, for lack of Quakerism in action."[3]

Hugh Doncaster had thought about the address for over a year, not when he was sitting at his desk but when he was working on his farm in England, "with a hoe in my hand and a bent back, and the sweat dripping into my eyes." He had steadfastly refused to write out anything in advance, believing that his message should not take final form until he was face to face with his listeners. Then the spirit interacting between them and himself would determine the words. It required great faithfulness to trust that when he was on the platform confronting nine hundred people, he would be given the insight to speak directly to their needs. Yet it was his very dependence on the leading of the spirit that made Hugh Doncaster's address a fitting introduction to the deliberations of the worship-sharing groups and round tables.

A documentary film of the *Phoenix*, released by the Canadian Broadcasting Company, was shown at the Conference. It made many American representatives uncomfortable. They still felt that it was wrong, under any circumstances, to defy the law. Other Americans felt overtaken by a deepening dilemma. They began to wonder whether Christian commitment wasn't all or nothing.

Quaker Life pointed out that none of the money contributed to the Friends United Meeting, the Friends General Conference or the American Friends Service Committee had gone to support A Quaker Action Group which, the editorial explained, "is an independent organization consisting of a few individuals who have the daring to . . . relieve the suffering of civilian casualties of war. . . . Most of us lack this kind of daring. We are afraid our fellow citizens will think we lack loyalty to our country or we have secret sympathies for the Communists. . . . But there is still one who . . . spoke of giving 'a cup of cold water.' Can you think of a more likely 'cup of cold water' than medical supplies for civilian casualties of war regardless of whether they thirst on friendly or enemy soil?"[4]

Roland L. Warren, Professor of Community Theory at Brandeis University, described the feeling of loss he experienced at the break of a silent meeting. "In a sense, and only partially, we have known each other in that which is eternal, but as we rise from the meeting we begin to lose contact with one another. And it has always seemed to be one of the important aspects of Quaker experience to keep that contact, to strive to carry through in one's total living that sense of God's pervasive presence and that sense of sharing this presence with one's fellow men at the deepest level. . . ."

As a Quaker International Affairs Representative in Germany, Roland Warren had been an interpreter between East and West, passing to and fro through the Wall, communicating to people, who were never allowed to meet face to face, the views of those on the other side. Patiently, impartially he brought to each group an awareness of the difficulties encountered by the other. Through him, each came to sense the possibility of flying over the divisive Wall into the spiritual unity of all mankind.

Roland Warren recognized all the difficulties involved in the Quaker approach. "We have been opposed to 'forcing people to do good.' . . . But at the same time . . . we often supported legislative measures which force certain people to act in certain ways which we think are good. Do we not need to seek further clarity on this question of the use of coercion to get other men to behave in certain ways which we think do justice to the intrinsic worth of still other men?"[5]

An unforgettable message electrified a worship service. Everett Cattell, President of Malone College, and Maurice Creasey, Director of Studies at Woodbrooke, had spoken briefly. Silence followed the singing of the hymn "Breathe on Me, Breath of God." Suddenly, this was broken by a cry from the body of the Meeting: "I'm a Negro in a ghetto. I can't hear you. . . . I'm a burnt child in Vietnam. I can't hear you. . . . I'm a mother in a South American slum. I can't hear you. . . . I'm an American soldier in Vietnam, under orders to kill. I can't hear you. . . ."[6]

U Thant, Secretary General of the United Nations, gave the principal address. "Accompanying spouses" of the Conference representatives, who had been holding their own "Greensboro Gathering" were invited to attend.

Reporting on these two conferences in the Greensboro *News*, Joseph Knox wrote, "Just who did they think they were, anyway, this handful of presumptuous people, assuming responsibility for sufferers of all the calculated cruelties people inflict on people? Why, there are more Baptists in North Carolina alone than Quakers in all the world! During days I met with them to report . . . I came to see them as a small band of conspirators, . . . fussing among themselves to live their preachments, needling the conscience of the world to be about the business of the Sermon on the Mount. . . . One small measure of their worldwide prestige was the appearance here of U Thant. Effectively, this Burmese Buddhist . . . was only an extension of their own voice crying out for goodwill and peace on earth. They invited him. He accepted. Could Baptists, Presbyterians, Methodists or whoever have gotten him to Greensboro? Would they have thought to ask? Would they have wanted him? . . . these Quakers must be dreadfully embarrassing to Christians. They must also be embarrassing to governments, who surely wish they would just hush up and go away . . . they say the jungle war (in Vietnam) has solved and will solve nothing. . . . Just stop fighting."[7]

U Thant told his audience that as long as governments are unwilling to surrender any part of their sovereignty to serve the common good of the international community, it is futile to expect the United Nations to develop a supranational authority. The United Nations can be an effective instrument for keeping the peace, he declared, "provided the super powers are willing to keep the peace, either by throwing their weight on its side, or by refraining from active opposition. This . . . is related to the larger question of . . . fashioning a new world. . . . I believe that both in Vietnam and in the Middle East there will be no solution . . . if the human factor is ignored."

U Thant urged that the People's Republic of China be included in the United Nations, warning that the progress it has made in the development of nuclear weapons surprised qualified observers. "It bodes little good for the interests of world peace and security to perpetuate the isolation of China," he declared, "and keep her cut off from normal contacts with the rest of the world. I believe the time must come when China can play its part as a member of the international community on equal terms with others, and the sooner this happens the better.

"The peace that we have to seek in order to save succeeding generations from the scourge of war must therefore be a peace that will envelop the whole of humanity. . . . No man can save himself or his country or his people unless he consciously identifies himself with, and deliberately works for, the whole of mankind."[8]

Replying on Friends' behalf, Douglas Steere made what is surely the greatest Quaker understatement of all time: "Quakers are not an easy group to speak in the name of, for in matters of strategy and conduct, they have always had a considerable current of diversity." He illustrated this point by describing how some North Carolina Quakers met the approach of the Civil War by moving north; others were Abolitionists; some used their homes as stations on the Underground Railroad and still others, though sympathetic with the slaves, disapproved of breaking the law.

"We have this same diversity in strategy today," Douglas Steere explained, "and should not be surprised at it or see in it anything but a condition of vigor and growth. . . . Back of these differences, however, there is a common ground of spiritual concern. . . . Woolman's word is again utterly adequate, 'Love was the first motion.'"

The authentic Quaker witness, Douglas Steere said, was "a capacity to break ideological situations down into human faces . . . to quicken our responsibility for each other as . . . pilgrims living together on this earth who are capable of answering from the seed of God that is in every soul."

He closed hopefully. "We are nearer to a break-through on the abandonment of massive war as an instrument of settling international conflicts than ever before . . . the biological morality of the world in the present balance of terror is slowly moving over to an acknowledgement that another way *must* be found . . . we must . . . be joined to all the living . . . the day we work for not only will break, but is breaking. . . ."[9]

At the conclusion of Douglas Steere's response, U Thant hurried back to New York.

Floyd Moore commented afterward, "Most of the Friends who heard U Thant speak had no idea how relieved the security agents and Conference officials were when they saw him safely into a small, private plane that flew him to New York in an hour over territory which took heavy toll from George Fox and early Friends."

When the Conference was over, Marjorie Nelson went home to say good-by to her father. They had a few beautiful days together on his boat, cruising around Lake Huron. She repeated for him phrases from the Conference: "The world is dying, literally dying for lack of Quakerism in action" and "to be joined to all the living" —she, Marge, was about to be joined to the living in Vietnam and also to the dying—"the day we work for not only will break, but is breaking. . . ."

The last night aboard, they brought their sleeping bags up on deck. They spoke little. Accustomed, as evangelical Friends, to verbalizing prayer, they realized, as they looked at the stars, that no words could express what they felt.

Marge was thinking of Beryl, waiting in Hong Kong to make his testimony on the *Phoenix*. It might be costly. She was thinking of her mother and her Uncle Bill, a Colonel in the Air Force, who was missing in Vietnam. Suddenly she realized that she was leaving her father to carry all this alone.

She rolled over so that her face was close to his. "Do you mind?" she asked. "I never really thought what it was going to mean to you. With Beryl over there, too. I never really thought—it might be dangerous. Do you mind?"

He reached out and put his arm around her. "Honey," he said, "you know I want you to do what you feel is right."

Six months later, when she was a prisoner, it was the recollection of these words that gave Marge comfort. In accepting the call to go to Vietnam, running the risk which had now become reality, she had had her father's blessing.

39 Joined to All the Living

On the gatepost of the house in Quang Ngai, where Quaker Service-Vietnam was located, a notice explained the motivation of the people inside. Under the red-and-black star, in both Vietnamese and English, the notice stated: "Quakers believe in the dignity and equality of all men. For over 300 years we have been guided by this principle and opposed to the use of military force to resolve conflict. We seek to alleviate human suffering wherever it may occur and to serve those in need without regard to their race, religion or political views."

Strange words, in a country where large-scale suffering and death were regarded as the only fitting response to political views.

In 1966, the Service Committee opened a day care center and kindergarten in Quang Ngai, six miles inland from the South China Sea, about midway between Saigon and Hanoi. Here, children aged two and one-half to six, who were living in temporary refugee shelters, could get a meal, a bath, clean clothes, love and medical attention. Here, against the sound of gunfire and explosions, they were encouraged to behave like children—to laugh and play.

In Saigon, American Quaker volunteers were working in social welfare agencies which were not political or connected with the war. Other young Service Committee workers in VISA—Voluntary International Service Assignments—were teaching and providing recreation in refugee camps. Friends' appeals to the United States Government for permission to initiate relief projects in North Vietnam had been rejected.

There were also American Quaker missionaries in South Vietnam, who were helping refugees and preaching to them of salvation through the atoning blood of Jesus Christ. Oregon Yearly Meeting of Friends Church supported three workers, one of them in Hue, the others in outlying villages. They had no connection with the Service Committee, which their Yearly Meeting had disavowed some years earlier. "The American Friends Service Committee consistently refuses to give relief in the name of Jesus Christ," Oregon Friends declared, "and thus it removes the *Christian* basis for its service activities. The Friends Service Committee leaders have repeatedly expressed as the basis for their peace philosophy the universal goodness of man, or as they so often state, 'that of God in every man' which, to us, is contrary to the teaching of Romans the first chapter and other Scriptures . . . if Oregon Yearly Meeting were to continue the association it would be an indication of a similarity of beliefs and policies. . . ."[1]

There was, therefore, no contact between the American Friends Service Committee workers and the American Evangelical Friends missionaries. The sum of both efforts was pitifully small, in view of the needs of the Vietnamese people. In 1967 alone, there were one hundred thousand civilian casualties. Roughly a quarter of the injured were children under sixteen. The Provincial Hospital in Quang Ngai was so crowded that patients had to double up in bed. The hospital could amputate an arm or a leg, but it could not provide artificial ones or help the amputee return to active life.

So, in the fall of 1967, Friends opened a Rehabilitation Center in an unused building opposite the Quang Ngai Provincial Hospital and installed an American, British and Dutch staff, who received only maintenance and ten dollars a month for pocket money. These workers immediately began to train Vietnamese apprentices in physiotherapy and the making of artificial limbs, which were badly needed because so many of the war-injured required amputations. Limb parts had been ordered from Britain. They were held up by a dock strike. Improvising, the Director of the Quaker Prosthetic Service, Joseph Clark, made a limb for the Center's first patient, a twelve-year-old orphan whose leg had been amputated below the knee. Homeless, he spent his days on the veranda of the hospital's surgical ward, running about on his knees, begging food from passing Americans. A week after his new leg was fitted, bursting with pride, he walked out of the Quaker Center on two legs.

Next to commitment and courage, the most essential qualification for members of Quaker Service-Vietnam was ingenuity. Sandbags were cut up into slings and sheets for treatment tables. Frozen juice cans became splints for children's hands. The members of the staff, who were responsible for keeping the place running, performed miracles with scrounged materials. It was a red-letter day when the wing of a plane which had been shot down was donated to Quaker Service. This was quickly turned into splints and artificial limbs. There were no wheel chairs, so the staff carried the patients piggyback. Before Dr. Nelson arrived, the nurse was giving all the medical care in a makeshift dispensary.

It took a certain flexibility of outlook for Quakers to accept the fact that by going into a war zone they became dependent on the military. Supplies had to travel by U. S. Government transport. Building materials for an addition to the Rehabilitation Center could only be obtained at the American Naval Base in Da Nang. American Army authorities offered the Friends guns and ammunition and were surprised when all weapons were refused. Not only that—the Friends did not wish to be rescued, they said, should they be captured, since this might endanger the life of someone else. What baffling people!

It was steaming hot when Marjorie Nelson reached Quang Ngai. The patients with bomb injuries and horrible-looking napalm burns, who waited on the hospital veranda for admission, were covered with flies. Some of the children, Marge was told, just stayed there, although they'd been discharged to make room for worse cases. Their parents had been killed. They had no place to go.

The team was shorthanded. One of the physical therapists, Dorothy Weller, was ill with encephalitis. During the summer, she had written humorously to Philadelphia of "trying to maintain diplomatic relations with these Viet mosquitoes, but, believe me, it's hard to maintain the proper Quaker attitude toward them. They don't seem to understand that when I get into bed all buttoned up beneath the mosquito netting, they are supposed to be outside."[2] Before long, one of those mosquitoes carrying a strain of encephalitis got Dorothy Weller.

Her colleague, Sally Squires, a member of Radnor, Pennsylvania, Meeting, showed Marge around the Provincial Hospital. "Sights I've seen this week would make any American go hysterical from pain," she told Marge.

Injured civilians, just evacuated from the war zone, huddled in the corridors of the hospital waiting to be treated, or lay on the ground outside in pools of blood and excreta. The place smelled of neglected people, too weak to shoo the flies off their wounds. Why they didn't all die from infection was something a Western mind couldn't grasp. The agony, the senseless, needless horror, the insufficiency of everything that was needed for proper treatment almost did make Marge break down at first. She had seen bad injuries on the emergency service at home, but few were intentionally inflicted. Many of these patients had been hit by American anti-personnel bombs, which drove millions of metal slivers into their skin, covering them from head to foot with cuts and blinding them when they entered the eye.

Katie Maendel, the rehab nurse, showed Marge the leg fracture of a seven-year-old boy, whom she carried around in her arms. It wasn't healing, she said, touching it tenderly. He and his little brother had been brought in with a batch of refugees after their family and their whole village had been wiped out in an air strike. The little one died of starvation a few days later. She had worked over the wound of this one—they didn't know his name—but the infection seemed to be in the bone. Would he recover? She looked pleadingly at Marge, begging to be told that the little guy's chances were better than she thought.

But Marge couldn't reassure Katie. Maybe back in the States a team of orthopedic surgeons, operating in a first-class hospital, could save the little Nameless One, as Katie called him, from osteomyelitis. In Quang Ngai, there weren't any orthopedic surgeons.

Marge didn't even stop to unpack. She went right to work. "Bac-si"—doctor—the people she treated called her softly. Stoical, gentle people, they murmured apologetically, "*Dau Qua, Dau Qua*" —it hurts too much.

She fell into bed that first night. Tomorrow, she'd unpack and try to make her room home. But she had to learn to sleep through the thud of mortars and bombs and machine-gun fire. How near was that explosion? After a few nights, she got a little used to it. Even in sleep, one was tense and alert here.

Yet no matter how close the war was or how many patients were waiting, after breakfast the members of the team took half an hour for worship. It seemed to Marge that the gathered silence meant more in Vietnam than it did at home. Silence was the antithesis of war, the solace of God's presence. If peace ever came, it would have the sound of Friends worshiping.

The monsoons set in a week after Marge arrived. Torrential rains, hurled by high winds, drove water through the glassless windows of the Quaker Day Care Center till it was waist-high on the ground floor. This was the worst flood in Quang Ngai's history. Furniture had to be carried upstairs. Outside, only the roof of the Center's little Citroen showed. The water finally went down but the patient load kept rising. Fighting was becoming more intense. As Marge worked day after day without a break, she came to know these patients and it struck her that the most important thing she had to give them was a laugh, a smile.

What people who are suffering really require, she thought, is people who love them, yes, and people who care for them, yes.

But even beyond this it seems as though part of it as well is people who bring them *joy.*

She was working hard to learn the language. By Christmas, she had acquired a fair-sized vocabulary. It wasn't enough. In letters from home, people kept asking what the Vietnamese themselves thought about the war. Although Marge had been in the country almost three months, she didn't feel she could answer this question until she spoke Vietnamese more fluently.

When she woke up, much too early, on Christmas morning, it was raining. She couldn't get back to sleep. Was Kokomo having a white Christmas? At home, the three of them would be running down to see the tree—she and Keith and Beryl. She pictured her brothers, not as they were now—Keith settling down after his tour of duty in the Navy and Beryl on the *Phoenix* in Hong Kong—but years ago, when they were all three still safe at home, small children, tumbling downstairs in their pajamas on Christmas morning to see what was under the tree.

They had a happy, interesting childhood. Home was a place where people of other races and nationalities were made welcome. Marge's mother even went to school and learned Spanish so she could communicate with the migrant workers who came to Kokomo to pick tomatoes and work in the canneries. They needed befriending. The Nelsons visited back and forth with Black families as unself-consciously as they did with whites.

But growing up in a deeply religious home could be frustrating. Unlike some contemporary Friends, who adopted the social standards of their community, Earl and Elda Nelson were still strict about things like smoking, drinking and dancing. When Marge decided to go to the Junior High prom, her parents said No. Marge had her heart set on it. Later, her parents told her that they had talked the matter over; they were no less opposed to dancing. If, in spite of this, she still wished to go to the prom, they would help her. And they went the extra mile—Marge's mother made a beautiful dress; her father took her downtown and helped her pick out costume jewelry to go with it. He drove her to the dance.

Had she had a good time? he asked on the way home. No, not really.

This Christmas, Earl Nelson was being needled by his neighbors, who demanded to know what his son Beryl thought he was doing, giving aid and comfort to the enemy? The *Phoenix* had tried to take another shipment of medical supplies to Haiphong but the

North Vietnamese refused clearance because, they claimed, she would be endangered by the "intensive, barbaric bombing of North Vietnam by U.S. warplanes." Then, hoping instead to deliver the cargo to the South Vietnamese Red Cross and the United Buddhist Church, the crew sailed the *Phoenix* to Da Nang, where the port authorities wouldn't let her dock, either. South Vietnamese sailors towed her out into the South China Sea. Completely frustrated in her mercy mission, the *Phoenix* returned to Hong Kong with her cargo.

Questioned there about his reasons for sailing to North Vietnam, Beryl Nelson said simply that in his Sunday school at Friends Church in Kokomo, Indiana, he had been taught to love his enemies. That was all he was trying to do.

When this report reached Indiana, the reaction was mixed. Some Friends feared that the voyage of the *Phoenix* "cast discredit on the name of Quakers and served to aid the enemies of our government."[3]

But those Friends who had taught Beryl in Sunday school and who knew his sincerity faced the realization that they could no longer teach their children the Bible unless they were willing to live by its precepts, even when it upset their political beliefs and made them vulnerable.

Earl Nelson was interviewed by the Associated Press. What, the reporter inquired, did his fellow workers at the Chrysler plant think of his son's action?

"Even the fathers of some of the boys fighting over there have told me they're in favor of anything that will get some communication going," he answered. And he pointed out that his brother Bill, who was missing after flying two hundred missions in Vietnam, "didn't like the war any better than anybody else." Then Earl Nelson gave the reporter his definition of patriotism: "It means working for the best interest of your country at all times and I can't believe waging war is ever in the best interest."[4]

Marge had more than her family on her mind this Christmas morning. She was thinking a great deal these days about Bob Perisho, the boy from Minnesota who was taking his Ph.D. at Yale. They had worked together in YFNA—the Young Friends of North America—which included people from all varieties of Quaker background. Bob came from the Midwest, too, and, like Marge, had been brought up an evangelical Friend. Like her, he had come to feel at home in unprogramed Meetings when he went to Scattergood

School, which was maintained by Iowa Conservative Friends, and to Haverford College. He could also attend Mass with his roommates and worship comfortably. Marge felt drawn to this quiet, thoughtful physicist, who approached religion as he did an experiment, without presuppositions—something to be discovered through experience. Like George Fox, Bob "knew God experimentally," and like a good scientist, he felt called to communicate his findings to others.

Although YFNA only met twice a year, it meant more to those who attended than their Meetings at home—more than anything else in their lives. They'd come from anywhere in the United States to Kansas City or Indianapolis or Chicago just to spend the weekend together in some Friends Meetinghouse, worshiping, talking about their own and the world's problems, preparing frugal meals, sleeping on the Meetinghouse floor—but not much. Who needs sleep when there won't be another chance to talk for six months?

They'd arrive feeling discouraged about the present, hopelessly baffled about their future. In those few days together they'd catch a vision of what they wanted to do with their lives and *could* do—far greater things than they'd ever dreamed of before. They became more aware of their own identity here than at home or in college. They had what they felt was an authentic encounter with God—inward, yet shared.

They asked each other why they never had this experience with their contemporaries who were not Friends, although they saw them all the time and were much closer, really. They certainly didn't have the same experience with older Friends in their home Meetings.

The members of YFNA strove to conduct their Meetings for Business truly under the leading of the Spirit, which meant that they never adopted a minute until they could do it corporately, with the wholehearted assent of every member. This took time. Opposing views were stated, respectfully considered, meditated upon, refined, adjusted until the whole group sincerely felt that its action was in accordance with the will of God. These Young Friends were not acting in response to individual Light nor in obedience to a set of values determined for the community by part of it. They had the sense that in each new situation, they were propelled together by divine guidance.

Everyone wanted to stay in YFNA as long as possible. Of course, when a Young Friend finished grad school or got married, it was time to leave. Making the break was hard. Marge had thought that here in Quaker Service there would be the same spirit; that working and living together, Friends would feel a strong bond, too. They did, but the premises were different. Marge was sure that to be happily married she would have to choose a man who shared her YFNA experience, like Bob Perisho. But Bob was a long, long way from here, probably just getting to Minnesota for Christmas.

As a Bac-si, Marge said to herself reprovingly, jumping out of bed, I'd diagnose my ailment like this: touch of homesickness.

When she opened the door, her spirits rose, for there was a sock stuffed with presents and a card from Father Christmas. The English members of the team had evidently been his messengers. Later, Marge found another sock. That one came from Santa Claus!

Christmas afternoon, she went for a bicycle ride with Kees Willink, the Dutch occupational therapist who had just joined the team. Like Marge, he was interested in botany. They traveled north, across the river, past the rice fields, then eastward toward the sea. At the foot of a mountain, they decided to walk up, stopping to make friends on the way with some children who were picking flowers and, farther on, with a group of Buddhist monks working in the fields. The monks invited Marge and Kees to visit the large pagoda on the summit and the cemetery, where the young monk who had recently immolated himself was buried.

Marge thought of Norman Morrison. She had never met him. But she had seen his picture in the newspaper after his death—a smiling, completely forthright face.

"Why," Marge asked Kees, "is it considered right, as it is in America, to make people die in a war but wrong if they choose to die in the cause of peace?"

Kees shook his head. He had no explanation.

When they got back to the Center, Christmas dinner was ready—turkey, cranberry sauce and all. It was a different Christmas from any Marge had ever known but, she thought during the silence before the meal, she was where she wanted to be, where God had led her to be.

The day after Christmas everything was the same—newly injured patients waited resignedly for help. The fighting went right on, heavier than before. The noise from the planes and helicopters, the deafening gunfire continued without a let-up. But a truce had been declared for Tet, the Lunar New Year, at the end of January. People could live in peace for a few days, usher in a new, hopefully better year. All the patients wanted to go home, even those who were too sick. The Vietnamese staff dwindled away. Home was the place to be at New Year. After Tet, everyone promised, they'd come back.

With the truce and the decreased patient load, this seemed a good time for members of the Quaker staff to take some time off. Four had already gone. Marge decided to spend a few days in Hue, staying with her friend, Sandra Johnson, a teacher from Cambridge, Massachusetts, who was working there with International Voluntary Service. After almost four months in Quang Ngai, it was time she had a break, Marge told herself. So she went to Hue just before Tet.

The twelve Friends who remained at the Center had their first good night on January 29. The guns went silent, observing the truce. Instead of the deadly racket, there were fireworks, celebrating the New Year.

At four o'clock on the morning of the thirty-first, the Friends were wakened by artillery and tank fire right outside their house. The house was not the target, though. The prison next door, with thirteen hundred people locked inside, was being shelled. Next to the prison, little houses, made out of eucalyptus branches, bamboo and cow dung, were crowded with refugees. Just before daybreak, their thatched roofs caught fire and went up in black smoke. News came through that the Viet Cong were using the truce to launch an offensive on Da Nang and Hue as well.

Marge, the Friends thought at once, *their Bac-si*—had she been caught in the attack on Hue? Was she all right?

The whole Quaker team rushed to the hospital to help, never stopping during that whole grim day to eat or drink. "You will not believe," Kees Willink, the Dutch worker reported later, "the circumstances we had to work in. There was gauze, but there were no scissors . . . I was helping our nurse, Katie. I cut off clothing from bodies to locate an injury with my pen knife, cut bandages with the same tool. Within a couple of minutes my hands were sticky and covered red with blood. . . . And still more and more patients were coming in, and still bombing and shooting was going on in town. People walking in in a condition that you wonder how they are able to put one foot in front of the other without falling."[5]

When, exhausted, the members of the team went to bed that night, they still had had no word from Marge.

By the next day, there were so many casualties that no more

patients could fit into the hospital. They were left on the ground outside, which also served as the only available toilet facility. There, in the open air, with intravenous bottles hanging from the bushes, minor surgery was performed.

The next day and the next, the Quakers went on doggedly. There was no news of Marge. They tried to make contact, but she had disappeared. Their Vietnamese friends brought word that Sandra Johnson and another woman—probably Marge, they figured—had been seen leaving Hue in the custody of a Viet Cong cadre. If the other woman really was Marge, then she had been captured. They couldn't put her from their minds. They heard that one of the Oregon Quaker missionaries, Jerry Sandoz, who was also in embattled Hue, had been rescued by U. S. Marines after eight harrowing days.

Huddled on the floor all night, with shells bursting around them, the members of the team asked each other how long they could hold out here. They were determined not to forsake their Vietnamese friends. But they were far too understaffed, since the team members who had gone on vacation hadn't been able to get back. The doctor was missing. There was no word from Philadelphia. The Center was cut off from the outside world.

They kept going for eleven days. On Sunday, during their Meeting for Worship with the racket going on outside, it came to Richard Johnson, the Field Director, that it was neither wise nor prudent to let the staff in his charge remain in Quang Ngai. The fighting made all but first aid impossible. If Quang Ngai fell to the Viet Cong, the Quakers would probably not be roughly treated. But they might be an embarrassment to their South Vietnamese friends—indeed, a mortal danger. And they were certainly in great danger from gunfire themselves.

No one wanted to leave. It was heartbreaking to think of what would happen to the Center they had built and to the people who had come to depend on them. One Vietnamese apprentice said, "Now this happens, it is as if I am having an accident."[6]

The Friends went to Hong Kong, where they were joined by the staff members who had not been able to get back to Quang Ngai. Everyone was accounted for except Marjorie Nelson. A representative from the Philadelphia office of the Service Committee came over to confer. As the fighting seesawed, they weighed all the arguments for and against returning to Vietnam. Finally they decided to send a reconnoitering group. Five team members left for

Quang Ngai on March 4. They found their Center in a deplorable state, but it was obvious that they were needed more than ever. Although it would be months before they could function there again, they were determined to reactivate Quaker Service-Vietnam.

Meanwhile, in Philadelphia, the Yearly Meeting convened for its 1968 sessions. As they came together, Friends recalled that just a year ago Marjorie Nelson had been present, begging them to support the *Phoenix*. Now she was missing in Vietnam. It was seven weeks since she had left Quang Ngai.

A few Friends expressed reservations about renewing Quaker Service-Vietnam because it demanded cooperation with the American military and the Saigon Government. But Colin Bell declared, "I do not believe that acts of love can ever be totally silenced or overlaid by evil or totally misunderstood. There would be a special poignancy for us all if the AFSC could not help refugees, created in large part by our own nation's bombs and napalm—if, as it were, sufferers from our violence were off limits to our love!"[7]

After nineteen years as Executive Secretary of the Service Committee, Colin Bell was scheduled to be succeeded by Dr. William Lotspeich, who had given up the chairmanship of the Department of Physiology in the University of Rochester Medical School to join the Service Committee. But that March William Lotspeich was forced by illness to resign. He died eight months later at the age of forty-eight. To all who knew him, he communicated his awareness of the presence of God.

At those sessions of Philadelphia Yearly Meeting, Friends were acutely concerned about the mounting needs of their Black neighbors. The Yearly Meeting was already contributing to the Chester Project, which sought to give Black high school students a sense of identity by helping them learn about their heritage. Public housing, citizen participation in urban renewal and education of the white community were the major fields of effort. The Yearly Meeting sent a letter to the largest banks in Philadelphia concerning the problems of consumer credit. The poor, they explained, were often cheated by unscrupulous salesmen.

A committee was appointed to "examine the total picture of the urban crisis and make a comprehensive study of the committees presently working in these areas, so that the most efficient use of money and personnel can be made."

Friends were reminded that they have a deep responsibility to face up to the problems of prejudice and racial violence in themselves, their Meetings and communities. "We cannot be content unless we begin to change the social order. Funds must be found to make those changes possible."[8]

A sense of urgency seized the Yearly Meeting as it expressed its wholehearted intention of supporting the non-violent Poor People's Campaign for Jobs and Income, which the Reverend Martin Luther King, Jr., was planning to hold in Washington in June. He hoped the Campaign would move those in power to proceed more energetically toward eliminating hunger and poverty, "to redeem the soul of America."

On the last afternoon of Yearly Meeting, a message was brought up to the Clerk's desk. Glancing at it, the Clerk suddenly forgot his Quaker decorum. Jubilantly waving the little slip of paper, he made for the microphone. "Radio Hanoi has just announced that Marjorie Nelson and Sandra Johnson, held by the National Liberation Front for the past fifty-two days, will shortly be released!"

40 A Loaf of Bread

The Friends General Conference was held at Cape May, New Jersey, from June 21 to 28, 1968. On the Saturday evening, James Farmer, the guest speaker—who couldn't guess then that he was to be Assistant Secretary of Health, Education and Welfare in the Nixon administration—discussed the needs of his people. Blacks rioted, he said, because they felt they were being manipulated. They needed to control their own destiny.

On Sunday, Friends delighted in Meeting for Worship on the jetty—a cherished tradition at Cape May Conferences. One could almost forget the discomfort of the rocky seat as one experienced the exhilaration of the salt breeze blowing through the soul. But the following day, Friends catapulted from their ethereal experience to a sickening awareness. Out of Washington came news that the Poor People's Campaign had not obtained more food for the hungry.

Barely a week after Philadelphia Yearly Meeting voiced support for the Reverend Martin Luther King, Jr.'s plan to hold the Campaign, he had been assassinated. His plan was nevertheless carried out by the Reverend Ralph Abernathy. Caravans of poor people came from all over the United States to press Congress and the Administration for legislation that would improve their lot. They called their encampment of plywood shacks in West Potomac Park, Resurrection City, U.S.A. When the Department of the Interior refused to extend their permit before they had succeeded in securing a promise of assistance, three hundred demonstrators marched to the Capitol, where 260 were arrested, charged with unlawful assembly. "If Resurrection City is destroyed," they said, "we still have a resurrection in our hearts, and nobody can take that away from us."[1] But they still didn't have enough to eat.

William Penn House, the Florida Avenue Friends Meeting and other Quaker groups as well as individuals offered hospitality to the members of the Southern Christian Leadership Conference, which sponsored the Campaign. A Quaker dentist treated the participants free of charge.

At Cape May, a few Friends urged the whole General Conference to adjourn to Washington and join the demonstrators. After prayerful consideration, Friends decided that it was their responsibility to remain and search for long-range ways in which the Society of Friends could serve.

That Sunday evening, Gilbert White, Chairman of the American Friends Service Committee and Professor of Geography at the University of Chicago, spoke of "the great sense of power" that Americans have and "the great sense of anxiety. . . . Many of the instruments for social change now in use are essentially conservative. We are moving into a time when more revolutionary efforts will be called for. . . . Can Friends—with our peculiar assets of faith in the capacities of ordinary people, our commitment to a way of love, and our practical experience in working across ethnic, religious, and national boundaries—contribute to constructive action by others while testifying to it in our daily lives? I believe we can."

Bronson Clark, the new Executive Secretary of the Service Committee, urged Friends to listen to the poor and alienated, to pay attention to youth, to provide a climate of forgiveness and love. The Associate Executive Secretary, Stephen G. Cary, was not present. He was serving a sentence of fourteen days in a District of Columbia jail for demonstrating with the Poor People.

In his statement to the Judge of the Court of General Sessions, Stephen Cary had said, "Your Honor, I want to say first of all that I respect the law and do not take casually a decision to violate it. . . . There are two reasons that compel my conscience . . . I consider it absolutely intolerable that in this rich country of ours any child . . . should have to go to bed hungry . . . the Congress can talk righteously about refusing to be coerced, but the fact remains that it is wicked and wrong that food stamps are not made available without charge to those who have no funds to pay for them. The rich are subsidized with crop payments; the rich can coerce Congress with their lobbies; our nation can pour thirty billion dollars a year into destroying a poor peasant culture ten thousand miles away, but the poor in America must continue to starve. . . . I believe that the options are running out for our country. . . . We who are white and affluent must therefore either stand behind responsible leadership who crusade for change in peaceful, non-violent ways, or we shall shortly be confronted with irresponsible leadership, who crusade for change with revolutionary violence. When this happens—and if we fail now I deeply believe that it will—our choice will be between repression and insurrection, and neither of these is to me a viable option for a free society."[2]

At Cape May, youth was demanding attention. It pressed the Conference to take corporate action in support of the campaign. This resulted in "a called meeting for worship, petition and witness on Friday, June 28, 1968, in Washington, D.C. . . . to bring about a shift in priorities of American resources—to reduce drastically war and military expenditures and increase funds to meet human needs; a public vigil adjacent to the Capitol grounds; and a meeting for worship and petition on the Capitol grounds." This last was illegal, and Friends knew that anyone who participated in it was subject to arrest.

Over against the excited urgency to go to Washington and jail, a little serenity was provided by Euell Gibbons, the Quaker naturalist, who pointed out the edible riches on the Cape May beaches and in the surrounding fields. In the spirit of George Fox, who reminded men of "the living God that clothes earth with grass and herbs and causes the trees to grow and bring forth fruit for you, and makes the fishes of the sea to breathe and live,"[3] Euell Gibbons wrote in *Beachcomber's Handbook*, "The primitive and the modern, the wild and the domestic, the savage and the civilized can be blended together harmoniously in my food, my life, and my very soul."

In Washington, on the day of the vigil, 250 Friends gathered across the street from the Capitol grounds. Thirty-five crossed to a terrace of the Capitol to hold a Meeting for Worship, near some members of the Southern Christian Leadership Conference, who were singing and praying. The Blacks were arrested. The Quakers were disregarded, although they were breaking the same law. Feeling that they were getting preferential treatment, the Quakers joined the Black group. Then the police arrested them, too. Charged with unlawful assembly, Friends were given sentences of from three to fourteen days in jail.

Two weeks later, eighty people, sponsored by A Quaker Action Group and the Young Friends of North America, each carried a loaf of bread and an explanatory letter to 435 congressmen in support of a proposed amendment that would eliminate the ceiling on Food Stamp funds.

"How," these concerned young people had asked one another, "are we going to present a small picture to dramatize the issue of abundance and hunger, of large farm subsidies and small welfare payments, of rich and poor people, of the need for substantial Congressional action. . . . How could we encourage people to work on Congress for legislation to end hunger? So we carried bread and a letter to tell these things, hoping that the story of Jesus sharing five loaves with the multitude could be repeated." The loaves had been baked by members of Friends Meetings and Washington churches. One loaf had a note attached. "I hope this tastes good—it is the first bread I have baked."[4]

The congressmen liked the bread. But poor people still didn't have enough to eat.

Marjorie Nelson was in Washington, too, calling on senators, congressmen, military representatives, and members of the State Department. She thought the senators believed that the United States should negotiate an end to the war but that most of them were "unwilling or felt unable to do much to encourage negotiations."[5]

Everyone was eager to hear her story. She had gone from Quang Ngai to Hue during Tet to visit Sandra Johnson. While she was there, the National Front of Liberation took the city. She and Sandra were alone in Sandra's house. They spent four days in a makeshift bomb shelter with hardly any food. Then Viet Cong soldiers came and took them away to the mountains, along with some American service men. They walked for a night and a day. Marge's shoes weren't suitable and she raised bad blisters. At the end of two weeks, the two girls were taken to another camp, where they were treated kindly, but all they had to eat was rice. Marge developed dysentery. Although she felt ill, she managed to make friends with her captors—her hosts, she called them—because she was deeply interested in their way of life and could speak their language enough to communicate. The Viet Cong understood that Marge and Sandra had come to Vietnam to help their countrymen, not to kill and destroy.

After fifty-two days of captivity, the two women were sent out of the camp with an escort under cover of night and given assistance in getting to Hue. There they spoke to the first Americans they saw and explained who they were. They were driven to military headquarters.

"Throughout the whole experience, I felt the presence of God," Marge later told Friends. "I feel this experience was a demonstration of what love can do. In spite of language, cultural and ideological barriers, meaningful communication was possible."[6]

After reporting to Quaker Service-Vietnam in Hong Kong and visiting Beryl on the *Phoenix*, Marge flew to Detroit with Sandra, arriving on April 12 to what Marge described as "a rather tumultuous welcome." Bob Perisho had come from New Haven to greet her.

Now, Marge was spending the summer in the Rehabilitation Center of the University of Pennsylvania Hospital, learning more about prosthetics, for she had decided to return to Vietnam and finish her term of service. The Quaker Center in Quang Ngai had reopened and she was needed. New civilian amputees, missing one or both legs, were arriving there at the rate of fifty a month.

On August 4, three American fliers, who had been captured by the North Vietnamese, arrived in New York. They had been released in Hanoi for repatriation in the care of three Americans, one of whom was Stewart Meacham, Peace Secretary of the Service Committee.

There was another part of the world in which Friends felt called to alleviate suffering. The war between Nigeria and Biafra had dislodged thousands from their homes. Crops could not be planted. It was estimated that there were eight hundred thousand refugees. Babies were dying fast. The Service Committee launched an appeal for two hundred thousand dollars to help these war victims.

By contrast, in East Africa, Friends were flourishing. The Yearly Meeting had thirty-two thousand members. In addition to the 120-bed hospital at Kaimosi and five rural dispensaries, new buildings had just been added to the Lugulu Health Center. The Friends World Conference of 1967 had expressed overwhelming concern for the right sharing of the world's resources—to narrow the gap between the "have" and "have-not" nations. The American Section of the World Committee proposed an experimental program in economic development, "Partnership for Productivity." David H. Scull was appointed chairman of the international Quaker group which undertook, through capital investment and management assistance, to encourage the establishment of small businesses in western Kenya. Friends hoped that the financial backing and personal service they were giving would attract support from other sources.

Another result of the concern felt at the World Conference for the right sharing of the world's resources was the establishment of the One Per Cent More Fund. Friends committed themselves to give one per cent more of their income than they were already contributing for the alleviation of want in all parts of the world. They hoped this might encourage their governments to do likewise.

At home, the Associated Executive Committee of Friends on Indian Affairs was rounding out one hundred years of service. In the beginning, it built schools and Meetinghouses for the tribes in Oklahoma. The boarding school it opened for Seneca, Shawnee and Wyandotte children was called "Friends' Godly Experiment in the Wilderness."

In 1968, Friends in the Northwest were concerned about the fishing rights of the Indians on Puget Sound—the Muckleshoot, Puyallup and Nisqually tribes. Just as a century and a half earlier Friends in the East had defended the Senecas against the efforts of land companies to evict them from reservations which the government had guaranteed by treaties, so now these Friends defended Indians who were having difficulties with sportsmen and the state of Washington Game Department. The sportsmen resented the fact that the Indians had fishing rights, which were stipulated in treaties. Fish were becoming scarce due to pollution of the rivers by sewage and the refuse from pulp mills. Dams kept the salmon and steelhead trout from reaching their spawning grounds. The number of fish was reduced; the number of disgruntled sportsmen multiplied.

A study group, appointed by the Service Committee, spent eighteen months clarifying the issues. The National Congress of American Indians published the conclusions under the title *An Uncommon Controversy*. Fishing, this study claimed, is not only economically important to the Indians but also central to their cultural identity. The report urged that members of the tribes be included in planning and carrying out conservation programs.

Friends at the other end of the continent had a continuing concern for the Passamaquoddy and Penobscot tribes. On their reservations in Maine, Work Camps were conducted by the New England Regional Office of the Service Committee. College-age young people helped the Indians with building and repairs. They made recreational equipment and played with the children. Between Work Camps, George I. Bliss, the executive secretary of the New England office, and later his successor, Robert A. Lyon, faithfully kept in touch with the Indians by visiting them in the winter months. They went from shack to shack, listening to people's troubles. These tribes were wards not of the federal government, but of the state of Maine. Through their representatives, Friends sought to bring the needs of the Indians to the attention of the state.

In 1968, Wayne Newell, an engaging young Passamaquoddy who had happy boyhood memories of a Friends' Work Camp on his reservation, joined the New England Service Committee staff in order to help his people to help themselves. Friends felt that the appointment of an Indian to undertake work that had formerly been done by whites promised to renew the self-respect of the Indians. During the first five months of his work for the Service Committee, Wayne Newell organized teen-age activities, secured improved health care and initiated the study of Passamaquoddy history and language. He was named to the Maine Education Advisory Council to help frame legislation for the education of the Indian children. Special intelligence tests were conducted on the reservations. "In the past," Wayne Newell said, "testing was done on the same level with other children who had a much better use of the English language. . . . I feel that for the first time the Indian children were being tested fairly.

"Under the Department of Health and Welfare, the Indians of Maine had no voice in their matters. There was paternalism in the greatest degree. Under this system, which lasted for 175 years, apathy was the natural result. . . . Even before I joined the AFSC staff, I was deeply concerned in the role that Passamaquoddies were being given in determining their own affairs. . . . Surely the day is coming when our elected representative to the State Legislature will be a full member and not just a figurehead. . . . At present, the representative cannot vote, he cannot sit as a regular member and gets a token fee which doesn't cover his telephone bill. To change this it would take a two-thirds majority of the House and Senate. Amendments are hard to come by in Maine but my hopes are high that we might at least break the ice this year."[7]

Young Friends were suddenly coming to Meeting sporting broadbrims and bonnets. Since genuine Quaker beavers had long ago disappeared from attics because they were so often favored by moths, the young men of 1968 had to settle for Amish hats, which were still being made. Only a knowledgeable Friend knew the difference. Bonnets were easier to acquire. Some still existed, and a clever girl could make some kind of imitation.

In the nineteenth century, it was the young Friends who prevailed upon their elders to abandon the peculiarities of Quaker dress and speech. Now the young revived them in order to recall to their elders the testimony of simplicity. Unfortunately, some older Friends could remember the plain dress of a superlatively fastidious and courteous grandparent. A broadbrim or bonnet failed to make the desired impression when it was teamed with frayed blue jeans, bare feet and the absence of amenities.

A few young Friends were also reverting to plain speech, "so I can try to speak to the spiritual conditions of others," one of them explained, "in a loving and helpful way." He had begun the practice in 1967 after Philadelphia Yearly Meeting affirmed support for the *Phoenix*. "I had long been concerned with vigorous outreach," this young Friend said, "but at this session, when tears of joy flowed freely from more than just me among the young people . . . my concept of outreach was radically altered. . . . But I reject as against the spirit and letter of its original purpose the use of plain speech by Quakers only among Friends. It builds walls around those who rate and those who do not. It should be used all the time or dropped entirely."[8]

Young Friends were in earnest about simplicity. Some went to live in a farmhouse they called New Swarthmoor, near Utica, New York. They reduced their material wants and possessions to a minimum, picked apples and did other odd jobs to maintain themselves on a subsistence level, walked four miles to Meeting and four miles back again, and paid pastoral visits to Friends all over the country, communicating their concern. They didn't think of New Swarthmoor as their permanent home but as a place to which one might come to rethink and readjust one's values.

They maintained that a generation gap does not exist among Friends. Ideally, this should always have been true, for Friends insisted on the worth of the individual. But there was a period when older Friends kept younger ones well in their place simply because this was the general temper of the times. Meetings had always been intended to function as a whole—old and young—under divine leading. Yet in an era when seniority mattered most, this respect for the views of younger Friends was lost. When the separated Yearly Meetings in New England reunited, the Clerk of the Wilburite group, Henry Perry, recalled that in 1914 when he was thirty years old, he made a proposal at Yearly Meeting which, if accepted, would have thawed relations between his people and the Gurneyites much earlier. But the then clerk observed indulgently, "Always nice to hear from the young folks," and passed on to other business, leaving matters as frozen as before.

Relations between the generations had altered markedly since that time. If anything, elders were deferring to the young in an exaggerated effort to restore balance.

A number of young Friends were becoming intrigued with the concept of fighting the Lamb's War. This figure, popular with early Friends, had been recalled by Hugh Barbour in his book *The Quakers in Puritan England* and was enthusiastically pursued by T. Canby Jones, who found it particularly applicable to the present.

Defined by Hugh Barbour, "The Lamb's War is the worldwide struggle of the Spirit, God's victory over evil within and without men." For the earliest Quakers, the Lamb's War had two sides: "the intense . . . word of judgment that they brought to . . . merchants . . . about their cheating . . . judges about their cruelty and disregard for legal rights, noblemen about their love of titles and status, clergymen about their salaries and security. . . . Then as today, there was argument about how effective shock tactics were. . . . But the Friends' aim was to shock men into awareness. Even specific Testimonies against silver buckles or against saying "you" to noblemen and "thee and thou" to workingmen, were used and pressed, not for their own sake so much as to remind men how much their pride was tied up in social customs."

In the seventeenth century, the Lamb's War plunged each new Quaker into a long and bitter spiritual struggle. "Early Friends preached with fire because they had been through it.

"The blending of the inner and the outer Lamb's War today . . . can remind men that non-violence . . . is the necessary way, whether it succeeds or not, because the battle is in men's hearts, and any other war or struggle is the wrong battle against the wrong evil in the wrong way. Violence, at the same time, should not shock us in others. . . . God knows we have enough anger and violence inside ourselves . . . we may need to recognize it more often and be less afraid that it is there while we learn to live above it. This is Fox's ocean of darkness above which stands the ocean of light."[9]

T. Canby Jones referred to the Lamb's War as "a concept the early Friends found in the Book of Revelation. That book is chiefly concerned with a cosmic and final spiritual conflict in which all evil and sin and disobedience in all ages and all cultures will be overcome. . . . Obviously, the Christian peace testimony is an inescapable corollary and expression of love without limits . . . those called to live peaceable revolution and fight the Lamb's War envision a new humanity, new heavens, a new earth, which they see already coming to birth."[10]

In 1667, Robert Barclay, a young Scot, joined Friends, "not by strength of arguments . . . for when I came into the silent assemblies of God's people, I felt a secret power among them, which touched my heart." Yet it wasn't until 1968, when D. Elton Trueblood, Professor at Large at Earlham College, published *Robert Barclay* after a lifetime of research that a full-length interpretation of this scholar's works appeared.

"As iron sharpeneth iron," Barclay wrote of the Meeting for Worship, "the seeing of one another, when both are inwardly gathered unto the life, giveth occasion for the life secretly to rise, and pass from vessel to vessel. And as many candles lighted, and put in one place do greatly augment the light, and make it more to shine forth, so when many are gathered together into the same life, there is more of the glory of God, and his power appears to the refreshment of each individual."[11]

41 Quaker Hospitality

The Friends Meetinghouse in Cambridge, Massachusetts, stands between Craigie House, Henry Wadsworth Longfellow's Brattle Street home, and the Charles River. Of warm rose brick with white trim and a slate roof, overhung by trees, the Meetinghouse hovers close to the earth. Inside, there is nothing to divert the eye except the view through the clear windows of a wide lawn, oaks and sycamores. There is no altar and since Cambridge Friends do not have a pastor, no lectern. The traditional Quaker benches are ranged around a fireplace.

At the end of the hour of worship on First-day (Sunday), Eighth Month (August) 11, 1968, there was none of the handshaking with which Friends customarily break Meeting.[1] Instead, a Harvard professor, acting as Clerk, introduced to the assembled Friends and attenders Frederick Rutan, who was, the Clerk explained, absent from the army without leave because he could not, in conscience, go to Vietnam.

Frederick—he preferred to be called Eric—was sitting on one of the front benches beside a tall, white-haired Friend with handsome features and outdoor coloring—a beautiful woman, as Quakers say, although they are not referring to externals but to the spirit shining through a face. In this Friend, inward and outward beauty were uncommonly joined.

Eric stood up to acknowledge the introduction. He was tall, likable-looking. His army crew cut had hardly grown out enough to alarm anyone. When he sat down again, he glanced at the tiny, unruffled girl on his other side. His mother was in the row behind. A widow, she had come alone to this strange place to see her fugitive son.

Meeting had not been broken, the Clerk explained, because Friends intended to continue worshiping in support of this objector to war as long as he remained among them. Then the Clerk read a statement authorized by the Monthly Meeting: "We who oppose all war are associating ourselves with certain young men who have refused to comply with the draft or to fight in Vietnam. We are citizens of this country whose just laws and democratic way of life we are deeply committed to preserving. Even such laws as seem to us harmful and unjust are normally observed by us, even while we seek to bring about their repeal by lawful and democratic means." The Clerk glanced toward the door, as if expecting the police to burst in. "Our objective," he read on, "in extending our hospitality and support to these men who face arrest and prosecution, is to convey to them a measure of encouragement. For though many of them do not fully share our beliefs and ideals, we are satisfied that their disobedience is motivated by genuine principles and ideals which command our respect."

Nodding at Eric, the Clerk indicated that this was the moment for his statement. The Meetinghouse was crowded right up to the last bench, but the intensity of the silence as Eric stood fumbling with his papers was almost audible.

"My name is Frederick Newman Rutan," he read, "age twenty-two. I have been in the Army for ten months. My present rank is Specialist Fourth Class. But I have been AWOL since June ninth at which time I was supposed to report to Oakland Army Base to be transported to Vietnam." He spoke harshly of the army and what it demanded. "Therefore, it is a happy moment for me," he said, looking far from happy, "to accept sanctuary in order to take a stand against the war."

For ten months, he had been under military discipline. For two, he had been hiding, no one knew where, and sick. Suddenly, he was standing before a couple of hundred sympathetic people, declaring views he had long been obliged to suppress. At the same time, he was presenting himself for arrest. Bewildered, obviously not accustomed to speaking in public, he still communicated deep sincerity. He had, he said, attended Eastern Nazarene College in Wollaston, Massachusetts, his home town. At the end of a year, he dropped out. "I just wanted some time to put my life in order and find myself." He was immediately drafted. "I was very confused and bitter. I definitely wanted to avoid the possibility of having to kill." He thought he could do this by enlisting. When he got into the army, a soldier who had been in Vietnam told him about the killing of children, which he had witnessed. Eric decided to apply for CO classification. "I will be taken back to the Army," he concluded bitterly. "I want all to see that the Army cannot stifle free and opposing attitudes just because it represents an imposing and oppressive authority and makes it damn difficult and sacrificial to try and buck it."

When Eric sat down, the Friend beside him flashed a quick, reassuring smile his way.

Reflecting on what he had said about the killing of children in Vietnam, a number of people recalled the article that had recently appeared in Look, "To Make Children Whole Again," which described the Quaker Rehabilitation Center in Quang Ngai. Heartrending pictures told the story of children whose arms and legs had been blown off by artillery shells and land mines. An oriental madonna-like face, sorrowful, patient, bore the caption, "Who dares say what thoughts are in the mind of a 12-year-old girl as she watches her own artificial leg being made?"

A young man had got to his feet and was explaining that he was a divinity student; that he spoke for the New England Resistance, the group to which Eric had appealed while he was in hiding and which had asked Cambridge Meeting to help him. Other Resisters, mostly men and women in their twenties, sat near Eric, also encountering Quaker worship for the first time. Their spokesman communicated their determination to oppose the war by combining "moral opposition with physical obstruction," a tactic repugnant to Friends. "So, as we say," the divinity student concluded, expressing disappointment, "we do our thing and the Quakers do theirs."

The Resisters had wanted to chain themselves to Eric so the police would have to arrest them, too, but the Quakers didn't want a chain in their Meetinghouse. They had been refusing military service for over three hundred years, always trying to accept the consequences with grace. They hoped the Resisters wouldn't stage any physical obstruction when the police arrived. Two or three had threatened . . . and Eric—what would he do? He'd told someone he intended to go limp.

A Friends Meetinghouse is not a sanctuary. In Quaker eyes, no *place* is holy, only the aspiration which may be experienced in it. Eric was, therefore, not being offered sanctuary—asylum—but hospitality—a meal and spiritual support. Friends didn't intend to interfere with his arrest which, they assumed, would take place as soon as his whereabouts were made known. They'd called a press conference in the Friends Center across the way. The Clerk and overseers—those Friends appointed by the Monthly Meeting to be responsible for the right ordering of this witness—left, taking Eric with them. It was dinnertime, but the rest settled back into silence.

A porte-cochere connects the Meetinghouse with the Friends Center. Under the eaves of its gable roof, children of the First-day School have carved in handsome block letters words which no one can fail to read in passing: *Walk cheerfully over the world, answering that of God in every one.* George Fox sent this message to Friends from prison about the time that Mary Fisher and Ann Austin and the *Speedwell* voyagers landed on the other side of the Charles River.

Reporters from the Boston papers were waiting in the Friends Center. The clerk handed them the statements that had just been read. By this act, Cambridge Friends announced Eric's presence among them. He stood on the lawn to be photographed. In the Center kitchen, some of the women of the Meeting were preparing dinner for him, his mother, his girl, Janet, his companions from the Resistance and the Quaker overseers.

As the reporters sped out of Longfellow Park with their scoop, Friends braced themselves for the arrival of the police. Three Friends stood at the end of the driveway—one to receive the officers, the other two to carry the news of their arrival to the Center and the Meetinghouse. It was beautiful weather. After standing expectantly for an hour at the point where the driveway meets Longfellow Park, the first watch thought they could use chairs.

Word quickly got around Harvard Square. In no time, the Meetinghouse lawn swarmed with types very different from those ordinarily seen there on First-day. Mini-miniskirts, which were still a shock, abundant hair, bare feet, guitars—never had Longfellow Park witnessed anything like this. The young Friends thought it was great, but some of the weighty ones were appalled by the appearance of the premises.

Longfellow Park is one of Cambridge's finest residential sections. Apart from the Friends Meetinghouse and the Mormon Church at the other end, it is composed of stately homes, whose owners aren't necessarily in accord with the views of Friends even while they respect their uprightness and altruism. Not all the neighbors—perhaps none—would understand why Friends felt called to extend hospitality to an AWOL soldier right at *their* front doors. Someone from the Meeting went around to explain. Someone else picked up the candy wrappers and Coke cans that already speckled the lawn.

Most of the young people who suddenly arrived didn't know what a Quaker was. Ordinarily, they wouldn't have been caught dead in a place of worship. They came because this was where the action was and they opposed the draft and the war. They claimed, as Friends do, that the state does not have authority over their consciences, but few of them would have relegated that authority, as Friends do, to God.

The Friends who had continued to worship finally went home or over to the Center to eat. Others, having finished lunch, returned to the Meetinghouse. Suddenly they were struck motionless under the porte-cochere, their hearts pounding, as a police siren coming down Brattle Street shrieked. But it grew fainter, rushing toward the Square. Relieved, they went in.

All afternoon they pondered their responsibility for the mass of seeking, disturbed young people who had suddenly come here. The seeking seemed soul-sized.

"If a boy is asked to die for a cause in which he does not believe," someone said presently, groping for words, "it is altogether necessary for him to find a cause in which he *does* believe enough to die for it. Whatever else Eric's statement reveals, he didn't know how to live as well as not know how to die." The Friend paused, looking out through the tall windows at the ancient oaks and sycamores and the mass of young people beneath them. "How much discipline are we putting ourselves under? Or do we suppose discipline is only for those who are trained to kill? Is the Meeting disciplined enough to speak to Eric's condition? Will he leave us healed of his confusion, prepared better to live or die?"

From time to time, throughout the bright afternoon, little groups of those seeking young people quietly entered and sat down near Eric, betraying in the way they carried themselves their feeling that, because it was short, this time together was precious.

Not all of them were solemn. On the far corner of the lawn under an oak tree, a little group sat, singing to guitars. The young Friends taught their visitors a Quaker song:

> Stand in the light, wherever you may be! In your old leather
>   breeches and shaggy, shaggy locks
> You're walking in the glory of the light, George Fox.

"If we give you a pistol, will you fight for the Lord?"
"You can't kill the devil with a gun or a sword."
"Will you swear on the Bible?" "I will not," said he,
"For the truth is as holy as the Book to me."

"Stand in the light," the women in the Center kitchen echoed, joining in the refrain, while they stirred spaghetti and meatballs, "stand in the light, wherever you may be!"

The police didn't come. At dusk, the Meetinghouse lights were turned on. Toward midnight, Friends went home and returned with cots, which they put up in the First-day School for the men of the Resistance who wanted to stay near Eric. Janet was given the guestroom in the Center. Eric's mother went home.

The Meetinghouse consists of one big room. Friends didn't know where to put Eric. The basement! Besides the furnace, its dim recesses contain the American Friends Service Committee's clothing room. There, on weekdays, Friends and their friends volunteer to sort, clean, mend and pack clothing donated for relief, not a hundred yards from Craigie House where, in the winter of 1775, Rhode Island Quakers pleaded with General Washington for permission to distribute clothing to the needy behind the lines.

So Friends bedded Eric down between the bales of castoffs and the sewing machines. Alongside the button boxes, he stretched out on a cot, waiting for the authorities to come and get him.

The Friend at the end of the driveway was spending the ten to midnight watch meditating under the street lamp. Suppose the officers came now—what would he do? He had no idea. It was a test he wasn't prepared for. When his relief arrived, he realized that he wouldn't have to confront the police. He was free to go home! But he still wondered—what would he have said? He was forced to come to grips with questions he'd never asked himself before.

At daybreak one of the overseers who had participated in the nightlong worship hurried home to Lincoln to milk her cow. Then she rushed back to Longfellow Park. Three sleepy Friends sat at the end of the driveway. So the police hadn't come! The Friends were poring over the morning paper. There was Eric, looking grave, with the Meetinghouse in the background. "Cambridge Quakers Shelter AWOL Soldier" was the caption.

People began arriving from all over Boston and the suburbs. They had heard the news on the radio or TV. They wanted to add their weight to the witness. Protestant ministers, rabbis, nuns in their new, short habits filled the Meetinghouse benches. Others came who didn't go for religion. To their surprise, they felt easy here. The place made no demands. There were no symbols to rebel against; no words to repeat which they might not believe. There was only the healing silence, interrupted from time to time by people who felt deeply moved—ordinary, searching people, like themselves—telling simply what lay on their hearts. The passionate longing for peace that hung over the countryside had found a focus. The ache all these people brought with them, remembering someone in Vietnam or the doom that threatened their children, received a promise of surcease.

A church historian from Oxford looked at Eric sitting there, surrounded by Friends, waiting for doom to catch up with him. *Wherefore*, the Englishman recalled, *seeing we also are compassed about with so great a cloud of witnesses, let us lay aside every weight* . . .

That morning, the women who provided breakfast had asked themselves whether they should plan on lunch. Now they left the Meetinghouse to go over to the Center and prepare supper. Overseers came in after work, and those who had been there all day went home. All night long, Friends sat in the Meetinghouse, sometimes two or three, sometimes only one. The coffee urn on the library table in the Center was kept filled. But it wasn't slumber proof. At dawn, a very tall Friend was discovered stretched under the table, his hat over his eyes, dead to the world.

Eric came up from the clothing room and sat in the Meetinghouse, restless, constantly glancing toward the door. Then it was night again, then day, then night. The police didn't come. Time seemed to blur into eternity. A cricket, stuck in the hot air register, chirped against the silence. Friends spoke of George Fox's counsel, *Know one another in that which is eternal.* Never had there been such luxury of time to meditate, to examine one's self, one's real motives. Friends who had trouble all their lives "centering down" for an hour on First-day found themselves reveling in this great, long, continuous Meeting. They brought their children to let them see that real Meeting isn't Sunday clothes and rushing so as not to be late. Couples dropped in for half an hour around midnight to worship together. Meeting was always there, waiting to be tuned in on.

Friends had a great deal to think about—Eric, all the Erics in the world who had to put their lives in order before they'd barely begun them, who were trying to find their relation to their fellow men, to create something better than the status quo without being destroyed in the process. Friends thought, too, about the risks they were taking. Going to jail didn't just belong to the quaint Quaker past, like bonnets and thee and thy; it was very much part of now. The Charles Street jail, which one passed going from Harvard Square into Boston, looked like a huge Lion's Den. There was a great deal to think about.

The Resisters were searching just as diligently. "If I weren't at bottom an agnostic," one of them declared, breaking the silence, "I would say God moves in strange ways, or at least that history does. Our involvement in Vietnam has led thousands of young men's minds, like a catalyst. We really dropped out of America. We were really close to being walking dead people. We saw no American dream worth striving for. But finally, the impotence of being an individual in technocracy melted before the choice, 'Will I go?' or 'Will I not go?' We moved from the limbo of alienation into some kind of rebirth. We could say 'no' and by saying 'no' be true to ourselves."

A girl with long, blond hair that covered her face, who lived up on Brattle Street, had stopped in for a few minutes on her way to the beach. Listening, she changed her mind. She'd stay. What fun would it be, working on her suntan, when people her age—

"I must live in the present," the Resister was saying, "and the present as my future, not allowing myself to dwell on what may come in harassment or prison or whatever. I have no choice but to be me and find fulfillment in that realization."

The fellow sat down. The girl with the blond hair shivered. Then the silence enfolded her.

Each day that passed made the inevitable conclusion harder for Friends to face. They were growing very fond of Eric and Janet. Even the barefoot companions no longer seemed incongruous. Someone with that rare Quaker combination of humor and religious insight spoke of the Burning Bush and God's command to Moses, "Put off thy shoes from off thy feet, for the place whereon thou standest is holy ground."

Friends' responsibility for Eric wouldn't end with his arrest. If possible, they'd visit him in the stockade, help him appeal for CO classification, attend his court-martial, testify to his sincerity.

Those who held Meeting in the wee hours of the morning brought their toothbrushes so they could go straight to work, just as in the seventeenth century when Quaker worship was unlawful, Friends took their nightcaps with them to Meeting because they knew that by bedtime they'd be in jail.

On the tenth morning, a Radcliffe girl came running across the lawn. "The Russians have invaded Czechoslovakia!" she shouted.

The enormity of this new assault on man's freedom seemed beyond anyone's power to grasp in the summer sunshine. Friends instinctively resorted to the silence. Some recalled the many efforts to communicate to the Russians the Quaker belief in the sacredness of every individual.

In Czechoslovakia, this morning, Friends wouldn't be allowed to sit quietly, upholding a young man's right to refuse what the government decreed. In Czechoslovakia, they'd simply be mowed down by tanks. Even worship would be denied them. To be a Christian or a Jew under the Soviets was more of a hardship than Americans could understand.

Friends remembered that the testimony they were making here against war was only part of the Quaker Peace Testimony. The other was to change their country's outlook, peaceably but radically, so that war on people would be replaced by war on want and injustice—The Lamb's War. It began with overcoming evil in one's self. To protest was futile without simultaneously furnishing creative solutions. This might prove "damn sacrificial," as Eric put it, but for Americans it was permissible and, for Friends, it was mandatory. Because they were allowed to pray "Give us this day our daily bread," they were obliged to answer that prayer.

At mealtimes, more and more strangers seemed to be turning up. They weren't all there to worship or to express their solidarity. Friends knew that, in some instances, they were being used. "But if someone's hungry," the Friend who was spending her vacation from the Harvard Library cooking in the Center kitchen argued, "what difference does it make?"

While it was true that some people were dropping in to get a meal for free that they could easily have paid for, others—also strangers, many of them—arrived laden with food. It wasn't for Friends to pass judgment on the motives of those who came.

As they sat down at the long tables which had been put up in the Center parlor and bowed their heads before the meal, Friends thought of Jesus washing the feet of his disciples, of his saying, "Ye are my friends if ye do whatsoever I command you." They were to wait on each other, not judge; to share their meals, not only with the starving Biafrans but also with sufferers in Nigeria.

One would have thought, sitting down to dinner in the Center parlor, that this was one long, hilarious house party. An unaccountable joy seemed to pervade the "community of conscience" as it became ever more tightly knit. There was fun, there was a lot of joking. The conversation could be heated, too, as when the Resisters expressed their anger over the way the hippies had been treated when they were arrested on the Cambridge Common.

"This is Fascism!" one fellow exclaimed.

The Friend clearing the dishes stood still. He had escaped from the Nazis in his youth. "I've lived under Fascism," he said, waving a plate in his emotion, "and this," he declared with authority, trying to keep his voice calm, "is not Fascism."

As the number of meals increased, garbage disposal became an acute problem. The city of Cambridge would only collect so much. Amused by the odd dilemma which their religious conviction had unexpectedly led to, Friends carried bulging cans home under cover of night and brought empty ones back in the morning.

After two weeks—day and night—the Resisters and young Friends were just about talked out, sung out and, as Friends often say of themselves after Meeting for Business that has dragged on too long, "meetinged out." They wanted to *do* something. So they took Janet's scooter apart. All that second Saturday, they worked on the scooter in the yard behind the Center, tuning it up, polishing, putting it back together.

Cambridge can be pretty hot in the summertime. As Friends entered the third week of their effort on Eric's behalf, the strain began to be felt. To sit in the Meetinghouse for ten minutes was to be fighting sleep. Some of the Overseers went on vacation. There were fewer hands to do the work and more mouths to feed.

A Unitarian dropped in at the Meetinghouse one afternoon. Her son, Chris, was applying for Conscientious Objector status, she told the Overseer, perhaps feeling she must explain why she had come. She was not used to sitting still with no minister to direct her thoughts. But she settled down on a back bench. There were only a few people. She studied their faces, their clothes; she thought up a grocery list, counted the squares of the paneling along the wall, struggled to stay awake.

She must have dozed off, for suddenly she was alone in the Meetinghouse, except for the cricket. Startled, she sat upright. There was no one else to keep the Meeting going. She was needed here to hold Meeting with the cricket, to keep the light from going out. Tomorrow, she said to herself, not knowing why, because she had

QUAKER HOSPITALITY 401

an appointment to have her hair done, but her son, Chris—Tomorrow afternoon, she'd return.

When tomorrow afternoon arrived, she wasn't needed.

At eleven o'clock that morning of Eighth Month 29, a Friend in his early thirties, an engineering professor at M.I.T., was sitting calmly at the end of the driveway with two teen-agers. An unmarked car drove into Longfellow Park and stopped five feet away.

The Feds! the Friend said to himself. What made him think so? He couldn't figure it, but he knew. What was he going to say? Panic gripped him. He hadn't prepared a speech. He simply had to trust that he would respond in the right way.

Two men in plain clothes jumped out of the car, flashing badges. They were policemen, all right, a lieutenant and a sergeant. They looked prepared for trouble. Was Frederick Rutan here?

The messengers sped to the Meetinghouse and Center with the news.

The Friend stood up, trying to walk cheerfully toward the officers, trying to answer not the badges on their shirts but "that of God" in their hearts. "Yes," he heard himself saying.

The lieutenant waved a paper at him. It was a warrant for Eric's arrest.

"He's in the Meetinghouse," the Friend said, trying to make his voice sound the way it would have if he were directing any other stranger, only he knew it didn't. "I'll take you in. But we've been holding a Meeting for Worship here for the past eighteen days and nights. Won't you give us five minutes to finish it up?"

The lieutenant looked embarrassed, as if rocks or bottles were a greeting he knew how to respond to, but this—

At the door of the Meetinghouse, the lieutenant and sergeant didn't look up. They were searching for Eric. They didn't read the words carved by the children under the eaves of the porte-cochere.

"Won't you come in," the Friend asked, "and join us?"

So it came about that two police officers entered the Friends Meetinghouse and sat down on a back bench, joining in the living silence.

At the front of the room, near the fireplace, Eric was sitting just where he'd sat on the first morning, with Janet on one side of him and the beautiful woman on the other.

No one in the hushed room gave any sign that the police officers were different from all the others who'd come here to worship for the past two and a half weeks. The silence continued, unbroken by their entrance, a deep, prayerful silence, pulsing with concern for Eric and all his contemporaries, those who were fighting and those who couldn't.

Would he force the police to use force? Would he go limp?

It could only have been a minute later but it seemed forever before the Executive Secretary of the Meeting rose and spoke quietly of Friends' willingness to suffer rather than to kill anyone, since to kill a person was to kill part of God. This Friend had devoted his whole life to communicating this belief. His touching simplicity must have reached the two visitors on the back bench for they didn't move. When he sat down, the silence became an overwhelming urgency. Time was running out.

The Friend beside Eric stood up and spoke of the loving nature of God and the brotherhood of all people—black and yellow and red and white. Everyone who took part in this religious witness had shared something significant, she thought. They had somehow been faithful.

"It is from such waiting on the spirit that the wisdom and strength we need must come," she said. Then she settled on the bench again, leaving unuttered the question that was in every Friend's mind: Had they spoken to Eric's condition? Was he leaving after all this time with them, healed of his confusion, prepared better to live or die? They hadn't let the Resistance "do their thing" in this confrontation. Had Friends done theirs?

Eric turned to the beautiful woman. "Do they have a warrant?" he whispered.

She nodded.

The lieutenant caught her eye. His raised eyebrow seemed to ask, "Is it okay now?"

Sadly, slowly, the Friend nodded again.

The two officers got to their feet and marched up the aisle. They presented Eric with the warrant. They didn't lay hands on him. He glanced at the warrant. Janet reached out and touched his arm. Eric stood up. With a quick backward look at Janet, he faced the door and walked out with the officers.

For another quarter of an hour, silence enfolded the company in the Meetinghouse. Then Friends shook hands.

42 Who Shall Live?

At the beginning of 1969, within a space of four days, President Courtney C. Smith of Swarthmore College departed this life tragically, and President Richard M. Nixon of the United States was inaugurated, declaring to the nation that elected him, "Our destiny lies not in the stars but in earth itself, in our own hands."[1]

On January 16, President Smith walked up the stairs of the building in which, for over a week, protesting Black students had occupied the Admissions office. His strength had been spent in dealing with the disruption. On the stairs, he suffered a heart attack and died soon afterward.

Out on the chilly campus, other students responded to the news by sitting down together under the bare elms, expressing their grief in the silence which, at this Quaker college, denoted the highest reverence. They had loved and believed in their President.

When he came to Swarthmore fifteen years earlier, there were virtually no Black students. Under his leadership, they had been admitted in a larger proportion than to most other colleges. But Courtney Smith had also concentrated on a variety of college problems while to the Black students, all that seemed important was getting their brothers and sisters in. Their "non-negotiable demands," when they seized the office, were for a larger number of Blacks to be admitted, regardless of academic standing, and Black administrators who would be subject to the Black students' approval.

"We felt," Clinton Etheridge, Chairman of the Swarthmore Afro-American Students Society, told *Life* magazine, "Swarthmore could be in the vanguard of both social *and* academic excellence. Swarthmore could play a role in cultivating black brainpower. And not by lowering standards. Look, you can always get a good rap here. . . . But there are a lot of agile black minds going to waste out there for lack of a little college support."

He criticized white liberals. "They automatically think they understand the racial scene, but they don't. White men like Courtney—a very good guy—are molding your mind from above, making all decisions from a life style that isn't yours . . . we're moving toward two societies, what's the point in adopting the integrationist ethic?"

Separatism was a concept Friends could not assent to in 1969.

Four days after the death of Courtney Smith, President Nixon was inaugurated. After the election, he had been interviewed by a reporter from the London *Observer*, to whom he said, "On my mother's side of the family, we were Quakers. Her name was Milhous and she came from a Quaker family that left County Kildare in Ireland in 1729. My father was Irish, too. His family was Methodist, but when he married my mother, he became a Quaker. . . . As a human being, I hold certain principles with which I have been imbued, and which I learned as a lad and a young man in the simple school of life. As a public servant, I am a pragmatist. I believe that in regulating the affairs of human beings, more can be done by the intelligent application of good will, good temper and the understanding that we all have to make concessions to live together, than by trying to impose this or that political doctrine on the community as a whole, either by force or propaganda."[2]

During the campaign, the Friends Committee on National Legislation had tried to arrange a meeting between the Republican candidate and a few representative Friends, but Richard Nixon's secretary indicated that it was not possible to schedule such a meeting. After the election, representatives from the American Section of the Friends World Committee, the Friends Committee on National Legislation, Philadelphia Yearly Meeting and Washington Friends wrote to the President-elect, proposing a pastoral visit. The letter assured him that while Quaker testimonies would be presented, there would be no political overtones to the visit. A telegraphed reply said, "President-elect Richard Nixon regrets that present demands upon his time will not allow him to schedule the requested appointment with you. We thank you for your kind letter and extend to you our best wishes."[3]

Before the President took up residence in the White House, the Friends Meeting of Washington was concerned about ministering to his spiritual needs. He had not made the Florida Avenue Meeting his place of worship when he was a congressman and Vice-President. Friends assumed that as President he would wish to attend a Friends Meeting like the one to which he belonged in East Whittier, California. This was programed and employed a pastor. Since the Florida Avenue Meeting was unprogramed and non-pastoral, Friends wondered whether they should provide some alternative to the traditional Meeting for Worship in order to strengthen and uphold the President during his term of office.

The President resolved the issue when he introduced religious services at the White House.

In Biafra that spring, thousands of Ibo refugees were dying for lack of food. It was estimated that by August the death toll might reach two million. Quaker workers quietly rushed food and medical care to both Biafra and Nigeria. The program was not widely publicized because Friends wished to help the sufferers without becoming involved in the political struggle. In Biafra, American Quakers cooperated with the Mennonites, in Nigeria with British Friends. Although the two groups of Americans were very close, stationed directly behind the lines on each side, their only channel of communication was via Philadelphia.

In the Middle East, Paul and Jean Johnson, who had given the better part of their lives to the search for peace there, were shuttling back and forth between political groups in Israel and the Arab countries, endeavoring to reconcile them, maintaining cheerfulness in the face of repeated disappointment. From time to time, they were joined by other Friends. Landrum Bolling, President of Earlham College, made several journeys to the area, valiantly seeking solutions to the sticky international problems. He edited a book entitled *Search for Peace in the Middle East*. The Service Committee, urged by both Jews and Arabs to explore every possible approach, had appointed a working party to prepare this book which was eventually translated into Hebrew and Arabic. One member of the working party was Don Peretz, now Director of the Southwest Asian and North African Studies Program at Harpur College in Binghamton, New York. As a young Quaker worker in the Gaza Strip twenty years earlier, he had written home jubilantly, "Napoleon failed to take Acre after subjecting it to a 60-day artillery bombardment and siege. Beethoven took the town in two hours just the other Saturday night." But now even Beethoven couldn't bring harmony to the Middle East.

Members of this working party listened to people in many walks of life, to high officials in Jordan, Israel, Lebanon, the United Arab Republic, at the UN and in many world capitals. As they listened to "the cries of real people overcome by real fears and frustrations—and explainable hatreds," they almost despaired. But "an inner imperative, linked to the ancient Quaker testimony against war" kept them at it, although they felt "incapable of communicating the depth of human anguish experienced on both sides." In conclusion they wrote, "our basic concern is not with politics, power, or sovereignty. . . . The real issue, significant for everyone, is whether the sterile negatives of today's life in the Middle East, by which all men are imperilled, can be converted to a pattern of human cooperation not yet known or seen among men. Of all places on the face of the earth, Jerusalem should be the city where peace is made manifest in real terms . . . there are no hopeless situations, only hopeless men . . . we find hopeful men on both sides of the tragedy who are deeply concerned for the human condition and for the spirits of men."[4]

Forty workers, appointed by the Board of Missions of Friends United Meeting, were trying to bring "reconciliation to a broken world," in East Africa, the Middle East, Jamaica and Latin America as well as to the American Indians in the West. "Perhaps the world isn't any more broken than it has been for a long time," the Board of Missions conceded. "But . . . it shows its cracks more. Fissures divide haves from have-nots, east from west, young from old, and these breaks in fellowship are secondary to the primary separation —man from God."

"Man and the Economy" was the subject which another Quaker working party wrestled with. "Our purpose," it said, "is . . . to ask how the economy can serve all men by providing them the basics of life . . . nations with far less wealth have . . . substantially reached the goal of eliminating poverty." These specialists pointed out that the need was not so much for "financial sacrifices, if any, but the overturning of old presuppositions, old fears, old ways of proceeding and old privileges."[5]

Meanwhile, a group of doctors and scholars was addressing itself to a different, deeply baffling problem—the ethical implications of man's control over birth and death. *Who Shall Live?* the group asked in its published reflections. What contribution did the beliefs of the Society of Friends have to make to the question of abortion? This working party soon discovered that the question was only part of Friends' whole concern for the quality of life. They had to consider not only abortion, but also their attitudes toward contraception, sexual morality and "the ethical issues implicit in . . . prolonging the life of the dying. . . . What was a right course of action yesterday may not be the right one today; and what seems right today may not be appropriate in tomorrow's situation. . . . Perhaps a healthy perspective on death would lead us to devote our resources to making our lives better rather than longer."[6]

Generations before they were faced with the moral dilemmas arising from modern medical practices, Friends had tried to make their lives better rather than longer. For over three centuries, they had contributed to the quality of American life. This history was reviewed in a book which appeared in March of 1969, *The Quiet Rebels* by Margaret H. Bacon. It communicated to present-day youth the possibility of dissenting from the Establishment and achieving reform while remaining within the American system.

Cambridge, Massachusetts, Friends traveled to Fort Devens to attend Eric Rutan's court-martial. He was sentenced to six months in the stockade. The Conscientious Objector status he requested was never granted, but when he had served his sentence, he was assigned to non-combatant duty. On a weekend pass, he rushed home and married Janet. In Atlanta, Georgia, another young soldier who, like Eric, was not a Quaker, also appealed for sanctuary. Atlanta Monthly Meeting offered "hospitality and moral support" with the understanding that "non-violence shall prevail . . . there shall be no secrecy." The soldier was arrested the next morning and sentenced to six months in Fort Leavenworth. Three members of the armed forces, who wished to resign, appealed to Orange Grove Monthly Meeting in Pasadena. The Meeting then wrote to the commandant of the Marine Corps, "In no sense is the Meeting attempting to interfere with due process of law, hindering appropriate authorities from taking individuals into custody or concealing fugitives from justice."

Friends provided hospitality in the Meetinghouse for the three men and their supporters. At night, the benches became beds. Food was donated. "Beyond the discussions, beyond the bongos and rock music, beyond the problems of life style, there has emerged a strange and beautiful community, a community of the concerned," Orange Grove Meeting affirmed. "Young people who had rejected the Church and religion have found a new dynamic in the silent worship; they have discovered Quakerism."[7]

One of the soldiers, Timothy Springer, asked to be married under the care of Orange Grove Meeting, but before the wedding could take place, he was arrested and placed in the stockade at Fort Ord. Friends were unable to obtain permission for holding a marriage in the base chapel during visiting hours. Three months later, on June 3, 1969, they attended Timothy Springer's court-martial. When the court adjourned for the day, Friends gathered under a Monterey pine outside the Judge Advocate's office and held a Meeting for Worship, in the course of which the couple, attended by a military guard, was married. There was no time to prepare a scroll so the certificate was written on a sheet of yellow foolscap.

"One Friend made reference to the incongruity of this quiet meeting on a United States Army base, in the midst of all this destructive power. He hoped that the bugle, like this marriage, was sounding the end of the old way of life and heralding the dawn of a new day. . . . And then the Army's prosecuting attorney rose to speak. He said that he had been married for ten years and knew the joys and responsibilities of married life. He wanted Tim and Monica and all the Meeting to know that, regardless of how the case turned out, there was nothing personal in his role as prosecutor. He wished them happiness and gave his blessing to the marriage."[8]

The following day, Tim Springer was found guilty of desertion and given a dishonorable discharge.

In San Francisco, Madge T. Seaver, former Clerk of Pacific Yearly Meeting, listened to Joan Baez, the singer, talk about her Quaker upbringing and its failure to satisfy her when she became adult. For her and for her husband, David Harris, contemporary Quakerism apparently did not carry the concepts of non-violence and brotherhood far enough. "I hated Quaker meetings for worship, which I had to attend from the time I was tiny until I was sixteen, but the silence didn't hurt. I prefer unimposed silences. I always loved the spontaneous silences in my family—sitting quietly in the woods, for instance. . . .

"David will probably go to prison in June. He talks of delay because I'm pregnant, but I tell him that the sooner he goes, the sooner he'll be out and meeting his child. . . .

"What is the young Friend rebelling against?" Joan Baez asked Madge Seaver. "And how is he rebelling? . . . I'd like to say to him . . . If you have the nerve to rebel, you should be brave enough to be honest with your parents, to trust them to see that you count. If you want them to consider that you're real, *be real*. . . . What kind of world will my children grow up in?"[9]

Quaker educators were asking what kind of world the students faced who were currently enrolled in fifty-eight schools and fifteen colleges under the care of Friends. The objective of Quaker education was to prepare them for contributing positively to that world rather than for taking exams. Howard Brinton claimed that a Quaker education should be devoted "not so much to absorbing many facts as to sensing the meaning and goal of life, not so much to thought and research as to insight and meditation."[10]

According to Thomas S. Brown, Executive Director of the Friends Council on Education, a Quaker school should provide "an atmosphere within which all the members of the community deal honestly and openly and creatively with the basic human question, 'What is the meaning of my life?' "[11]

"The enduring strength of Quakerism," Douglas Heath, Professor of Psychology at Haverford College declared, "lies in the reciprocal and integral combination of both its individualistic and communal traditions. . . . The assertion of student 'freedom' or 'right to self-determination' is difficult for a Quaker to moderate who is sympathetic to such a belief but as only one of his basic beliefs. . . . A Friends school, deeply aware of the Quaker assumption that a mature individuality develops out of corporate experiences, will not abandon too readily its customs and institutions in response to anarchistic demands of its students. . . . Customs and institutions . . . are replaced usually by a vacuum. And life then does become more barren and meaningless for the young."[12]

Friends World College, the newest and most experimental Quaker institution of higher learning, conducted programs in North and Latin America, Africa, India, Europe and Japan. Students pursued independent study. Barrington Dunbar, a member of New York Yearly Meeting, was appointed coordinator of Afro-American studies.

Leanore Goodenow, who made Scattergood School in West Branch, Iowa, a vital place after it had been closed for years, stated her educational philosophy when she retired. With profoundly meaningful simplicity she said, "You live with youngsters and they grow."

In 1969, Haverford, the first college in the United States to be established by Friends, was still pioneering: Students were represented on the Board of Managers and at faculty meetings. Guilford College began a new curriculum, designed to provide an educational experience that is interdisciplinary and conducive to independent thought and study. Members of the Wilmington College faculty were offering courses at the Lebanon State Prison, making it possible for inmates, who previously had no educational opportunities beyond high school, to earn college credit within the prison. Pacific Oaks College was developing leaders for work with young children, cultivating new insights in human relationships and education.

Malone College in Canton, Ohio, was planning "education for 2000 A.D. in a context of firm Christian commitment." Friends University in Wichita, Kansas, also evangelical in emphasis, had shifted from the semester system to the four-quarter plan and a work-study program. William Penn College in Oskaloosa, Iowa, was, in the words of President Duane Moon, "pleased to be identified with a higher education that seeks to meet, in a genuine way, the total educational needs of youth."[13]

President Paul S. Smith of Whittier College was named Director of the Richard Nixon Institute of Human Affairs, a graduate school. David C. Le Shana, author of *Quakers in California*, became President of George Fox College. President Landrum R. Bolling of Earlham College appeared before the Committee on Science and Aeronautics of the United States House of Representatives to present the needs of liberal arts colleges in educating scientists.

That summer, while four hundred thousand young people were attending the Woodstock Music and Art Festival, five hundred of their contemporaries were taking part in Friends Service Committee projects all over the United States and overseas—acting as aides in institutions, helping in community enterprises and participating in Work Camps. At the same time, a group of the youngest Service Committee staff workers, deeply troubled about the prevalence of hunger in their own country, went into fifteen states to discover whether the food programs offered by the federal government for the alleviation of hunger were reaching the people who needed them.

They called their program CRASH—Call to Research and Act to Stop Hunger. Originally designed by a Radcliffe student, a Catholic nun, an architecture student and high school students from suburban Chicago, Pennsylvania and Michigan, CRASH was eventually carried out by two hundred people. Teams moved into areas where the Service Committee already had some involvement. They stayed from six to eight weeks, interviewing officials, food program participants, interested citizens. Convinced that "the United States of America is not only financially able but morally obligated to assure that no one . . . suffer from hunger or malnutrition" and that "no human being should be made to feel he has to divest himself of all dignity in order to physically survive,"[14] they went from door to door.

The Senate Select Committee on Hunger and Human Needs estimated that an additional four billion dollars a year was needed. "We have a long, long way to go before we succeed in eliminating hunger in America," Senator George McGovern, Chairman of the Senate Select Committee, stated.

CRASH found that food stamps were not available to all those who needed them; that migratory workers and Indians were often unable to procure food to which they were entitled by law; that many communities could not provide school lunches because the schools had no cafeterias. At the end of the summer, the participants in the CRASH program compiled a report. They called it *hunger —why?* It made specific recommendations for the improvement of existing programs and for the simplification of procedures, which many deprived people could not understand or follow.

That same summer, young Friends traveled across the country in peace caravans. At the Friends General Conference in Wilmington, Ohio, they heard Kenneth E. Boulding, Professor of Economics at the University of Colorado, say that "The great problem is the right balance between heroic and economic, inward and outward, self-legitimation and community identification. . . . The wholly inward, whether religious or hippie, leads to an illusion. The wholly community-identified leads to authoritarianism and sterility."[15] George Sawyer, the Quaker Director of Indianapolis Legal Service, spoke of "The Stranger Among You." "White America," he said, "with its limited democracy, limited to Whites only, has, with its tool of unchristian Christianity, created the conditions under which she now stands in awesome fear of the Black Stranger."

The National Black Economic Development Conference had recently issued the Black Manifesto, demanding massive "reparations" from white churches and synagogues. Friends United Meeting urged its members to meet any confrontation with "respectful listening" and an understanding spirit. "It is imperative that the Christian community should not be 'turned off' by the new militancy," Lorton Heusel, the General Secretary, observed. "The concern for self-determination and independence, the shocking demands and the 'no strings attached' policy proclaimed by the Blacks may be difficult for us to hear. But behind the militancy we must surely discern the cry of desperation . . . the agony of accumulated hurts and deprivation."[16]

At the 1969 sessions of Friends United Meeting, a National Fund for Urban Economic Development was authorized. Individual members were urged to commit 1 per cent of their income toward programs of economic development on behalf of the deprived.

In harmony with this proposal, Samuel R. Levering, together with a Mennonite and a member of the Church of the Brethren, issued "A Call to Simple Living." Samuel Levering, like his model, John Woolman, was a Quaker apple grower who scaled down his material wants so that he could devote half his time to peace and other concerns. "The ultimate value is persons," he said. "Across the lives of all of us come times when we could make the difference in the life of someone between deprivation, spiritual, moral, mental, material, and the beginnings of what is needed to live effectively and well. You can't dodge it. It's there. It's the kind of thing we are called to do."[17]

Attending the Friends United Meeting sessions, as usual, was Levi T. Pennington, President Emeritus of Pacific—now George Fox—College, who was about to turn ninety-four. This rare Friend, large in body, mind and spirit, combined a deep evangelical fervor with understanding of non-pastoral Quakers. He was still amusing members of both branches with his limitless fund of stories while deftly prodding their consciences.

"Silent at a Fort in Darien," thirteen Americans, sponsored by A Quaker Action Group, held a vigil before the gate of Fort Gulick in the Panama Canal Zone to express their concern over United States military, political and economic influence in Latin America. "Our hearts go out to the poor and the oppressed, but our aid has gone to wealthy oligarchies and military dictators," these protestors claimed. They recommended that American economic assistance to Latin-American countries be channeled through the UN and that our military involvement in those countries be terminated.[18]

Marjorie Nelson returned to Quang Ngai in August 1968 to spend another year with Quaker Service-Vietnam. In addition to working in the Rehabilitation Center and the Provincial Hospital, as she had done before her capture, she was now going to the prison every Friday afternoon to care for the women and children there. She brought them milk and vitamins and managed to see from fifteen to eighteen patients in an afternoon. Like most Quakers,

Marge had always had a concern for prisoners. Now that she had been one herself, she understood their feelings. But, she maintained, she had been better treated than the prisoners she visited.

Fighting continued to rage around the area. "How can men justify a war like this?" she wrote home. "Perhaps it's because they don't see and they don't know. Their view of the war is in missions flown, 'enemy structures destroyed, x number of VC dead, etc., civilian casualties were light.' My view is that one of those 'enemy structures' had a bomb shelter containing a family of four—result: father and one child dead, mother with one leg blown off above the knee. 'Civilian casualties were light' but one of those casualties was a 14-year-old boy who will never walk again."[19]

His name was Tho. Paralyzed from the chest down, he was brought to the Provincial Hospital. He had been shot during the Allied "Bold Mariner" attack on his home in the Ban Tan Gan Peninsula. His older brother was missing. His parents were arrested. His mother, about eight months pregnant, was put in the prison next door to the Quaker Center. She was allowed out to have her baby, then taken back in again. Marge visited her every week. Tho's father was sent to a political prison. So Tho had no relatives to look after him in the hospital.

One day, an American doctor arrived, sent by the Committee of Responsibility to Save War-burned and War-injured Vietnamese Children. His assignment was to select seventy-five children who might profit from a stay in American hospitals. Marge showed him Tho, the young paraplegic. When Tho was asked whether he wished to be sent to the United States for treatment, he had no one to turn to for help in making the decision except Marge. After he decided to go, Marge asked the Committee doctor to send Tho to a hospital on the east coast so that she could visit him when she went home.

She left Quang Ngai at the end of September 1969. Her father and Bob Perisho came from the States to take her home. But first, Marge announced her engagement to Bob. A Vietnamese "formal asking ceremony" was arranged by Marge's Vietnamese friends and members of the Quaker team. Marge later described the ceremony to her friends in America. "The bridegroom-to-be arrives at the home of the bride with relatives and friends bearing gifts of gold, food and drink . . . the oldest male member of the groom's family solemnly asks the oldest male member of the bride's family if her family agrees to this betrothal. After agreement, these two men present themselves to the family altar to request the assent of the ancestors. In turn, the two oldest female members of the respective families do the same, followed by the bridegroom and finally the bride. . . . We modified a bit, not having a family altar, and substituted a few moments of silent Quaker worship. Then Keith Brinton read an explanation in Vietnamese about the Quaker wedding ceremony and the custom of having a wedding certificate which everyone present signed. Then the guests sat down to a feast of roast pig and many Vietnamese delicacies while Bob and I circulated so he could get acquainted with my friends there."

It was a happy ending to Marge's Vietnam experiences, but her last view of Quang Ngai as she and Earl Nelson and Bob Perisho took off from the Airport was "a foggy one," for she had dissolved in tears. "A part of my heart will always remain there," she said, "in that patch of land and water—Quang Ngai."[20]

That summer, in a colorful ceremony involving feathers, Levinus K. Painter of Collins Monthly Meeting, New York, was adopted by the Six Nations and given the Indian name, Ha-Dant'-Tah-Nies, which means, "he preaches." This was in recognition of the help he gave the Senecas when their land was taken away for the construction of the Allegheny River Reservoir at Kinzua, Pennsylvania.

The *Friends Journal*, whose predecessor, the *Friends Intelligencer*, confidently prophesied twenty years earlier that beards would not enhance the future scene, now rejoiced in an undulant, rubicund florescence to which was annexed its new editor. Alfred Stefferud had succeeded Frances Browin. As the first issues in a new format came off the press, faithful readers concluded that the literary quality of the magazine lived up to the excellence of the editorial beard.

43 Fair to the Present

In the General Epistle issued by New York Yearly Meeting at its 274th annual sessions, held at Silver Bay in July 1969, Friends observed sadly that "Some young Friends, both by their words and their way of life, seem to be saying, 'I hurt,' and Friends could see no way to relieve this pain, short of re-ordering the society which has created it." The Yearly Meeting focused attention on police practices, court procedures, and conditions in local jails. "Under the Omnibus Crime Control Act, the appropriations have stressed weaponry rather than creative prevention of disorder. Unless national priorities are rechanneled into basic social reforms, we are concerned that the country will become further divided."

Gently prodded by Barrington Dunbar, the Yearly Meeting authorized the creation of a fifty-thousand-dollar Development Fund to provide housing, education, job training, community organization, and legal aid to Black people in the New York Yearly Meeting area. The fund was to be administered by a Yearly Meeting committee, the majority of whose members were Black.

Barrington Dunbar found himself "in the odd position of a black man seeking desperately to relate to a . . . religious community that seems to reflect so much of the immorality of a racist society. . . . Black people living in the ghettos of American cities . . . cannot hear Friends who profess the way of love and nonviolence, but yet maintain a destructive silence in obvious situations of social injustice."

Meanwhile, Philadelphia Yearly Meeting was one of the religious bodies which was being confronted by the Black Manifesto. This was addressed to "The White Christian Churches and the Jewish Synagogues in the United States of America and All Other Racist Institutions." Muhammad Kenyatta, Pennsylvania Field Director of the Black Economic Development Conference, demanded half a million dollars from Philadelphia Yearly Meeting as reparations for Friends' part in four centuries of exploitation of Black people.

At an adjourned session of Philadelphia Yearly Meeting, held in the Arch Street Meetinghouse on October 11, Friends expressed a desire to contribute to those in need up to the limit of their resources. But the demand for "reparations" brought varying responses. Some Friends considered assent to the demand an appropriate acknowledgement of white guilt. Others felt that designating any resources they might share with their Black brothers as reparations did not reflect their true feelings. Hadn't Quakers freed their slaves a century before the Emancipation Proclamation? Hadn't they recompensed them for their services?

Now and Then, whose "Letters from the Past" had been appearing for twenty-eight years now, recalled that the Friendly Association for Regaining and Preserving Peace with the Indians by Pacific Measures, the oldest Quaker committee for social concerns, "appealed successfully not to any sense of corporate guilt on the part of its donors, but to their generosity in connection with fair claims of Indians for wrongs done them at the hands of others."

Seven years after the Friendly Association was formed, John Woolman expressed some thoughts "under a feeling of universal Love . . .

"Suppose an inoffensive youth, forty years ago, was violently taken from Guinea, sold here as a slave, and laboured hard till old age, and hath children who are now living. Though no sum may properly be mentioned as an equal reward for the total deprivation of liberty; yet if the sufferings of this man be computed at no more than fifty pounds, I expect candid men will suppose it within bounds, and that his children have an equitable right to it."

Woolman worked out the interest on £50, computed at 3 per cent for forty years, "adding the Interest to the Principal once in ten years," and found that it totaled £140. "Now when our minds are thoroughly divested of all prejudice in relation to the difference of colour, and the love of Christ, in which there is no partiality, prevails upon us, I believe it will appear that a heavy account lies against us as a Civil Society for oppressions against people who did not injure us; and . . . it would appear that there was considerable due them."[1]

At the adjourned session of Philadelphia Yearly Meeting in 1969, some Friends proposed not only handing over all the assets of the Yearly Meeting to the Black Economic Development Conference, but urged that their Meetinghouses be sold for the purpose as well. Others, who had spent years as the stewards of Meeting funds, disbursing them in accordance with the wishes of the donors, or who had been the trustees of Meetinghouse property, felt they would be less than faithful if they used the resources entrusted to them for any purpose other than the one originally specified. Moreover, after they had given everything away, how would they pay their bills? Other Friends pointed out that the Black Economic Development Conference only represented one group of disadvantaged people. What about all the rest who were not making demands?

Friends who never understood how the Quaker Separations could possibly have taken place now realized that such a thing might conceivably happen again. They were all seeking to do the right thing according to their Light, but the Light appeared differently to different people and, in their busy lives, there wasn't time for the slow deliberation and willingness to listen to each other that are characteristic of a true Quaker Meeting for Business.

The Clerk called for a period of silence so that Friends might seek God's will together. At that juncture, more than a few moments of prayerful quiet were needed to bring them into unity. Most of the visitors were not acquainted with the Quaker method of settling differences. They had simply come to press their demands. And some Friends forgot that a Meeting for Business is a Meeting for Worship. More intent on scoring their point than, with divine assistance, working toward agreement, all of these returned to the debate as soon as the silence was over. The afternoon was advancing and there was other business on the agenda. Leisure for the most important thing in life—sensing the leading of the Spirit—simply wasn't available.

The Blacks' demand for half a million dollars without strings or oversight led some Friends to fear that Quaker funds might be used for activities which ran counter to Quaker testimonies—perhaps even, one or two suggested, for the purchase of guns. Black Friends rose to plead passionately with their fellow members for the chance to determine their own destiny, to experiment, to make some mistakes and learn from them.

A century and a quarter earlier, Lucretia Mott, understanding this craving for money of one's own, had written, "How glad I was that I stopped at that colored school! I left fifty cents to be divided among the children, about three or four cents each, and the teacher proposed that it be laid out in books for them, which was not just what I intended. Those pious primers! I wanted the little things made happy in spending of their own, as they listed. . . ."[2]

Many responses to the Black Manifesto, involving large financial commitments, were proposed at the adjourned session of Philadelphia Yearly Meeting but no action could be taken because there was no sense of the Meeting. And so the matter was held over.

It seemed to some of the Friends present that the wrong issues had been raised, that neither a confession of guilt nor payment of the large sum demanded would materially improve the sad lives of most of their Black brothers. An entirely new, imaginative approach was called for, a kind of partnership had to be created which had never existed, one which conferred dignity on Blacks. Nothing else would absolve whites of their continuing guilt. It could only be accomplished when Friends were ready to put themselves in their brothers' place.

There was another item on the agenda that also strained Friends' unity. Fifteenth Street in Philadelphia was about to be widened. Buildings which now housed the Service Committee, the Wider Quaker Fellowship, the Green Circle Program and several Yearly Meeting Committees were going to be demolished. Money received from the condemnation of the properties was earmarked for rebuilding. It had been proposed that the Race Street Meetinghouse, which was built by Hicksite Friends in 1856 and which was no longer functional, should be torn down at the same time and that a smaller Meetinghouse, suitable for use on weekdays by non-Quaker groups in the Center City, be erected on the site, along with an office building for various Quaker Committees and the editorial offices of the *Friends Journal*.

The Race Street Meetinghouse, not an architectural treasure, was nevertheless a storehouse of associations for some older Friends. They had been married there. It was the place where the Service Committee was formed in 1917. Rufus Jones, Henry Cadbury and many another overworked committeeman had been known to stretch out on a bench for a little nap in what they thought was an invisible corner of the balcony. Part of some Friends' past would be destroyed if this Meetinghouse came down. But they kept their feelings to themselves because the feelings were personal.

Strenuous opposition came, however, from Friends who felt that when people were hungry money should not be put into bricks and mortar. Younger members recalled that early Friends worshiped in the woods—why have a Meetinghouse at all? But if you happened to be old and arthritic, in the wintertime—Besides, in Center City where were the woods?

Action on this item also had to be deferred because there was, as yet, no sense of the Meeting.

Four days later, when Friends from all over the United States joined the Vietnam Moratorium March in Washington, one of them, Edwin Bronner, viewed the route with an historian's memory. "While walking up Pennsylvania Avenue Saturday afternoon, surrounded by thousands of my fellow Americans bent on influencing our government to change its policy, my thoughts went to other persons and groups that have traveled on that historic highway . . . my mind centered on those who, though in the minority, turned out to be right, while the majority was wrong. I thought of Abraham Lincoln, who went up and down that avenue, the last time in a coffin. I remembered that he voted against the Mexican War forty-seven times. . . . There were . . . the valiant souls who demanded equal rights for women. . . . Quaker women, and many others . . . marched on Pennsylvania Avenue in 1913 and the fact that a 'silent majority' opposed their campaign did not dissuade them. . . .

"There was unpleasantness around us on Pennsylvania Avenue some of the time. Most of us were quiet, peaceful, and cooperative. Some were noisy, militant, abrasive. I remembered that not all persons who have been right in our history were respectable, cooperative, and lovable. Benjamin Lay, the dwarf who needled Quakers . . . came to mind—Benjamin Lay, who sprinkled Friends with pig's blood, to remind them of the blood of slaves . . .

"Finally, my mind moved to a recent novel, Jessamyn West's *Except for Me and Thee* . . . the saga of the Birdwells, patterned on her Milhous ancestors. . . . These Quaker ancestors of Jessamyn West heard the clear call to a higher law than the Fugitive Slave Law of 1850, and obeyed the still small voice within them.

"Those of us who cry out against the war in Vietnam, who demonstrate in Washington . . . may not be in the majority and we may not all be lovable, but we do feel we are obeying a 'higher law,' and we know we are following in the footsteps of our Quaker ancestors."[3]

Joseph Elder, Professor of Sociology at the University of Wisconsin, was in North Vietnam, bringing equipment for open-heart surgery to a hospital in Hanoi. The U. S. State Department had granted the American Friends Service Committee permission to send twenty-five thousand dollars' worth of medical equipment in his care. He brought 250 letters from the wives of American prisoners and also their gift of vitamins for North Vietnamese children. The authorities decided to distribute the vitamins among the American prisoners instead of giving them to their own children. They refused to furnish Joseph Elder with a list of the prisoners, which he offered to deliver to the prisoners' wives. American pilots were, the officials maintained, volunteer aggressors, distinct from draftees. Joseph Elder had an interview with Foreign Minister Nguyen Duy Trinh. The Vietnamese have fought outsiders for four thousand years, the Minister told him, and will continue to fight as long as foreigners remain in their country.

Oscar and Olive Marshburn of Whittier, California, were in Korea, encouraging the Seoul Friends Meeting. Floyd H. Sidwell of Columbiana, Ohio, was also in Korea, helping the Leper Colony at Tan Dong, which almost starved when the barley crop failed. Seoul Friends, unable to give the lepers enough support, appealed to American Friends. The lepers obviously needed an agricultural expert to advise them. A Joint Committee for Korea, representing Ohio Yearly Meeting (Conservative) and Lake Erie Yearly Meeting sent Floyd Sidwell to assist the lepers. "Conservation of soil and water is an unknown practice to all but a few Koreans," he reported. "A program of grass management is a necessity before advance will be made in their livestock and food production. The floods develop because there is little on the hills and mountains to hold the water."[4]

On October 27, Anna Brinton died at the age of eighty-four. To generations at Pendle Hill and in Pacific Yearly Meeting, she had been both a great Friend and a friend. Sylvia Shaw Judson, who translated Anna Brinton's character into sculpture, also captured it in words.

"Pendle Hill was my first contact with Quakers, and a lecture in the library at Upmeads was my introduction to Anna. She had gone all the way to the Metropolitan Museum to obtain slides of Japanese art to show to a group of trainees who were going to work for the Service Committee in Japan, so that they would respect Japanese culture. It was knowing Anna that made me realize that I could be both an artist and a Quaker, something which I had previously doubted. Once we went together to an Austrian exhibit at the Chicago Art Institute and as we were leaning over a case of lovely, useless enamels, she whispered, 'Isn't it fortunate that all the world has not been Quaker!' "⁵

Since 1936, when Anna and Howard Brinton became Directors of Pendle Hill, the students were concerned with the prevention of war and the function of religion in social change. In 1969, when Dan Wilson was completing seventeen years as Director, a course was in progress called "Meeting for the Quest and the Questions." This was a search for "my own integrity, joy in being human, where I am needed in the world, and how to prepare for radical living." An Australian member of the staff, Margaret Walpole, commented, "We at Pendle Hill believe this Quaker study center is having a sort of renaissance: that is a way of saying the vision of its founders is as strong as ever, maybe stronger. . . . Those who come to Pendle Hill feel that they have climbed to a mountain-top out of the valley of their previous lives."⁶

After a separation of one hundred and forty years, the two Baltimore Yearly Meetings were again one. "There is a sense of peace and rightness which is the result of differences reconciled and parts made whole," the reunited Yearly Meeting declared at the 297th annual session. "We continue to strive for love and understanding with a vision, borrowed from Kenneth Boulding, of our various shades of Quakerism merging like a rainbow into a shaft of pure white light."⁷

Throughout the United States, adherents to the various shades of Quakerism were longing for some rapprochement. The day when they would merge into a single shaft of light was far away; their theological differences were too great. But Friends were beginning to see that these differences did not preclude an honest confrontation in a spirit of love and respect under the guidance of the Holy Spirit. With great faith and courage, an Ad Hoc Committee of Friends Concerned for Renewal called for a conference of all branches to be held in St. Louis in 1970 to consider "The Future of Friends." David C. Le Shana was appointed chairman. The concern arose among evangelical Friends but their desire was to have every Yearly Meeting in the United States represented as well as the Evangelical Friends Alliance, the Friends United Meeting, the Friends General Conference and the Friends World Committee.

"We are all so far from the truth, we are all so fallible, standing under the judgment and forgiveness of God, that we ought to be able to be reconciled to God and to one another," Richard P. Newby, pastor of University Friends Church in Wichita, Kansas, observed.[8]

Fifty years earlier, Rufus Jones had defined as "the most central feature of Quaker faith . . . that the living Christ sweeps onward . . . and carries His true 'seed' on into fresh experiences, enlarged ideas, growing faiths, greater deeds, and more daring missions."[9]

Over New Year, New Swarthmoor, the Young Friends community in Clinton, New York, held "an open gathering to seek together about the things which the next ten years may hold for us as individuals, as a religious society, and as a nation . . . everyone is invited—feel free to come, with food or wood if you have any, or just your loving self if you don't. . . . Things must have gotten crowded sometimes in the Old Swarthmoor too, but we doubt that that interfered much with the deep peace Friends found there. . . . Maybe our name is ill-chosen. We really haven't any prospect of seeing the birth in the near future of a movement that even poorly reflects the one which made such vital use of the Fell home in Northwest England. But perhaps we can at least grow a little in that direction."

It was hard to imagine, but people who were now in their seventies and eighties had once been Young Friends, too. In 1920, four hundred of them held an International Conference and the message they sent out from Jordans, England, the resting place of Penn, might almost have come from New Swarthmoor: "The sacredness of personality demands a fundamental change in our social and economic system. . . . We are called to live as citizens of the new world while still in the old . . . our individual lives and corporate fellowship must be founded deep in unity with God. Quakerism for us means just that God-conscious life, and we desire to pass on to others the vision we have seen."

This they did. Many who were young in those days became Friends pastors and workers—Milton Hadley, Ward Applegate, Glenn Reece, Norval Webb, Russell Rees, Hugh Moore, Harold Tollefson, Raymond Wilson and many, many more. Even they caught their vision from Friends who were young before them and who were still, in the 1970s, passing it on—nonagenarians like Levi Pennington in Newberg, Oregon, whose father lost his home because he assumed another man's debt; like Thomas Perry in Westerly,

Rhode Island, the grandson of Charles. Winter and summer, he faithfully worshiped in the old Wilburite Meetinghouse, helping to keep a small flame alive. Lavina Edgerton in Barnesville, Ohio, the daughter of Thomissey, sat serene and upright on the lawn at Yearly Meeting time with a crowd of fascinated First-day schoolers at her feet. About to enter her hundredth year, she was recounting for yet another rising generation the adventures of a Quaker among the Indians. In these Friends, the Light shone with special beauty.

As 1969 departed and Friends prayed that the new decade would bring peace to the world, they could turn back a full century to that tiny old lady who embodied such great wisdom and compassion. "Take a cheerful view of the past," Lucretia Mott urged in 1869, "be hopeful for the future, and be *fair* to the present."[10]

Yet, old or young, the Publishers of Truth who have been cited here for their part in the American epic during 315 years are not the foremost Friends. The heart of Quakerism has always been in the lives of those who were anonymous, whose diligence in love illuminated their homes, their fields, their Meetings, their neighborhoods, their classrooms, their offices, and, throughout this long history, their prison cells. "It is the silent help from the nameless to the nameless which is their contribution to the promotion of brotherhood." Their answer to the question, "Who shall live?" embraces all mankind.

44 So Long as We Both Shall Live

Early on Easter morning, 1970, a large company of well-wishers gathered in the Race Street Meetinghouse, Philadelphia, to witness the marriage of Marjorie Nelson to Robert Perisho. Although April was only two days away, the driving rain froze as it came down. The Meetinghouse corridors buzzed with people parking umbrellas and exuberantly greeting friends. But once they entered the Meeting room, they joined the living silence which those who arrived early had prepared. This was a Meeting for Worship. In accordance with custom, there was no music, there were no flowers.

Three men and three women occupied the raised facing benches, which formed what was called "the ministers' gallery" in the old days. Then, the gallery was reserved on one side for women ministers in somber silks and wearing bonnets, and the other side for men ministers, whose coats had no collars and who kept their broadbrims on during Meeting except when someone offered prayer or they themselves felt moved to speak. The Friends who sat there today were not necessarily recorded ministers. They were not segregated by sex and they wore contemporary clothes. These were the Overseers, appointed "to see that the wedding is accomplished with dignity, reverence and simplicity."[1]

Guests filled all the benches. Many had known Bob when he was a student at Haverford and Marge when she was taking her internship at the Pennsylvania Hospital. They had been anxious when she was missing in Vietnam. Now, here she was, about to enter the Meeting on the arm of the man she had hoped, during her captivity, that she might live to marry.

Without fanfare, in the meaningful silence, the couple came in together. A Quaker bride is not given away. She gives herself to the bridegroom and he gives himself to her. The guests remained seated, silently watching Marge and Bob walk to the front of the Meeting and sit down on the narrow marriage bench at the bottom of the gallery. They were followed by two young Friends. The bridesmaid wore an everyday dress and a Quaker bonnet; the best man wore his version of plain Quaker attire. These two took their places on either side of the bride and groom.

When Marge's Vietnamese friends heard that she was going home to be married, they made her a present of white silk with the symbol of happiness woven in it. A dressmaker in Quang Ngai made the silk into a traditional Vietnamese wedding gown, full length, narrow, dropping straight from the mandarin neck. It was slit at the hem on either side so that lace-edged pantalets were just visible. Marge wore nothing on her head. She carried a little bunch of violets and lilies of the valley—a couple of months later, she might have picked them herself in the woods at Pendle Hill.

A Quaker wedding may take place as well on Easter as on any other day since, like Christmas, Easter is not traditionally observed by Friends. Christ, they maintain, is born and risen in men's hearts every day. The mysterious birth of the Seed, the silent growth in the dead husk—these are nativity and resurrection, a daily celebration.

Yet there is nothing to deter a Friend from joining with those who celebrate holydays. "He who keeps not a day may unite in the same Spirit, in the same life, in the same love, with him that keeps a day; and he who keeps a day may unite in heart and soul with the same Spirit and life in him who keeps not a day; but he that judgeth the other because of either of these errs from the Spirit, from the love, from the life, and so breaks the bond of unity."[2]

In the deeply reverent silence, a young Friend from Ireland offered prayer. Then there was silence again until Bob and Marge felt moved to stand and make their promises to each other before the assembled company. Bob took Marge's hand and said with great solemnity, "In the presence of God and these our friends, I take thee, Marjorie Nelson, to be my wife, promising with divine assistance to be unto thee a loving and faithful husband so long as we both shall live." He put the ring on her finger.

Marge's whole heart was in her eyes as she said more softly, "In the presence of God and these our friends, I take thee, Robert Perisho, to be my husband," and went on to make the identical promise. When she had slipped a ring on Bob's finger, they kissed and sat down.

The bridesmaid and best man got up to fetch a little table from the aisle. It held the scroll on which the marriage certificate was engrossed. The table was placed in front of Bob and Marge. He signed the certificate first, then Marge did, using her new name. All the guests—adults and children—were witnesses to the marriage and later, during the reception, they would sign the certificate. Now, it was handed up to one of the Overseers. Standing in his place, he read so that everyone present could hear, "Whereas . . ." The long, legal document stated that after Robert Clarence Perisho and Marjorie Ellen Nelson had "declared their intentions of marriage with each other to Central Philadelphia Monthly Meeting of the Religious Society of Friends . . . and having the consent of parents, their proposed marriage was allowed by that Meeting." The certificate described how the two had said their vows and signed their names, "she, according to the custom of marriage, assuming the surname of her husband. . . . And we, having been present at the marriage, have as witnesses set our hands the day and year above written."

When the Overseer had finished reading the certificate, he sat down and the Meeting settled once more into silence. After a time, Marge's father, who was sitting on one of the front benches with Beryl, rose and read some Quaker sentiments regarding marriage. "The family is the standing witness that man is not intended to live alone; that he becomes what he is meant to be as his character is trained in unselfishness by responsibility for others, and by the claims and duties of a common life."

The silence was interspersed with messages coming from every part of the Meetinghouse, from young Friends, who were under the weight of the world's agony even on this happy occasion, and from older Friends, for whom the ceremony was a reliving of their own wedding. Life, with all its vicissitudes, had, on balance, been so satisfying for most of the older Friends that they could hardly identify with these troubled youngsters. They had known hard times, too. They had grown up during one or other of the world wars or during the Depression but not under the threat of nuclear extinction. Older Friends spoke with assurance and hope.

Nevertheless, as they thought of the immediate future—tomorrow—they felt apprehensive. Tomorrow, at the 290th annual gathering of Philadelphia Yearly Meeting, the Black Manifesto, with its demands for half a million dollars in "reparations" would be considered again. Friends were still divided about the proper response to the demands. Unity seemed completely out of reach.

It came suddenly to one of these Friends, as insight does sometimes during Meeting—a thought which seems inappropriate and yet is actually the fulfillment of the worshiper's highest aspiration— it came to this Friend that unity was out of reach perhaps because the issue was only money, when it should have been Friends' entire substance. Since when did Quakers bestow money unaccompanied by friendship? Barrington Dunbar once said that the Society of Friends in the United States might yet play a significant role by giving sacrificially of its manpower as well as of its financial resources. Might not Friends volunteer to stand in for Blacks on their jobs, in a one-to-one relationship, freeing them to get more education? A white housewife with time on her hands might go out and clean someone else's house so that the Black woman, whose job it was, could collect her day's pay while going to school and preparing herself for an occupation she considered dignified. Wouldn't a Quaker student be glad to work the way through school for a Black classmate? Such a partnership would make life more significant. There was no limit to what a retired person might do, teamed up with an ambitious younger one. Imaginative, sacrificial giving had always been the genius of Friends. What were they waiting for now?

The Friend tried to put extraneous thoughts aside, to center down, to support through prayer the young couple who were making a new beginning, who had the gifts and the will to fashion a better world society and Society of Friends.

The moment had come for the young couple to walk out of the Meeting as man and wife. They started gravely, but as they reached the door, they almost skipped through it. They were married! For another little while, Friends remained to worship. Then the silence was broken as they shook hands and greeted one another. They filed out to felicitate the bride and groom, who were waiting for them in the Cherry Room across the corridor. Everyone signed the certificate.

The simplest collation, beautifully spread on a side table—coffee in silver urns and doughnuts on Waterford glass platters—made this a Quakerly reception. Marge had baked the wedding cake herself.

Laughter and chatter and gay greetings replaced solemnity. But suddenly everyone in the Cherry Room was jolted back sharply to the other reality. Three little wedding guests were congratulating the bridal couple. They were Vietnamese children—a boy in a wheel chair, another whose face was bandaged and a girl with napalm burns. The boy in the wheel chair was Tho. He had been sent to the Pennsylvania Hospital, where he underwent a series of amazingly successful operations and where Marge could visit him when she was in Philadelphia. The other boy had been struck by artillery shell fragments, which tore away his face. With reconstruction surgery, his mouth and cheek were being rebuilt. The little girl's face was scarred from burns. These were three of the children who had been taken to the United States for medical care by the Committee of Responsibility. A young lady from Saigon, who acted as their interpreter, brought them to the wedding.

Friends, who could hardly bear to look at these young victims of *their* country's artillery and *their* country's napalm, also knew that the three children were among the more fortunate. Thousands and thousands of sufferers would never have medical care. All Friends' efforts to bring their concern for terminating the war before their government had not been successful. What more could they do, what more could they do?

The children's eyes brightened when Marge spoke to them in their own language. She was their friend from home.

When the reception was over, the newly married couple drove away from the Meetinghouse, sent off in a whirl by a crowd of gay contemporaries. They were showered, not with rice and confetti but with snowflakes.

The older guests came down the wavy brick walk cautiously, skidding a little, trying to integrate in their hearts the confusing contradictions of life, the overwhelming joy and devastating sorrow. This Meetinghouse, in which so many memories and associations were stored, might not be here much longer. Friends had just witnessed a beautiful beginning but also a sad ending to normal existence, when it had barely begun. Spring was supposed to be here and they were heading into a driving blizzard. Yet, through it all, in the ground of their beings, they joyfully experienced resurrection. This was Easter morning 1970.

In 1670, George Fox sent a message to Friends. It was, he noted, "a cruel, bloody, persecuting time, but the Lord's power went over all." Only a few months before, he and Margaret had stood "in the meeting house at Broad Mead in Bristol, the Lord joining us together in the honourable marriage, in the everlasting covenant and immortal Seed of life." Now Margaret was a prisoner in Lancaster Castle again.

Fox was in London. He had gone "to the meeting in Gracechurch Street though I was but weak." Then, "in the motion of life," he wrote to Friends, "Be not amazed at the weather . . . though the waves and storms be high, yet your faith will keep you to swim above them, for they are but for a time, and the Truth is without time. . . . And do not think that anything will outlast the Truth, which standeth sure, and is over that which is out of the Truth; for the good will overcome the evil; and the light, darkness; and the life, death. . . . So be faithful, and live in that which doth not think the time long."

References

ABBREVIATIONS USED IN REFERENCES

AF	*American Friend*
AFSC	American Friends Service Committee
AFSERCO	*AFSERCO News*
Besse	Joseph Besse, *Collection of the Sufferings of the People Called Quakers*, 1753
BFHA	*Bulletin of the Friends Historical Association*
Bowden	James Bowden, *History of the Society of Friends in America*, 1850–54
BQ	W. C. Braithwaite, *Beginnings of Quakerism*
FI	*Friends Intelligencer*
FOL	Elizabeth Gray Vining, *Friend of Life*
FJ	*Friends Journal*
FMTB	Clarence E. Pickett, *For More Than Bread*
GIML	Raymond J. Jeffreys, *God Is My Landlord*
JGF	*The Journal of George Fox*, Cambridge edition, 1952
JJW	*The Journal and Major Essays of John Woolman*, edited by Phillips P. Moulton, 1971
LPQ	Rufus M. Jones, *Later Periods of Quakerism*
QAC	——, *Quakers in the American Colonies*
QASIA	Thomas E. Drake, *Quakers and Slavery in America*
QL	*Quaker Life*
SPQ	W. C. Braithwaite, *The Second Period of Quakerism*
TR	"A True Relation of the Voyage of the *Woodhouse*"
WFTCP	Elizabeth Gray Vining, *Windows for the Crown Prince*

REFERENCES

CHAPTER 1

1. FMTB, p. 133.
2. AF, July 10, 1947.
3. Ibid.
4. FOL, p. 282.
5. Ibid., p. 301.
6. FMTB, p. 135.
7. AF, July 10, 1947.
8. Ibid.
9. Ibid.
10. Isaac Penington, Letter XVI.

CHAPTER 2

1. Gerard Croese, *History of the Quakers*, Vol. II, p. 124.
2. Ibid.
3. At a Council held at Boston, July 11, 1656.
4. Ibid.
5. George Bishop, *New England Judged*, 1702, p. 7.
6. Ibid., p. 12.

CHAPTER 6

7. Colony Records of Massachusetts, Vol. I, 1, p. 279.
8. Humphrey Norton, *New England's Ensign*, p. 14.
9. JGF, p. 242.
10. Ibid., p. 263.
11. Kenneth L. Carroll, *Quaker History*, Vol. 57, No. 2.
12. Colony Records of Massachusetts, Vol. IV, Pt. 1, p. 277.
13. Besse, Vol. II, p. 206.

CHAPTER 3

1. FI, Sixth Month 1, 1940.
2. FMTB, p. 173.
3. Ibid., p. 139.
4. Ibid., p. 135.
5. Ibid., pp. 140–41.
6. Ibid., pp. 166–67.
7. Ibid., p. 155.
8. Mary Hoxie Jones, FI, Sixth Month 15, 1940.
9. New York *Times*, June 4, 1940.
10. AFSERCO, November 1940.
11. FI, Sixth Month 29, 1940.
12. Ibid., Eighth Month 10, 1940.
13. Ibid., Sixth Month 1, 1940.
14. Ibid.

CHAPTER 4

1. JGF, p. 2.
2. Ibid., p. 7.
3. Ibid., p. 4.
4. Ibid., pp. 3–11.
5. Ibid., p. 103.
6. Ibid., p. 104.
7. TR.
8. Bowden, Vol. I, p. 61.
9. TR.
10. Ibid.
11. Ecclesiastical Records of New York, II, p. 156.
12. Bowden, p. 313.
13. Ibid., p. 314.
14. TR.

CHAPTER 5

1. Bowden, p. 19, quotation from Bancroft.
2. QAC, p. 20.
3. Mary Hoxie Jones, *The Standard of the Lord Lifted Up*, p. 14.
4. Bowden, Vol. I, p. 67.
5. Humphrey Norton, *New England's Ensign*, p. 22.
6. Colony Records of Massachusetts, Bowden, p. 46.
7. Plymouth Records, Vol. 2, p. 156; quoted in QAC, p. 57.
8. *New England's Ensign*, p. 2.
9. Henry Fell to Margaret Fell, QAC, p. 64.
10. *New England's Ensign*, p. 69; QAC, p. 73.
11. Ibid., p. 60; QAC, p. 66.
12. Bowden, p. 122.
13. Ibid., p. 120.
14. George Bishop, *New England Judged*, p. 168.
15. Bowden, p. 342.
16. Ibid., p. 344.
17. Ibid., p. 346.
18. Ibid., p. 123.
19. Ibid., p. 124.
20. Ibid.
21. Ibid., p. 346.
22. William Penn's Testimony Concerning Josiah Coale, 1671.
23. Gerard Croese, *History of the Quakers*, p. 52.
24. Bowden, p. 125.
25. Colony Records of Massachusetts, Vol. I, Pt. 1, p. 345; QAC, p. 76.
26. *New England Judged*, p. 84.
27. Besse, Vol. II, p. 198.
28. Colony Records of Massachusetts, Vol. IV, Pt. 1, p. 367.
29. Besse, Vol. II, p. 197.
30. Ibid., p. 191.

CHAPTER 6

1. George Bishop, *New England Judged*, p. 127.
2. Ibid., p. 131.

3. Ibid., p. 476.
4. Colony Records of Massachusetts, Vol. IV, Pt. 1, p. 384.
5. William Starbuck, *History of Nantucket*, p. 20.
6. Ibid.
7. Ibid.
8. *Memoir of John Taylor*, p. 21; QAC, p. 86.
9. Besse, Vol. II, p. 206.
10. BQ, p. 404.
11. Samuel Deane, *History of Scituate, Massachusetts*, p. 372.
12. *New England Judged*, p. 296.
13. QAC, p. 96.
14. Francis Howgill, *Works*, p. 259; QAC, p. 93.
15. JGF, p. 411.
16. Ibid.
17. John Greenleaf Whittier, *Works*, p. 408.
18. Besse, Vol. II, p. 225.
19. Besse, Vol. II, p. 226.
20. Swarthmore MSS, in Bowden, p. 369.
21. MS Letter of Josiah Coale, in Bowden, p. 369.
22. Henry J. Cadbury, BFHA, Vol. 35, No. 1, p. 23.
23. Ibid.
24. QAC, p. 54n.
25. *New England Judged*, p. 351.
26. Colony Records of Massachusetts, Vol. IV, Pt. 2, p. 2.
27. Bowden, Vol. I, p. 345.
28. George Fox, *A Collection of Many Select and Christian Epistles*, 1698, Epistle 153.
29. George Rofe, Letter to Richard Hubberthorne, QAC, p. 54n.

CHAPTER 7

1. Francis Howgill in Edward Burrough, *The memorable works of a son of thunder*, 1672.
2. Geoffrey Nuttall, *Early Quaker Letters*, No. 324.
3. George Fox, *A Collection of Many Select and Christian Epistles*, 1698, Epistle 131.
4. JGF, p. 511.
5. Ibid., p. 492.
6. Ibid., p. 555.
7. Ibid., p. 557.
8. SPQ, p. 64.
9. Ibid., p. 69.
10. Tolles and Alderfer, *The Witness of William Penn*, p. 88.
11. SPQ, pp. 70–73.
12. JGF, p. 578.
13. Ibid., p. 594.
14. Ibid., p. 593.
15. Ibid., p. 609.
16. Ibid., p. 595.
17. George Fox, *Gospel Family Order*, 1676.
18. Ibid.
19. JGF, p. 614.
20. Ibid., p. 617.
21. Ibid.
22. Archives of Rhode Island Historical Society; QAC, p. 114.
23. JGF, pp. 625, 628–29.
24. Ibid., p. 631.
25. Ibid., p. 632.
26. Ibid., p. 643.
27. Ibid., p. 664.
28. Ibid., p. 665.
29. JGF, p. 685.
30. Henry J. Cadbury, *George Fox's Later Years*, Epilogue to JGF, p. 718.
31. Bowden, Vol. I, p. 395.
32. QAC, p. 366.
33. Allen C. Thomas, *History of Friends in America*, p. 84.
34. Ibid., p. 85.
35. Ibid.
36. Rufus M. Jones, *The Story of George Fox*, p. 157.
37. Bowden, Vol. II, p. 60.
38. Edwin B. Bronner, *William Penn's "Holy Experiment,"* p. 27.
39. Bowden, Vol. II, p. 17.
40. Broadside in Friends Historical Library, Swarthmore College.
41. Bowden, Vol. II, pp. 21–23.

CHAPTER 8

1. QASIA, p. 11.
2. Ibid., p. 10.
3. QAC, p. 441.
4. QASIA, p. 12.
5. Edwin B. Bronner, *William Penn's "Holy Experiment,"* p. 152.
6. SPQ, p. 163.
7. QASIA, p. 19.
8. Ibid., p. 22.
9. *William Penn's "Holy Experiment,"* p. 206.
10. Ibid.
11. QAC, p. 499.
12. Ibid., p. 125.
13. QASIA, p. 30.
14. QAC, p. 157.
15. Ibid., p. 159.
16. QASIA, p. 36.
17. JJW, pp. 32, 33.
18. QASIA, p. 45.
19. Frederick B. Tolles, *Meeting House and Counting House*, p. 216.
20. William Bartram, *Travels*, Introduction.
21. *William Penn's "Holy Experiment,"* p. 257.
22. Sydney V. James, *A People Among Peoples*, p. 178.
23. QAC, p. 503.
24. JJW, p. 35.
25. Ibid., p. 38.
26. Ibid., p. 92.
27. Ibid., pp. 92, 93.
28. Ibid., pp., 95, 96, 108, 109, 111, 112.
29. Ibid., p. 133.
30. Ibid., pp. 124, 127, 133, 134.
31. Ibid., pp. 164, 165.

CHAPTER 9

1. JGF, p. 197.
2. Letter from Moses Brown to William Wilson, in Historical Society of Pennsylvania; Henry J. Cadbury, *Quaker Relief During the Siege of Boston*, p. 17.
3. George W. Greene, *The Life of Nathanael Greene, Major-General in the Army of the Revolution*, Vol. 1, pp. 142-43.
4. Letter from Moses Brown to William Wilson in *Quaker Relief During the Siege of Boston*, p. 18.
5. William Rotch, *Memorandum written in the 80th year of his age*, pp. 3-5.
6. Minutes of New England Yearly Meeting for Suffering, I, 38; quoted in *Quaker Relief During the Siege of Boston*.
7. QAC, p. 566.
8. Thomas Gilpin, *Exiles in Virginia*, p. 233.
9. QASIA, p. 91.
10. Ibid., p. 93.
11. W. E. Burghardt Du Bois, *The Suppression of the African Slave-Trade to the United States of America*, p. 226.
12. Rotch, *Memorandum*.
13. Mack Thompson, *Moses Brown, Reluctant Reformer*, p. 274.
14. Frederick B. Tolles, *George Logan of Philadelphia*, p. 287.
15. Ibid., Introduction, XII.
16. LPQ, p. 407.
17. Kenneth S. P. Morse, *A History of Conservative Friends*, p. 2.
18. Henry Harvey, *History of the Shawnee Indians, from the year 1661 to 1854*, p. 119.

CHAPTER 10

1. Walt Whitman, *November Boughs*.
2. Walt Whitman, *Leaves of Grass*, No. 37.
3. Horace Traubel, *With Walt Whitman in Camden*, Vol. 2, p. 19.

4. Walt Whitman, *Song of Myself*, No. 1.
5. Ibid., No. 48.
6. Ibid., No. 6.
7. *November Boughs*.
8. Ibid.
9. LPQ, Vol. 1, p. 84.
10. Bliss Forbush, *Elias Hicks, Quaker Liberal*, p. 120.
11. Ibid., p. 121.
12. E. W. Emerson and W. E. Forbes, *The Journals of Ralph Waldo Emerson*, Vol. II, p. 177.
13. *Elias Hicks, Quaker Liberal*, p. 193.
14. Ibid., p. 189.
15. Ibid., p. 194.
16. Ibid., p. 226.
17. John Comly, *Journal*, p. 310.
18. *November Boughs*.
19. Ibid.
20. *Elias Hicks, Quaker Liberal*, p. 266.
21. LPQ, p. 522.

CHAPTER 11

1. *Journal of Negro History*, Vol. VIII, No. 2, H. N. Sherwood, "Paul Cuffe."
2. Ibid., Vol. XXI, No. 2, Henry J. Cadbury, "Negro Membership in the Society of Friends."
3. Ibid., Vol. VIII, No. 2.
4. Ibid.
5. Edward Stabler, *Memoirs*.
6. William Lloyd Garrison, *The Story of His Life by His Children*, Vol. 1, p. 25.
7. *Life, Travels and Opinions of Benjamin Lundy*, compiled under the direction and on behalf of his children, 1847, p. 15.
8. LPQ, p. 563n.
9. Ellen Larned, *History of Windham County*, 1880, Vol. II, p. 491; BFHA, Vol. 22, No. 1.
10. *History of Windham County*, Vol. II, p. 497.
11. George B. Thayer, *Pedal and Path*, p. 209.
12. Ibid., p. 213–14.

CHAPTER 12

1. George Fox, *A Collection of Many Select and Christian Epistles*, 698, Epistle 216.
2. JGF, p. 621.
3. Joseph John Gurney, *A Journey to North America*, p. 1.
4. Ibid., p. 400.
5. Winthrop S. Hudson, *Religion in America*, p. 136.
6. David E. Swift, *Joseph John Gurney*, p. 193.
7. *A Journey to North America*, p. 171.
8. Joseph John Gurney, *A Winter in the West Indies*.
9. *Journal of the Life of John Wilbur*, p. 123.
10. Ibid.
11. LPQ, p. 531.
12. *Joseph John Gurney*, p. 241.
13. Ibid., p. 229.
14. JGF, p. 624.
15. LPQ, p. 529.
16. Ralph M. Hower, *History of Macy's of New York*, p. 26.
17. JGF, p. 169.
18. David C. Le Shana, *Quakers in California*, pp. 49, 50.
19. Ibid., p. 50.
20. Christina H. Jones, *American Friends in World Missions*, p. 27.
21. Western Meeting for Sufferings, Minute 21, July 1863, quoted in LPQ, p. 730.
22. Ethan Foster, *Conscript Quakers*, pp. 7, 8.
23. Ibid., p. 15.
24. Rufus M. Jones, *Eli and Sybil Jones*, p. 170.
25. Samuel T. Pickard, *Life and*

CHAPTER 16

Letters of John Greenleaf Whittier, p. 441.
26. Ibid.

CHAPTER 13

1. Errol T. Elliott, Quakers on the American Frontier, p. 57.
2. Rayner W. Kelsey, Friends and the Indians, p. 166.
3. Louis T. Jones, The Quakers of Iowa, p. 207.
4. Thomas C. Battey, The Life and Adventures of a Quaker Among the Indians, p. 59.
5. Ibid., p. 63.
6. Ibid., p. 240.
7. Ibid., p. 253.
8. The Quakers of Iowa, p. 210.
9. David C. Le Shana, Quakers in California, p. 54.
10. Quakers on the American Frontier, p. 126.
11. Arthur G. Dorland, The Quakers in Canada, p. 209.
12. Quakers in California, p. 58.
13. Ibid.
14. The Quakers of Iowa, p. 166.
15. Quakers in California, pp. 60, 61.
16. Rufus M. Jones, Finding the Trail of Life, p. 148.
17. LPQ, p. 921.
18. Quakers in California, p. 138.
19. Charles W. Cooper, Whittier, Independent College in California, p. 15.
20. Quakers in California, p. 119.
21. Lawrence McK. Miller, "Friends General Conference" in American Quakers Today, p. 45.
22. Pendle Hill Bulletin, No. 172.
23. "A Tribute to Eternity . . . as expressed through the life of Anna Cox Brinton."
24. American Friends Fellowship Council Conference, 1936, Washington, D.C.
25. Elbert Russell, The History of Quakerism, p. 543.
26. A Message from the Society of Friends in France, August 1937.

CHAPTER 14

1. AF, January 10, 1946.
2. GIML, p. 3.
3. Ibid., p. 7.
4. Ibid., p. 9.
5. Robert Barclay, Apology, 1678.
6. Rhode Island Colony Records, II, pp. 495–99; QAC, p. 179.
7. Richmond P. Miller, FI, First Month 25, 1941.

CHAPTER 15

1. Thomas R. Kelly, A Testament of Devotion, pp. 29, 30.
2. Ibid., p. 92.
3. Douglas V. Steere, A Biographical Memoir, p. 27.
4. FMTB, p. 172.
5. Ibid., p. 183.
6. Ibid., p. 178.
7. Ibid., p. 174.
8. FI, "Letter from the Past," 42.
9. JGF, p. 687.
10. Francis Howgill, A Lamentation for the Scattered Tribes, 1658.
11. Henry J. Cadbury, "A Liberal Approach to the Bible," Journal of Religious Thought.
12. AFSC Board of Directors, June 1941.
13. Preamble to the Charter of the United Nations.
14. FI, "Letter from the Past," 16.
15. GIML, p. 10.
16. Ibid., p. 13.

CHAPTER 16

1. FMTB, p. 234.
2. Christina H. Jones, American Friends in World Missions, p. 213.

3. Walter R. Williams and Myrtle M. Williams, *Me and My House*, p. 164.
4. AFSERCO, December 1941.
5. Raymond Booth, FI, Second Month 14, 1942.
6. *American Friends in World Missions*, p. 252.
7. Walter Balderston, FI, Fourth Month 11, 1942.
8. Thomas R. Bodine, FI, Sixth Month 6, 1942.
9. AFSERCO, June 1942.
10. Kathleen Hambly Hanstein, *Historical Summary of the Refugee Service of the American Friends Service Committee*, April 1967.
11. JGF, p. 611.
12. Anna Griscom Elkinton, FI, Fifth Month 17, 1941.
13. GIML, p. 14.
14. A Message from the American Friends Service Committee to the Society of Friends and to Our Fellow Christians.
15. FI, Eighth Month 29, 1942.

CHAPTER 17

1. GIML, p. 16.
2. Gilbert F. White, FJ, April 15, 1967.
3. AFSERCO, March 1944.
4. Bliss Forbush, *The Sheppard and Enoch Pratt Hospital, A History*, pp. 16, 239.
5. FMTB, p. 328.
6. Douglas V. Steere, FI, Fifth Month 9, 1942.

CHAPTER 18

1. William Penn, Preface to the First Frame of Government for Pennsylvania.
2. FMTB, p. 184.

3. GIML, p. 20.
4. Ibid., p. 29.
5. Frederick B. Tolles, *Quakerism and Politics*.
6. FI, Eleventh Month 6, 1943.
7. AFSERCO, May–June 1944.
8. Ibid., February 1944.
9. Ibid., September 1944.
10. GIML, p. 35.
11. Ibid., p. 47.
12. Ibid., p. 57.
13. Ibid., p. 61.
14. Ibid., p. 64.

CHAPTER 19

1. FI, "Letter from the Past," 52.
2. Winston S. Churchill, *The Second World War, Triumph and Tragedy*, p. 344.
3. AFSERCO, May 1945.
4. GIML, p. 87.
5. AFSERCO, June–July 1945.
6. Walter R. Williams and Myrtle M. Williams, *Me and My House*, pp. 149–51.
7. Statement of the American Friends Service Committee and the Friends Committee on National Legislation made before the House Commitee on Post-War Military Policy, June 7, 1945, by D. Robert Yarnall.

CHAPTER 20

1. General Court of Massachusetts Senate Bill 511, 1945.
2. FI, "Letter from the Past," 69.
3. Ibid.
4. New England Yearly Meeting, 1945, Minute 73.
5. FI, Seventh Month 28, 1945.
6. GIML, p. 76.
7. FI, Ninth Month 29, 1945.

CHAPTER 23

8. A Message from German Friends to Friends in America, Ninth Month 29, 1945.
9. Roger C. Wilson, *Quaker Relief,* p. 227.
10. GIML, p. 80.

CHAPTER 21

1. Theodore Dreiser, *The Bulwark,* p. 319.
2. FI, Sixth Month 1, 1946.
3. Rufus M. Jones, "Are We Ready?" Address before joint gathering of Arch, Race, and Twelfth Street Meetings in Philadelphia, February 27, 1944.
4. AFSC Meeting, Philadelphia, May 3 and 4, 1946.
5. JGF, p. 66.
6. M. R. Brailsford, *Quaker Women,* p. 24.
7. John Bellers, *Some Reasons against Puting of Fellons to Death,* 1699.
8. Besse, Vol. 1, p. 470.
9. John Bellers, *Some Reasons for an European State,* 1710.
10. —— *An Essay Towards the Improvement of Physick,* 1714.
11. —— *An Epistle to the Quarterly Meeting of London and Middlesex,* 1718.
12. —— Broadside, *To the Criminals in Prison,* undated.
13. JJW, pp. 23–25.
14. William Guest, *Stephen Grellet,* p. 79.
15. AFSERCO, January–February 1946.
16. Ibid.
17. FMTB, p. 197.
18. Ibid., p. 300.
19. GIML, p. 106.
20. Ibid., p. 101.
21. Ibid., p. 107.

CHAPTER 22

1. WFTCP, p. 15.
2. Ibid., p. 16.
3. FOL, p. 304.
4. FMTB, p. 236.
5. WFTCP, p. 11.
6. Ibid., p. 20.
7. Ibid., p. 21.
8. Ibid., p. 23.
9. Ibid., pp. 29, 30.
10. FMTB, p. 239.
11. Ibid., p. 237.
12. Ibid., p. 239.
13. Ibid., p. 240.
14. WFTCP, p. 40.
15. Ibid., pp. 48–50.
16. FJ, January 1, 1967, reprinted from *Christian Science Monitor.*

CHAPTER 23

1. Levinus K. Painter, AF, December 26, 1946.
2. Douglas and Dorothy Steere, *Friends Work in Africa,* p. 32.
3. Levinus K. Painter, *The Hill of Vision,* p. 20.
4. Ibid., p. 25.
5. Ibid., p. 44.
6. Ibid., p. 45.
7. Elizabeth Emerson, *Emory Rees, Language Pioneer,* p. 21.
8. Alta Hoyt, quoted in *The Hill of Vision,* p. 47.
9. Mary Hoxie Jones, in *Then and Now,* p. 53.
10. JGF, p. 10.
11. Ibid., p. 19.
12. AFSC Report of the Nobel Prize.
13. FMTB, p. 200.
14. AFSC *Bulletin,* November 1947, p. 7.
15. Roy McCorkel, FI, Fifth Month 14, 1949.
16. FI, Ninth Month 21, 1946.
17. FMTB, p. 339.

18. John S. Hoyland, *Digging for a New England*, 1936, pp. 221–23.
19. FI, Twelfth Month 18, 1940.
20. AFSC *Bulletin*, November 1947, p. 7.

CHAPTER 24

1. Ecclesiastical Records of New York, Vol. 1, p. 412.
2. Ibid., p. 433.
3. Ibid.
4. Ibid., p. 530.
5. JGF, p. 620.
6. FMTB, p. 406.
7. FOL, p. 309.
8. FMTB, p. 262.
9. Ibid., p. 263.
10. Ibid., p. 264.
11. AFSC Report.
12. Rufus M. Jones, *Eli and Sybil Jones*, p. 190.
13. Ibid., p. 189.
14. Ibid., p. 192.
15. Christina H. Jones, *American Friends in World Missions*, p. 153.
16. FOL, p. 59.
17. *Eli and Sybil Jones*, p. 313.

CHAPTER 25

1. Anna Davis Hallowell, *James and Lucretia Mott*, p. 110.
2. Ibid., p. 40.
3. Ibid., p. 294.
4. Ibid., p. 121.
5. LPQ, p. 569.
6. *James and Lucretia Mott*, p. 130.
7. Otelia Cromwell, *Lucretia Mott*, p. 166.
8. Ibid., p. 167.
9. *James and Lucretia Mott*, p. 353.
10. Ibid., p. 351.
11. Ibid., p. 388.
12. *Lucretia Mott*, p. 170.
13. Swarthmore Monthly Meeting *Newsletter*, October 1947.
14. JGF, p. 313.
15. Mary Hoxie Jones, *A Biographical Sketch*, p. 50.
16. FOL, p. 312.
17. *A Biographical Sketch*, p. 51.
18. Ibid., p. 50.
19. Rufus M. Jones, "A New Installment of the Heroic Spirit."
20. J. Floyd Moore, *Rufus Jones, Luminous Friend*, p. 13.
21. Rufus M. Jones, *A Call to What Is Vital*, p. 142.

CHAPTER 26

1. FI, Tenth Month 23, 1948.
2. Baltimore Monthly Meeting, Stony Run, *Newsletter*.
3. FI, Sixth Month 26, 1948.
4. FMTB, p. 266.
5. Ibid., p. 261.
6. Frederick B. Tolles, *Quaker Testimonies in Daily Life*.
7. FMTB, p. 281.
8. FI, Ninth Month 10, 1949.
9. FMTB, p. 283.
10. Ibid., p. 231.
11. W. W. Cadbury and Mary Hoxie Jones, *At the Point of a Lancet*, Foreword.
12. Errol T. Elliott, *Quakers on the American Frontier*, p. 318.
13. JGF, p. 420.

CHAPTER 27

1. FI, Eighth Month 20, 1949.
2. Martha E. Hadley, *The Alaskan Diary of a Pioneer Quaker Missionary*, Background Note.
3. Ibid., p. 197.
4. AF, June 23, 1949.
5. FI, Ninth Month 17, 1949.
6. FI, Eleventh Month 5, 1949.
7. JJW, p. 44.
8. *Memoirs of the Religion, Life and Labors of Edward Hicks*, p. 330.

CHAPTER 30   439

9. Eleanore Price Mather, *Edward Hicks, Primitive Quaker*, Pendle Hill Pamphlet 170.
10. New York *Times*, August 28, 1960.
11. FI, Twelfth Month 10, 1949.

CHAPTER 28

1. AFSC *Bulletin*, January–February 1950.
2. Ibid.
3. WFTCP, p. 315.
4. FI, Fifth Month 5, 1951.
5. FI, First Month 6, 1951.
6. FI, Fifth Month 5, 1951.
7. AFSC *Bulletin*, February–April 1948.
8. FI, First Month 6, 1951.
9. Ibid.
10. FMTB, p. 410.
11. Christina H. Jones, *American Friends in World Missions*, p. 182.
12. Ibid., p. 116.
13. WFTCP, pp. 291, 292.
14. Ibid., p. 306.
15. Ibid., p. 312.
16. Ibid., p. 318.

CHAPTER 29

1. JGF, p. 104.
2. AF, September 11, 1952.
3. BQ, p. 158.
4. Ibid., p. 297.
5. FI, Sixth Month 7, 1952.
6. *Oxford Times*, August 8, 1952.
7. "The Third World Conference of Friends," FI, Ninth Month 20, 1952.
8. Bernard Canter, "Undertones of the World Conference," FI, Ninth Month 20, 1952.
9. *Friends Face Their Fourth Century*, p. 7.
10. Ibid., p. 72.
11. Ibid., p. 26.

12. Ibid., p. 27.
13. Ibid., p. 28.
14. Ibid., p. 80.
15. Ibid., p. xviii.
16. AF, September 11, 1952.
17. FI, Ninth Month 13, 1952.

CHAPTER 30

1. JGF, p. 11.
2. Ibid., p. 27.
3. Ibid., p. 35.
4. Ibid., p. 36.
5. Ibid., p. 103.
6. Frederick B. Tolles, *Quakers and the Atlantic Culture*, p. 4.
7. JGF, p. 104.
8. Ibid., p. 106.
9. Francis Howgill, *A Lamentation for the Scattered Tribes*.
10. JGF, p. 109.
11. Ernest E. Taylor, *The Valiant Sixty*, p. 43.
12. Norman Penney, *First Publishers of Truth*, p. 244.
13. BQ, p. 156.
14. Robert Proud, *History of Pennsylvania*.
15. SPQ, p. 444.
16. JGF, p. 114.
17. Elfrida Vipont Foulds, *The Story of Quakerism Through Three Centuries*, p. 34.
18. Ibid., p. 35.
19. JGF, p. 374.
20. Swarthmore MSS iv, 41, quoted by Geoffrey Nuttall in Introduction to JGF, xxxvi.
21. Letter from Thomas Curtis to George Fox, 1664, quoted in SPQ, p. 226.
22. Elisabeth Brockbank, "The Story of Quakerism in the Lancaster District," quoted in Elfrida Vipont Foulds, *The Birthplace of Quakerism*.
23. Margaret Fell, *Works*, p. 8.
24. William Hubben, FI, Ninth Month 29, 1952.

CHAPTER 31

1. AFSC Report, "Integration of Washington Schools."
2. Ibid.
3. Bliss Forbush, FI, First Month 1, 1955.
4. Florence L. Kite, FI, Fourth Month 12, 1952.
5. Ibid.
6. Bliss Forbush, FI, First Month 1, 1955.
7. Ibid.
8. FJ, November 24, 1956.

CHAPTER 32

1. *Speak Truth to Power* by Stephen G. Cary, James E. Bristol, Amiya Chakravarty, A. Burns Chalmers, William B. Edgerton, Harrop A. Freeman, Robert Gilmore, Cecil E. Hinshaw, Milton Mayer, A. J. Muste, Clarence E. Pickett, Robert Pickus, Norman J. Whitney; pp. 67–70.
2. Ibid., pp. 38, 39.
3. *Meeting the Russians* by Wroe Alderson, Stephen G. Cary, William B. Edgerton, Hugh W. Moore, Clarence E. Pickett, Eleanor Zelliot; p. 15.
4. Ibid., p. 25.
5. Ibid., p. 24.
6. Ibid., p. 74.
7. Ibid., p. 94.
8. Philadelphia Yearly Meeting (Arch Street) 1955, Minutes.
9. Philadelphia Yearly Meeting (Race Street) 1955, Minutes.
10. Philadelphia Yearly Meeting (Arch and Race Streets) 1955, Minutes.
11. Milton and Alexandra Zimmerman, FJ, July 9, 1955.
12. FI, Sixth Month 11, 1955.
13. New York Yearly Meeting, 1955, Minutes.
14. Ibid.
15. Ibid.
16. FI, "Letter from the Past," 152.
17. FJ, June 30, 1956.
18. FJ, April 28, 1956.
19. Joanna Grant, *Black Protest*, p. 277.
20. FJ, May 5, 1956.
21. Ibid.
22. Ibid.
23. New England Yearly Meeting, 1956, Minute 34.

CHAPTER 33

1. Albert Bigelow, *The Voyage of the Golden Rule, an Experiment with Truth*, p. 42.
2. Ibid., p. 58.
3. Ibid., p. 45.
4. FJ, December 28, 1957.
5. FJ, May 17, 1958.
6. *The Voyage of the Golden Rule*, p. 118.
7. Ibid., p. 169.
8. Ibid., p. 172.
9. Earle Reynolds, *The Forbidden Voyage*, p. 32.
10. Ibid., p. 34.
11. *The Voyage of the Golden Rule*, p. 195.
12. Ibid., p. 200.
13. Ibid., p. 238.
14. FJ, August 9, 1958.
15. *The Forbidden Voyage*, p. 78.
16. Ibid., jacket.
17. Ibid., p. 281.
18. Ibid., p. 278.
19. Ibid., p. 279.
20. *The Voyage of the Golden Rule*, p. 178.

CHAPTER 34

1. Robert L. Wixom, "Little Rock Friends," FJ, November 9, 1957.

CHAPTER 36 441

2. JJW, pp. 65–69.
3. Robert L. Wixom, "Letter from Little Rock," FJ, May 17, 1958.
4. Frederick B. Tolles, "Philadelphia Yearly Meeting, 1758," FJ, April 26, 1958.
5. John Woolman, *A Plea for the Poor*, 1763.
6. JJW, pp. 53, 54.
7. Edwin H. Cady, *John Woolman*, p. ix.
8. FJ, October 15, 1967.
9. FJ, September 1, 1966.

CHAPTER 35

1. FJ, February 21, 1959.
2. FJ, January 1, 1963.
3. FJ, September 1, 1961
4. FJ, November 14, 1959.
5. Elizabeth Gray Vining, personal letter.
6. FJ, September 1, 1961.
7. FJ, January 15, 1962.
8. FJ, April 16, 1960.
9. FJ, June 1, 1969.
10. Ibid.
11. JGF, p. 399.
12. Mildred Binns Young, FJ, December 1, 1960.
13. FJ, "Letter from the Past," 185.
14. JGF, p. 400.
15. Ralph K. Beebe, *A Garden of the Lord*, p. 169.
16. Ibid., p. 170.
17. Ibid., p. 171.
18. Ibid., p. 182.
19. Jack Willicuts, Report, ibid., p. 191.

CHAPTER 36

1. FJ, June 1, 1962.
2. Ibid.
3. AFSC Report.
4. FJ, "Letter from the Past," 204.
5. Dorothy Horton McGee, *Herbert Hoover*, p. 217.
6. FJ, "Letter from the Past," 212.
7. Ibid.
8. FJ, December 15, 1966.
9. Earlham School of Religion, Annual Report of the Dean, 1966.
10. FJ, October 26, 1957.
11. Hugh Barbour, *Quakers in Puritan England*, p. 159.
12. T. Canby Jones, "The Bible: Its Authority and Dynamics in George Fox and Contemporary Quakerism," *Quaker Religious Thought*, Vol. iv, No. 1, Spring 1962.
13. FJ, April 1, 1963.
14. FJ, January 15, 1963.
15. Frederick B. Tolles, *Meeting House and Counting House*, p. 15.
16. FJ, July 1, 1964.
17. FJ, October 1, 1964.
18. *Quaker Monthly*, "Letter from America," 1965.
19. FJ, January 15, 1965.
20. William Penn, *Some Fruits of Solitude*, Maxims 1 and 2.
21. Charter of SIECUS.
22. David Mace, "A Quaker Portrait: Mary Steichen Calderone," FJ, March 15, 1971.
23. FJ, April 15, 1964.
24. FJ, September 15, 1970.
25. FJ, April 15, 1965.
26. QL, July 1965.
27. Arthur O. Roberts in *American Quakers Today*, p. 69.
28. Douglas V. Steere, "Extracts from a Roman Journal," FJ, November 1, 1965.
29. William Huntington, "Thoughts from Turtle Bay," FJ, November 1, 1965.
30. Isabel C. Barrows, *A Moral Citadel*.

31. Harold Loukes, "The Troubles of a Pacifist," *The Student Movement*, Spring 1935

CHAPTER 37

1. Proceedings of Philadelphia Yearly Meeting, 1967.
2. Ibid.
3. Walter Ludwig, "Look Northward, Friend," FJ, April 1, 1967.
4. Proceedings of Philadelphia Yearly Meeting, 1967.
5. Lee Huntington, "It Is Going to Cost Much to Be a Quaker," FJ, June 15, 1967.

CHAPTER 38

1. J. Floyd Moore, *Friends in the Carolinas*, p. 5.
2. QL, July 1965.
3. Report of the Fourth World Conference of Friends, p. 50.
4. QL, June 1967.
5. Report of the Fourth World Conference of Friends, p. 74.
6. Ibid., Minutes of Fifth Plenary Session.
7. Ibid., press reviews.
8. Ibid., p. 102.
9. Ibid., p. 113.

CHAPTER 39

1. Ralph K. Beebe, *A Garden of the Lord*, p. 85.
2. Quaker Service-Vietnam Report, no. 5, July 11, 1967.
3. QL, October 1967.
4. Ibid.
5. American Friends Service Committee Report, March 5, 1968.
6. Ibid.
7. Colin W. Bell, "The Listening Heart," AFSC Annual Meeting, October 28, 1967.
8. Proceedings of Philadelphia Yearly Meeting, 1968.

CHAPTER 40

1. *Pendle Hill Bulletin*, 198.
2. FJ, December 15, 1968.
3. George Fox, Epistle 292, 1672.
4. Carl Zietlow, Report of Quaker Direct Action Corps, August 1968.
5. Marjorie Nelson, Prism no. 4, Letters from Quang Ngai.
6. AFSC *Newsletter*, Spring 1968.
7. AFSC Maine Indian Program, September 1968.
8. FJ, October 15, 1968.
9. Hugh Barbour, *The Lamb's War*.
10. T. Canby Jones, Address delivered at the 10th Anniversary of Earlham School of Religion.
11. Robert Barclay, *Apology*, 1678.

CHAPTER 41

1. This is a composite of impressions recorded by participants in the "Hospitality and Support" at the Friends Meeting at Cambridge, August 1968.

CHAPTER 42

1. President Richard M. Nixon, "Inaugural Address."
2. Boston Sunday *Globe*, November 17, 1968.
3. FJ, January 1, 1969.
4. *Search for Peace in the Middle East* by Landrum R. Bolling, William E. Barton, Colin W. Bell, Alan W. Horton, Paul and Jean Johnson, Frances Neely, Hanna Newcombe, Don Peretz.

CHAPTER 44

5. Jane Reinheimer Motz, *Man and the Economy*.
6. *Who Shall Live?* by Henry J. Cadbury, Lorraine K. Cleveland, John C. Cobb, Elizabeth Conrad Corkey, Richard L. Day, Johan W. Eliot, J. Russell Elkinton, Joseph Stokes, Jr.
7. FJ, April 1, 1969.
8. FJ, September 1, 1969.
9. FJ, June 1, 1969.
10. Howard H. Brinton, *Quaker Education in Theory and Practice*.
11. Thomas S. Brown, *Strange Fire*, the 16th Ward Lecture, Guilford College.
12. Douglas H. Heath, *To Educate for Today's Needs, Why a Friends School?*
13. QL, November 1969.
14. *hunger-why?*, Report from a Special AFSC Team.
15. FJ, August 1, 1969.
16. QL, October 1969.
17. Ibid., July–August 1969.
18. FJ, April 15, 1969.
19. Marjorie Nelson, Prism No. 8, Letters from Quang Ngai.
20. Ibid., No. 10.

CHAPTER 43

1. John Woolman, *A Plea for the Poor*.
2. Anna Davis Hallowell, *James and Lucretia Mott*, p. 262.
3. FJ, December 15, 1969.
4. Floyd H. Sidwell, "Visit to Korea."
5. "A Tribute to Eternity . . . as expressed through the life of Anna Cox Brinton."
6. FJ, December 15, 1968.
7. Proceedings of Baltimore Yearly Meeting, 1968.
8. QL, December, 1970.
9. LPQ, p. 530.
10. Otelia Cromwell, *Lucretia Mott*, p. 190.

CHAPTER 44

1. Philadelphia Yearly Meeting, *Faith and Practice*.
2. Isaac Pennington, *Works*, 1681, Pt. 1.

INDEX

Abdulhadi, Amin Bey, 222
Abernathy, Ralph, 381
Acadians, 69
Acheson, Dean, 272
Acre, 242, 243, 244
Addams, Jane, 3, 207
Adrian, Mich., 199–200
Adrianople, Turkey, 24
AEC (Atomic Energy Commission), 309 ff.
Africa and Africans, 16, 91, 96, 209–12. *See also* East Africa
AFSC. *See* American Friends Service Committee
Airlift Seminar, 241
Akihito, Prince, 202–7, 264–65, 329–30
Alabama, 302, 351
Alaska, 17, 251–52
Albemarle Sound, 56
Algerians, 328–29
Algonquin Indians, 30, 35
Allegheny River Reservoir, 414
Allen, Robert S., 14
American Anti-Slavery Society, 228
American Association of University Women, 323
American Bible Society, 211, 335
American Christian Committee for Refugees, 12
American Civil War, 113–16, 316
American Colonization Society, 96, 100, 102
American Friend, 254
American Friends Board of Missions, 16, 17, 209, 264, 327
American Friends Service Committee (AFSC), 126–27, 160–63, 173–74, 197–99, 200, 212–17, 238, 249–50, 253, 259 ff., 286, 288, 329 ff., 341, 354, 357–59, 361 ff., 369, 386, 410, 418 (*see also* Philadelphia, Pa.; specific branches, countries, persons, projects); and Middle East problems, 242–44, 300–1, 326; and Nobel Prize, 212–14, 339; and Spanish Civil War, 2, 162–63, 238; and World War I, 3, 126–27, 160–62; and World War II, 1 ff., 12 ff., 144, 145, 154 ff., 172–73, 181, 238
American Joint Distribution Committee, 12
American Revolution, 75–80
Amesbury, Mass., 108, 115, 116, 122
Amsterdam, Holland, 16, 237–39
Andover, Mass., 185–86, 234
Andrew, John A., 224

Andros, Sir Edmund, 65
Annapolis, Md., 9
Apache Indians, 120
Applegate, Ward, 422
Arabs, 2, 223, 242–44, 284, 405–6. *See also* specific countries
Arapaho Indians, 120
Archdale, John, 362
Arizona, 120, 250–51
Arkansas, 316–19
Army Appropriations Bill, 164–65
Arnold, Joseph, 66
Associated Executive Committee of Friends on Indians, 386
Association of Reform Rabbis of New York, 360
Athenagoras, Archbishop, 222
Atkinson, Margaret, 239–40
Atlanta, Ga., 331–32, 407
Atomic Energy Commission (AEC), 309 ff.
Auburndale, Mass., 302–5
Audland, John, 278, 279
Audubon, John James, 119
Austin, Ann, 7–8, 23, 24, 303
Austin, Tex., 293
Austin-McCormack House (San Francisco), 349
Austria, 7, 11, 13, 148, 241, 326
Aymara Indians, 335
Azzam Pasha, 222–23

Bacon, Margaret H., 407
Baden-Baden, Germany, 163–64
Baez, Joan, 408
Bailey, Gerald, 262
Bailey, Mabel, 242
Bailey, Moses, 242, 284, 342
Bainton, Roland H., 212, 343
Baker, Daniel, 247
Balch, Emily Greene, 207–8
Balderston, Martha and Robert W., 11
Baltimore, Charles Calvert, 3rd Lord, 60–61
Baltimore, Md., 98, 99, 113, 125, 291–93, 352; Association of Friends to Assist and Advise Friends in Southern States, 117
Baltimore Yearly Meeting, 74, 84, 92, 94, 113, 126, 292, 421
Banks, Nathaniel P., 224
Bantu, the, 209–12
Baptists, 29, 90, 108, 246, 296, 308, 318
Barbados, 7, 52–53
Barbour, Hugh, 343, 389

INDEX 445

Barcelona, Spain, 16
Barclay, Robert, 57, 58, 61, 90, 133, 390
Barnard, Hannah, 90
Bartram, John, 67–68
Bartram, William, 68
Bastogne, Belgium, 179
Batista, Fulgencio, 327
Battey, Thomas C., 118–19
Bayly, Charles, 9
Bayly, Mary Fisher. See Fisher, Mary
Bayly, William, 24
Beacon Hill Friends House (Boston), 302
Bean, Catherine, 112–13
Bean, Hannah, 112–13, 122 ff.
Bean, Joel, 112–13, 120, 122 ff.
Bear Creek, Iowa, 121, 123
Beards, 257–58
Beiss, Adolf, 240
Belcher, Jonathan, 184
Belgium, 12, 16, 148, 215
Belgrade, Yugoslavia, 259–60
Bell, Colin W., 260, 339, 357–58, 379
Bellers, John, 193–95, 196
Bellingham, Richard, 7, 41
Belsen, Germany, 189
Benezet, Anthony, 69, 73, 80
Bengal, India, 181
Bergraav, Eivind, 222
Berkeley, Calif., 286
Berlin, Germany, 1, 3, 5–6, 13 ff., 180, 189, 241–42, 252
Bernadotte, Count Folke, 224, 242
Bethel College, 14
Biafra, 385, 405
Bible (New and Old Testaments, Scriptures), 86, 132, 143, 170, 211–12, 229, 335
Bible societies, 91, 105, American, 211, 335
Biddle, Francis, 137
Biddle, Owen, 89
Bigelow, Albert, 306–7, 311, 312
Birth and death, 406–7
Bishop, George, 34, 41
Black Beaver (Indian), 119
Blackburn, Elisha, 210
Blackburn, Virginia, 210
Black Manifesto, 411–12, 415, 417–18, 426
Blacks (Negroes, racial problems), 95–102, 117, 173–74, 248–50, 271, 284, 287–93, 299, 301–2, 316–17, 330–32, 351, 379–80, 383, 411–12, 415–18, 426–27 (see also Slavery; specific countries); Conscientious Objectors and, 165; and Friends World Conference at Guilford College, 337–38; at Swarthmore, 403
"Blanket Nickels," 329

Bliss, George I., 345, 386–87
Bloomingdale Asylum, 166
Bodine, Thomas R., 158–59
Bok, Curtis and Nellie, 249
Boland, Frederick, 332
Bolivia, 17, 335–37
Bolling, Landrum R., 405, 410
Bond, Archibald A., 264
Boston, Mass., 7–11, 24, 30 ff., 37–41 ff., 75 ff., 98 ff., 184–85, 224, 229; 1st Friends school in area, 345; statue of Mary Dyer, 184, 302, 321–22
Boulding, Kenneth E., 309–10, 411, 421
Bowden, James, 45
Bowles, Gilbert, 151, 313, 315
Bowles, Luanna J., 203
Bowles, Minnie, 151
Bowne, John, 44, 219
Bowne House (New York City), 219
Boxer Uprising, 246
Braddock, Edward, 69
Bradford, William, 62
Brandywine, Penna., 79
Brantingham, Barbara and John, 246
Braunschweig, Germany, 239–40
Breda, Declaration of, 39, 57
Brend, William, 10, 31, 35
Brethren, Church of the, 133, 308
Brigflatts, England, 277
Brinton, Anna Cox, 127–28, 348, 349, 420–21
Brinton, Howard H., 127–28, 201, 239, 270, 344, 349, 409, 420–21
Bristol, England, 49, 428
British, the. See England and the English
British and Foreign Anti-Slavery Society, 229
Brocksopp, Joan, 41
Bronner, Edwin B., 64, 69, 343–44, 345, 419
Brooklyn, N.Y., 87–88
Brooks, Arle, 136
Brotherton Indians, 119
Browin, Frances, 414
Brown, Henry, 229
Brown, John and wife, 231
Brown, Moses, 77–78, 80, 82, 89, 90
Brown, Moses, School, 90
Brown, Thomas S., 409
Brüning, Heinrich, 15
Bryn Mawr College, 18, 125, 341
Buber, Martin, 243
Buck, Pearl, 172
Bucks County, Pa., 61, 68
Budapest, Hungary, 179
Buffalo, N.Y., 356
Buffum, Arnold, 101
Buffum, Joshua, 35, 36
Bulgaria, 148

Bullitt, William, 141
Bulwark, The, 191
Bunche, Ralph, 242, 285
Bundelkhand, Nepal, 182
Bunker Hill, Battle of, 76
Bunting, Samuel J., 263, 297
Burke-Wadsworth bill, 133
Burleigh, Charles G., 102
Burling, William, 66
Burlington, N.J., 57, 60
Burma Road, 164
Burnyeat, John, 53
Burrough, Edward, 41–42, 280
Business of Our Lives, The, 303–5
Butler, Esther H., 246

Cadbury, Barrow, 272
Cadbury, Emma, 129
Cadbury, Henry Joel, 130, 184–85, 253, 261–62, 297, 340–42, 349, 418; and acceptance of Nobel Prize, 212–13; addresses Institutes of International Affairs, 14; as "Now and Then," 142–43 (*see also* "Now and Then"); at Oxford conference, 271–72
Cadbury, Lydia, 349
Cadbury, William Warder, 246
Cairo, Egypt, 222–23, 243, 326
Calcutta, India, 172, 198
Calderone, Mary Steichen, 347
Calhoun, John C., 105
California, 111, 124–25, 127, 201, 251, 286. *See also* specific places
California Yearly Meeting, 17, 126, 251, 252
Call to Persons of Good Will, A, 145–46
Calvert, Charles, 3rd Lord Baltimore, 60–61
Cambridge, Mass., 76–77, 130, 391–402; Friends School, 345–46
Cambridge, University of, 7
Camm, John, 279
Camm, Thomas, 279
Cammsgill, England, 279
Canada and Canadians, 17, 80, 121, 239, 246, 355–56
Canaday, John, 257
Canada Yearly Meeting, 121
Canterbury, Conn., 97–102
Canton, Ohio, 410
Cape May, N.J., 381–82, 383
Carolina, 56. *See also* North Carolina; South Carolina
Carolina Friends School, 346
Cart and Whip Act, 44–45
Cary, Steven G., 382–83
Casablanca, Morocco, 149, 163
Castillo, Fortunato, 264
Castle, Edgar B., 222–23

Castro, Fidel, 327
Catholics, 16, 18, 237, 302, 318, 351–52
Caton, William, 214
Catt, Carrie Chapman, 227
Cattell, Catherine, 181–82, 246
Cattell, Everett, 181, 182, 351, 365
Cayuga Indians, 120
Cedergren, Elsa, 262
Ceresole, Pierre, 216
Chaco War, 336
Chalkley, Thomas, 64
Chalons-sur-Marne, France, 161
Chamberlain, Neville, 1
Channing, William Ellery, 91
Chapel Hill, N.C., 346
Charles II, King of England, 39, 41–43, 45, 57, 58, 61, 280, 333
Charlotte, N.C., 332
Chautauqua, N.Y., 126
Chengtu, China, 246
Chester Project, 379
Chetsingh, Ranjit M., 271
Cheyenne Indians, 120
Chiang Kai-shek, 153
Chiang Kai-shek, Mme., 198
Children, 137, 141–42, 197 (*see also* Education and schools; specific countries, wars); Gurney on American, 105; Navajo, 250
Chilson, Arthur, 209, 210
China, 2, 17, 137, 151, 152–53, 164, 171, 198, 245–47, 350, 366; Emily Balch's poem on, 208; Tibet invasion, 328
Chou En-Lai, 272
Christian Quakers, 62
Christison, Wenlock, 40–41
Churchill, Sir Winston, 141, 179
Church World Service Refugee Program, 327
Civilian Public Service Camps, 137, 144–45, 164 ff. *See also* Conscientious Objectors
Civilian Training Center for Women, 147
Clarens, Switzerland, 285
Clark, Bronson, 147, 382
Clark, Eleanor, 147
Clark, Joseph, 370
Clarke, Walter, 65
Clarkson, Robert, 9
Clay, Henry, 99, 105, 107
Clement, Emma, 199
Cleveland, Grover, 353
Cleveland, Ohio, 323
Clothing: Quaker dress, 191–92 (*see also* Hats); for relief, 18–19 (*see also* specific countries)
Coale, Josiah, 33–34, 34–35, 43, 47

INDEX

Coal miners, 162
Coddington, William, 30, 65
Coffin, Addison and Vestal, 363
Coleman, Elihu, 65
Coleman, Isaac, 39
Coleman, Milton and Rebecca, 182
Coleridge, Samuel Taylor, 68
College Park Association of Friends, 124–25, 126, 127
Colleges, 14–15, 125, 409–10. *See also* specific schools
Comanche Indians, 120
Comly, John, 92, 93
Committee of Responsibility . . . , 413, 428
Committee on Foreign Relief Appeals in the Churches, 12
Communion, 237
Communists and Communism, 269, 271, 359. *See also* Loyalty oath; specific countries
Concord, Mass., 76
Coney, James, 156–57
Conference of Young Friends. *See* Young Friends
Conferences for Diplomats, 285
Congregationalists, 108, 308
Congress, U. S., 12, 82–83, 104, 170, 201, 383–84 (*see also* Friends Committee on National Legislation; House of Representatives); Senate, 411
Congress of the Confederacy, 80
Connecticut, 33, 102, 174 (*see also* specific places); Black Law, 101, 102
Connecticut Valley Quarterly Meeting, 303
Conscience Bay Meeting (St. James, N.Y.), 359–60
Conscientious Objectors, 127, 133–38, 144–45, 164–68, 188, 193, 253–55, 391–402, 407–8
Cooper, Wilmer A., 343
Cooperstown, N.Y., 145
Coordinating Council for French Relief, 12, 16
Cope, Joshua A., 241
Cope, Robert, 156
Copeland, John, 30–31, 32, 35, 41
Copijara, Bolivia, 335, 336
Cordier, Andrew, 223
Cork, Ireland, 49
Corn, 67
Cornell, Ezra, 125
Cornell University, 125
Corsica, 163
Cotton, John, 10
Council House Friends Meeting, 120
Cousins, Norman, 314
Cox, Catherine Bean, 112–13, 313

Craigie House (Cambridge), 76
Crandall, Almira and Pardon, 101
Crandall, Prudence, 97–102, 293, 303
CRASH, 410–11
Creasey, Maurice, 365
Crenshaw House (Los Angeles), 349
Cromwell, Oliver, 3, 32
Crooks, Kenneth, 264
Cuba(ns), 17, 263–64, 327–28
Cuban Friends Service Committee, 327
Cudworth, James, 33
Cuffe, Alice, 95
Cuffe, John, 95
Cuffe, Paul, 95–97
Czechoslovakia, 148, 399

Dalai Lama, 328
Dale, Alma G., 121
Da Nang, Vietnam, 374, 377
Dangerfield, Daniel, 231
Dartmouth, Mass., 95
Dartmouth, Nova Scotia, 80
Davis House (Washington, D.C.), 284–85
"Day of Broken Glass," 12
Dean, Vera Micheles, 15
Declaration of Breda, 39, 57
Declaration of 1660, 333, 334, 335
De Hartog, Jan, 347
De Hartog, Marjorie, 347
Delaware, 60–61, 75, 80, 177; Yearly Meeting for Pennsylvania, New Jersey, and, 63, 67
Delaware Indians, 61, 119
Delhi, India, 328
Denison, Major General, 35
Denison College, 14
Denmark, 107, 148
Derby, England, 23, 193
Des Moines, Iowa, 349
Detroit, Mich., 346
DeVol, Charles, 153, 181
DeVol, George F., 246
DeVol, Isabella French, 246
DeVol, W. E., 152–53, 181
Dew, Joseph, 83
Dewey, John, 254
Dewsbury, William, 23, 25
Dickinson, John, 89
Dien Bien Phu, Vietnam, 285
Dillwyn, George, 89
Diplomats, Conferences for, 285
Doncaster, L. Hugh, 363–64
Dos Passos, John, 254
Douglas Island, 251
Dover, N.H., 37
Dowdney, Richard, 26
Dreiser, Theodore, 191
Drummond, James, 283

Dumbarton Oaks Charter, 172
Dun, Angus, 238
Dunbar, Barrington, 409, 415, 427
Dunkirk, France, 12, 81–82
Durand, William, 9
Durham, N.C., 346
Dyer, Mary, 10–11, 30, 37 ff., 303; grandson Samuel, 185; statue, 184, 302, 320–22, 361
Dyer, William, 30
Dykstra, Clarence A., 137
Dynamic kernels. *See* Wheat
Dynamic Peace, 145–46

Earlham College, 104, 125, 164, 342–43
Earlham School of Religion, 343
East Africa, 17, 385
East Africa Yearly Meeting, 209, 351, 385
East India Company, 247
Eastman, Fred, 12
Easton, Nicholas, 54
Easton, Md., 56
Eddy, Thomas, 166
Eden, Anthony, 272
Edgerton, Lavina, 423
Edgerton, William B., 260, 296
Edinburgh Conference on Faith and Order, 238
Edmundson, William, 53, 60, 362
Education and schools, 89–90, 117, 152, 158–59, 297, 345–47, 408–10 (*see also* specific countries, schools); and "Churkendoose," 322–23; Indians, 250, 386, 387; Prudence Crandall and, 97–102; and "Rimi," 323–24; and segregation, 287–93, 330–31
Egypt, 151, 180, 242, 243, 326. *See also* specific places
Eichenberg, Fritz, 332–33
Eisenhower, Milton S., 158
Eisenhower, President Dwight D., 163, 180, 295, 299, 306, 308, 311, 316, 334
El Alamein, Egypt, 163
Elder, Joseph, 419–20
Elizabeth II, Queen of England, 268–69
Elk Falls, Kans., 102
Elkinton, Anna Griscom, 156–57
Elkinton, Howard W., 172, 173
Elkinton, J. Passmore, 156, 187
Elliott, Errol T., 16, 116, 121, 246–47, 267
Ellis, Zenos H., 184, 302
Emancipator (paper), 98
Embargo Act (1810), 83
Embree, Elihu, 98
Emerson, Ralph Waldo, 91
Endicott, John, 3, 32, 37, 40, 42, 43, 322
England and the English (Great Britain and the British), 7 ff., 12, 13, 20–24, 39 ff., 47–52, 56 ff., 61 ff., 67, 73–74, 75–76 ff., 92, 103 ff., 122, 127, 141, 142, 147, 148, 153, 163, 164, 169, 179, 189, 196, 245, 328, 334 (*see also* specific persons, places); and Cuffe plan, 96; Declaration of 1660, 333; evacuation of children in World War II, 17; Friends pilgrimage, 274–83; Friends War Victims Relief Committee, 137; and Gregorian calendar, 27; and Joel and Hannah Bean, 125; and mission to Gestapo, 5; and Nigeria, 405; and Nova Scotia, 69; Oxford Conference of Friends, 267–73; and Palestine, 221, 223 ff.; and red-and-black star, 180; and sex, 346–47; Toleration Act, 62–63; and UN, 171, 179; and War of 1812, 83; and World Council of Churches Assembly, 238
Eniwetok-Bikini area, 309 ff.
Episcopalians, 108, 318
Escolme, Edward, 170, 190
Eskimos, 251–52
Etheridge, Clinton, 403
Evangelical Friends Alliance, 351
Evangelism (revivalists), 90, 104, 120, 123, 344
Evans, Harold, 142, 223–24, 254–55, 260
Evans, Sylvia, 260
Evans, William Bacon, 297, 348–49

Fair employment, 249
Fairfax, Jean, 217, 241
Fair Hill Boarding School (Sandy Spring, Md.), 89
Faith and Practice, 138–39, 234, 297
Farmer, James, 381
Farmville, Va., 330–31
Farnsworth, Richard, 276, 280–81
Federal Council of Churches of Christ in America, 238
Fell, Henry, 247
Fell, Isabel, 58
Fell, Judge, 23, 48, 280–81, 282
Fell, Margaret (Fox), 23, 25, 32–33, 47, 48–49, 51–52, 56, 57, 64, 280–81, 282–83, 428–29
Ferris, Benjamin, 91
Finland (Finnish), 186, 215–16, 240–41, 267
Finney, Charles G., 91
Firbank Fell, England, 277–78
Fisher, Dorothy Canfield, 12
Fisher, Geoffrey Francis, 221–22
Fisher, Martha, 51
Fisher, Mary, 7–8, 23, 24, 278, 303
Fisher's Island, 55
Five Years Meeting, 126, 156, 157, 185,

INDEX

209, 238, 264, 351
Fletcher, Elizabeth, 268
Florida Avenue Meeting (Washington, D.C.), 171, 333–34, 381, 404–5
Flushing, N.Y., 44, 55, 218–20
Folger, Herschel, 154
Folger, Timothy, 72
Food programs, 383–84, 410–11. *See also* specific countries
Forbush, Bliss, 86, 239, 291, 292
Ford, Henry, 170, 174 ff., 179, 180, 187, 189–90
Ford, Jefferson, 212
Ford Motor Company, 187, 190
For More Than Bread, 14
Fort Detrick, 334
Fort Devens, 407
Fort Gulick (Panama), 412
Fort Leavenworth (Kans.), 407
Fosdick, Harry Emerson, 222, 254
Foster, Ethan, 113–15, 304
Foster, Henry, 303
Foulds, Elfrida Vipont, 274, 280–81
Fowler, Robert, 23–24, 25–28, 311
Fox, George, 7, 9, 11, 20–23 ff., 37, 41, 43, 45, 48–49, 51–57 ff., 75, 103, 109, 143, 193, 212–13, 214, 219, 234, 247, 267, 268, 286, 307, 326, 362, 394, 397, 428–29; death, 63; and Jamaica, 156; and John Perrot, 47; Jones on Puritanism of, 343; and lobbying, 171; and mental illness, 165; in *Quakerama*, 303; Quaker pilgrimage to places associated with, 274–83; on tradesmen, 111–12; Whitman and, 87
Fox, George, College (formerly Friends Pacific Academy), 125–26, 410, 412
Fox, Margaret Fell. *See* Fell, Margaret Fox
Fox Indians, 120
France and the French, 68–69, 81–82, 82–83, 88, 129, 180, 285, 334; and World War I, 127, 160–61, 357; and World War II, 12–13, 15–16, 141, 142, 148, 149, 155–56, 163, 180, 181, 198
Franco, Francisco, 162–63
Franconia, S.S., 7, 11
Franco-Prussian War (1870), 180
Frankford Hospital (Philadelphia), 166
Frankfurt, Germany, 188–89
Franklin, Benjamin, 66
Frawley, Margaret, 180
Free Quakers, 78
French, Paul Comly, 145
French and Indian War, 68–69, 88
French Indochina, 148. *See also* Vietnam
Friend, The (periodical), 298
Friendly Association for Regaining and Preserving Peace with the Indians, 416

Friendly Persuasion, The, 191
Friend of Life, 226, 234
Friends Ambulance Unit. *See* specific places
Friends Board of Missions. *See* American Friends Board of Missions
Friends Committee on National Legislation, 169–70, 171–72, 350–51, 404
Friends Concerned for Renewal (committee), 421
Friends General Conference, 126, 147–48, 185, 239, 303, 364, 381–83, 411
Friends Hospital (Philadelphia), 166
Friends Intelligencer, 257–58, 263, 267, 298. *See also* "Now and Then"
Friends Journal, 208, 298–99, 414
Friends Pacific Academy. *See* Fox, George, College
Friends Relief Service, 189
Friends Service Council, 212, 217
Friends Service Unit, 245–46
Friends United Meeting, 351, 364, 406, 411–12
Friends University (Wichita), 410
Friends War Problems Committee, 147, 169
Friends War Victims Relief Committee, 137
Friends World College, 346, 409
Friends World Committee, 129, 209, 221, 262, 337–38, 351–52, 404
Friends World Conferences, 127, 129, 267–73, 362–67, 385–86
Fry, Elizabeth, 107, 197, 347, 348
Fry, Elizabeth, House, 349
Fugitive Slave Laws, 113, 231
Fuller, William, 9
Furcolo, John Foster, 321–22
Furnas, Paul J., 144

Gage, Thomas, 75, 76
Gale, David, 307
Gandhi, Mahatma, 221
Garrison, William Lloyd, 98, 99, 100
Gaza Strip, 242–44
Geist, Raymond (Consul General), 5, 6
Geneva, Switzerland, 149, 240, 285, 326
Genius of Universal Emancipation, The, 98, 99
George VI, King of England, 179
George School, 291
Georgia, 79, 99
Germantown, Md., 311
Germantown, Pa., 58, 60
Germany (Germans), 11, 12 ff., 140 ff., 151, 160 ff., 169, 172, 179, 180, 188–89, 198, 216, 235, 239–40, 241–42, 253, 365; George Fox in, 58; and Germantown, 60; Order of Merit to Pickett,

284; and Oxford conference, 269 ff.;
  Quaker mission to Gestapo, 1-6, 7, 11
Gibara, Cuba, 263-64
Gibbons, Euell, 383
Gibbons, Sarah, 26, 31-32
Gilpin, Thomas, 79
Glen Mills, Pa., 147
Gloucester, Mass., 77
Goebbels, Joseph, 5
Goering, Hermann, 5
Golden Rule (ketch), 306-14, 315
Goldsmith, Ralph, 42
Goodenow, Leanore, 409
Governor's Island, 113, 114
Grant, Ulysses S., 118
Great Choptank River, 53-54
Greece, 148, 151
Green Circle Program, 322-23
Greene, John, 302
Greene, Nathanael, 77
Greensboro, N.C., 337-38, 362-67. *See also* Guilford College
Grellet, Stephen, 92, 196-97, 347
Grew, Joseph G., 187
Griffith, Helen, 250, 303
Grinnell College, 14
Griscom, John, 197
Gromyko, Andrei A., 253, 296
Guatemala, 17
Guilford College (formerly New Garden Boarding School), 115-16, 117, 125, 337-38, 362-67, 409
Gurney, Joseph John, and Gurneyites, 103-7 ff., 126, 303-4. *See also* specific meetings
Guzman, Juan, 264

Hadley, Martha, 252
Hadley, Milton, 422
Hague, The, Holland, 207, 353
Haiphong, Vietnam, 354, 356, 373-74
Hamilton, Alice, 3
Hammarskjold, Dag, 349
Handel, Georg Friedrich, 257
Hanoi, Vietnam, 419-20
Harriman, Averell, 299
Harris, David, 408
Harris, Elizabeth, 9
Harris, Sarah, 99-100
Harris, Thomas, 32
Harris, William T., 232
Harrison, Agatha, 262
Harvey, Henry, 84-85
Harvey, T. Edmund, 177
Hats, 8 ff., 32, 42, 51, 81, 387-88
Havana, Cuba, 16-17
Haverford College, 18, 125, 140, 357-59, 409
Haverhill, Mass., 111-12

Hawaiian Islands (Sandwich Islands), 112-13, 151; Honolulu, 126, 310-15; Pearl Harbor, 150, 152
Hayden, Perry, 132-33, 145, 148-49, 149-50, 157, 163, 170-71, 174-76, 179, 180, 187-88, 190, 199, 200
Hayden, Elizabeth (Mrs. Perry), 157, 199
Hayes, Rutherford B., 119
Hazard, Thomas, 66
Heard, Gerald, 141
Heath, Douglas, 409
Helena, Ark., 316
Helsinki, Finland, 240, 241
Hempstead, N.Y., 27
Hershey, Lewis B., 137, 144
Hertzog, Isaac, 222, 223
Heusel, Lorton, 411-12
Heydrich, Richard, 5-6
Hicks, Edward, 5, 92, 256-57, 286
Hicks, Elias, and Hicksites, 79, 86-94, 106, 110, 117, 118, 126, 227 ff. *See also* specific Meetings
Hilty, Hiram, 264, 327
Hilty, Janet, 264
Hirohita, Emperor, 202 ff., 265
Hiroshima, Japan, 186, 190, 205
Historic Peace Churches, 133, 137, 144, 145
Hitler, Adolf, 1 ff., 13, 147, 163, 180
Hoag, Enoch, 120
Hobson, William, 121-22
Ho Chi Minh, 285
Hodgson, Robert, 26, 27-28, 34, 43-44
Holder, Christopher, 26, 30-31, 32, 34, 37, 41, 55
Hole, Edgar T., 209
Hole, Francis D., 345
Holland and the Dutch (Netherlands), 5, 12, 26-27, 58, 60, 107, 148, 218, 219, 237-39
Holmes, Jesse H., 174
Holmes, John Haynes, 254
Hominy Friends Meeting, 120
Honduras, 17
Honey Creek Meeting, Iowa, 84, 122, 124
Hong Kong, 354, 378
Honolulu, Hawaii, 126, 310-15
Hooton, Elizabeth, 41, 45, 53, 193
Hoover, Herbert, 3, 122-23, 125-26, 161, 162, 179, 341-42
Hoover, Hulda, 122
Hoover, Jesse, 122
Hoover, Lou Henry (Mrs. Herbert), 126, 341, 342
Hopi Indians, 250-51
Hopkins, Johns, 125
Hopkinton, R.I., 113

INDEX 451

Hopper, Isaac T., 197
Hoskins, Lewis, 259
Hospital, The, 347
Hospitals, 347. See also Mental Illness; specific countries
House of Refuge, 197
House of Representatives, 104, 182-83, 326, 345, 410
Houston, Tex., 347
Hotchkiss, Willis R., 209
Howard University, 174
Howe, William, 77, 79
Howgill, Francis, 109, 131, 143, 278, 279
Hoyland, John S., 217
Hsüchou, China, 245
Hubben, William, 298
Hubberthorne, Richard, 44, 46, 282
Hudson, N.Y., 82
Hue, Vietnam, 369, 377, 378, 384
Hull, Spahr, 318-19
Hungary (Hungarians), 148, 214, 326
Hunnicutt, Anna, 251-52
Hunt, John, 79
Hunt, Patricia, 284
Huntington, William R., 261, 307, 312-13, 329, 352
Huolto, Suomen, 240
Hutchinson, Anne, 29-30, 37, 321

Illinois, 113. See also specific places
India, 17, 91, 172, 255-56, 272, 328. See also specific places
India Famine Relief Committee, 172
Indiana, 84, 113, 119, 191
Indiana Yearly Meeting, 84, 94, 113, 121, 126, 316
Indians, American, 2, 9, 17, 29, 35, 54, 55, 58, 59, 60, 64, 68-70, 72-73, 89, 117-20, 177, 386-87, 416 (see also specific tribes); Bolivian, 335-37; Levinus Painter adopted by, 414; Work Campers and, 250-51, 386
Indian Territory, 118
Indochina, French, 148. See also Vietnam
Institutes of International Affairs, 14-15
International Committee for the Assistance of Child Refugees, 12
International Congress of Women, 207
International Fellowship of Reconciliation, 216
International Labor Office, 266
International Service Seminars, 174, 327
International Student House (Washington, D.C.), 17-18
International Work Camps. See Work Camps
Interracial Youth Camps, 174
Iowa, 84, 113. See also specific places

Iowa Yearly Meeting, 113, 123-24 ff., 156
Ireland, the Irish, 48, 49, 79
Ishikawa, Pastor, 154
Israel (Palestine), 2, 16, 17, 151, 221-25, 242-44, 284, 405-6
Italy and Italians, 148, 163, 180, 198, 267, 290; Rimini, 323-24; Rome, 16, 351-52

Jackson, Elizabeth, 252
Jackson, Elmore, 252, 253, 262, 301, 326
Jackson, Robert, 137
Jahn, Gunnar, 213
Jamaica, 17, 53, 156-57, 264
James II, King of England, 61
Japan and Japanese, 2, 17, 148, 150, 151-52 ff., 157-59, 179, 182, 186, 187, 238, 285; Elizabeth Vining and Prince Akihito, 202-7, 264-66, 329-30; and Oxford conference, 267, 269
Japan Yearly Meeting, 152
Jefferson, Thomas, 81
Jerusalem, 221-24, 225, 243, 244, 406
Jessup, Lois, 221, 252
Jessup, Philip, 220-21, 252
Jews, 1, 2, 13, 16, 18, 155, 198, 318, 326 (see also Israel); in Friends schools, 290; Peter Stuyvesant and, 218; in Russia, 296
Jodl, Alfred, 180
Johns Hopkins University, 125
Johnson, Eric, 181
Johnson, Jane, 230
Johnson, Jean, 300, 405
Johnson, Mordecai, 339
Johnson, Paul, 300, 301, 326, 405
Johnson, Richard, 1
Johnson, Sandra, 377, 378, 380, 384
Johnson administration, 355
Jones, A. Willard, 225, 242
Jones, Christina H., 225, 242
Jones, Eli and Sybil, 115, 224-26, 304
Jones, Elizabeth, 4-5, 234
Jones, James, 115
Jones, Louis T., 123
Jones, Lowell, 225
Jones, Mary Hoxie, 4-5, 30, 234-35
Jones, Rufus M., 94, 107, 109-10, 124, 127, 140, 153-54, 177, 186, 192, 212, 221-22 ff., 246, 248, 290, 357, 358-59, 418, 422; on Benjamin Lundy, 98; on Dynamic Peace, 145; and Elizabeth Vining, 202, 234; gets Roosevelt Medal, 163; Howard Brinton on, 344; illness, death, 234-36; on mission to Gestapo, 2, 4-5, 6, 7, 11; in *Quakerama,* 304; at 25th anniversary of AFSC, 160-63; and Wider Quaker Fellowship, 128;

Wilmer Cooper on, 343
Jones, Rufus, House (Des Moines), 349
Jones, Sarah (Sallie) Coutant, 225, 235
Jones, Sylvester, 263–64
Jones, T. Canby, 343, 389
Jones, Thomas E., 144, 389–90
Jonesboro, Tenn., 98
Jordan, 300–1, 405
Jordans, England, 127, 422
Judson, Sylvia Shaw, 286–87, 302, 321, 322, 420–21

Kaifu, Chuzo, 152
Kaimosi, Kenya, 209–10, 337–38, 385
Kake, Alas., 251
Kansas, 84, 118
Kansas Yearly Meeting, 17, 121, 126, 351
Kashmir, 221
Kaw Indians, 120
Keene, J. Calvin, 174
Keith, George, 58, 62
Kelly, Harry F., 199
Kelly, Lael, 140
Kelly, Thomas Raymond, 140–41
Kempthorn, Simon, 7
Kendal, England, 279–80
Kennedy, John F., 334, 339, 340
Kennedy, Mrs. John F., 339
Kenya, 2, 209–12, 267, 299, 337–40, 351, 385
Kenyatta, Muhammad, 415
Khrushchev, Nikita, 285, 332–33
Kickapoo Friends Center, 120
Kicking Bird, Chief, 119
Kiev, Russia, 296
King, Francis T., 117
King, Martin Luther, Jr., 301, 302, 331, 351, 380, 381
Kinzua, Pa., 414
Kiowa Indians, 118–19, 120
Knoxville, Tenn., 288
Korea, 259, 262, 269, 272, 285, 420
Kotzebue, Alas., 251–52
Kraus, Hertha, 18
Ku Klux Klan, 117

Lachmund, Margarethe, 271
Lafayette, Marie du Motier, Marquis de, 81
Lake Erie Yearly Meeting, 420
Lake George, N.Y., 299
Lake Mohonk Conferences, 353
Lake Success, N.Y., 261ff.
Lamb's War, 389–90, 399
Lancashire, England, 23
Lancaster, England, 281–83; Castle, 48, 49, 282–83, 428–29
Language, 267; plain, 10, 192, 388
La Paz, Bolivia, 335, 337

Lapland, 186, 198, 216
LARA, 205
Latin America, 412. *See also* specific countries
Launceston, England, 9
Lay, Benjamin, 66–67, 419
Lea, Robert, 220
Leaves of Grass, 87
Lebanon, 301, 405
Leddra, William, 10, 40
Leeds, Hadassah Moore, 297
Leeds, Morris, 297
Leningrad, Russia, 295
Lepers, 420
Le Shana, David C., 410, 421
Levering, Samuel R., 412
Levering Act, 286
Lexington, Mass., 76
Liberator (paper), 98 ff.
Lie, Trygve, 221
Light Within (Inner Light), 47, 86, 90, 122, 126, 135, 417
Lincoln, Abraham, 112, 113–14, 304, 339–40, 419
Lincoln Castle (England), 193
Lion's Den (Boston prison), 11, 32, 41
Lisbon, Portugal, 16, 149
Littleboy, Gerald, 273
Littleboy, Wilfrid E., 267
Little Rock, Ark., 316–19
Litu, Joeli, 209, 211, 212
Lloyd, Thomas, 63
Loe, Thomas, 279
Logan, George, 82–83
Logan, James, 67
Logan Act, 83
Lokka, Finland, 216
London, England, 17, 21 ff., 47 ff., 229, 282, 428 (*see also* London Yearly Meeting); Friends World Conference delegates in, 268–69; Fox's death in, 63; and mentally ill people, 165–66; and prison reform, 193–95, 196–97; Rufus Jones speaks in Westminster, 127
London Yearly Meeting, 61, 65, 75, 80, 105, 122, 239
Long Island, 54–56, 219–20. *See also* specific places
Longstreth, Walter C., 136
Los Angeles, Calif., 349
Lost Creek, Tenn., 84
Lotspeich, William D., 324–25, 379
Louisiana, 302
Lower, Thomas, 57
Lowry, Ann Gidley, 220
Loyalty oath, 286
Lugulu, Kenya, 209, 385
Luhr, China, 246

INDEX

Lundy, Benjamin, 98, 229
Lung'aho, Thomas, 299, 338
Lutherans, 108, 218
Luxembourg, 12
Lynn, Mass., 75
Lyon, Robert A., 327, 386–87

MacArthur, Douglas, 259
McCallin, Myrtle, 323
McCarthy, Joseph, 286
Mace, David, 347
McGovern, George, 411
McKim, Miller, 230
McNamara, Robert S., 340
Macy, Charles, 111
Macy, Rowland Hussey, 111–12
Macy, Thomas, 38–39, 227
Madagascar, 267
Madison, Dolley, 96
Madison, James, 83, 95–96
Maendel, Katie, 372, 377
Maine (Mayn), 37, 386–87
Malagasy Friends, 363
Malik, Yakov, 252
Malone College, 410
Manchester College, 14
Manpower bill, 147
Marblehead, Mass., 77
Margherita, Signorina, 323, 324
Marion, Ind., 211
Marion, N.C., 238
Maris, Albert B., 357
Maritime Commission, 172
Marne Valley (France), 160–61
Marriage, 124, 424–28. *See also* specific persons
Marseilles, France, 16, 181
Marshall Islands, and nuclear protest, 306–15
Marshburn, Olive and Oscar, 420
Martha's Vineyard, 30, 34–35
Martin, Zenas L., 263
Maryland, 9, 33, 34, 43, 47, 53, 60, 228, 288. *See also* specific places
Marysville, Calif., 111
Mason-Dixon line, 60, 228
Massachusetts, 8–11, 23, 29–31ff., 37, 75, 95, 107, 184–86, 320–22. *See also* specific places
Massachusetts General Hospital, 165
Mather, Eleanore Price, 257
May, Samuel, 100–1
Meacham, Stewart, 308, 385
Meade, William, 49, 50, 51, 195
Medical experiments, 165, 188
Meetings for Sufferings, 75 ff., 113
Mendenhall, Nereus, 115–16, 117
Mennonites, 12, 133, 405
Mental illness, 165–67

Methodists, 90, 108, 155, 246, 308, 318
Mexico, 173, 264
Mexico City, 16–17
Miami, Fla., 327–28
Michener, James, 232–33
Michigan, 199–201. *See also* specific places
Milford Haven, Wales, 82
Military service. *See* Conscientious Objectors; specific wars
Millbrook, N.Y., 89
Mills College, 14, 127
Milner, Clyde A., 337, 338
Ministers, ministry, 7, 22, 55, 56, 62, 108–9, 123, 268
Minneapolis, Minn., 320
Minnesota, University of, 165, 188
Minott, George, 264
Minthorn, H. J., 126
Mirabeau, Honoré Riquetti, Comte de, 81
Missions and missionaries, 17, 119–20, 151–53, 209–12, 224–26, 245–47, 251–52, 263–64, 369–70 (*see also* specific agencies, persons); Bolivian, 335–37
Mississippi Delta, 2
Mitchell, Morris, 346
Modoc Indians, 118
Mohammed IV, Sultan of Turkey, 3, 24
Mohonk Mountain House (New Paltz, N.Y.), 353
Monomonee Indians, 119
Montana, 155
Montgomery, Ala., 301–2, 351
Months of the year, 298–99
Moon, Duane, 410
Moore, Hugh, 422
Moore, J. Floyd, 235–36, 338, 362, 367
Moore, Mrs. (teacher), 324
Morecambe Bay (England), 281
Morgan, Arthur E., 200, 240
Morgan, Cadwalader, 63
Morgan, Lucy, 200, 240
Morgan, Rita, 329
Morocco, 328, 329
Morrison, Norman, 332, 352–53, 376
Moscow, Russia, 171, 296
Moslems, 221ff. *See also* Arabs
Mott, Anna, 231
Mott, James, 227–29
Mott, John R., 208, 222
Mott, Lucretia, 47, 101, 227–32, 423
Mount Pleasant, Ohio, 84, 94, 98
Muckleshoot Indians, 386
Muhlenberg College, 14
Munich, Germany, 1
Murphy, Frank, 137
Music, 172–73, 244, 257
Mussolini, Benito, 147, 180

Mysticism, 343, 344

Nagasaki, Japan, 186, 190
Nanking, China, 152–53, 246
Nantucket Island, 39, 64–65, 72, 78, 79–82, 110, 111
Narragansett, R.I., 44
Narragansett Indians, 29, 30, 44
National Black Economic Development Conference, 411, 416, 417
National Catholic Welfare Conference, 205
National Conference of Quaker Men, 264
National Congress of American Indians, 386
National Council of Christians and Jews, 323
National Council of Churches, 347
National Fund for Urban Economic Development, 412
National Mental Health Foundation, 167
National Park Service, 164
Navajo Indians, 120, 150
Nayler, James, 280–81
Nebraska, 118
Negroes. *See* Blacks; Slavery
Nehru, Jawaharlal, 198, 255, 256, 272
Nelson, Beryl, 356, 362, 368, 373–74, 385, 426
Nelson, Earl, 367–68, 373, 374, 413, 414, 426
Nelson, Marjorie Ellen, 356, 361–62, 367–68, 371–79, 380, 383, 412–14; wedding, 424–28
Nepal, 181–82
Netherlands. *See* Holland and the Dutch
New Amsterdam, 26–27, 43, 218–19
New Bedford, Mass., 82
Newberg, Oreg., 122, 125–26
Newby, Richard P., 422
New Castle, Del., 59, 177
New Delhi, India, 256
Newell, Wayne, 387
New England, 7–11, 23 ff., 29–36, 37–46, 75 ff., 105, 119, 289, 302. *See also* New England Yearly Meeting; specific states
New England Resistance, 393
New England Yearly Meeting, 44, 46, 54, 60, 103, 106–7 ff., 113, 130–31, 220, 233–34, 235, 302–5, 388–89; 1st school, 89, 90; reunited after Separation, 185–86; and slavery, 65–66, 72, 74
New Garden, N.C., 82
New Garden Boarding School. *See* Guilford College
New Garden Meetinghouse (Greensboro, N.C.), 363

Newgate Prison (London), 9, 196–97, 280
New Haven, Conn., 18, 33
New Jersey (East and West Jersey), 56, 57, 66, 75, 76, 80, 177, 195–96; Yearly Meeting for Pennsylvania, New Jersey, and Delaware, 63, 67
Newlin, Algie I., 239, 240
Newlin, Eva, 240
New London, Conn., 334
Newman, Mary, 322
New Mexico, 250
New Paltz, N.Y., 353
Newport, R.I., 10, 28, 30, 43, 44, 54, 65, 66, 72, 103 ff.
New Swarthmoor (N.Y.), 388, 422
New York (state), 119, 120, 209, 289. *See also* New York Yearly Meeting; specific places
New York City, 7, 75, 79, 112, 166, 191, 197, 252–53, 326, 359. *See also* Flushing, N.Y.; New Amsterdam; United Nations
New York Hospital, Westchester Division, 166
New York Yearly Meeting, 66, 74, 92, 94, 113, 121, 126, 220, 299–300, 355, 356, 415
Ngaira, Joseph, 211
Nguyen Duy Trinh, 420
Nicholson, Joseph, 41
Nigeria, 385, 405
Nine Partners School (Millbrook, N.Y.), 89, 227
Nisqually Indians, 386
Nitobe, Inazo, 151
Nixon, E. D., 302
Nixon, Richard M., 201, 403, 404–5
Nixon, Richard, Institute of Human Affairs, 410
Nobel Prize, 207, 212–14, 339
Non-Violent Action Against Nuclear Weapons, 306, 311
Norfolk, Va., 95
North Africa, 163. *See also* specific places
North American Conference on Church and Family, 347
North Carolina, 98–99, 115, 117, 174, 256, 317, 362–67. *See also* North Carolina Yearly Meeting
North Carolina, University of, 14
North Carolina Yearly Meeting, 74, 98–99, 115, 332, 363
North Dakota, 155
Norton, Humphrey, 25–26, 31, 41
Norway, 148, 212, 213
Norwich, England, 103, 105
Nottingham, England, 23

INDEX

Nova Scotia, 69, 80
"Now and Then," 142-43, 178-79, 300, 334-35, 340, 416
Nuclear weapons protests, 306-15, 339-40
Nuttall, Geoffrey F., 343
Nyack, N.Y., 18

Oakwood School (Poughkeepsie, N.Y.), 89
Office of Scientific Research and Development, 165
Ohio, 83-84, 119
Ohio Yearly Meeting, 17, 84, 94, 122, 351, 420, 423
Oklahoma, 386
Oklahoma, University of, 14
Old-Believers, 296
One Per Cent More Fund, 385-86
Onondaga Indians, 119
Open housing, 249-50
Orange Grove Monthly Meeting, 315, 407
Oregon Yearly Meeting, 17, 126, 251, 335, 336, 351, 369-70
Orthodox Yearly Meetings, 93-94, 118. See also specific Meetings
Osage Indians, 120
Osborn, Charles, 98
Osborne, Irene, 288
Oskaloosa, Iowa, 410
Oslo, Norway, 212, 213
Overbrook, Pa., 323
Owl, W. David, 177
Oxford, England, and Oxford University, 267-73, 279
Oyster Bay (Long Island), 54

Pacific Coast Association of Friends, 127, 201
Pacific College. See Fox, George, College
Pacific Oaks College, 410
Pacific Yearly Meeting, 201, 286
Painter, Levinus K., 210, 414
Palestine. See Israel
Panama Canal Zone, 412
Panmunjom, Korea, 272, 285
Panyushkin, Alexander, 214
Paris, France, 180
Parks, Rosa, 301, 302
Parliament House (Nantucket), 65
Pasadena, Calif., 154, 201, 315, 407
Passamaquoddy Indians, 119, 386-87
Pastorius, Francis Daniel, 60
Patapsco State Forest, Md., 145
Patuxent, Md., 33, 34
Paul VI, Pope, 352
Pauling, Linus, 339

455

"Peaceable Kingdom" (Hicks), 5, 256-57
Pearl Harbor, 150, 152
Pearson, Drew, 14
Peck, Jim, 312
Pemberton, Israel, 69, 75, 79
Pemberton, John, 75, 79
Pendle Hill (Lancashire, England), 23, 267, 274-75
Pendle Hill (Wallingford, Pa.), 127-28, 181, 420, 421
Penington, Mary, 52
Penn, Admiral Sir William, 58, 156, 179
Penn, Gulielma, 52, 56, 63
Penn, Hannah Callowhill, 63
Penn, Lady, 178-79
Penn, Thomas, 68
Penn, William, 49-51, 52, 56 ff., 60-61 ff., 68, 156, 169, 194, 196, 219-20, 256, 270, 279; buried at Jordans, 127; on Josiah Coale, 35; and lobbying, 171; and naming of Polaris sub, 340; on Seekers, 277-78; 300th anniversary of birth, 177-78
Penn, William, Charter School, 61, 62
Penn, William, College, 125, 410
Penn, William, House (Washington, D.C.), 381
Pennington, Levi T., 412, 422
Pennsylvania, 2, 58-59, 60-62 ff., 66-70 ff., 80, 88-89, 196, 228, 279 (see also specific places); in Revolution, 75, 76, 79; and school integration, 289; and 300th anniversary of Penn's birth, 177-78
Pennsylvania, New Jersey, and Delaware, Yearly Meeting for, 63, 67
Pennsylvania Hall, 228-29
Pennsylvania Hospital, 166, 427
Penobscot Indians, 119, 386-87
Pentagon, 333-34, 340, 352-53
Peretz, Don, 244, 405
Perisho, Marjorie. See Nelson, Marjorie Ellen
Perisho, Robert Clarence (Bob), 374-76, 385, 413, 414, 424-28
Perrot, John, 47
Perry, Charles, 113-15, 304
Perry, Henry, 388-89
Perry, Julianna, 11
Perry, Temperance Foster, 113
Perry, Thomas, 304, 422-23
Perryville, R.I., 109
Perth Amboy, N.J., 66
Pétain, Henri Philippe, 13, 163
Peterson, Jerome, 243
Phelps, Nicholas, 35-36
Philadelphia, Pa., 1, 2, 7, 13, 60, 61,

73, 75, 76, 79, 83, 92, 119, 136, 141, 145, 151, 205, 228–29 ff., 306; Acadians in, 69; fair employment, 249; Friends Committee on National legislation in, 171–72; open housing, 249–50; Society for Relieving Distressed Prisoners, 196; yellow fever in, 82
Philadelphia Yearly Meeting, 67, 79, 91–93, 94, 233–34, 239, 301, 319, 349, 355, 356–57, 379–80, 415, 426; and Green Circle Program, 322; and liquor for Indians, 64; Mission Board, 17, 152, 186–87 (*see also* specific missions); proposes pastoral visit to Nixon, 404; reunited after Separation, 297–99; and school integration, 291; and slavery, 71, 74; 300th anniversary of Penn's birth, 177–78
Philanthropist (paper), 98
Philleo, Calvin, 102
Philleo, Prudence. *See* Crandall, Prudence
Phillips Academy, 185–86
Phoenix (ketch), 310–12, 314–15, 354–56, 359, 362, 364, 368, 373–74, 385
Pickering, Aquilla, 125
Pickering, Hannah, 125
Pickering, Ont., 121
Pickett, Clarence Evan, 1–2, 13–14, 15, 141–42, 151, 167, 169, 181, 248, 254–55, 262, 287, 349, 358; and Dynamic Kernels, 199, 200; on Elizabeth Vining and Japanese prince, 203; Germany gives Order of Merit to, 284; and Palestine-Arab problems, 221, 223, 242, 243, 244–45; retires as Secretary of Service Committee, 259; and Soviets, 253; at Washington dinner, 339
Pickett, Lilly, 243, 339, 349
Piscataqua River, 37, 39
"Plain speech," 10, 192, 388
Plea for the Poor, A, 197
Plymouth, Mass., 30–31, 33, 35
Point Shirley, Mass., 77
Poland, 148, 198, 214
Polaris submarines, 334, 340
Poor People's Campaign, 380, 381, 382–83
Porter, Elmer, 190
Portsmouth, England, 25
Portsmouth, N.H., 37
Portsmouth, R.I., 89
Portugal (Portuguese), 3; Lisbon, 16, 149
Potawatomi Indians, 120
Poughkeepsie, N.Y., 89
Pratt, Enoch, 166–67
Preparatory Department of Friends College, 126
Presbyterians, 90, 108, 318

President's War Relief Control Board, 172
Preston Patrick, England, 279
Prince Edward County, Va., 330–31
Princeton, N.J., 80
Prisons and prisoners, 193–97, 313–14, 349–50, 410, 415. *See also* Conscientious Objectors; specific persons, prisons
Protestantism, 16, 18, 108, 344. *See also* specific sects
Providence, R.I., 29, 82, 90, 122, 130
Puget Sound, 386
Pulitzer Prize, 232
Purdy, Alexander, 342–43
Puritans and Puritanism, 7 ff., 29, 37, 343–44. *See also* specific places
Pusan, Korea, 285
Puyallup Indians, 386

Quaker Act, 9, 282
Quaker Action Group, A, 354, 356, 364, 383, 412
Quakerama, The, 303–5
Quaker Hill (Richmond, Ind.), 18, 169
Quaker House (Atlanta, Ga.), 331
Quaker House (New York City), 220–21, 252, 253, 261, 262
Quakerism, A View from the Back Benches, 354
Quaker Life, 364
Quaker Men, National Conference of, 264
Quaker Peace Testimony, 17, 81–82, 135, 138, 147, 332, 333, 334, 340, 399
Quaker Theological Discussion Group, 324–25
Quang Ngai, Vietnam, 361, 369–78, 379, 385, 393, 412–14
Quapaw Indians, 120
Quiet Eye, The, 286–87, 321
Quietism, 89, 90

Racial problems, 173–74 (*see also* specific groups); "Churkendoose" and, 322–23
Ralston Relief Cereal, 200
Ramallah, Israel, 225
Ranters, the, 47–48
Rawlins, Gladys, 322
Reading, England, 273
Red Cross, 12, 16, 162, 214, 326, 355
Redding, Earl, 327
Reeb, James, 351
Reece, Glenn, 422
Reed College, 14
Rees, Russell, 422
Reese, Deborah, 210–11
Reese, Emory, 210–11, 212
Reese, William, 172–73

INDEX

Replogle, Charles, 251
Replogle, Delbert, 242
Replogle, May, 251
Replogle, Ruth, 242
Revivalists. *See* Evangelism
Reynaud, Paul, 15, 16
Reynolds, Barbara, 315
Reynolds, Earle, 310, 311, 314-15, 354
Reynolds, Reginald, 257
Rhoads, Esther B., 187, 203, 204-5
Rhode Island, 9-10, 26 ff., 29 ff., 44, 65, 66, 80, 103, 134 (*see also* specific places); and Revolution, 76-78
Richardson, John, 64
Richmond, Ind., 18, 84, 104, 169, 209, 264. *See also* Earlham College
Richmond Declaration of Faith, 126
Rimini, Italy, 323-24
Rindge, N.H., 345
Roberts, Arthur O., 351
Roberts, Owen J., 178
Robinson, Clifton J., 132, 200
Robinson, Richard, 277
Robinson, William, 10, 34, 37 ff., 303
Rocky Mountain Yearly Meeting, 351
Rofe, George, 43-44, 46, 282, 303
Rome, Italy, 16, 351-52
Rommel, Erwin, 163
Roosevelt, Eleanor, 12, 167
Roosevelt, President Franklin D., 1, 12 ff., 133, 134, 137, 141, 179-80
Roper, Richard, 47
Ross, Betsy, 78
Ross, Isabel, 280
Rotch, Benjamin, 82
Rotch, William, 72, 78, 81, 82, 96
Rough Rocks Friends Meeting, 120
Rous, John, 32-33, 41, 49, 52, 56
Rowntree, John Wilhelm, 138
Rushland, Pa., 255
Russell, Elbert, 129, 238
Russia (Soviet Union), 214-15, 221, 241, 252-53, 261, 269, 285, 324, 326, 332-33, 334; Quaker delegates to, 295-97; Sputnik, 308; and World War II, 148, 163, 171, 179, 186
Russian Orthodox Church, 296
Rustin, Bayard, 255-56, 271
Rutan, Frederick (Eric), 391-402, 407
Rye, N.Y., 55

Sac Indians, 120
Saigon, Vietnam, 369
St. Croix, 107
St. James, N.Y., 359-60
St. Louis, Mo., 158, 421
St. Peter's (Rome), 352
Salem, Mass., 29, 31-32, 35, 36, 75, 77
Salem, N.J., 57

Salisbury, Mass., 38-39
Salter, William, 43
Samms, Carrie and Robert, 251
Sandiford, Ralph, 66
San Dimas, Calif., 145
Sandoz, Jerry, 378
Sandwich, Mass., 9, 33, 35
Sandy Spring, Md., 89, 346
San Francisco, Calif., 158, 180, 295, 311, 315, 349, 408; Grace Cathedral, 320
San Jose, Calif., 124
San Pedro, Calif., 306-7
Sawyer, George, 411
Sayre, Francis B., 221
Scattergood, Thomas, 166
Scattergood School, 18
School Affiliation Service, 323-24
Scosthrop, Richard, 247
Scull, David H., 287, 385
Search for Peace in the Middle East, 405
Seaside, Jamaica, 156-57
Seattle, Wash., 155
Seaver, Madge, 408
Sedbergh, England, 277, 280
Seekers, 277-78, 279
Sein, Encario M., 262
Sein, Heberto M., 262-63
Sein, Margaretta Marriage, 262
Selective Service Act, 134 ff., 144, 169
Selleck, Florence and George A., 240, 241
Selma, Ala., 351
Seminole Indians, 68
Senate Select Committee on Hunger and Human Needs, 411
Seneca Falls, N.Y., 227, 229, 232
Seneca Indians, 119, 120, 386, 414
Seoul, Korea, 420
Severn, Md., 34
Seward, William Henry, 114
Sex education, 346-47
Shaffer, Alice, 188-89, 241-42
Shaffer, Leslie, 129
Shanghai, China, 16, 153
Sharpless, Edith, 152
Sharpless, Evi, 156
Shattuck, Samuel, 32, 35-36, 42, 303
Shawnee Indians, 84-85, 119, 120, 386
Shelter Island, 36, 39, 55
Sheppard, Moses, 166
Sheppard and Enoch Pratt Hospital, 167
Sheppard Asylum, 166-67
Sherrill, Henry Knox, 222
Sherwood, Orion, 307
Shillitoe, Thomas, 93-94, 104
Short Creek, Ohio, 84
Shrewsbury, N.J., 56
Sidwell, Floyd H., 420
Sidwell Friends School, 289

Sierra, Juan, 264
Sierra Leone, 96
Silver Bay, N.Y., 299, 415
Simpson, William, 268
Sky Island (Nyack, N.Y.), 18
Slater, Eleanor, 18
Slavery, 36, 45–46, 52–53, 60, 65–67, 70–72, 73–74, 80, 82, 89, 91, 96–97 ff., 105, 107, 108, 112 ff., 121, 227, 271, 294–95; abolished, 116; in Arkansas, 316–17; Underground Railroad, 113, 115, 230, 363
Smallpox, 77–78, 82
Smiley, Albert K., 353
Smiley, Keith, 353
Smith, Al, 341
Smith, Bradford, 328
Smith, Courtney, 403
Smith, Lillian, 316
Smith, Paul S., 410
Smith, Richard, 8, 66
Smith, Sarah, 197
Society for the Reformation of Juvenile Delinquents (formerly Society for Prevention of Pauperism), 197
Sollmann, Wilhelm, 15
Southampton, N.Y., 8
South Carolina, 79, 99
Southern Christian Leadership Conference, 381, 383
South Florida Desegregation Consulting Center, 323
South Kingstown, R.I., 66
Southland Institute (Helena, Ark.), 316–17
Southwick, Cassandra, 32, 35, 36
Southwick, Daniel, 36
Southwick, Josiah, 35–36
Southwick, Laurence, 32, 35, 36
Southwick, Provided, 36
Soviet Union. *See* Russia
Spain, 2, 12, 148, 162–63, 238
Speak Truth to Power, 294–95
Speedwell (ship), 8, 23, 24
Spellman, Francis Cardinal, 222
Springer, Timothy, 407–8
Squires, Sally, 371
Stabler, Edward, 97
Stage, Robert, 43–44
Stalin, Joseph, 147
Stalingrad, Russia, 163
Stamps, 218, 227, 232; food, 383–84
Standard of the Lord Lifted Up, The, 30
Stanton, Edwin McMasters, 114
Stanton, Elizabeth Cady, 227, 229
Star, red-and-black, 180, 181, 354, 369
Starbuck, Edward, 39
Starbuck, Mary, 64–65
State Department, U.S., 334, 354, 419

Steere, Douglas, 128, 140, 167, 186, 239–40, 241, 351–52, 366–67
Stefferud, Alfred, 414
Stephenson, Marmaduke, 10, 37–38, 39, 303
Stettinius, Edward, 180
Still, William, 230
Stimson, Henry Lewis, 163
Stone, I. F., 349
Story, John, 57
Story, Thomas, 64
Street, Guilford B., 254
Streit, Clarence, 15
Stringer, Hannah, 51
Stubbs, John, 52, 247
Student Peace Service, 15
Stuyvesant, Peter, 26, 27, 218, 219
Suez Canal, 326
Susquehanna Indians, 34, 43
Swallow (ship), 7, 8, 303
Swarthmoor Hall (Ulverston, England), 23, 32, 57, 69, 280–81
Swarthmore, Pa., 129, 160
Swarthmore College, 18, 125, 231, 233, 403
Switzer, L. Glenn, 264
Sylvester, Nathaniel, 36
Syria, 16, 151

Takahashi, Tane, 203, 205
Talleyrand, Charles-Maurice de, 81
Tamayo, Miguel, 264
Tamplin, Carroll, 335, 336
Tan Dong, Korea, 420
Tappan, Arthur, 99, 101–2
Tarkington, Booth, 163
Taunton, Mass., 95
Taxes, 136–37, 356–57
Taylor, Ernest E., 274
Taylor, Joseph W., 125
Tecumseh, Mich., 132, 145, 174–76, 179, 190, 200–1
Tel Aviv, Israel, 242
Temple, Sir Thomas, 37
Tennessee, 115
Testament of Devotion, 140
Texas, 172–73, 249
Thayer, George B., 102
Tho (Vietnamese boy), 413, 427
Thoreau, Henry, 108
Thurston, Thomas, 33, 34
Tibet, 328
Timbres, Harry, 214
Timbres, Rebecca, 214
Tito, Josip Broz, 261
Tokyo, Japan, 152, 179, 202–7, 329–30
Toleration Act (1689), 62–63
Tollefson, Harold, 422
Tolles, Frederick B., 67, 83, 171, 191,

243, 276, 319, 344
Tolstoi, Count Leo, 332, 333
Tompkins, Oliver S., 270
Tougaloo College, 250
Toulouse, France, 155–56
Townsend, Naomi, 250
Trueblood, D. Elton, 134, 239, 390
Truman, Harry S., 186, 254, 255, 284
Tuba City, Ariz., 250
Tucker, Robert W., 348–49
Tuke, Esther, 74
Tuke, William, 74, 166
Tunisia, 163, 328, 329
Turkey, Sultan of, 3, 24
Turner, Nat, 98
Tuttle, Kenneth, 188
Twain, Mark, 102

Underground Railroad, 113, 115, 230, 363
Unionist, The (paper), 102
Unitarians, 91, 108
United Arab Republic, 405
United Nations (UN), 146, 169, 178 ff., 215, 218, 220–21, 223, 252, 260, 295, 296, 326, 334, 339, 366, 405; and aid to Latin America, 412; and Kashmir, 272; Khrushchev at, 332; and Korea, 259; at Lake Success, 261–63; Pope at, 352
United Society of Friends Women, 264
UNRRA, 180
Untermeyer, Louis, 254
Updegraff, David B., 123
Upsall, Nicholas, 8–9
Urbana-Champaign, Ill., Meeting, 334
U Thant, 365, 366, 367
Utica, N.Y., 388

Vail, James G., 11, 142, 172, 222–23, 224
Valiant Sixty, 47, 278–79
Valtin, Rolf, 232
Van Buren, Martin, 104
Van Doren, Carl, 254
Van Paassen, Pierre, 254
Vassalboro, Maine, 82
Vatican II, 351–52
Versailles, Treaty of, 13, 147
Vichy, France, 163
Vienna, Austria, 1, 16, 162, 241, 326
Vietnam and Vietnamese, 285–86, 350–51, 352–53, 354–56, 359, 360, 361, 368, 369–79, 384–85, 412–14, 425; children, Majorie Nelson's wedding guests, 427–28; Elder takes medical supplies to, 419–20; soldiers refuse to fight in, 391–402, 407–8
Vincent, Mabel, 264

Vining, Elizabeth Gray, 202–7, 226, 234, 259, 264–66, 329–30
Virginia, 33, 43, 47, 53, 56, 74, 98, 99, 115, 287, 288. *See also* specific places
Virginia Beach Friends School, 346
Virginia Yearly Meeting, 74
VISA, 369
VISTA, 217
Voltaire, François Marie Arouet de, 60
Voorhis, Jerry, 201
Vyshinsky, Andrei, 272

Wales, 48, 82
Wallingford, Pa. *See* Pendle Hill
Walpole, Margaret, 421
Walsh, Richard J., 172
Walton, George A., 299; on mission to Gestapo, 2, 5, 7, 11
Walton, J. Barnard, 129
Wanton, Edward, 40
Wanyama, Petro, 209
Wapakoneta, Ohio, 84
Waring, Thomas, 345
War of 1812, 83, 96
Warren, Roland L., 364–65
Washington (state), 386
Washington, D.C., 17–18, 171, 186–87, 255, 284–85, 287 ff., 307–8, 333–34, 339–42, 352–53, 381ff., 419 (*see also* specific agencies, Presidents); Japanese cherry trees, 154; Poor People's Campaign, 380, 381, 382–83
Washington, George, 69, 76, 77, 79
Washington University, 158
Waterloo, N.Y., 229
Watertown, Mass., 78
Waugh, Dorothy, 26–27, 31–32, 278
Waugh, Jane, 278
Weatherhead, Mary, 26–27, 31
Webb, Norval, 422
Weddings. *See* Marriage
Welcome (ship), 59, 279
Weller, Dorothy, 371
Wellesley College, 14, 207–8
Wensleydale, England, 276–77
West, Benjamin, 80
West, Jessamyn, 191, 419
West Branch, Iowa, 18, 112, 113, 122–23
Westbury, N.Y., 346
West China Union University, 246
Westerly, R.I., 109, 422–23
Western Yearly Meeting, 113, 126
West India Company, 219
West Indies, 105, 107. *See also* specific islands
Westtown School, 89
West Virginia, 2
Wetherald, William, 121
Wharton, Edward, 38, 40

Wheat (Dynamic Kernels program), 132–33, 145, 148–50, 157, 163, 170–71, 174–76, 179, 180, 187–88, 189–90, 199–201
White, Gilbert F., 163–64, 285, 382
White House, 307, 339–40. *See also* specific Presidents
White Plains, N.Y., 166
Whitewater, Ind., 84, 316–17
Whitman, Walt, 86–88, 92–93, 106
Whitney, Eli, 82
Whitney, Norman, 318, 319
Whittier, Calif., 125–26, 154
Whittier College, 14, 201, 410
Whittier, John Greenleaf, 111, 122, 229, 286; and jailing of Garrison, 99; poetry quoted, 42, 108, 115, 116, 224–25, 304; in *Quakerama*, 304; town named for, 125
Who Shall Live?, 406–7
Wichita Indians, 120
Wichita, Kans., 118, 410
Widders, Robert, 281–82
Wider Quaker Fellowship, 128–29
Wight, Isle of, 25
Wilbur, John, and Wilburites, 103 ff., 303–4
Wilder, Thornton, 254
Wilkinson, John, 57
Willebrand, Bishop, 352
William II, King of Netherlands, 107
William III, King of England, 63
Williams, Myrtle M., 182
Williams, Roger, 29, 30
Williams, Walter R., 181–82
Williamson, Passmore, 230
Willink, Kees, 376, 377
Willoughby, George, 307
Wilmington College, 125, 409–10
Wilmington, Ohio, 411
Wilmington Yearly Meeting, 126
Wilson, Dan, 421
Wilson, E. Raymond, 147, 169–70
Wilson, George, 43
Wilson, Louise, 346
Winchester, Va., 79
Windows for the Crown Prince. See Vining, Elizabeth Gray
Winthrop, John, Jr., 30, 37
Wolfeboro, N.H., 18
Woman's Foreign Missionary Association, 151–52
Woman's Rights Convention, 227
Women, 22, 37, 55, 56, 92, 147, 419; Dutch, 26; Gurney on, 105; halfway house for, 349; Lucretia Mott and, 227 ff.; mental hospital attendants, 167
Women's International League for Peace and Freedom, 207
Wood, Carolena, 3
Wood, Richard R., 298
Woodhouse (ship), 10, 11, 23–24, 25–28, 30, 31, 311
Woolman, John, 66, 70–74, 96–97, 106, 195, 197, 271, 283, 316, 317–18, 319–20, 412, 416; marriage, 255; in *Quakerama*, 303; in *Quiet Eye*, 286
Woolman, John, Memorial Association, 255
Woolman, John, School (Calif.), 346
Woolman, Mary, 74
Woolman, Sarah Ellis, 73, 74, 255
Worcester, England, 57, 143
Wordsworth, William, 68
Work Camps, 215–17, 240, 241, 248, 249, 250–51, 284, 386, 410
World Affairs Seminar (Little Rock), 317, 318
World Conference Against Atomic and Hydrogen Weapons, 299
World Conference of Friends. *See* Friends World Conferences
World Council of Churches, 237–39
World War I, 3, 13, 31, 127, 147, 160–62, 208
World War II, 1–6, 12–19, 148–50, 151–59, 163–65 ff., 169 ff., 179–80 ff., 186, 241. *See also* specific countries
Wright brothers, 252
Wyalusing, Pa., 73–74
Wyandotte Friends Meeting, 120
Wyandotte Indians, 386

Yale University (Yale College), 18, 105
Yalta Conference, 179, 241
Yarnall, D. Robert, 142, 182–83, 264; on mission to Gestapo, 2, 4, 7, 11
Yarnall, Elizabeth, 4
Yealand Conyers, England, 281–82
Yellow fever, 82
York, England, 74; Castle, 7; Retreat, 166
York, James, Duke of, 219
Yorkshire, England, 23
Young Friends, 127, 273, 422; of North America (YFNA), 374, 375–76, 383
Young people (students), 127, 273, 302–3, 353, 387–88, 410–11, 422 (*see also* Education and schools; Work Camps; specific countries); "Airlift Seminar," 241; International Student House, 17–18; Interracial Youth Camps, 174; Student Peace Service, 15; World Affairs Seminar, 317, 318; YFNA, 374, 375–76, 383
Yugoslavia, 148, 259–61, 326–27
Yungblut, John, 331

Zaki, Abdul Hamid, 243
Zante, 24

www.ingramcontent.com/pod-product-compliance
Lightning Source LLC
Chambersburg PA
CBHW021825220426
43663CB00005B/133